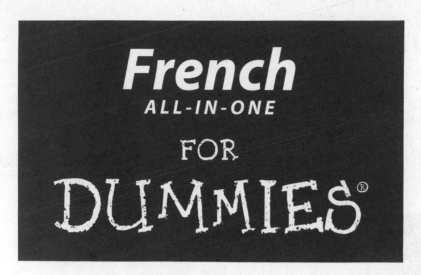

French
ALL-IN-ONE
FOR
DUMMIES®

by Eliane Kurbegov with Dodi-Katrin Schmidt, Michelle M. Williams, Dominique Wenzel, Zoe Erotopoulos, and Laura K. Lawless

WILEY

John Wiley & Sons, Inc.

French All-in-One For Dummies®

Published by
John Wiley & Sons, Inc.
111 River St.
Hoboken, NJ 07030-5774
www.wiley.com

WILEY

About the Authors

Eliane Kurbegov has been teaching French at secondary and post-secondary levels in Florida and is currently serving as Campus Curriculum Coordinator and High School World Language Chair at Discovery Canyon Campus in Colorado. Eliane is a French native speaker who was twice honored by the French government with the prestigious *Palmes académiques* for her contributions to the promotion of the French language and culture. Eliane has authored many publications for a variety of educational purposes and thoroughly enjoys sharing her love of the French language and francophone cultures.

Dodi-Katrin Schmidt has been a writer, translator, and editor for over a decade. Aside from translating German, French, and English texts of various kinds, including linguistic handbooks, film reviews, travel guides, and children's books, she has been involved in developing language textbooks, language courses, teachers' handbooks, and grammar companions for video language courses. Dodi has been teaching for more than two decades at high school, adult education, and college levels in Europe as well as the United States. She also writes test items for various national language tests and recorded textbook and test material. Together with her husband, she travels a great deal, and they continually house and entertain foreign students and former students in their home in Princeton, New Jersey.

Michelle M. Williams is an editor at a major educational publisher. A former French teacher, she has taught students ranging from 2 years old to adults in both the public and private sectors. She is a firm believer in making the language fun and accessible to all who want to learn. Her most rewarding experience, however, is watching and listening to her son Nathaniel learn to speak and sing in French.

Dominique Wenzel has been a freelance teacher of French and a translator for 15 years. Born and raised in France, she received a master's degree from the University of Paris-Sorbonne and studied at the University of Chicago on a postgraduate Fulbright scholarship. Her students include business professionals, children, and adults of all levels and interests. She travels regularly to France. Dominique raised two bicultural, bilingual children who are both active in the international field.

Zoe Erotopoulos holds an MA, MPhil, and PhD in French and Romance Philology from Columbia University. Her French teaching experience ranges from elementary to advanced level courses, including literature and theater. Dr. Erotopoulos has taught at a number of institutions, including Columbia

University, Reid Hall in Paris, and Trinity College in Hartford, Connecticut. For the past 15 years, she has been teaching in the Department of Modern Languages and Literatures at Fairfield University in Fairfield, Connecticut.

Laura K. Lawless is the author of seven language instruction books (four French and three Spanish). She also teaches French, Spanish, and English on the Internet and has a website of vegetarian recipes and information.

Dedication

I dedicate this work to all those who love French, including my colleagues all over the United States who work hard to share their passion for the French language and cultures, and also to my wonderful American family who wholeheartedly espoused my French legacy as a means to enrich their own lives. —Eliane Kurbegov

Author's Acknowledgments

I extend my greatest thanks to Senior Project Editor Alissa Schwipps for her patient, supportive, and professional guidance in the writing of this book. Her probing questions for clarification have undoubtedly improved the quality and depth of the explanations and examples I provided. I also thank Copy Editors Danielle Volrol and Megan Knoll and Technical Editors Carrie Klaus and Jenny Darnall whose suggestions consistently presented the learners' perspective and helped me focus on their needs rather than on my understanding of the language and culture. —Eliane Kurbegov

Publisher's Acknowledgments

We're proud of this book; please send us your comments at `http://dummies.custhelp.com`. For other comments, please contact our Customer Care Department within the U.S. at 877-762-2974, outside the U.S. at 317-572-3993, or fax 317-572-4002.

Some of the people who helped bring this book to market include the following:

Acquisitions, Editorial, and Vertical Websites

Senior Project Editor: Alissa Schwipps

Acquisitions Editor: Michael Lewis

Senior Copy Editor: Danielle Voirol

Copy Editor: Megan Knoll

Assistant Editor: David Lutton

Editorial Program Coordinator: Joe Niesen

Technical Editors: Jenny Darnall, Carrie Klaus

Vertical Websites: Melanie Orr, Josh Frank

Editorial Manager: Christine Meloy Beck

Editorial Assistants: Rachelle Amick, Alexa Koschier

Art Coordinator: Alicia B. South

Cover Photo: © iStockphoto.com/ Matthew Dixon

Cartoons: Rich Tennant (`www.the5thwave.com`)

Composition Services

Senior Project Coordinator: Kristie Rees

Layout and Graphics: Carl Byers, Carrie A. Cesavice, Joyce Haughey, Corrie Niehaus, Christin Swinford

Proofreaders: The Well-Chosen Word, Rebecca Denoncour, Melanie Hoffman

Indexer: Potomac Indexing, LLC

Illustrator: Elizabeth Kurtzman

Audio Produced by: Her Voice Unlimited, LLC (`hervoice@iquest.net`)

Special Help

Elaine Wiley

Publishing and Editorial for Consumer Dummies

Kathleen Nebenhaus, Vice President and Executive Publisher

David Palmer, Associate Publisher

Kristin Ferguson-Wagstaffe, Product Development Director

Publishing for Technology Dummies

Andy Cummings, Vice President and Publisher

Composition Services

Debbie Stailey, Director of Composition Services

Contents at a Glance

Table of Contents

Book V: Going Back in Time 485

Introduction

··

Whether you're studying French in school, traveling to francophone (French-speaking) regions on business, or just exploring a different culture, learning the language has many advantages. Whatever your reason for wanting to pick up some French, *French All-in-One For Dummies* can help.

This book is a broad guide to acquiring French as a second (or third or fourth) language, covering topics ranging from vocabulary and pronunciation to grammar, sentence construction, and culture. The back of the book is straight reference, offering mini French-English dictionaries and extensive tables that show verbs conjugated in various tenses and moods. And to bring the real world into your living room (or car or wherever), this book comes with audio dialogues complete with translations and pronunciation guides. We even provide a Fun & Games section in the book so you can take a break from instruction by applying and testing your skills in a fun way.

So whether you choose to express yourself with some key words and phrases or to challenge yourself by becoming familiar with more complex rules of usage, it's all up to you. **Laissez les bons temps rouler !** (leh-sey ley bohN tahN rooh-ley!) (*Let the good times roll!*)

About This Book

French All-in-One For Dummies isn't like a class that you have to drag yourself to twice a week for a specified period of time. You can use this book however you want to, whether your goal is to discover some phrases to help you get around when you visit a francophone country, to say "Hello, how are you?" to your French-speaking neighbor, or to get a little extra grammar help in your French class. We even include French-Canadian terms and pronunciation differences to help make your French well-rounded. Go through this book at your own pace, reading as much or as little at a time as you like. You don't have to trudge through the chapters in sequential order, either; just read the sections that interest you. Cross-references throughout the book allow you to easily find any support material you need.

Listening comprehension is a huge part of any language study, so along with this book, you get audio tracks of the French alphabet and lots of the dialogues that appear in the text. We highlight these dialogues as they appear throughout the book; you can also flip to Appendix E for a complete listing of the audio tracks.

Conventions Used in This Book

To make this book easy to navigate, we've set up some conventions:

- French terms are usually set in **boldface** to make them stand out (however, in standalone example sentences, we sometimes boldface only key words we want to highlight). Translation of the French terms is set in *italic*.

- The pronunciation, which is set in parentheses, follows the French terms in Books I and II. Hyphens connect syllables in the same word. See Chapter 1 of Book I for a pronunciation key that shows how the letters sound.

- Because French nouns are typically preceded by an article, we include those articles in the word lists throughout this book, even though the English translation may not use the article. Furthermore, because articles indicate a noun's grammatical gender, they're helpful bits of information when you're learning a language. The definite articles are **le** (luh), masculine singular; **la** (lah), feminine singular; **l'** (l), an abbreviation of either **le** or **la**; and **les** (ley), plural; these are the equivalents of the English word *the*. The indefinite articles are **un** (uhN), masculine singular; **une** (ewn), feminine singular; and **des** (dey), plural; these are equivalent to the English words *a, an,* or *some*. When the article is plural or abbreviated, however, you can't tell the gender. In those instances, we add a gender designation: (m) for masculine and (f) for feminine.

- We sometimes put alternate word endings in parentheses at the end of a masculine noun or adjective to show feminine or plural forms. In general, an added **-e** makes a word feminine, an **-s** makes it plural, and an **-es** makes it feminine plural. For example, **ami(e/s/es)** (ah-mee) (*friend*) stands for four forms: the masculine singular **ami**, the feminine singular **amie**, the masculine plural **amis**, and the feminine plural **amies**.

- A space appears before two-part punctuation marks — question marks, exclamation points, and colons — in French.

So that you can make fast progress in French, this book includes a few elements to help you along:

- **Talkin' the Talk dialogues:** The best way to learn a language is to see and hear how it's used in conversation, so we include dialogues throughout the book. The dialogues come under the heading "Talkin' the Talk" and show you the French words, the pronunciation, and the English translation. Many of the dialogues come with an audio track so that you can hear them spoken as you read along.

- **Words to Know blackboards:** Memorizing key words and phrases is also important in language learning, so we collect the important words from a Talkin' the Talk dialogue in a chalkboard with the heading "Words to Know."

✔ **Fun & Games activities:** If you don't have actual French speakers to practice your new language skills on, you can use the Fun & Games activities in Appendix D to reinforce what you read. These games are fun ways to gauge your progress.

Also note that, because each language has its own way of expressing ideas, the English translations that we provide for the French terms may not be literal. We want you to know the gist of what's being said, not just the words that are being said. For example, the phrase **C'est normal** (sey nohr-mahl) can be translated literally as *It's normal,* but the phrase really means *It's no big deal.* This book gives the more natural translation — or sometimes both.

Foolish Assumptions

To write this book, we had to make some assumptions about who you are and what you want from a book called *French All-in-One For Dummies.* Here are the assumptions that we've made about you:

✔ You're a French student looking for an in-depth, easy-to-use reference.

✔ You know no or very little French — or if you took French back in school, you don't remember much of it.

✔ You want to have a choice of learning words, phrases, and sentence constructions on topics of personal interest and in any order that tickles your fancy.

✔ You want to have fun and pick up a little French at the same time.

If any of these statements applies to you, you've found the right book!

How This Book Is Organized

This book is divided by topic into five smaller, individual books, and then each one of these books is divided into chapters. A sixth book provides several helpful appendixes. The following sections tell you what types of information you can find in each book.

Book 1: Speaking in Everyday Settings

This book lets you get your feet wet by giving you some French basics: how to pronounce words, what the accent marks mean, and so on. We even boost your confidence by reintroducing you to some French words that you probably already know. Finally, we outline the basics of French grammar that you may need to know when you work through later chapters in the book. But mainly, you just find out what is essential in ordinary and routine situations such as greeting people, asking for directions, or buying some food.

Book II: Exploring and Wandering About

In this book, you stretch outside local or familiar settings. We give you the tools you need to take your French on the road, whether you're going to a local French restaurant or to a museum in France. This part covers all aspects of travel in French-speaking parts of the world, and it even has a chapter on how to handle emergencies.

Book III: Building the Grammatical Foundation for Communication

If you're looking for small, easily digestible pieces of information about how to structure sentences in French, this book is for you. You can read about the various parts of speech, including nouns, adjectives, adverbs, and verbs. Then you get to move on to slightly more involved topics, such as conjugating verbs in French. Pretty soon, you'll be constructing your very own French sentences.

Book IV: Getting Down to Detail and Precision in Your Communication

This book exposes you to more advanced grammatical skills that allow you to express yourself more clearly and in a variety of ways. You discover how to use adjectives, adverbs, and prepositions to give or ask for specific information. You start looking toward the future and even find out how to express nuances and wishes like the French do: by putting your verbs in the subjunctive mood.

Book V: Going Back in Time

If you get tired of discussing everything in the present and the future and want to walk down memory lane, this book is what you need. It shows you how to use past tenses to tell when and where you were born or to tell stories of past events and how things used to be. It also shows you how to form fancy past tenses to express what you had done before something else happened or what you would've done if you'd known better.

Book VI: Appendixes

This book includes important information that you can use for reference. Appendix A features verb tables, which show you how to conjugate both regular verbs and those verbs that stubbornly don't fit the regular pattern. Appendix B is a French-to-English mini-dictionary, and Appendix C is an English-to-French mini-dictionary. If you encounter a French word that you don't understand or you need to say something in French that you can't find quickly elsewhere in the book, look for it here. Appendix D can entertain and amuse you with its Fun & Games activities, and Appendix E lists the audio tracks that come with this book so that you can find the dialogues easily and follow along.

Icons Used in This Book

You may be looking for particular information while reading this book. To make certain types of information easier to find, we've placed the following icons in the left-hand margins throughout the book:

This icon highlights tips that can make learning French easier.

This icon points out interesting information that you ought not forget.

To help you avoid linguistic, grammatical, and cultural faux pas, we use this icon.

Languages are full of quirks that may trip you up if you're not prepared for them. This icon points to discussions of these peculiar grammar rules. Because Books III, IV, and V are nearly all grammar, you see this icon only in Books I and II.

If you want information and advice about culture and travel, look for this icon. It draws your attention to interesting tidbits about the countries and regions where French is spoken.

The audio CD that comes with this book gives you the opportunity to listen to real French speakers so you can get a better understanding of what French sounds like. This icon marks the book text that you can find on the CD. If you're using a digital version of this book, go to http://booksupport.wiley.com to download the audio tracks.

Where to Go from Here

Learning a language is all about jumping in and giving it a try — no matter how bad your pronunciation is at first. So make the leap! Start at the beginning, pick a chapter that interests you, or listen to a few dialogues on the CD. Before long, you'll be able to respond **Oui !** (wee!) (*Yes!*) when people ask **Parlez-vous français ?** (pahr-ley vooh frahN-sey?) (*Do you speak French?*).

If you've never been exposed to French before, you may want to read the chapters in Book I before you tackle the later chapters. Book I gives you some of the basics that you need to know about the language, such as some key expressions and words, how to pronounce the various sounds, and the fundamentals of French sentence structure.

Book I

Speaking in Everyday Settings

In this book . . .

You have to start somewhere, but we bet you know a lot more French than you realize. Don't think so? Then check out Chapter 1 and see how many French words and idioms you already use. In this book, we warm you up with the basics of pronunciation and parts of speech. Then we engage you in some French small talk and place you in common situations where you pick up the language quite naturally.

Here are the contents of Book I at a glance:

Chapter 1

Warming Up with Some French Fundamentals

In This Chapter

▶ Looking at French words related to English

▶ Exploring pronunciation patterns

▶ Noting differences in Canadian French

*L*earning a new language can be challenging. Not only do you need to pick up a whole new vocabulary, but you also need to twist your head around different grammar rules and twist your tongue — and ears — around different pronunciation rules. But here's a little news that may make the task seem a little less daunting: You already know quite a few French words and expressions. How? Because the English language has borrowed many French words and expressions, and French has absorbed some English words, too.

In this chapter, you explore some French words and phrases that have the same spellings and meanings as their English counterparts as well as words that are close in spelling and meaning. But not every word that resembles an English word shares its meaning, so we also tell you which words to watch out for. In addition, we include some French expressions that you probably already know and understand. We also cover pronunciation so you can accustom your ear, tongue, and brain to the French spoken in Europe (France, Belgium, Luxembourg, Monaco, and Switzerland) as well as the French that's uniquely Canadian.

Starting with What You Already Know

With just a narrow stretch of water between them, the people of England and France have historically been very close, even if they weren't always the friendly allies they are today. In fact, French was the language of the English court for a very long time. The Normans who invaded England in 1066 with William the Conqueror were French, as were some of the most prominent people in English history. French became the language of the nobility after

William took the English throne and didn't lose its prestige until the Hundred Years' War in the 14th and 15th centuries.

What does this have to do with your learning French? Well, today, about 35 percent of English vocabulary is of French origin, so you already know an impressive amount of French, whether you realize it or not. The only pitfall is that English words sometimes have different meanings from their French counterparts and almost certainly have different pronunciations.

Friendly allies: The perfect matches

Several French words are spelled the same and have the same meanings as their English counterparts. The only thing that may be different is the pronunciation (for pronunciation guidelines, check the later section "Practicing Some Basic Pronunciation"). Take a look at these **bons alliés** (bohN zah-lyey) (*friendly allies*). The first two examples are adjectives, and the rest are nouns (**le**, **la**, and **l'** mean *the*):

- **excellent** (ehk-seh-lahN)
- **important** (aN-pohr-tahN)
- **le bureau** (luh bew-roh)
- **le client** (luh klee-yahN)
- **le concert** (luh kohN-sehr)
- **la condition** (lah kohN-dee-syohN)
- **le courage** (luh kooh-razh)
- **le cousin** (luh kooh-zaN)
- **la culture** (lah kewl-tewr)
- **le garage** (luh gah-razh)
- **le guide** (luh geed)
- **le moment** (luh moh-mahN)
- **la nation** (lah nah-syohN)
- **l'orange** (f) (loh-rahNzh)
- **le parent** (luh pah-rahN)
- **la question** (lah kehs-tyohN)
- **la radio** (lah rah-dyoh)

 ✔ **le restaurant** (luh rehs-toh-rahN)

 ✔ **la route** (lah rooht)

 ✔ **le sport** (luh spohr)

 ✔ **la surprise** (lah sewr-preez)

Kissing cousins: A clear resemblance

Some French words, although not identical in spelling to their English counterparts, look similar. Sometimes the resemblance is just obvious. For example, the French word **succès** means *success,* and the French word **adresse** means *address.*

Changing part of a French word sometimes gives you its English equivalent or at least something very close to it. If the change works, you don't have to waste time looking up those words in a dictionary. Try the following rules:

 ✔ Change the **-ique** ending of a French word to *-ic:* **fantastique** → *fantastic,* **musique** → *music*

 ✔ Change the **ê** in the French word to *eas* or *es:* **fête** → *feast,* **forêt** → *forest*

 ✔ Change the **-ment** ending of a French word to *-ly:* **probablement** → *probably,* **sérieusement** → *seriously*

 ✔ Change the **-té** ending of the French word to *-ty:* **charité** → *charity,* **liberté** → *liberty*

 ✔ Change the **-aire** ending of the French word to *-ary:* **exemplaire** → *exemplary,* **dromadaire** → *dromedary*

 ✔ Change the **-eur** ending of a French word to *-or* in professions: **acteur** → *actor,* **professeur** → *professor*

 ✔ Change the **-ie** ending of a French noun to *y* or *c:* **comédie** → *comedy,* **magie** → *magic* (noun)

 ✔ Change the **-que** ending of a French noun to *c* or *ck:* **banque** → *bank,* **chèque** → *check*

Here are some words that fit into the kissing-cousins category:

 ✔ **nécessaire** (ney-sey-sehr) (*necessary*)

 ✔ **ordinaire** (ohr-dee-nehr) (*ordinary*)

 ✔ **le kiosque** (luh kyuhhsk) (*kiosk*)

 ✔ **l'aéroport** (m) (lah-ey-roh-pohr) (*airport*)

- **la lampe** (lah lahmp) (*lamp*)
- **l'allée** (f) (lah-ley) (*alley*)
- **la lettre** (lah leh-truh) (*letter*)
- **l'Américain** (m) (lah-mey-ree-kaN) (*American*); **l'Américaine** (f) (lah-mey-ree-kehn) (*American — female*)
- **la mémoire** (lah mey-mwahr) (*memory*)
- **l'âge** (m) (lahzh) (*age*)
- **le miroir** (luh mee-rwahr) (*mirror*)
- **l'artiste** (m/f) (lahr-teest) (*artist*)
- **la nationalité** (lah nah-syoh-nah-lee-tey) (*nationality*)
- **la cathédrale** (lah kah-tey-drahl) (*cathedral*)
- **la classe** (lah klahs) (*class*)
- **le papier** (luh pah-pyey) (*paper*)
- **la chambre** (lah shahN-bruh) (*chamber, bedroom*)
- **le poème** (luh poh-ehm) (*poem*)
- **la démocratie** (lah dey-moh-krah-see) (*democracy*)
- **le sénateur** (luh sey-nah-tuhr) (*senator*)

Sometimes a French word is used in English with a slightly different meaning, but with a little reasoning, you can still figure out what it means in the context of the sentence. For example, *matinee* in English refers to a daytime or early show at the movies or at the theater. In French, **la matinée** (lah mah-tee-ney) means *morning,* which is, of course, the early part of a day.

False friends: Deceptive lookalikes

Some French words are **faux amis** (foh zah-mee) (*false friends*) — they look similar to English words, but they don't have the same meaning. Misusing these words can cause a lot of confusion. For example, if you tell people that your young adult son or daughter is in **collège** (koh-lehzh), they'll probably look at you strangely, because the French word **collège** means *middle school.* You use the French word **l'université** (f) (lew-nee-vehr-see-tey) when you want to say *college.*

The following list shows some of these easy-to-confuse words:

- ✔ **actuellement** (ahk-tew-ehl-mahN): This word means *now*, not *actually*. The French word for *actually* is **en fait** (ahN feht).

- ✔ **assister à** (ah-sees-tey ah): This word means *to attend*, not *to assist*. The French word for *to assist* is **aider** (ey-dey).

- ✔ **attendre** (ah-tahN-druh): This word means *to wait for*, not *to attend*. The French word for *to attend* is **assister à** (ah-sees-tey ah).

- ✔ **la bague** (lah bahg): This word means *ring* (the kind you wear on your finger), not *bag*. The French word for *bag* is **le sac** (luh sahk).

- ✔ **blesser** (bleh-sey): This word means *to wound* or *to hurt*. The French word for *to bless* is **bénir** (bey-neer).

- ✔ **la cave** (lah kahv): The word **cave** means *cellar* in French. The word for *cave* is **la grotte** (lah gruhht).

- ✔ **formidable** (fohr-mee-dah-bluh): This word means *wonderful* or *tremendous*, not *fearsome* or *daunting*. To say *formidable* in French, you use the word **redoutable** (ruh-dooh-tah-bluh).

- ✔ **la lecture** (lah lehk-tuhr): This word means *a reading*, as in a reading of Balzac's novels. The word for *lecture* is **la conférence** (lah kohN-fey-rahNs).

- ✔ **la librairie** (lah lee-brey-ree): This word means *bookstore*, not *library*. The French word for *library* is **la bibliothèque** (lah bee-blee-oh-tehk).

- ✔ **la place** (lah plahs): This word means *square*, *seat at the theater*, or *seat on the bus*, not *place*. The French word for *place* is **le lieu** (luh lyuh) or **l'endroit** (m) (lahN-drwah).

- ✔ **rester** (reh-stey): This word means *to stay* or *to remain*, not *to rest*. The French word for *to rest* is **se reposer** (suh ruh-poh-zey).

- ✔ **sympathique** (saN-pah-teek): This word means *nice*. To say *sympathetic* in French, you say **compatissant(e)** (kohN-pah-tee-sahN[t]).

- ✔ **la veste** (lah vehst): This word means *jacket* in French, not *vest* or *waistcoat*. The French word for *vest* is **le gilet** (luh zhee-leh).

If a French word looks like something you know but makes no sense, guess at another meaning within the context.

French words borrowed from English

English isn't the only language that has nicked a few words. French has borrowed many words from English and continues to do so — in spite of the loud protest by purists, who condemn this trend as a sign of cultural contamination and name this shameful mix **franglais** (frahN-gleh). Here's a list of some of the terms borrowed from English and absorbed into the French language. Note the different pronunciations:

- **cool** (koohl)
- **le budget** (luh bewd-zheh)
- **le business** (luh beez-nehs)
- **le camping** (luh kahN-peeng)
- **le chewing-gum** (luh shweeng-guhhm)
- **le fast food** (luh fahst foohd)
- **le hamburger** (luh ahm-boohr-guhr)
- **le jet set** (luh jeht seht)
- **le job** (luh johb); **la job** [Québec] (lah johb)
- **le manager** (luh mah-nah-zhehr)
- **le marketing** (luh mahr-kuh-teeng)
- **le parking** (luh pahr-keeng)
- **le shopping** (luh shoh-peeng)
- **le steak** (luh stehk)
- **le week-end** (luh wee-kehnd)
- **le podcasting** (luh puhhd-kahs-teeng)
- **l'e-mail** (lee-mail)
- **l'iPad** (lee-pahd)
- **l'iPhone** (lee-fuhhn)

Talkin' the Talk

Listen to this conversation between two young French people making plans for the weekend. They use several words borrowed from English. (Track 3)

Thomas: **Sylvie, qu'est-ce que tu fais ce week-end ?**
seel-vee, kehs kuh tew fey suh wee-kehnd?
Sylvie, what are you doing this weekend?

Sylvie: **Oh, du shopping probablement. Tu veux venir avec moi ?**
oh, dew shoh-peeng proh-bah-bluh-mahN. tew vuh vuh-neer ah-vehk mwah?
Oh, I'll probably go shopping. Do you want to come with me?

Thomas: **Okay, cool. Et après, on va aller manger dans un fast-food.**
oh-keh, koohl. ey ah-preh, ohN vah ah-ley mahN-zhay dahN zhuN fahst-food.
Okay, cool. And afterward, we'll go eat in a fast food place.

Sylvie: **J'espère qu'on va trouver un parking !**
zheh-spehr kohN vah trooh-vey uhN pahr-keeng!
I hope we'll be able to find a parking place.

Thomas: **Pendant la matinée, pour sûr ! Plus tard, ce n'est pas certain.**
pahN-dahN lah-mah-tee-ney, poohr sewr! plew tahr, suh ney pah sehr-taN.
In the morning, for sure! Later, it's not certain.

Sylvie: **Au lieu de conduire en auto, on peut prendre l'autobus.**
oh lyuh duh kohN-dweer ahN noh-toh, ohN puh prahN-druh loh-toh-bews.
Instead of driving, we can take the bus.

Thomas: **Excellente idée ! J'ai un article de magazine sur l'environnement à te montrer.**
eyk-sey-lahN tee-dey! zhey uhN nahr-tee-kluh duh mah-gah-zeen sewr lahN-vee-roh-nuh-mahN ah tuh mohN-trey.
Excellent idea! I have a magazine article on the environment to show you.

Sylvie: **Super ! Rendez-vous à l'arrêt d'autobus, Boulevard Jean Jaurès, dans dix minutes !**
sew-pehr! rahN-dey-vooh ah lah-rey doh-toh-bews, booh-luh-vahr zhahN zhoh-reys, dahN dee mee-newt!
Super! Let's meet at the bus stop, Boulevard Jean Jaurès, in ten minutes!

Thomas:	**Je finis de vérifier mes e-mails et j'arrive. Attends-moi !**
	zhuh fee-nee duh vey-ree-fee-ey mey zee-meyl ey zhah-reev. ah-tahN-mwah!
	I'll finish checking e-mails, and I'll be there. Wait for me!

Practicing Some Basic Pronunciation

Whenever anyone hears a foreign language spoken at normal speed, the words — which don't make sense to begin with — create a muddle of sounds almost impossible to reproduce. One of the hardest parts of speaking French is overcoming your fear of not sounding French. After you overcome this fear of sounding funny, however, the rest can be fun. To that end, this section includes the information you need to know to pronounce French correctly.

Knowing the French alphabet

The French alphabet has the same 26 letters as the English alphabet. Of course, the names of most of the letters are pronounced differently. Table 1-1 lists the letters and gives you their names in French, which you may find useful if you have to spell your name over the phone or write down an address. You can hear the French alphabet on Track 1.

Table 1-1		The French Alphabet	
Letter	*Pronunciation*	*Letter*	*Pronunciation*
A	ah	N	ehn
B	bey	O	oh
C	sey	P	pey
D	dey	Q	kew
E	uh	R	ehr
F	ehf	S	ehs
G	zhey	T	tey
H	ahsh	U	ew
I	ee	V	vey
J	zhee	W	dooh-bluh vey

Letter	Pronunciation	Letter	Pronunciation
K	kah	X	eeks
L	ehl	Y	ee-grehk
M	ehm	Z	zehd

Letter perfect: Sounding French

French is a Romance language — and that's *Romance* as in Ancient Rome, not love. *Romance languages,* which also include Spanish, Italian, Romanian, and Portuguese, share the same origin and thus the same characteristics. One of the most important characteristics of the Romance languages is that their sound is based mostly on vowels, unlike the Anglo-Saxon languages (English and German), which are based on consonants.

The emphasis on vowels helps give French its soft, smooth, even, and musical character. French words certainly contain consonants, but compared to the consonants in English, French consonants are much softer — and at the ends of words, they often aren't pronounced at all. Read on to find out how to pronounce French vowels and consonants.

The upcoming tables, which help you pronounce French sounds, include English words where the French and English pronunciations are the same or nearly so. However, French also includes sounds that don't exist in English. In those cases, we give you tips on how to pronounce the particular sound.

The vowel sounds

French vowel sounds, which you see in Table 1-2, are the most difficult for English-speakers to pronounce. They're shorter than in English and usually end a syllable. Almost all of them have an English equivalent.

Table 1-2		French Vowel Sounds	
French	**Symbol**	**As in English**	**French Word**
a â à	ah	c<u>a</u>rd	**la tasse** (lah tahs) (*cup*) **la pâtisserie** (lah pah-tees-ree) (*pastry shop*) **là-bas** (lah-bah) (*over there*)
e eu	uh	d<u>u</u>ll (approximate)	**le petit** (luh puh-tee) (*little one*) **la fleur** (lah fluhr) (*flower*)

(continued)

Table 1-2 *(continued)*

French	Symbol	As in English	French Word
é ez er	ey	m<u>ay</u>	**les cafés** (m) (ley kah-fey) (*coffee houses*) **le nez** (luh ney) (*nose*) **parler** (pahr-ley) (*to speak*)
è ê ai ei et	eh	s<u>e</u>t	**la mère** (lah mehr) (*mother*) **la fenêtre** (lah fuh-neh-truh) (*window*) **clair** (klehr) (*clean, light-colored*) **la neige** (lah nehzh) (*snow*) **le secret** (luh suh-kreh) (*secret*)
i î y	ee	f<u>ee</u>t	**vite** (veet) (*quickly*) **le gîte** (luh zheet) (*shelter*) **le/les pays** (luh/ley pey-ee) (*country/ countries*)
o ô au eau	oh	b<u>oa</u>t	**le mot** (luh moh) (*word*) **les côtes** (f) (ley koht) (*ribs*) **aujourd'hui** (oh-zhoohr-dwee) (*today*) **l'eau** (f) (loh) (*water*)
o	uhh	l<u>o</u>ve	**la pomme** (lah puhhm) (*apple*) **les bottes** (f) (ley buhht) (*boots*)
ou où	ooh	y<u>ou</u>	**l'amour** (m) (lah-moohr) (*love*) **où** (ooh) (*where*)
oi oy	wah	<u>wa</u>tch	**la soie** (lah swah) (*silk*) **moyen** (mwah-yaN) (*average*)
u	ew	No English equivalent	**salut** (sah-lew) (*hello*)

 Represented in French by the letter **u**, the sound we write as *ew* doesn't exist in English, and getting it right takes a little practice. Here's a little trick to help you: Say *ee* with the tip of your tongue against your front bottom teeth. Then, keeping your tongue against your bottom teeth, round your lips. The sound coming out of your mouth is the French *ew*.

The mute e

When the letter **e** appears at the end of a word or between two consonants, it usually isn't pronounced; it's silent. For example, you don't pronounce the **e** at the end of **grande** (grahNd) (*tall*) or in the middle of **samedi** (sahm-dee) (*Saturday*).

The nasal sounds

The nasal sound, which is very common in French, is fairly easy to pronounce. Imagine you have a cold and pronounce the sounds *ah, oh,* and *un* (without the *n*) through your nose. They come out nasalized. Here's a phrase that contains all the nasal sounds in French: **Un bon vin blanc** (uhN bohN vaN blahN) (*a good white wine*).

Although English has no true equivalent for the French nasal sounds, we include some words in English that come close in Table 1-3. When you read these "equivalents," don't focus on the word itself; focus on how the vowel sound changes ever so slightly as your mouth prepares to make the *n* or *ng* sound that follows.

Book I

Speaking in Everyday Settings

Table 1-3		**French Nasal Sounds**	
French	*Symbol*	*Approximate English Equivalent*	*French Word*
an **am** **en** **em**	ahN	p<u>o</u>nd	**grand** (grahN) (*big, large*) **ambitieux** (ahN-bee-syuh) (*ambitious*) **l'enfant** (m/f) (lahN-fahN) (*child*) **l'employé(e)** (m/f) (lahN-plwah-yey) (*employee*)
un	uhN	<u>u</u>ncle	**brun** (bruhN) (*brown*)
ain **in** **aim** **im**	aN	sl<u>a</u>ng	**le pain** (luh paN) (*bread*) **le matin** (luh mah-taN) (*morning*) **la faim** (lah faN) (*hunger*) **impossible** (aN-poh-see-bluh) (*impossible*)
oin	waN	tw<u>a</u>ng	**loin** (lwaN) (*far*)
ien	yaN	<u>Ya</u>nkee	**le chien** (luh shyaN) (*dog*)
on **om**	ohN	wr<u>o</u>ng	**bon** (bohN) (*good*) **le nom** (luh nohN) (*name*)

Consonants

French consonants are pronounced almost like in English, except you don't linger on them; let them explode and move on to the vowel that follows. Because the consonants are said so quickly, you need to articulate them clearly; otherwise, they get lost and the word is hard to understand.

The French **r** often scares English-speakers, but don't be intimidated. You just have to pronounce it with your throat. Imagine that you've got something stuck in your throat and you're trying to get it out, but make the sound as soft and gentle as you can.

The consonants at the end of a word aren't usually pronounced. Consider these examples: **l'argent** (m) (lahr-zhahN) (*money*), **vingt** (vaN) (*twenty*), and **les fruits** (ley frwee) (*fruit*). Of course, this rule has some exceptions. A letter **c**, **r**, **f**, or **l** at the end of a word usually *is* pronounced (think of the word *careful* to help you remember). Here are some examples of these consonants: **chic** (sheek) (*chic, stylish*), **neuf** (nuhf) (*nine, new*), **cher** (shehr) (*dear, expensive*), and **avril** (ah-vreel) (*April*).

French has two different **h**'s: the *mute* **h** and the *aspirated* **h** — neither of which you pronounce. We discuss the difference between these **h**'s in the later section "The liaison."

Table 1-4 lists some consonants whose sounds in French can change, depending on the vowel or the consonant that follows. Also note that the letter **s** is pronounced as an *s* at the beginning of a word, but it's pronounced as a *z* when it's between two vowels.

Table 1-4	Tricky French Consonants		
French Letter	*Symbol*	*As in English*	*French Word*
c (in front of **a, o, u**)	k	<u>c</u>ollege	**le collège** (luh koh-lehzh) (*middle school*)
c (in front of **e, i**) **ç** (in front of **a, o, u**)	s	<u>s</u>ole	**le ciel** (luh syehl) (*sky*) **le garçon** (luh gahr-sohN) (*boy*)
ch	sh	<u>sh</u>ip	**le chapeau** (luh shah-poh) (*hat*)
g (in front of **a, o, u**) **gu** (in front of **e** and **i**)	g	<u>g</u>reed	**le gâteau** (luh gah-toh) (*cake*) **la guerre** (lah gehr) (*war*) **la guitare** (lah gee-tahr) (*guitar*)
g (in front of **e, i**) **j**	zh	lei<u>s</u>ure	**le genou** (luh zhuh-nooh) (*knee*) **le jour** (luh zhoohr) (*day*)
gn	ny	ca<u>ny</u>on	**la montagne** (lah mohN-tah-nyuh) (*mountain*)

French Letter	Symbol	As in English	French Word
s (at the beginning of a word) **ss** (between two vowels)	s	<u>s</u>ole	**le soleil** (luh soh-lehy) (*sun*) **le poisson** (luh pwah-sohN) (*fish*)
s (between two vowels)	z	civili<u>z</u>ation	**la civilisation** (lah see-vee-lee-zah-syohN) (*civilization*)

Accent marks

French has five accent marks, or *diacritical marks,* as grammarians like to call them. The accent affects only the letter on which it stands, and even then, it doesn't change the pronunciation unless the letter is an **e** or a **c** (refer to Tables 1-2 and 1-4 for basic pronunciation of vowels and consonants).

The accent mark can change the pronunciation of the letter or simply distinguish one word from another. In both cases, omitting an accent mark is like misspelling a word. The following list explains each of the five French accent marks:

- ✐ **l'accent aigu** (lahk-sahN tey-gew) (*the sharp accent*): The accent mark ´ appears only over the letter e. é. Its sound closely resembles the *a* in the word *take:* **le café** (luh kah-fey) (*coffee, café*).

- ✐ **l'accent grave** (lahk-sahN grahv) (*the grave accent*): The accent mark ` can appear over *e, a,* or *u:* **è, à, ù**. However, it affects sound only in the letter *e.* The **è** is an open *eh* sound, as in the English word *set* or in the French word **la mère** (lah mehr) (*mother*).

  Over the letters *a* and *u,* this accent distinguishes between two words otherwise spelled the same. For example, the word **à** (ah) is a preposition meaning *to, in,* or *at.* Without the accent, **a** (ah) is a form of the verb **avoir** (ah-vwahr) and means *has.* The accent plays a similar role with the letter *u.* The word **où** (ooh) means *where,* but the word **ou** (ooh) means *or.*

- ✐ **l'accent circonflexe** (lahk-sahN seehr-kohN-flehks) (*the circumflex accent*): When the accent mark ^ appears over *a, e, i, o,* or *u,* it represents a letter (usually an **s**) that was dropped from the French word centuries ago but that may still remain in the related English word. Here are some examples: **l'hôpital** (m) (loh-pee-tahl) (*hospital*), **le château** (luh shah-toh) (*castle, chateau*), **la forêt** (lah foh-reh) (*forest*), and **l'intérêt** (m) (laN-tey-reh) (*interest*). Over an *e,* this hat-like accent mark changes the sound of the vowel from *uh* to *eh* — the same sound as **è** but somewhat elongated.

✔ **le tréma** (luh trey-mah) (*dieresis*): The accent mark ¨ indicates that back-to-back vowels are pronounced separately from each other. Check out the following words: **naïf** (nah-eef) (*naïve*), **Noël** (noh-ehl) (*Christmas*).

✔ **la cédille** (lah sey-deey) (*the cedilla*) or **c cédille** (sey sey-deey) (*c cedilla*): This accent appears only under the letter *c* (**ç**). The cedilla indicates that you pronounce the *c* as an *s*. If the letter *c* does not have the cedilla under it and is followed by *a, o,* or *u,* then you pronounce it as you would the letter *k,* as in the English word *can.* Check out this French command: **Commençons** (koh-mahN-sohN) (*Let's begin*).

Making it musical: Stringing together words and phrases

French is a rhythmic, flowing language. French doesn't stress one syllable over another like English does. Every syllable in a word or group of words is pronounced with the same emphasis, except for the last syllable in a phrase. That last syllable isn't louder, but it's a little longer.

The musicality of the French language also comes from the effects of **liaison** (lyey-zohN) (linking sounds from juxtaposed words) and *elision* (eliminating the sound of a vowel to avoid two similar repeated vowel sounds), which allow a continuous flow of utterances. We discuss all these sound effects in the following sections.

Don't stress

In French, every syllable is of equal importance in volume and stress — hence, the absence of stressed syllables in the pronunciations in this book. For example, in the English word *photography* (fuh-*tahg*-ruh-fee), you say the second syllable with more force. But in the French word **la photographie** (lah foh-toh-grah-fee) (*photography*), you don't stress any one particular syllable.

Although the volume doesn't change from syllable to syllable, French does elongate some vowel sounds: That emphasis is on the last syllable in a group of words. In the sentence **J'aime la photographie** (*I like photography*), there's a slight elongation of **-phie**.

In words that have similar spellings in French and in English, remembering to unstress the syllable you're used to pronouncing with more force may take quite a bit of practice. It's like ironing a stubborn pleat out of a pair of trousers!

The liaison

When listening to a French conversation, have you ever thought that it sounded like a great big, long word? Probably. That's because of a French phenomenon called the **liaison**. **Faire la liaison** (fehr lah lyey-zohN) (*to make* *a liaison*) means linking the last consonant of a word — which is usually unpronounced — with the vowel that begins the next word. Check out these examples:

> **C'est un petit appartement.** (sey tuhN puh-tee tah-pahr-tuh-mahN.) (*It's a small apartment.*) Here, the **t** from **c'est** links to the beginning of **un**, and the final **t** from **petit** links to the beginning of **appartement**.

> **Vous êtes mon ami depuis six ans.** (vooh zeht mohN nah-mee duh-pwee see zahN.) (*You have been my friend for six years.*) In this sentence, the **s** from **vous** links to the beginning of **êtes**, the **n** from **mon** links to **ami**, and the **x** from **six** links to **ans**.

A **liaison** never appears with the conjunction **et** (ey) (*and*). In **un livre et un crayon** (uhN lee-vruh ey uhN kreh-yohN) (*a book and a pencil*), for example, you don't pronounce the **t** in **et**, even though the word **un** begins with a vowel.

Whether you form a **liaison** with a word that begins with **h** depends on whether the **h** is *mute* or *aspirated*. The **h** isn't pronounced in either case. Here are the differences:

- **Mute *h:*** With a mute **h**, you treat the word like it begins with a vowel, so you make a **liaison**. For example, to say *the men,* you say **les hommes** (ley zuhhm), pronouncing the **s** that appears at the end of **les**.

- **Aspirated *h:*** No **liaison** occurs between the article **les** and a word that begins with an aspirated **h**, like in **les héros** (ley ey-roh) (*the heroes*). If the **liaison** were permitted here, **les héros** would sound like **les zéros** (ley zey-roh) (*the zeros*). The aspirated **h** still doesn't make a sound, but it acts like a consonant in that it prevents **liaison**.

  Aspirated **h**'s happen infrequently. Here's a list of some common words that begin with an aspirated **h** in French: **le homard** (luh oh-mahr) (*lobster*), **le handicapé/la handicapée** (luh/lah ahN-dee-kah-pey) (*handicapped person*), **les haricots** (ley ah-ree-koh) (*beans*), **les hors-d'œuvre** (ley ohr-duh-vruh) (*hors d'oeuvres, appetizers*).

  Not only do you avoid making a **liaison** with an aspirated **h**, but you also don't form contractions (elisions). You'll know you've encountered a word that has an aspirated **h** when you see or hear the singular definite article **le** or **la** rather than **l'** before singular a word that starts with **h**. See the next section for details.

The elision: Forming contractions

An *elision* occurs when a word ending with an **e** or an **a** is followed by a word that starts with a vowel or a mute **h**. The first **e** or **a** disappears and is replaced by an apostrophe. This rule contributes to the easy flow of the French language. Usually only articles or pronouns are elided. The most common words that require elision are **je** (*I*), **me** (*me*), **te** (*you* singular, used as an object), **le** (*the/it/him*), **la** (*the/it/her*), and **que** (*that*).

Here are some examples showing elisions:

je + **aime** → **j'aime** (zhehm) (*I like*)

je + **habite** → **j'habite** (zhah-beet) (*I live*)

la + **école** → **l'école** (ley-kuhhl) (*the school*)

le or la + **enfant** → **l'enfant** (lahN-fahN) (*the child*)

la + **histoire** → **l'histoire** (lee-stwahr) (*the story, history*)

If a word starts with an aspirated **h**, the words remain separate — you don't use elision. For example, **le hockey** (luh oh-keh) (*hockey*) doesn't become **l'hockey**. See the preceding section for info on mute and aspirated **h**'s.

Exploring Canadian French

The French language in Canada, especially Québec, is unique in the world. This is due to the turbulent history of the French settlers in Canada starting in the late 1500s and early 1600s. When the French lost their territories called **Nouvelle-France** (new-vehl frahNs) (*New France*) to the English in the eighteenth century, the split had a lasting effect on the language. Many words from that time later became obsolete in France but remained in use in Canada. On the other hand, the language of the people in those territories encountered a strong English influence. And in the twentieth century, French-Canadians distinguished themselves with their efforts to go back to their roots by restoring the authenticity of their language.

In this section, we explore how this interplay of old and new, French and English has resulted in the unique vocabulary and sounds of Canadian French.

Looking at unique French-Canadian words and phrases

The French spoken by approximately 7 million French-Canadians (5 million in the province of Québec) has developed unique features over time. It comprises seventeenth-century French words, words borrowed from English, *anglicisms* (English words made to sound French or translated literally into French), and original French words created to reflect emerging concepts. Here are some characteristics of Canadian French:

✔ **Historic French words:** Canadian French uses old French words, such as **dispendieux** (dee-spahN-dyuh) (*expensive*) and **char** (shahr) (*car*), that have been lost in France and other French-speaking regions.

✔ **New words:** French-Canadian speakers have created French words for new concepts, whereas their European counterparts just used the English words in their French. For example, French-Canadians prefer the word **courriel** (kooh-ryehl) (a blend of the words **courrier** and **électronique** — *electronic mail*) to the word **e-mail** (ee-meyl). French-Canadians also invented **magasinage** (mah-gah-zee-nahzh), which comes from the French noun **magasin** (mah-gah-zaN) (*store*), for the idea of shopping.

✔ **French-English mash-ups:** Canadian French includes many expressions that combine French and English words, such as **C'est du fun** (sey dew fuhn) (*It's fun*). This expression is **C'est amusant** (sey tah-mew-zahN) in other French-speaking regions.

✔ **Literal translations of English idioms:** Canadian French uses expressions that are direct translations from English, such as **le chien-chaud** (luh shyaN-shoh) (*hot dog*). That would be **la saucisse** (lah soh-sees) or **le hot dog** (luh oht-dohg) elsewhere.

✔ **French-sounding English words:** Canadian French borrowed English words and made them sound French, as in **l'Arena** (lah-rey-nah) (*the skating rink*) and **checker** (tsheh-key) (*to check*).

✔ **An extra là:** French-Canadian speakers often add the syllable **là** (which adds no particular meaning to the sentence) after many words, especially at the end of a sentence, as in the phrase **C'est bien ça là** (sey byaN sah lah) (*that's it*). The word just adds a little emphasis.

Speaking French with a Canadian accent

The sound of Canadian French tends to differ from standard French French in the following ways:

✔ Canadian French is less clearly articulated, with less lip movement. The clear *ah* sound from standard French may border on an *aN* sound in Canadian French.

✔ It has a slower pace than standard French.

✔ It includes some stress on syllables, probably picked up from English.

In addition, some change in consonant sounds occurs:

✔ The **t** and **d** sounds shift to *ts*.

✔ Both **k** and **g** followed by **i** or **e** become *palatalized* (pronounced with the tongue touching the *hard palate*, or roof of the mouth).

✔ Nasal vowels tend to lose the nasal element.

Play Track 2 to hear the alphabet with a French-Canadian pronunciation.

Talkin' the Talk

Listen to the dialogue between Margie and Marc. Note the stretched-out vowel sounds and the slower pace in the dialogue. (Track 4)

Margie: **Dis, Marc, qu'est-ce que tu vas faire en fin de semaine ?**
          dee, mahrk, kehs kuh tew vah fehr ahN faNd suh-mehn?
          Hey, Marc, what are you going to do this weekend?

Marc: **Je vais voir mes vieux chums Yves et Michael.**
          zhvey vwahr mey vyuh tchahNm eev ey mee-kah-ehl.
          I'm going to see my old friends Yves and Michael.

Margie: **Ah ouai, tes compagnons de hockey !**
          Ah wey, tey kohM-pah-nyohN duh oh-key.
          Oh yeah, your hockey pals!

Marc: **C'est bien ça là. On va faire une partie de hockey à l'Aréna et manger des chiens-chauds.**
          sey byaN sah lah. ohN vah fehr ewn pahr-tee duh oh-key ah lah-rey-nah ey mahN-zhey dey shyaN-shoh.
          That's it. We're going to play a hockey game at the skating rink and eat some hot-dogs.

Margie: **Moi, j'vais magasiner à Montréal.**
          mwa, zh-vey mah-gah-zee-ney ah mohN-rey-ahl.
          I'm going shopping in Montreal.

Marc: **C'est un peu dispendieux à Montréal, tu penses pas ?**
          sey tuhN puh dee-spahN-dyuh ah mohN-rey-ahl, tew pahNs pah?
          It's a little expensive in Montreal, don't you think?

Margie: **En ce moment, il y a des spéciaux. Je reçois des courriels à ce propos.**
          ahNs moh-mahN, eel ee ah dey spey-syoh. zhuh ruh-swah dey kooh-ryehl ah suh proh-poh.
          At the moment, there are sales. I receive e-mails about those.

Marc: **Ah ouai ! C'est plus de fun alors !**
          ah wey! sey plews duh fuhn ah-lohr!
          Oh yeah! It's more fun that way!

Chapter 2

Un, Deux, Trois: Numbers, Dates, and Times

• •

• •

Counting and being able to express and understand numbers are essential parts of everyday life. You need numbers when you reveal your age, buy food, read recipes, make sense of bus or train schedules, or ask for a movie ticket. One of the most important uses of numbers is to specify dates and time. How else would you keep track of appointments or plan visits and trips? In this chapter, we show you how to do all of that — use numbers, dates, and time — one step at the time.

Numbers: Counting Your Lucky Stars

In French, as in English, you have to distinguish cardinal numbers from ordinal numbers. You use cardinal numbers such as 1, 2, and 3 to indicate a number of inanimate objects or living beings. You use them in prices (as in 200 euros), in time (as in 2 o'clock), in phone numbers, in measurements, and in telling how many people are coming to your party. You need ordinal numbers to indicate the position or order of an event, object, or person relative to others — as in naming the first or second time you saw that movie, the fifth time someone called you, or the third person who arrived. With what follows, you can handle almost any number-related situation.

Cardinal numbers

Most of the time, you can use plain old cardinal numbers from 0 to around 100 to express the number of units of something: how much money you have in your wallet, how many hours you have to wait before your plane takes off, how many sheep you have to count before you fall asleep, and so on. Fortunately, French numbers follow a pattern, much like numbers in English.

Counting up to 20

The following list shows the numbers **un** (uhN) (*one*) through **vingt** (vaN) (*twenty*):

- 1 **un** (uhN)
- 2 **deux** (duh)
- 3 **trois** (trwah)
- 4 **quatre** (kah-truh)
- 5 **cinq** (saNk)
- 6 **six** (sees)
- 7 **sept** (seht)
- 8 **huit** (weet)
- 9 **neuf** (nuhf)
- 10 **dix** (dees)
- 11 **onze** (ohNz)
- 12 **douze** (doohz)
- 13 **treize** (trehz)
- 14 **quatorze** (kah-tohrz)
- 15 **quinze** (kaNz)
- 16 **seize** (sehz)
- 17 **dix-sept** (dee-seht)
- 18 **dix-huit** (deez-weet)
- 19 **dix-neuf** (deez-nuhf)
- 20 **vingt** (vaN)

The pronunciation of some numbers changes when the number is followed by a vowel, a mute **h** (check out the mute **h** in Chapter 1 of Book I), or a consonant:

✔ When a number ending in **-s** or **-x** is followed by a vowel or mute **h**: In these instances, the final **s** and **x** make a *z* sound: **deux enfants** (duh zahN-fahN) (*two children*) and **trois enfants** (trwah zahN-fahN) (*three children*), for example.

✔ When the numbers **six**, **huit**, and **dix** are followed by a consonant: The final consonants of these numbers aren't pronounced: **six livres** (see lee-vruh) (*six books*), **huit personnes** (wee pehr-suhhn) (*eight people*), and **dix films** (dee feelm) (*ten films*), for example.

✔ When the numbers **neuf** and **dix-neuf** are followed by a vowel or mute **h**: In these cases, the final **f** makes the *v* sound: **neuf artistes** (nuhv arh-teest) (*nine artists*), for example. The final **t** in **vingt** (20) is pronounced before another number, as in **vingt-cinq** (vaNt-saNk) (25).

Counting from 21 to 69

After you count to **vingt** (20), you're ready to go higher. After all, if you want to make a special purchase, like an exceptional bottle of wine, it will surely cost more than 20 euros!

You form the numbers 21 through 69 in French much as you do in English, counting up from each tens number until you hit the next tens number and then starting over. You use **et un** (*and one*) for numbers ending in 1 but use a hyphen to attach digits 2 through 9:

✔ 21 **vingt et un** (vaNt ey uhN)

✔ 22 **vingt-deux** (vahNt-duh)

✔ 23 **vingt-trois** (vahNt-trwah)

✔ 30 **trente** (trahNt)

✔ 31 **trente et un** (trahNt ey uhN)

✔ 32 **trente-deux** (trahNt-duh)

✔ 40 **quarante** (kah-rahNt)

✔ 41 **quarante et un** (kah-rahNt ey uhN)

✔ 42 **quarante-deux** (kah-rahNt-duh)

✔ 50 **cinquante** (saN-kahNt)

✔ 51 **cinquante et un** (saN-kahNt ey uhN)

✔ 52 **cinquante-deux** (saN-kahNt-duh)

✔ 60 **soixante** (swah-sahNt)

✔ 61 **soixante et un** (swah-sahNt ey uhN)

✔ 62 **soixante-deux** (swah-sahNt-duh)

Counting from 70 through 99

The number 70 in French is 60 + 10. The number 71 is 60 + 11, 72 is 60 + 12, and so on until you get to 80. For example:

- 70 **soixante-dix** (swah-sahNt-dees)
- 71 **soixante et onze** (swah-sahN tey ohNz)
- 72 **soixante-douze** (swah-sahNt-doohz)

The number 80 is 4×20, although the word "times" isn't used; you instead say **quatre-vingts** (*four twenties*). The number 81 is $4 \times 20 + 1$, 82 is $4 \times 20 + 2$ and so on, until you get to 90, which is $4 \times 20 + 10$. The number 91 is $4 \times 20 + 11$. (Notice that you don't use the conjunction **et** in the number 81 and higher. Also when another number follows 80, the **s** in **vingt** is dropped.) Here are some examples:

- 80 **quatre-vingts** (kah-truh-vaN)
- 81 **quatre-vingt-un** (kah-truh-vaN-uhN)
- 82 **quatre-vingt-deux** (kah-truh-vaN-duh)
- 90 **quatre-vingt-dix** (kah-truh-vaN-dees)
- 91 **quatre-vingt-onze** (kah-truh-vaN-ohNz)
- 92 **quatre-vingt-douze** (kah-truh-vaN-doohz)

If you travel to Switzerland or to Belgium, you may be happy to know that those countries commonly use the old — and easier — forms of **septante** (sehp-tahNt) (70) and **nonante** (noh-naNt) (90) rather than the French **soixante-dix** and **quatre-vingt-dix**. Some parts of Switzerland use the forms **huitante** (wee-tahNt) or **octante** (ohk-tahNt) for 80.

Counting from 100 on up

After you hit 100, counting to a thousand or even hundreds of thousands is a breeze. Just indicate the number of hundreds or thousands and count up as you do in English. For example:

- 100 **cent** (sahN)
- 101 **cent-un** (sahN-uhN)
- 102 **cent-deux** (sahN-duh)
- 200 **deux cents** (duh sahN)
- 201 **deux cent un** (duh sahN uhN)

- 202 **deux cent deux** (duh sahN duh)
- 1,000 **mille** (meel)
- 2,000 **deux mille** (duh meel)
- 3,000 **trois mille** (trwah meel)
- 1,000,000 **un million** (uhN mee-lyohN)
- 1,000,000,000 **un milliard** (uhN mee-lyahr)

The French word **billion** (bee-lyohN) means 1,000,000,000,000 (*trillion*), not 1,000,000,000 (*billion*). If you want to say *billion,* use **milliard**.

In the preceding list, notice that you drop the **s** in **cents** when another number follows it. Also, the number **mille** doesn't use an **s**, even when it refers to several thousands. Finally, **un** doesn't precede **cent** or **mille** when you say *one hundred* or *one thousand*.

Ordinal numbers

Ordinal numbers are pretty important when you need to give or follow directions. To recognize ordinal numbers, remember that except for **premier** (m) (pruh-myey) (*first*) and **première** (f) (pruh-myehr) they all have **-ième** (ee-ehm) after the number — just like the *-th* ending in English. Also, English uses the superscript *th* (or *st* or *rd*) to indicate ordinal numbers (5th, for example), but in French, the superscript is the letter **e**: 9e, 4e, and so on.

The French word for *first* has both masculine and feminine forms. The word is **premier** when it accompanies a masculine noun, as in **premier film** (pruh-myey feelm) (*first movie*), and **première** when it accompanies a feminine noun, as in **première fois** (pruh-myehr fwa) (*first time*).

Table 2-1 lists the ordinal numbers from 1st through 20th, but you can go as high as you like. Here are the rules for forming ordinal numbers:

- If the cardinal number ends in an **-e**, drop the **-e** before adding **-ième**. For example, **quatre** becomes **quatrième** (kah-tree-ehm) (*fourth*), and **seize** becomes **seizième** (seh-zee-ehm) (*sixteenth*).
- For the number **cinq** (saNk), add a **u** before **-ième**: **cinquième** (sahN-kee-ehm) (*fifth*).
- For the number **neuf**, the **f** changes to **v**: **neuvième** (nuh-vee-ehm) (*ninth*).

Table 2-1		Ordinal Numbers from 1er through 20^e			
Abbrev.	*French*	*Pronunciation*	**Abbrev.**	*French*	*Pronunciation*
1^e	**premier** **première**	(pruh-myey) (pruh-myehr)	11^e	**onzième**	(ohN-zee-ehm)
2^e	**deuxième**	(duh-zee-ehm)	12^e	**douzième**	(dooh-zee-ehm)
3^e	**troisième**	(trwah-zee-ehm)	13^e	**treizième**	(treh-zee-ehm)
4^e	**quatrième**	(kah-tree-ehm)	14^e	**quatorzième**	(kah-tohr-zee-ehm)
5^e	**cinquième**	(saN-kee-ehm)	15^e	**quinzième**	(kaN-zee-ehm)
6^e	**sixième**	(see-zee-ehm)	16^e	**seizième**	(seh-zee-ehm)
7^e	**septième**	(seh-tee-ehm)	17^e	**dix-septième**	(dee-seh-tee-ehm)
8^e	**huitième**	(wee-tee-ehm)	18^e	**dix-huitième**	(dee-zwee-tee-ehm)
9^e	**neuvième**	(nuh-vee-ehm)	19^e	**dix-neuvième**	(deez-nuh-vee-ehm)
10^e	**dixième**	(dee-zee-ehm)	20^e	**vingtième**	(vaN-tee-ehm)

In France, the ground floor of a building is called the **rez-de-chaussée**. The first floor (**premier étage**) is one flight of stairs up. So when you take an elevator down to the lobby in a hotel or other building, don't press the first floor button; you'll end up at what Americans consider the second floor.

Approximating quantities

Sometimes you want to approximate the numbers instead of being exact. If you were speculating on someone's age, for example, you may say that a woman is fortyish or looks about 40. You can do the same in French by adding the suffix **-aine** (ehn) to the cardinal numbers. You do so only for **dix**, **douze**, **quinze**, **vingt**, **trente**, **quarante**, **cinquante**, **soixante**, and **cent**. Note that the **-x** ending of **dix** becomes **-z** before you add the suffix and that any cardinal number ending in **-e** loses the **-e**. Here are some examples:

- **dix** (*10*) → **une dizaine** (ewn dee-zehn) (*about 10*)
- **quinze** (*15*) → **une quinzaine** (ewn kaN-zehn) (*about 15*)
- **vingt** (*20*) → **une vingtaine** (ewn vaN-tehn) (*about 20*)
- **cent** (*100*) → **une centaine** (ewn sahN-tehn) (*about 100*)

Note that the French word **douzaine** is an approximation (*about a dozen*) rather than a definite dozen. **Dizaine** and **quinzaine** are much more common than **douzaine**.

To talk about an approximate quantity of something, add the preposition **de** (duh) (*of*) and the noun. Use the abbreviated form **d'** before a noun that begins with a vowel or a mute **h**:

> **Je voudrais une dizaine de croissants.** (zhuh vooh-drey ewn dee-zehn duh krwah-sahN.) (*I would like about 10 croissants.*)

> **Il y a une vingtaine d'étudiants dans la classe.** (eel ee ah ewn vahN-tehn dey-tew-dyahN dahN lah klahs.) (*There are about 20 students in the class.*)

You can refer to approximate numbers by using the words **à peu près** (ah puh preh) or **environ** (ahN-vee-rohN), both of which mean *approximately*. For example, **J'ai environ quatre-vingts livres dans mon bureau** (zhey ahN-vee-rohN kah-truh-vaN lee-vruh dahN mohN bew-roh.) (*I have approximately 80 books in my office*).

Talkin' the Talk

Take a look at this conversation between two young French siblings. They're quarreling over their collector's cards.

Jojo: **Suzie, où sont mes cartes de football ?**
sew-zee, ooh sohN mey kart duh fooht-buhhl?
Suzie, where are my football cards?

Suzie: **Oh, voilà trois cartes !**
oh, vwah-lah trwah kahrt!
Oh, there are 3 cards!

Jojo: **Comment ? J'ai une centaine de cartes !**
koh-mahN? zhey ewn sahN-tehn duh kahrt!
What? I have about 100 cards!

Suzie: **Je sais, mais moi, j'ai seulement ces trois cartes.**
zhuh sey, mey mwah, zhey suhl-mahN sey trwah kahrt.
I know, but I have only these 3 cards.

Jojo: **Je te prête une trentaine de mes cartes et tu en as trois ?**
Zhuh tuh preht ewn trahN-tehn duh mey kahrt ey tew ahN nah trwah?
I lend you about 30 cards and you have 3 of them?

Suzie:	**Oh ! Voilà encore une dizaine de cartes. Je crois que les autres sont dans ma chambre.**
	oh! vwah-lah ahN-kohr ewn dee-zehn duh kahrt. zhuh krwah kuh ley zoh-truh sohN dahN mah shahN-bruh.
	Oh! There are about 10 more cards. I think the rest are in my room.

Jojo:	**Tu crois ? Mes cartes doivent rester ensemble. C'est la centième fois que je te dis ça.**
	tew krwah? mey kahrt dwahv rey-stey ahN-sahN-bluh. sey lah sahN-tee-ehm fwah kuh zhuh tuh dee sah.
	You think? My cards have to stay together. This is the hundredth time I've told you that.

Suzie:	**Oh ! Écoute, c'est la première fois que tu me prêtes tes cartes !**
	oh! ey-koot, sey lah pruh-mee-ehr fwah kuh tew muh preht tey kahrt!
	Oh! Listen, this is the first time you've lent me your cards!

Jojo:	**Et la dernière fois aussi. Tu es impossible !**
	ey lah dehr-nee-ehr fwah oh-see. tew ey zaN-poh-see-bluh!
	And the last time, too. You are impossible!

Using the Calendar and Dates

France, the United States, and many other countries around the world use a similar calendar, one that has 7 days and 12 months. However, many countries present the date differently. In American English, the month comes first, followed by the day of the month, followed by the year. In French, the day of the month comes first, followed by the month, followed by the year. For example, French presents the date May 8, 2013, as **le 8 [huit] mai 2013 [deux mille treize]** (luh wee mey duh meel trehz), and writes it 8-5-2013. Imagine how embarrassing it would be if you were invited to an important event on 8-5-2013 and you showed up on August 5, 2013!

Even though a week has seven days, the French refer to a week as **huit jours** (wee zhoohr) (*8 days*) and to two weeks as **quinze jours** (kaNz zhoohr) (*15 days*). The reason is that if you count from Monday to Monday and you include both Mondays, you have 8 days; if you continue counting to the following Monday (the third Monday), you have 15 days.

Recounting the days of the week

On a French calendar, Monday is the first day of the week. The days of the week aren't capitalized:

- **lundi** (luhN-dee) (*Monday*)
- **mardi** (mahr-dee) (*Tuesday*)
- **mercredi** (mehr-kruh-dee) (*Wednesday*)
- **jeudi** (zhuh-dee) (*Thursday*)
- **vendredi** (vahN-druh-dee) (*Friday*)
- **samedi** (sahm-dee) (*Saturday*)
- **dimanche** (dee-mahNsh) (*Sunday*)

When referring to a particular day, state the day without an article: **Je travaille samedi** (zhuh trah-vahy sahm-dee) (*I work [this] Saturday*). But if you want to say *I work on Saturdays,* you have to place the definite article **le** (luh) (*the*) in front of the day of the week, like this: **Je travaille le samedi** (zhuh trah-vahy luh sahm-dee.) (*I work [on] Saturdays.*). Placing the definite article **le** in front of the day of the week is like adding an *s* to the day in English.

Knowing the names of the months

Just like the days of the week, the months of the year aren't capitalized in French. Here are the months in French:

- **janvier** (zhahN-vyey) (*January*)
- **février** (fey-vryey) (*February*)
- **mars** (mahrs) (*March*)
- **avril** (ah-vreel) (*April*)
- **mai** (mey) (*May*)
- **juin** (zhwaN) (*June*)
- **juillet** (zhwee-yeh) (*July*)
- **août** (ooht) (*August*)
- **septembre** (sehp-tahN-bruh) (*September*)
- **octobre** (ohk-tuhh-bruh) (*October*)
- **novembre** (noh-vahN-bruh) (*November*)
- **décembre** (dey-sahN-bruh) (*December*)

To say that something is happening in a certain month, you use the preposition **en** (ahN) (*in*) in front of the month. Here are some examples:

> **Mon anniversaire est en décembre.** (mohN nah-nee-vehr-sehr ey tahN dey-sahN-bruh.) (*My birthday is in December.*)

> **En janvier, je pars pour la Martinique.** (ahN zhaN-vyey, zhuh pahr poohr lah mahr-tee-neek.) (*In January, I leave for Martinique.*)

> **Je reviens en avril.** (zhuh ruh-vyaN ahN nah-vreel.) (*I'm coming back in April.*)

Setting specific dates

When expressing a specific date, use the following construction:

> **Le** + cardinal number + month + year

You use this formula to express all dates, except for the first of the month, when you use the ordinal number. Here are a couple of examples:

> **C'est le 6 [six] avril 2000 [deux mille].** (sey luh see zah-vreel duh meel.) (*It's April 6, 2000.*)

> **C'est le premier mai.** (sey luh pruh-myey mey.) (*It's the first of May.*)

Remembering the seasons

The seasons in French are masculine and, unlike in English, require the definite article:

- **le printemps** (luh praN-tahN) (*spring*)
- **l'été** (ley-tey) (*summer*)
- **l'automne** (loh-tuhhn) (*fall*)
- **l'hiver** (lee-vehr) (*winter*)

Pay attention to prepositions. To express *in the spring,* say **au printemps** (oh praN-tahN) (*in the spring*). But to say *in the summer, in the fall,* and *in the winter,* say **en été** (ahN ney-tey), **en automne** (ahN noh-tuhhn), and **en hiver** (ahN nee-vehr).

Talkin' the Talk

 Juliette is talking to her friend Corinne about her sister's upcoming wedding. (Track 5)

Juliette: **Ma sœur va se marier au printemps.**
mah suhr vah suh mah-ryey oh praN-tahN.
My sister is getting married in the spring.

Corinne: **Ah oui. Quand exactement ?**
ah wee. kahN tehg-zahk-tuh-mahN?
Oh, yes. When exactly?

Juliette: **Le 6 [six] avril.**
luh see zah-vreel.
April 6.

Corinne: **C'est quel jour ?**
sey kehl zhoohr?
What day is it?

Juliette: **C'est un samedi.**
sey tuhN sahm-dee.
It's a Saturday.

Corinne: **Combien de personnes avez-vous invitées ?**
kohN-byaN duh pehr-suhhn ah-vey-vooh aN-vee-tey?
How many people did you invite?

Juliette: **Une centaine de personnes.**
ewn sahN-tehn duh pehr-suhhn.
About 100 people.

Words to Know

ma sœur	mah suhr	my sister
se marier	suh mah-ryey	to get married
C'est quel jour ?	sey kehl zhoohr?	What day is it?
C'est un samedi.	sey tuhN sahm-dee.	It's a Saturday.
Quand exactement ?	kahN tehg-zahk-tuh-maN?	When exactly?
Quel jour ?	kehl zhoohr?	What day?

Celebrating holidays

Each French-speaking country has celebrations that come from the unique history and traditions of that country. Here are a few examples:

- **Maple syrup festivals:** Among French Canadians, celebrating around the old tradition **la cabane à sucre** (lah kah-bahn ah sew-kruh) (*sugar shack*) is still customary. When Canada was first being settled, **sirop d'érable** (see-roh dey-rah-bluh) (*maple syrup*) was much appreciated during the cold winter months, when you could invite friends and neighbors and cook everything imaginable with maple syrup. Today, people still gather for *sugaring off* parties or festivals in the spring. They head for the woods to tap maple trees for sap that they then boil down in **cabanes à sucre** to make maple syrup and maple sugar.

- **April Fool's Day:** In France, people celebrate April Fool's Day under the sign of a fish. That tradition goes back to 1564, when the French king Charles IX ruled that the celebration of the New Year would take place on January 1 rather than on April 1. Because April also marked the opening of fishing season, people started giving fake New Year's gifts — often fish — to their friends on the old holiday date. To this day, a favorite joke among French children is to pin a paper fish on someone's back without the other person's noticing and then shout "**poisson d'avril**" (pwah-sohN dah-vreel) (*April fish*).

- **Labor Day:** Not everyone in the world celebrates **La Fête du Travail** (lah feht dew trah-vay) (*Labor Day*) on the same day. Francophone Europe celebrates the day on May 1; people go out into the country and pick the first flowers of spring, usually **le muguet** (luh mew-guey) (*lily of the valley*).

✔ **Saints' days:** Another use of the word **fête** is based on Catholicism, which was predominant in France for many centuries. French calendars generally include a saint's name for each day of the year so that a person named Sandrine (sahN-dreen), for example, may celebrate her **fête** on Saint Sandrine's feast day. To wish Sandrine a happy saint's day, you say **bonne fête** (buhhn feht). Note, however, that French Canadians use **bonne fête** to wish someone a happy birthday as well as a happy saint's day. To wish someone a happy birthday in France, you say **bon anniversaire** (buhhn ah-nee-vehr-sehr).

✔ **Mardi Gras or Carnival: Mardi Gras** (mahr-dee grah) (*Fat Tuesday*) or **Carnaval** (kahr-nah-vahl) is known across the world. It's a huge celebration in New Orleans because of that region's French Cajun heritage, but many other francophone regions of the world also celebrate it with parades, street dancing, masked balls, and outrageous costumes.

In the province of Québec, **Carnaval** takes on a slightly different look with its **jeux de neige** (zhuh duh nehzh) (*snow games*), its **sculptures de glace** (skewl-tewr duh glahs) (*ice sculptures*), its **promenades en traîneau** (pruhhm-nahd ahN trey-noh) (*sleigh rides*), its **patinage artistique** (pah-tee-nahzh ahr-tees-teek) (*ice skating*), and especially its **Bonhomme Carnaval** (buhhn-uhhm kahr-nah-vahl) (*Carnaval snowman*), who is the symbol of the festivities during this joyous period of the year.

✔ **Christmas dinner:** In many French-speaking countries, folks celebrate Christmas Eve with a long **réveillon** (rey-vey-ohN), a dinner that features a multitude of courses. In Québec, this meal includes the **tourtière** (toohr-tyehr) (*meat pie*), while in France, it includes **la dinde** (lah daNd) (*turkey*). The essential ending to a proper **réveillon** is the famous **Bûche de Noël** (bewsh duh noh-ehl) (*Yule Log*), a delicious rolled chocolate cake that looks like a log to remind everyone it's winter.

In addition, many French-speaking countries celebrate national holidays. They all fall in July, with the exception of Switzerland's:

✔ **le premier juillet** (luh pruh-myey zhwee-yeh): July 1, the Canadian national holiday

✔ **le 14 [quatorze] juillet** (luh kah-tohrz zhwee-yeh): July 14, the French national holiday (the day the Bastille prison was overtaken, known as Bastille Day in the U.S.)

✔ **le 17 [dix-sept] juillet** (luh dee-seht zhwee-yeh): July 17, the Belgian national holiday

✔ **le premier août** (luh pruh-myey ooht): August 1, the Swiss national holiday

On the Clock: Telling Time

One of the most important and frequent uses of numbers is, of course, to tell time. To ask what time it is, say **Quelle heure est-il ?** (kehl uhr ey-teel?). The French use both the familiar 12-hour clock as well as the official 24-hour clock to tell time.

You probably abbreviate time in the *hour:minute* format: 12:15 or 3:35, for example. In France, instead of using a colon to separate the hour from the minutes, you use a lowercase *h*. For example, 11:30 becomes 11h30. Whether you're using the 12-hour system or the 24-hour system, you abbreviate the same way. For example, 10h30 can mean 10:30 a.m. or 10:30 p.m., and 22h30 means 10:30 p.m.

Using the 12-hour clock

To express the time in French by using the 12-hour system, you begin with **il est** (eel ey) (*it is*). Add a number representing the hour and then the word **heure(s)** (uhr) (*hour[s], o'clock*). Write the singular **heure** when it's 1:00 a.m. or 1:00 p.m., and write the plural **heures** for all other hours. Here are some examples:

> **Il est huit heures.** (eel ey weet uhr.) (*It's 8 o'clock.*)
>
> **Il est neuf heures.** (eel ey nuhv uhr.) (*It's 9 o'clock.*)
>
> **Il est une heure.** (eel ey ewn uhr.) (*It's 1 o'clock.*)

Of course, the time isn't always exactly on the hour. Therefore, you need a way to indicate time past and before the hour, too. To indicate time past the hour, you can simply follow the phrase **il est . . . heure(s)** with the number of minutes it is past the hour. To express time before the hour (10 minutes to/till 8:00, for example), you add the word **moins** (mwaN), which means *minus*. Consider these examples:

> **Il est huit heures dix.** (eel ey weet uhr dees.) (*It's 8:10.*)
>
> **Il est huit heures moins dix.** (eel ey weet uhr mwaN dees.) (*It's 7:50; It's 10 till 8:00. Literally: It's 8:00 minus 10.*)
>
> **Il est dix heures moins vingt-cinq.** (eel ey dee zhuhr mwaN vaN-saNk.) (*It's 9:35; It's 25 till 10:00. Literally: It's 10:00 minus 25.*)

Alternatively, you can use these French phrases to express common 15-minute time increments:

✔ **et quart** (ey kahr) (*quarter after*): For example, **Il est neuf heures et quart** (eel ey nuh vuhr ey kahr) (*It's 9:15; It's a quarter past nine*).

✔ **et demi(e)** (ey duh-mee OR eyd-mee) (*half past*): For example, **Il est huit heures et demie** (eel ey weet uhr ey duh-mee) (*It's 8:30; It's half past 8:00*).

✔ **moins le quart** (mwaN luh kahr) (*quarter till*): For example, **Il est neuf heures moins le quart** (eel ey nuhv uhr mwaN luh kahr) (*It's quarter till 9:00*).

To distinguish between a.m. and p.m. in the 12-hour clock, use these phrases after the time:

✔ **du matin** (dew mah-taN) (*in the morning*)

✔ **de l'après-midi** (duh lah-preh-mee-dee) (*in the afternoon*)

✔ **du soir** (dew swahr) (*in the evening*)

✔ **midi** (mee-dee) (*noon*)

✔ **minuit** (mee-nwee) (*midnight*)

Here are a couple of examples:

> **Il est 10 [dix] heures du matin.** (eel ey deez uhr dew mah-taN.) (*It's 10:00 in the morning.*)

> **Il est 10 [dix] heures du soir.** (eel ey deez uhr dew swahr.) (*It's 10:00 in the evening.*)

Both **midi** and **minuit** are masculine, so when you say *half past noon* or *half past midnight*, you don't add an **e** to the word **demi**: **Il est midi et demi** (eel ey mee-dee ey duh-mee.) (*It's half past noon.*) You add an **e** to the word **demi** when using it with any other hour because **heure** is feminine: **Il est deux heures et demie** (eel ey duhz urh ey duh-mee).

Using the 24-hour routine

European countries and French-speaking Canada commonly use the 24-hour clock, or military time, for all transportation schedules, concert times, store hours, appointment times, and any other scheduled events. When you use the 24-hour clock, you don't need to distinguish between a.m. and p.m. If you're accustomed to the 12-hour system, telling time by the 24-hour clock may be a little confusing. Here's what you need to know: You count up from 1:00 a.m. to 12:00 p.m. (noon) just as you're used to, but instead of starting over again at 1:00 p.m., you keep counting up: 13:00, 14:00, and so on until you hit 23:59, which is one minute before midnight (0:00). So 13:00 is 1:00 p.m., 14:00 is 2:00 p.m. and so on.

When you see a time such as **15h** in an itinerary or a TV guide, quickly subtract 12 hours from the number 15, and you get 3 p.m. When you want to say a time such as 3 p.m. in the 24-hour system, add 12 hours to the number 3, and you get **15 [quinze] heures** (kaNz uhr).

To say what exact time it is in the 24-hour system, simply add the number of minutes to the hour. Here are some examples:

> **Il est onze [11] heures quinze.** (eel ey ohNz uhr kaNz.) (*It's 11:15 a.m.*)

> **Il est seize [16] heures dix.** (eel ey sehz uhr dees.) (*It's 4:10 p.m.; It's 16:10.*)

Take a look at Table 2-2 to see all this timely information spelled out.

Table 2-2	French Times on the 24-Hour Clock	
Time	*Heure*	*Abbreviation*
midnight	**minuit**	0h00
1 a.m.	**une heure**	1h00
2 a.m.	**deux heures**	2h00
3 a.m.	**trois heures**	3h00
4:15 a.m.	**quatre heures et quart** **quatre heures quinze**	4h15
5:30 a.m.	**cinq heures et demie** **cinq heures trente**	5h30
6:45 a.m.	**six heures quarante-cinq**	6h45
noon	**midi**	12h00
1 p.m.	**treize heures**	13h00
2 p.m.	**quatorze heures**	14h00
3 p.m.	**quinze heures**	15h00
4:05 p.m.	**seize heures cinq**	16h05
5:17 p.m.	**dix-sept heures dix-sept**	17h17
6:55 p.m.	**dix-huit heures cinquante-cinq**	18h55

Talkin' the Talk

 Pierre and Claire are running late. (Track 6)

Pierre: **Claire, quelle heure est-il ?**
            klehr, kehl uhr ey-teel?
            Claire, what time is it?

Claire: **Il est dix heures dix.**
            eel ey dee zuhr dees.
            It's 10:10 am.

Pierre: **Il est dix heures dix ?**
            eel ey dee zuhr dees?
            It's 10:10 a.m.?

Claire: **Oui, nous sommes en retard.**
            wee, nooh suhhm zahN ruh-tahr.
            Yes, we're late.

Pierre: **Oh non ! Allons-y ! Dépêchons-nous !**
            oh nohN! ahl-ohN-zee! dey-pehsh-ohN-nooh!
            Oh no! Let's go! Hurry up!

Words to Know

Il est . . . heures	ee ley . . . uhr	It's . . . o'clock
Quelle heure est-il ?	kehl uhr ey-teel?	What time is it ?
être en retard	eh-traN ruh-tahr	to be late
Allons-y !	ah-lohN-zee!	Let's go!
Dépêchons-nous !	dey-pey-shohN-nooh!	Let's hurry up!

Chapter 3

Greetings, Goodbyes, and Small Talk

In This Chapter

▶ Greeting people in formal and familiar settings

▶ Asking and answering casual questions

▶ Making small talk

▶ Saying goodbye

*T*o mingle with speakers of French, one of the first things you need to know is how to greet people properly. In this chapter, you discover a variety of common greetings and how to adapt them for formal or informal settings.

Whether you're conversing with someone you just met or chatting with an old acquaintance, small talk is a key part of many conversations. Although it can lead to more serious discussion, small talk generally deals with innocent subjects, such as what you do for a living, your interests, the weather, and so on. It's a wonderful way to get acquainted with someone, and it allows you to decide whether you want to pursue a conversation with the stranger next to you on the plane or go back to the book you're reading. This chapter helps give you the information you need to **parler de tout et de rien** (pahr-ley duh tooh ey duh ryaN) (*talk about everything and nothing*).

Finally, when it's time to take your leave, you need to know which expressions are appropriate for the occasion and which expressions to use if you want to explore the relationship further. We end this chapter with a few goodbyes — but not without first telling you how to ask for someone's contact information.

Addressing Someone Formally or Informally

In French, you can vary the level of formality in your speech by how you say the word *you*. Depending on whom you're addressing, you can use the informal **tu** (tew) or the more formal **vous** (vooh). You need to know when one or the other is appropriate because if you say the wrong thing, at best, you sound a little funny; at worst, you offend someone.

In general, use the formal **vous** when you address somebody you've never met, a superior, or an older person. As you get to know that person better, you may both switch to **tu**. Use the familiar **tu** when you speak to a friend, a child, or an animal. In addition, members of the same family, whatever their age, use the **tu** form.

The environment in which you find yourself also determines the correct form of address. For example, if you're a young person traveling on the train in France and you meet other young people, you would address one another as **tu**. On the other hand, if you're in a store, you'd address the clerk with **vous**, even if she looks a lot younger than you. Also keep in mind that the **vous** form is used to address one person on a formal level, but it's also a plural form used to address any number of people formally or informally.

If you're not sure which form to use, use **vous** until the person you're addressing asks you to use the **tu** form. Then you avoid a **faux pas** (foh pah) (*social blunder.* Literally: *false step*). **Il faut se vouvoyer** (eel foh suh vooh-vwa-yey) means *We must be formal and use the "vous" form of verbs when saying "you."* If you become friendly with someone, then you can address the person with his or her name and say **On peut se tutoyer** (ohN puh suh tew-twa-yey) (*You can be familiar and use "tu" when saying "you"*). Refer to Chapter 3 of Book III for more on **tu** and **vous**.

In a formal situation, it's polite to add **monsieur** (muh-syuh) (*mister, sir*) to address a man and **madame** (mah-dahm) (*ma'am, missus*) to address a woman, even after the simplest of expressions like **bonjour** (bohN-zhoohr) (*good day, hello*) and **merci** (mehr-see) (*thank you*). The French government recently decided that the word **mademoiselle** (mahd-mwah-zehl) (*miss*), which was used to refer to unmarried women, is discriminatory and no longer appropriate in current society. It's no longer used in official communications, but you may still hear the word in conversation. Remember that **monsieur**, **madame**, and **mademoiselle** can be used without the person's name and are used that way most of the time.

Greetings: Formal and Friendly

Greetings are the first steps in establishing contact with someone, whatever the language. This section presents plenty of very simple French greetings that you may use to help you meet people.

A smile often does the job in the United States, but in Europe, you're better off acknowledging someone with **Bonjour, monsieur** (bohN-zhoohr muh-syuh) or **Bonjour, madame** (bohN-zhoohr mah-dahm). The French reserve a smile for responding to something funny or nice rather than offering a welcoming hello.

Saying hello

Nothing in a foreign language is easier than saying hello. Actually, the French language has a saying for referring to something that's really a cinch: **C'est simple comme bonjour** (sey saN-pluh kuhhm bohN-zhoohr) (*It's as easy as saying hello*). So go ahead and practice these greetings:

- **Bonjour !** (bohN-zhoohr!): This literally means *Good day!* but you can use it when first greeting someone in the morning or afternoon, as long as the sun is shining.

- **Salut !** (sah-lew!) (*Hi! or Bye!*). This is the most informal of all hellos and is also a way of saying goodbye. Although you can use it at any time of day, you can't use it with just anybody. Use this word only with children and people you're familiar with.

In Québec, people also say **bonjour** when leaving, giving it the true meaning of *good day.* On the other hand, when the Québécois say **bienvenue** (byaN-vuh-new) (*welcome*) to you, they often mean *You're welcome* when you just thanked them. In France, the word **bienvenue** is used only to welcome someone and extend hospitality, not as a reply to **merci** (mehr-see) (*thanks*).

Introducing yourself and others

After you greet people, you may need to introduce yourself and find out their names.

In French, when you want to say *My name is,* you use a reflexive form of the verb **appeler** (ahp-ley) (*to call*). Thus, **je m'appelle** (zhuh mah-pehl) literally means *I call myself.* The following table shows all the forms of **appeler** in the present tense. (Refer to Chapter 3 of Book III for detailed information on French verbs, and refer to Chapter 4 of Book III for reflexive verbs.)

Conjugation	Pronunciation	Translation
je m'appelle	zhuh mah-pehl	*my name is*
tu t'appelles	tew tah-pehl	*your name is*
il/elle/on s'appelle	eel/ehl/ohN sah-pehl	*his/her/its name is*
nous nous appelons	nooh nooh zah-plohN	*our names are*
vous vous appelez	vooh vooh zah-pley	*your names are*
ils/elles s'appellent	eel/ehl sah-pehl	*their names are*

You may use either of these phrases to tell someone your name:

- ✔ **Je m'appelle . . .** (zhuh mah-pehl . . .) (*My name is . . .*)
- ✔ **Je suis . . .** (zhuh swee . . .) (*I am . . .*)

To ask someone else his or her name, you can use these phrases:

Comment vous appelez-vous ? (koh-mahN vooh zah-pley-vooh?) (*What's your name?* or *What are your names ?* — plural or singular formal)

Comment tu t'appelles ?/Comment t'appelles-tu ? (koh-mahN tew tah-pehl?/koh-mahN tah-pehl-tew?) (*What's your name?* — singular familiar)

Or if you want to know who that person over there is, you ask

Comment s'appelle . . . ? (koh-mahN sah-pehl . . . ?) (*What's . . . name?*)

Et lui, qui est-ce ? (ey lwee, kee ehs?) (*And who is he?*)

Et elle, qui est-ce ? (ey ehl, kee ehs?) (*And who is she?*)

And you receive the answer **C'est . . .** (sey. . .) (*That is . . .*).

To introduce someone, say any of the following:

- ✔ **Je vous présente . . .** (zhuh vooh prey-zahNt . . .) (*Let me introduce . . . to you.* — plural or singular formal)
- ✔ **Je te présente . . .** (zhuh tuh prey-zahNt . . .) (*Let me introduce . . . to you.* — singular familiar)
- ✔ **Voici . . . /Voilà . . .** (vwah-see . . ./vwah-lah . . .) (*Here is . . . /There is . . .*)

After you introduce yourself or someone else, the other person, if a man, typically says **Enchanté !** (ahN-shahN-tey!) or, if a woman, **Enchantée !** (pronounced the same). In either case, the meaning is the same: *Delighted!*

Talkin' the Talk

 Marc Sauval and his wife Christine, entrepreneurs from Québec, are meeting their French counterpart, Claire Rivet, for the first time. (Track 7)

Marc:	**Bonjour, madame. Je m'appelle Marc Sauval.**
	bohN-zhoohr, mah-dahm. zhuh mah-pehl mahrk soh-vahl.
	Hello, ma'am. My name is Marc Sauval.
Claire:	**Ah, Monsieur Sauval. Je suis Claire Rivet. Enchantée !**
	ah, muh-syuh soh-vahl. zhuh swee klehr ree-vey. ahN-shahN-tey!
	Ah, Mr. Sauval. I am Claire Rivet. Delighted to meet you!
Marc:	**Madame Rivet, je vous présente ma femme, Christine.**
	mah-dahm ree-vey, zhuh vooh prey-zahNt mah fahm, kree-steen.
	Mrs. Rivet, let me introduce you to my wife, Christine.
Claire:	**Enchantée, madame !**
	ahN-shahN-tey, mah-dahm!
	Delighted, ma'am!
Christine:	**Enchantée !**
	ahN-shahN-tey
	Delighted!

Asking "how are you?"

Another thing that accompanies hellos is the traditional "How are you?" Beware that when the French ask this question, they'll actually expect an answer! Here are a few phrases to ask this question:

Comment allez-vous ? (koh-mahN tah-ley-vooh?) — plural or singular formal

Ça va ? (sah vah?) — informal

Comment ça va ? (koh-mahN sah vah?) — informal

Here are some ways to answer those questions:

Pas mal, merci. (pah mahl mehr-see.) (*Not bad, thank you.*)

Bien, merci. (byaN, mehr-see.) (*Fine, thank you.*)

Très bien, merci. (trey byaN, mehr-see.) (*Very well, thank you.*)

Making Small Talk

You can ask a yes-or-no question in French in numerous ways: You can make the tone of your voice rise at the end of a sentence, or you can place **est-ce que** (ehs kuh) in front of the sentence, or you can invert the subject and the verb. (See Chapter 5 of Book III for details on question structures.) Here are examples that show you each type of questioning:

Vous habitez près d'ici ? (vooh zah-bee-tey prey dee-see?) (*Do you live near here?*)

Est-ce que vous allez souvent au cinéma ? (ehs kuh vooh zah-ley sooh-vahN oh see-ney-mah?) (*Do you often go to the movies?*)

Faites-vous beaucoup de voyages ? (feht-vooh boh-kooh duh vwah-yahzh?) (*Do you go on a lot of trips?*)

When you make small talk, however, you probably want to ask questions that elicit more than a yes-or-no answer. With the information in this section, you'll be able to ask basic questions and use expressions that are an important part of every conversation.

Using key question words

To get specific information, you need to know these key question words:

- ✔ **à quelle heure** (ah kehl uhr) (*at what time*)
- ✔ **combien de** (kohN-byaN duh) (*how many*)
- ✔ **combien** (kohN-byaN) (*how much*)
- ✔ **comment** (koh-mahN) (*how*)

- **où** (ooh) (*where*)

- **pourquoi** (poohr-kwah) (*why*)

- **qu'est-ce que** (kehs kuh) (*what*)

- **quand** (kahN) (*when*)

- **quel(s)/quelle(s)** (kehl) (*which, what*)

- **qui** (kee) (*who*)

You can use these question words on their own, just as in English, or you can use them in sentences. For example, you can ask about where someone lives and someone's age with these questions:

> **Où habitez-vous ?** (ooh ah-bee-tey-vooh?) (*Where do you live?* — plural or singular formal)
>
> **Quel âge avez-vous ?** (kehl ahzh ah-vey-vooh?) (*How old are you?* — plural or singular formal)
>
> **Quel âge as-tu ?** (kehl ahzh ah-tew?) (*How old are you?* — singular familiar)

The age questions here use forms of the verb **avoir** (ah-vwahr) (*to have*) instead of **être** (eh-truh) (*to be*), so the literal translation is *What age do you have?* The answer uses the verb **avoir** as well: **J'ai douze ans** (zhey doohz ahN) (*I am 12.* Literally: *I have 12 years*).

Saying the magic words: Polite expressions

A kind word goes a long way. Saying *please, thank you,* and *excuse me* as well as a few other universal phrases marks you as a considerate person and one worth getting to know. Use the following expressions liberally:

- **Excusez-moi.** (eks-kew-zey-mwah.) (*Excuse me.*)

- **Pardon.** (pahr-dohN.) (*Excuse me, sorry.*)

- **Je suis désolé(e).** (zhuh swee dey-zoh-ley.) (*I'm sorry.*)

- **Ce n'est pas grave !** (suh ney pah grahv!) (*That's okay!*)

- **Merci.** (mehr-see.) (*Thank you.*)

- **De rien.** (duh ryaN.) (*You're welcome.* Literally: *It's nothing.*)

- **Je vous en prie.** (zhuh vooh zahN pree.) (*You're welcome.*)

- **S'il vous plaît.** (seel vooh pley.) (*Please.*)

Talkin' the Talk

After arriving in Paris from New York on an all-night flight, Amanda gets on her connecting flight to Nice. Exhausted, she collapses in her seat and is about to fall asleep when a young man addresses her. (Track 8)

Patrick: **Pardon, madame. Quel est le numéro de votre place ?**
pahr-dohN, mah-dahm. kehl ey luh new-mey-roh duh vuhh-truh plahs?
Excuse me, ma'am. What is your seat number?

Amanda: **Je ne sais pas. Attendez ! Oh, c'est le 24B. Excusez-moi. Je suis désolée.**
zhuhn sey pah. ah-tahN-dey! oh, sey luh vaNt-kah-truh bey. ek-skew-zey-mwah. zhuh swee dey-zoh-ley.
I don't know. Wait! Oh, it's number 24B. Excuse me. I'm sorry.

After Amanda moves to her assigned seat, their conversation continues.

Patrick: **Ce n'est pas grave ! Je m'appelle Patrick. Et vous ?**
suh ney pah grahv! zhuh mah-pehl pah-treek. ey vooh?
That's okay! My name is Patrick. And you?

Amanda: **Enchantée, monsieur. Je m'appelle Amanda.**
ahN-shahN-tey, muh-syuh. zhuh mah-pehl ah-mahN-dah.
Delighted, sir. My name is Amanda.

Patrick: **Enchanté, madame. Où allez-vous ?**
ahN-shahN-tey, mah-dahm. ooh ah-ley-vooh?
Delighted, ma'am. Where are you going?

Amanda: **Je vais d'abord à Nice, puis à Toulon voir ma fille.**
zhuh veh dah-bohr ah nees, pwee ah tooh-lohN vwahr mah feey.
I'm going to Nice first, then to Toulon to see my daughter.

Patrick: **Vous venez souvent en France ?**
vooh vuh-ney sooh-vahN ahN frahNs?
Do you often come to France?

Amanda:	**Oh oui, j'adore la France.**
	oh wee, zhah-dohr lah frahNs.
	Oh yes, I love France.

Patrick:	**Combien de temps restez-vous en France ?**
	kohN-byaN duh tahN reh-stey vooh ahN frahNs?
	How long are you staying in France?

Amanda:	**Un mois. Et vous, pourquoi allez-vous à Nice ?**
	uhN mwah. ey vooh, poohr-kwah ah-ley-vooh ah nees?
	A month. And you, why are you going to Nice?

Patrick:	**Pour le travail.**
	Poohr luh trah-vahy.
	For work.

Words to Know

Quel est le numéro ?	kehl ey luh new-mey-roh?	What is the number?
attendez	ah-tahN-dey	(you) wait
je vais/vous allez	zhuh vey/vooh zah-ley	I go/you go
souvent	sooh-vahN	often
j'adore	zhah-dohr	I love, adore
le travail	luh trah-vahy	work

Could you repeat that, please?

When you're just learning a foreign language, you may need to let the person speaking to you know that you're having a little difficulty understanding or responding. Instead of saying "Huh?" try these expressions:

Je ne comprends pas. (zhuhn kohN-prahN pah.) (*I don't understand.*)

Je ne sais pas. (zhuhn sey pah.) (*I don't know.*)

Peux-tu parler plus lentement, s'il te plaît ? (puh-tew pahr-ley plew lahNt-mahN, seel tuh pley?) (*Can you speak more slowly, please? — singular familiar*)

Pouvez-vous parler plus lentement, s'il vous plaît ? (pooh-vey vooh pahr-ley plew lahNt-mahN, seel vooh pley?) (*Can you speak more slowly, please? — plural or singular formal*)

Peux-tu répéter, s'il te plaît ? (puh-tew rey-pey-tey seel tuh pley?) (*Can you repeat [that], please? — singular familiar*)

Pouvez-vous répéter, s'il vous plaît ? (pooh-vey vooh rey-pey-tey seel vooh pley?) (*Can you repeat [that], please? — plural or singular formal*)

Stating your preferences

One of the ways in which people get to know each other is by expressing likes and dislikes. When you say that you like to travel, that you hate waiting in line, or even that you love a certain film, you use *verbs of preference.* These verbs include the following:

- ✔ **aimer** (eh-mey) (*to like, to love*)
- ✔ **aimer mieux** (eh-mey myuh) (*to like better, to prefer*)
- ✔ **adorer** (ah-doh-rey) (*to adore*)
- ✔ **préférer** (prey-fey-rey) (*to prefer*)
- ✔ **détester** (dey-teh-stey) (*to hate*)

Aimer, **adorer**, and **détester** are all regular **-er** verbs; in Chapter 3 of Book III, we explain how to conjugate regular verbs, including verbs like **préférer**, which has regular endings but a stem change: The accent on the second **e** changes from an **é**, to **è**, except for in the **nous** and **vous** forms. Here's the conjugation of **préférer**:

Conjugation	Pronunciation	Translation
je préfère	zhuh prey-fehr	*I prefer*
tu préfères	tew prey-fehr	*you prefer*
il/elle/on préfère	eel/ehl/ohN prey-fehr	*he/she/it/one prefers*
nous préférons	nooh prey-fey-rohN	*we prefer*
vous préférez	vooh prey-fey-rey	*you prefer*
ils/elles préfèrent	eel/ehl prey-fehr	*they prefer*

To say that you like or hate something in French, you use the definite article *the* — **le** (luh), **la** (lah), and **les** (ley) — even though the article may not be necessary in English. Check out these examples:

> **J'aime le café au lait.** (zhehm luh kah-fey oh leh.) (*I like coffee with milk.*)
>
> **Nous préférons les films étrangers.** (nooh prey-fey-rohN ley feelm zey-trahN-zhey.) (*We prefer foreign films.*)
>
> **Ils détestent le bruit.** (eel dey-tehst luh brwee.) (*They hate noise.*)

Talking about what you do

In French, when you state your profession, you just say **Je suis . . .** (zhuh swee . . .) (*I am . . .*) and then name the profession. For example, **Je suis professeur** (zhuh swee proh-feh-suhr) means *I am a teacher, professor.* To identify someone else's profession, use the construction **Il/Elle est . . .** (eel/ehl ey . . .) (*He/She is . . .*). **Il est ingénieur** (eel ey taN-zhey-nyuhr), for example, means *He is an engineer.* Notice that in these constructions, you don't use the article **un** (uhN) (*a, an*), as you do in English (I am *a* teacher, for example, or he is *an* engineer).

You use the same construction to describe yourself or someone else: **Je suis optimiste** (zhuh swee zohp-tee-meest) (*I am optimistic*), for example, or **Il est intelligent** (eel ey taN-teh-lee-zhahN) (*He is intelligent*).

Although not exhaustive by any means, this list includes many common occupations:

- ✔ **le professeur** (luh proh-feh-suhr) (*high school teacher, college professor*)
- ✔ **l'informaticien/l'informaticienne** (laN-fohr-mah-tee-syaN/laN-fohr-mah-tee-syehn) (*computer scientist*)
- ✔ **le/la secrétaire** (luh/lah suh-krey-tehr) (*secretary*)
- ✔ **le médecin** (luh meyd-saN) (*physician*)
- ✔ **l'infirmier/l'infirmière** (laN-feer-myey/laN-feer-myehr) (*nurse*)
- ✔ **l'avocat/l'avocate** (lah-voh-kah/lah-voh-kaht) (*lawyer*)
- ✔ **l'ingénieur** (m) (laN-zhey-nyuhr) (*engineer*)
- ✔ **le serveur/la serveuse** (luh sehr-vuhr/lah sehr-vuhz) (*waiter/waitress*)
- ✔ **le/la dentiste** (luh/lah dahN-teest) (*dentist*)
- ✔ **le retraité/la retraitée** (luh ruh-treh-tey/lah ruh-treh-tey) (*retired person*)
- ✔ **l'homme d'affaires/la femme d'affaires** (luhhm dah-fehr/lah fahm dah-fehr) (*businessman/businesswoman*)

- ✔ **l'architecte** (m/f) (lahr-shee-tehkt) (*architect*)
- ✔ **le PDG** (luh pey dey zhey) (*CEO*. Literally: an acronym for **Président Directeur Général**)

Some professions have only one form for both the masculine and the feminine. As a rule, words that end in **-e** — for example, **dentiste** — are the same regardless of gender. Some professions don't have a feminine form because the gender designation is a remnant of the days when certain professions were mostly filled by men. But don't be surprised if you hear a native speaker of French say **la professeure** (lah proh-fey-suhr) or the abbreviation **la prof** (lah pruhhf), even though official dictionaries list the noun as masculine (**le professeur/ le prof**).The feminine noun **la professeure** is even found in official documents nowadays. In Québec, you hear French-Canadians call a female writer **l'écrivaine** (ley-kree-vehn) with the feminine spelling **-e** at the end instead of the masculine form of the profession, **l'écrivain** (ley-kree-vaN). The ongoing debate about this evolution of the French language reflects changing trends in society.

The following are some useful job-related expressions:

Quel est votre métier ? (kehl ey vuhh-truh mey-tyey?) (*What is your profession?*)

Qu'est-ce que vous faites dans la vie ? (kehs kuh vooh feht dahN lah vee?) (*What do you do for a living?*)

Pour quelle entreprise/compagnie travaillez-vous ? (poohr kehl ahN-truh-preez/kohN-pah-nyee trah-vah-yey-vooh?) (*What company do you work for?*)

Voyagez-vous souvent pour votre travail ? (vwah-yah-zhey-vooh sooh-vahN poohr vuhh-truh trah-vahy?) (*Do you travel often for your job/work?*)

Votre métier est intéressant. (vuhh-truh mey-tyey ey taN-tey-reh-sahN.) (*Your profession is interesting.*)

Talkin' the Talk

On the flight to Nice, newly acquainted Amanda and Patrick talk about work. (Track 9)

Amanda: **Où travaillez-vous ?**
ooh trah-vah-yey-vooh?
Where do you work?

Patrick: **Mon bureau est à Paris, mais je vais souvent à Nice
                en voyage d'affaires.**
                mohN bew-roh ey tah pah-ree, mey zhuh vey sooh-
                vahN ah nees ahN vwah-yahzh dah-fehr.
                *My office is in Paris, but I often go to Nice on business
                trips.*

Amanda: **Quel est votre métier ?**
                kehl ey vuhh-truh mey-tyey?
                What is your profession?

Patrick: **Je suis informaticien. Je travaille pour une compagnie
                d'informatique.**
                zhuh swee zaN-fohr-mah-tee-syaN. zhuh trah-vahy
                poohr ewn kohN-pah-nyee daN-fohr-mah-teek.
                *I'm a computer scientist. I work for a computer sci-
                ence company.*

Amanda: **C'est une grande compagnie ?**
                sey tewn grahNd kohN-pah-nyee?
                Is it a large company?

Patrick: **Non, elle est très petite. Il y a seulement dix
                employés.**
                nohN, ehl ey treh puh-teet. eel ee ah suhl mohN dee
                zahN-plwah-yey.
                No, it's very small. There are only ten employees.

Words to Know

le voyage d'affaires	luh vwah-yahzh dah-fehr	business trip
mon bureau	mohN bew-roh	my office
une compagnie	ewn kohN-pah-nyee	a company
un employé/ une employée	uhN nahN-plwah-yey/ ew nahN-plwah-yey	an employee

Chatting about the weather

A great topic for small talk is, of course, **le temps** (luh tahN) (*the weather*). In fact, one way to designate small talk in French is with the phrase **parler de la pluie et du beau temps** (pahr-ley duh lah plwee ey dew boh tahN) (Literally: *to talk about the rain and the nice weather*). In countries of great weather contrasts, like Canada, weather is a constant topic of conversation. In more temperate climates, like that of France, the weather is still a favorite topic, especially if you want to complain about it.

Of course, you can't talk about the weather without knowing the names of the seasons: **le printemps** (luh praN-tahN) (*spring*), **l'été** (m) (ley-tey) (*summer*), **l'automne** (m) (loh-tuhhn) (*fall*), and **l'hiver** (m) (lee-vehr) (*winter*).

You can ask about the weather with the question **Quel temps fait-il ?** (kehl tahN fey-teel) (*What's the weather like?*). To answer this question, you use **Il fait . . .** (eel fey . . .) (*It's . . .*) and plug in any of the following terms:

- **beau** (boh) (*nice*)
- **doux** (dooh) (*mild*)
- **mauvais** (moh-veh) (*bad*)
- **chaud** (shoh) (*warm, hot*)
- **frais** (freh) (*cool*)
- **froid** (frwah) (*cold*)
- **du soleil** (dew soh-lehy) (*sunny*)
- **du vent** (dew vahN) (*windy*)

To indicate that it's raining or snowing, you say **Il pleut** (eel pluh) (*It's raining*) or **Il neige** (eel nehzh) (*It's snowing*).

Notice that all the weather phrases start with **il**. Although you may be familiar with **il** as the masculine singular pronoun *he* — **il habite** (eel ah-beet) (*he lives*), for example — this **il** doesn't refer to a male person or a masculine object. Instead, it's impersonal, like the English *it*.

You can also say what the temperature is. Remember that throughout most of the world, the temperature is stated in degrees Celsius (centigrade). So when you hear **La température est de 25 [vingt-cinq] degrés** (lah tahN-pey-rah-tewr ey duh vaNt-saNk duh-grey) (*The temperature is 25 degrees*), think 25 degrees Celsius, which is a rather comfortable 77 degrees Fahrenheit.

Talkin' the Talk

The captain of the plane Patrick and Amanda are on makes an announcement about the weather in Nice, prompting a conversation between the two acquaintances.

Captain: **À Nice, il fait beau et chaud et la température est de 30 [trente] degrés.**
Ah nees, eel fey boh ey shoh ey lah tahN-pey-rah-tewr ey duh trahNt duh-grey.
In Nice, the weather is nice and warm, and the temperature is 30 degrees.

Patrick: **À Nice, il fait toujours beau !**
Ah nees, eel fey tooh-zhoohr boh!
In Nice, the weather is always nice!

Amanda: **Même en hiver ?**
mehm ahN nee-vehr?
Even in winter?

Patrick: **En hiver, il pleut un peu, mais il fait doux. Et à New York ?**
ahN nee-vehr, eel pluh uhN puh, mey zeel fey dooh. ey ah New York?
In winter, it rains a little, but it's mild. And in New York?

Amanda: **En hiver, il fait très froid et il neige, et en été il fait très chaud et humide.**
ahN nee-vehr, eel fey trey frwah ey eel nehzh, ey ahN ney-tey eel fey trey shoh ey ew-meed.
In winter, it's very cold and it snows, and in summer, it's very hot and humid.

Patrick: **Et au printemps et en automne ?**
ey oh praN-tahN ey ahN noh-tuhhn?
And in spring and fall?

Amanda: **Le temps est agréable.**
luh tahN ey tah-grey-ah-bluh.
The weather is pleasant.

Words to Know

toujours	tooh-zhoohr	always
même	mehm	even
un peu	uhN puh	a little
agréable	ah-grey-ah-bluh	pleasant

Saying Goodbye

When you're done talking and are ready to part company, you have to decide whether you want to stay in touch. If you do, you can exchange some personal contact information before saying your goodbyes. The kind of expressions you use depends on how friendly you got and whether you plan to meet again.

Deciding to keep in touch

If you feel you got to know your new acquaintances, you may want to give your **coordonnées** (koh-ohr-doh-ney) (*address and phone number*). You can use these phrases:

- ✔ **Moi, j'habite rue Leclerc. Et vous ?** (mwah, zhah-beet rew luh-clehr. ey vooh?) (*I live on Leclerc Street. How about you?*)

- ✔ **Où habitez-vous ?** (ooh ah-bee-tey-vooh?) (*Where do you live?*)

- ✔ **Je vous donne mon numéro de téléphone.** (zhuh vooh duhhn mohN new-mey-roh duh tey-ley-fuhhn.) (*Here's my phone number.*)

- ✔ **Donnez-moi votre numéro de téléphone, s'il vous plaît.** (duhh-ney-mwah vuhh-truh new-mey-roh duh tey-ley-fuhhn seel vooh pley.) (*Give me your phone number, please.*)

- ✔ **Je mets votre adresse e-mail dans mon iPod.** (zhuh mey voh-trah-drehs ee-meyl dahN mohN nee-puhhd.) (*I'm putting your e-mail address on my iPod.*)

In this day and age, you're likely to give an e-mail address. The French language has a word for it: **l'adresse électronique** (lah-drehs ey-lehk-troh-neek). But saying **e-mail** (ee-meyl) is so much more convenient; it's even been Frenchified as **le mél** (luh mehl)! Of course, French also has a word for the @ sign: **arobase** (ah-roh-bahz) or, more commonly, **à** (ah) (*at*); the dot is **point** (pwaN), which means, among many other things, the period at the end of a sentence.

Canada has the same telephone system as the United States: a local area code — **l'indicatif** (m) (laN-dee-kah-teef) — followed by the seven digits of a personal phone number. In France, each time you make a call, even locally, you have to dial the two-digit area code (which begins with a zero, like 01 or 02) followed by eight numbers that are stated in groups of two: 04 94 37 08 56, for example. To call a French number from the United States, dial 011, the code for France (33), and then the number directly, skipping the 0 of the area code: 011 33 4 94 37 08 56, for example. For more information on numbers, see Chapter 2 of Book I.

Formal and familiar goodbyes

When you leave, you can use one of these expressions for goodbye:

- ✔ **Bonsoir !** (bohN-swahr!) (*Good evening!*) You use this greeting in the late afternoon and the evening to say hello or goodbye.

- ✔ **Au revoir !** (ohr-vwahr!) (*Goodbye!*) Like its English counterpart, you can use this term any time of day or night.

- ✔ **Bonne nuit !** (buhhn nwee!) (*Good night!*) Say this only when you're retiring for the night or when you're putting a child to bed. It essentially means *sleep well*.

- ✔ **À bientôt !** (ah byaN-toh!) (*See you soon!*) Say this when you expect to see the person again in the near future.

- ✔ **À tout à l'heure !** (ah tooh tah luhr!) (*See you later!*) Use this phrase only when you'll see the person again the same day.

- ✔ **À demain !** (ah duh-maN!) (*See you tomorrow!*)

- ✔ **Bonne journée !** (buhhn zhoohr-ney!) (*Have a good day!*)

- ✔ **Bonne soirée !** (buhhn swah-rey!) (*Have a good evening!*) Say this only when your company has plans for the rest of the evening.

If you're much younger than the person you met or if you feel that you're not on a best-friends basis, be sure to use the appropriate title (see the earlier section "Addressing Someone Formally or Informally" for details). In formal situations, you can never overuse the **monsieur** or **madame** titles.

Talkin' the Talk

Amanda and Patrick are still chatting, and the conversation becomes more personal. (Track 10)

Patrick: **On peut se tutoyer ?**
ohN puh suh tew-twa-yey?
Can we be familiar with each other?

Amanda: **Oui, bien sûr.**
wee, byaN sewr.
Yes, of course.

Patrick: **Si tu veux bien, donne-moi ton numéro de téléphone.**
see tew vuh byaN, duhhn-mwah tohN new-mey-roh duh tey-ley-fuhhn.
If you don't mind, give me your phone number.

Amanda: **D'accord. C'est le 01-88-66-12-22 [zéro un – quatre-vingt-huit – soixante-six – douze – vingt-deux].**
dah-kohr. sey luh zey-roh uhN–kah-truh-vaNt-weet–swah-sahNt-sees–doohz–vaNt-duh.
Okay. It's 01-88-66-12-22.

Patrick: **Tu voudrais dîner avec moi un soir ?**
tew vooh-drey dee-ney ah-vek mwah uhN swahr?
Would you like to have dinner with me one evening?

Amanda: .   **Volontiers, si je suis libre.**
voh-lohN-tyey, see zhuh swee lee-bruh.
Gladly, if I'm free.

Patrick: **Je connais des bistros et des cafés très sympa.**
zhuh koh-ney dey bee-stroh ey dey kah-fey trey saN-pah.
I know some very nice bistros and cafes.

Amanda: **Et moi, j'ai hâte de sortir à Nice. Merci, c'est gentil de m'inviter.**
ey mwah, zhey aht duh sohr-teer ah nees. mehr-see, sey zhahN-tee duh maN-vee-tey.
And I can't wait to go out in Nice. Thanks, it's nice of you to invite me.

Patrick: **Pas de quoi. Je te présenterai aussi à des copains et à des copines.**
pahd kwah. zhuh tuh prey-sahN-tuh-rey oh-see ah dey koh-paN ey ah dey koh-peen.
Don't mention it. I'll also introduce you to some [male and female] friends.

Chapter 4

Getting Personal: Discussing Your Home, Family, and Daily Routine

In This Chapter

▶ Talking about where you live and what you own

▶ Sharing info about your family and entourage

▶ Describing your daily routine

*I*f you're like most people, home and family are at the center of your life, and they provide numerous topics for conversation. Just try counting the number of times a day you mention your home and family to your coworkers or friends. The same is true of people everywhere, which is why these topics are often the first you tackle when you learn a new language.

Furthermore, these topics of conversation are often the first things people who don't know you ask about. They may ask you where you live, whether you have siblings, whether you're married or single, and so on. With the vocabulary and information in this chapter, you'll be ready to answer these questions and perhaps even ask a few of your own.

Describing Where You Live

"Where you live" can be the country, the state, the city, or the geographical location you come from. Or it can be the neighborhood in a certain city or even whether you live in an apartment, a house, or a dorm. This section helps you describe where you live in a variety of ways.

Your neck of the woods: Cities and states

When you meet new people and you want to tell them where you live, you may start by telling them your city or hometown. Unless you live in a big city like New York or San Francisco, you may also name the state to better help them locate where you come from. You can say

> **J'habite à New York.** (zhah-beet ah nooh york.) (*I live in New York.*)
>
> **J'habite à Lafayette, en Louisiane.** (zhah-beet ah lah-fah-yeht, ahN looh-ee-zyahn.) (*I live in Lafayette, Louisiana.*)
>
> **J'habite à Tucson, en Arizona.** (zhah-beet ah tew-suhhn, ahN nah-ree-zoh-nah.) (*I live in Tucson, Arizona.*)
>
> **J'habite à Boulder, au Colorado.** (zhah-beet ah bowl-duhr, oh koh-loh-rah-doh.) (*I live in Boulder, Colorado.*)

In French, two verbs correspond to the English *to live:* **habiter** (ah-bee-tey) and **vivre** (vee-vruh). Sometimes these verbs are interchangeable, but **habiter** refers to space, whereas **vivre** refers to time as well as space. For example, to say "We live in the 21st century," you use **vivre: Nous vivons au vingt-et-unième siècle** (nooh vee-vohN oh vaN-tey-ew-nee-ehm syeh-kluh). But when you talk about where you live, you use the verb **habiter**. This verb is followed by the preposition **à** (ah) when you name a city, by the preposition **en** (ahN) when you name a feminine state, and by **au** (oh) when you name a masculine state.

To use the verb **habiter** in all its forms of the present tense, look at this table. The verb **résider** (rey-zee-dey) (*to reside*) follows the same conjugation. (You can find the conjugation of the irregular verb **vivre** in Appendix A.)

Conjugation	Pronunciation	Translation
j'habite	zhah-beet	*I live*
tu habites	tew ah-beet	*you live*
il/elle/on habite	eel/ehl/ohNn ah-beet	*he/she/it/one lives*
nous habitons	nooh zah-bee-tohN	*we live*
vous habitez	vooh zah-bee-tey	*you live*
ils/elles habitent	eel/ehl zah-beet	*they live*

Your pied à terre: Your home

To be precise about how you live, you can tell people whether you live in town, in the country, in a house, or in an apartment:

Nous habitons à la campagne/en ville. (nooh zah-bee-tohN ah lah kahN-pah-nyuh/ahN veel.) (*We live in the country/city.*)

Nous habitons en banlieue. (nooh zah-bee-tohN ahN bahN-lyuh.) (*We live in the suburbs.*)

J'habite dans une maison. (zhah-beet dahN zewn mey-zohN.) (*I live in a house.*)

J'habite dans un appartement. (zhah-beet dahN zuhN nah-pahr-tuh-mahN.) (*I live in an apartment.*)

J'habite dans un studio. (zhah-beet dahN zuhN stew-dyoh.) (*I live in a studio.*)

Je réside dans un dortoir universitaire. (zhuh rey-zeed dahN zuhN dohr-twahr ew-nee-vehr-see-tehr.) (*I reside in a university dorm.*)

J'ai une chambre au premier étage. (zhey ewn shahN-broh pruh-myey rey-tahzh.) (*I have a room on the first floor.*)

The French consider the first floor of a house or apartment to be the ground floor, **le rez-de-chaussée** (luh reyd-shoh-sey) (*street level*), and they start counting floors after that. Therefore, what you'd consider to be the *second floor* is actually the first floor — **le premier étage** (luh pruh-myey-rey-tahzh). In France; the *third floor* is the second — **le deuxième étage** (luh duh-zee-ehm ey-tahzh) — and so forth.

To describe your house or apartment, you need to know **les pièces de la maison** (ley pyehs duh lah mey-zohN) (*the rooms of a house*). Read on for details about various rooms.

Le salon: The living room

The French have two names for the living room: **le salon** (luh sah-lohN), which is a more formal living room, and **la salle de séjour** (lah sahl duh sey-zhoohr) — **le séjour** (luh sey-zhoohr) for short — meaning a casual family room. The French also use the Anglicism **le living** (luh lee-veeng). Here's a list of furnishings that you'd normally find in a living room:

- ✔ **un sofa/un canapé** (uhN soh-fah/uhN kah-nah-pey) (*sofa/couch*)
- ✔ **un fauteuil** (uhN foh-tohy) (*armchair*)
- ✔ **un tapis** (uhN tah-pee) (*rug*)
- ✔ **une moquette** (ewn moh-keht) (*wall-to-wall carpet*)
- ✔ **une table de salon** (ewn tah-bluh duh sah-lohN) (*coffee table*)
- ✔ **une lampe** (ewn lahmp) (*lamp*)
- ✔ **des rideaux** (dey ree-doh) (*curtains, drapes*)
- ✔ **une télévision/une télé** (ewn tey-ley-vee-zyohN/ewn tey-ley) (*TV*)

With these terms, you can say things like

> **J'ai seulement une télévision. Elle est dans le salon.** (zhey suhl-mahN ewn tey-ley-vee-zyohN. ehl ey dahN luh sah-lohN.) (*I have only one television. It's in the living room.*)

> **J'ai un fauteuil très confortable.** (zhey uhN foh-tohy trey kohN-fohr-tah-bluh.) (*I have a very comfortable armchair.*)

La cuisine: The kitchen

La cuisine (lah kwee-zeen) (*the kitchen*) is the heart of many homes. Not only is it the place to prepare and eat home-cooked meals, but it's also where family and friends gather to discuss their day, make plans for the weekend, or talk about the weather. Here's a list of what you may find in a typical **cuisine**:

- **une cuisinière** (ewn kwee-zee-nyehr) (*stove*)
- **un réfrigérateur/un frigo** (uhN rey-free-zhey-rah-tuhr/uhN free-goh) (*refrigerator/fridge*)
- **un évier** (uhN ney-vyey) (*kitchen sink*)
- **un comptoir** (uhN kohN-twahr) (*counter*)
- **un four à micro-ondes** (uhN foohr ah mee-kroh-ohNd) (*microwave oven*)
- **un lave-vaisselle** (uhN lahv-vey-sehl) (*dishwasher*)
- **une table de cuisine** (ewn tah-bluh duh kwee-zeen) (*kitchen table*)
- **des chaises** (dey shehz) (*chairs*)

Here are some kitchen-related sentences:

> **J'ai une petite cuisine.** (zhey ewn puh-teet kwee-zeen.) (*I have a little kitchen.*)

> **J'ai une table de cuisine et des chaises modernes.** (zhey ewn tah-bluh duh kwee-zeen ey dey shehz moh-dehrn.) (*I have a kitchen table and some modern chairs.*)

> **J'ai aussi un lave-vaisselle haut de gamme.** (zhey oh-see uhN lahv-vey-sehl oh duh gahm.) (*I also have a top-of-the-line/high-end/fancy dishwasher.*)

In France, the kitchen isn't usually counted in the number of the rooms in a house. If you're looking to rent an apartment or a house and see **un appartement à trois pièces** (uhN nah-pahr-tuh-mahN ah trwah pyehs) in the French classifieds, it means a 4-room apartment, indicating a living room, two bedrooms, and a kitchen.

La chambre: The bedroom

Your **chambre** (shahN-bruh) (*bedroom*) is your own personal space that reflects your personality and taste. It's also where you can go when you need some privacy. Here's a list of some of the things you may find in a bedroom:

- ✔ **un lit** (uhN lee) (*bed*)
- ✔ **des lits jumeaux** (dey lee zhew-moh) (*twin beds*)
- ✔ **un lit d'une personne** (uhN lee dewn pehr-suhhn) (*single bed*)
- ✔ **un lit de deux personnes** (uhN lee duh duh pehr-suhhn) (*double bed*)
- ✔ **une commode** (ewn koh-muhhd) (*dresser*)
- ✔ **une armoire** (ewn ahr-mwahr) (*armoire*)
- ✔ **une table de nuit** (ewn tah-bluh duh nwee) (*nightstand*)
- ✔ **un réveil** (uhN rey-vehy) (*alarm clock*)
- ✔ **une couverture** (ewn kooh-vehr-tewr) (*blanket*)
- ✔ **un oreiller** (uhN noh-rey-yey) (*pillow*)
- ✔ **des draps** (dey drah) (*sheets*)

In describing your room, you can say

> **J'adore mon lit.** (zhah-dohr mohN lee.) (*I love my bed.*)
>
> **J'ai besoin d'un réveil.** (zhey buh-zwaN duhN rey-vehy.) (*I need an alarm clock.*)
>
> **J'achète des draps en soie.** (zhah-sheht dey drah ahN swah.) (*I buy silk sheets.*)

La salle de bains: The bathroom

In French, **la salle de bains** (lah sahl duh baN) (*bathroom*) and **les toilettes** (ley twah-leht) (*toilet*) are different. **La salle de bains** literally means *the room of baths,* or a place to bathe. It doesn't necessarily have a toilet. If you're looking for the restroom, be sure to ask for either **les toilettes** or **les W.C.** (ley vey sey*) (water closet*). Note that the letter **w** (dooh-bluh vey) in **W.C.** is pronounced like a French **v** (vey) to give it a shorter form.

Here are some things you commonly find in **la salle de bains**:

- ✔ **une baignoire** (ewn beh-nwahr) (*bath tub*)
- ✔ **un bidet** (uhN bee-deh) (*bidet*)

- **une douche** (ewn doohsh) (*shower*)
- **un lavabo** (uhN lah-vah-boh) (*sink*)
- **une serviette** (ewn sehr-vyeht) (*towel*)
- **un miroir** (uhN mee-rwahr) (*mirror*)
- **une brosse** (ewn bruhhs) (*hairbrush*)
- **un peigne** (uhN peh-nyuh) (*comb*)
- **un rasoir** (uhN rah-zwahr) (*razor*)
- **une brosse à dents** (ewn bruhhs ah dahN) (*toothbrush*)
- **du dentifrice** (dew dahN-tee-frees) (*toothpaste*)
- **du savon** (dew sah-vohN) (*soap*)

If you're missing an important item in the bathroom either at somebody's house or in a hotel room, use the question **Où est . . . ?** (ooh ey . . . ?) (*Where is . . . ?*) For example, **Où est la serviette ?** (ooh ey lah sehr-vyeht?) (*Where is the towel?*).

Talkin' the Talk

Suzanne, a student at the Sorbonne, is looking for a roommate to share her rent and other expenses. She has posted an ad and found another student, Agnès, who is interested in sharing the apartment. The two meet to discuss the situation. (Track 11)

Suzanne: **Où habites-tu maintenant ?**
ooh ah-beet-tew maN-tuh-nahN?
Where do you live now?

Agnès: **J'habite en banlieue mais je voudrais être plus près de l'université. Où se trouve l'appartement ?**
zhah-beet ahN bahN-lyuh mey zhuh vooh-drey eh-truh plew preh duh lew-nee-vehr-see-tey. ooh suh troohv lah-pahr-tuh-mahN?
I live in the suburbs, but I'd like to be closer to the university. Where is the apartment located?

Suzanne: **L'appartement se trouve dans le 5ᵉ [cinquième] arrondissement, près de la Sorbonne.**
lah-pahr-tuh-mahN suh troohv dahN luh saNk-ee-ehm ah-rohN-dees-mahN, preh duh lah sohr-buhhn.
The apartment is in the 5th district, near the Sorbonne.

Agnès :   **Combien de pièces y a-t-il ?**
kohN-byaN duh pyehs ee ah-teel?
How many rooms are there?

Suzanne: **Il y a trois pièces: un séjour, deux chambres et la cuisine.**
eel ee ah trwah pyehs: uhN sey-zhoohr, duh shahN-bruh ey lah kwee-zeen.
There are three rooms: a living room, two bedrooms, and the kitchen.

Agnès: **Est-ce que l'appartement est meublé ?**
ehs kuh lah-pahr-tuh-mahN ey muh-bley?
Is the apartment furnished?

Suzanne: **Oui, il y a un canapé, un fauteuil, une table de salon et une télévision dans le séjour et un lit, une armoire et une table de nuit dans la chambre.**
wee, eel ee ah uhN kah-nah-pey, uhN foh-tohy, ewn tah-bluh duh sah-lohN ey ewn tey-ley-vee-zyohN dahN luh sey-zhoohr ey uhN lee, ewn ahr-mwahr ey ewn tah-bluh duh nwee dahN lah shahN-bruh.
Yes, there's a sofa, a chair, a coffee table, and a television in the living room and a bed, an armoire, and a nightstand in the bedroom.

Agnès: **Est-ce que la cuisine est aménagée ?**
ehs kuh lah kwee-zeen ey tah-mey-nah-zhey?
Is the kitchen equipped?

Suzanne: **Oui, il y a un frigo, une cuisinière et un four à micro-ondes.**
wee, eel ee ah uhN free-goh, ewn kwee-zee-nyehr ey uhN foohr ah mee-kroh-ohNd.
Yes, there's a fridge, a stove, and a microwave.

Agnès: **Combien est le loyer ?**
kohN-byaN ey luh lwah-yey?
How much is the rent?

Suzanne: **550 [cinq cent cinquante] euros par mois.**
saNk sahN saNk-ahNt uh-roh pahr mwah.
550 euros a month.

Agnès: **C'est parfait !**
sey pahr-fey!
It's perfect!

Mentioning What You Own

In talking about where and how you live, you may want to mention your most valued personal possessions, such as your collection of posters or your special hats. The following list gives you some words for talking about your stuff:

- **des livres** (dey lee-vruh) (*some books*)
- **des bandes dessinées** (dey bahNd dey-see-ney) (*some comic books*)
- **des bijoux** (dey bee-zhooh) (*some jewelry*)
- **des souvenirs** (dey sooh-vuh-neer) (*some souvenirs*)
- **des photos** (dey foh-toh) (*some photos*)
- **des albums** (dey zahl-buhhm) (*some albums*)
- **des posters** (dey poh-stehr) (*some posters*)
- **une radio** (ewn rah-dyoh) (*a radio*)
- **un mobile/un cellulaire** (uhN moh-beel/uhN sehl-lew-lehr) (*a cell phone*)
- **un journal intime** (uhN zhoohr-nahl aN-teem) (*a diary*)
- **une bicyclette/un vélo** (ewn bee-see-kleht/uhN vey-loh) (*a bicycle/a bike*)
- **une voiture/une auto** (ewn vwa-tewr/ewn oh-toh) (*a car*)
- **une table de ping-pong** (ewn tah-bluh duh ping-pong) (*a ping-pong table*)
- **un billiard** (uhN bee-yahr) (*a billiard table*)
- **des skis** (dey skee) (*some skis*)
- **des patins** (dey pah-taN) (*some skates*)
- **des vêtements** (dey veht-mahN) (*some clothes*)

Explaining what you have

To talk about what you have, you can use the verb **avoir** (*to have*). Look at the conjugation of this verb:

Conjugation	Pronunciation	Translation
j'ai	zhey	*I have*
tu as	tew ah	*you have*
il/elle/on a	eel/ehl/ohNn ah	*he/she/it/one has*
nous avons	nooh zah-vohN	*we have*
vous avez	vooh zah-vey	*you have*
ils/elles ont	eel/ehl zohN	*they have*

Here are some example sentences about possessions that use **avoir**:

J'ai une petite voiture italienne. (zhey ewn puh-teet vwah-tewr ee-tah-lyehn.) (*I have a little Italian car.*)

Tu as une guitare ? (tew ah ewn gee-tahr?) (*Do you have a guitar?*)

Mon copain a des trophées de tennis dans sa chambre. (mohN koh-paN ah dey troh-fey duh tey-nees dahN sah shahN-bruh.) (*My friend has tennis trophies in his room.*)

Noting what's yours, mine, and ours

When you talk about possessions, you'll likely use possessive adjectives, such as *my, our, your,* and so on. For example, you may say, "My room is very small" or "Your bikes are in the garage." You use possessive adjectives the same way in French as you do in English. Here's an important difference, however: Because French nouns have a gender, the possessive adjectives change to agree with the gender (masculine or feminine) and number (singular or plural) of the noun, just as the articles **le/la/les** (luh/lah/ley) (*the*) do. Table 4-1 shows you how to say *my* as well as *your* (to another person in a familiar setting). Refer to Chapter 2 of Book III for more on gender and possessive words.

Table 4-1	Possessive Adjectives		
In English	*Masculine Singular (or Singular before a Vowel or Mute h)*	*Feminine Singular*	*Masculine/ Feminine Plural*
my	**mon** (mohN)	**ma** (mah)	**mes** (mey)
your	**ton** (tohN)	**ta** (tah)	**tes** (tey)

Here are some examples and guidelines for using these possessive adjectives:

✔ Before a masculine singular noun or any singular noun starting with a vowel or mute **h**, use **mon/ton**:

Mon/ton mobile est sur la table. (mohN/tohN moh-beel ey sewr lah tah-bluh.) (*My/your cell phone is on the table.*)

Mon/ton ordinateur est neuf. (mohN/tohN nohr-dee-nah-tuhr ey nuhf.) (*My/your computer is new.*)

✔ Before a feminine singular noun that doesn't start with a vowel or mute **h**, use **ma/ta**:

ma/ta radio (mah/tah rah-dyoh) (*my/your radio*)

✔ Before any plural noun, use **mes/tes**:

   Mes/tes souvenirs (mey/tey sooh-vuh-neer) (*my/your souvenirs*)

Talkin' the Talk

Suzanne and Agnès now talk about the personal possessions they'll have in their shared apartment. (Track 12)

Suzanne: **Tu as beaucoup de choses à apporter ?**
tew ah boh-kooh duh shohz ah ah-pohr-tey?
Do you have a lot of things to bring?

Agnès: **J'ai mes livres, mes vêtements et ma guitare.**
zhey mey lee-vruh, mey veht-mahN ey mah gee-tahr.
I have my books, my clothes, and my guitar.

Suzanne: **Moi, j'ai un petit piano numérique.**
mwah, zhey uhN puh-tee pyah-noh new-mey-reek.
I have a little digital piano.

Agnès :   **Cool. Ah ! J'ai aussi une collection de photos à mettre au mur.**
koohl. ah! zhey oh-see ewn koh-lehk-syohN duh foh-toh ah meh-troh mewr.
Cool. Oh! I also have a collection of photos to put on the wall.

Suzanne: **C'est bien. Tu as probablement des bijoux comme moi.**
sey byaN. tew ah proh-bah-bluh-mahN dey bee-zhooh kuhhm mwah.
You probably have jewelry like me.

Agnès: **Pas beaucoup. Mais je suis assez sportive et j'ai des patins à glace et des skis.**
pah boh-kooh. mey zhuh swee ah-sey spohr-teev ey zhey dey pah-taN ah glahs ey dey skee.
Not a lot. But I am pretty athletic, and I have ice skates and skis.

Suzanne: **Il y a un grand placard dans ta chambre. Ça ira.**
eel ee ah uhN grahN plah-kahr dahN tah shahN-bruh. sah ee-rah.
There is a big closet in your room. It'll be fine.

Agnès:	**Et toi, tu as beaucoup de choses dans l'appartement ?** ey twah, tew ah boh-kooh duh shohz dahN lah-pahr-tuh-mahN? *How about you, do you have a lot of things in the apartment?*
Suzanne:	**Oui, j'habite là depuis deux ans.** wee, zhah-beet lah duh-pwee duh zahN. *Yes, I've been living there for two years.*

Your Entourage: Talking about Your Family

No matter where you go, a common topic of conversation is family. People may ask you whether you have brothers and sisters, grandparents, cousins, children, and so on. In French, these make up your **entourage** (ahN-tooh-rahzh), all the people who are a part of your life. Here are some terms for your immediate family:

- **mon mari** (mohN mah-ree) (*my husband*)
- **ma femme** (mah fahm) (*my wife*)
- **mon père** (mohN pehr) (*my father*)
- **ma mère** (mah mehr) (*my mother*)
- **mes parents** (mey pah-rahN) (*my parents*)
- **mon fils** (mohN fees) (*my son*)
- **ma fille** (mah feey) (*my daughter*)
- **mes enfants** (mey zahN-fahN) (*my children*)
- **mon frère** (mohN frehr) (*my brother*)
- **ma sœur** (mah suhr) (*my sister*)

When you talk about aunts, uncles, grandparents, and others beyond Mom and Dad and brothers and sisters, use these words:

- **mes grands-parents** (mey grahN-pah-rahN) (*my grandparents*)
- **mon grand-père** (mohN grahN-pehr) (*my grandfather*)
- **ma grand-mère** (mah grahN-mehr) (*my grandmother*)

- **mes petits-enfants** (mey puh-tee-zahN-fahN) (*my grandchildren*)
- **mon neveu** (mohN nuh-vuh) (*my nephew*)
- **ma nièce** (mah nyehs) (*my niece*)
- **mon cousin/ma cousine** (mohN kooh-zaN/mah kooh-zeen) (*my cousin*)
- **mon oncle** (m) (mohN nohN-kluh) (*my uncle*)
- **ma tante** (mah tahNt) (*my aunt*)

Many American households consider pets to be part of the family, and people in the French-speaking world would agree. All you have to do is look at classic comic books like *Tintin* or *Astérix,* which are products of French-speaking Belgium — a main character is always accompanied by his dog. Here are some examples of common house pets:

- **mon chien** (mohN shyaN) (*my dog*)
- **mon chat** (mohN shah) (*my cat*)
- **mon oiseau** (mohN nwah-zoh) (*my bird*)
- **mon poisson rouge** (mohN pwah-sohN roohzh) (*my goldfish*)
- **mon lapin** (mohN lah-paN) (*my rabbit*)

In English, you can refer to a whole family by making the last name plural: the Millers or the Whites, for example. In French, however, you can't add an *s* to a proper name. Instead, you use the plural article **les** (*the*) before the name. So **Monsieur et Madame Texier** (muh-syuh ey mah-dahm tehk-syey) (*Mr. and Mrs. Texier*), for example, are **les Texier** (ley tehk-syey).

Talkin' the Talk

Stéphane and Julie are former pen pals who are planning to meet someday. Julie Skypes him with some news. This is the conversation from their online video call. (Track 13)

Julie: **Salut, Stéphane. Je viens de recevoir un chien. Il est tout jeune et tout mignon.**
sah-lew stey-fahn. zhuh vyaN duh ruh-suh-vwahr uhN shyaN. eel ey tooh zhuhn ey tooh mee-nyohN.
Hi, Stephane. I just got a dog. He's very young and very cute.

Stéphane:	**Bonjour, Julie. Montre-moi ton chien ! Ah, le voilà ! Comment il s'appelle ?**
	bohN-zhoohr zhew-lee. mohN-truh-mwah tohN shyaN! ah, luh vwah-lah! koh-mahN eel sah-pehl?
	Hello, Julie. Show me your dog! Ah, there he is! What's his name?

Julie:	**Il s'appelle Chouchou. C'est mon bébé !**
	eel sah-pehl shooh-shooh. sey mohN bey-bey!
	His name is Chouchou (Honey). He's my baby!

Stéphane:	**Moi aussi, j'ai un chien, un gros chien. Mais il est dehors en ce moment, en train de jouer avec le chat.**
	mwah oh-see, zhey uhN shyaN, uhN groh shyaN. mey eel ey duh-ohr ahN suh moh-mahN, ahN traN duh zhooh-ey ah-vehk luh shah.
	I have a dog, too, a big dog. But he's outside at the moment, playing with the cat.

Julie:	**Je vais donner un bain à Chouchou. Á blentôt.**
	zhuh vey duhh-ney uhN baN ah shooh-shooh. ah byaN-toh.
	I'm going to give Chouchou a bath. Talk to you soon.

Stéphane:	**Au revoir, Julie ! Au revoir, Chouchou !**
	Ohr-vwar zhew-lee! ohr-vwar shooh-shooh!
	Bye, Julie! Bye, Chouchou!

Your Daily Routine

Whether your daily routine is boring, normal, or totally off the beaten path, it's *your* daily routine, and it's important to you. This section introduces you to a variety of ways to describe that routine from morning to evening, from preparing yourself for the day ahead to going to bed.

Beginning the day

As you get ready to start the day, you wake up, get up, wash, brush your teeth, style your hair, get dressed, and so on. To express all those actions that concern only you, you have to use reflexive verbs in French.

A *reflexive verb* is one in which the subject performs the action on itself. For example, in the English sentence *I cut myself,* the subject (*I*) is performing an action (*cut*) and the receiver of that action is *myself,* which refers back to the subject. Reflexive verbs are much more common in French than they are in English. For example, to say *I wake up* in French, you say **je me réveille** (zhuh muh rey-vey) (Literally: *I wake myself up*).

Reflexive verbs have an added pronoun — the reflexive pronoun — before the verb (check out Chapter 3 of Book IV for details). In the infinitive (dictionary) form, the sign of a reflexive verb is the pronoun **se** (suh), which means *oneself,* but it can also fill in for *myself, yourself,* and so on, depending on the subject of the sentence. Many reflexive verbs are just regular **-er** verbs; the only thing to remember when conjugating them is to put the appropriate reflexive pronoun before the verb.

Here's the conjugation of the reflexive verb **se réveiller** (suh rey-vey-ey) (*to wake up*):

Conjugation	Pronunciation	Translation
je me réveille	zhuh muh rey-vey	*I wake up*
tu te réveilles	tew tuh rey-vey	*you wake up*
il/elle/on se réveille	eel/ehl/ohN suh rey-vey	*he/she/it/one wakes up*
nous nous réveillons	nooh nooh rey-vey-ohN	*we wake up*
vous vous réveillez	vooh vooh rey-vey-ey	*you wake up*
ils/elles se réveillent	eel/ehl suh rey-vey	*they wake up*

After you wake up, you have to get out of bed. In French, you use the reflexive verb **se lever** (suh luh-vey) (*to get up*). Here's the conjugation of **se lever**:

Conjugation	Pronunciation	Translation
je me lève	zhuh muh lehv	*I get up*
tu te lèves	tew tuh lehv	*you get up*
il/elle/on se lève	eel/ehl/ohN suh lehv	*he/she/it/one gets up*
nous nous levons	nooh nooh luh-vohN	*we get up*
vous vous levez	vooh vooh luh-vey	*you get up*
ils/elles se lèvent	eel/ehl suh lehv	*they get up*

In addition to **se réveiller** and **se lever**, you may need the following reflexive verbs to describe your morning routine:

- ✔ **se laver** (suh lah-vey) (*to wash*)
- ✔ **se doucher** (suh dooh-shey) (*to shower*)
- ✔ **se baigner** (suh bey-nyey) (*to bathe*)

> ✔ **se raser** (suh rah-zey) (*to shave*)
>
> ✔ **se brosser les dents** (suh broh-sey ley dahN) (*to brush your teeth*)
>
> ✔ **se brosser les cheveux** (suh broh-sey ley shuh-vuh) (*to brush your hair*)
>
> ✔ **se peigner (les cheveux)** (suh pey-nyey [ley shuh-vuh]) (*to comb [your hair]*)
>
> ✔ **s'habiller** (sah-bee-yey) (*to get dressed*)
>
> ✔ **s'en aller** (sahN nah-ley) (*to leave*)

Book I

Speaking in Everyday Settings

You can use a number of these reflexive verbs to describe your daily routine or someone else's. Here are some examples:

> **Je me réveille à huit heures.** (zhuh muh rey-vey ah weet uhr.) (*I wake up at 8 o'clock.*)
>
> **Il se douche.** (eel suh doohsh.) (*He takes a shower.*)
>
> **Elle s'habille.** (ehl sah-beey.) (*She's getting dressed.*)

Because reflexive verbs are used for personal matters such as washing hair and brushing teeth, you don't need possessive adjectives before parts of the body in French. The reflexive pronoun shows that you're doing an action to yourself, so that the possessive adjective (*my, your, his, her*) would be redundant:

> **Nous nous brossons les dents.** (nooh nooh broh-sohN ley dahN.) (*We brush our teeth.*)
>
> **Elles se lavent les mains.** (ehl suh lahv ley maN.) (*They're washing their hands.*)

Ending the day

As you end the day, you once again become absorbed in yourself, and you have to use some reflexive verbs for the actions you perform at bedtime. You can see how to say *to shower* and *to brush your teeth* in the preceding section, but add the following terms to your list of reflexive verbs:

> ✔ **se déshabiller** (suh dey-zah-bee-yey) (*to get undressed*)
>
> ✔ **se reposer** (suh ruh-poh-zey) (*to rest*)
>
> ✔ **se coucher** (suh kooh-shey) (*to go to bed*)
>
> ✔ **s'endormir** (sahN-dohr-meer) (*to fall asleep*)

Doing chores

In French, you can do any number of household chores with the verb **faire** (fehr) (*to do, to make*). **Faire** is a handy verb because you use it in many expressions. You sometimes use it in place of **jouer** (zhooh-ey) (*to play*) when talking about sports and instruments. You also use it when talking about the weather, travel, and other things. Look at the conjugation of the verb **faire**.

Conjugation	Pronunciation	Translation
je fais	zhuh fey	*I do/make*
tu fais	tew fey	*you do/make*
il/elle/on fait	eel/ehl/ohN fey	*he/she/it/one does/makes*
nous faisons	nooh fuh-zohN	*we do/make*
vous faites	vooh feht	*you do/make*
ils/elles font	eel/ehl fohN	*they do/make*

Here's a list of household chores and errands that use **faire**:

- **faire le lit** (fehr luh lee) (*to make the bed*)
- **faire le café** (fehr luh kah-fey) (*to make [the] coffee*)
- **faire le ménage** (fehr luh mey-nahzh) (*to do the housework*)
- **faire la cuisine** (fehr lah kwee-zeen) (*to cook*)
- **faire la vaisselle** (fehr lah vey-sehl) (*to do the dishes*)
- **faire la lessive** (fehr lah ley-seev) (*to do the laundry*)
- **faire les courses** (fehr ley koohrs) (*to do errands*)

And here are some example sentences:

> **Papa fait la cuisine le dimanche.** (pah-pah fey lah kwee-zeen luh dee-mahNsh.) (*Dad cooks on Sundays.*)
>
> **Je fais mon lit dès que je me réveille.** (zhuh fey mohN lee dey kuh zhuh muh rey-vehy.) (*I make my bed as soon as I wake up.*)

As handy as **faire** is, it can't do everything. For things like vacuuming and cleaning the bathroom, you need a few other verbs: To say *vacuum* in French, use the verb **passer** (pah-sey) (*to pass*), which is a regular **-er** verb, followed by the word for *vacuum cleaner*, **l'aspirateur** (m) (lah-spee-rah-tuhr): **Il passe l'aspirateur** (eel pahs lah-spee-rah-tuhr) (*He is vacuuming*).

Another regular verb associated with cleaning is the verb **ranger** (rahN-zhey) (*to arrange, to straighten up, to tidy up*): **Je range ma chambre** (zhuh rahNzh mah shahN-bruh) (*I tidy up my room*).

Enjoying meals

Just like in the United States, where people may eat "dinner" in the middle of the day (common in the South) or in the evening, people in the francophone world use different names for their meals. So whereas the French use the term **dîner** (dee-ney) (*dinner*) for an evening meal and **souper** (sooh-pey) (*supper*) for a light after-theater or after-movie meal, the Québécois use the term **dîner** for their midday meal and **souper** for their evening meal.

When you're talking about eating and drinking in French, you need to know the verbs **manger** (mahN-zhey) (*to eat*), **prendre** (prahN-druh) (*to take*), and **boire** (bwahr) (*to drink*). Check out Chapter 3 of Book III or the verb tables in Appendix A, which show you how to conjugate regular and irregular verbs.

Here are some examples of **manger** and **boire** in action:

> **Nous mangeons des légumes tous les jours.** (nooh mahN-zhohN dey ley-gewm tooh ley zhoohr.) (*We eat vegetables every day.*)

> **Je bois du café le matin.** (zhuh bwah dew kah-fey luh mah-taN.) (*I drink coffee in the morning.*)

In English, when you talk about what's on the menu at mealtime, you use the verb *to have*: "We're having soup and sandwiches," for example, or "They're having salad." In French, however, you use the verb **prendre,** which means *to take*:

> **Pour le petit déjeuner, je prends du pain et de la confiture.** (poohr luh puh-tee dey-zhuh-ney, zhuh prahN dew paN ey duh lah kohN-fee-tewr.) (*For breakfast, I have bread and jam.* Literally: *For breakfast, I take bread and jam.*)

This section explains the kinds of foods eaten during a typical meal in France. You can find information on grocery shopping and cooking in Chapter 7 of Book I and info on dining out in Chapter 2 of Book II.

A bounty for breakfast

The word for *breakfast* is **le petit déjeuner** (luh puh-tee dey-zhuh-ney) in France and **le déjeuner** (luh dey-zhuh-ney) in Québec. The traditional French breakfast is usually made up of the following:

- ✔ **le café** (luh kah-fey) (*coffee*): If you don't like your coffee black, you can drink **le café au lait** (luh kah-fey oh leh) (*coffee with hot milk, usually served in a bowl*) or **le café crème** (luh kah-fey krehm) (*coffee with a little milk*).

- ✔ **le thé nature** (luh tey nah-tewr) (*plain tea*): If plain tea isn't your cup of tea, opt for **le thé au lait** (luh tey oh leh) (*tea with milk*), **le thé au citron/le thé citron** (luh tey oh see-trohN/luh tey see-trohN) (*tea with lemon*), or **la tisane** (lah tee-zahn) (*herbal tea*).

✔ **le pain** (luh paN) (*bread*) or **le pain grillé** (luh paN gree-yey) (*toast*): You can also get **les tartines** (ley tahr-teen) (*slices of bread with some kind of spread*), often with **le beurre** (luh buhr) (*butter*) or **la confiture** (lah kohN-fee-tewr) (*jam*).

✔ **un croissant** (uhN krwah-sahN) (*a croissant*): A French breakfast may include pastries like **le pain au chocolat** (luh paN oh shoh-koh-lah) (*a chocolate-filled croissant*), **le chausson aux pommes** (luh shoh-sohN oh puhhm) (*an applesauce-filled danish*), or **le pain aux raisins** (luh paN oh rey-zaN) (*raisin bread*).

Eating lunch

The word for *lunch* is **le déjeuner** (luh dey-zhuh-ney) in France and **le dîner** (luh dee-ney) in Québec and other French-speaking countries. Common lunch items include

✔ **un sandwich** (uhN sahN-dweesh) (*a sandwich*)

✔ **une salade** (ewn sah-lahd) (*a salad*)

✔ **une soupe** (ewn soohp) (*soup*)

✔ **une omelette** (ewn ohm-leht) (*an omelet*)

Dinner time!

The word for the evening meal is **le dîner** (luh dee-ney) in France and **le souper** (luh sooh-pey) in Québec and other francophone countries. French families usually eat dinner around 7:30 or 8:00 p.m. The French are more formal when sitting down to dinner, and even on a weekday, the dinner consists of at least an appetizer, a main dish, and a cheese platter.

L'entrée (lahN-trey) (*the appetizer, starter*) begins the meal and can be anything from soup to **pâté** (pah-tey) (*pâté, a meat paste*) to a tomato salad. The *main dish*, or **le plat principal** (luh plah praN-see-pahl), usually consists of **viande** (vyahNd) (*meat*), **volaille** (voh-lahy) (*poultry*), or **poisson** (pwah-sohN) (*fish*) and some **légumes** (ley-gewm) (*vegetables*). **Le plat principal** is usually followed by a salad, a cheese platter, and a dessert.

Snacking between meals

After coming home from school, children enjoy **le goûter** (luh gooh-tey) (*midafternoon snack*), which usually consists of bread with butter, jam, or chocolate. If you suddenly find yourself hungry between meals, you can always have **un casse-croûte** (uhN kahs-krooht) (*a snack*. Literally: *break the crust*), such as a crêpe at a stand in Paris, a hot dog sold by a street vendor in Montréal, or anything in between.

Having fun and relaxing on the weekend

People enjoy some activities on the weekend wherever they live: sports, hobbies, family time, going to movies, and so on. The following sentences give you some idea of how to talk about your weekend activities in French:

> **Moi, le week-end, je joue au tennis avec un copain.** (mwah, luh wee-kehnd, zhuh zhooh oh teh-nees ah-vehk uhN koh-paN.) (*On weekends, I play tennis with a friend.*)

> **Je fais la grasse matinée le samedi matin.** (zhuh fey lah grahs mah-tee-ney luh sahm-dee mah-taN.) (*I sleep late on Saturday mornings.*)

> **Je vais au cinéma ou au concert le samedi soir.** (zhuh vey oh see-ney-mah ooh oh kohN-sehr luh sahm-dee swahr.) (*I go to the movies or to a concert on Saturday nights.*)

When you say "on Mondays," "on Tuesdays," or "on the weekend," you mean that you regularly do something on that day or on weekends. In French, you don't translate "on," but you use the word **le** (*the*) in front of the day or the word **week-end**, as in **Le samedi, j'ai une classe de yoga** (luh sahm-dee zhey ewn klahs duh yoh-gah) (*On Saturdays, I have a yoga class*). Also remember that in Québec, you often hear **la fin de semaine** (lah faN duh suh-mehn) (*the end of the week*) rather than **le week-end**.

Here are some other things you may do in your free time:

> **Je lis mes magazines favoris.** (zhuh lee mey mah-gah-zeen fah-voh-ree.) (*I read my favorite magazines.*)

> **Je regarde les sports à la télé.** (zhuh ruh-gahrd ley spohr ah lah tey-ley.) (*I watch sports on TV.*)

> **Je fais toujours une longue randonnée en montagne.** (zhuh fey tooh-zhoor ewn lohNg rahN-doh-ney ahN mohN-tah-nyuh.) (*I always go for a long hike in the mountains.*)

> **Je fais du vélo à la campagne.** (zhuh fey dew vey-loh ah lah kahN-pah-nyuh.) (*I bike in the countryside.*)

> **Je fais un bon petit dîner pour ma famille.** (zhuh fey uhN bohN puh-tee dee-ney poohr mah fah-meey.) (*I make a good little dinner for my family.*)

> **Je fais du jardinage.** (zhuh fey dew zhahr-dee-nahzh.) (*I take care of the garden.*)

Talkin' the Talk

Once in a while, former pen pals Stéphane and Julie Skype each other. This is one of their conversations.

Julie: **Salut, Stéphane. Ça va aujourd'hui ?**
              sah-lew stey-fahn. sah vah oh-zhoohr-dwee?
              Hi, Stephane. How are you today?

Stéphane: **Bonjour, Julie. Ça va mais j'ai plein de choses à faire aujourd'hui.**
              bohN-zhoohr, zhew-lee. sah vah mey zhey plaN duh shoz ah fehr oh-zhoohr-dwee.
              Hello, Julie. I'm fine, but I have lots of things to do today.

Julie: **Ah oui, pourquoi ?**
              ah wee, poohr-kwah?
              Oh, why is that?

Stéphane: **D'habitude j'aime faire la grasse matinée le samedi mais je dois aider mes parents à nettoyer la maison.**
              dah-bee-tewd zhehm fehr lah grahs mah-tee-ney luh sahm-dee mey zhuh dwah ey-dey mey pah-rahN ah ney-twah-yey lah mey-zohN.
              Usually I like to sleep late on Saturdays, but I have to help my parents to clean the house.

Julie: **Je fais ça tous les week-ends avec mes parents. Mon travail c'est toujours de nettoyer les salles de bain.**
              zhuh fey sah tooh ley wee-kehnd ah-vehk mey pah-rahN. mohN trah-vay sey tooh-zhoohr duh ney-twah-yey ley sahl duh baN.
              I do that every weekend with my parents. My job is always to clean the bathrooms.

Stéphane: **Passer l'aspirateur, laver les fenêtres, ce n'est pas mon truc. Je préfère lire mes magazines ou jouer à des jeux vidéo.**
              pah-sey lahs-pee-rah-tuhr, lah-vey ley fuh-neh-truh, suh ney pah mohN trewk. zhuh preh-fehr leer mey mah-gah-zeen ooh zhooh-ey ah dey zhuh vee-dey-oh.
              Vacuuming, washing windows, that's not my thing. I prefer to read my magazines and play video games.

Julie: **Je comprends. Tu vas quand même faire autre chose ce week-end, non ?**
zhuh kohM-prahN. tew vah kahN mehm fehr oh-truh shohz suh wee-kehnd, nohN?
I understand. Still, you're going to do other things this weekend, right?

Stéphane: **Heureusement ! Mes cousins arrivent de Paris cet après-midi.**
uh-ruhz-mahN! mey kooh-zaN ah-reev duh pah-ree seht ah-prey-mee-dee.
You bet! My cousins arrive from Paris this afternoon.

Julie: **Super ! Qu'est-ce que vous allez faire ?**
sew-pehr! kehs kuh vew zah-ley fehr?
Great! What are you going to do?

Stéphane: **Ce soir, on va sortir au restaurant avec mes parents. Demain, on va faire une randonnée et un pique-nique.**
suh swar, ohN vah sohr-teer oh reh-stoh-rahN ah-vehk mey pah-rahN. duh-maN, ohN vah fehr ewn rahn-doh-ney ey uhN peek-neek.
Tonight we're going out to the restaurant with my parents. Tomorrow we're going for a hike and a picnic.

Julie: **Ah ! Des activités en plein-air. Super ! Il fait beau chez toi ?**
ah! dey zahk-tee-vee-tey ahN plaNn ehr. sew-pehr! eel fey boh shey twah?
Oh! Outdoor activities. Great! Is the weather nice where you live?

Stéphane: **Il fait un temps splendide ici en automne. Les Parisiens adorent ça.**
eel fey uhN taN splahN-deed ee-see ahN noh-tuhhn. ley pah-ree-zyaN ah-dohr sah.
The weather is splendid here in autumn. Parisians love it.

Julie: **Je dois te quitter. Maman m'appelle. Au revoir, Stéphane. Amuse-toi bien !**
zhuh dwaht kee-tey. mah-mahN mah-pehl. ohr-vwahr, stey-fahn. ah-mewz-twah byaN!
I have to leave. Mom is calling me. Bye, Stephane. Have fun!

Stéphane: **Salut, Julie. À un de ces jours !**
sah-lew, zhew-lee. ah uhNd sey zhoohr!
Bye, Julie. See you around!

Chapter 5

Talking Business and Politics

• •

In This Chapter

▶ Mastering office-related vocab

▶ Calling on communication terms

▶ Chiming in on current issues

• •

Many people work and communicate with colleagues and partners from around the world. This chapter introduces you to workplace terms and phrases you may encounter while conducting business, working in an office, or communicating via phone, fax, or e-mail with a French-speaking colleague.

This chapter also introduces you to terms and phrases you need while communicating about business, current events, and politics. The French are well-known for their argumentative natures, which is why you often see animated discussions in which everyone wants to explain his or her point of view and, if possible, convince others to agree.

The right to disagree is an inalienable right in French society, which may explain why the right of workers to go on strike is so protected there (and why France sees so many strikes).

Getting Along at the Office

If you're traveling to France or another French-speaking country for business — or you're just meeting with French colleagues via teleconference or conversing online — rest assured that everyone wants to make the encounter pleasant. Here are some of the professionals and staff members you may encounter:

✔ **le président-directeur général (PDG)** (luh prey-zee-dahN-dee-rehk-tuhr zhey-ney-rahl [pey dey zhey]) (*the head of the company who functions as CEO, chairman, and managing director*)

✔ **le gérant/la gérante** (luh zhey-rahN/lah zhey-rahNt) (*manager [of a restaurant, hotel, shop]*)

✔ **le directeur/la directrice** (luh dee-rehk-tuhr/lah dee-rehk-trees) (*manager [of a company, business]*)

✔ **le personnel** (luh pehr-suhh-nehl) (*staff, employees*)

✔ **le/la propriétaire** (luh/lah proh-pree-ey-tehr) (*owner*)

Some French business practices may be different from your own. Knowing about and respecting these differences not only impresses your French-speaking counterparts but also brings you closer to achieving your goals.

During the 1980s, French businesses experienced an entrepreneurial explosion. The media and public utilities were privatized, and some of the newer and larger businesses were reorganized by American management consultants. These reorganized businesses tend to be more flexible and have a less centralized decision-making process than the older, family-owned businesses. Still, you may not find the same atmosphere of teamwork that prevails in the United States and Canada. Expect **le président-directeur général** to make most decisions. Employees below the **PDG** follow a strict chain of command, with the junior staff handing problems over to superiors.

Eyeing office supplies and equipment

Whether you're in your home office or abroad conducting business, your office includes things that are indispensable for working efficiently and accurately. Look around the office, and you'll see some very familiar **fournitures de bureau** (foohr-nee-tewr duh bew-roh) (*office supplies*), **matériel de bureau** (mah-tey-ree-ehl duh bew-roh) (*office equipment*), and **mobilier de bureau** (moh-bee-lyey duh bew-roh) (*office furniture*) that you can't do without:

✔ **les agrafes** (ley zah-grahf) (*staples*)

✔ **l'agrafeuse** (f) (lah-grah-fuhz) (*stapler*)

✔ **le bureau** (luh bew-roh) (*desk*)

✔ **les ciseaux** (ley see-zoh) (*scissors*)

✔ **le classeur à tiroirs** (luh klah-suhr ah tee-rwahr) (*file cabinet*)

✔ **la corbeille à papiers** (lah kohr-behy ah pah-pyey) (*wastepaper basket*)

✔ **le crayon** (luh krey-ohN) (*pencil*)

✔ **les élastiques** (m) (ley zey-lah-steek) (*rubber bands*)

✔ **les enveloppes** (f) (ley zahN-vluhhp) (*envelopes*)

✔ **les fichiers** (m) (ley fee-shyey) (*files*)

✔ **la gomme** (lah guhhm) (*eraser*)

✔ **la photocopieuse** (lah foh-toh-koh-pyuhz) (*copy machine*)

- ✔ **le ruban adhésif** (luh rew-bahN ah-dey-zeef) (*tape*)
- ✔ **le siège/la chaise de bureau** (luh syehzh/lah shehz duh bew-roh) (*office chair*)
- ✔ **le stylo** (luh stee-loh) (*pen*)
- ✔ **le tableau d'affichage** (luh tah-bloh dah-fee-shahzh) (*bulletin board*)
- ✔ **le télécopieur** (luh tey-ley-koh-pyuhr) (*fax machine*)
- ✔ **les trombones** (m) (ley trohN-buhhn) (*paper clips*)

Talking tech: Using computers and the Internet

Electronic communication is par for the business course in many countries, and the francophone world is no exception. In French, the World Wide Web is sometimes called **la toile** (lah twahl), which literally means *the web*. More often, French-speaking people call it **Le Web** (luh web).

Here are some handy computer and Internet-related terms to help you navigate electronic communication:

- ✔ **le clavier** (luh klah-vyey) (*keyboard*)
- ✔ **le curseur** (luh kewr-suhr) (*cursor*)
- ✔ **le fichier** (luh fee-shyey) (*file*)
- ✔ **l'icône** (f) (lee-kohn) (*icon*)
- ✔ **l'imprimante** (f) (laN-pree-mahNt) (*printer*)
- ✔ **le logiciel** (luh loh-zhee-syehl) (*software*)
- ✔ **le matériel** (luh mah-tey-ryehl) (*hardware*)
- ✔ **le moniteur** (luh moh-nee-tuhr) (*monitor*)
- ✔ **le mot de passe** (luh moh duh pahs) (*password*)
- ✔ **le navigateur** (luh nah-vee-gah-tuhr) (*web browser*)
- ✔ **l'ordinateur** (m) (lohr-dee-nah-tuhr) (*computer*)
- ✔ **la page d'accueil** (lah pahzh dah-kuhy) (*home page*)
- ✔ **le portable** (luh pohr-tah-bluh) (*laptop*)
- ✔ **le pseudo** (luh psuh-doh) (*username*)
- ✔ **le réseau** (luh rey-zoh) (*network*)
- ✔ **le serveur** (luh sehr-vuhr) (*server*)
- ✔ **la souris** (lah sooh-ree) (*mouse*)

- ✔ **surfer le Web** (sewr-fey luh wehb) (*to surf the web*)

- ✔ **le système d'exploitation** (luh see-stehm dehk-splwah-tah-syohN) (*operating system*)

- ✔ **télécharger** (tey-ley-shahr-zhey) (*to download/to upload*)

A French keyboard is set up differently from the one you're used to. Although French and English use the same letters of the alphabet, French includes accents over vowels as well as the **cédille** (*cedilla*) under the letter **c** (See Chapter 1 of Book I for accent marks). So French keyboards include keys that allow for the quick typing of these characters. On an American computer equipped with Windows, you can type letters with accents using special Alt codes. For example, you can type **é** by pressing Alt+130 on your numeric keypad. But on a French keyboard, you just press the key featuring **é**. Because Canada has bilingual laws, the keyboard layout commonly used in Canada allows you to type all accented French characters while serving all English functions.

Communicating at Work

The way people communicate in the professional and business world has been revolutionized by laptops, smartphones, tablets, and the Internet. Nowadays, people have effective and superfast means of establishing contact, including e-mailing one another at the click of a key.

Placing and taking calls

Although texting has become standard communication among friends and relatives, making phone calls is still important when you're discussing business, scheduling appointments with doctors or dentists, planning a big party, or making a reservation at a nice restaurant. These terms are relevant when using the phone:

- ✔ **appeler** (ahp-ley) (*to call*)

- ✔ **faire un coup de téléphone** (fehr uhN kooh duh tey-ley-fuhhn) (*to make a phone call*)

- ✔ **donner un coup de fil** (duhh-ney uhN kooh duh feel) (*to make a phone call — familiar phrase*)

- ✔ **composer un numéro** (kohN-poh-zey uhN new-mey-roh) (*to dial a number*)

✔ **raccrocher** (rah-kroh-shey) (*to hang up*)

✔ **répondre** (rey-pohN-druh) (*to answer*)

✔ **parler** (pahr-ley) (*to talk*)

✔ **écouter** (ey-kooh-tey) (*to listen*)

✔ **poser une question** (poh-zey ewn keh-styohN) (*to ask a question*)

✔ **la ligne est occupée** (lah lee-nyey toh-kew-pey) (*the line is busy*)

✔ **sur l'autre ligne** (sewr loh-truh lee-nyuh) (*on the other line*)

Next, we help you manage the conversation.

Making appointments: Being mindful of business hours

In European francophone countries, it's polite to schedule appointments several weeks in advance. However, some businesses may not confirm an appointment until the last minute. Here are some considerations to keep in mind when trying to set up an appointment:

✔ Don't plan on doing business in France during the two weeks before and after Christmas or Easter. Also avoid the months of July and August, when many stores, theaters, restaurants, and businesses close for an annual vacation.

✔ Generally speaking, businesses are open from 8:00 or 9:00 a.m. to noon and from 2:00 p.m. to 5:00 or 6:00 p.m. Monday through Friday. Many businesses don't open on Mondays until 2:00 p.m. and are open Saturdays from 9:00 a.m. to noon or 1:00 p.m. Even though businesses may be open on Saturdays, don't try to schedule appointments then. Saturday is usually reserved for sales meetings and conferences.

✔ You may also have trouble scheduling appointments in Belgium on **Bourse** (boohrs) days, which are Mondays in Antwerp and Wednesdays in Brussels, because businesspeople meet professional colleagues for lunch then.

✔ Europeans often take a longer lunch break than their North American counterparts. **Le déjeuner** (luh dey-zhuh-ney) (*lunch*) lasts anywhere from one and a half to two hours, and business lunches are also more common than business dinners. Lengthy and lavish lunches are usually reserved for a first meeting or for celebrating the closing of a deal.

Don't be the first to initiate business conversation at a meal. Let your host decide whether to discuss business right away or to wait until the after-meal coffee has been served.

Opening the conversation

After you dial a phone number, someone will probably answer the phone and greet you. Generally, you should expect the two words: **allô** (ah-loh) (*hello*) and **bonjour** (bohN-zhoohr) (*good morning, good day*). Sometimes, the person answering the phone also introduces him- or herself. Here are some terms to understand:

- **Allô, bonjour.** (ah-loh, bohN-zhoohr.) (*Hello, good morning.*)
- **C'est madame Girard à l'appareil.** (sey mah-dahm zhee-rahr ah lah-pah-rehy.) (*This is Madam Girard.*)
- **Vous désirez ?** (vooh dey-zee-rey?) (*How may I help you?*)
- **Un instant, s'il vous plaît.** (uhN naN-stahN, seel vooh pley.) (*One moment, please.*)
- **Ne quittez pas, s'il vous plaît.** (nuh kee-tey pah, seel vooh pley.) (*Please stay on the line.*)
- **Veuillez patienter, s'il vous plaît.** (vuh-yey pah-syahN-tey, seel vooh pley.) (*Please hold.*)
- **Qui est à l'appareil ?** (kee ey tah lah-pah-rehy?) (*Who is calling?*)
- **C'est de la part de qui ?** (sey duh lah pahr duh kee?) (*Who is calling?*)
- **Je vous le/la passe.** (zhuh vooh luh/lah pahs.) (*I'm transferring your call to him/her.*)

When you initiate a call, you may use the following phrases:

- **Bonjour, monsieur/madame.** (bohN-zhoohr, mah-dahm/muh-syuh.) (*Hello, sir/madam.*)
- **Je voudrais parler à . . .** (zhuh vooh-drey pahr-ley ah . . .) (*I would like to talk to . . .*)
- **Pourrais-je parler à . . . ?** (pooh-rehzh pahr-ley ah . . . ?) (*May I speak to . . . ?*)
- **Je voudrais demander rendez-vous.** (zhuh vooh-drey duh-mahN-dey rahN-dey-vooh.) (*I would like to make an appointment.*)
- **J'aimerais laisser un message.** (zhehm-rey leh-sey uhN mey-sahzh.) (*I would like to leave a message.*)

Getting clarification

You may run into problems during the call. Perhaps the connection is bad, or you lost it entirely, or the person's voice is muffled. You can explain the situation using the following phrases:

- **Nous avons été coupés.** (nooh zah-vohN ey-tey kooh-pey.) (*We've been cut off.*)

- **Je ne vous entends pas très bien.** (zhuhn vooh zahN-tahN pah trey byaN.) (*I don't hear you well.*)

- **Je n'ai pas compris.** (zhuh ney pah kohN-pree.) (*I didn't understand.*)

- **Pourriez-vous répéter, s'il vous plaît ?** (pooh-ryey-vooh rey-pey-tey, seel vooh pley?) (*Could you repeat, please?*)

Ending the call

Here are some phrases to use when you're ready to end the call, including thanking the person on the other end and saying good-bye:

- **Merci, je rappellerai.** (mehr-see, zhuh rah-pehl-rey.) (*Thanks, I'll call back.*)

- **Je vous remercie, monsieur/madame.** (zhuh vooh ruh-mehr-see, muh-syuh/mah-dahm.) (*I thank you, sir/madam.*)

- **Ça va comme ça. Tout est bien.** (sah vah kuhhm sah. tooh tey byaN.) (*That's fine.*)

- **C'est parfait.** (sey pahr-fey.) (*That's perfect.*)

- **Au revoir, monsieur/madame.** (ohr-vwahr, muh-syuh/mah-dahm.) (*Goodbye, sir/madam.*)

Talkin' the Talk

Dan Thompson, an American consultant, calls to set up an appointment with Monsieur Seiffert, the CEO of a chain of French **supermarchés** (sew-pehr-mahr-shey) (*supermarkets*). Monsieur Seiffert's secretary, **la secrétaire** (lah suh-krey-tehr), answers.

La secrétaire: **Compagnie France Supermarché, bonjour.**
kohN-pah-nyee frahNs sew-pehr-mahr-shey, bohN-zhoohr.
Hello, France Supermarket Company.

Dan: **Bonjour, madame. Dan Thompson à l'appareil. Passez-moi Monsieur Seiffert, s'il vous plaît.**
bohN-zhoohr, mah-dahm. dan tomp-sun ah lah-pah-rehy. pah-sey mwah muh-syuh see-fehr, seel vooh pley.
Hello, madam. This is Dan Thompson calling. Please transfer me to Mr. Seiffert.

La secrétaire: **Un instant. Ne raccrochez pas. Il est dans son bureau. Je vous le passe.**
uhN naN-stahN. nuh rah-kroh-shey pah. eel ey dahN sohN bew-roh. zhuh vooh luh pahs.
One moment. Don't hang up. He's in his office. I'll transfer you to him.

M. Seiffert: **Allô, Monsieur Thompson ?**
ah-loh, muh-syuh tomp-sun?
Hello, Mr. Thompson?

Dan: **Allô, Monsieur Seiffert, bonjour. Je vais être à Nice le 14 [quatorze] juin. Je voudrais fixer un rendez-vous pour discuter de votre stratégie de marketing.**
ah-loh, muh-syuh see-fehr, bohN-zhoohr. zhuh vey zeh-truh ah nees luh kah-tohrz zhwaN. zhuh vooh-drey feek-sey uhN rahN-dey-vooh poohr dee-skew-tey duh vuhh-truh strah-tey-zhee duh mahr-keh-teeng.
Hello, Mr. Seiffert. I'm going be in Nice on June 14. I would like to arrange a meeting to discuss your marketing strategy.

M. Seiffert: **Ah, bon. Un instant. Je consulte mon calendrier. Ça va, je suis libre le 14 [quatorze] juin à 15h30 [quinze heures trente].**
ah, bohN. uhN naN-stahN. zhuh kohN-sewlt mohN kah-lahN-dree-yey. sah vah, zhuh swee lee-bruh luh kah-tohrz zhwaN ah kaN zuhr trahNt.
Good. One moment. I'll consult my calendar. Okay, I'm free June 14 at 3:30 p.m.

Dan: **Très bien. Le 14 [quatorze] juin à 15h30 [quinze heures trente].**
treh byaN. luh kah-tohrz zhwaN ah kaN zuhr trahNt.
Very well. June 14 at 3:30 p.m.

M. Seifert: **Au revoir.**
ohr-vwahr.
Good bye.

Words to Know

. . . à l'appareil.	. . . ah lah-pah-rehy.	This is . . . calling.
Passez-moi . . .	pah-sey mwah . . .	Transfer me to . . .
un instant	uhN-naN-stahN	one moment
Ne raccrochez pas.	nuh rah-kroh-shey pah.	Don't hang up.
Il est/n'est pas dans son bureau.	eel ey/ney pah dahN sohN bew-roh.	He's in/out of his office.
Je vous le/la passe.	zhuh vooh luh/lah pahs.	I'll transfer you to him/her.
un rendez-vous	uhN rahN-dey-vooh	an appointment
Je consulte mon calendrier.	zhuh kohN-sewlt mohN kah-lahN-dree-yey.	I'll check my calendar.
Je suis libre . . .	zhuh swee lee-bruh . . .	I'm free . . .

Sending an e-mail or fax

With the Internet, the world has gotten smaller. Now you can stay in touch with business partners as well as with your family and friends via **le courrier électronique/le mél** (luh kooh-ryey ey-lehk-troh-neek/luh meyl) (*e-mail*). Sending an e-mail is generally as quick and easy as it is in English. (Flip to the earlier section "Talking tech: Using computers and the Internet" for a primer on computer-related terminology.)

Figuring out the steps for sending an attachment can be a bit tricky. Although specific instructions vary, in general, to send **une pièce jointe** (ewn pyehs zhwaNt) (*an attachment*), you do the following: Click on the icon **Insertion** (aN-sehr-syohN) (*Insert*), click on **Pièce jointe** (pyehs zhwaNt) (*Attachment*), and choose the correct *file,* or **fichier** (fee-shyey). Click on the button **Joindre** (zhwaN-druh) (*Attach*). Finally, click on **Envoyer** (ahN-vwah-yey) (*Send*).

To send a document that includes privileged information such as a signed contract, you can easily send **une télécopie/un fax** (ewn tey-ley-koh-pee/uhN fahks) (*a fax*). As in the United States, faxing is still common in small businesses or in hospitals because of patient confidentiality. If you're dialing from the United States, enter the international access code (011) followed by the country code (33 for France) followed by the receiving fax machine's number, skipping the 0 of the area code. Then press Send.

Talkin' the Talk

Monsieur Laroche is asking his secretary, Madame Rosier, to send a contract to a prospective client. (Track 14)

M. Laroche: **Madame Rosier, je vous prie d'envoyer un nouveau contrat à Monsieur Bouchard tout de suite.**
mah-dahm roh-zyey, zhuh vooh pree dahN-vwah-yey uhN nooh-voh kohN-trah ah muh-syuh booh-shahr tooh-dsweet.
Mrs. Rosier, please send a new contract to Mr. Bouchard right away.

Mme Rosier: **Oui, Monsieur Laroche. Est-ce que je l'envoie par courriel ou par fax ?**
wee, muh-syuh lah-rohsh. ehs kuh zhuh lahN-vwah pahr kooh-ryehl ooh pahr fahks?
Yes, Mr. Laroche. Should I send it by e-mail or by fax?

M. Laroche: **Il vaut mieux lui téléphoner et lui demander.**
eel voh myuh lwee tey-ley-foh-ney ey lwee duh-mahN-dey.
It would be better to call and ask him.

Mme Rosier: **Je vais peut-être faire les deux mais lui demander de nous faxer la page avec sa signature.**
zhuh vey puh-teh-truh fehr ley duh mey lwee duh-mahN-dey duh nooh fahk-sey lah pahzh ah-vehk sah see-nyah-tewr.
I may do both but ask him to fax us the page with his signature.

M. Laroche:	**Bonne idée ! Rappelez-lui aussi qu'il faudra nous envoyer le contrat signé par la poste dans les plus brefs délais.**
	buhhn ee-dey! rahp-ley-lwee oh-see keel foh-drah nooh zahN-vwa-yey luh kohN-trah see-nyey pahr lah puhhst dahN ley plew brehf dey-ley.
	Good idea! Remind him also that he will have to send us the signed contract by postal mail as soon as possible.
Mme Rosier :	**Oui, monsieur. Je m'en occupe.**
	wee, muh-syuh. zhuh mahN noh-kewp.
	Yes, sir. I'll take care of it.

Opening and closing a business letter

The most common form of address used when writing a business letter is **Monsieur, Madame** (mohN-syuh, mah-dahm) (*To whom it may concern*). With individuals who bear a professional title, **monsieur** (*sir*) or **madame** (*madam*) is followed by the professional title:

- **Monsieur le Directeur** (mohN-syuh luh dee-rehk-tuhr) (*Dear sir*)

  Madame la Directrice (mah-dahm lah dee-rehk-trees) (*Dear madam*)

- **Monsieur le docteur** (mohN-syuh luh dohk-tuhr) (*Dear doctor*)

  Madame le docteur (mah-dahm luh dohk-tuhr) (*Dear doctor*)

- **Monsieur le professeur** (mohN-syuh luh proh-feh-suhr) (*Dear professor*)

  Madame le professeur (mah-dahm luh proh-feh-sur) (*Dear professor*)

There may or may not be separate masculine and feminine forms of the professional title. In France, as per **l'Académie française** (the official moderator of the French language), there's still only **le professeur** and **le docteur**, so in formal writing, you should follow the official format. In Canada, however, most titles do exist in two forms. There, you may well see, for example, **Madame la professeure** (mah-dahm lah proh-feh-suhr).

Formal closings in e-mails tend to be short. Here are a few examples that are all equivalents of a simple *Sincerely:*

- **Avec mes salutations les plus cordiales** (ah-vehk mey sah-lew-tah-syohN ley plew kohr-dyahl)
- **Bien à vous** (byaN nah vooh)
- **Bien cordialement** (byaN kohr-dyahl-mahN)
- **Cordialement** (kohr-dyahl-mahN)
- **Cordiales salutations** (kohr-dyal sah-lew-tah-syohN)
- **Sincères salutations** (saN-sehr sah-lew-tah-syohN)

In formal letters, closings can be quite a bit longer and more flowery, such as the following:

> **Veuillez agréer, madame/monsieur, l'expression de mes sentiments distingués.** (vuh-yey zah-grey-ey, mah-dahm/muh-syuh, leyk-sprey-syohN duh mey sahN-tee-mahN dee-staN-gey.) (Literally: *Please accept the expression of my most distinguished sentiments.*)

Sending mail the old-fashioned way

Although many people prefer to communicate over the Internet these days, sometimes you need to send a postcard or a package through the regular postal mail. With the vocabulary and advice we share in this section, going to **la poste** (lah pohst) (*the post office*) will be a breeze.

Here are some general postal terms and services:

- **l'affranchissement** (m) (lah-frahN-shees-mahN) (*postage*)
- **la boîte postale** (lah bwaht poh-stahl) (*post office box*)
- **le code postal** (luh kuhhd poh-stahl) (*zip code*)
- **le courrier** (luh kooh-ryey) (*mail*)
- **le/la destinataire** (luh/lah deh-stee-nah-tehr) (*addressee*)
- **l'enveloppe** (f) (lahN-vluhhp) (*envelope*)
- **l'envoi spécial** (m) (lahN-vwah spey-syahl) (*special delivery*)
- **l'expéditeur/l'expéditrice** (lehk-spey-dee-tuhr/lehk-spey-dee-trees) (*sender*)
- **le facteur** (luh fahk-tuhr) (*the letter carrier*)
- **la lettre express** (lah leh-truh ehk-sprehs) (*express letter*)

✔ **la lettre recommandée** (lah leh-truh ruh-kuhh-mahN-dey) (*registered letter*)

✔ **le paquet/le colis** (luh pah-keh/luh koh-lee) (*package*)

✔ **le timbre** (luh taN-bruh) (*stamp*)

The postal service in France is a publicly owned company and constitutes the second largest postal company in Europe. It's one of the largest employers in France. When you visit France, you can't help but notice the bright yellow signs that indicate the post office as well as the bright yellow **boîtes aux lettres** (bwah toh leh-truh) (*mailboxes*). The postal service provides many services besides just mailing letters. You may purchase money orders, stamps, and phone cards; use a pay phone; send a fax; open a bank account; take out a loan; or invest money!

Discussing Events around the Water Cooler

Knowing what's going on locally as well as in the rest of the country and world is a matter of great importance for many people. The French, Belgian, Swiss, and Canadian media devote a lot of time to the economy and politics. What is the state of the economy? What is the latest scandal among politicians? Which topics are being debated? When you're informed, you, too, can join discussions during your breaks at the office, at lunchtime, or just about any time.

Keeping current: News and headlines

Whether you buy the paper at the local **kiosque** (kee-uhhsk) (*newsstand*) or go online to see what's happening in the world, the first things you see are the **gros titres** (groh tee-truh) (*the headlines*). Then you may read an article or listen to a podcast **sur un sujet d'actualité** (sewr uhN sew-zhey dahk-tew-ah-lee-tey) (*on a current topic*), such as the following:

✔ **culture** (kewl-tewr) (*culture*)

✔ **économie** (ey-koh-noh-mee) (*economy*)

✔ **emploi** (ahN-plwa) (*jobs*)

✔ **immobilier** (ee-moh-bee-lyey) (*real estate*)

✔ **météo** (mey-tey-oh) (*weather*)

✔ **politique** (poh-lee-teek) (*politics*)

✔ **santé** (sahN-tey) (*health*)

✔ **sciences** (syahNs) (*science*)

✔ **services** (sehr-vees) (*services*)

✔ **société** (soh-syey-tey) (*society*)

✔ **sport** (spohr) (*sport*)

Here are some terms related to journalism and the publication and layout of a **journal** (zhoor-nahl) (*newspaper*), **newsletter** (news-leht-uhr) (*newsletter*), or **magazine** (mah-gah-zeen) (*magazine*):

✔ **le quotidien** (luh koh-tee-dyaN) (*the daily [paper]*)

✔ **l'hebdomadaire** (m) (lehb-doh-mah-dehr) (*the weekly [paper/ magazine]*)

✔ **l'édition imprimée/électronique** (f) (ley-dee-syohN aN-pree-mey/ ey-leyk-troh-neek) (*printed/electronic version*)

✔ **à la une** (ah lah ewn) (*on page one*)

✔ **le dossier** (luh doh-syey) (*file/set of articles, columns, or features*)

✔ **les nouvelles** (f) (ley noo-vehl) (*the news*)

✔ **la presse** (lah prehs) (*the press*)

✔ **le reportage** (luh ruh-pohr-tahzh) (*report/set of articles/commentary*)

✔ **la rubrique** (lah rew-breek) (*section/column*)

A nose for news outlets

Three major newspapers published daily in France are **Le Monde** (luh mohNd), **Le Figaro** (luh fee-gah-roh), and **Libération** (lee-bey-rah-syohN). Each one has a particular political bias. These large daily newspapers don't publish on Sundays, but many French people buy the appropriately named **Le Journal du Dimanche** (luh zhoor-nahl dew dee-mahNsh) on Sunday.

The most popular daily newspaper, **L'Équipe** (ley-keep) (*The Team*) covers sports, and it *is* sold every day. Other popular publications include serious weekly magazines like **L'Express** (leyk-sprehs) and less serious ones like **La presse people** (lah prehs pee-pehl), a sensationalist tabloid-type magazine.

The French-speaking world has many television channels, both private and public. TV5Monde is a global television network broadcast worldwide like CNN is. It includes many editions, such as TV5Monde Europe, TV5Monde Afrique, and TV5 Québec Canada. TV5Monde États-Unis has news programs and movies subtitled in English.

French television channels have traditionally devoted a lot of time to local and international news. However, like everywhere else, more and more people in France want to catch up on the news on their own schedule. **La télé de rattrapage** (lah tey-ley duh rah-trah-pahzh) (*the TV of catching up*), a system of broadcasting television news on the Internet for a few weeks after its live airing, has become popular.

Wherever you watch your news, keep these key words in mind:

- **le blog** (luh blohg) (*blog*)
- **la chaîne** (lah shehn) (*channel*)
- **le communiqué de presse** (luh koh-mew-nee-key duh prehs) (*newsbrief*)
- **l'émission** (f) (ley-mee-syohN) (*broadcast*)
- **les informations** (f) (ley zaN-fohr-mah-syohN) (*news bulletin*)
- **le journal télévisé** (luh zhoor-nahl tey-ley-vee-zey) (*TV news*)
- **le podcast** (luh pohd-kahst) (*podcast*)
- **le programme** (luh proh-grahm) (*program*)
- **la vidéo** (lah vee-dey-oh) (*video*)

Following politics

Politics is in the air everywhere in France. Criticizing the government and asking for reforms has been a favorite activity among the French ever since the French Revolution of 1789. Here are some important words for talking politics:

- **la campagne présidentielle** (lah kahN-pah-nyuh prey-zee-dahN-syehl) (*presidential campaign*)
- **le candidat** (luh kahN-dee-dah) (*candidate*)
- **le débat** (luh dey-bah) (*debate*)
- **le discours** (luh dee-skoohr) (*speech*)
- **l'élection** (f) (ley-leyk-syohN) (*election*)
- **la polémique** (lah poh-ley-meek) (*polemic/controversy*)
- **le premier ministre** (luh pruh-myey mee-nees-truh) (*prime minister*)
- **le président** (luh prey-see-dahN) (*president*)

France has a democratic government with a president who heads the state and a prime minister who heads the government. But unlike the United States, whose political system has only two major parties, France has a multi-party system that includes many parties from the left (**la gauche**), from the center (**le centre**), and from the right (**la droite**); a few examples are **le Parti Communiste**, **le Parti Socialiste**, **l'Alliance Centriste**, and **le Front National.** This setup provides many options for political affiliations and sets the stage for interesting discussions.

Talkin' the Talk

During their lunch break, Didier and Jacqueline discuss the possibility that Sarkozy, the former president of France, will come back to politics after a scandal. (Track 15)

Didier: **Sarkozy veut revenir à la politique.**
sahr-koh-zee vuh ruh-vuh-neer ah lah poh-lee-teek.
Sarkozy wants to come back to politics.

Jacqueline: **Ah non ! Il y a trop de scandales dans sa vie politique et personnelle.**
ah-nohN! eel ee ah troh duh skahN-dahl dahN sah vee poh-lee-teek ey pehr-soh-nehl.
Oh no! There are too many scandals in his political and personal life.

Didier: **Sa vie personnelle n'a rien à voir avec la fonction publique.**
sah vee pehr-soh-nehl nah ryaN ah vwahr ah-vehk lah fohNk-syohN pew-bleek.
His personal life has nothing to do with public function.

Jacqueline: **Tu peux penser ce que tu veux. Moi, je ne veux pas le voir dans notre gouvernement.**
tew puh pahN-sey suh kuh tew vuh. mwah, zhuhn vuh pah luh vwahr dahN noh-truh gooh-vehr-nuh-mahN.
You can say what you want. I don't want to see him in our government.

Didier: **Ton orientation politique me surprend toujours.**
tohN noh-ryahN-tah-syohN poh-lee-teek muh sewr-prahN tooh-zhoohr.
Your political orientation always surprises me.

Chapter 6

Shopping at a Store and Online

In This Chapter

▶ Browsing through department stores

▶ Getting assistance while shopping

▶ Making online purchases

*L*e **shopping** (luh shoh-peeng) (*shopping*) — what a fun thing to do wherever you are! And when you're in a foreign country, you probably want to bring back a special souvenir, like a bottle of perfume, a designer scarf or handbag, or a CD full of songs that remind you of your travels. Whether you're in Paris, Montréal, Geneva, or Brussels, you're in a shopper's paradise! Although what you buy in these places won't come cheap, you'll have your selection of the best of the best. And after all, **une fois n'est pas coutume** (ewn fwah ney pah kooh-tewm) (*once isn't a habit,* or *once [in a while] does no harm*).

This chapter explains what you need to know to shop, including how to compare items, how to ask for assistance, what to say when you want to try something on, and more. And if you're the kind of shopper who prefers to hunt for deals from a cozy chair, we've got you covered; this chapter also helps you tackle online shopping.

Checking Out Department Stores

Where you go shopping depends on what you want to buy. For some items, a discount store or an upscale boutique is the better choice. For many of your needs, though, department stores are the answer. France has several upscale department stores throughout the country, such as **Le Printemps** (luh praN-tahN) and **Les Galeries Lafayette** (ley gah-luh-ree lah-fah-yeht). Québec has its own unique department stores as well as well-known American stores like Nordstrom.

Pay attention to opening hours. Canada is pretty much the same as the United States in this regard, but in France, some stores may be closed on Sundays and even Mondays (though Monday is usually a safe shopping day for department stores). Many stores used to close at lunchtime, and this custom still holds in some places, especially outside big cities. Before you go shopping, call ahead to find out the store's hours. These questions can help:

À quelle heure ouvrez-vous/fermez-vous ? (ah kehl uhr ooh-vrey-vooh/fehr-mey-vooh?) (*At what time do you open/close?*)

Êtes-vous ouverts le dimanche ? (eht-vooh zooh-vehr luh dee-mahNsh?) (*Are you open on Sundays?*)

Navigating the store

Most stores have familiar layouts. Here are the terms you need to know to find your way around a store:

- **le rez-de-chaussée** (luh reyd-shoh-sey) (*the ground floor*)
- **le premier étage** (luh pruh-myey rey-tahzh) (*the first floor*)
- **le deuxième étage** (luh duh-zyehm ey-tahzh) (*the second floor*)
- **le troisième étage** (luh trwah-zyehm ey-tahzh) (*the third floor*)
- **le sous-sol** (luh sooh-suhhl) (*the basement*)
- **l'escalier roulant** (m) (leh-skah-lyey rooh-lahN) (*the escalator*)
- **l'ascenseur** (m) (lah-sahN-suhr) (*the elevator*)
- **les cabines** (f) **d'essayage** (ley kah-been deh-sey-yahzh) (*fitting rooms*)
- **les toilettes** (f) (ley twah-leht) (*restrooms*)

The French consider the first floor to be the ground floor and start numbering after the ground floor. So what a French store calls the first floor may actually be what you consider the second floor.

Inside a store, you find the wide variety of **rayons** (reh-yohN) (*departments*) you're accustomed to. Here are a few of them:

- **beauté** (boh-tey) (*beauty*)
- **chaussures** (shoh-sewr) (*shoes*)
- **homme** (uhhm) (*men*)
- **femme** (fahm) (*women*)
- **enfant** (ahn-fahn) (*children*)

- ✔ **électro-ménager** (ey-leyk-troh-mey-nah-zhey) (*appliances*)

- ✔ **jouets** (zhooh-ey) (*toys*)

- ✔ **lingerie** (laN-zhuh-ree) (*lingerie*)

- ✔ **luxe** (lewks) (*luxury goods*)

- ✔ **meubles** (muh-bluh) (*furniture*)

- ✔ **prêt-à-porter** (prey-tah-pohr-tey) (*ready-to-wear*)

Asking for assistance

If you're looking for a specific item, you may need personal assistance. In a department store, you'll probably hear **une vendeuse** (ewn vahN-duhz) (*a saleswoman*) or **un vendeur** (uhN vahN-duhr) (*a salesman*) ask **Je peux vous aider ?** (zhuh puh vooh zey-dey?) (*May I help you?*). If you're just browsing, you can say **Non, merci, je regarde** (nohN, mehr-see, zhuh ruh-gahrd) (*No, thank you, I'm just looking*).

If you do need help, you can use any of the following phrases:

- ✔ **Je voudrais un renseignement.** (zhuh vooh-drey uhN rahN-seh-nyuh-mahN) (*I'd like some information.*)

- ✔ **Je cherche . . . .** (zhuh shehrsh . . . .) (*I'm looking for . . . .*)

- ✔ **Pouvez-vous m'aider, s'il vous plaît ?** (pooh-vey-vooh mey-dey, seel vooh pley?) (*Can you help me, please?*)

The French language doesn't distinguish between *I can* and *I may*. Both are **je peux** (zhuh puh). The verb is the irregular **pouvoir** (pooh-vwahr), which you conjugate in the present tense as follows:

Conjugation	Pronunciation	Translation
je peux	zhuh puh	*I can/may*
tu peux	tew puh	*you can/may*
il/elle/on peut	eel/ehl/ohN puh	*he/she/it/one can/may*
nous pouvons	nooh pooh-vohN	*we can/may*
vous pouvez	vooh pooh-vey	*you can/may*
ils/elles peuvent	eel/ehl puhv	*they can/may*

In formal settings such as offices or stores, you may hear the phrase **puis-je** (pweezh) (*may I*), as in **Puis-je vous aider ?** (pweezh vooh zey-dey?) (*May I help you?*). **Puis** is an old form of the verb **pouvoir** that's always used in question form: **puis** followed by a hyphen and the pronoun **je** (*I*).

The verb **pouvoir** is always followed by an infinitive. When the sentence has an object pronoun like **me** (muh) (*me*) — or **m'** before a vowel sound — you place the pronoun before the infinitive (for more on object pronouns, go to Chapter 3 of Book IV). Here are some examples:

> **Est-ce que vous pouvez me renseigner ?** (ehs kuh vooh pooh-vey muh rahN-sey-nyey?) (*Can you give me some information?*)

> **Pouvez-vous m'aider ?** (pooh-vey-vooh mey-dey?) (*Can you help me?*)

Object pronouns, which receive the action of the verb, include **me** (*me/to me*), **te** (singular familiar *you/to you*), **nous** (*us/to us*), and **vous** (plural or singular formal *you/to you*). In the sentence "He shows me a sweater," the pronoun *me* is the object of the verb because *me* receives or is subjected to the action. You can read more on pronouns in Chapter 3 of Book IV.

If no salesclerk is in sight, you can look for **les renseignements** (ley rahN-seh-nyuh-mahN) (*the information counter*) or look for **le service clients** (luh sehr-vees klee-yahN) (*customer service*). Most likely, someone there speaks English, but if not, the following phrases and responses can help you find your way around:

> **Pardon, madame, où sont les parfums ?** (pahr-dohN, mah-dahm, ooh sohN ley pahr-fuhN?) (*Excuse me, ma'am, where are the perfumes?*)

> **Ici, au rez-de-chaussée.** (ee-see, oh reyd-shoh-sey.) (*Here, on the ground floor.*)

> **Les vêtements pour dames, s'il vous plaît.** (ley veht-mahN poohr dahm, seel vooh pley.) (*Ladies' clothes, please.*)

> **C'est au troisième étage.** (sey toh trwah-zyehm ey-tahzh.) (*It's on the third floor.*)

Identifying specific objects in a display

Periodically, you want to draw attention to a particular item. If you don't know what the item is called — a fairly common situation when you're learning a language — you can always point to it and use these demonstrative adjectives (more on those in Chapter 2 of Book III):

- ✔ **ce** (suh) (*this, that*): Use **ce** in front of masculine singular nouns: **ce CD** (suh sey-dey) (*this/that CD*) for example.

- ✔ **cet** (seht) (*this, that*): Use **cet** in front of masculine singular nouns that begin with a vowel or a mute **h**: **cet ordinateur** (seht ohr-dee-nah-tuhr) (*this/that computer*).

- ✔ **cette** (seht) (*this, that*): Use **cette** in front of feminine singular nouns: **cette veste** (seht vehst) (*this jacket, that jacket*), for example.

✔ **ces** (sey) (*these, those*): Use **ces** in front of plural nouns, whether masculine or feminine: **ces jeux vidéo** (sey zhuh vee-dey-oh) (*these/those video games*), for example.

Notice that the demonstrative adjectives mean both *this* and *that* in the singular and *these* and *those* in the plural. If you need to distinguish between two items (this suit and that suit, for example, or these boots and those boots), you add the suffixes **-ci** (-see) and **-là** (-lah) to the nouns:

✔ Adding the suffix **-ci** to a noun translates as *this* or *these*.

✔ Adding the suffix **-là** to a noun translates as *that* or *those*.

Check out these examples:

Cette robe-ci est plus jolie que cette robe-là. (seht ruhhb-see ey plew zhoh-lee kuh seht ruhhb-lah.) (*This dress is prettier than that dress.*)

Ces magasins-ci sont plus chers que ces magasins-là. (sey mah-gah-zaN-see sohN plew shehr kuh sey mah-gah-zaN-lah.) (*These stores are more expensive than those stores.*)

Shopping for Clothes

Shopping for clothes or shoes is a common occurrence. Whether you're looking for something for yourself or for a loved one, you have to consider all sorts of criteria: size, fit, color, fabric, and so on. This section breaks down these various categories as well as lots of different clothing items you may be looking for. Now if you could just keep your sister from regifting that sweater. . . .

Item by item: Naming what's on the rack

Here's a list of **vêtements pour dames** (veht-mahN poohr dahm) (*women's clothes*) and **vêtements pour hommes** (veht-mahN poohr uhhm) (*men's clothes*) that may come in handy:

✔ **une chemise** (ewn shuh-meez) (*shirt*)

✔ **un chemisier** (uhN shuh-mee-zyey) (*blouse*)

✔ **une chemise de nuit** (ewn shuh-meez duh nwee) (*nightgown*)

✔ **un complet** (uhN kohN-pley) (*man's suit* [France])

✔ **un costume de bain** (uhN koh-stewm duh baN) (*bathing suit* [Québec])

✔ **un blazer** (uhN blah-zehr) (*blazer*)

- ✔ **un habit** (uhN nah-bee) (*man's suit* [Québec])
- ✔ **un imperméable** (uhN naN-pehr-mey-ah-bluh) (*raincoat*)
- ✔ **une jupe** (ewn zhewp) (*skirt*)
- ✔ **un jean** (uhN jeen) (*jeans*)
- ✔ **un manteau** (uhN mahN-toh) (*coat*)
- ✔ **un maillot de bain** (uhN mah-yoh duh baN) (*bathing suit* [France])
- ✔ **un pantalon** (uhN pahN-tah-lohN) (*pair of pants or slacks*)
- ✔ **un pardessus** (uhN pahr-duh-sew) (*overcoat*)
- ✔ **une robe** (ewn ruhhb) (*dress*)
- ✔ **une robe de chambre** (ewn ruhhb duh shahN-bruh) (*dressing gown/a robe*)
- ✔ **des sous-vêtements** (m) (dey sooh-veht-mahN) (*underwear*)
- ✔ **un tailleur** (uhN tah-yuhr) (*woman's suit*)
- ✔ **une veste** (ewn vehst) (*jacket*)
- ✔ **une veste de sport** (ewn vehst duh spuhhr) (*sports jacket*)
- ✔ **un veston** (uhN veh-stohN) (*suit jacket*)

And here are some accessories:

- ✔ **une ceinture** (ewn saN-tewr) (*belt*)
- ✔ **un chapeau** (uhN shah-poh) (*hat*)
- ✔ **des chaussettes** (f) (dey shoh-seht) (*socks*)
- ✔ **une cravate** (ewn krah-vaht) (*tie*)
- ✔ **un foulard** (uhN fooh-lahr) (*scarf*)

French has borrowed many English words for clothes; here are a few, though keep in mind that some have a different meaning from the English version you're used to:

- ✔ **le jogging** (luh zhoh-geeng) (*warm-up suit*)
- ✔ **le pull** (luh pewl) (*sweater*)
- ✔ **le slip** (luh sleep) (*underpants*)
- ✔ **le sweat** (luh sweet) (*sweatshirt*)
- ✔ **le tee-shirt** (luh tee-shuhrt) (*t-shirt*)

When shopping for **une paire de chaussures** (ewn pehr duh shoh-sewr) (*a pair of shoes*), use these terms:

✔ **les baskets** (m) (ley bah-skeht) (*sneakers*)

✔ **les tennis** (m) (ley tey-nees) (*sneakers, tennis shoes*)

✔ **les bottes** (f) (ley buhht) (*boots*)

✔ **les chaussons** (m) (ley shoh-sohN) (*slippers* [Québec])

✔ **les pantoufles** (f) (ley pahN-tooh-fluh) (*slippers*)

✔ **les chaussures à talons** (f) (ley shoh-sewr ah tah-lohN) (*high-heeled shoes*)

✔ **les sandales** (f) (ley sahN-dahl) (*sandals*)

Finding the right fit

In Canada, clothing sizes are the same as in the United States. In Europe, you may find different ways of measuring, depending on the country. Here are the rough equivalents for sizes of women's clothes — just add 30 to the Canadian/U.S. size to get the French size:

Canadian/U.S. Size	French Size
2	32
4	34
6	36
8	38
10	40
12	42
14	44
16	46
18	48
20	50

For men's jacket and suit sizes, use the following approximate conversions — add 10 to the Canadian/U.S. size to get the French size:

Canadian/U.S. Size	French Size
34	44
36	46
38	48
40	50
42	52
44	54
46	56
48	58
50	60

Of course, if everything else fails, you can always ask for **petit** (puh-tee) (*small*), **moyen/médium** (mwah-yaN/mey-dyuhhm) (*medium*), **large** (lahrzh) (*large*), or **extra-large** (ehk-strah lahrzh) (*extra-large*).

The French word for *size* is **la taille** (lah tahy). But often you don't even have to say the word, as these examples show:

> **Je fais du 36 [trente-six].** (zhuh fey dew trahNt-sees.) (*I'm a 36.*)

> **Je voudrais essayer une robe en 40 [quarante].** (zhuh vooh-drey ey-sey-yey ewn ruhhb ahN kah-rahNt.) (*I'd like to try a dress in a 40.*)

> **Est-que vous l'avez en plus petit ?** (ehs kuh vooh lah-vey ahN plew puh-tee?) (*Do you have it smaller?*)

La taille refers only to sizes in clothing; **la pointure** (lah pwaN-tewr) is what you use for shoe sizes.

To describe how something fits, you use the phrase **Ça . . . va** (sah . . . vah) (*It fits . . .*). Between **Ça** and **va**, you indicate whom the piece of clothing fits. Here are some examples:

> **Ça me va.** (sah muh vah.) (*It fits me.*)

> **Ça te va bien.** (sah tuh vah byaN.) (*It fits you well* — singular familiar)

> **Ça vous va très bien.** (sah vooh vah trey byaN.) (*It fits you very well* — plural or singular formal.)

To say that something fits *me, you, him, her, us,* or *them,* you have to use indirect object pronouns in front of the verb **va**. These pronouns are **me** (muh) (*me*), **te** (tuh) (*you,* singular familiar), **lui** (lwee) (*him/her*), **nous** (nooh) (*us*), **vous** (vooh) (*you,* plural or singular formal), and **leur** (luhr) (*them*). See Chapter 3 of Book IV for more on object pronouns.

You can also use the following terms to more specifically describe the fit of an item of clothing:

- ✔ **ample** (ahN-pluh) (*loose*)
- ✔ **étroit(e)** (ey-trwah/ey-trwaht) (*tight*)
- ✔ **large** (lahrzh) (*wide* [*shoes*])
- ✔ **serré(e)** (seh-rey) (*tight*)
- ✔ **trop court(e)** (troh koohr/koohrt) (*too short*)

✔ **trop grand(e)** (troh grahN/grahNd) (*too big*)

✔ **trop long(ue)** (troh lohN/lohNg) (*too long*)

✔ **trop petit(e)** (troh puh-tee/puh-teet) (*too small*)

French adjectives have different spellings depending on the gender and number of the noun they describe. You generally add **-e** to make an adjective feminine and **-s** to make it plural. For example, you say **un pantalon court** (uhN pahN-tah-lohN koohr) but **une robe courte** (ewn ruhhb koohrt). For more on adjectives, refer to Chapter 2 of Book IV.

Here are some examples:

Ce pantalon est trop court. (suh pahN-tah-lohN ey troh koohr.) (*This pair of pants is too short.*)

Cette jupe est trop courte. (seht zhewp ey troh koohrt.) (*This skirt is too short.*)

Ces baskets sont étroits. (sey bah-skeht sohN tey-trwah.) (*These sneakers are tight.*)

Ces chaussures sont étroites. (sey shoh-sewr sohN tey-trwaht.) (*These shoes are tight.*)

Talkin' the Talk

Cécile is shopping for a dress and has spotted one that she likes. The saleswoman approaches her. (Track 16)

La vendeuse: **Je peux vous aider, madame ?**
zhuh puh vooh zey-dey, mah-dahm?
Can I help you, ma'am?

Cécile: **Oui, s'il vous plaît. Avez-vous cette robe en 36 [trente-six]?**
wee, seel vooh pley. ah-vey-vooh seht ruhhb ahN trahNt-sees?
Yes, please. Do you have this dress in size 36?

La vendeuse: **Attendez un instant. Oui, nous l'avons. La voilà.**
ah-tahN-dey uhN naN-stahN. wee, nooh lah-vohN. lah vwah-lah.
Wait a moment. Yes, we have it. There it is.

Cécile: **Est-ce que je peux l'essayer ?**
ehs kuh zhuh puh ley-sey-yey?
May I try it on?

La vendeuse: **Mais bien sûr, madame. Les cabines d'essayage sont au fond à gauche.**
mey byaN sewr, mah-dahm. ley kah-been dey-sey-yahzh sohN toh fohN ah gohsh.
But of course, ma'am. The fitting rooms are in the back on the left.

A few minutes later, Cécile comes out of the fitting room with the dress on and asks the saleswoman's opinion.

Cécile: **Qu'est-ce que vous en pensez ?**
kehs kuh vooh zahN pahN-sey?
What do you think of it?

La vendeuse: **Je ne sais pas. Elle est un peu trop grande, je crois.**
zhuhn sey pah. ehl ey uhN puh troh grahNd, zhuh krwah.
I don't know. It's a little too big, I think.

Cécile: **Moi, je trouve qu'elle ne me va pas du tout. Est-ce que vous l'avez en plus petit ?**
mwah, zhuh troohv kehl nuh muh vah pah dew tooh. ehs kuh vooh lah-vey ahN plew puh-tee?
I think it doesn't fit me at all. Do you have it in a smaller size?

La vendeuse: **Non, je suis désolée. C'est la plus petite taille.**
nohN, zhuh swee dey-zoh-ley. sey lah plew puh-teet tahy.
No, I'm sorry. It's the smallest size.

Cécile: **Tant pis !**
tahN pee!
Oh well!

Words to Know

attendez un instant	ah-tahN-dey uhN naN-stahN	wait a moment
au fond	oh fohN	in the back
à gauche	ah gohsh	on the left
un peu	uhN puh	a little
trop	troh	too much
je trouve/pense	zhuh troohv/pahNs	I think
pas du tout	pah dew tooh	not at all
tant pis	tahN pee	too bad, oh well

Talking about color

When you're picking out clothes, what's more important than the color? Most color-related adjectives have to agree with the nouns they describe. Here's a list of colors in their masculine and feminine singular forms — the feminine endings are in parentheses:

- **beige** (behzh) (*beige*)
- **blanc(he)** (blahN/blahNsh) (*white*)
- **bleu(e)** (bluh) (*blue*)
- **gris(e)** (gree/greez) (*gray*)
- **jaune** (zhohn) (*yellow*)
- **marron** (mah-rohN) (*brown*)
- **mauve** (mohv) (*mauve purple*)
- **noir(e)** (nwahr) (*black*)

✔ **orange** (oh-rahNzh) (*orange*)

✔ **rose** (rohz) (*pink*)

✔ **rouge** (roohzh) (*red*)

✔ **vert(e)** (vehr/vehrt) (*green*)

✔ **violet(te)** (vee-oh-ley/vee-oh-leht) (*violet purple*)

To make the adjective plural, you usually add an **-s**, unless it already ends in that letter. The colors **orange** and **marron**, however, are invariable; they don't change to agree with nouns.

The color adjective always follows the noun, as in these examples:

un pantalon noir (uhN pahN-tah-lohN nwahr) (*black pants*)

des chaussures marron (dey shoh-sewr mah-rohN) (*brown shoes*)

une jupe verte (ewn zhewp vehrt) (*a green skirt*)

When you add the word **clair** (klehr) (*light*) or **foncé** (fohN-sey) (*dark*) to a color, the color adjective becomes invariable. You no longer need to worry about making the adjective feminine or plural. For example, a dark blue dress is **une robe bleu foncé** (ewn ruhhb bluh fohN-sey).

Talkin' the Talk

Vincent is looking for a sports jacket. He enters **une boutique de vêtements pour hommes** (ewn booh-teek duh veht-mahN poohr uhhm) (*a men's clothing store*). He is immediately greeted by **le vendeur** (luh vahN-duhr) (*the clerk*) and presents his request. (Track 17)

Vincent: **Je cherche une veste.**
zhuh shehrsh ewn vehst.
I'm looking for a jacket.

Le vendeur: **Quel genre de veste voulez-vous, monsieur ? Un blazer ? Un veston habillé ?**
kehl zhahNr duh vehst vooh-ley-vooh, muh-syuh? uhN blah-zehr? uhN veh-stohN ah-bee-yey?
What type of jacket do you want, sir? A blazer? A dressy suit jacket?

Vincent: **Non, plutôt une veste de sport.**
nohN, plew-toh ewn vehst duh spohr.
No, rather, a sports jacket.

Le vendeur: **En quelle taille ?**
ahN kehl tahy?
In what size?

Vincent: **En général, je porte du 50 [cinquante].**
ahN zhey-ney-rahl, zhuh pohrt dew saN-kahNt.
Usually, I wear a 50.

Le vendeur: **Nous avons ce modèle, ou celui-ci en pure laine.**
nooh-zah-vohN suh moh-dehl, ooh suh-lwee-see ahN pewr lehn.
We have this style, or this one in pure wool.

Vincent: **Je préfère une couleur plus foncée — bleu foncé, peut-être.**
zhuh prey-fehr ewn kooh-luhr plew fohN-sey — bluh fohN-sey, puh-teh-truh.
I prefer a darker color — dark blue, perhaps.

Vincent chooses a jacket and tries it on.

Le vendeur: **Oh, elle vous va à merveille ! Et elle est très à la mode.**
oh, ehl vooh vah ah mehr-vehy! ey ehl ey trey zah lah muhhd.
Oh, this one looks great on you! And it's very much in fashion.

Vincent: **Oui, vous avez raison et elle est en solde ! Alors je la prends.**
wee, vooh zah-vey rey-zohN ey ehl ey tahN suhhld! ah-lohr zhuh lah prahN.
Yes, you're right, and it's on sale! Then I'll take it.

Words to Know

habillé	ah-bee-yey	dressy
foncé(e)	fohN-sey	dark
Ça vous va à merveille.	sah vooh vah ah mehr-vehy.	It looks great on you.
à la mode	ah lah muhhd	in fashion, in style
les soldes	ley suhhld	sales [France]

In France, *sales* (**les soldes**) are regulated by the government. Stores may hold sales only during state-sanctioned periods in January and July. Because absolutely everything — from trivial to designer items — is available at an increasingly steep discount as time goes by during the traditional **soldes**, locals go as far as taking time off from work to take advantage of them. So watch out! In hard economic times, the French government has been known to relax rules and allow stores to hold unofficial sales. These are advertised as **Promotions** (*Promotions*) or **Soldes exceptionnelles** (*Exceptional sales*).

Choosing the right fabric

When you're shopping for clothing, you may have a particular *fabric* — **le tissu** (luh tee-sew) — in mind. Being able to express your preference to the salesclerks gives them the information they need to direct you to the right area. Here's a list of common fabrics:

- **le corduroy** (luh kohr-dew-rwah) (*corduroy* [Québec])
- **le coton** (luh koh-tohN) (*cotton*)
- **le cuir** (luh kweer) (*leather*)
- **la flanelle** (lah flah-nehl) (*flannel*)
- **la laine** (lah lehn) (*wool*)
- **le lin** (luh laN) (*linen*)
- **la soie** (lah swah) (*silk*)
- **le velours** (luh vuh-loohr) (*velvet, velours*)
- **le velours côtelé** (luh vuh-loohr koht-ley) (*corduroy* [France])

When talking about fabrics, you use **en** after the verb or **de** after the noun, as in these examples:

Cette veste est en laine. (seht vehst ey tahN lehn.) (*This jacket is in [made of] wool.*)

Est-ce que ces chaussures sont en cuir ? (ehs kuh sey shoh-sewr sohN tahN kweer?) (*Are these shoes in [made of] leather?*)

Je voudrais un foulard de soie. (zhuh vooh-drey uhN fooh-lahr duh swah.) (*I'd like a silk scarf.*)

Narrowing Your Options

When you're seriously shopping, you eventually need to decide what to buy. What's your priority? Quality? Price? This section helps you discuss these concepts.

Comparing items, more or less

Very few stores offer only one version of an item. Usually, you find various brands, package sizes, prices, and levels of quality in every product category. So how do you discuss these differences?

To make a comparison between two objects (or two people), the French language uses the following constructions for almost all adjectives:

- ✔ **plus . . . que** (plew . . . kuh) (*more . . . than*)
- ✔ **moins . . . que** (mwaN . . . que) (*less . . . than*)
- ✔ **aussi . . . que** (oh-see . . . kuh) (*as . . . as*)

Here are a few examples of comparisons:

Ce pull est plus chaud que ce tee-shirt. (suh pewl ey plew shoh kuh suh tee-shuhrt.) (*This sweater is warmer than this t-shirt.*)

Cet imperméable est aussi cher que ce manteau de laine. (seh taN-pehr-mey-ah-bluh ey toh-see shehr kuh suh mahN-toh duh lehn.) (*This raincoat is as expensive as this wool coat.*)

Ce pantalon est moins court que l'autre. (suh pahN-tah-lohN ey mwaN koohr kuh loh-truh.) (*This pair of pants is shorter than the other one.*)

You can't use the **plus . . . que** comparative construction for **bon** (bohN) (*good*). Just as you don't say *gooder* or *more good* in English, you don't say **plus bon** in French. Instead, you use **meilleur(e)** (mey-yuhr) for the masculine or feminine form of *better* or *best*.

- ✔ **meilleur(e)** (meh-yuhr) (*better*)

     Le cuir est meilleur que le caoutchouc. (luh kweer ey mey-yuhr kuh luh kah-ooh-tchooh.) (*Leather is better than rubber.*)

- ✔ **le/la meilleur(e)** (luh/lah mey-yuhr) (*the best*)

     On trouve le meilleur chocolat en Suisse. (ohN troohv luh mey-yuhr shoh-koh-lah ahN swees.) (*The best chocolate is found in Switzerland.*)

Considering price

How important is it for you to understand prices when you shop for clothes, food, books, music, gadgets, and so on? Pretty important, you say? Well, in that case, you need to remember that French and French-Canadian stores use a comma where U.S. stores would use a decimal point. In addition, French puts the currency sign after the number. Remember, the French currency is the euro, or €. The Canadian dollar uses the same dollar sign as the U.S. dollar. Here are some examples:

French/French-Canadian System	*U.S. System*
1,50 €	$1.50
24,95 $	$24.95

Note: Canadian websites usually allow you to click on **français** or **anglais** and pick the language in which you want to navigate the site. Therefore, even if the site is actually French-Canadian, you may be able to see prices in the U.S. format if you choose the English option.

To ask a person for a price, such as in a souvenir shop that doesn't display prices or from a street vendor, use **Combien coûte/coûtent . . .** ? (kohN-byaN kooht . . . ?) (*How much does . . . cost?*) or **Ça fait combien ?** (sah fey kohN-byaN?) (*How much is this?*), as in the following questions:

   Combien coûte ce chapeau ? (kohN-byaN kooht suh shah-poh?) (*How much does this hat cost?*)

   Combien coûtent ces cartes ? (kohN-byaN kooht sey kahrt?) (*How much do these cards cost?*)

   Ça fait combien, ce parapluie ? (sah fey kohN-byaN, suh pah-rah-plwee?) (*How much is this umbrella?*)

Talkin' the Talk

Nicole Verdier is shopping for shoes. She finds a pair she likes that fit her perfectly.

Nicole: **Combien coûtent ces chaussures ?**
kohN-byaN kooht sey shoh-sewr?
How much are these shoes?

La vendeuse: **Cinquante euros.**
saN-kahNt uh-roh.
Fifty euros.

Nicole: **C'est un peu cher, mais elles sont très jolies.**
sey tuhN puh shehr, mey ehl sohN trey zhoh-lee.
It's a little expensive, but they're very pretty.

La vendeuse: **Vous pouvez revenir la semaine prochaine quand nous aurons des soldes.**
vooh pooh-vey ruh-vuh-neer lah suh-mehn proh-shehn kahN nooh zoh-rohN dey suhhld.
You can come back next week when we're having sales.

Nicole: **Je dois absolument acheter des chaussures aujourd'hui. Allez, je les prends.**
zhuh dwah ahb-soh-lew-mahN ahsh-tey dey shoh-sewr oh-zhoohr-dwee. ah-ley, zhuh ley prahN.
I absolutely must buy shoes today. Okay, I'll take them.

La vendeuse: **C'est une très bonne décision, madame.**
sey tewn trey buhhn dey-see-zyohN, mah-dahm.
It's a very good decision, ma'am.

Words to Know

Combien coûte/ coûtent . . . ?	kohN-byaN kooht . . . ?	How much is/ are . . . ?
absolument	ahb-soh-lew-mahN	absolutely
aujourd'hui	oh-zhoohr-dwee	today

Making the Most of Online Shopping

Nowadays, most large stores offer online shopping. To use these services, you just need to know some terminology. This section presents the words and phrases you need to navigate an online shopping site, create an account, and place an order.

Entering the site

Although most shopping sites make spending your money easy — usually too easy — finding your way to all the available goodies can be trickier when the site isn't in your native language. Here's a handy primer to help you decode the homepage:

- **Abonnez-vous à notre newsletter.** (ah-boh-ney-vooh ah noh-truh news-leh-tuhr.) (*Subscribe to our newsletter.*)
- **accueil** (ah-kuhy) (*welcome*)
- **aide** (ehd) (*help*)
- **application iPhone** (ah-plee-kah-syohN ee-fuhhn) (*iPhone app*)
- **contact** (kohN-tahkt) (*contact [us]*)
- **Découvrez l'achat à domicile.** (dey-kooh-vrey lah-shah ah doh-mee-seel.) (*Discover home shopping.*)
- **Recevez par e-mail toutes les exclusivités de nos membres.** (ruh-suh-vey pahr ee-meyl tooht ley zehk-sklew-zee-vee-tey duh noh mahN-bruh.) (*Receive exclusive offers for our members by e-mail.*)
- **service à la clientèle** (sehr-vees ah lah klee-ahN-tehl) (*customer service*)

Browsing the site

After you've discovered an online shopping site, you're ready to get down to business. The following terms help you use the site to browse your options or search for specific items:

- **les aubaines** (f) (ley zoh-behn) (*bargains*)
- **le catalogue en ligne** (luh kah-tah-luhhg ahN lee-nyuh) (*online catalog*)
- **couleurs disponibles** (m) (kooh-luhr dee-spoh-nee-bluh) (*available colors*)
- **des prix choc** (m) (dey pree shuhhk) (*exceptional prices*)

✔ **existe en deux coloris** (eyg-zeest ahN duh koh-loh-ree) (*exists in two colors/patterns*)

✔ **les idées** (f) **cadeaux** (ley zee-dey kah-doh) (*gift ideas*)

✔ **les listes** (f) **de marriage** (ley leest duh mah-ryahzh) (*wedding registries*)

✔ **les nouveautés** (f) (ley nooh-voh-tey) (*new items*)

✔ **une offre spéciale** (ewn uhh-fruh spey-syahl) (*special offer*)

✔ **notre prix** (m) (noh-truh pree) (*our price*)

✔ **par marque** (pahr mahrk) (*by name brand*)

✔ **par prix** (pahr pree) (*by price*)

✔ **les promotions** (f) (ley proh-moh-syohN) (*promotions, sale items*)

✔ **le rabais** (luh rah-bey) (*discount*)

✔ **rechercher un article** (ruh-shehr-shey uhN nahr-tee-kluh) (*search for an item*)

✔ **suivant** (swee-vahN) (*next*)

These terms can help you keep track of the items you've looked at and perhaps marked for purchase:

✔ **gérer mon abonnement** (zheh-rey mohN nah-buhhn-mahN) (*managing my subscription*)

✔ **mes articles préférés** (mey zahr-tee-kluh prey-fey-rey) (*my favorite items*)

✔ **mes derniers articles vus** (mey dehr-nyey zahr-tee-kluh vew) (*my last items viewed*)

✔ **mon panier** (mohN pah-nyey) (*my basket/cart*)

Checking out online

Usually, Internet shopping requires that you **créer un compte** (krey-ey uhN kohNt) (*create an account*) with the online retailer before you actually buy anything. In addition to your basic contact info (see Chapter 3 of Book I), you need these terms for your **inscription** (aN-skreep-syohN) (*registration*):

✔ **l'adresse courriel** (f) (lah-drehs kooh-ryehl) (*e-mail address*)

✔ **le mot de passe** (luh moh duh pahs) (*password*)

Checking out online is pretty much the same everywhere: You choose your payment option, see the final price, and get a projected delivery date and a confirmation number. Here are some words and phrases to help you complete your online purchase:

- **annuler** (ah-new-ley) (*to cancel*)
- **la carte bancaire** (lah kahrt bahN-kehr) (*debit/bank card*)
- **la carte cadeau** (lah kahrt kah-doh) (*gift card*)
- **la carte de crédit** (lah kahrt duh krey-dee) (*credit card*)
- **commander** (koh-mahN-dey) (*to order*)
- **le compte PayPal** (luh kohNt pey-pahl) (*PayPal account*)
- **la date de validité** (lah daht duh vah-lee-dee-tey) (*expiration date*)
- **le délai de livraison** (luh dey-ley duh lee-vrey-zohN) (*delivery schedule*)
- **la détaxe** (lah dey-tahks) (*tax*)
- **les frais** (m) **de retour** (ley frey duh ruh-toohr) (*return fees*)
- **l'envoi** (m) (lahN-vwah) (*shipping*)
- **gratuit** (grah-twee) (*free of charge*)
- **imprimer** (aN-pree-mey) (*print*)
- **le numéro de référence** (luh new-mey-roh duh rey-fey-rahNs) (*reference number*)
- **le paiement sécurisé** (luh pey-mahN sey-kew-ree-zey) (*secure payment*)
- **le prix total de la commande** (luh pree toh-tahl duh lah koh-mahNd) (*total amount of order*)
- **le remboursement** (luh rahN-boohr-suh-mahN) (*reimbursement*)
- **suivre mes commandes** (swee-vruh mey koh-mahNd) (*managing my orders*)
- **valider la commande** (vah-lee-dey lah koh-mahNd) (*to confirm your order*)

Chapter 7

Buying, Preparing, and Tasting Foods

In This Chapter

▶ Visiting local markets

▶ Frequenting neighborhood food shops

▶ Shopping at big supermarkets

▶ Trying out recipes

▶ Enjoying meals

Food varies greatly from one francophone country to another, and cuisine is also unique in each region within a country. Cuisine often depends on the geographical features of the area and which natural products are native to it. In southeastern France, Provence is a Mediterranean region where olives, garlic, tomatoes, and herbs grow in abundance, so most **Provençal** (proh-vahN-sahl) dishes include these ingredients. Provence is also by the sea, so no wonder that a fish soup, **bouillabaisse** (booh-yah-behs), is one of the specialties of the region. On the other hand, the region called **Bourgogne** (boohr-goh-nyuh) has wonderful red Burgundy wine; you can expect, then, that one of the specialties of the region is **bœuf bourguignon** (buhf boohr-gee-nyohN), beef braised in red wine.

You must know a lot of terms that describe foods so you know what they are and what you can use them for. If you're looking for poultry, you wouldn't want to order **lapin** (lah-paN) and find out later you bought rabbit meat. Being able to discuss foods will surely improve your table manners and your dinner conversations and engage your palate in new ways. This chapter introduces you to essential phrases to help you enjoy food at levels you may never before have imagined.

Fresh Food, Fresh Air: Going to Food Markets

Outdoor markets are a delight. They're especially nice in small country villages, where you can enjoy the local fare and delight in the noises, smells, and accents. But big cities have wonderful markets, too. Certain districts in Paris have a market most days of the week in the morning, rain or shine. Montréal is famous for its outdoor all-day markets during the summer months. Cities and small town squares also have **les halles** (ley ahl) (*indoor markets*).

What better way to try out your French than going to a food market? After all, you can point to what you want and maybe find out the right word from a friendly vendor. This section introduces you to foods you can expect to find at an outdoor market.

What you find at fresh food markets

You find fruit, vegetables, meat, fish, cheese, condiments, and even bread at local food markets in addition to freshly cut flowers and many other things.

Les fruits: Fruit

Here's a list of **fruits** (frwee) (*fruit*) you may find at **le marché** (luh mahr-shey) (*the market*):

- **la banane** (lah bah-nahn) (*banana*)
- **la pomme** (lah puhhm) (*apple*)
- **la poire** (lah pwahr) (*pear*)
- **la pêche** (lah pehsh) (*peach*)
- **l'abricot** (m) (lah-bree-koh) (*apricot*)
- **la cerise** (lah suh-reez) (*cherry*)
- **le raisin** (luh reh-zaN) (*grape*)
- **la prune** (lah prewn) (*plum*)
- **la figue** (lah feeg) (*fig*)
- **la framboise** (lah frahN-bwahz) (*raspberry*)
- **la fraise** (lah frehz) (*strawberry*)
- **l'ananas** (m) (lah-nah-nah) (*pineapple*)

- ✓ **l'orange** (f) (loh-rahNzh) (*orange*)
- ✓ **le melon** (luh muh-lohN) (*cantaloupe*)
- ✓ **la pastèque** (lah pah-stehk) (*watermelon*)

Les légumes: Vegetables

Your mother always told you to eat your vegetables. Here's a list of **légumes** (ley-gewm) (*vegetables*) you may find very fresh at a local market:

- ✓ **les pommes** (f) **de terre** (leypuhhm duh tehr) (*potatoes*)
- ✓ **les haricots verts** (m) (ley ah-ree-koh vehr) (*green beans*)
- ✓ **les petits pois** (m) (ley puh-tee pwah) (*peas*)
- ✓ **les épinards** (m) (ley zey-pee-nahr) (*spinach*)
- ✓ **les asperges** (f) (ley zah-spehrzh) (*asparagus*)
- ✓ **le chou** (luh shooh) (*cabbage*)
- ✓ **les choux de Bruxelles** (m) (ley shooh duh brew-sehl) (*Brussels sprouts*)
- ✓ **le chou-fleur** (luh shooh-fluhr) (*cauliflower*)
- ✓ **les poireaux** (m) (ley pwah-roh) (*leeks*)
- ✓ **les champignons** (m) (ley shahN-pee-nyohN) (*mushrooms*)

In France, vendors don't appreciate your touching their fruit or vegetables. You can, however, ask for something specific, such as a very ripe melon or a melon that you'll eat within a couple of days, and they'll oblige.

Les fruits de mer et le poisson: Seafood and fish

For those of you who love what comes out of the sea, here's a list of **fruits de mer** (frwee duh mehr) (*seafood*) and **poissons** (pwa-sohN) (*fish*) you can find at a market:

- ✓ **la truite** (lah trweet) (*trout*)
- ✓ **le saumon** (luh soh-mohN) (*salmon*)
- ✓ **le thon** (luh tohN) (*tuna*)
- ✓ **l'espadon** (m) (leh-spah-dohN) (*swordfish*)
- ✓ **les sardines** (f) (ley sahr-deen) (*sardines*)
- ✓ **les crevettes** (f) (ley kruh-veht) (*shrimp*)
- ✓ **le homard** (luh oh-mahr) (*lobster*)

- **les moules** (f) (ley moohl) (*mussels*)
- **les huîtres** (f) (ley zwee-truh) (*oysters*)
- **les coquilles Saint-Jacques** (f) (ley koh-keey saN-zhahk) (*scallops*)

Les viandes: Meats

You can also find meat at the market. Here's a list of **viandes** (vyahNd) (*meat*):

- **le poulet** (luh pooh-ley) (*chicken*)
- **le canard** (luh kah-nahr) (*duck*)
- **le lapin** (luh lah-paN) (*rabbit*)
- **le porc** (luh pohr) (*pork*)
- **l'agneau** (m) (lah-nyoh) (*lamb*)
- **le veau** (luh voh) (*veal*)
- **le bœuf** (luh buhf) (*beef*)

Les fromages: Cheeses

France is known for its wonderfully delicious **fromages** (froh-mahzh) (*cheeses*), and most French people eat **le fromage** with every meal. France is said to have a different cheese for each day of the year. In fact, France has many sayings about the importance of cheese, such as this one: **Un repas sans fromage est comme une journée sans soleil** (uhN ruh-pah sahN froh-mahzh ey kuhhm ewn zhoohr-ney sahN soh-lehy) (*A meal without cheese is like a day without sun*).

France has numerous hard and soft cheeses. Many soft French cheeses are characterized by a strong smell — the older the cheese, the stronger the smell. These cheeses are made with raw milk, which has bacteria that multiply and develop the flavor as cheese ages. If you prefer less smelly cheeses, pick a hard cheese or, if you're cautiously ready for new tastes, start with **fromage frais/jeune** (froh-mahzh frey/zhuhN) (*fresh/young cheese*). This type of cheese hasn't been allowed to ripen for more than a few weeks and therefore hasn't had a chance to develop much of a smell.

You'll find cheeses from the **terroir** (tehr-wahr) (*local area*) at your local market. If you're buying cheese for a party you're giving, know that it's customary to have different types of cheeses made with goat's milk, cow's milk, or sheep's milk to offer after the meal. Some popular cheeses are **le chèvre** (luh shehv-ruh) (*chèvre, goat cheese*), **le camembert** (luh kah-mahN-behr) (*Camembert*), **le brie** (luh bree) (*Brie*), **le Roquefort** (luh rohk-fohr) (*Roquefort*), and **le gruyère** (luh gree-yehr) (*Gruyère* or *Swiss cheese*).

Specifying how much you want

The French adopted the metric system in the 18th century, and it's now used in the majority of countries around the world. If you travel to France, or to any other country for that matter, being familiar with the metric system is very handy, especially when you want to buy something scrumptious at the market.

The basic metric unit of weight is the gram, and you usually buy fruit, vegetables, cheese, or meat in grams. Table 7-1 lists values related to the gram.

Table 7-1	Measuring Food in Metric	
French	*Translation*	*Conversion*
un gramme (uhN grahm)	*1 gram (g)*	453.60 g = 1 lb.
un kilogramme (uhN kee-loh-grahm) **un kilo** (uhN kee-loh)	*1 kilogram (kg)*	1kg = 1,000 g, about 2.2 lbs.
un demi-kilo (uhN duh-mee-kee-loh)	*half a kilogram*	½ kg = 500 g, about 1.1 lbs.

If you want a pound of something, ask for **une livre de . . .** (ewn lee-vruh duh . . .) *(a pound of . . .)* or **un demi-kilo de . . .** (uhN duh-mee-kee-loh duh . . .) *(a half kilogram of . . .)* — a half kilo is just slightly more than a pound:

> **Je voudrais une livre de fraises bien mûres.** (zhuh vooh-drey ewn lee-vruh duh frehz byaN mewr.) (*I would like a pound of well-ripened strawberries*).

> **Vous pouvez me donner un demi-kilo de bananes pas trop mûres ?** (vooh pooh-vey muh duhh-ney uhN duh-mee-kee-loh duh bah-nahn pah troh mewr?) (*Can you give me a half kilo of bananas that aren't too ripe?*)

In addition to buying foods by weight, you can buy some items by the slice, chunk, or other unit of measurement, as follows:

> **Je voudrais quatre cuisses de poulet, s'il vous plaît.** (zhuh vooh-drey kah-truh kwees duh pooh-ley, seel vooh pley.) (*I would like four chicken drumsticks, please.*)

> **Je voudrais cinq oranges.** (zhuh vooh-drey sank oh-rahNzh.) (*I would like five oranges.*)

> **Je vais prendre une barquette de champignons.** (zhuh vey prahN-druh ewn bahr-keht duh shahN-pee-nyohN.) (*I'll take a container of mushrooms.*)

Talkin' the Talk

Friday morning is **le jour du marché** (luh zhoohr dew mahr-shey) (*market day*) for Madame Arnaud. She takes her nephew Thibaud along with her to go shopping at the local outdoor market. (Track 18)

Mme Arnaud: **Thibaud, qu'est-ce que tu aimes comme fruits ?**
tee-boh, kehs kuh tew ehm kuhhm frwee?
Thibaud, what kind of fruit do you like?

Thibaud: **Tous ! Mais à cette saison, je préfère les pêches.**
toohs! mey ah seht sey-zohN, zhuh prey-fehr ley pehsh.
All of them! But at this time of year, I prefer peaches.

Madame Arnaud and Thibaud wait in line at the fruit stand. When their turn comes, Madame Arnaud addresses **le vendeur** (luh vahN-duhr) (*the vendor*).

Mme Arnaud: **Donnez-moi un kilo de pêches, s'il vous plaît.**
duhh-ney-mwah uhN kee-loh duh pehsh, seel vooh pley.
Give me 1 kilo [2.2 pounds] of peaches, please.

Le vendeur: **Voilà madame, et avec ça ?**
vwah-lah mah-dahm, eh ah-vehk sah?
Here you are, ma'am. Anything else? Literally: And with that?

Mme Arnaud: **Je voudrais aussi un demi-kilo d'abricots et un demi-kilo de raisins.**
zhuh vooh-dreh oh-see uhN duh-mee-kee-loh dah-bree-koh eh uhN duh-mee-kee-loh duh reh-zaN.
I would also like a half kilo of apricots and a half kilo of grapes.

Le vendeur: **Très bien madame. C'est tout ?**
trey byaN mah-dahm. sey tooh?
Very well, ma'am. Is that all?

Mme Arnaud: **C'est tout, merci. Ça fait combien ?**
sey tooh, mehr-see. sah fey kohN-byaN?
That's all, thank you. How much is it?

Le vendeur: **Huit euros.**
weet uh-roh.
Eight euros.

Words to Know

je préfère	zhuh prey-fehr	I prefer
donnez-moi	duhh-ney mwah	give me
je vais prendre	zhuh vey prahN-druh	I'll take
Ça fait combien ?	sah fey kohN-byaN?	How much is it?
Et avec ça ?	ey ah-vehk sah?	And with that?

Buying Food at the Store

When you don't have time to go to the outdoor market or you can't find what you need at a little store, the supermarket comes in handy. France has some huge **supermarchés** (sew-pehr-mahr-shey) (*supermarkets*) that line the highways as you enter a city. Some of them are so large that they're called **hypermarchés** (ee-pehr-mahr-shey) (*hypermarkets*). There, you can find absolutely everything: food, clothes, computers, and all sorts of appliances.

The big stores are certainly convenient, but if you visit France and have some time on your hands, go discover the little neighborhood food stores. You're sure to enjoy them. We discuss stores, both large and small, in this section.

Shopping at neighborhood food stores

A fairly large number of people — mostly older — still go shopping for food every morning in France. Because supermarkets are sometimes far from the city center, the French do their daily shopping in the neighborhood stores, which are conveniently close to each other. People walk from store to store buying everything they need for the day's meals — vegetables, fruit, cheese, bread, and meat. French refrigerators are often smaller than American ones, too, so buying food in smaller quantities is helpful.

Following are some of **les petits magasins** (ley puh-tee mah-gah-zaN) (*the little [food] stores*) that you find in most neighborhoods throughout France:

✔ **la boulangerie** (lah booh-lahN-zhree) (*the bakery*): **La boulangerie** sells bread and bread products, like **des croissants** (dey krwah-sahN) (*croissants*) and **du pain aux raisins** (dew paN oh reh-zaN) (*sweet rolls with raisins and vanilla custard*).

✔ **la pâtisserie** (lah pah-tees-ree) (*the confectioner's shop*): These shops specialize in cakes and pastries. They don't sell bread.

✔ **la boucherie** (lah booh-shree) (*the butcher shop*): Here you can find fresh cuts of all sorts of meats like beef, veal, lamb, goat, and chicken.

✔ **la charcuterie** (lah shahr-kew-tree) (*the deli, butcher shop*): These shops specialize in pork and prepared foods.

✔ **la poissonnerie** (lah pwah-sohn-ree) (*the fish store*): These shops sell fresh fish and seafood.

✔ **la crèmerie** (lah krehm-ree) (*the dairy shop*): This is where you can buy cheese and other dairy products.

✔ **le marchand de fruits et légumes** (luh mahr-shahN duh frwee ey ley-gewm) (*the produce vendor*): These stores have all kinds of fresh fruits and vegetables.

Allons à la boulangerie-pâtisserie ! Let's go to the bakery!

Very often in France, a single store functions as a bakery and a pastry shop. It's then called a **boulangerie-pâtisserie** (booh-lahN-zhree-pah-tees-ree). Here's a list of some of their products:

✔ **la baguette** (la bah-geht) (*baguette*)

✔ **le pain paysan** (luh paN pey-ee-zahN) (*country bread*)

✔ **le pain de seigle** (luh paN duh seh-gluh) (*rye bread*)

✔ **le petit pain** (luh puh-tee paN) (*roll*)

✔ **la brioche** (lah bree-ohsh) (*sweet bun made with egg and butter*)

✔ **le croissant au beurre** (luh krwah-sahN oh buhr) (*butter croissant*)

✔ **le croissant aux amandes** (luh krwah-sahN oh zah-mahNd) (*croissant filled with almond paste*)

✔ **le pain au chocolat** (luh paN oh shoh-koh-lah) (*chocolate-filled croissant*)

✔ **le gâteau** (luh gah-toh) (*cake*)

✔ **la tarte** (lah tahrt) (*tart*)

✔ **la pâtisserie** (lah pah-tees-ree) (*pastry*)

✔ **l'éclair** (m) **au chocolat/à la vanille** (ley-klehr oh shoh-koh-lah/ah lah vah-neey) (*chocolate/vanilla eclair*)

It's also not unusual for the French of all ages, especially in big cities, to buy bread twice a day because every **quartier** (kahr-tyey) (*neighborhood*) has its **boulangerie**. French bread is made without preservatives and doesn't keep well, so buying in small quantities more often makes better sense. Plus, French bread tastes so good when it's freshly baked!

Allons à la boucherie-charcuterie ! Let's go to the meat shop!

Often in France, a single store functions as a butcher shop and as a deli. It's
then called a **boucherie-charcuterie** (booh-shree-shahr-kew-tree). Here's a
list of some of products:

- ✔ **la viande** (lah vyahNd) (*meat*)
- ✔ **le jambon** (luh zhahN-bohN) (*ham*)
- ✔ **le saucisson** (luh soh-see-sohN) (*sausage*)
- ✔ **le salami** (luh sah-lah-mee) (*salami*)

Allons à la crèmerie ! Let's go to the dairy store!

The French are so fond of cheese and other dairy products that they have
special stores for that, too. Here's a list of some of their products other than
cheese:

- ✔ **le yaourt** (luh yah-oohr) (*yogurt*)
- ✔ **la crème fraîche** (lah krehm frehsh) (*a thick, tangy type of half and half*)
- ✔ **les œufs** (m) (ley zuh) (*eggs*)
- ✔ **le lait** (luh ley) (*milk*)
- ✔ **le beurre** (luh buhr) (*butter*)

Enjoying a wider selection at the grocery or supermarket

When you just need to pick something up quickly on the way home, you
can stop at an **épicerie** (ey-pee-sree) (*grocery store*). There are many in every
quartier (kahr-tyey) (*neighborhood*).

The Québecois and other French-Canadians have a special word for a grocery
store. They use **dépanneur** (dey-pah-nuhr), from the verb **dépanner**, which
means *to help out*. The same word is used in France for the driver of a
tow-truck.

Here are some things you can find at **l'épicerie**:

- ✔ **les céréales** (f) (ley sey-rey-ahl) (*cereals*)
- ✔ **les biscuits** (m) (ley bee-skwee) (*cookies*)
- ✔ **le vin** (luh vaN) (*wine*)
- ✔ **l'eau minérale** (f) (loh mee-ney-rahl) (*mineral water*)

CULTURAL WISDOM

Mineral water accompanies most meals in France. The French drink a lot of mineral water, not only when they're out but also at home, even when the local water is good. They believe in the virtues of mineral water, and they have choices — some types are **gazeuses** (gah-zuhz) (*bubbly, carbonated*) and others are **plates** (plaht) (*flat, without carbonation*), and the taste isn't always the same.

Here are several terms related to packaging:

- ✔ **un paquet de café** (uhN pah-key duh kah-fey) (*a package of coffee*)
- ✔ **une tablette de chocolat** (ewn tah-bleht duh shoh-koh-lah) (*a chocolate bar*)
- ✔ **une bouteille de bière** (ewn booh-tehy duh byehr) (*a bottle of beer*)
- ✔ **une boîte de petits pois** (ewn bwaht duh puh-tee pwah) (*a can of peas*)
- ✔ **un bocal de cornichons** (uhN boh-kahl duh kohr-nee-shohN) (*a jar of pickles*)

As life gets faster for the French, more **supermarchés** (sew-pehr-mahr-shey) (*supermarkets*) have emerged. These are a lot like our supermarkets. All the specialty stores are present here as departments. Here's a list of some words you need to recognize:

- ✔ **le chariot** (luh shah-ryoh) (*shopping cart*)
- ✔ **le rayon** (luh rey-yohN) (*department*)
- ✔ **la caisse** (lah kehs) (*the cash register*)
- ✔ **passer à la caisse** (pah-sey ah lah kehs) (*to check out*)
- ✔ **le caissier/la caissière** (luh keh-syey/lah keh-syehr) (*the cashier*)
- ✔ **le sac à provisions** (luh sahk ah proh-vee-zyohN) (*shopping bag*)
- ✔ **la buvette** (lah bew-veht) (*snack bar*)

Talkin' the Talk

Yvonne takes her American friend Lisa to the supermarket. They're planning to make a delicious dinner tonight at Yvonne's house.

Yvonne: **Je veux te faire un dîner très français ce soir. Je vais prendre deux escalopes de veau à la boucherie.**
zhuh vuh tuh fehr uhN dee-ney trey frahN-sey suh swar. zhuh vey prahN-druh duh zey-skah-luhhp duh voh ah lah booh-shree.
I want to make you a very French dinner this evening. I'm going to get two veal scaloppini in the meat department.

Lisa: **Si tu veux ! Mais je vais t'aider.**
see tew vuh! mey zhuh vey teh-dey.
If you want! But I'm going to help you.

Yvonne: **D'accord ! Attends ! Voilà la crème fraîche. Un petit
pot, ça suffit.**
dah-kohr! ah-tahN! vwah-lah lah krehm frehsh. uhN
puh-tee poh, sah sew-fee.
*Okay! Wait! There's the cream. A little container,
that's enough.*

Lisa: **Le veau à la crème, c'est avec des champignons ?**
luh voh ah lah krehm, sey ah-vehk dey
shahN-pee-nyohN?
*Is veal scaloppini in cream sauce served with
mushrooms?*

Yvonne: **Oui, c'est ça. J'achète toujours mes champignons frais
au marché.**
wee, sey sah. zhah-sheht tooh-zhoohr mey shahN-
pee-nyohN frey oh mahr-shey.
*Yes, that's right. I always buy my mushrooms fresh at
the market.*

Lisa: **Ah oui ? Et les légumes aussi sans doute ?**
ah wee? eh ley ley-gewm oh-see sahN dooht?
Really? And the vegetables, too, no doubt?

Yvonne: **Bien sûr ! En ce moment c'est la saison des asperges.
Tu aimes ça ?**
byaN sewr! ahn suh moh-mahN, sey lah sey-zohN dey
zah-spehrzh. tew ehm sah?
*Of course! At the moment it's asparagus season. Do
you like that?*

Lisa: **J'adore les asperges blanches. On va se régaler.**
zhah-duhhr ley zah-spehrzh blahNsh. ohN vah suh
rey-gah-ley.
I love white asparagus. We're going to enjoy.

Yvonne: **Je voudrais aussi une bouteille d'eau minérale et une
bonne bouteille de vin blanc.**
zhuh vooh-drey oh-see ewn booh-tey doh mee-ney-
rahl eh ewn buhhn booh-tey duh vaN blahN.
*I would also like a bottle of mineral water and a good
bottle of white wine.*

Lisa: **Permets-moi d'acheter le vin blanc. Mais on va dans un magasin de vin pour ça.**
pehr-mey-mwah dah-shtey luh vaN blahN. mey zohN vah dahN zuhN mah-gah-zaN duh vaN poohr sah.
Allow me to buy the white wine. But let's go to a wine store for that.

Yvonne: **Merci, tu es bien gentille. Mais ils ont de très bons vins ici.**
mehr-see, tew eh byaN zhahN-tee. mey zeel zohN duh trey bohN vaN ee-see.
Thanks, you're really nice. But they have very good wines here.

Lisa: **Ah bon ! Quel vin est-ce que tu voudrais ?**
ah bohN! kehl vaN ehs kuh tew vooh-drey?
All right! Which wine would you like?

Yvonne: **Une bouteille de Riesling si tu veux ? Ou un Bordeaux ?**
ewn booh-tey duh reez-leeng see tew vuh? ooh uhN bohr-doh?
A bottle of Riesling if you want? Or a Bordeaux?

Lisa: **Je te laisse choisir.**
zhuh tuh lehs shwah-zeer.
I'll let you choose.

Yvonne: **Bon, je crois que nous avons tout ce qu'il faut. Passons à la caisse !**
bohN, zhuh crwah kuh nooh zah-vohN tooh skeel foh. pah-sohN zah lah kehs!
Good, I think we have all we need. Let's check out!

Making Your Own Meals

What prompted Julia Child to write her first French cookbook was her realization that the French seemed to trust their intuition and creativity rather than solid instructions and precise measurements while creating a dish — thus the need to write easy-to-follow recipes for ordinary people.

But you don't have to be Julia Child or Paul Bocuse to make a few simple dishes. You just need to understand the recipe's ingredients, measurements, and instructions. Look up some **recettes** (ruh-seht) (*recipes*) online, get the freshest ingredients you can find, and read on for some common expressions and measurements found in recipes for all kinds of food.

Reading the ingredients

When following a recipe for the first time, understanding some common **ingrédients** (ley zaN-grey-dyahN) (*ingredients*) is helpful. This section lists some herbs, spices, cooking liquids, condiments, and baking ingredients. You can find the names of meats, fish, fruits, and vegetables in the earlier section "What you find at fresh food markets."

Herbs, spices, and onions

French cooking isn't heavy on spices, but you do see plenty of fresh herbs. Here's a list of **les herbes** (ley zehrb) (*herbs*), **les épices** (ley zey-pees) (*spices*), and other flavorful ingredients, such as onions and garlic:

- **le sel** (luh sehl) (*salt*)
- **le poivre** (luh pwah-vruh) (*pepper*)
- **le basilic** (luh bah-zee-leek) (*basil*)
- **le laurier** (luh loh-ryey) (*bay leaves*)
- **le persil** (luh pehr-seel) (*parsley*)
- **le cerfeuil** (luh sehr-fuhy) (*chervil*)
- **la ciboulette** (lah see-booh-leht) (*chives*)
- **le clou de girofle** (luh clooh duh zhee-ruhh-fluh) (*clove*)
- **le cumin** (luh kew-maN) (*cumin*)
- **la menthe** (lah mahNt) (*mint*)
- **le thym** (luh taN) (*thyme*)
- **l'ail** (m) (lahy) (*garlic*)
- **l'échalote** (f) (ley-shah-luhht) (*shallot*)
- **l'oignon** (m) (loh-nyohN) (*onion*)

Liquids and condiments

Here are **les condiments** (kohN-dee-mahN) (*condiments*) and cooking liquids:

- **le bouillon** (luh booh-yohN) (*bouillon*)
- **la mayonnaise** (lah mah-yoh-nehz) (*mayonnaise*)
- **la moutarde** (lah mooh-tahrd) (*mustard*)
- **l'huile d'olive** (f) (lweel doh-leev) (*olive oil*)
- **le lait de coco** (luh ley duh koh-koh) (*coconut milk*)

Baking ingredients

You use these ingredients for baking:

- **la farine** (lah fah-reen) (*flour*)
- **le sucre en poudre** (luh sew-krahN pooh-druh) (*white sugar*)
- **le sucre glace** (luh sew-kruh glahs) (*powdered sugar*)
- **l'extrait** (m) **de vanille** (lehk-strey duh vah-nee) (*vanilla extract*)

Wines and liqueurs

The French use a multitude of **vins** (vaN) (*wines*) and **liqueurs** (lee-kuhr) (*liqueurs*) in cooking everything from fish and seafood dishes such as **moules marinières** (moohl mah-ree-nyehr) (*mussels steamed in wine-based broth*) to meat dishes such **bœuf bourguignon** (buhf boohr-gee-nyohN) (*beef cooked in red wine from the Burgundy region*) or **coq au vin** (kohk oh vaN) (*chicken in red wine sauce*), not to mention desserts such as **soufflé au grand marnier** (sooh-fley oh grahN mahr-nyey) (*Grand Marnier soufflé*). The soufflé can be a main dish or a dessert; it's made from whipped egg whites combined with a base and baked to a puffed state. For the Grand Marnier soufflé, the base is a Cognac brandy spiced with orange peels and sugar syrup.

Many regional main dishes and desserts are made with **vins** or **liqueurs** from the **terroir** (tehr-wahr) (*local area*). For example, **kirsh** (keersh), which is made in the northeastern part of Alsace, a region rich in cherry trees, is a clear brandy distilled from cherry juice. In Normandy and Brittany, north-western regions rich in apple trees, **calvados** (kahl-vah-dohs) (*apple brandy*) rules. Here are a few other types of brandy:

- **l'armagnac** (m) (lahr-mah-nyahk) (*grape brandy*)
- **le grand marnier** (luh grahN mahr-nyey) (*orange brandy*)
- **le cognac** (luh koh-nyahk) (*variety of brandy named after the French city of Cognac*)

The French like to refer to various parts of the country by the names of the regions that were the provinces that belonged to various members of royalty before the French Revolution (1789) — check out `www.cartes france.fr/carte-france-region/carte-france-regions.html` for a map. So when you hear **un vin d'Alsace** (uhN vaN dahl-zahs), **un vin de Bourgogne** (uhN vaN duh boohr-goh-nyuh), **un vin de Provence** (uhN vaN duh proh-vahNs), or **un Champagne** (uhN shahN-pah-nyuh), know that they refer to wines from a specific region, such as Alsace, Bourgogne, Provence, or Champagne. Some wines or brandies are named after cities such as **Bordeaux** (bohr-doh) or **Cognac** (koh-nyahk).

Measuring ingredients

To make a French recipe, you need to know the measurement terms. Earlier in "Specifying how much you want," we introduce you to the metric units of measurement — **grammes et kilogrammes** — for solid foods.

Most recipes outside the United States measure dry ingredients by weight rather than volume. You can look up measurement conversions for each ingredient online, but calculations are a hassle. If you plan to do much cooking or baking, consider getting a digital kitchen scale that offers metric measurements.

Table 7-2 shows liquid metric measurements, their abbreviations, and their approximate equivalents in the U.S. system.

Table 7-2	Liquid Measurements	
Measurement and Abbreviation	*Equivalent in Litres*	*U.S. Equivalent*
1 millilitre (1 ml)	**1/1,000 litre**	0.03 fluid oz. (a little under ¼ teaspoon)
1 centilitre (1 cl)	**1/100 litre**	0.34 fluid oz. (about 2 teaspoons)
1 décalitre (1 dl)	**1/10 litre**	3.5 fluid oz. (a little under ½ cup)
1 litre (1 lt)	**1 litre**	1.06 quarts (about 4¼ cups)

Here are some other measurements you may see in French recipes:

✔ **cuillère à café** (abbreviated as **c. à c.**) (kwee-yehr ah kah-fey) (*teaspoon [t]*)

✔ **cuillère à soupe** (abbreviated as **c. à s.**) (kwee-yehr ah soohp) (*tablespoon [T]*)

- **gousse** (f) **d'ail** (goohs dahy) (*clove of garlic*)
- **botte** (f) **de persil** (buhht duh pehr-seel) (*sprig of parsley*)
- **sachet** (m) (sah-shey) (*package*)

In Canada, you may find the following measurements:

- **une tasse** (ewn tahs) (*a cup*)
- **une cuillère à thé** (abbreviated as **c. à thé**) (ewn kwee-yehr ah tey) (*a teaspoon*)
- **une cuillère à table** (abbreviated as **c. à table**) (ewn kwee-yehr ah tah-bluh) (*a tablespoon*)

Francophone countries, including Canada, measure temperatures using the Celsius scale. Use the following table if you're using a metric recipe in the United States:

Celsius	*Fahrenheit*	*Heat*
190–270°C	375–518°F	Hot to very hot
165–190°C	325–375°F	Medium hot
120–150°C	250–300°F	Low
Below 120°C	Below 250°F	Very low

Peeling, cutting, mixing, and cooking

Not only do you have to know the ingredients in a recipe, but you also have to understand the instructions. The verbs used to give instructions are either in the imperative **vous** form (see Chapter 4 of Book III for information) or in the infinitive (dictionary) form. Here are a few examples of recipe instructions:

- **faites/faire chauffer** (feht/fehr shoh-fey) (*heat up*)
- **faites/faire sauter** (feht/fehr soh-tey) (*sauté*)
- **coupez/couper** (kooh-pey) (*cut*)
- **épluchez/éplucher** (ey-plew-shey) (*peel*)
- **égoutez/égouter** (ey-gooh-tey) (*drain*)
- **ajoutez/ajouter** (ah-zhooh-tey) (*add*)
- **mélangez/mélanger** (mey-lahn-zhey) (*mix*)
- **mettez/mettre** (meh-tey/meh-truh) (*put*)

> ✔ **retirez/retirer du feu** (ruh-tee-rey dew fuh) (*remove from stove/burner*)
>
> ✔ **lavez/laver** (lah-vey) (*wash*)
>
> ✔ **hachez/hacher** (ah-shey) (*chop*)
>
> ✔ **salez/saler** (sah-ley) (*add salt*)
>
> ✔ **poivrez/poivrer** (pwah-vrey) (*add pepper*)

Eating Throughout the Day

People eat quite a few meals throughout the day. You start with breakfast, perhaps have a snack mid-morning, take lunch in the middle of the day, have another snack in the afternoon, and finally eat dinner. Here are a few names to remember:

> ✔ **le petit déjeuner** (luh puh-tee dey-zhuh-ney) (*breakfast*)
>
> ✔ **un en-cas** (uhN ahN-kah) (*an in-between-meals tiding-you-over snack*)
>
> ✔ **le déjeuner** (luh dey-zhuh-ney) (*lunch in France*)
>
> ✔ **le goûter** (luh gooh-tey) (*a midafternoon or after-school snack*)
>
> ✔ **le dîner** (luh dee-ney) (*dinner in France but lunch in Québec and Belgium*)
>
> ✔ **le souper** (luh sooh-pey) (*supper in France but dinner in Québec and Belgium*)

In Québec and Belgium, meals have slightly different names from the ones the French use. There, **le dîner** (luh dee-ney) is lunch and **le souper** (luh sooh-pey) is the evening meal. In France, **le dîner** is the evening meal and **le souper** is a light, late-night dinner for those who spent the evening at the theater, for example. The word **souper** comes from **la soupe** because a light dinner is often a dish of soup. So if you're invited to **un dîner**, clarify when you're expected, or you just might miss it entirely.

Starting the day with breakfast French style

Contrary to popular belief, the French don't have **croissants** every day for breakfast. **Croissants** and **brioches** require a trip to a **boulangerie** or **café**; that's more for people who are vacationing and for relaxing weekends.

An ordinary way to start the day in French homes is with **du pain grillé** (dew pahN gree-yey) (*toast*) or **un bol de céréales** (uhN buhhl duh sey-rey-ahl) (*a bowl of cereal*). If there's time to run out to the corner store, families get fresh **baguette** (bah-geht) for breakfast. Otherwise, they simply make toast or eat **des tartines** (dey tahr-teen) (*bread and butter*) with **de la confiture** (duh lah kohN-fee-tewr) (*jam*) or **du miel** (dew myehl) (*honey*). Coffee or hot chocolate is usually served in **un bol** (uhN buhhl) (*a bowl*), which looks like a small salad bowl to an American. In Canada, **pain doré** (paN doh-rey) (*French toast. Literally: golden bread*) or pancakes are accompanied by **du sirop d'érable** (dew see-roh dey-rah-bluh) (*maple syrup*) as well as blueberries, which the Canadians call **bleuets** (bluh-ey) from their blue color; the French call them **myrtilles** (meer-tee-yuh).

Here are a few more words to help you talk about a French **petit déjeuner** (puh-tee dey-zhuh-ney) (*breakfast*):

- ✔ **une tartine au beurre** (ewn tahr-teen oh buhr) (*a slice of bread with butter*)

- ✔ **une tartine au miel** (ewn tahr-teen oh myehl) (*a slice of bread with honey*)

- ✔ **un bol de café** (uhN buhhl duh kah-fey) (*a bowl of coffee*)

- ✔ **un bol de chocolat chaud** (uhN buhhl duh shoh-koh-lah shoh) (*a bowl of hot chocolate*)

- ✔ **un verre de lait** (uhN vehr duh ley) (*a glass of milk*)

- ✔ **un verre de jus d'orange** (uhn vehr duh zhew doh-rahNzh) (*a glass of orange juice*)

When saying a glass or a cup of something, just use the preposition **de** to express *of* before the noun: **un verre *d'*eau** (uhN vehr doh) is a glass of water, and **une tasse *de* thé** (ewn tahs duh tey) is a cup of tea. However, when talking about vague amounts of something like *some* butter, you have to use the partitive article **du, de la, de l'**, or **des** to express *some*, even when the word *some* is omitted in English: **de l'eau** (duh loh) is (some) water, **du café** (dew kah-fey) is (some) coffee, **de la confiture** (duh lah kohN-fee-tewr) is (some) jam, and **des croissants** (dey krwah-sahN) is (some) croissants. Refer to Chapter 2 of Book III for more information on articles.

Preparing lunch

Lunch is still a main meal for most French people. At home, a lunch often includes an appetizer, a main dish, a salad, some cheese, and a dessert, which may just be a piece of fruit. In school cafeterias, a lunch looks pretty much the same as a homemade lunch. At work, people who still have the traditional two hours off for lunch can go to a café or to a deli for a sandwich and a salad. Here are some words to discuss **le déjeuner** (luh dey-zhuh-ney) (*lunch*):

- ✔ **l'entrée** (f) (lahN-trey) (*first course, appetizer*)

- ✔ **la soupe** (lah soohp) (*soup*)

- ✔ **la salade** (lah sah-lahd) (*salad*)

- ✔ **la quiche** (lah keesh) (*quiche — pastry crust with eggs, cheese, cream, and fillings such as ham, bacon, or vegetables*)

- ✔ **l'omelette** (f) (luhhm-leht) (*omelet*)

- ✔ **le sandwich au jambon** (luh sahN-dweesh oh zhahN-bohN) (*ham sandwich*)

The French word **entrée** (ahN-trey) (*entrance, way in*) is a false friend. Because it leads into the meal, the **entrée** of a French meal is the first course, not the main course, as it is in the United States. What Americans call the *entree,* the French call **le plat principal** (luh plah praN-see-pahl) (*the main course*).

Serving dinner

A meal is quite a ceremony and cannot be rushed in France. When you get invited to someone's home for dinner, expect to spend a few hours enjoying various parts of the meal and making a lot of conversation. The evening starts with an **apéritif** (ah-pey-ree-teef) (*before-dinner drink meant to stimulate your appetite*). For example, your host may offer you a glass of **kir** (keer) (*dry white wine and cassis liqueur*) to sip while waiting for dinner to be ready. Here are the various courses of the meal in order:

- ✔ **les amuse-bouche** (m) (ley zah-mewz-boosh) (*appetizers. Literally: amuse the mouth*)

- ✔ **les hors d'œuvre** (m) (ley ohr-duh-vruh) (*hors d'oeuvres. Literally: outside the work/main meal*)

- ✔ **l'entrée** (f) (lahN-trey) (*first course, starter*)

- ✔ **le plat (principal)** (luh plah praN-see-pahl) (*main dish*)

- ✔ **la salade verte** (lah sah-lahd vehrt) (*green salad*)

- ✔ **le fromage** (luh froh-mahzh) (*cheese*)

- ✔ **le dessert** (luh dey-sehr) (*dessert*)

- ✔ **le café** (luh kah-fey) (*coffee*)

- ✔ **le digestif** (luh dee-zheh-steef) (*an after-dinner drink such as cognac or sherry to help you digest your food*)

Talkin' the Talk

Guy and Michelle Soucy are a Canadian couple who are visiting their French friends Marc and Sophie in Paris. They're getting ready to sit down for dinner. (Track 19)

Marc: **Guy et Michelle, venez au salon. Je vais vous servir un kir.**
          gee ey mee-shehl, vuh-ney oh sah-lohN. zhuh vey vooh sehr-veer uhN keer.
          Guy and Michelle, come to the living room. I'm going to serve you a kir.

Michelle: **Je vais aider Sophie à finir le repas.**
          zhuh vey zey-dey soh-fee ah fee-neer luh ruh-pah.
          I'm going to help Sophie finish the meal.

Sophie: **Tu peux apporter les hors-d'œuvre au salon, si tu veux.**
          tew puh ah-pohr-tey ley ohr-duh-vruh oh sah-lohN, see tew vuh.
          You can bring the hors d'oeuvres to the living room, if you want.

Guy: **Ce melon au jambon fumé a l'air délicieux.**
          suh muh-lohN oh zhaN-bohN few-mey ah lehr dey-lee-syuh.
          This melon with smoked ham looks delicious.

Sophie: **Oui, le mélange du melon sucré et du jambon salé est vraiment bon.**
          wee, luh mey-lahNzh dew muh-lohN sew-krey ey dew zhahN-bohN sah-ley ey vrey-mahN bohN.
          Yes, the blending of the sweet melon and the salty ham is really good.

Marc: **À votre santé, chers amis !**
          ah voh-truh sahN-tey, shehr zah-mee!
          To your health, dear friends!

Michelle: **À la vôtre ! L'an prochain, vous allez venir chez nous au Québec et je vous ferai une tourtière.**
          ah lah voh-truh! lahn proh-shaN, vooh zah-ley vuh-neer shey nooh oh key-behk ey zhuh vooh fuh-rey ewn toohr-tyehr.
          To yours! Next year, you'll come visit us in Québec, and I'll make you a tourtière.

Guy:	**Je ne connais pas très bien mais je sais que c'est une sorte de tarte aux pommes de terre.**
	zhuhn koh-ney pah trey byaN mey zhuh sey kuh sey tewn sohrt duh tahrt oh puhhm duh tehr.
	I don't know it very well, but I know it's a kind of tart with potatoes.

Michelle:	**Oui, mais on peut la faire de différentes façons avec de la viande comme du bœuf, du porc ou du veau. On peut aussi la faire avec du poisson.**
	wee, mey ohN puh lah fehr duh dee-fey-rahNt fah-sohN ah-vehk duh lah vyahNd kuhhm dew buhf, dew pohr ooh dew voh. ohN puh oh-see lah fehr ah-vehk dew pwah-sohN.
	Yes, but you can make it different ways with meat like beef, pork, or veal. You can also make it with fish.

Marc:	**Bon, il faut peut-être faire deux tourtières, une à la viande pour moi et une au poisson pour Sophie.**
	bohN, eel foh puh-teh-truh fehr duh toohr-tyehr, ewn ah lah vyahNd poohr mwah eh ewn oh pwah-sohN poohr soh-fee.
	Well, you may have to make two tourtières, one with meat for me and one with fish for Sophie.

Sophie:	**Toi alors ! Quel gourmand !**
	twah ah-lohr! kehl goohr-mahN!
	Oh, you! What a glutton!

Notice the use of the word **on** in this dialogue. This pronoun is called impersonal because it can represent anybody. It's often used to talk about people in general, as in **On mange le dîner à midi au Québec** (ohN mahNzh luh dee-ney ah mee-dee oh key-behk) (*They/People in general eat lunch at noon in Québec*). However, it's also frequently used instead of **nous** (nooh) (*we*) in familiar settings: **On mange ?** (ohN mahNzh?) (*Should we eat?*).

Le melon *au jambon*, **l'omelette** *au fromage*, **la quiche** *aux champignons*, and **la tourtière** *à la viande* are examples of how you can add a detail of what a dish is made with. You just add **à** + **le/la/les** (which may contract to **au** or **aux**, as we explain in Chapter 2 of Book III) and the name of the ingredient(s).

Book II
Exploring and Wandering About

The 5th Wave   By Rich Tennant

"It says children are forbidden from running, touching objects, or appearing bored during the tour."

In this book . . .

At some point, you may find yourself traveling to a country in which French is spoken, and that's what this book is all about. We cover all aspects of travel, from planning a trip and going through customs to handling emergencies and seeking medical assistance. We also help you exchange money, use public transportation, and reserve a hotel room.

Here are the contents of Book II at a glance:

Chapter 1

Making Plans and Discovering New Places

In This Chapter

▶ Planning a trip

▶ Inviting your friends out (and accepting their invitations)

▶ Vistiting cities of all sizes

▶ Vacationing for adventure or relaxation

▶ Mastering French directions

*W*hen you visit a new region or a new town, you want to enjoy as much of the local entertainment as possible. That may mean attending museums, concerts, and plays; going out dancing; spending long, lazy days at the beach; or trekking through mountains and valleys.

Exploring new places is fun, but to find those places, you'll likely have to ask someone where to go. This chapter gives you expressions that can help you discuss where you want to go and how to get there. Along with helping you organize a variety of trips and activities, this chapter also covers the vocabulary you need to handle bureaucratic matters so that your trip can be the getaway you always dreamed of.

Preparing For Your Trip

What better way to get away, relax, and perhaps seek adventure than **voyager** (vwah-yah-zhey) (*to travel*)? Planning your travels is the first step to a fulfilling experience. Whatever you're looking for — adventure, history, nature, or cultural enlightenment — France and other French-speaking countries have it all.

Making travel plans

When you plan your trip, you're likely to hear the questions **Où voulez-vous aller ?** (ooh vooh-ley-vooh zah-ley?) (*Where do you want to go?*). To answer this question, you simply say **Je voudrais aller à . . .** (zhuh vooh-drey zah-ley ah . . .) (*I'd like to go to . . .*) and fill in your destination city. If you want to specify a country, you may have to use a preposition other than **à** — see Chapter 1 of Book IV for details.

If you're working with a travel agent, you may also hear **Quand voulez-vous partir ?** (kahN vooh-ley-vooh pahr-teer?) (*When do you want to leave?*) and **Quand voulez-vous revenir ?** (kahN vooh-ley-vooh ruh-vuh-neer?) (*When do you want to come back?*) Here's another variation: **Vous voulez rester pour combien de jours ?** (vooh vooh-ley reh-stey poohr kohN-byaN duh zhoohr?) (*How many days do you want to stay?*) If you're reserving seats, your agent will ask **Pour combien de personnes ?** (poohr kohN-byaN duh pehr-suhhn?) (*For how many people?*). To answer, simply say **Pour . . . personnes** (poohr . . . pehr-suhhn) (*For . . . people*). Refer to Chapter 2 of Book I for information on numbers and dates.

Talkin' the Talk

Anne Brasse is at a Parisian travel agency to book a flight to Nice for her and her husband. (Track 20)

Anne: **Bonjour, monsieur.**
          bohN-zhoohr, muh-syuh.
          Good morning, sir.

Agent: **Bonjour, madame. Vous désirez ?**
          bohN-zhoohr, mah-dahm. vooh dey-zee-rey?
          Good morning, ma'am. Can I help you?

Anne: **Nous voudrions prendre l'avion pour Nice en décembre.**
          nooh vooh-dree-yohN prahN-druh lah-vyoN poohr nees ahN dey-sahN-bruh.
          We'd like to take a flight to Nice in December.

Agent: **C'est pour combien de personnes ?**
          sey poohr kohN-byaN duh pehr-suhhn?
          For how many people?

Anne: **Pour deux personnes, monsieur.**
          poohr duh pehr-suhhn, muh-syuh.
          For two people, sir.

Agent: **Et pour quelle date ? Vous voulez rester pour combien de jours ?**
ey poohr kehl daht? vooh vooh-ley reh-stey poohr kohN-byaN duh zhoohr?
And for which date? How many days do you want to stay?

Anne: **Dix jours : du 22 [vingt-deux] décembre au 2 [deux] janvier.**
dee zhoohr: dew vahNt-duh dey-sahN-bruh oh duh zhahN-vyey.
Ten days: from December 22 to January 2.

Book II

Exploring and Wandering About

Agent: **Vous avez de la chance. J'ai encore deux places. Votre nom ?**
vooh zah-vey duh lah shahNs. zhey ahN-kohr duh plahs. vuhh-truh nohN?
You're in luck. I still have two seats. Your name?

Anne: **Anne et Michel Brasse : B, R, A, deux S, E.**
ahn ey mee-shehl brahs: bey, ehr, ah, duh zehs, uh.
Anne and Michel Brasse: B, R, A, two S's, E.

Agent: **C'est le vol Air France 6002 [six mille deux] qui part à 10 [dix] heures de Charles de Gaulle. Ca vous convient ?**
sey luh vohl ehr frahNs see meel duh kee pahr ah deez uhr duh shahrl duh gohl. sah vooh kohN-vyaN?
It's Air France flight 6002, which leaves at 10 a.m. from Charles de Gaulle [Airport]. Does that suit you?

Anne: **Oui, c'est parfait. À quelle heure est-ce qu'il arrive ?**
wee, sey pahr-fey. ah kehl uhr ehs keel ah-reev?
Yes, that's perfect. What time does it arrive?

Agent: **Il arrive à Nice à 11h30 [onze heures trente].**
eel ah-reev ah nees ah ohNz uhr trahNt.
It arrives in Nice at 11:30 a.m.

Anne: **Bon. Pouvez-vous réserver deux sièges pour nous ?**
bohN. pooh-vey-vooh rey-zehr-vey duh syehzh poohr nooh?
Good. Can you reserve two seats for us?

Agent: **Mais oui, bien sûr.**
mey wee, byaN sewr.
Yes, of course.

Considering passports and visas

The requirements to enter countries can vary. If you're a U.S. citizen, you need **un passeport valide** (uhN pahs-pohr vah-leed) (*a valid passport*), and depending on how long you stay, you may also need a visa. For example, a visa is required if you plan to stay in Europe for more than three months. Here are some terms and phrases that can get you the information you need:

- ✔ **le consulat français** (luh kohN-sew-lah frahN-sey) (*the French consulate*)

- ✔ **Est-ce qu'il faut un visa pour aller en/au/aux . . . ?** (ehs keel foh uhN vee-zah poohr ah-ley ahN/oh/oh . . . ?) (*Does one need a visa to go to . . . ?*)

- ✔ **Je veux rester . . . jours/semaines en/au/aux . . .** (zhuh vuh reh-stey . . . zhoohr/suh-mehn ahN/oh/oh . . .) (*I want to stay . . . days/weeks in . . .*)

The second example uses the impersonal construction **il faut**, which you can read about in the later section "Following commands: Going, turning, taking, and crossing."

Check the expiration date on your passport early because getting it renewed can take weeks. If you've never had a passport, apply for your passport at least six weeks before you want to leave.

Don't let the need for documentation scare you away from traveling. If you're traveling to Europe, you can hop from country to country within the continent to your heart's desire; in most cases, you won't even be asked to show your passport.

Packing your belongings

When you pack for your trip, you want to bring comfortable clothes and shoes (refer to Chapter 6 of Book I for clothing terms). You may also want to bring your **lunettes de soleil** (lew-neht duh soh-lehy) (*sunglasses*), your **rasoir** (rah-zwahr) (*razor*), and so on. Here are some of those miscellaneous items:

- ✔ **ma brosse à dent** (mah bruhhs ah dahN) (*my toothbrush*)

- ✔ **ma trousse de premier secours** (mah troohs duh pruh-myey suh-koohr) (*my first-aid kit*)

- ✔ **ma trousse de voyage** (mah troohs duh vwah-yahzh) (*my travel bag*)

- ✔ **mes tennis/mes baskets** (m) (mey tey-nees/mey bah-skeht) (*my sneakers*)

- ✔ **mon appareil photo** (mohN nah-pah-rehy foh-toh) (*my camera*)

- ✔ **mon dentifrice** (mohN dahN-tee-frees) (*my toothpaste*)

- ✔ **mon gel aseptisant** (mohN zhehl ah-sehp-tee-zahN) (*my sanitizing gel*)

- ✔ **mon lecteur de livres numériques** (mohN leyk-tuhr duh lee-vruh new-mey-reek) (*my e-book reader*)

- ✔ **mon roman** (mohN roh-mahN) (*my novel*)

- ✔ **mon sac à dos** (mohN sahk ah doh) (*my backpack*)

To talk about your stuff, you use possessive adjectives. Check out Chapter 2 of Book III for **mon/ma/mes** (mohN/mah/mey) (*my*) and other possessives.

As you're packing, keep in mind the local expectations regarding appropriate attire. When you visit religious sites in France, such as cathedrals and churches, you don't see locals wearing clothing that's too revealing (very short shorts or skirts, for example, or low-cut tank tops), and you shouldn't dress that way, either.

Book II

Exploring and Wandering About

Talkin' the Talk

Lynne and her husband, David, have never been to the south of France. She calls her friend Anne, who lives in France, to ask about what type of clothing to take. (Track 21)

Lynne: **Anne, je fais mes valises. Qu'est-ce que tu me conseilles comme vêtements ?**
ahn, zhuh fey mey vah-leez. kehs kuh tew muh kohN-sehy kuhhm veht-mahN?
Anne, I'm packing my suitcases. What kind of clothes should I bring? [Literally: *What do you advise me about clothes?*]

Anne: **C'est facile. Des choses légères mais un pull pour le soir.**
sey fah-seel. dey shohz ley-zhehr mey uhN pewl poohr luh swahr.
That's easy. Light things but a sweater for the evening.

Lynne: **Okay. Alors, je vais prendre mes shorts et mes t-shirts pour la plage.**
oh-key. ah-lohr, zhuh vey prahN-druh mey shohrt ey mey tee-shuhrt poohr lah plahzh.
Okay. So I'm going to take my shorts and my t-shirts for the beach.

Anne:	**Et peut-être ta robe rouge et ta jupe noire pour sortir. Dis à David d'apporter son costume et sa cravate.**
	ey puh-teh-truh tah ruhhb roozh ey tah zhewp nwahr poohr sohr-teer. dee ah dah-veed dah-pohr-tey sohN koh-stewm ey sah krah-vaht.
	And maybe your red dress and your black skirt for going out. Tell David to bring his suit and his tie.

Lynne:	**Ah oui, et ses chaussures.**
	ah wee, ey sey shoh-sewr.
	Oh yes, and his shoes.

Anne:	**Voilà. Mais ne prenez pas trop de choses.**
	vwah-lah. mey nuh pruh-ney pah trohd shohz.
	That's it. But don't take too many things.

Lynne:	**Et nos sandales et nos baskets, ça suffit ?**
	ey noh sahN-dahl ey noh bah-skeht, sah sew-fee?
	And our sandals and our sneakers, is that enough?

Anne:	**Oui. N'oubliez pas vos lunettes de soleil !**
	wee. nooh-blee-yey pah voh lew-neht duh soh-lehy!
	Yes. Don't forget your sunglasses!

Seeing the Sites with the Locals

Who knows better than you what is worth visiting in your area? Just as you'd be happy to show family and friends what you like most about where you live, your friends or acquaintances are in a good position to guide you when you visit their turf. Try to befriend some of the local people before you venture out on your own.

Extending an invitation for fun

Wherever you go, you're sure to find plenty of local color and attractions to explore. Here are some verbs to describe common activities:

- **aller au café** (ah-ley oh kah-fey) (*to go to the café*)
- **aller aux brocantes** (ah-ley oh broh-kahNt) (*to go to rummage sales*)
- **boire un pot** (bwahr uhN poh) (*to have a drink*)

✔ **chercher des souvenirs** (shehr-shey dey sooh-vuh-neer) (*to look for souvenirs*)

✔ **faire du lèche-vitrine** (fehr dew lehsh-vee-treen) (*to go window-shopping. Literally: to lick the shop windows*)

✔ **faire du vélo** (fehr dew vey-loh) (*to go for a bike ride*)

✔ **se balader** (suh bah-lah-dey) (*to take a stroll*)

✔ **visiter un musée** (vee-zee-tey uhN mew-zey) (*to visit a museum*)

✔ **voir une exposition** (vwahr ewn ehk-spoh-zee-syohN) (*to see an exibit*)

Regardless of the activity, inviting a friend to come along always makes things more fun. By using the **tu** (tew) form — the singular informal *you* form — you may ask your friend what he's doing, whether he wants to go out, and, if so, where. Here are a few questions that may come in handy:

Qu'est-ce que tu fais [ce soir] ? (kehs-kuh tew fey [suh swahr]?) (*What are you doing [this evening]?*)

Veux-tu sortir ? (vuh-tew sohr-teer?) (*Do you want to go out?*)

Qu'est-ce que tu veux faire ? (kehs-kuh tew vuh fehr?) (*What do you want to do?*)

Tu as envie de sortir quelque part ? (tew ah ahN-vee duh sohr-teer kehl-kuh pahr?) (*Do you want to go out somewhere?*)

Ça te dit de sortir un peu ? (sah tuh dee duh sohr-teer uhN puh?) (*Do you feel like going out a bit?*)

On sort aujourd'hui ? (ohN sohr?) (*Should we go out today?*)

Où veux-tu aller ? (ooh vuh-tew ah-ley?) (*Where do you want to go?*)

Veux-tu aller en ville ? (vuh-tew ah-ley ahN veel?) (*Do you want to go to town?*)

When you plan activities with a friend, you can just start with **je voudrais** (zhuh vooh-drey) (*I'd like*) and end with whatever verb corresponds to your chosen activity. For example, you can say **Je voudrais aller au café boire un pot.** (zhuh vooh-drey zah-ley oh kah-fey bwahr uhN poh.) (*I'd like to go to the cafe to have a drink.*)

Check out these example invitations for specific activities:

Tu voudrais faire du vélo ? (tew vooh-drey fehr dew vey-loh?) (*Would you like to go for a bike ride?*)

Tu veux aller voir la nouvelle exposition au musée ? (tew vuh zah-ley vwahr lah nooh-vehl eyk-spoh-zee-syohN oh mew-zey?) (*Do you want to see the new exhibit at the museum?*)

On pourrait aller au marché aux puces. (ohN pooh-rey ah-ley oh mahr-shey oh pews.) (*We could go to the flea market.*)

On va se promener ? (ohN vah suh prohm-ney?) (*Shall we go for a walk?*)

The impersonal pronoun **on** (rather than **nous**) is often used among relatives and friends to say *we*. *On* translates as *one, people* in general. Don't hesitate to use it when suggesting or asking about going out — just remember to follow it with a verb conjugated in the third person singular. You can check out verb conjugations in Chapter 3 of Book III.

Accepting and declining invitations

When you're bored or when you want to go out, you gladly accept your friends' invitations. But when don't feel like being social, you may want to decline an invitation and perhaps even reschedule. With these phrases, you can do all three:

Je veux bien. (zhuh vuh byaN.) (*I'd like to very much.*)

J'aimerais vraiment aller au cinéma. (zhehm-rey vreh-mahN tah-ley oh see-ney-mah.) (*I'd really like to go to the movies.*)

J'aimerais/Je voudrais voir le nouveau film de . . . (zhehm-rey/zhuh vooh-drey vwahr luh nooh-voh feelm duh . . .) (*I'd like to see the new film by . . .*)

Je n'ai pas envie de sortir. (zhuh ney pah zahN-vee duh sohr-teer.) (*I don't feel like going out.*)

Peut-être demain/la semaine prochaine. (puh teh-truh duh-maN/lah suh-mehn proh-shehn.) (*Perhaps tomorrow/next week.*)

Considering Some Big-City Destinations

When you visit a new place, you don't want to just sit in your hotel room; you want to go out, explore the city, and partake in everything it has to offer. You can visit the museums or go to the little boutiques and look for unusual presents to take back home. Of course, you can also sit at a café and do a little people-watching like French people do. This section explores some fun activities to pursue in cities such as Paris and Montréal.

Au musée : At the museum

You can visit many museums in Paris. The most famous is **Le Louvre** (luh looh-vruh). Originally built as a royal fortress, the Louvre is now home to artifacts dating from 5,000 BC to 1848, including some of the most famous sculptures and paintings in the world, such as the Winged Victory of Samothrace, the Venus de Milo, and Leonardo da Vinci's **La Joconde** (lah zhoh-kohNd) (*the Mona Lisa*). You can also see original 12th-century fortress foundations and drawbridge supports. Another famous museum, **Le Musée D'Orsay** (luh mew-zey dohr-sey), once a railway station, is home to the world's finest collection of van Gogh paintings (well, outside the van Gogh museum in Amsterdam) as well as to an impressive collection of Impressionist art.

Museums in Paris are closed on different days. The Louvre is closed on Tuesdays, for example, and **Le Musée D'Orsay** is closed on Mondays. Be sure to check out the hours before you go. (Check out the admission fees, too. Some museums have free admission on certain days. Admission to the Louvre, for instance, is free on the first Sunday of the month and on July 14, France's national holiday.)

If you're going to a museum, check into discounts. Students, young children, large families, and senior citizens often get a price break. Or consider buying a museum pass, a **Carte Musées et Monuments** (kahrt mew-zey ey moh-new-mahN). These passes, available at museum ticket offices, tourist offices, and subway stations, can add to your savings. For more information, contact the **Association InterMusées** (ah-soh-syah-syohN aN-tehr-mew-zhey) online at www.intermusees.fr.

As you tour these remarkable places, you may encounter signs such as the following:

- ✔ **photos au flash interdites** (foh-toh oh flash aN-tehr-deet) (*no flash photography*)
- ✔ **défense d'entrer** (dey-fahNs dahN-trey) (*no admittance*)

Au parc : At the park

Large cities like Paris and Montréal can surprise you with the number of parks they have. On nice days, parks attract people of all ages — families with young children who want nothing more than to run around, young people in love who crowd the benches, and people taking their daily stroll.

Book II

Exploring and Wandering About

Some Parisian parks are called **jardins** (zhahr-daN) (*gardens*). Tourists and locals alike spend many hours walking, reading, and playing tennis at the **Jardin du Luxembourg** (zhahr-daN dew lewk-sahN-boohr), which has a small bronze **Statue de la Liberté** (stah-tew duh lah lee-behr-tey) (*Statue of Liberty*). The **Jardin des Tuileries (**zhahr-daN dey twee-luh-ree), adjacent to the Louvre, is filled with statues by famous French sculptors and features tree-lined promenades and fountains. Other parks are called **bois** (bwah) (*wood*), like the **Bois de Vincennes** (bwah duh vaN-sehn), with its **zoo** (zoh) (*zoo*), its **musée** (mew-zey) (*museum*), its **château** (shah-toh) (*royal castle*), and its **quatre lacs** (kah-truh lahk) (*four lakes*). The **Bois de Vincennes** is known for its **course de chevaux** (koohrs duh shuh-voh) (*horse races*). The **Bois de Boulogne** (bwah duh booh-luhh-nyuh), which is at least twice as large as Central Park, offers tons of sports and leisure activities on the weekend.

Canada is known for its nearly unlimited land, so you shouldn't be surprised that many parks in Québec offer striking land expanses filled with natural wonders. For example, the **Bois de l'île Bizard** (bwah duh leel bee-zahr) in Montréal features not only woods but also **plages** (plahzh) (*beaches*) and **marais** (mah-rey) (*marshlands*). The **Parc du Mont-Royal** (pahrk dew mohN-rwah-yahl) (*Mount Royal Park*), also in Montréal, spreads over 529 acres of land. This park was designed by Frederick Law Olmsted, the same landscape architect who designed New York City's Central Park. It offers a magnificent view over the city and many opportunities for free and affordable outdoor sports for all ages, especially in winter.

Au marché aux puces : At the flea market

Shopping at French flea markets can be tons of fun, with lots of open stalls selling everything from junk to vintage clothing and valuable antiques. On a not-so-busy day, vendors are more inclined to bargain with you over prices. Otherwise, if you're really interested, stick around and show genuine respect for the goods. Doing so makes it easier to negotiate. Try out your French with the following questions:

- ✔ **Vous voulez combien pour . . . ?** (vooh vooh-ley kohN-byaN poohr . . . ?) (*How much do you want for . . . ?*)

- ✔ **Ça vaut combien ?** (sah voh kohN-byaN?) (*How much is it?*)

- ✔ **Est-ce que vous pouvez me faire un petit prix ?** (ehs kuh vooh pooh-vey muh fehr uhN puh-tee pree?) (*Can you give me a better price?*)

A **marché aux puces** can take many shapes and forms, depending on where it takes place. The **Marché de Saint Ouen** in Paris is one of the largest flea markets in the world and includes very serious **antiquaires** (ahN-tee-kehr) (*antique dealers*).

Be careful in very busy places like big weekend flea markets. They're breeding grounds for pickpockets.

The flea market is home to all kinds of good stuff, often including the following:

- ✔ **la bague** (lah bahg) (*ring*)
- ✔ **le bouquin** (luh booh-kaN) (*book*)
- ✔ **le bric-à-brac** (luh bree-kah-brahk) (*knicknack*)
- ✔ **la carte** (lah kahrt) (*map/card*)
- ✔ **le collier** (luh koh-lyey) (*necklace*)
- ✔ **la cravate** (lah krah-vaht) (*tie*)
- ✔ **l'écharpe** (f) (ley-shahrp) (*winter scarf*)
- ✔ **le foulard** (luh fooh-lahr) (*scarf*)
- ✔ **le jouet** (luh zhooh-ey) (*toy*)
- ✔ **le miroir** (luh mee-rwahr) (*mirror*)
- ✔ **le portefeuille** (luh pohrt-fuhy) (*wallet*)
- ✔ **le sac (à main)** (luh sahk [ah maN]) (*[hand]bag*)
- ✔ **le tableau** (luh tah-bloh) (*painting*)
- ✔ **le vase** (luh vahz) (*vase*)

A **brocante** (broh-kahNt) is a rummage sale just like the ones in the United States. People get together and bring their used items to sell at whatever prices they can get.

Book II

Exploring and Wandering About

Talkin' the Talk

Nathalie and Mike are two students in Paris. It's a nice day, and Nathalie feels like going out. She calls her friend Mike.

Nathalie: **Allô, Mike. C'est Nathalie. Dis, tu as envie d'aller à une brocante près d'ici ?**
ah-loh, mahyk. sey nah-tah-lee. dee, tew ah ahN-vee dah-ley ah ewn broh-kahNt prey dee-see?
Hello, Mike. This is Nathalie. Say, do you feel like going to a rummage sale near here?

Mike:	**Pourquoi pas ? Je peux voir si quelqu'un a une lampe Belle Époque à vendre.**
	poohr-kwah pah? zhuh puh vwahr see kehl-kuhN ah ewn lahNp behl ey-puhhk ah vahN-druh.
	Why not? I can see whether someone has a Belle Époque lamp to sell.
Nathalie:	**Tu es prêt ? On y va tout de suite ?**
	tew ey prey? ohN nee vah toohd sweet?
	Are you ready? Should we go right away?
Mike:	**J'ai une idée ! On va à la brocante et puis après, on va se promener au Jardin du Luxembourg.**
	zhey ewn ee-dey! ohN vah ah lah broh-kahNt et pwee ah-prey, ohN vah suh prohm-ney oh zhahr-daN dew lewk-sahN-boohr.
	I have an idea! Let's go to the rummage sale and then afterward go for a walk to the Luxembourg Gardens.
Nathalie:	**Oui, parfait. On peut acheter un sandwich et des boissons à une charcuterie du coin et faire un pique-nique.**
	wee, pahr-fey. ohN puh ahsh-tey uhN sahNd-wish ey dey bwah-sohN ah ewn shahr-kew-tree dew kwaN ey fehr uhN peek-neek.
	Yes, perfect. We can buy a sandwich and some drinks at a neighborhood deli and have a picnic.

Touring Small Towns

Visiting the big cities is a must, but don't ignore the smaller towns in France, Belgium, Switzerland, and Québec. They hold many secrets and many unique, quaint, and charming features, such as local cuisines and customs. This section gives you a peek at some of these finds.

Finding hidden treasures in France

Many towns and villages in francophone countries will mesmerize you. During spring and summer in France, the **village fleuri/ville fleurie** (vee-lahzh fluh-ree/veel fluh-ree) contest is great motivation for every **commune** (koh-mewn) (*township*) to put forward its best beautification efforts. Inhabitants go to amazing lengths to make their villages competitive by adorning their houses with gorgeous flowers and creating beautiful landscapes sculpted according to a distinctive regional trait, such a barrel or a bottle of Champagne. Look for the sign **Ville fleurie** or **Village fleuri** at the entrance of a town. These signs have anywhere from one to four flowers, depending on where the town placed in this year's contest: the more flowers, the higher the ranking.

In addition, many French villages have some noteworthy historical attribute: a manor, a castle, an old church, a special museum, or whatever. If you're lucky, you may be able to catch a reenactment of a historical event in a **Son et Lumière** (sohN ey lew-myehr) (*Sound and Light show*) taking place at an authentic period site.

Here are some words to help you find some interesting places:

Book II

Exploring and Wandering About

- ✔ **les bords** (m)/**les rives** (f) (ley bohr/ley reev) (*riverbanks*)
- ✔ **le château** (luh shah-toh) (*castle*)
- ✔ **la croisière** (lah krwah-zyehr) (*cruise*)
- ✔ **l'église** (f) **[du Moyen Age]** (ley-gleez [dew mwah-yaNn ahzh]) (*church [from the Middle Ages]*)
- ✔ **la mairie** (lah meh-ree) (*city hall*)
- ✔ **le manoir** (luh mah-nwahr) (*manor*)
- ✔ **le rampart** (luh rahN-pahr) (*rampart*)
- ✔ **la rivière** (lah ree-vyehr) (*river*)

Enjoying the old-world charm of Québec

The province of Québec is known for its wintry landscapes and festivals as well as its sports activities, such as ice hockey, ice fishing, snowshoeing, and snowmobile races. But it also has many old towns where European and American influences have blended. For example, Quebec City (Québec's capital) has kept its small-town feel. In its **Vieux-Québec** (vyuh key-behk) (*Old Québec*) — declared a World Heritage Site by UNESCO (the United Nations Educational, Scientific, and Cultural Organization) — you walk on narrow cobblestone streets dating back to the 1600s. You can tour the town on foot or by **calèche** (kah-lehsh) (*horse-drawn carriage*). Here's a list of words that can help you identify some of what the **Québécois** (key-bey-kwah) towns offer:

- ✔ **les chutes** (f) (ley shewt) (*waterfalls*)
- ✔ **la compétition sportive** (lah kohN-pey-tee-syohN spohr-teev) (*sports event or competition*)

- **le festival d'hiver** (luh feh-stee-vahl dee-vehr) (*winter festival*)

- **le fleuve Saint-Laurent** (luh fluhv saN-loh-rahN) (*Saint Lawrence River*)

- **le patrimoine historique** (luh pah-tree-mwahn ee-stoh-reek) (*historical heritage*)

- **la pêche** (lah pehsh) (*fishing*)

- **la piste** (lah peest) (*trail, runway, track*)

- **le stade de hockey** (luh stahd duh oh-key) (*hockey stadium*)

- **la vieille ville** (lah vyehy veel) (*old town*)

Talkin' the Talk

A French couple is visiting Quebec City during the Winter Festival. (Track 22)

Julie: **Regarde, Luc, voilà le célèbre Château Frontenac.**
ruh-gahrd, lewk, vwah-lah luh sey-leh-bruh shah-toh frohN-tuh-nak.
Look, Luc, there's the famous Château Frontenac.

Luc: **On entre ? Je voudrais voir l'intérieur de l'hôtel.**
ohN nahN-truh? zhuh vooh-drey vwahr laN-tey-ryuhr duh loh-tehl.
Should we enter? I'd like to see the inside of the hotel.

Julie: **Bien sûr. Allons-y ! Mais admirons d'abord la vue sur le fleuve Saint-Laurent.**
byaN sewr. ah-lohN-zee! mey ahd-mee-rohN dah-bohr lah vew sewr luh fluhv saN-loh-rahN.
Of course. Let's go! But let's first admire the view over the Saint Lawrence River.

Luc: **C'est magnifique, n'est-ce pas ? Demain, on va faire une croisière sur le fleuve.**
sey mah-nee-feek, nehs pah? duh-maN, ohN vah fehr ewn krwah-zyehr sewr luh fluhv.
Magnificent, isn't it? Tomorrow, we'll go for a cruise on the river.

Julie: **J'espère qu'on va voir des baleines.**
zhehs-pehr kohN vah vwahr dey bah-lehn.
I hope we see some whales.

Luc:	**Sûrement.** sewr-mahN. *Surely.*
Julie:	**Après la visite de l'hôtel, je voudrais faire un tour en calèche et aller dans les petites boutiques.** ah-preh lah vee-zeet duh loh-tehl, zhuh vooh-drey fehr uhN toohr ahN kah-lehsh ey ah-ley dahN ley puh-teet booh-teek. *After the hotel visit, I'd like to take a carriage tour and go to the little boutiques.*
Luc:	**N'oublie pas que nous voulons voir les chutes de Montmorency.** nooh-blee pah kuh nooh vooh-lohN vwahr ley shewt duh mohN-moh-rahN-see. *Don't forget we want to see the Montmorency Falls.*
Julie:	**Oui, cet après-midi. Mais passons d'abord un peu de temps en ville. C'est si charmant !** wee, sehh ah-preh-mee-dee. mey pah-sohN dah-bohr uhN puh duh tahN ahN veel. sey see shahr-mahN! *Yes, this afternoon. But let's first spend some time in town. It's so charming!*

The **Château Frontenac** is a hotel located on the bank of the Saint Lawrence River in the heart of Quebec City's historic district. It was built in the shape of a castle by New York architect Bruce Price in the 19th century and named after a French count, **le comte de Frontenac** (luh kohNt duh frohN-tuh-nahk), who led the French settlers in this part of Canada in the 17th century. The **chutes de Montmorency** (shewt duh mohN-moh-rahN-see) (*Montmorency Falls*) are located about 12 kilometers (about 7.5 miles) from downtown Quebec City and are a popular side trip for Quebec City visitors. They're a site of great natural beauty and historical significance, with a cable car that runs up to the **manoir** (mah-nwahr), an old villa built around 1780.

À l'Aventure ! Looking for an Active Vacation

If you can't sit still and you love adventure, the francophone world has a lot to offer. Quebec, thanks to its huge territory and varied landscape, offers lots of outdoor activities — equestrian riding, biking, rafting, and kayaking — and it hosts sports events all year round. France boasts cycling tours and hiking, camping, and fishing throughout the countryside.

Getting active outdoors

The French don't tend to be exercise addicts. They'll often tell you that they get their daily exercise by walking to work or to the stores. However, they love to take off to natural settings on long weekends and during **vacances** (vah-kahNs) (*vacations*). The tourism industry in France is quite ingenious and offers many opportunities for active vacations, including the following:

- ✔ **la ballade en VTT/véhicule tout terrain** (lah bah-lahd ahN vey-tey-tey/ vey-ee-kewl tooh teh-raN) (*ride in an all terrain vehicle*)
- ✔ **le chemin balisé** (luh shuh-maN bah-lee-zey) (*marked path*)
- ✔ **les courses** (f) **en traîneau** (ley koohrs ahN treh-noh) (*sled races*)
- ✔ **l'escalade** (f) (leh-skah-lahd) (*climbing*)
- ✔ **la piste cyclable** (lah peest see-klah-bluh) (*bicycle path*)
- ✔ **les randonnées** (f) **en montagne** (ley rahN-doh-ney ahN mohN-tah-nyuh) (*hikes in the mountains*)
- ✔ **le séjour à thème** (luh sey-zhoohr ah tehm) (*theme vacation*)
- ✔ **la spéléologie** (lah spey-ley-oh-loh-zhee) (*spelunking, cave exploration*)
- ✔ **les vacances actives** (f) (ley vah-kahNs ahk-teev) (*active vacations*)
- ✔ **les vacances** (f) **de ski** (ley vah-kahNs duh skee) (*skiing vacations*)
- ✔ **le voyage à vélo** (luh vwah-yahzh ah vey-loh) (*bicycle trip*)

France has several mountain ranges where you can enjoy active vacations: **les Alpes** (ley zahlp) at its borders with Switzerland and Italy, **les Pyrénées** (ley pee-rey-ney) at its border with Spain, **les Vosges** (ley vohzh) at its border with Germany, and **le Jura** (luh zhew-rah) at its border with Switzerland. Québec has the **Laurentides** (loh-rahN-teed), tall mountains along its borders with Maine, New Hampshire, and Vermont.

Watching sports events

A trip to France in July means you hear about the famous **Tour de France** (toohr duh frahNs) bicycle race all over the news. If you stay in an area that the cyclists pass, be prepared for roads to be closed to the general traffic. You can mingle with the bystanders and wait (free of charge) for the riders — including the one in the **maillot jaune** (mah-yoh zhohn) (*yellow jersey,* marking the overall time leader) and the one in the **maillot vert** (mah-yoh vehr) (*green jersey,* marking the points leader). The **Tour** attracts riders and teams from all over the world. It includes many **étapes** (ey-tahp) (*stages*) spanning several weeks across France, ending on **les Champs-Élysées** (ley shahN-zey-lee-zey), right by the **Arc de Triomphe** (ahrk duh tree-ohNf) in Paris.

Other popular French **sports-spectacles** (spohr-spehk-tah-kluh) (*spectator sports*) are **le foot(ball)** (luh fooht[-bohl]) (*soccer*), **les courses de chevaux** (ley koohrs duh shuh-voh) (*horse races*), and **les courses automobiles** (ley koohrs oh-toh-moh-beel) (*auto races*).

In Quebec City, you may attend one of the biggest sports events in the world, the **Pentathlon des neiges** (pahN-taht-lohN dey nehzh) (*Snow Pentathlon*). The five sports represented are **la course à pied** (lah koohrs ah pyey) (*running*), **le vélo** (luh vey-loh) (*bicycling*), **le ski de fond** (luh skee duh fohN) (*cross-country skiing*), **le patin à glace** (luh pah-taN ah glahs) (*ice skating*), and **la course à raquettes** (lah koohrs ah rah-keht) (*snowshoeing*). Another option is going to the **Coupe du Monde de surf des neiges** (koohp dew mohNd duh suhrf dey nehzh) (*World Cup of Snowboarding*). Other popular Canadian sports are **le hockey (sur glace)** (luh oh-key [sewr glahs]) (*[ice] hockey*) and *soccer,* which the Québécois call **le soccer** (luh soh-kuhr).

Indulging in Relaxing Activities

Sometimes, the best vacation is just kicking back. You can do that in many areas of the francophone world. Guadeloupe, Martinique, France, Switzerland, Belgium, and Québec have lots of casual and fancy resorts. Whether you're at the beach, by a pool, or camping near a lake, you're sure to have a good time if you know some of the language we present next.

Catching some sun at the beach

Allons à la plage ! (ah-lohN zah lah plahzh!) (*Let's go to the beach!*) Nothing is more relaxing than a day spent lounging on the sand or playing in the water. **La Côte d'Azur** (lah koht dah-zewr) (*the Azure Coast*), also known as the French Riviera, is situated on the southern coast of France, along the Mediterranean Sea. Its numerous beaches are quite crowded during July and August. Here are some water-related activities to try:

- ✔ **la natation** (lah nah-tah-syohN) (*swimming*)
- ✔ **la planche à voile** (lah plahNsh ah vwahl) (*windsurfing*)
- ✔ **la plongée sous-marine** (lah plohN-zhey sooh-mah-reen) (*scuba diving*)

✔ **la plongée libre** (lah plohN-zhey lee-bruh) (*snorkeling*)

✔ **le ski nautique** (luh skee noh-teek) (*water skiing*)

✔ **la voile** (lah vwahl) (*sailing*)

To talk about doing the preceding activities, you use the verb **faire** (fehr) (*to do, to make*) plus the preposition **de** (duh) and the appropriate definite article — **le** for masculine nouns or **la** for feminine, as in **faire de la voile** (*to go sailing*). Check out Chapter 3 of Book III for the conjugation of the irregular verb **faire**.

Topless sunbathing is accepted on most French beaches. So is **nudisme/naturisme** (new-dee-zmuh/nah-tew-ree-zmuh) (*nudism*), and you can find many **plages nudistes** (plahzh new-deest) (*nudist beaches*). Before disrobing completely, look around to see what's acceptable.

With a couple of towels, some sunblock, a refreshing drink, and these vocabulary words, you're all set to spend a day at the beach:

✔ **l'algue** (f) (lahlg) (*seaweed*)

✔ **le banc de sable** (luh bahN duh sah-bluh) (*sandbank*)

✔ **le bord de la mer/au bord de la mer** (luh bohr duh lah mehr/oh bohr duh lah mehr) (*the seashore/by the seashore*)

✔ **le bronzage** (luh brohN-zahzh) (*suntan*)

✔ **bronzer** (brohN-zey) (*to tan*)

✔ **le château de sable** (luh shah-toh duh sah-bluh) (*sand castle*)

✔ **les coquillages** (m) (ley koh-kee-yahzh) (*seashells*)

✔ **le coup de soleil** (luh kooh duh soh-lehy) (*sunburn*)

✔ **la lotion/crème solaire** (lah loh-syohN/ krehm soh-lehr) (*sunblock/sunscreen*)

✔ **le maillot de bain** (luh mah-yoh duh baN) (*bathing suit*)

✔ **la mer** (lah mehr) (*the sea*)

✔ **le sable** (luh sah-bluh) (*sand*)

✔ **la vague** (lah vahg) (*wave*)

✔ **la serviette** (lah sehr-vyeht) (*towel*)

If you see a sign posted that reads **Baignade interdite** (beh-nyahd aN-tehr-deet), beware. That means *No swimming!*

Talkin' the Talk

Madame Lafarge and her two sons Gaston and Henri are spending the day at the beach.

Gaston et Henri: **Maman ! Nous allons nager.**
mah-mahN! nooh zah-lohN nah-zhey.
Mom! We're going swimming.

Mme. Lafarge: **Attendez ! Vous oubliez la crème solaire.**
ah-tahN-dey! vooh zooh-blee-yey lah krehm soh-lehr.
Wait! You're forgetting suncreen.

Gaston: **Oh, maman ! Dépêche-toi !**
oh, mah-mahN! dey-pehsh-twah!
Oh, Mom! Hurry up!

Henri: **Gaston, regarde les très grandes vagues !**
gah-stohN, ruh-gahrd ley treh grahNd vahg!
Gaston, look at those really big waves!

Gaston: **C'est super ! Maman, as-tu mon tuba et mes palmes ? Nous allons faire de la plongée libre.**
sey sew-pehr! mah-mahN, ah-tew mohN tew-bah ey mey pahlm? nooh zah-lohN fehr duh lah plohN-zhey lee-bruh.
It's great! Mom, do you have my snorkel and flippers? We're going snorkeling.

Mme. Lafarge: **Oui, ils sont dans le sac. Je vais bronzer. Amusez-vous bien !**
wee, eel sohN dahN luh sahk. zhuh veh brohN-zey. ah-mew-zey-vooh byaN!
Yes, they're in the bag. I'm going to tan. Have fun!

Book II

Exploring and Wandering About

Camping out

Camping is a great way to get away from it all. France offers approximately 11,000 campsites. Traditionally, July and August are when the French — especially the Parisians — head to the hills, so to speak. Highways are jammed with cars and campers escaping from the city. Along the French Riviera, traffic has been known to be stalled for hours as cars wind their way to the coast.

Just like hotels and restaurants, French campsites are classified according to a star ranking system: from one to four stars based on the level of amenities. Most campgrounds have showers and restaurants as well as separate sites for bicycles and tent campers. Many campsites are situated along the beaches. If you plan to go, making reservations well in advance is a good idea, especially for the months of July and August. Off-road camping is illegal.

Here are some expressions to help you figure out what campsites offer:

- **animé** (ah-nee-mey) (*with activities*)
- **avec accès direct à la mer** (ah-vehk ahk-sey dee-rehkt ah lah mehr) (*with direct access to the sea*)
- **avec piscine couverte/ouverte** (ah-vehk pee-seen kooh-vehrt/ooh-vehrt) (*with indoor/outdoor pool*)
- **les douches** (f) (ley doohsh) (*showers*)
- **insolite** (aN-soh-leet) (*unusal*)
- **naturiste** (nah-tew-reest) (*naturist/nudist*)
- **les toilettes** (f) (ley twah-leht) (*the toilets*)
- **les services** (m) (ley sehr-vees) (*the facilities*)

Watch for the expression **à proximité de** (ah prohk-see-mee-tey duh). It tells you that the site is in the vicinity of something special, such as castles, beaches, **falaises** (fah-lehz) (*cliffs*), or **vignobles** (vee-nyoh-bluh) (*vineyards*).

The following words and phrases pertaining to camping and fishing are useful in case you want to pursue these fun-filled activities:

- **les allumettes** (f) (ley zah-lew-meht) (*matches*)
- **attraper** (ah-trah-pey) (*to catch*)
- **la canne à pêche** (lah kahn ah pehsh) (*fishing pole*)
- **faire un feu de camp** (fehr uhN fuh duh kahN) (*start a campfire*)

> ✔ **monter la tente** (mohN-tey lah tahNt) (*to pitch the tent*)

> ✔ **pêcher** (peh-shey) (*to fish, to go fishing*)

> ✔ **le poisson** (luh pwah-sohN) (*fish*)

> ✔ **le sac de couchage** (luh sahk duh kooh-shahzh) (*sleeping bag*)

Talkin' the Talk

Étienne and Christine are going camping. Christine has been napping in the car. (Track 23)

Étienne: **Lève-toi ! Nous sommes arrivés.**
lehv-twah! nooh sohm zah-ree-vey.
Get up! We're here.

Christine: **Oh ! C'est très joli, n'est-ce pas ?**
oh! sey trey zhoh-lee, nehs pah?
Oh! It's very pretty, isn't it?

Étienne: **Oui. Montons la tente.**
wee. mohN-tohN lah tahNt.
Yes, let's pitch the tent.

Christine: **D'accord. Quels services y a-t-il ?**
dah-kohr. kehl sehr-vees ee ah-teel?
Okay. What facilities are there?

Étienne: **Il y a des toilettes et des douches.**
eel ee ah dey twah-leht ey dey doohsh.
There are toilets and showers.

Christine: **Voilà les sacs de couchage.**
vwah-lah ley sahk duh kooh-shahzh.
Here are the sleeping bags.

Étienne: **Merci. Peux-tu trouver les allumettes ?**
mehr-see. puh-tew trooh-vey ley zah-lew-meht?
Thanks. Can you find the matches?

Christine: **Oui, les voilà.**
wee, ley vwah-lah.
Yes, here they are.

Étienne: **Bon. Je vais faire un feu de camp.**
bohN. zhuh vey fehr uhN fuh duh kahN.
Good. I'll start a campfire.

After their campsite is set up, the friends talk about how to spend their afternoon.

Étienne: **Christine, je vais pêcher.**
kree-steen, zhuh vey peh-shey.
Christine, I'm going fishing.

Christine: **Je n'aime pas pêcher. Je vais lire mon livre.**
zhuh nehm pah peh-shey. zhuh vey leer mohN lee-vruh.
I don't like fishing. I'm going to read my book.

Étienne: **J'espère attraper des poissons pour le dîner.**
zheh-spehr ah-trah-pey dey pwah-sohN poohr luh dee-ney.
I hope to catch some fish for dinner.

Christine: **Tu as ta canne à pêche ?**
tew ah tah kahn ah pehsh?
Do you have your fishing pole?

Étienne: **Oui et des vers aussi.**
wee ey dey vehr oh-see.
Yes, and some worms, too.

Christine: **Dégoûtant ! Va-t'en !**
dey-gooh-tahN! vah-tahN!
Disgusting! Go away!

Finding Your Way Around

The most common question anyone in a new place must ask repeatedly is *Where is . . . ?* This section helps you ask for and understand directions so you don't spend your vacation wandering around lost.

Asking where things are with où

Where questions follow this construction:

> **où** + verb + subject

The verb **être** (*to be*) is the verb most often connected with **où**, as these examples show (check out Chapter 3 of Book III for the complete conjugation of the verb **être**):

> **Où est le Louvre ?** (ooh ey luh looh-vruh?) (*Where is the Louvre?*)
>
> **Où est la place Victor Hugo ?** (ooh ey lah plahs veek-tohr ew-goh?) (*Where is Victor Hugo Square?*)
>
> **Où sont les toilettes ?** (ooh sohN ley twah-leht?) (*Where is the bathroom?*)

But **où** also frequently pairs with the verb **se trouver** to ask *where* questions:

> **Où se trouve le Louvre ?** (ooh suh troohv luh looh-vruh?) (*Where is the Louvre [located]?* Literally: *Where does the Louvre find itself?*)
>
> **Où se trouve la place Victor Hugo ?** (ooh suh troohv lah plahs veek-tohr ew-goh?) (*Where is Victor Hugo Square?*)
>
> **Où se trouvent les toilettes ?** (ooh suh troohv ley twah-leht?) (*Where is the bathroom?*)

You use this sentence structure for all verbs you choose to connect with **où**:

> **Où va ce bus ?** (ooh vah suh bews?) (*Where is this bus going?*)
>
> **Où mène cette rue ?** (ooh mehn seht rew?) (*Where does this road lead?*)

Explaining where you are and where you're going

Prepositions are often little words, like *to, in,* and *at,* that indicate a relationship between one thing and another in a sentence. They're also a key element in answering *where* questions: Where are you going? To the zoo. Where is the concert? In the park. Where's Alice? At the museum.

Book II

Exploring and Wandering About

Fortunately, you have to remember only one French preposition for these concepts in most cases: **à** (ah), which means *to, in,* or *at.* How you use **à**, though, depends on the context of the answer.

As a rule, you use the preposition **à** when you want to say that you're going to or staying in a city or town. For example

> **Je vais à Lille.** (zhuh vey zah leel.) (*I'm going to Lille.*)

> **Ils sont à Montréal.** (eel sohN tah mohN-rey-ahl.) (*They're in Montréal.*)

When you want to talk about going to or staying at places in general, such as museums, cathedrals, or churches, you need to add the definite article — **le** (luh), **la** (lah), or **les** (ley), all of which mean *the* — after **à**. Note that **à** contracts with the masculine singular **le** and the plural **les**. The following list shows these combinations and provides a sample sentence that uses that construction:

- ✔ **à + le = au**

    > **Sylvie va au musée.** (seel-vee vah oh mew-zey.) (*Sylvie is going to the museum.*)

- ✔ **à + la = à la**

    > **Guy veut aller à la cathédrale.** (gee vuh tah-ley ah lah kah-tey-drahl.) (*Guy wants to go to the cathedral.*)

- ✔ **à + l' = à l'**

    > **Les Martin vont à l'église St. Paul.** (ley mahr-taN vohN tah ley-gleez saN pohl.) (*The Martins go to St. Paul Church.*)

- ✔ **à + les = aux**

    > **Allez aux feux d'artifice !** (ah-ley zoh fuh dahr-tee-fees!) (*Go to the fireworks!*)

The preposition you use in saying *in* or *to* a country depends on the gender and number of the country. With masculine singular countries like **le Canada** (luh kah-nah-dah), you say **Je vais au Canada** (zhuh vey zoh kah-nah-dah) (*I'm going to Canada*). And with plural countries like **les États-Unis** (ley zey-tah-zew-nee), you say **Je vais aux États-Unis** (zuh vey oh zey-tah-zew-nee) (*I'm going to the United States*).

However, with feminine singular countries like **la Belgique** (lah behl-zheek), you use **en** (ahN), not **à la**: **Je vais en Belgique** (zhuh vey zahN behl-zheek) (*I'm going to Belgium*). Continents, like **l'Afrique** (lah-freek) (*Africa*) and **l'Amérique** (lah-mey-reek) (*America*), are all feminine, so you say **Je vais en Afrique/Amérique** (zhuh vey zahN ah-freek/ah-mey-reek). To read more about prepositions to use with geographical areas such as regions, countries, islands, and continents, see Chapter 1 of Book IV.

Talkin' the Talk

John and Ann are in their hotel lobby inquiring about directions to go to the Cathedral of Notre Dame. **Le réceptionniste** (luh rey-seyp-syoh-neest) (*the desk clerk*) helps them.

Le réceptionniste: **Bonjour, monsieur. Je peux vous aider ?**
bohN-zhoohr, muh-syuh. zhuh puh vooh zey-dey?
Hello, sir. Can I help you?

John: **Nous voulons savoir où se trouve la cathédrale de Notre-Dame.**
nooh vooh-lohN sah-vwahr ooh suh troohv lah kah-tey-drahl duh nuhh-truh-dahm.
We want to know where the Cathedral of Notre Dame is.

Le réceptionniste: **Notre-Dame se trouve à l'Ile de la Cité.**
nuhh-truh-dahm suh troohv ah leel duh lah see-tey.
Notre Dame is on the Ile de la Cité.

John: **Est-ce que c'est loin d'ici ? Nous voulons aller à pied.**
ehs kuh sey lwaN dee-see? nooh vooh-lohN zah-ley ah pyey.
Is it far from here? We want to walk.

Le réceptionniste: **Non, c'est à 15 [quinze] minutes peut-être. Sortez de l'hôtel, tournez à gauche et continuez tout droit.**
nohN, sey tah kahNz mee-newt puh-teh-truh. sohr-tey duh loh-tehl, toohr-ney ah gohsh ey kohN-tee-new-ey tooh drwah.
No, it's maybe 15 minutes [from here]. Leave the hotel, turn left, and keep going straight ahead.

John: **Et ensuite ?**
ey ahN-sweet?
And then?

Le réceptionniste: **Traversez le Pont Neuf et la cathédrale est à gauche.**
trah-vehr-sey luh pohN nuhf ey lah kah-tey-drahl ey tah gohsh.
Cross the Pont Neuf, and the cathedral is on the left.

Book II

Exploring and Wandering About

John:	**Merci beaucoup.**
	mehr-see boh-kooh.
	Thank you very much.
Le réceptionniste:	**Je vous en prie.**
	zhuh vooh zahN pree.
	You're welcome.

Understanding directions

Whenever and wherever you travel, you're bound to need directions at some point. Understanding a few basic expressions can give you the general idea of where to go.

Following commands: Going, turning, taking, and crossing

When someone directs you somewhere, that person is giving you a command. In a command, it's understood that you're being addressed, but French has two ways to say *you* — the singular informal **tu** (tew) and the plural or formal **vous** (vooh). In addition, there's the **nous** (nooh) (*we*) command that you use to say "Let's!"

The command, or *imperative,* form of a verb comes from the **tu**, **nous**, or **vous** form of the present tense. You omit the **tu**, **nous**, or **vous** in front of the verb (just as you drop the *you* and *we* in English). See what we mean in the following examples:

> **Tu** form: **Va au cinéma.** (vah oh see-ney-mah.) (*Go to the movies.*)

> **Vous** form: **Allez tout droit.** (ah-ley tooh drwah.) (*Go straight ahead.*)

> **Nous** form: **Traversons le pont.** (trah-vehr-sohN luh pohN.) (*Let's cross the bridge.*)

For **-er** verbs, the **tu** form of the verb in a command appears without the final **-s** that you usually see in the present tense conjugation. For example, for the verb **trouver**, you write the statement **Tu trouves** (tew troohv) (*You find*), but the command form is **Trouve !** (troohv!) (*Find!*), without the **tu** and without the **-s**. Check out Chapter 4 of Book III for more information on commands.

When you ask directions from people you don't know or don't know well, you'll probably find that they address you with a polite **vous**. Here are some verbs in the **vous** form that will come in handy:

✔ **tournez** (toohr-ney) (*turn*)

> **Tournez à droite/à gauche à la rue . . .** (toohr-ney ah drwaht/ah gohsh ah lah rew . . .) (*Turn right/left on . . . Street.*)

✔ **prenez** (pruh-ney) (*take*)

> **Prenez la deuxième rue à droite/à gauche.** (pruh-ney lah duh-zee-ehm rew ah drwaht/ah gohsh.) (*Take the second street on the right/ on the left.*)

✔ **montez** (mohN-tey) (*go up*)

> **Montez la rue . . .** (mohN-tey lah rew . . .) (*Go up . . . Street.*)

✔ **descendez** (dey-sahN-dey) (*go down*)

> **Descendez le boulevard . . .** (dey-sahN-dey luh boohl-vahr . . .) (*Go down . . . Boulevard.*)

✔ **suivez** (swee-vey) (*follow*)

> **Suivez l'avenue . . .** (swee-vey lahv-new . . .) (*Follow . . . Avenue.*)

✔ **continuez à** (kohN-tee-new-ey ah) (*continue on*)

> **Continuez à la rue . . .** (kohN-tee-new-ey ah lah rew . . .) (*Continue on . . . Street.*)

✔ **allez tout droit** (ah-ley tooh drwah) (*go straight*)

> Well, this phrase can stand by itself — no example necessary.

✔ **traversez** (trah-vehr-sey) (*cross*)

> **Traversez le pont.** (trah-vehr-sey luh pohN.) (*Cross the bridge.*)

Book II

Exploring and Wandering About

Commands tend to sound a bit bossy, but luckily, French gives you a way out of sounding pushy. You can use just one form for everybody — **il faut** (eel foh) (*one has to*). This impersonal form exists only in the **il** (eel) (*it*) form. The form **il faut** never changes: Simply put the infinitive of any verb after this phrase, as these examples show. Whether the subject is translated as *I*, *you*, or *we* depends on the context:

> **Il faut retourner à l'hôtel.** (eel foh ruh-toohr-ney ah loh-tehl.) (*I/you/we have to go back to the hotel.*)

> **Il faut aller au centre-ville.** (eel foh tah-ley oh sahN-truh veel.) (*I/you/we have to go downtown.*)

> **Il faut prendre un taxi.** (eel foh prahN-druhN tahk-see.) (*I/you/we have to take a cab.*)

Specifying left, right, near, far, and other relationships

Directions generally explain where things are located in relation to each other. The following prepositional phrases help you be precise about locations:

- **à côté de** (ah koh-tey duh) (*next to*)
- **à droite de** (ah drwaht duh) (*to the right of*)
- **à gauche de** (ah gohsh duh) (*to the left of*)
- **dans** (dahN) (*in, inside*)
- **derrière** (deh-ryehr) (*behind*)
- **devant** (duh-vahN) (*in front of*)
- **en face de** (ahN fahs duh) (*across from, in front of*)
- **entre** (ahN-truh) (*between*)
- **loin (de)** (lwaN [duh]) (*far [from]*)
- **près (de)** (preh [duh]) (*near [to], close* [to])
- **sous** (sooh) (*under, underneath*)
- **sur** (sewr) (*on, on top of*)

Check out these example sentences with some of these prepositions:

> **Le restaurant est entre la poste et l'hôtel de ville.** (luh reh-stoh-rahN ey tahN-truh lah pohst ey loh-tehl duh veel.) (*The restaurant is between the post office and town hall.*)

> **Le cinéma est en face de l'hôtel.** (luh see-ney-mah ey tahN fahs duh loh-tehl.) (*The movie theater is across from the hotel.*)

> **La boulangerie se trouve à côté du musée.** (lah booh-lahN-zhree suh troohv ah koh-tey dew mew-zey.) (*The bakery is next to the museum.*)

Occasionally, the place you're looking for (or being asked about) is actually right in front of you or close enough to point to. After all, if you've never been to a particular location before, you may not recognize that you've already arrived. Similarly, if you're giving directions to your companion as you go along, you'll very likely announce your arrival with *Here is the . . .* or a similar expression. To create these expressions, you use the words **voici** (vwah-see) (*here*) and **voilà** (vwah-lah) (*there*):

> **Voici la poste/le musée/l'université !** (vwah-see lah pohst/luh mew-zey/ lew-nee-vehr-see-tey!) (*Here's the post office/the museum/the university!*)

> **Voilà le bois !** (vwah-lah luh bwah!) (*There are the woods!*)

CULTURAL WISDOM

Counting the districts of Paris

Paris has 20 districts called **arrondissements** (ah-rohN-dees-mahN), numbered in a clockwise spiral pattern as in the following figure. The higher the number, the farther from the center the district is; the smaller the number, the closer to the center the district is. The first district is in the heart of Paris and includes the Louvre. When you speak with people who live in Paris, you often hear them use ordinal numbers to indicate which section of the city a particular place is in. For example, if someone says **Dans quel arrondissement est le restaurant ?** (dahN kehl ah-rohN-dees-mahN ey luh reh-stoh-rahN?) (*In which district is the restaurant?*), the response may be **Il est dans le deuxième** (eel ey dahN luh duh-zee-ehm) (*It's in the second [district]*). Check out the ordinal numbers like **deuxième** in Chapter 2 of Book I.

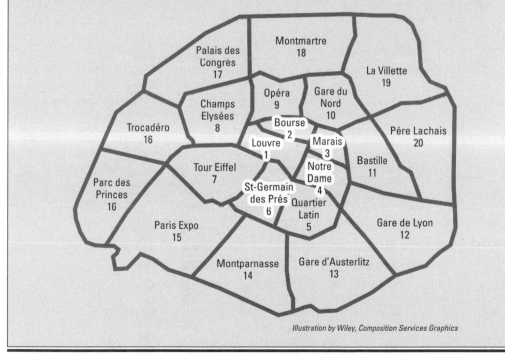

Illustration by Wiley, Composition Services Graphics

Book II

Exploring and Wandering About

GRAMMATICALLY SPEAKING

Theoretically, the difference between **voici** and **voilà** is that **voici** refers to something very close to you (*here*), and **voilà** refers to something farther away from you (*there*). Many people use them interchangeably, so don't worry too much about which one you use. In addition, you may use these two words after **le/la/les** without naming what you're pointing at: **Ah ! Le/la voilà !** (ah! luh/lah vwah-lah!) (*Ah! There it is!*) or **Les voilà !** (ley vwah-lah!) (*There they are!*)

Going north, south, east, and west

If you're unfamiliar with a place, directions that use local landmarks may not do you much good. And when the person giving you directions doesn't know *your* exact location (if you're asking for directions over the phone, for example), he or she can't very well tell whether you need to turn right or left to get to your destination. In those cases, using north, south, east, and west is easier. An added bonus of using cardinal directions is that doing so makes taking unplanned side trips — exploring the countryside, for example — that much easier. Here are some compass points:

- **nord** (nohr) (*north*), **nord-est** (nohr-ehst) (*northeast*), and **nord-ouest** (nohr-ooh-ehst) (*northwest*)

- **sud** (sewd) (*south*), **sud-est** (sew-dehst) (*southeast*), and **sud-ouest** (sewd-ooh-ehst) (*southwest*)

- **est** (ehst) (*east*)

- **ouest** (wehst) (*west*)

When you ask for or give directions by using cardinal points, always place **au** (oh) (*to the*) in front of a direction that begins with a consonant and **à l'** (ah l) (*to the*) in front of a direction that begins with a vowel. Here are some examples:

Le marché aux puces est au nord de Paris. (luh mahr-shey oh pews ey toh nohr duh pah-ree.) (*The flea market is north of Paris.*)

Ce quartier est à l'est de Montréal. (suh kahr-tyey ey tah lehst duh mohN-rey-ahl.) (*This neighborhood is east of Montréal.*)

Talkin' the Talk

Julie asks her French friend Cécile about the location of the Versailles castle.

Julie: **Cécile, où est le château de Versailles ?**
sey-seel, ooh ey luh shah-toh duh vehr-sahy?
Cécile, where is the palace of Versailles?

Cécile: **Il se trouve au sud-ouest de Paris.**
eel suh troohv oh sewd-ooh-ehst duh pah-ree.
It's southwest of Paris.

Julie: **C'est loin ?**
sey lwaN?
Is it far?

Cécile:	**Ton hôtel est à l'est, n'est-ce pas ? C'est à une heure en voiture, à peu près. Allons ensemble samedi.**
	tohN noh-tehl ey tah lehst, nehs pah? sey tah ewn uhr ahN vwah-tewr, ah puh preh. ah-lohN zahN-sahN-bluh sahm-dee.
	Your hotel is in the east, right? It's one hour by car, roughly. Let's go together on Saturday.
Julie:	**Très bonne idée !**
	trey buhhn ee-dey!
	That's a very good idea!
Cécile:	**Okay. Il faut se téléphoner avant samedi.**
	oh-key. eel foh suh tey-ley-fuhh-ney ah-vahN sahm-dee.
	Okay. We have to telephone each other before Saturday.
Julie:	**Très bien. Au revoir, Cécile.**
	treh byaN. ohr-vwahr, sey-seel.
	Great. Bye, Cécile.

Covering distances in time and space

People also use the prepostion **à** (ah) (*at, to, in*) to indicate how far away something is, as in the following:

À deux minutes. (ah duh mee-newt.) (*It takes only two minutes./It's two minutes away.*)

À cent mètres. (ah sahN meh-truh.) (*Only 100 meters farther./It's in about 100 meters.*)

C'est à cent mètres [d'ici]. (sey tah sahN meh-truh [dee-see].) (*It's 100 meters [from here].*)

C'est à deux kilomètres. (sey tah duh kee-loh-meh-truh.) (*It's two kilometers away./It's two kilometers from here.*)

Checking directions or your location

What if you get lost on your way to Versailles? Or maybe you just want to make sure that you're on the right track, wherever you may be going. Here are some helpful questions that you can ask in either situation:

Est-ce que c'est la bonne route pour . . . ? (ehs kuh sey lah buhhn rooht poohr . . . ?) (*Is this the right way to . . . ?*)

Où va cette rue ? (ooh vah seht rew?) (*Where does this street go?*)

Comment s'appelle cette ville ? (koh-mahN sah-pehl seht veel?) (*What's the name of this town?*)

Pourriez-vous m'indiquer comment aller . . . ? (pooh-ree-ey-vooh maN-dee-key koh-mahN tah-ley . . . ?) (*Could you tell me how to get to . . . ?*)

Getting clarification when you don't understand

If you don't understand the directions just because the person giving them is talking too fast, mumbling, or has a pronounced accent, don't give up! Instead, say that you don't understand and ask the person to repeat the information more slowly. That's when the following phrases can help you:

- **Pardon. Je ne comprends pas.** (pahr-dohN. zhuh nuh kohN-prahN pah.) (*Pardon. I don't understand.*)

- **Excusez-moi ! Est-ce que vous pouvez répéter, s'il vous plaît ?** (eyk-skew-zey-mwah! ehs kuh vooh pooh-vey rey-pey-tey, seel vooh pley?) (*Excuse me. Can you repeat that, please?*)

- **[Parlez] plus lentement.** ([pahr-ley] plew lahNt-mahN.) (*[Speak] more slowly.*)

- **Qu'est-ce que vous avez dit ?** (kehs kuh vooh zah-vey dee?) (*What did you say?*)

- **Pouvez-vous épeler le nom de cette rue ?** (pooh-vey-vooh zeyp-ley luh nohN duh seht rew?) (*Can you spell out the name of this street?*)

- **Pouvez-vous écrire ces directions ?** (pooh-vey-vooh ey-kreer sey dee-rehk-syohN?) (*Can you write down these directions?*)

Of course, you should say **merci** (mehr-see) (*thank you*) or **merci beaucoup** (mehr-see boh-kooh) (*thank you very much*) whenever someone tries to help. In reply, you may hear **De rien** (duh ryaN) (*Don't mention it*), **Il n'y a pas de quoi** (eel nyah pah duh kwah) (*It's nothing*), or **Je vous en prie** (zhuh vooh zahN pree) (*You're welcome*).

Talkin' the Talk

Vivianne is looking for **Le Panthéon** (luh pahN-tey-ohN) (*the Pantheon*), an 18th-century church and mausoleum in Paris. She asks **un agent de police** (uhN nah-zhahN duh poh-lees) (*a police officer*) for directions. (Track 24)

Vivianne:	**Excusez-moi, s'il vous plaît. Comment est-ce qu'on peut aller au Panthéon ?** eyk-skew-zey-mwah, seel vooh pley. koh-mahN ehs kohN puh tah-ley oh pahN-tey-ohN? *Excuse me, please. How can I get to the Pantheon?*
Agent de Police:	**Montez la rue Saint-Jacques et prenez la troisième rue à droite.** mohN-tey lah rew saN-zhahk ey pruh-ney lah trwah-zyehm rew ah drwaht. *Go up St. Jacques Street and take the third street on the right.*
Vivianne:	**Bon. La troisième à droite. Elle s'appelle comment, cette rue ?** bohN. lah trwah-zyehm ah drwaht. ehl sah-pehl koh-mahN, seht rew? *Okay. The third on the right. What's the name of that street?*
Agent de Police:	**C'est la rue Pierre et Marie Curie. Tournez à gauche à la rue d'Ulm et continuez tout droit. Le Panthéon est à votre droite.** sey lah rew pyehr ey mah-ree kew-ree. toohr-ney ah gohsh ah lah rew dewlm ey kohN-tee-new-ey tooh drwah. luh pahN-tey-ohN ey tah vuhh-truh drwaht. *It's Pierre and Marie Curie Street. Turn left on Ulm Street and continue straight. The Pantheon is on your right.*
Vivianne:	**Je ne comprends pas. Pouvez-vous répéter, s'il vous plaît ?** zhuh nuh kohN-prahN pah. pooh-vey-vooh rey-pey-tey, seel vooh pley? *I don't understand. Could you please repeat [that]?*

Book II

Exploring and Wandering About

Agent de Police: **Tournez à gauche à la rue d'Ulm et continuez tout droit. Le Panthéon est à votre droite.**
toohr-ney ah gohsh ah lah rew dewlm ey kohN-tee-new-ey tooh drwah. luh pahN-tey-ohN ey tah vuhh-truh drwaht.
Turn left on Ulm Street and continue straight. The Pantheon is on your right.

Vivianne: **Merci beaucoup.**
mehr-see boh-kooh.
Thank you very much.

Chapter 2

Enjoying a Night on the Town

In This Chapter
▶ Going out to eat
▶ Taking in a movie, show, or concert
▶ Hitting the clubs

Y ou can enjoy so much nighttime entertainment wherever you go if you know where — and how — to find it. Whether you're planning an evening at a show, a special dining experience, or a night out dancing, this chapter gives you the questions, words, and expressions to make the most of your evening out.

Dining Out

What better way to enjoy what you're eating than to start with an empty stomach? Then you can say **J'ai faim** (zhey faN) (*I'm hungry*) or **J'ai soif** (zhey swahf) (*I'm thirsty*), and the glorious world of French gastronomy is yours! If you're really hungry, you can say **Je meurs de faim** (zhuh muhr duh faN) (*I'm famished. Literally: I'm dying of hunger*). This section gives you the lowdown on eating at a restaurant, from deciding where to eat to picking up the check.

Finding a restaurant

In France, Belgium, Luxembourg, and Switzerland, look for small family-run bistros or cafés, where you're sure to get local specialties of good quality at reasonable prices. If you're watching your budget, consider the **brasseries** (brah-suh-ree) (*casual restaurants*) as well as **routiers** (rooh-tyey) (*roadside cafés*) and **auberges** (oh-behrzh) (*inns*), and be on the lookout for **menus** (muh-new) (*fixed-price meals*). If money is no object, you'll prefer ordering **à la carte** (ah lah kahrt) (*item by item*) at a fine restaurant.

French food is one of the most famous and the most praised cuisines in the world, and you don't have to go to Paris to enjoy it. You can find French restaurants and specialty food shops in many larger metropolitan areas in the United States, although they're often expensive. But just across the border, you can find total satisfaction at reasonable prices in Montréal, Québec's largest city.

To find a restaurant, consult the **Guide Michelin** (geed meesh-laN) (*The Michelin Guide*), the restaurant-lover's bible. A new edition of this internationally known red book — the one with stars for food quality and forks for the level of formality — is published annually and can make or break a restaurant overnight.

Making a restaurant reservation

In big cities like Paris or Montréal, many popular or well-known restaurants require a reservation — as much as two months in advance in some cases! So whenever you plan to dine out casually with friends or go to a fancy restaurant, phone ahead and reserve a table. To do so politely, you have to use the conditional conjugation of verbs. This conjugation expresses wish, possibility, and supposition and is used to make polite requests, as in *I'd like some water, please* or *Could you please pass the salt?* Check out Chapter 6 of Book IV for more on the conditional mood.

One verb you use quite often in the conditional is **vouloir** (vooh-lwahr) (*to want*), which means *would like* in its conditional form. You use this verb to make a reservation: **Je voudrais faire une réservation** (zhuh vooh-drey fehr ewn rey-zehr-vah-syohN) (*I'd like to make a reservation*) or **Je voudrais réserver une table** (zhuh vooh-drey rey-zehr-vey ewn tah-bluh) (*I'd like to reserve a table*). The following table shows how to conjugate the conditional tense of **vouloir**:

Conjugation	Pronunciation	Translation
je voudrais	zhuh vooh-drey	*I would like*
tu voudrais	tew vooh-drey	*you would like*
il/elle/on voudrait	eel/ehl/ohN vooh-drey	*he/she/one would like*
nous voudrions	nooh vooh-dree-yohN	*we would like*
vous voudriez	vooh vooh-dree-yey	*you would like*
ils/elles voudraient	eel/ehl vooh-drey	*they would like*

Pouvoir (pooh-vwahr) (*to be able to*) is another very important verb you use to make polite requests. In its conditional form, this verb means *may* or *could,* as in **Pourriez-vous (me/nous) recommander un bon restaurant, s'il vous plaît ?** (pooh-ryey vooh [muh/nooh] ruh-kuhh-mahN-dey uhN bohN reh-stoh-rahN, seel vooh pley?) (*Could you recommend a good restaurant [to me/to us], please?*). The following table shows the conditional tense for the verb **pouvoir:**

Conjugation	Pronunciation	Translation
je pourrais	zhuh pooh-rey	*I could*
tu pourrais	tew pooh-rey	*you could*
il/elle/on pourrait	eel/ehl/ohN pooh-rey	*he/she/one could*
nous pourrions	nooh pooh-ryohN	*we could*
vous pourriez	vooh pooh-ryey	*you could*
ils/elles pourraient	eel/ehl pooh-rey	*they could*

Talkin' the Talk

Mr. Miller is visiting Paris with his wife, and they've decided to dine at a very nice restaurant. Mr. Miller gets on the phone and talks to **la réceptionniste** (lah rey-sehp-syoh-neest) (*the receptionist*) to reserve a table.

Mr. Miller:	**Bonjour, je voudrais réserver une table.** bohN-zhoohr, zhuh vooh-drey rey-zehr-vey ewn tah-bluh. *Hello, I'd like to reserve a table.*
La réceptionniste:	**Bien sûr, monsieur. Pour quand ?** byaN sewr, muh-syuh. poohr kahN? *Of course, sir. For when?*
Mr. Miller:	**Pour lundi prochain.** poohr luhN-dee proh-shaN. *For next Monday.*
La réceptionniste:	**Ah, je suis désolée, monsieur. Nous sommes fermés le lundi.** ah zhuh swee dey-zoh-ley, muh-syuh, nooh suhhm fehr-mey luh luhN-dee. *Oh, I'm sorry, sir. We're closed on Mondays.*

Mr. Miller:	**Alors mardi.** ah-lohr mahr-dee. _Tuesday, then._
La réceptionniste:	**D'accord. Pour déjeuner ou pour dîner ?** dah-kohr. poohr dey-zhuh-ney ooh poohr dee-ney? _Very well. For lunch or dinner?_
Mr. Miller:	**Pour dîner.** poohr dee-ney. _For dinner._
La réceptionniste:	**Pour combien de personnes ?** poohr kohN-byaN duh pehr-suhhn? _For how many people?_
Mr. Miller:	**Pour deux personnes.** poohr duh pehr-suhhn. _For two people._
La réceptionniste:	**Et à quelle heure ?** ey ah-kehl uhr? _And at what time?_
Mr. Miller:	**À 20h00 [vingt heures].** Ah vaNt uhr. _At 8:00 p.m._
La réceptionniste:	**C'est à quel nom ?** sey tah kehl nohN? _What is the name?_
Mr. Miller:	**Miller — M, I, deux L, E, R.** mee-lehr — ehm, ee, duh zehl, uh, ehr. _Miller — M, I, two L's, E, R._
La réceptionniste:	**Très bien, monsieur. Une table pour deux personnes mardi 16 [seize] à 20h00 [vingt heures]. À bientôt.** treh byaN, muh-syuh. ewn tah-bluh poohr duh pehr-suhhn mahr-dee sehz ah vaNt uhr. ah byaN-toh. _Very well, sir. A table for two Tuesday the 16th at 8:00 p.m. See you soon._

You may be asked to spell your name when you make any kind of reservation. Whenever you spell a word in French that includes a double consonant, such as *tt,* say **deux T** (duh tey) (*two T's*) instead of repeating the letter. You can check the pronunciation of the letters of the alphabet in Chapter 1 of Book I.

Perusing the menu

In most restaurants in France, you can order from a **menu à prix fixe** (muh-new ah pree feeks) (*set-price menu*). The **prix fixe** menu generally costs less and often offers several set menus, each with a selection of an appetizer, a main dish, and cheese and/or dessert. Alternatively, you can order **à la carte** (ah lah kahrt), with a stated price for each dish. When you order **à la carte**, you can choose anything on the menu. Following is a sample of some of the menu items you may find in a French restaurant. Remember, different restaurants may give these things different names, so if you're unsure, ask the **serveur** (sehr-vuhr) (*waiter*) or **serveuse** (sehr-vuhz) (*waitress*).

French law requires that all restaurants post their menus — with prices — outside, so you won't have any costly surprises when you get in.

Starters

Here are **les entrées** (ley zahN-trey) (*appetizers*) you may find on a French menu:

- ✔ **les crudités** (f) (ley krew-dee-tey) (*mixed raw vegetables*)
- ✔ **les escargots** (m) (ley zeys-kahr-goh) (*snails*)
- ✔ **le pâté/la terrine** (luh pah-tey/lah teh-reen) (*pâté, meat paste*)
- ✔ **la quiche lorraine** (lah keesh loh-rehn) (*quiche with bacon*)
- ✔ **le saumon fumé** (luh soh-mohN few-mey) (*smoked salmon*)
- ✔ **la soupe à l'oignon** (lah soohp ah loh-nyohN) (*onion soup*)

Because it leads into the meal, the **entrée** (ahN-trey) (Literally: *entrance, way in*) of a French meal is the first course, not the main course as it is in the United States. What Americans call the *entree,* the French call **le plat principal** (luh plah praN-see-pahl) (*the main course*).

Le plat principal

In a French meal, a main dish often consists of meat or fish accompanied by vegetables. However, **le plat principal** may also be a salad or a vegetarian dish. Here are some common dishes in French restaurants:

Book II

Exploring and Wandering About

- **la brochette d'agneau** (lah broh-sheht dah-nyoh) (*skewer of lamb*)

- **la choucroute alsacienne** (lah shooh-krooht ahl-zah-syaNn) (*sauerkraut with sausages and bacon — a specialty from the Alsace region*)

- **le coq au vin** (luh cohk oh vaN) (*chicken cooked in wine sauce*)

- **l'entrecôte grillée** (f) (lahN-truh-koht gree-yey) (*grilled prime rib*)

- **les lasagnes** (f) **aux épinards** (ley lah-zah-nyuh oh zey-pee-nahr) (*spinach lasagne*)

- **les pâtes** (f) **aux fruits de mer** (ley paht oh frwee duh mehr) (*pasta with seafood*)

- **la salade niçoise** (lah sah-lahd nee-swahz) (*Mediterranean-style salad with eggs, tuna, and raw vegetables*)

- **le steak au poivre** (luh stehk oh pwah-vruh) (*steak in pepper sauce*)

Although meat and fish dishes come with veggies, you can order side dishes of **le riz** (luh ree) (*rice*), **les pâtes** (ley paht) (*pasta*), or **les pommes de terre** (ley puhhm duh tehr) (*potatoes*). You can check out specific words for meat, fish, veggies, and more in Chapter 7 of Book I.

What a difference an accent can make! **Le pâté** (luh pah-tey) is a meat paste, usually made from pork meat and spices, which is eaten as an appetizer with bread. On the other hand, **les pâtes** (ley paht) are pastas. So watch how that accent mark changes the pronunciation, or you may be surprised by what you receive!

Desserts

The French like a salad, often **la salade verte** (lah sah-lahd vehrt) (*salad with lettuce only. Literally: green salad*), and a piece of cheese after dinner. But after that, a dessert typically follows a formal dinner. Here are **les desserts** (ley dey-sehr) (*desserts*) you often see on French menus:

- **la crème caramel** (lah krehm kah-rah-mehl) (*caramel custard*)

- **la crème brûlée** (lah krehm brew-ley) (*custard topped with a hard crust of caramelized sugar*)

- **la crêpe** (lah krehp) (*crêpe, a thin pancake*)

- **le gâteau au chocolat** (luh gah-toh oh shoh-koh-lah) (*chocolate cake*)

- **la glace** (lah glahs) (*ice cream*)

- **la tarte aux pommes** (lah tahr toh puhhm) (*apple tart*)

The French eat ice cream, and they eat apple pie, but they don't eat them together — even though people in the United States use the French phrase **à la mode** (ah lah muhhd) (*in fashion*) to indicate pie with a scoop of ice cream. French apple pies are also very different from their American counterparts. They're very thin and don't have a top crust; they look more like what Americans would call a tart. Crêpes were originally a specialty from the Bretagne region, which has many **crêperies** (krehp-ree), or restaurants specializing in crêpes with all kinds of fillings, making them appropriate for the main dish or for dessert. Dessert crêpes are everywhere at street stands and in cafés and restaurants. Choices include the crêpe **au sucre** (oh sew-kruh) (*with sugar*), **à la confiture** (ah lah kohN-fee-tewr) (*with jam*), **au Nutella** (oh new-teh-lah) (*with chocolate-hazelnut spread*), **au Grand Marnier** (oh grahN mahr-nyey) (*with orange liqueur*), and many more.

Coffee

When you order coffee from a café or a restaurant in France, you get **un express** (uhN nehk-sprehs) (*an espresso*) in a small cup. If you want milk in your coffee, you have to order **un café crème** (uhN kah-fey krehm) (*coffee with milk*). Of course, you can also order one of the following:

- **un déca/un décaféiné** (uhN dey-kah/uhN dey-kaf-fey-ee-ney) (*a decaf coffee*)
- **un double express** (uhN dooh-blehk-sprehs) (*a double espresso*)
- **un grand crème** (uhN grahN krehm) (*a large coffee with milk*)

Large doesn't mean large in the American sense here. Rather, it more exactly means *double;* a large is the equivalent of two small espresso cups. Also, even though **crème** (krehm) means *cream,* **café crème** isn't coffee with cream but rather coffee with frothy milk. The French word for *milk* is **le lait** (luh ley), and in many places, whether you ask for a **café crème** or a **café au lait** (kah-fey oh ley), you get the same thing. Once in a while, a **café au lait** is served with milk **sur le côté** (sewr luh koh-tey) (*on the side*). In France, coffee with milk is usually reserved for breakfast.

Placing your order

When it's time to order, the waiter asks you these kinds of questions:

Qu'est-ce que vous voulez boire ? (kehs kuh vooh vooh-ley bwahr?) (*What do you want to drink?*)

Qu'est-ce que vous voulez comme boisson ? (kehs kuh vooh vooh-ley kuhhm bwah-sohN?) (*What do you want as a drink?*)

Avez-vous choisi ? (ah-vey-vooh shwah-zee?) (*Have you decided?*)

Que désirez-vous comme plat principal ? (kuh dey-zee-rey-vooh kuhhm plah praN-see-pahl?) (*What will you have as a main course?*)

If you want to ask the waiter what kinds of selections are available, you use the question **Qu'est-ce que vous avez comme . . . ?** (kehs kuh vooh zah-vey kuhhm . . . ?) (*What do you have as . . . ?*). Take a look at these examples:

Qu'est-ce que vous avez comme boisson ? (kehs kuh vooh zah-vey kuhhm bwah-sohN?) (*What do you have as a drink?*).

Qu'est-ce qu'il y a comme boisson ? (kehs keel ee ah kuhhm bwah-sohN?) (*What is there as a drink?*)

Qu'est-ce que vous avez comme vin ? (kehs kuh vooh zah-vey kuhhm vaN?) (*What kind of wine do you have?* Literally: *What do you have as wine?*)

Qu'est-ce que vous avez comme entrée ? (kehs kuh vooh zah-vey kuhhm ahN-trey?) (*What do you have as an appetizer?*)

You may want to ask the waiter a few questions about the dishes on the menu. Actually, the more sophisticated the restaurant, the less likely you are to understand its menu. The names of dishes are almost as elaborate as their preparation. And don't think that you're the only one who doesn't understand: The average French restaurant-goer doesn't, either. Your best bet is to ask the waiter. You can also ask for the waiter's recommendation by saying **Qu'est-ce que vous recommandez/suggérez ?** (kehs kuh vooh ruh-kuhh-mahN-dey/sewg-zhey-rey?) (*What do you recommend/suggest?*).

When you're all set and ready to order, you need to have these phrases handy:

- ✔ **Comme entrée, je prends . . .** (kuhhm ahN-trey, zhuh prahN . . .) (*For the first course [appetizer], I'll have . . .*)
- ✔ **Je voudrais . . .** (zhuh vooh-drey . . .) (*I'd like . . .*)
- ✔ **Pour moi . . .** (poohr mwah . . .) (*For me . . .*)
- ✔ **Et ensuite . . .** (ey ahN-sweet . . .) (*And then . . .*)
- ✔ **Et comme boisson . . .** (ey kuhhm bwah-sohN . . .) (*And to drink . . .*)
- ✔ **Et comme dessert . . .** (ey kuhhm dey-sehr . . .) (*And for dessert . . .*)

Don't address the waiter as **garçon** (gahr-sohN), which is considered condescending because it means *boy*. Use **monsieur** (muh-syuh) (*sir*) or **madame** (mah-dahm) (*ma'am*) instead.

Talkin' the Talk

Julie, a young woman from Québec, and her friend Mike, visiting from the United States, have spent a long morning sightseeing in **le vieux Montréal** (luh vyuh mohN-rey-ahl) (*the old Montreal*). They're getting hungry, and the street is lined with restaurants.

Julie: **Je meurs de faim.**
zhuh muhr duh faN.
I'm starving.

Mike: **Moi aussi ! Tu veux un sandwich ?**
mwah oh-see! tew vuh uhN sahN-dweesh?
Me, too! Do you want a sandwich?

Julie: **Oh non, il y a un tas de bons petits restaurants pas chers ici. Et puis je suis fatiguée.**
oh nohN, eel ee ah uhN tah duh bohN puh-tee reh-stoh-rahN pah shehr ee-see. ey pwee zhuh swee fah-tee-gey.
Oh no, there are plenty of inexpensive little restaurants here. And I'm tired.

Mike: **Bon, d'accord. Alors, on mange à la terrasse de ce bistrot ici.**
bohN, dah-kohr. ah-lohr, ohN mahNzh ah lah tey-rahs duh suh bee-stroh ee-see!
Well, okay. Let's eat at a table outside this bistro here.

They sit down on the terrace and **le serveur** (luh sehr-vuhr) (*the waiter*) brings them the menu.

Le serveur: **Vous voulez boire quelque chose ?**
vooh vooh-ley bwahr kehl-kuh shohz?
Would you like something to drink?

Julie: **Un verre de vin blanc, s'il vous plaît.**
uhN vehr duh vaN blahN, seel vooh pley.
A glass of white wine, please.

Mike: **Et pour moi, une bière.**
ey poohr mwah, ewn byehr.
And for me, a beer.

Book II

Exploring and Wandering About

A few minutes later, the waiter comes back with the drinks.

Le serveur: **Voilà vos boissons. Vous avez choisi ?**
vwah-lah voh bwah-sohN. vooh zah-vey shwah-zee?
Here are your drinks. Have you decided?

Julie: **Oui, je voudrais le poulet avec des pommes de terre et une salade verte.**
wee, zhuh vooh-drey luh pooh-leh ah-vehk dey puhhm duh tehr ey ewn sah-lahd vehrt.
Yes, I'd like the chicken with potatoes and a green salad.

Mike: **Moi, je prends le steak-frites.**
mwah, zhuh prahN luh stehk-freet.
Me, I'll have the steak with fries.

Words to Know

un verre de vin blanc	*uhN vehr duh vaN blahN*	*a glass of white wine*
Vous avez choisi ?	*vooh zah-vey shwah-zee?*	*Have you decided?*
je prends le steak-frites	*zhuh prahN luh stehk-freet*	*I'll have the steak with fries*

When your food comes, your server may say **Bon appétit !** (buhhn ah-pey-tee!) (*Enjoy your meal!*) or **Régalez-vous !** (rey-gah-ley-vooh!) (*Enjoy the food!*). To share your dish with your companions, you can say **Goûtez !** (gooh-tey!) (*Taste!*) or **Servez-vous !** (sehr-vey-vooh!) (*Help yourself!*).

Paying the bill

After you finish your meal, it's time to pay the bill. But don't expect a waiter in France to bring you the check before you ask for it — that's considered pushy and impolite. To get your check, call the waiter and say **L'addition, s'il vous plaît** (lah-dee-syohN, seel vooh pley) (*Check, please*).

In France, the tax and tip are included in the price list: **le pourboire est compris** (luh poohr-bwahr ey kohN-pree) or **le service est compris** (luh sehr-vees ey kohN-pree) (*the tip is included*). What you see is what you get, and there's no expectation to pay more. Of course, you may tip an extra euro or two if you so desire, especially in a very good restaurant, but in cafés and ordinary restaurants, you don't have to. Even in the most elegant restaurant, you'd never leave more than 5 percent of your total bill. In Canada, a tax is added to your check, and the waiter does expect to be tipped.

Le pourboire (luh poohr-bwahr) (*the tip*) is a funny word in French. It literally means *in order to drink.* This very old word dates back to the 17th century, when it was customary to give a tip so the recipient could go and buy himself a drink (alcoholic, supposedly). The name has remained, but its function has changed.

If you like to carry cash, that's one easy way to pay your bill. If you prefer to use your credit or debit card, which usually gives you the most favorable exchange rate, you'd be wise to carry a Visa or Mastercard; credit cards like Discover and American Express aren't universally accepted in Europe. Be sure to have a numeric pin code if you plan to get a cash advance on your credit card at an ATM. (You can find more info on money transactions in Chapter 3 of Book II)

Book II

Exploring and Wandering About

Talkin' the Talk

Julie and Mike are thoroughly enjoying their meal and relaxing when the waiter comes along.

Le serveur: **Vous voulez un dessert ?**
vooh vooh-ley uhN deh-sehr?
Would you like dessert?

Julie: **Non, merci. Deux cafés seulement et l'addition.**
nohN, mehr-see. duh kah-fey suhl-mahN ey
lah-dee-syohN.
No, thank you. Just two coffees and the check.

The waiter comes back with the check, and Mike takes out his credit card.

Mike: **Vous prenez les cartes de crédit ?**
vooh pruh-ney ley kahrt duh krey-dee?
Do you take credit cards?

Le serveur: **Bien sûr, monsieur.**
byaN sewr, muh-syuh.
Of course, sir.

Finding the restrooms

Before leaving the restaurant, you may want to visit the restroom, in which case you ask **Où sont les toilettes, s'il vous plaît ?** (ooh sohN ley twah-leht, seel vooh pley?) (*Where are the restrooms?*). In French restaurants, the restrooms are usually located **en bas** (ahN bah) (*downstairs*). Don't forget to take some change along with you; you often have to pay to get in! In most places, the pictogram is self-explanatory, but you may also see **Dames** (dahm) (*Women*) or **Hommes** (uhhm) (*Men*) written on the door.

Experiencing the Nightlife

Whatever your muse inspires you to do for **divertissement nocturne** (dee-vehr-tees-mahN nohk-tewrn) (*nighttime entertainment*), you'll find plenty of opportunities to indulge yourself in any large francophone city. You can find cultural activities like a **vernissage** (vehr-nee-sahzh) (*gallery opening*); watch a play; or attend classical, jazz, rock, or pop concerts in Paris, Geneva, Brussels, or Montréal. You can partake of dinner cruises on the **Seine** (sehn) River or go to a famed club like the **Moulin Rouge** (mooh-laN roohzh) in Paris, or you can simply enjoy a great dinner before catching a good movie. This section introduces you to the terms necessary to explore these types of experiences.

Spending an evening at the theater

French theater has been world famous for centuries and offers something for every taste and budget, from classical productions to the **avant-garde** (ah-vahN-gahrd) (*modern*). Paris alone has nearly 130 theaters. The most famous is one of the national theaters of France, **La Comédie Française** (lah kuhh-mey-dee frahN-sehz), which Louis XIV established in 1680 and which stages performances of the classic plays of perhaps the greatest playwrights of the 17th century — **Pierre Corneille** (pyehr kohr-nehy), **Jean Racine** (zhahN rah-seen), and **Jean-Baptiste Poquelin** (zhahN-bah-teest pohk-laN), better known as **Molière** (moh-lyehr).

You should make reservations at one of the national theaters, unless you plan on trying to pick up some last-minute "rush" tickets, which are usually on sale (and at a discount to students) 45 minutes before the show starts.

Consider using one of the many known ticket services in Paris, which eliminate the need to go to the theater box office in advance. Some services offer discount tickets, especially for same-day performances, though there are restrictions. Check out **Kiosque-Théâtre** (kyuhhsk-tey-ah-truh), which is considered the best discount box office, selling discount tickets the day of the show, and **Alpha FNAC: Spectacles** (ahl-fah fnahk spehk-tah-kluh).

Going to the theater is an occasion, so people dress the part: Men wear dark suits, and women wear dresses. Opening nights call for more formal attire, such as tuxedos and evening gowns. Also, remember that tipping the usher (usually a euro or two) as well as the attendant in the public restrooms (0.20 to 0.40 euros) is customary. The attendant is such a familiar character of the French scene that she has a special name: **dame pipi** (dahm pee-pee).

Here are some key words to discuss your evening at the theater:

- ✔ **le balcon** (luh bahl-kohN) (*the balcony*)
- ✔ **le billet** (luh bee-yeh) (*the ticket*)
- ✔ **la comédie** (lah kuhh-mey-dee) (*comedy*)
- ✔ **les costumes** (ley koh-stewm) (*the costumes*)
- ✔ **le décor** (luh dey-kohr) (*the décor/scenery*)
- ✔ **l'éclairage** (m) (ley-kleh-rahzh) (*the lighting*)
- ✔ **l'entracte** (m) (lahN-trahkt) (*the intermission*)
- ✔ **monter une pièce** (mohN-tey ewn pyehs) (*to put on a play*)
- ✔ **la pièce** (lah pyehs) (*the play*)
- ✔ **la représentation/le spectacle** (lah ruh-prey-zahN-tah-syohN/luh spehk-tah-kluh) (*the performance*)
- ✔ **le rideau** (luh ree-doh) (*the curtain*)
- ✔ **la scène** (lah sehn) (*the stage*)
- ✔ **la tragédie** (lah trah-zhey-dee) (*tragedy*)

Book II

Exploring and Wandering About

Here are some questions that you may want to ask or that someone may ask you:

Aimez-vous le théâtre ? (ey-mey-vooh luh tey-ah-truh?) (*Do you like the theater?*)

Voulez-vous aller au théâtre ? (vooh-ley-vooh zah-ley oh tey-ah-truh?) (*Do you want to go to the theater?*)

Quelle pièce voulez-vous voir ? (kehl pyehs vooh-ley-vooh vwahr?) (*What play do you want to see?*)

Qu'est-ce qu'on joue ? (kehs kohN zhooh?) (*What's playing?*)

Combien coûtent les billets ? (kohN-byaN kooht ley bee-yeh?) (*How much do the tickets cost?*)

À quelle heure commence le spectacle ? (ah kehl uhr koh-mahNs luh spehk-tah-kluh?) (*What time does the show start?*)

Talkin' the Talk

Elise, a French student, and Steven, an American exchange student, are discussing going to the theater.

Elise: **Je voudrais aller au théâtre ce soir. Ça te dit ?**
zhuh vooh-drey zah-ley oh tey-ah-truh suh swahr. sah tuh dee?
I'd like to go to the theater tonight. Care to join me?

Steven: **Oui, volontiers. Qu'est-ce qu'on joue ?**
wee, voh-lohN-tyey. kehs kohN zhooh?
Sure. What's playing?

Elise: **Tartuffe, une comédie de Molière.**
tahr-tewf, ewn kuhh-mey-dee duh moh-lyehr.
Tartuffe, a comedy by Molière.

Steven: **Je ne connais pas beaucoup le français. Ça va me plaire ?**
zhuh nuh koh-ney pah boh-kooh luh frahN-sėh. sah vah muh plehr?
I don't know a lot of French. Will I like it?

Elise: **Oui, bien sûr. C'est rigolo.**
wee, byaN sewr. sey ree-goh-loh.
Yes, of course. It's funny.

Later, Elise is buying tickets **au guichet** (oh gee-shey) (*at the box office*) from **le caissier** (luh key-syey) (*the ticket seller*).

Elise: **Bonsoir. Je voudrais deux places à l'orchestre, s'il vous plaît.**
bohN-swahr. zhuh vooh-drey duh plahs ah lohr-keh-struh, seel vooh pley.
Good evening. I'd like two orchestra seats, please.

Le caissier: **Tout est complet à l'orchestre.**
Tooh tey kohN-pley ah lohr-keh-struh.
The orchestra seats are sold out.

Elise: **Au balcon, s'il vous plaît.**
oh bahl-kohN, seel vooh pley.
The balcony, please.

Le caissier: **Il y a deux places au premier rang au balcon.**
                eel ee ah duh plahs oh pruh-myey rahN oh bahl-kohN.
                There are two seats in the front row of the balcony.

Elise: **C'est parfait ! Combien coûtent les billets ?**
                sey pahr-fey! kohN-byaN kooht ley bee-yey?
                That's perfect! How much are the tickets?

Le caissier: **60 [soixante] euros, s'il vous plaît.**
                swah-sahNt uh-roh, seel vooh pley.
                Sixty euros, please.

Elise: **Le lever du rideau est à quelle heure ?**
                luh luh-vey dew ree-doh ey tah kehl uhr?
                What time does the curtain go up?

Le caissier: **Dans une demi-heure.**
                dahN zewn duh-mee-uhr.
                In half an hour.

Elise: **Merci, monsieur.**
                mehr-see, muh-syuh.
                Thank you, sir.

Words to Know

rigolo	ree-goh-loh	funny
la place	lah plahs	seat
à l'orchestre	ah lohr-keh-struh	orchestra seats
tout est complet	tooh tey kohN-pley	sold out
le premier rang	luh pruh-myey rahN	front row
le rideau se lève	luh ree-doh suh lehv	the curtain goes up

Heading to the movies

Are you **un cinéphile** (uhN see-ney-feel) (*a movie buff*)? Then we've got good news for you! A great way to experience the language and practice your skills is to watch a film made in French. The following terms may come in handy when you're talking about the movie theater or films in general:

- ✔ **l'acteur/l'actrice** (lahk-tuhr/lahk-trees) (*actor/actress*)
- ✔ **le cinéaste** (luh see-ney-ahst) (*filmmaker*)
- ✔ **les effets spéciaux/les trucages** (ley zeh-feh spey-syoh/ley trew-kahzh) (*special effects*)
- ✔ **le générique** (luh zhey-ney-reek) (*credits*)
- ✔ **le guichet** (luh gee-shey) (*ticket window*)
- ✔ **le long-métrage** (luh lohN-mey-trahzh) (*feature film*)
- ✔ **le metteur-en-scène/le réalisateur** (luh meh-tuhr-ahN-sehn/luh rey-ah-lee-zah-tuhr) (*director*)
- ✔ **la séance** (lah sey-ahNs) (*the showing*)
- ✔ **la vedette** (lah vuh-deht) (*movie star*)

Foreign-language films marked **VO (version originale)** (vey oh [vehr-syohN oh-ree-zhee-nahl]) are shown in their original language with French subtitles. **VF (version française)** (vey ehf [vehr-zyohN frahN-sehz]) means that the film has been dubbed in French.

Most people have a favorite film genre. If someone asks you **Quels genres de films aimez-vous ?** (kehl zhahNr duh feelm ey-mey-vooh?) (*What kinds of films do you like?*), you can use the following list to indicate the ones you favor:

- ✔ **un dessin animé** (uhN deh-saN ah-nee-mey) (*a cartoon, animated movie*)
- ✔ **un documentaire** (uhN doh-kew-mahN-tehr) (*a documentary*)
- ✔ **un film d'amour** (uhN feelm dah-moohr) (*a romance film*)
- ✔ **un film d'aventures** (uhN feelm dah-vahN-tewr) (*an adventure film*)
- ✔ **un film d'épouvante/d'horreur** (uhN feelm dey-pooh-vahNt/doh-ruhr) (*a horror film*)
- ✔ **un film d'espionnage** (uhN feelm dehs-pyoh-nahzh) (*a spy film*)
- ✔ **un film de science-fiction** (uhN feelm duh syahNs-feek-syohN) (*a science-fiction film*)
- ✔ **un film policier** (uhN feelm poh-lee-syey) (*a detective film*)
- ✔ **un western** (uhN weh-stehrn) (*a western*)

Invented by French brothers **Auguste** (oh-gewst) and **Louis** (looh-ee) **Lumière** (lew-myehr), the cinema had its debut in Paris. The French film industry has always seen itself as an artistic venue first and an industry second. The French cinema is so popular that over 300 films are shown in Paris per week, more than in any other city in the world. **Le Festival de Cannes** (luh feh-stee-vahl duh kahn) (*the Cannes Film Festival*) is an international film festival that takes place every May in Cannes, which is in the south of France. **La Palme d'Or** (lah pahlm dohr) (*the Golden Palm*) is awarded each year to the director of the best feature film in the competition. Each year, more than 1,000 films from around the globe are submitted to the festival in hopes of being selected.

Many theaters show a series of previews followed by commercials for as long as a half hour before the show. Therefore, if you don't want to miss the previews, get there early. **Les séances** (ley sey-ahNs) (*the showings*) are posted in the lobby of the movie theaters. You can also look them up online.

Talkin' the Talk

The following dialogue joins Madame and Monsieur Dumont as they try to decide what to do today. (Track 25)

M. Dumont: **Qu'est-ce qu'on fait ce soir ?**
kehs kohN fey suh swahr?
What shall we do tonight?

Mme Dumont: **Je voudrais aller au concert à la cathédrale Notre-Dame.**
zhuh vooh-drey zah-ley oh kohN-sehr ah lah kah-tey-drahl noh-truh-dahm.
I'd like to go to the concert at the Notre Dame cathedral.

M. Dumont: **Ah non, pas de concerts ! Tu veux aller au cinéma ?**
ah nohN, pah duh kohN-sehr! tew vuh zah-ley oh see-ney-mah?
Oh no, no concerts! Do you want to go to the movies?

Mme Dumont: **Ah oui, super ! Un film d'aventures ou un film policier !**
ah wee, sew-pehr! uhN feelm dah-vahN-tewr ooh uhN feelm poh-lee-syey!
Yes, great! An adventure or a detective film!

M. Dumont:	**J'aime mieux les documentaires. Mais à toi de décider.** zhehm myuh ley doh-kew-mahN-tehr. mey ah twah duh dey-see-dey. *I like documentaries better. But you decide.*
Mme Dumont:	**Merci, mon chéri. Je voudrais voir un film policier !** mehr-see mohN shey-ree. zhuh vooh-drey vwahr uhN feelm poh-lee-syey! *Thanks, my darling. I'd like to see a detective film!*

Words to Know

j'aime mieux	zhehm myuh	I prefer
C'est à toi de décider.	sey tah twah duh dey-see-dey.	It's for you to decide.
je voudrais voir	zhuh vooh-drey vwahr	I'd like to see

In France, **l'Académie des arts et techniques du cinéma** (lah-kah-dey-mee dey zahr ey teyk-neek dew see-ney-mah) gives out prizes like the Oscars. The award is called the **César** (sey-zahr) after the sculptor César Baldaccini, and the statuettes look like the artist himself.

After your movie is over, you can rate it with the following phrases:

- **Quel film super !** (kehl feelm sew-pehr!) (*What a great movie!*)

- **Quel navet !** (kehl nah-vey!) (*What a dud!*)

- **Le meilleur film de l'année !** (luh mey-yuhr feelm duh lah-ney!) (*The best movie of the year!*)

- **Le pire film de l'année !** (luh peer feelm duh lah-ney!) (*The worst movie of the year!*)

Going to concerts

It's often said that music is a universal language. If you're feeling overwhelmed by having to speak French all the time, try going to a concert. While there, you don't have to talk for a couple of hours, and you can relax and enjoy the music without worrying about making someone understand you. Here are some general terms and different kinds of musical performances that may interest you:

- ✔ **la musique classique** (lah mew-zeek klah-seek) (*classical music*)
- ✔ **la musique moderne** (lah mew-zeek moh-dehrn) (*modern music*)
- ✔ **la musique rock/le rock** (lah mew-zeek rohk/luh rohk) (*rock music/rock*)
- ✔ **la musique de jazz/le jazz** (lah mew-zeek duh dzahz/luh dzahz) (*jazz music/jazz*)
- ✔ **la musique techno/la techno** (lah mew-zeek tehk-noh/lah tehk-noh) (*techno music/techno*)
- ✔ **un orchestre de chambre** (uhN nohr-keh-struh duh shahN-bruh) (*a chamber orchestra*)
- ✔ **le rap** (luh rahp) (*rap music*)
- ✔ **une symphonie** (ewn saN-fuhh-nee) (*a symphony*)

Don't shout **Encore !** (ahN-kohr!) (Literally: *Again!*) at a French concert unless you want the performers to play the entire piece again. Instead, say **Bis !** (bees!), which means that you want them to play some more.

The verb **jouer** (zhooh-ey) is a regular **-er** verb meaning *to play*. You use it with the preposition **de** (duh) or **à** (ah). (***Note:*** These prepositions aren't translated into English when they're paired with the verb **jouer**.) When **jouer** refers to playing musical instruments or music in general, you use the preposition **de** + the definite article **le** (luh), **la** (lah), or **les** (ley), depending on the gender and number of the instrument or the musical term. (For more on using prepositions after the verb **jouer**, check out Chapter 1 of Book IV.) Following are examples that use **jouer** with music in general:

Je joue du piano. (zhuh zhooh dew pyah-noh.) (*I play the piano.*)

Tu joues de la guitare. (tew zhooh duh lah gee-tahr.) (*You play the guitar.*)

Il joue du violon. (eel zhooh dew vyoh-lohN.) (*He plays the violin.*)

Elle joue du Chopin. (ehl zhooh dew shoh-paN) (*She plays Chopin.*)

Ils jouent du jazz. (eel zhooh dew dzahz) (*They play jazz.*)

Elles jouent de la flûte. (ehl zhooh duh lah flewt) (*They play the flute.*)

Book II

Exploring and Wandering About

Hitting a club

Most cities have plenty of nightclubs that offer everything from dancing to live music. What kind of **club** (kluhb) (*club*) do you want to go to? Here are a few options:

- **une disco/discothèque** (ewn dee-skoh/dee-skoh-tehk) (*a disco*)
- **une revue** (ewn ruh-vew) (*a revue, a show*)
- **une boîte de nuit** (ewn bwaht duh nwee) (*a nightclub*)

Many Parisian clubs are officially private, meaning they have the right to pick and choose their clientele. In general, word of mouth and weekly journals are the best guides to the current scene. To be admitted to one of the more exclusive clubs, you may need to accompany a regular customer. Here are some other things to know: Europeans tend to dress up more for a night on the town than their North American counterparts do. The drinking age in France is 18. Women often receive discounts or are admitted free. The best advice is not to go alone, unless you're looking for a lot of attention. Weeknight admission is much cheaper and not nearly as crowded.

Talkin' the Talk

Paul and Denise are finishing dinner and deciding what type of nightlife to pursue. (Track 26)

Paul:	**Veux-tu aller en boîte ? Nous pouvons danser.** vuh-tew ah-ley ahN bwaht? nooh pooh-vohN dahN-sey. *Do you want to go to a nightclub? We can go dancing.*
Denise:	**Non, merci. Je suis trop fatiguée.** nohN, mehr-see. zhuh swee troh fah-tee-gey. *No, thanks. I'm too tired.*
Paul:	**Bon. Allons au club pour regarder une revue.** bohN. ahl-ohN oh kluhb poohr ruh-gahr-dey ewn ruh-vew. *Okay. Let's go to a club to watch a show.*
Denise:	**D'accord. Faut-il réserver ?** dah-kohr. foht-eel rey-zehr-vey? *Okay. Is a reservation necessary?*

Paul: **Nous allons devoir faire la queue.**
nooh zah-lohN duh-vwahr fehr lah kuh.
We'll have to stand in line.

Denise: **À quelle heure commence le spectacle ?**
ah kehl uhr koh-mahNs luh spehk-tah-kluh?
What time does the show start?

Paul: **À 23h00 [vingt-trois heures].**
ah vaN-trwah zuhr.
At 11:00 p.m.

Denise: **Oh non ! C'est trop tard !**
oh nohN! sey troh tahr!
Oh no! That's too late!

Words to Know

aller en boîte	ah-ley ahN bwaht	to go to a club
danser	dahN-sey	to dance
Je suis trop fatigué(e).	zuh swee troh fah-tee-gey.	I'm too tired.
Faut-il réserver ?	foht-eel rey-zehr-vey?	Is a reservation necessary?
faire la queue	fehr lah kuh	to wait in line
C'est trop tard.	sey troh tahr.	It's too late.

Chapter 3

Money Matters

In This Chapter

▶ Paying attention to French currency

▶ Utilizing credit cards, ATMs, and traveler's checks

L'argent (lahr-zhahN) (*money*) makes the world go 'round, they say, and you need money to go around the world. If you have the opportunity and pleasure of traveling to a French-speaking country, you need to know what the currency is and how to complete lots of transactions, such as exchanging currency, using bank machines, cashing traveler's checks, and more. In this chapter, we give you the information and phrases you need to express your needs clearly through several kinds of transactions.

Getting Current with Currency

Unified Europe — the block of countries that are part of the European Union (EU) — has made it easier to cross the borders within the EU without the hassle of going through border checkpoints. Furthermore, many countries within the EU have a common currency, the *euro* (€), which has been legal currency since January 1, 1999 (though the coins and banknotes didn't go into circulation until January 1, 2002). Here's a list of French-speaking regions, territories, and countries that use the euro:

▶ **In Europe**: France, Monaco, Belgium, Luxembourg, and Corsica

▶ **In the Americas**: French Guiana, St. Pierre, and Miquelon

▶ **In the Caribbean**: Martinique, Guadeloupe, St. Barthélemy, and St. Martin

▶ **In the Indian Ocean**: Mayotte and La Réunion

Of course, not all French-speaking countries are part of the European Union, nor do they all use euros; we cover some of these other currencies in the later section "Beyond Europe and the euro: Looking at currency in other French-speaking countries." This section tells you what you need to know about money.

Familiarizing yourself with euros and cents

The euro, like other currencies, comes in the form of coins and bills (notes) in several denominations. The notes are the same for all countries in the euro zone. Each country, however, issues its own coins. Coins have a common front side, but the designs on the back are specific to the country of origin. Like the bills, though, all coins can be used anywhere.

Getting the bills straight

Euro bills come in seven different denominations: €5, €10, €20, €50, €100, €200, and €500. The bills increase in size with the denomination and are very colorful. The designs include European architecture, the name *euro* in Greek and Latin, and the 12 stars of the European flag on both sides of the bill. The front of each bill features windows, arches, and gateways, and the back depicts a map of Europe and a European bridge. Figure 3-1 shows the front and back of a euro bill.

Figure 3-1:
All euro bills are the same from country to country.

Illustration by Wiley, Composition Services Graphics

Looking at the coins

Euro coins come in denominations ranging from 1 **centime** (sahN-teem) (*cent*) to 50 **centimes** (sahN-teem) (*cents*), plus 1- and 2-euro coins. You find eight coins in all: €0.01, €0.02, €0.05, €0.10, €0.20, €0.50, €1, and €2.

Although the back sides of the coins differ by country, the coins can be used interchangeably throughout the countries that use the euro. The French coins include these three symbols (see Figure 3-2):

- **La Marianne** (lah mah-ree-ahn), representing the French Republic of **Liberté, Egalité, Fraternité** (lee-behr-tey, ey-gah-lee-tey, frah-tehr-nee-tey) (*Liberty, Equality, Fraternity*), is on €0.01, €0.02, and €0.05 coins.
- **La Semeuse** (lah suh-muhz) (*the Sower*), a theme carried over from the French franc, is on €0.10, €0.20, and €0.50 coins.

✔ **L'Arbre** (lahr-bruh) (*the Tree*) surrounded by a hexagon is on €1 and €2 coins. The tree symbolizes life, continuity, and growth, and the hexagon symbolizes France, which is also called **l'Hexagone** (lehg-zah-guhhn) (*the Hexagon*) because of its six-sided shape.

Figure 3-2:
La Marianne,
la Semeuse,
and l'Arbre.

La Marianne

The Sower

Tree

Illustration by Wiley, Composition Services Graphics

The coins vary in size, but they don't necessarily grow in proportion to the denomination.

When you do your banking or shopping, keep in mind that the French separate euros and **centimes**/cents with a comma, not with a period. For example, €100,00 in France is written as €100.00 in the United States.

Beyond Europe and the euro: Looking at currency in other French-speaking countries

Not all French-speaking countries use the euro. Table 3-1 lists the currencies of several countries where French is an official language. *Note:* This list doesn't include places where French is spoken but isn't an official language, as in many regions in Africa.

Table 3-1	Currency in Other French-Speaking Countries	
Country/Region	*Currency (in English)*	*Currency (in French)*
Switzerland	*Swiss franc* (CHF)	**le franc suisse** (luh frahN swees)
Québec, Canada	*Canadian dollar* (CAD)	**le dollar canadien** (luh doh-lahr kah-nah-dyaN)
Haiti	*Haitian gourdes* (HTG)	**la gourde haïtienne** (lah goohrd ah-ee-syehn)
Madagascar	*Malagasy ariary* (MGA)	**l'ariary malgache** (lah-ree-ah-ree mahl-gahsh)

(continued)

Table 3-1 *(continued)*		
Country/Region	*Currency (in English)*	*Currency (in French)*
Tahiti, New Caledonia, and Wallis-et-Futuna	*CFP* franc* (XPF)	**le franc pacifique** (luh frahN pah-see-feek)
Vanuatu	*Vanuatu vatu* (VUV)	**le Vanuatu vatu** (luh vah-new-ah-tew vah-tew)

* CFP stands for Cour de Franc Pacifique, translated as the Pacific Franc.

Exchanging money

Because the majority of member states of the European Union use the euro as the shared currency, you have only one exchange rate to deal with for most European countries. Wonderful, right? And perfect for travelers. When you have **une devise (étrangère)** (ewn duh-veez [ey-trahN-zhehr]) (*foreign currency*), you can go to any of the following convenient places to exchange money at a reasonable rate:

- ✔ **un bureau de change** (uhN bew-roh duh shahNzh) (*a currency exchange office*): These businesses are everywhere in big cities. However, check the rates and commissions first, because they can vary greatly. A bank is often a good alternative when no currency exchange office is available.

- ✔ **les banques** (ley bahNk) (*banks*): Banks are often the most convenient place to exchange currency, especially in smaller towns, because small towns are less likely to have a specific currency exchange office. Banks charge an additional fee, which may vary from bank to bank, to exchange currency.

- ✔ **la poste** (lah puhhst) (*the post office*): In France, you can change money in many post offices. They open at 8:00 a.m. and close at around 7:00 p.m. If you happen to walk into a post office that doesn't offer currency exchange, the postal clerks can direct you to the nearest place that does offer this service.

Places such as hotel lobbies may exchange currency, but their rates are usually less favorable. And although you may have to change a few dollars at the money exchange counter of the airport upon your arrival, you can usually get a better deal if you wait until you're in town to change money at a bank. On the other hand, you may get a reasonable exchange rate at an airport ATM — just be aware of any fee that your home bank may charge for using a foreign ATM.

Currency rates change with the state of a country's economy. To find current exchange rates, check with your bank. Alternatively, you can simply ask for the current exchange rate with this question: **Quel est votre taux** de change ? (kehl ey vuhh-truh toh duh shahNzh?) (*What is your exchange rate?*). Here are some other phrases that may come in handy:

Est-ce qu'on peut changer de l'argent ici ? (ehs kohN puh shahN-zhey duh lahr-zhahN ee-see?) (*Can one exchange money here?*)

Je voudrais changer des dollars américains pour . . . (zhuh vooh-drey shahN-zhey dey doh-lahr ah-mey-ree-kaN poohr . . .) (*I'd like to change U.S. dollars for . . .*)

Quels sont vos frais de change ? (kehl sohN voh frey duh shahNzh?) (*How much do you charge to change money?*)

Talkin' the Talk

Martin, a Canadian tourist, walks into a money exchange office in Nice to exchange his Canadian dollars into euros.

L'employée: **Bonjour, monsieur, vous désirez ?**
bohN-zhoohr, muh-syuh, vooh dey-zee-rey?
Hello, sir, what can I do for you?

Martin: **Bonjour, madame. Je voudrais changer cent dollars canadiens.**
bohN-zhoohr, mah-dahm. zhuh vooh-drey shahN-zhey sahN doh-lahr kah-nah-dyaN.
Hello, ma'am. I'd like to change one hundred Canadian dollars.

L'employée: **Très bien, monsieur. Un moment, s'il vous plaît . . . bon, ça fait 75 [soixante-quinze] euros. Voilà, et votre reçu.**
trey byaN, muh-syuh. uhN moh-mahN, seel vooh pley . . . bohN, sah fey swah-sahNt-kaNz uh-roh. vwah-lah, ey vuhh-truh ruh-sew.
Very well, sir. One moment, please . . . well, it's 75 euros. Here you are, and your receipt.

Martin: **Merci, et au revoir.**
mehr-see, ey ohr-vwahr.
Thank you, and good-bye.

L'employée: **Au revoir, monsieur.**
ohr-vwahr, muh-syuh.
Good-bye, sir.

Going to the bank

When you travel to another country, one of the first places you probably need to go is to **la banque** (lah bahNk) (*the bank*), where you can exchange currency, cash a traveler's check, or change large bills into smaller denominations. Of course, you may be able to bypass the bank altogether if you have an ATM card that allows you to access funds internationally. We tell you more about that later. Here, we cover banking hours, how to describe what you need, and how to open a bank account.

Entering the bank

Banking hours — **heures d'ouverture et de fermeture** (uhr dooh-vehr-tewr ey duh fehr-muh-tewr) (Literally: *hours of opening and closing*) — usually fall somewhere between 8:00 a.m. and 6:00 p.m. (You may see these times listed as **8h** and **18h**; flip to Chapter 2 of Book I for info on time notation in French.) Some banks close for lunch, which can last up to two hours. Many banks are open on **samedi matin** (sahm-dee mah-taN) (*Saturday morning*) and are closed on **dimanche et lundi** (dee-maNsh ey luhN-dee) (*Sundays and Mondays*). If you're going to do any banking, check your closest bank's hours as soon as you arrive at your city of destination.

French banks often buzz you in through two sets of doors for security reasons. The following terms can help you navigate the bank:

- **la caisse** (lah kehs) (*cash register*)
- **le caissier/la caissière** (luh key-syey/lah key-syehr) (*teller*)
- **le client/la cliente** (luh klee-yahN/lah klee-yahNt) (*customer*)
- **le guichet de change** (luh gee-sheh duh shahNzh) (*cashier's window*)

Explaining what you need

When you enter a bank, someone there may ask you how he or she can help you. You may hear one of these phrases, both of which mean *Can I help you?*

- **Vous désirez ?** (vooh dey-zee-rey?)
- **Je peux vous aider ?** (zhuh puh vooh zey-dey?)

Instead of waiting to be offered help, you can also just walk up to an employee and state what you want. Start your request with **Je voudrais . . .** (zhuh vooh-drey . . .) (*I'd like . . .*) and then add the specifics — for example, **changer des dollars en euros** (shahN-zhey dey doh-lahr ahN nuh-roh) (*to change dollars into euros*) or **encaisser un chèque** (ahN-key-sey uhN shehk) (*to cash a check*).

To say *I need something* in French, you express the idea as *I have need of something*. First, you pick the appropriate form of the verb **avoir** (ah-vwahr) (*to have*): **J'ai** (zhey) (*I have*). (Head to Chapter 3 of Book III for the conjugation table for **avoir**.) Then you add **besoin de** (buh-zwaN duh) (*need of*) and follow it with whatever you need. Altogether, it looks like this: **J'ai besoin de** + a noun or a verb in the infinitive form. Here are some examples that express need with various forms of **avoir**:

> **J'ai besoin d'une pièce d'identité.** (zhey buh-zwaN dewn pyehs dee-dahN-tee-tey.) (*I need identification.*)
>
> **Christine a besoin d'argent.** (kree-steen ah buh-zwaN dahr-zhahN.) (*Christine needs money.*)
>
> **Avez-vous besoin de changer des dollars ?** (ah-vey-vooh buh-zwaN duh shahN-zhey dey doh-lahr?) (*Do you need to change dollars?*)

Opening a French bank account

If you plan to reside in France for more than three months, you may open a **compte bancaire** (kohNt baN-kehr) (*regular French bank account*). If you plan to reside in France for less than 3 months, you may open a **compte non-résident** (kohNt nohN-rey-zee-dahN) (*nonresident's account*). Some bank accounts available to you are the **compte à vue** (kohNt ah vew) or **compte chèque** (kohNt shehk) (*checking account*).

To open an account, you may need a **certificat de naissance** (sehr-tee-fee-kah duh ney-sahNs) (*birth certificate*), a **carte de séjour** (kahrt duh sey-zhoohr) (*resident permit*), a **facture d'électricité** (fahk-tewr dey-leyk-tree-see-tey) (*an electricity bill*), or a proof of status such as **une carte d'étudiant** (ewn kahrt dey-tew-dyaN) (*a student card*) or a **contrat d'emploi** (uhN kohN-trah dahN-plwah) (*an employment contract*).

French banks charge **des frais** (dey frey) (*fees*) for a **carte bleue** (kahrt bluh) (*French debit card*) and for online banking. When using a **chèque** (shehk) (*check*) from your French bank account, know that it's illegal to write a post-dated or open-dated check.

Processing Transactions

Some of the easiest ways to get and exchange money are to use **une carte de crédit** (ewn kahrt duh krey-dee) (*a credit card*) or **un distributeur (de billets)** (uhN dee-stree-bew-tuhr [duh bee-yey]) (*an automated teller machine/ATM*). You may take some traveler's checks with you as a backup plan. This section discusses the various payment methods and transactions you may encounter abroad.

When you're conducting any type of transaction, you can use the impersonal **on** (ohN) (*one*) in French instead of always using **je** (zhuh) (*I*) or **nous** (nooh) (*we*). For example, you can ask **On peut payer ici ?** (ohN puh pey-yey ee-see?) (*Can we can pay here? Literally: Can one pay here?*) **On peut** sounds a lot better to French ears than the good old **je peux** (zhuh puh) (*I can*) or **nous pouvons** (nooh pooh-vohN) (*we can*) form. **On** is what you usually hear. Sometimes **on** also replaces the *they* form, maybe just to be more casual: **Ah, ils ouvrent !** (ah, eel zooh-vruh!) becomes **Ah, on ouvre !** (ah, ohN nooh-vruh!), both of which mean *Ah, they're opening!* For more on **on**, check out Chapter 3 of Book IV.

When writing or reading French numbers, understanding the placement of points and commas is crucial. A point marks the thousands, and a comma separates the cents: **€1.000,00** (*mille euros*) (1,000 euros). A comma marks the fractions in a percentage: 25,5% is twenty-five point five percent.

Charging purchases

When you travel abroad, always take a couple of credit cards; they're the most convenient means of paying for your purchases. Check with your credit card issuer about foreign transaction fees and alert the company that you'll be making purchases out of the country; otherwise, they may assume the charges are fraudulent and your card may be declined. Make sure you have the right PIN, too.

If you're used to making all your purchases with your debit or credit card, you'd be wise to carry a Visa or MasterCard because credit cards like Discover and American Express aren't universally accepted in Europe.

Credit cards are widely accepted in French-speaking countries, but some stores have a minimum purchase requirement. For example, they may not accept credit cards if you spend less than 20 euros. Your American debit or credit cards should work everywhere in France, in restaurants, in shops, and at ATMs, but be aware that some self-serve French fuel pumps in **hypermarché** (ee-pehr-mahr-shey) (*large supermarket*) or marina areas may take only the French credit card, which has **une carte à puce** (ewn kahrt ah pews) (*a chip*). If you can find an attendant somewhere on the premises, you can pay by manual card transaction or cash. Otherwise, don't waste your time; find another station.

After you charge your purchase, the clerk may ask you **Pouvez-vous signer ici ?** (pooh-vey vooh see-nyey ee-see?) (*Can you sign here?*).

Accessing ATMs

Before you head out, make sure you have some cash or locate an ATM. ATMs are called **DAB** (dey-ah-bey) or **distributeurs automatiques de billets** (dee-stree-bew-tuhr oh-toh-mah-teek duh bee-yey). You can usually find them at banks, in shopping areas, at train stations, and at post offices. In large cities, ATMs are everywhere. Many metro stations in Paris have them.

To decide whether to use a credit card or debit card to take money out of an ATM, do a little research before you leave home. You'll typically pay more in fees when using a credit card rather than a debit card. (You pay a flat rate for each transaction plus a conversion fee, so to save money, you may engage in fewer transactions while withdrawing larger amounts.) Also confirm with your card issuer that your debit card will work in Europe, and be sure to get a PIN code that includes numbers only.

You can access ATMs all day and night . . . unless, of course, they're temporarily out of order. But nothing is perfect, right? French ATMs basically work the same as they do in the United States. You can usually opt to see the prompts in English, but in case the machine doesn't give you a language choice, here are the French phrases you need to know to use an ATM:

- ✔ **Insérez votre carte svp.** (aN-sey-rey vuhh-truh kahrt seel vooh pley.) (*Insert your card, please.*)

- ✔ **Tapez votre code svp.** (tah-pey vuhh-truh kohd seel vooh pley.) (*Type your PIN, please.*)

- ✔ **Retrait d'espèces.** (ruh-trey dey-spehs.) (*Cash withdrawal.*)

- ✔ **Carte en cours de vérification.** (kahrt ahN koohr duh vey-ree-fee-kah-syohN.) (*Verifying your card.*)

- ✔ **Patientez svp.** (pah-syaN-tey seel vooh pley.) (*Wait, please.*)

- ✔ **Reprenez votre carte svp.** (ruh-pruh-ney vuhh-truh kahrt, seel vooh pley.) (*Take your card, please.*)

- ✔ **Prenez votre argent svp.** (pruh-ney vuhh-truh ahr-zhahN seel vooh pley.) (*Take your money, please.*)

- ✔ **Voulez-vous un reçu ?** (vooh-ley-vooh uhN ruh-sew?) (*Would you like a receipt?*)

- ✔ **N'oubliez pas votre reçu.** (nooh-blee-yey pah vuhh-truh ruh-sew.) (*Don't forget your receipt.*)

The letters **svp** stand for **s'il vous plaît** (seel vooh pley) (*please*).

Verbs such as **pouvoir** (pooh-vwahr) (*to be able to*), **vouloir** (vooh-lwahr) (*to want*), and **devoir** (duh-vwahr) (*to have to*) require an infinitive verb after them to express what you *can, want,* and *must do* or *have to do.* The infinitive is the form of the verb you find in a dictionary. Here are some ATM-related examples that show the conjugated verbs followed by infinitives:

> Tu **peux insérer** ta carte. (tew puh aN-sey-rey tah kahrt.) (*You can insert your card.*)

> Je **veux aller** au distributeur. (zhuh vuh zah-ley oh dee-stree-bew-tuhr.) (*I want to go to the ATM.*)

> Vous **devez taper** votre code. (vooh duh-vey tah-pey vuhh-truh kohd.) (*You have to type in your PIN.*)

You can find the present tense conjugations of **pouvoir** and **devoir** in Chapter 3 of Book III.

Talkin' the Talk

Julie bought a couple of travel guides and tells **le vendeur** (luh vahN-duhr) (*the salesman*) that she wants to pay with her credit card. Unfortunately, the store doesn't accept credit cards. (Track 27)

Julie: **Bonjour, monsieur, vous acceptez les cartes de crédit ?**
bohN-zhoohr, muh-syuh, vooh zahk-sehp-tey ley kahrt duh krey-dee?
Hello, sir, do you accept credit cards?

Le vendeur: **Ah, non, désolé.**
ah, nohN, dey-zoh-ley.
Oh, no, sorry.

Julie: **Zut ! Alors, où est-ce qu'il y a un distributeur près d'ici ?**
zewt! ah-lohr, ooh ehs keel ee ah uhN dee-stree-bew-tuhr preh dee-see?
Darn! Then where is there an ATM close to here?

Le vendeur: **Il y en a un en face.**
eel yahN nah uhN ahN fahs.
There is one across the street.

Julie: **Je reviens tout de suite. Pouvez-vous garder mes guides ?**
zhuh ruh-vyaN toohd sweet. pooh-vey-vooh gahr-dey mey geed?
I'll be back right away. Can you hold my guides?

Le vendeur:	**Avec plaisir. Ne vous inquiétez pas.**
	ah-vehk pley-zeer. nuh vooh zaN-kyey-tey pah.
	Gladly. Don't worry.
Julie:	**Merci, à tout de suite.**
	mehr-see, ah toohd sweet.
	Thank you, I'll be right back.

Cashing checks

Cashing **un chèque de voyage** (uhN shehk duh vwah-yahzh) (a *traveler's check*) is another task you can take care of in **la banque.** When you go to cash your checks, you can say **Je voudrais encaisser . . .** (zhuh vooh-drey zahN-key-sey . . .) (*I'd like to cash . . .*). You'll be asked to provide **une pièce d'identité** (ewn pyehs dee-dahN-tee-tey) (*an ID*) and **votre signature** (vuhh-truh see-nyah-tewr) (*your signature*).

In most establishments, cashing local checks is **gratuit** (grah-twee) (*free of charge*). If it isn't, go to another bank. Some stores accept local checks just as they would cash. If your traveler's checks aren't in the local currency, you have to pay a fee to get them exchanged into local money.

Book II

Exploring and Wandering About

Talkin' the Talk

Susan is in a bank, wanting to cash her traveler's checks. She speaks to **la caissière** (lah key-syehr) (*the teller*).

Susan:	**Bonjour, mademoiselle. Je voudrais encaisser mes chèques de voyage.**
	bohN-zhoohr, mahd-mwah-zehl. zhuh vooh-drey zahN-key-sey mey shehk duh vwah-yahzh.
	Hello, miss. I'd like to cash my traveler's checks.
La caissière:	**Ils sont en euros ?**
	eel sohN tahN nuh-roh?
	Are they in euros?
Susan:	**Oui, en euros.**
	wee, ahN nuh-roh.
	Yes, in euros.
La caissière:	**Bon. J'ai besoin d'une pièce d'identité.**
	bohN. zhey buh-zwaN dewn pyehs dee-dahN-tee-tey.
	Very well. I need identification.

Susan:	**J'ai mon passeport et une carte de crédit, c'est bon ?**
	zhey mohN pahs-pohr ey ewn kahrt duh krey-dee, sey bohN?
	I've got my passport and a credit card. Will that do?

La caissière:	**Le passeport, c'est parfait. Merci. Et votre signature, s'il vous plaît.**
	luh pahs-pohr, sey pahr-fey. mehr-see. ey vuhh-truh see-nyah-tewr, seel vooh pley.
	The passport, that's perfect. Thank you. And your signature, please.

Susan:	**Ah oui, bien sûr. Voilà.**
	ah wee, byaN sewr. vwah-lah.
	Oh yes, certainly. Here you go.

Making change

Large bills can be inconvenient. Pulling out a very large bill to pay for a very inexpensive item can make you feel conspicuous. In addition, some businesses may not accept bills over a certain amount, and you may be asked **Avez-vous de la (petite) monnaie ?** (ah-vey-vooh duh lah [puh-teet] moh-neh?) (*Do you have [small] change?*). The same question in Québec is **Avez-vous du p'tit change ?** (ah-vey-vooh dew ptee shahNzh?). Plus, having a variety of small bills makes keeping track of how much you're spending and how much change you should get back a little easier, which is helpful when you're still learning to count out a new and unfamiliar currency.

When you want to get some change, you can use these phrases:

- ✔ **J'ai besoin de monnaie.** (zhey buh-zwaN duh moh-ney.) (*I need change [coins].*)

- ✔ **Je voudrais faire du change.** (zhuh vooh-drey fehr dew shahNzh.) (*I'd like to get some change.* [Québec])

- ✔ **Je voudrais faire de la monnaie.** (zhuh vooh-drey fehr duh lah moh-ney.) (*I'd like to get some change.* [France])

 Be careful not to translate the English word *money* as **monnaie.** Although the words look and sound a lot alike (see the discussion of false friends in Chapter 1 of Book I), **monnaie** means *change.* The French word for *money* is actually **argent** (ahr-zhahN).

Chapter 4

Home Is Where Your Suitcase Is: Looking for Accommodations

In This Chapter

▶ Finding a place to stay

▶ Reserving a room

▶ Navigating check-in and check-out

*N*ot everybody is lucky enough to have good friends with whom they can stay when traveling abroad. You likely need to add booking accommodations to your trip-planning checklist, along with composing an itinerary of the sites you want to see. Even if you're traveling on business and are limited to hotels selected by your company, you may still have questions about the accommodations. On the other hand, you may want to live in the countryside as closely as possible to the way the locals live, in which case you want to look into renting a chalet, cottage, or guest house. In this chapter, you get the information you need to find accommodations, make reservations, check in and check out of your hotel, and make your needs known.

Considering Your Accommodation Options

A hotel is your home away from home — even if you just consider it a place to lay your head after a day on the go — so it's good to know how to secure the kind of lodging you want. This section covers various kinds of hotel choices as well as the interesting **gîtes** (zheet) rental experience.

Sticking to traditional hotels

When you're thinking about what you want in a hotel, price is a consideration, but price alone doesn't determine the quality of your stay. **Les hôtels** (ley zoh-tehl) (*hotels*) range from basic one-star accommodations — **un hôtel une étoile** (uhN noh-tehl ewn ey-twahl) (*a one-star hotel*) — to luxury five-star establishments — **un hôtel cinq étoiles** (uhN noh-tehl saNk ey-twahl) (*a five-star hotel*). Room prices vary according to amenities, size, rating, and location. Most hotels offer breakfast (usually a continental breakfast, which includes either a croissant or a roll with butter and jam as well as coffee or tea), but not all have a restaurant.

The names for different types of hotels may vary a little throughout the French-speaking countries. **Hôtel garni** (oh-tehl gahr-nee) means *bed and breakfast,* and in French-speaking Canada, **maison de logement** (mey-zohN duh lohzh-mahN) refers to a smaller hotel or tourist home, which in other countries is sometimes called **une pension (de famille)** (ewn pahN-syohN [duh fah-meey]) (*a boarding house*) or **une auberge** (ewn oh-behrzh) (*inn*).

France also offers exquisite **châteaux** (shah-toh) (*castles*) that have been refurbished into hotels. Sure, they tend to be on the expensive side, but the ambiance and high-quality service are hard to surpass if you're looking for something special.

Finally, for the young and young at heart, France has about 200 **auberges de jeunesse** (oh-behrzh duh zhuh-nehs) (*youth hostels*), well scattered throughout the country, with varying facilities. For details, contact your national youth hostel association or search online.

Vacation rentals: Staying at a gîte in France

Alternatives to traditional hotels, such as **les gîtes ruraux** (ley zheet rew-roh), have become increasingly popular. Depending on where you are, **les gîtes ruraux** may take the form of furnished holiday cottages or flats, farmhouse arrangements, chalets, or even former monasteries. If you travel with your extended family and really want to experience life **en province** (ahN proh-vaNs) (*outside of big cities*), **les gîtes ruraux** are an ideal choice because they offer the amenities you have in your own home (kitchen, laundry room, and so on) and give you a home that has the traditional character of the region. Staying in a **gîte** allows you to get to know the local butcher and baker and take some meals in a homey setting.

Most **gîtes** are for rent on a minimum weekly basis from Saturday to Saturday, though you can rent some for just a weekend. Here's a list of words to recognize when looking to rent a **gîte**:

- **location hebdomadaire** (loh-kah-syohN ehb-doh-mah-dehr) (*weekly rental*)

- **location week-end** (loh-kah-syohN wee-kehnd) (*weekend rental*)

- **gîte pour six à huit personnes** (zheet poohr sees ah weet pehr-suhhn) (*gîte for six to eight people*)

- ✔ **haute/moyenne/basse saison** (oht/mwah-yehn/bahs sey-zohN) (*high/ middle/low season*)

- ✔ **quatre chambres à coucher** (kah-truh shaN-brah kooh-shey) (*four bedrooms*)

The Association **Gîtes de France** (recognized by the French ministry of tourism) regulates and classifies the rural accommodations according to the quality of amenities they offer. It uses one to five **épis** (ey-pee) (*ears of wheat*) as a symbol to represent rankings. The **5 épis gîte** may be a historic house equipped with a hot tub, a pool, bikes, and all kinds of games. The following phrases relate to location and amenities:

- ✔ **à dix minutes de l'autoroute** (ah dee mee-newt duh loh-toh-rooht) (*ten minutes away from the highway*)

- ✔ **à 2 km [deux kilomètres] de l'épicerie** (ah duh kee-loh-meh-truh duh ley-pees-ree) (*two kilometers from the grocery store*)

- ✔ **à proximité de la boulangerie** (ah prohk-see-mee-tey duh lah booh-lahN-zhree) (*near the bakery*)

- ✔ **accès Internet/connexion wifi** (ak-sey aN-tehr-neht/koh-nehk-syohN wee-fee) (*Internet access/Wi-Fi connection*)

- ✔ **cuisine toute équipée** (kwee-zeen tooht ey-kee-pey) (*fully equipped kitchen*)

- ✔ **four au bois** (foohr oh bwah) (*wood-burning stove*)

- ✔ **grande cheminée** (grahNd shuh-mee-ney) (*big fireplace*)

- ✔ **piscine avec patio meublé** (pee-seen ah-vehk pah-tee-o muh-bley) (*pool with furnished patio*)

- ✔ **stationnement disponible devant le gîte** (stah-syuhhn-mahN dee-spoh-nee-bluh duh-vahn luh zheet) (*parking available in front of the gîte*)

- ✔ **télévision avec CD et DVD** (tey-ley-vee-zyohN ah-vehk sey-dey ey dey-vey-dey) (*television with CD and DVD*)

And these phrases address the price of various services:

- ✔ **le prix comprend l'eau et l'électricité** (luh pree kohN-prahN loh ey ley-lehk-tree-see-tey) (*the price includes water and electricity*)

- ✔ **drap de bain et serviette de toilette à 4 [quatre] euros par personne et par semaine** (drah duh baN ey sehr-vyeht duh twah-leht ah kahtr-uh-roh pahr pehr-suhhn ey pahr suh-mehn) (*bath and hand towel at 4 euros per person per week*)

- ✔ **nettoyage lors du départ — 50 [cinquante] euros** (ney-twah-yahzh lohr dew dey-pahr saN-kahNt uh-roh) (*cleaning fee upon departure — 50 euros*)

- ✔ **linge et serviettes fournis à un petit supplément** (laNzh ey sehr-vyeht foohr-nee ah uhN puh-tee sew-pley-mahN) (*linen and towels provided for a small supplement*)

✔ **lit de bébé et chaise haute disponibles gratuitement sur simple demande** (lee duh bey-bey ey shehz oht dee-spoh-nee-bluh grah-tweet-mahN sewr saN-pluh duh-mahNd) (*crib and highchair provided for free simply upon request*)

Not all properties advertised as **gîtes** on the Internet are regulated by the French ministry of tourism. So do your research diligently before paying **les arrhes** (ley zahr) (*a deposit*).

Don't be surprised to find numerous **gîte** sites in English on the Internet. Although the **gîte** concept originated after World War II to help impoverished villagers use their farms for profit, many British people have acquired, renovated, and converted farms or windmills along the western coast of France into bed and breakfasts or **gîtes** in the last 20 years. This practice has been especially prevalent since the 1994 completion of the Chunnel, which allows a quick crossing of the English Channel between France and England. In addition, after the huge success of the book *A Year in Provence* (Vintage, 1989) by British author Peter Mayle, many English people purchased properties in that southeastern region of France as well, some to run rental properties.

Making Hotel Reservations

You usually book a room online or through a travel agent, but just in case you call in person, you need to know what to say. This section includes some questions and phrases to get you started.

Confirming availability

When you call a hotel, you'll probably first be connected to **la réception** (lah rey-sehp-syohN) (*reception*). You can say something like the following to explain why you're calling:

Je voudrais retenir/réserver une chambre, s'il vous plaît. (zhuh voohdrey ruh-tuh-neer/rey-zehr-vey ewn shahN-bruh, seel vooh pley.) (*I'd like to reserve a room please.*)

Avez-vous une chambre libre ? (ah-vey-vooh ewn shahN-bruh lee-bruh?) (*Do you have a room available?*)

You also need to say how long you'll be staying. To tell the hotel clerk that you're staying from a certain date to a certain date, you use **du** (dew) (*from*) and **au** (oh) (*to*). For example, if you're staying from June 4 to June 9, you say **du quatre juin au neuf juin** (dew kah-truh zhwaN oh nuhf zhwaN). Alternatively, you can say **du 4 au 9 juin** (dew kaht-ruh oh nuhf zhwaN), which means the same thing. If you're staying from the first of the month or to the first of the month, say **du premier** (dew pruh-myey) (*from the first*) and **au premier** (oh pruh-myey) (*to the first*) — for example, **du premier au sept juillet** (dew pruh-myey oh seht zhwee-yeh) (*from the first to the seventh of July; from July 1 to July 7*). Chapter 2 of Book I has more info on discussing specific dates.

Specifying the kind of room you want

When you call to reserve a room, you have to tell the hotel staff what type of room you're interested in. Do you want a single or a double room? One bed or two? Do you want the room to overlook a particular feature, such as the garden, the beach, or the courtyard? To state the type of room you want, place any of these terms after the phrase **une chambre** (ewn shahN-bruh) (*a room*):

Book II

Exploring and Wandering About

- **à deux lits jumeaux** (ah duh lee zhew-moh) (*with two twin beds*)
- **à un lit/à deux lits** (ah uhN lee/ah duh lee) (*with one bed/with two beds*)
- **double** (dooh-bluh) (*double*)
- **pour deux/trois/quatre personnes** (poohr duh/trwah/kaht-ruh pehr-suhhn) (*for two/three/four people*)
- **simple** (saN-pluh) (*single*)

French has no direct translation for what English calls a double bed, a queen-size bed, or a king-size bed. So just ask for **un petit lit** (uhN puh-tee lee) (*a small bed*), **un grand lit** (uhN grahN lee) (*a big bed*), **un lit pour une personne** (uhN lee poohr ewn pehr-suhhn) (*a bed for one person*), or **un lit pour deux personnes** (uhN lee poohr duh pehr-suhhn) (*a bed for two people*).

Do you want a room that faces or looks onto somewhere beautiful? Then you use the expression **donner sur** (duhh-ney sewr) (*facing, overlooking*). To request a particular view, you say **Je voudrais une chambre qui donne sur . . .** (zhuh vooh-drey ewn shahN-bruh kee duhhn sewr . . .) (*I'd like a room that faces . . .*) and then specify any of the following:

- **la cour** (lah koohr) (*the courtyard*)
- **le lac** (luh lahk) (*the lake*)
- **le jardin** (luh zhahr-daN) (*the garden*)
- **la mer** (lah mehr) (*the sea*)
- **la montagne** (lah mohN-tah-nyuh) (*the mountain*)
- **la piscine** (lah pee-seen) (*the swimming pool*)
- **la plage** (lah plahzh) (*the beach*)

The verb **donner** (duhh-ney), whose literal meaning is *to give,* is a regular **-er** verb, which you conjugate the same way you conjugate the verb **parler** (pahr-ley) (*to speak*). For the conjugation of verbs, refer to Chapter 3 of Book III or look at the verb tables of Appendix A.

Asking about amenities

In addition to the sleeping arrangements and room location, think about the kinds of amenities you're looking for. Here's a list of expressions that tell you more about your accommodations:

- **la blanchisserie** (lah blahN-shee-sree) (*laundry service*)
- **la climatisation** (lah klee-mah-tee-zah-syohN) (*air conditioning*)
- **une connexion Wi-Fi** (ewn kohN-neh-ksyohN wee-fee) (a *Wi-Fi connection*)
- **la navette d'aéroport** (lah nah-veht dah-ey-roh-pohr) (*airport shuttle*)
- **la piscine** (lah pee-seen) (*swimming pool*)
- **la salle de gym** (lah sahl duh zheem) (*fitness room*)
- **le site historique** (luh seet ee-stoh-reek) (*historic site*)

In many countries, **un lavabo** (uhN lah-vah-boh) (*a bathroom sink*) and **une baignoire** (ewn beh-nwahr) (*a bathtub*) and/or **une douche** (ewn doohsh) (*a shower*) are separate from the toilet and the bidet, an arrangement that's wonderful, of course. However, some showers are hand-held in the bathtub with no curtain around it, and that method takes a bit of getting used to.

Many hotels and other types of lodgings have Internet access, which is pretty affordable and reliable. Often you find computers in the hotel lobby, which you may be able to use free of charge or for a small fee. If your hotel doesn't provide this service, don't worry. Numerous Internet cafés and **cybercafés** (see-behr-kah-fey) (*cybercafés*) are located throughout major cities. Most hotels also provide Internet jacks into which you can plug your Ethernet cable.

The voltage in Europe is 220 volts as opposed to 110 volts used in the United States and Canada. If you're bringing any type of electronic equipment (hair dryer, electric shaver, laptop, and so on), bring an adapter with you. You can purchase these items at any electronics store. If you forget your adapter, you can buy one in an electronics store or any **hypermarché** (ee-pehr-mahr-shey) (*large superstore*) in the country you're visiting.

Talking price

An important point to consider before booking a room is the price. When you ask about room prices, also consider asking whether a deposit is necessary and whether the establishment accepts credit cards. The following sequence of questions and answers may help you:

> **Quel est le prix de la chambre ?** (kehl ey luh pree duh lah shahN-bruh?) (*What is the price of the room?*)

> **Le prix est 250 [deux cent cinquante] euros par jour.** (luh pree ey duh sahN saN-kahNt uh-roh pahr zhoohr.) (*The price is 250 euros per day.*)

> **Est-ce qu'il faut un acompte/des arrhes ?** (ehs keel foh uhN nah-kohNt/ dey zahr?) (*Do you need a deposit?*)

> **Il faut un acompte/des arrhes de 20 [vingt] pour cent.** (eel foh uhN nah-kohNt/dey zahr duh vaN poohr sahN.) (*You need a 20 percent deposit.*)

> **Acceptez-vous des cartes de crédit ?** (ahk-sehp-tey-vooh dey kahrt duh krey-dee?) (*Do you accept credit cards?*)

> **Oui, bien sûr.** (wee, byaN sewr.) (*Yes, of course.*)

Book II

Exploring and Wandering About

The closer your hotel is to the center of the city, the more expensive it's likely to be. Remember to ask how much the **taxe municipale** (f) (tahks mew-nee-see-pahl) (*city tax*) is per day per person; it's typically not included in the hotel rate.

Talkin' the Talk

Mr. and Mrs. Dalton are tired from driving and decide to call it a day in Annecy, a small, beautiful French town close to the Swiss border. They stop at a pretty country inn.

Mr. Dalton: **Bonjour ! Nous voudrions une chambre avec des lits jumeaux.**
bohN-zhoohr! nooh vooh-dree-yohN ewn shahN-bruh ah-vehk dey lee zhew-moh.
Hello! We'd like a room with twin beds.

Le concierge: **Côté cour ou côté rue ?**
koh-tey koohr ooh koh-tey rew?
Looking out on the courtyard or the street?
(Literally: *Courtyard side or street side?*)

Mrs. Dalton: **Côté cour. Et avec salle de bains et une baignoire, s'il vous plaît. Quel est le prix ?**
koh-tey koohr. ey ah-vehk sahl duh baN ey ewn beh-nwahr, seel vooh pley. kehl ey luh pree?
On the courtyard. And with a bathroom and a bath-tub, please. What is the price?

Le concierge: **Je vérifie. Au rez-de-chaussée ça coûte 150 [cent cinquante] euros.**
zhuh vey-ree-fee. oh reyd-shoh-sey sah kooht sahN saN-kahNt uh-roh.
I'm checking. On the ground floor, that costs 150 euros.

Mrs. Dalton: **Et au premier étage ?**
ey oh pruh-myey rey-tahzh?
And on the second floor?

Le concierge: **Je regrette. Le premier étage est complet.**
zhuh ruh-greht. luh pruh-myey rey-tahzh ey kohN-pley.
I'm sorry. The second floor is booked.

Mr. Dalton: **Pas de problème. Le rez-de-chaussée nous convient bien.**
pahd proh-blehm. luh reyd-shoh-sey nooh kohN-vyaN byaN.
No problem. The ground floor suits us fine.

Words to Know

côté cour	koh-tey koohr	facing the courtyard
côté rue	koh-tey rew	facing the street
je vérifie	zhuh vey-ree-fee	I'm checking
le rez-de-chaussée	luh reyd-shoh-sey	ground floor
ça coûte	sah kooht	that costs
au premier étage	oh pruh-myey rey-tahzh	on the second floor
il nous convient	eel nooh kohN-vyaN	its suits us

Remember that the ground floor of a French hotel is called **rez-de-chaussée** (reyd-shoh-sey). The numbering starts on the next floor up. So if you request a **chambre au premier étage** (shahN-broh pruh-myey rey-tazh) (*room on the first floor*), what you'll get is a room on the second floor.

Checking into a Hotel

After a long trip, arriving at a hotel is probably your first highlight — and perhaps your first interaction with French. You may wonder how to address the hotel staff, especially when you arrive to inquire about a room and get ready to **remplir la fiche d'hôtel** (rahN-pleer lah feesh doh-tehl) (*check-in. Literally: fill out your hotel [registration] form*).

The titles **Monsieur** (muh-syuh) (*Sir, Mister/Mr.*) and **Madame** (mah-dahm) (*Ma'am, Missus/Mrs.*) are used in French much more than in English and don't sound as formal. In fact, adding them after **bonjour** (bohN-zhoohr) (*hello; good morning*) is considered polite, especially when you're addressing someone you don't know. The term **mademoiselle** (mahd-mwah-zehl) is becoming old-fashioned and politically incorrect; it's now viewed as a sexist term that emphasizes a woman's unmarried status.

Book II

Exploring and Wandering About

Filling out a registration form

When you arrive at a hotel, chances are you have to fill out **une fiche** (ewn feesh) (*a registration form*). This form may ask you for these items:

- ✔ **nom/prénom** (nohN/prey-nohN) (*[last] name/first name*)
- ✔ **lieu de résidence/adresse** (lyuh duh rey-zee-dahNs/ah-drehs) (*address*)
- ✔ **rue/numéro** (rew/new-mey-roh) (*street/number*)
- ✔ **ville/code postal** (veel/kohd poh-stahl) (*city/zip code*)
- ✔ **état/pays** (ey-tah/pey-ee) (*state/country*)
- ✔ **numéro de téléphone** (new-mey-roh duh tey-ley-fuhhn) (*telephone number*)
- ✔ **nationalité** (nah-syoh-nah-lee-tey) (*nationality*)
- ✔ **date/lieu de naissance** (daht/lyuh duh ney-sahNs) (*date/place of birth*)
- ✔ **numéro de passeport** (new-mey-roh duh pahs-pohr) (*passport number*)
- ✔ **numéro d'immatriculation de la voiture** (new-mey-roh dee-mah-tree-kew-lah-syohN duh lah vwah-tewr) (*license plate number*)
- ✔ **date de l'arrivée** (daht duh lah-ree-vey) (*date of arrival*)

✔ **date du départ** (daht dew dey-pahr) (*date of departure*)

✔ **signature** (see-nyah-tewr) (*signature*)

Should you tip hotel staff such as bellhops and housekeepers? A service charge is generally included in hotel and restaurant bills, so basic good service is already covered. However, if the service has been particularly good, you can leave an extra tip.

Talkin' the Talk

Carol is checking in at the front desk while Max brings in the luggage with the doorman's help. (Track 28)

Carol: **Nous prenons la belle chambre au troisième étage.**
nooh pruh-nohN lah behl shahN-broh trwah-zyehm ey-tahzh.
We'll take the beautiful room on the fourth floor.

Le réceptionniste: **Bon. Veuillez remplir cette fiche, s'il vous plaît ? Et j'ai besoin de vos passeports.**
bohN. vuh-yey rahN-pleer seht feesh, seel vooh pley? ey zhey buh-zwaN duh voh pahs-pohr.
Good. Would you fill out this form, please? And I need your passports.

Carol: **Les voilà . . . et la fiche.**
ley vwah-lah . . . ey lah feesh.
Here they are . . . and the (registration) form.

Le réceptionniste: **Merci, madame. L'ascenseur est à gauche. Je vous souhaite une bonne soirée.**
mehr-see, mah-dahm. lah-sahN-suhr ey tah gohsh. zhuh vooh sweht ewn buhhn swah-rey.
Thank you, ma'am. The elevator is on the left. Have a nice evening.

Carol: **Merci. À quelle heure fermez-vous la porte principale ?**
mehr-see. ah kehl uhr fehr-mey-vooh lah pohrt praN-see-pahl?
Thank you. What time do you close the main door?

Le réceptionniste: **À minuit, mais vous pouvez toujours sonner.**
ah mee-nwee, mey vooh pooh-vey tooh-zhoohr suhh-ney.
At midnight, but you can always ring.

Words to Know

veuillez remplir	vuh-yey rahN-pleer	please fill out
j'ai besoin de	zhey buh-zwaN duh	I need
l'ascenseur	lah-sahN-suhr	elevator
vous fermez	vooh fehr-mey	you close
la porte principale	lah pohrt praN-see-pahl	main door
vous pouvez sonner	vooh pooh-vey suhh-ney	you can ring

In the dialogue, Carol says **les voilà** as she gives the receptionist the passports. To say *Here it is* or *There it is* while handing something over or pointing at it, just use one of the articles — **le**, **la**, or **les** — before the word **voici** (vwah-see) (*here is*) or **voilà** (vwah-lah) (*there is*). For example, when turning in a form, say **La voilà** (lah vwah-lah) (*There it is*) because you're referring to a feminine noun, **la fiche**. When giving your passport to the clerk, say **Le voilà** (luh vwah-lah) (*There it is*) because you're referring to a masculine noun, **le passeport**. Genders of nouns can be difficult to remember, so if you're too tired to think about grammatical nuances, just say **voici** or **voilà** followed by **monsieur** or **madame**.

Requesting room essentials

You're settling into your hotel room, but you discover you need more towels, blankets, and pillows. Or maybe the light bulb is out, or the bathroom needs more toilet paper. If you need any of these items, you call down to the desk and say **Il nous faut . . .** (eel nooh foh . . .) (*We need. . .*) and add the articles from the following list, as appropriate:

- ✔ **une ampoule/des ampoules** (ewn ahN-poohl/dey zahN-poohl) (*a light bulb/light bulbs*)
- ✔ **des cintres** (m) (dey saN-truh) (*hangers*)
- ✔ **une/des couverture(s)** (ewn/dey kooh-vehr-tewr) (*a blanket/blankets*)
- ✔ **un fer à repasser** (uhN fehr ah ruh-pah-sey) (*an iron*)
- ✔ **un oreiller/des oreillers** (uhN noh-reh-yey/dey zoh-reh-yey) (*a pillow/pillows*)
- ✔ **du papier hygiénique/de toilette** (dew pah-pyey ee-zhyey-neek/duh twah-leht) (*toilet paper*)
- ✔ **du savon** (dew sah-vohN) (*soap*)
- ✔ **une/des serviette(s)** (ewn/dey sehr-vyeht) (*a towel/towels*)

When the impersonal expression **il faut** (eel foh) (*it is necessary*) is followed by a noun, you use it to say *I need* something. However, you can personalize this construction by adding an indirect object pronoun of your choice in front of **faut: me** (muh) (*to me*), **te** (tuh) (*to you,* singular familiar), **lui** (lwee) (*to him/to her*), **nous** (nooh) (*to us*), **vous** (vooh) (*to you,* plural or singular formal), and **leur** (luhr) (*to them*). (Check out the indirect object pronouns in Chapter 3 of Book IV). Look at the following examples but note that you can't translate these examples literally:

Il me faut des serviettes. (eel muh foh dey sehr-vyeht.) (*I need towels.*)

Il nous faut du savon. (eel nooh foh dew sah-vohN.) (*We need soap.*)

Pointing out problems

Even in the best of hotels, you may encounter a problem that you want quickly resolved so you can rest, unpack, and start your vacation. Just in case, here are a few sentences to tell the front desk attendant what the problem is:

Le robinet n'arrête pas de couler dans la salle de bains. (luh roh-bee-ney nah-reht pah duh kooh-ley dahN lah sahl duh baN.) (*The faucet doesn't stop running in the bathroom.*)

Le lavabo est bouché. (luh lah-vah-boh ey booh-shey.) (*The sink is clogged.*)

Il y a trop de bruit dans la chambre à côté. (eel ee ah troh duh brwee dahN lah shaN-brah koh-tey.) (*There's too much noise in the room next door.*)

La télévision ne marche pas. (lah tey-ley-vee-zyohN nuh mahrsh pah.) (*The television doesn't work.*)

Il n'y a pas de courant dans la chambre. (eel nyah pah duh kooh-rahN dahN lah shahN-bruh.) (*There is no [electric] power in the room.*)

Il fait trop froid/chaud. (eel fey troh frwah/shoh.) (*It's too cold/hot.*)

La chambre sent la fumée. (lah shahN-bruh sahN lah few-mey.) (*The room smells of smoke.*)

Je n'arrive pas à ouvrir/fermer la fenêtre. (zhuh nah-reev pah zah ooh-vreer/fehr-mey lah fuh-neh-truh.) (*I can't open/close the window.*)

Je ne sais pas comment allumer l'eau dans la douche. (zhuhn sey pah koh-mahN ah-lew-mey loh dahn lah doohsh.) (*I don't know how to turn on the water in the shower.*)

Il n'y a pas de lumière dans le couloir. (eel nyah pah duh lew-myehr dahN luh kooh-lwahr.) (*There's no light in the hallway.*)

Book II

Exploring and Wandering About

In many French hotels and public places, the lights in the hallways turn off automatically after a short time in order to save electricity. Just look on the wall for a small button, often illuminated, and press it to turn the lights back on.

Asking the front desk attendant for information

Even if you've arranged many aspects of your stay ahead of time, you may encounter some details you haven't taken care of. Maybe you didn't expect to arrive this late and would love some room service. Maybe you can't remember whether the hotel serves breakfast, or you just want to confirm whether breakfast is included in the room price. You may want some information regarding nearby restaurants or stores. Here are some sentences to take care of last minute details:

À quelle heure servez-vous le petit déjeuner ? (ah kehl uhr sehr-vey-vooh luh puh-tee dey-zhuh-ney?) (*At what time do you serve breakfast?*)

Le petit déjeuner est compris, n'est-ce pas ? (luh puh-tee dey-zhuh-ney ey kohN-pree, nehs pah?) (*Breakfast is included, right?*)

Est-ce que vous faites le service-repas ? (ehs kuh vooh feht luh sehr-vees ruh-pah?) (*Do you provide room service?*)

Jusqu'à quelle heure ? (zhews-kah kehl uhr?) (*Until what time?*)

Il y a un café/un restaurant/une charcuterie tout près ? (eel ee ah uhN kah-fey/uhN rey-stoh-rahN/ewn shahr-kewt-ree tooh preh?) (*Is there a café/restaurant/deli nearby?*)

Où est la station de métro la plus proche ? (ooh ey lah stah-syohN duh mey-troh lah plew pruhhsh?) (*Where is the nearest subway station?*)

Vous avez un plan de la ville ? (vooh zah-vey uhN plahN duh lah veel?) (*Do you have a map of the city?*)

Checking Out of a Hotel

For whatever reason, **l'heure de quitter la chambre** (luhr duh kee-tey lah shahN-bruh) (*the hotel checkout time*) is hardly ever convenient, but you probably realize that rooms have to be cleaned before the next guest arrives. Of course, before leaving, you have to **régler la note** (rey-gley lah nuhht) (*settle the bill*) or at least verify it to see whether you've accrued any additional charges during your stay. The following phrases can come in handy when you're ready to check out:

- ✔ **À quelle heure faut-il libérer/quitter la chambre ?** (ah kehl uhr foh-teel lee-bey-rey/kee-tey lah shahN-bruh?) (*At what time does one have to check out?*)

- ✔ **Ces frais supplémentaires sont corrects/incorrects.** (sey frey sew-pley-mahN-tehr sohN koh-rehkt/aN-koh-rehkt.) (*These additional charges are correct/incorrect.*)

- ✔ **J'ai une question en ce qui concerne la note.** (zhey ewn keh-styohN ahN skee kohN-sehrn lah nuhht.) (*I have a question regarding the bill.*)

- ✔ **Je voudrais un reçu.** (zhuh vooh-drey uhN ruh-sew.) (*I'd like a receipt.*)

- ✔ **Je voudrais m'enregistrer pour mon vol en ligne.** (zhuh vooh-drey mahN-ruh-zhee-strey poohr mohN vohl ahN lee-nyuh.) (*I'd like to check in online for my flight.*)

- ✔ **Pouvez-vous m'imprimer ma carte d'embarquement ?** (pooh-vey-vooh maN-pree-mey mah kahrt dahN-bahr-kuh-mahN?) (*Can you print my boarding pass?*)

You may have to remove your belongings from your room before you're ready to depart from your location. Fortunately, many hotels allow you to leave your luggage in the lobby or some other place until you leave. To find out whether your hotel offers this service, ask **Je peux laisser mes bagages ici jusqu'à . . . ?** (zhuh puh ley-sey mey bah-gahzh ee-see zhew-skah . . . ?) (*Can I leave my luggage here until . . . ?*).

Talkin' the Talk

Judy's plane is leaving in the evening, so she wants to spend her last day in town and get the luggage later.

Judy:	**À quelle heure faut-il libérer la chambre ?** ah kehl uhr foh-teel lee-bey-rey lah shahN-bruh? *At what time do we have to check out?* (Literally: *At what time is it necessary to vacate the room?*)

La réceptionniste:	**Avant midi, madame.** ah-vahN mee-dee, mah-dahm. *Before noon, ma'am.*
Judy:	**Je peux laisser mes bagages ici jusqu'à 16h00 [seize heures] ?** zhuh puh ley-sey mey bah-gahzh ee-see zhew-skah sehz uhr? *Can I leave my luggage here until 4:00 p.m.?*
La réceptionniste:	**Oui, vous pouvez les laisser ici. Voulez-vous la note maintenant ?** wee, vooh pooh-vey ley ley-sey ee-see. vooh-ley-vooh lah nuhht maN-tuh-nahN? *Yes, you can leave them here. Would you like the bill now?*
Judy:	**Oui, s'il vous plaît. Voyons, les coups de télé-phone, le minibar . . . très bien. Vous acceptez les cartes de crédit, n'est-ce pas ?** wee, seel vooh pley. vwah-yohN, ley kooh duh tey-ley-fuhhn, luh mee-nee-bar . . . trey byaN. vooh zahk-sehp-tey ley kahrt duh krey-dee, nehs pah? *Yes, please. Let's see, the phone calls, the mini-bar . . . very well. You accept credit cards, don't you?*
La réceptionniste:	**Oui, Visa ou MasterCard. Merci . . . et voici votre reçu.** wee, vee-zah ooh mah-stehr-kahrd. mehr-see . . . ey vwah-see vuhh-truh ruh-sew. *Yes, Visa or MasterCard. Thank you . . . and here is your receipt.*

Judy: **Merci. Pouvez-vous m'appeler un taxi, s'il vous plaît ?**
                             mehr-see. pooh-vey-vooh mah-pley uhN tahk-see, seel vooh pley?
                             Thank you. Can you call a taxi for me, please?

La réceptionniste: **Bien sûr.**
                             byaN sewr.
                             Of course.

Words to Know

je peux laisser	zhuh puh ley-sey	I can leave (behind)
ici	ee-see	here
jusqu'à	zhew-skah	until
la note	lah nuhht	bill
un coup de téléphone	uhN kooh duh tey-ley-fuhhn	telephone call

Chapter 5

Getting Around

*W*hen you travel, your first concern may be getting to your destination country, but as soon as you're there, you want to get around. This chapter can help you navigate the airport, train station, or subway system as well as rent a car or flag down a taxi. When you arrive in any French-speaking country, you're instantly immersed in the French language. The porter, the taxi driver, and the customs people all address you in French, so the topics in this chapter can help you make sense of your new surroundings.

Breezing through the Airport

You may feel like the biggest hurdle between you and your vacation is just making your way to **l'avion** (lah-vyohN) (*the plane*). You often need to arrive at **l'aéroport** (lah-ey-roh-pohr) (*the airport*) at least two hours before your departure just to check in and get through security. With the terms in this section, you'll be all set to proceed to the boarding gate as well as enjoy your flight and breeze through customs.

Finding your way around the airport

Because of their size and the number of people who go through them every day, airports can be overwhelming places, especially when you're unfamiliar with the layout and the language. Here are some important areas in the airport:

✔ **départs** (dey-pahr) (*departures*)

✔ **arrivées** (ah-ree-vey) (*arrivals*)

✔ **enregistrement des bagages** (ahN-reh-zhee-struh-mahN dey bah-gahzh) (*baggage check*)

Before you embark: A few travel tips

Nothing derails a trip faster than realizing you've forgotten to consider some important information about airport guidelines or your destination country. Here are a few things to keep in mind before you go:

✔ If you travel to Europe, make sure you're familiar with the metric system and its three most common units: the meter, the gram, and the liter. One kilometer equals 0.621 miles. For example, from the center of Paris to Versailles is about 21 kilometers, or approximately 13 miles.

✔ Before the day of your flight, verify how many pieces of luggage your airline allows you to bring and the maximum allotted weight of each. By adhering to the airline's regulations, you can avoid unpleasant surprises like being charged extra for your luggage.

✔ Don't joke around with immigration or customs officers. They're there for serious business, and if your jokes read the wrong way, your vacation may be in big trouble before it really starts.

Your first task when you go to the airport is to find **l'aérogare** (lah-ey-roh-gahr) (*the terminal*) for **la ligne aérienne** (lah lee-nyuh ah-ey-ryehn) (*the airline*) you're flying. Then look for **le numéro du vol** (luh new-mey-roh dew vohl) (*the flight number*). After you arrive at **le comptoir** (luh kohN-twahr) (*the airline ticket counter*), you must **enregistrer les bagages/les valises** (ahN-reh-zhee-strey ley bah-gahzh/ley vah-leez) (*check your bags/suitcases*). At that time, you receive **une carte d'embarquement** (ewn kahrt dahN-bahr-kuh-mahN) (*a boarding pass*). Then you can go to **la porte** (lah puhhrt) (*the gate*) and wait until called to board your plane.

Up, up, and away: Relaxing on the plane

After you're on the plane, sit back and relax. **Un steward/une hôtesse de l'air** (uhN stee-wahr/ewn oh-tehs duh lehr) (*flight attendant*) will be around to see to your comfort, offering reading material, pillows, beverages, and so on.

At different points during the flight, you may hear the following:

✔ **Attachez votre ceinture.** (ah-tah-shey vuhh-truh saN-tewr.) (*Fasten your seatbelt.*)

✔ **Restez assis.** (reh-stey ah-see.) (*Remain seated.*)

✔ **Ne fumez pas./Interdiction de fumer.** (nuh few-mey pah./aN-tehr-deek-syohN duh few-mey.) (*Don't smoke./No smoking.*)

✔ **Éteignez tout appareil électronique.** (ey-taN-nyey tooh tah-pah-rehy ey-lehk-troh-neek.) (*Turn off all electronic devices.*)

The pilot will also share when the plane is going to **décoller** (dey-koh-ley) (*to take off*), **atterrir** (ah-teh-reer) (*to land*), or **faire une escale** (fehr ewn eh-skahl) (*to stop over*).

Going through customs

Your first hurdle after you reach your destination is making it through **la douane** (lah dooh-ahn) (*customs*). Before you land, you'll be asked to fill out a customs form regarding the purpose and length of your stay if you're traveling abroad. The form also asks whether you have anything to declare. If you're traveling with your family, only one form is necessary for all of you.

After deboarding, look for signs directing you to **la douane**. Have **votre passeport** (vuhh-truh pahs-pohr) (*your passport*) and customs form handy as well as any other documents that may apply, such as student or work permits or an extended visa. A visa isn't needed for most European countries if you're planning to stay for less than three months.

Common customs questions include the following:

> **Quelle est la raison de votre voyage ?** (kehl ey lah reh-zohN duh vuhh-truh wvah-yahzh?) (*What is the reason for your trip?*)

> **Combien de temps restez-vous à/en/au/aux . . . ?** (kohN-byaN duh tahN reh-stey-vooh ah/ahN/oh/oh . . . ?) (*How long are you staying in . . . ?*)

When talking about staying in a city, you use **à** (ah) to express the English *in* or *to,* such as **à Paris** (ah pah-ree) (*in/to Paris*) or **à Bruxelles** (ah brewk-sehl) (*in/to Brussels*). For countries, you usually use **en** (ahN) for the country names ending in **e** or beginning with a vowel: **en France** (ahN frahNs), **en Suisse** (ahN swees), **en Italie** (ahN nee-tah-lee), and so on. For most other countries, you use **au** or **aux** (oh): **au Canada** (oh kah-nah-dah), **au Portugal** (oh puhhr-tew-gahl), **aux États-Unis** (oh zey-tah-zew-nee), and so on. For details on which prepositions to use with geographical locations, see Chapter 1 of Book IV.

Most likely, **le douanier/la douanière** (luh dooh-ah-nyey/lah dooh-ah-nyehr) (*the customs officer*) will only need to see your passport and customs form. Occasionally, though, you may be picked out for further questioning. In this case, you may hear the following questions:

> **Avez-vous quelque chose à déclarer ?** (ah-vey-vooh kehl-kuh shohz ah dey-klah-rey?) (*Do you have something to declare?*)

> **Pouvez-vous ouvrir votre sac ?** (pooh-vey-vooh ooh-vreer vuhh-truh sahk?) (*Can you open your bag?*)

After you answer the questions, **le douanier/la douanière** will stamp your passport, and you'll be on your way.

Book II

Exploring and Wandering About

Talkin' the Talk

Le douanier is the first person Nicola encounters in the French airport. She hands him her passport and her customs slip, and he starts **le contrôle des passeports** (luh kohN-trohl dey pahs-puhhr) (*the passport check*).

Le douanier: **Bonjour. Bienvenue en France. Allez-vous rester en France pendant tout votre séjour ?**
bohN-zhoohr. byaN-vuh-new ahN frahNs. ah-ley-vooh reh-stey ahN frahNs pahN-dahN tooh vuhh-truh sey-zhoohr?
Hello. Welcome to France. Are you going to remain in France for your whole stay?

Nicola: **Non, je vais aussi à Bruxelles et en Suisse.**
nohN, zhuh vey zoh-see ah brewk-sehl ey ahN swees.
No, I'm also going to Brussels and to Switzerland.

Le douanier: **Et la raison de votre voyage ?**
ey lah reh-zohN duh vuhh-truh vwah-yahzh?
And the reason for your trip?

Nicola: **C'est pour les affaires et le plaisir.**
sey poohr ley zah-fehr ey luh pley-zeer.
It's for business and pleasure.

Le douanier: **Combien de temps restez-vous en tout ?**
kohN-byaN duh tahN reh-stey-vooh zahN tooh?
How long are you staying altogether?

Nicola: **Deux semaines.**
duh suh-mehn.
Two weeks.

Le douanier: **Avez-vous quelque chose à déclarer ?**
ah-vey-vooh kehl-kuh shohz ah dey-klah-rey?
Do you have anything to declare?

Nicola: **Non, je n'ai rien à déclarer.**
nohN, zhuh ney ryaN nah dey-klah-rey.
No, I have nothing to declare.

Le douanier: **Pouvez-vous ouvrir votre sac ?**
pooh-vey-vooh ooh-vreer vuhh-truh sahk?
Can you open your bag?

Nicola: **Oui, monsieur. Voilà.**
wee, muh-syuh. vwah-lah.
Yes, sir. Here you go.

Le douanier: **Je vous souhaite un bon séjour !**
zhuh vooh sweht uhN bohN sey-zhoohr!
Have a nice stay! Literally: *I wish you a good stay.*

Nicola: **Merci, monsieur. Au revoir.**
mehr-see, muh-syuh. ohr-vwahr.
Thank you, sir. Good-bye.

Book II

Exploring and Wandering About

Words to Know

pendant	pahN-dahN	during, for
séjour	sey-zhoohr	stay
pour les affaires	poohr ley zah-fehr	for business
combien de temps	kohN-byaN duh tahN	how much time
en tout	ahN tooh	in all
rien à déclarer	ryaN nah dey-klah-rey	nothing to declare
je vous souhaite	zhuh vooh sweht	I wish you

Taking Buses, Subways, and Trains

The public transportation system in most major cities of Europe and Canada is excellent. This section gives you general information so you can research some fun and economical ways of getting to your favorite destinations. So head to **le guichet** (luh gee-shey) (*the ticket window*) and get ready to hop aboard!

When you get on the bus, or before you get on the train or subway, be sure to validate your ticket in a machine installed for that purpose. **Le contrôleur** (luh kohN-troh-luhr) (*the conductor, the ticket inspector*) gets on and checks everybody, and the fine for boarding without having validated your ticket can make traveling awfully expensive.

Boarding the bus

If you have time, **le bus** (luh bews) (*the bus*) is probably the most wonderful way not only to get an impression of the **quartiers** (kahr-tyey) (*neighborhoods*) of a city but also to experience that city's people a bit. Buses are clean and pleasant and usually run at frequent and regular intervals. The majority of bus stops in major cities are equipped with an electronic device or a schedule that shows when the next bus is expected. Also displayed at the bus stops are **les lignes de bus** (ley lee-nyuh duh bews) (*bus routes*) and neighborhood maps. Major cities have **des excursions en bus** (dey zehk-skewr-syohN ahN bews) (*bus tours*), which are a great and inexpensive way to see the city.

You can usually buy **un ticket** (uhN tee-key) (*a ticket*) from **le conducteur de bus** (luh kohN-dewk-tuhr duh bews) (*the bus driver*), but remember that large bills aren't welcome; it's best to have the correct change. Generally, buying tickets in **un carnet** (uhN kahr-ney) (*a book of ten*) is cheaper. You can purchase these books at metro stations or at any **distributeur automatique** (dee-stree-bew-tuhr oh-toh-mah-teek) (*automated ticket vending machine*). You may also purchase tickets at **le guichet** (luh gee-shey) (*the ticket window*). In many cities, the subway system is connected with the bus system, so you can use the same tickets. See Chapter 3 of Book II for details on money and the next section for info on the subway system.

Talkin' The Talk

Stéphane and Oriane are at a bus stop, and they're not sure whether they're reading the bus schedule correctly. Bus number 82 is arriving. Stéphane turns to **une jeune femme** (ewn zhuhn fahm) (*a young woman*) next to him for help. (Track 29)

Stéphane:	**Excusez-moi, madame. C'est bien le bus pour l'hôtel de ville ?** ehk-skew-zey-mwah, mah-dahm. sey byaN luh bews poohr loh-tehl duh veel? *Excuse me, ma'am. Is that the correct bus to city hall?*
La jeune femme:	**Non, il faut prendre le bus numéro 67 [soixante-sept].** nohN, eel foh prahN-druh luh bews new-mey-roh swah-sahNt-seht. *No, you have to take bus number 67.*
Stéphane:	**À quelle heure est-ce qu'il arrive ?** ah kehl uhr ehs keel ah-reev? *What time does it come?*

La jeune femme:	**Il passe tous les quarts d'heure, mais il est souvent en retard.** eel pahs tooh ley kahr duhr, mey eel ey sooh-vahN ahN ruh-tahr. *It comes every quarter hour, but it's often late.*
Stéphane:	**Et c'est à combien d'arrêts d'ici ?** ey sey tah kohN-byaN dah-rey dee-see? *And how many stops is it from here?*
La jeune femme:	**Ce n'est pas très loin. C'est le prochain arrêt. Ah, le voilà ! Il est à l'heure !** suh ney pah trey lwaN. sey luh proh-shaN nah-rey. ah, luh vwah-lah! eel ey tah luhr! *It's not very far. It's the next stop. Ah, there it is! It's on time!*
Stéphane:	**Merci beaucoup. Au revoir.** mehr-see boh-kooh. ohr-vwahr. *Thank you very much. Goodbye.*

Book II

Exploring and Wandering About

Words to Know

l'hôtel de ville	loh-tehl duh veel	city hall
il faut prendre	eel foh prahN-druh	you need to take
il passe	eel pahs	it passes
souvent	sooh-vahN	often
combien d'arrêts	kohN-byaN dah-rey	how many stops
d'ici	dee-see	from here
le prochain arrêt	luh proh-shaN nah-rey	the next stop

The adjective or pronoun **tout** (tooh) (*all, every*), which appears in the nearby dialogue, has four forms — **tout**, **toute**, **tous**, and **toutes** — because it agrees in gender and number with the noun it modifies or replaces. **Tous** and **toutes** mean *every* when they're connected with a time definition in the plural, as in these examples:

tous les quarts d'heure (tooh ley kahr duhr) (*every quarter of an hour*)

tous les jours (tooh ley zhoohr) (*every day*)

toutes les vingt minutes (tooht ley vaN mee-newt) (*every 20 minutes*)

When **tout** is connected with time definitions in the singular, however, it takes on a different meaning — *all* or *something in its entirety*, as these examples show:

toute la matinée (tooht lah mah-tee-ney) (*all morning long, the whole morning, the entire morning*)

toute la journée (tooht lah zhoohr-ney) (*all day long, the whole day, the entire day*)

Rapid transit: Using the subway

Le métro (luh mey-troh) (*the subway, metro, underground*) is a fast, economical way to get around the city. Paris, Brussels, Lille, Lyon, and Montréal all have very efficient subway systems. Big maps in each station make the systems easy to use, and the hours of operation (usually from 5:30 a.m. to 1:00 a.m.) make the **métro** very convenient. In these cities, the fare is standard no matter how far you travel. Here are some words that may come in handy:

- **la correspondance** (lah koh-reh-spohN-dahNs) (*transfer point, connection*)
- **la ligne** (lah lee-nyuh) (*[metro] line*)
- **la place/le siège** (lah plahs/luh syehzh) (*seat*)
- **le plan** (luh plahN) (*map*)
- **le quai** (luh key) (*platform*)
- **la sortie** (lah sohr-tee) (*the exit*)
- **la station de métro** (lah stah-syohN duh mey-troh) (*metro station*)
- **la voiture** (lah vwah-tewr) (*car, metro car, train car*)

You can buy subway tickets from machines or from an attendant at the **station de métro**. Most employees in the **métro** speak enough English to sell tickets and answer your questions. But just in case, here are some helpful phrases:

Un ticket, s'il vous plaît. (uhN tee-key, seel vooh pley.) (*One ticket, please.*)

Un carnet, s'il vous plaît. (uhN kahr-ney, seel vooh pley.) (*A book of [ten] tickets, please.*)

Comment aller à . . . ? (koh-mahN tah-ley ah . . . ?) (*How do I get to . . . ?*)

Quelle est la ligne pour . . . ? (kehl ey lah lee-nyuh poohr . . . ?) (*Which line is for . . . ?*)

Est-ce le bon sens pour aller à . . . ? (ehs luh bohN sahNs poohr ah-ley ah . . . ?) (*Is this the right direction to go to . . . ?*)

Est-ce qu'il faut prendre une correspondance ? (ehs keel foh prahN-drewn koh-reh-spohN-dahNs?) (*Do I need to transfer?*)

Où est la sortie, s'il vous plaît ? (ooh ey lah sohr-tee, seel vooh pley?) (*Where is the exit, please?*)

Talkin' the Talk

Mr. and Mrs. Meyer split up for the morning to see different museums, but now it's time to meet for lunch. Mr. Meyer wants to take the **métro**, but he thinks he needs a map and stops at a kiosk.

Mr. Meyer: **Bonjour. Est-ce que vous avez un plan de métro ?**
bohN-zhoohr. ehs kuh vooh zah-vey uhN plahN duh mey-troh?
Hello. Do you have a metro map?

L'employée **Le voici. Est-ce que je peux vous aider à trouver une ligne ?**
luh vwah-see. ehs kuh zhuh puh vooh zey-dey ah trooh-vey ewn lee-nyuh?
Here it is. Can I help you find a route?

Mr. Meyer: **Oui, pour la Grande Place, c'est quelle ligne ?**
wee, poohr lah grahNd plahs, sey kehl lee-nyuh?
Yes, to Grande Place, which route is it?

L'employée: **C'est direct avec la ligne 3 [trois].**
sey dee-rehkt ah-vehk lah lee-nyuh trwah.
You can go directly with route 3.

Mr. Meyer: **Combien de temps est-ce qu'il faut ?**
kohN-byaN duh tahN ehs keel foh?
How long does it take?

L'employée: **Disons . . . 20 [vingt] minutes.**
dee-zohN . . .vaN mee-newt.
Let's say . . . 20 minutes.

Mr. Meyer: **Merci beaucoup, madame.**
mehr-see boh-kooh, mah-dahm.
Thank you very much, ma'am.

> L'employée: **Je vous en prie.**
> zhuh vooh zahN pree.
> *You're welcome.*

Je vous en prie (zhuh vooh zahN pree), which appears in the nearby dialogue, is a formal way of saying *You're welcome*. The more casual expression is **Pas de quoi** (pahd kwah) (*No worries*), a phrase you can make more formal by not abbreviating it: **Il n'y a pas de quoi** (eel nyah pahd kwah) (*Don't mention it*). You can also say **De rien** (duh ryaN) (*It's nothing*).

Traveling by train

Although some European airlines (such as Irish companies Aer Lingus and Ryanair) have given trains a run for their money in the last few years, you can't find a better way to cross Europe than by rail. Trains in Europe are modern, clean, fast, and efficient. For long distance travel, trains are equipped with restaurants or café cars as well as **des couchettes** (dey kooh-sheht) (*berths, built-in beds*). A number of rail passes allow you to travel to the countries of your choice, but remember to purchase such passes ahead of time. Student and age discounts are available, so don't forget to ask for those.

For long-distance travel between France, Belgium, and the Netherlands, try the **Train à Grande Vitesse (TGV)** (traN ah grahNd vee-tehs [tey zhey vey]), a high-speed train that you can use only with reservations. It can take you across France in no time and is truly worth the experience. The **TGV Thalys** (tey-zhey-vey tah-lees) runs from Paris to Brussels to Amsterdam and back.

Also convenient, **l'Eurostar/Le Shuttle** (luh-roh stahr/luh shuh-tuhl) is a passenger Channel Tunnel link from London's Waterloo train station to Paris and Brussels. The **SNCF (Société Nationale des Chemins de Fer Français)** (ehs ehn sey ehf [soh-see-ey-tey nah-syoh-nahl dey shuh-maN duh fehr frahN-seh]) is the French National Railway Company. Paris alone has six major **gares** (gahr) (*train stations*).

Here are some useful phrases for when you're traveling by train:

✔ **à bord** (ah bohr) (*on board*)

✔ **à destination de** (ah deh-stee-nah-syohN duh) (*bound for*)

✔ **un [billet] aller-retour** (uhN [bee-yey] ah-ley-ruh-toohr) (*a round-trip [ticket]*)

✔ **un [billet] aller-simple** (uhN [bee-yey] ah-ley-saN-pluh) (*a one-way [ticket]*)

✔ **le bureau des objets trouvés** (luh bew-roh dey zohb-zheh trooh-vey) (*the lost and found*)

✔ **le compartiment** (luh kohN-pahr-tee-mahN) (*compartment*)

✔ **composter** (kohN-poh-stey) (*to validate [a ticket]*)

✔ **la consigne** (lah kohN-see-nyuh) (*baggage room*)

✔ **direct(e)** (dee-rehkt) (*direct, nonstop*)

✔ **les heures** (f) **de pointe** (ley zuhr duh pwaNt) (*rush hour, peak*)

✔ **l'horaire** (m) (loh-rehr) (*the schedule*)

✔ **l'indicateur [automatique]** (m) (laN-dee-kah-tuhr [oh-toh-mah-teek]) (*automated train schedule*)

✔ **la période creuse** (lah pey-ree-uhhd kruhz) (*off-peak*)

✔ **le quai** (luh key) (*platform*)

✔ **les renseignements** (m) (ley rahN-seh-nyuh-mahN) (*the information desk*)

✔ **la salle d'attente** (lah sahl dah-tahNt) (*waiting room*)

✔ **un tarif réduit** (uhN tah-reef rey-dwee) (*reduced fare*)

✔ **la voie** (lah vwah) (*track*)

Book II

Exploring and Wandering About

Getting help at the train station

Train stations are busy, noisy, and confusing, but you can usually find helpful people, such as the police and station employees, whom you can turn to for direction. You can use these questions with your traveling companions or other people at the station:

Pardon, où sont les guichets ? (pahr-dohN, ooh sohN ley gee-shey?) (*Pardon, where are the ticket windows?*)

Excusez-moi, où est la salle d'attente ? (ehk-skew-zey-mwah, ooh ey lah sahl dah-tahNt?) (*Excuse me, where is the waiting room?*)

Il arrive par quel train ? (eel ah-reev pahr kehl traN?) (*Which train is he arriving on?*)

Quelles places avez-vous ? (kehl plahs ah-vey-vooh?) (*Which seats do you have?*)

Quel est le nom de la gare ? (kehl ey luh nohN duh lah gahr?) (*What is the name of the train station?*)

Quelles sont les heures de pointe ? (kehl sohN ley zuhr duh pwaNt?) (*What are the peak hours?*)

Buying tickets and checking the schedule

When you're traveling, you undoubtedly need to ask questions about plane and train schedules. Here are a few questions and answers that may come in handy:

Quand voulez-vous partir ? (kahN vooh-ley-vooh pahr-teer?) (*When do you want to leave?*)

Où voulez-vous aller ? (ooh vooh-ley-vooh zah-ley?) (*Where do you want to go?*)

Voulez-vous un aller-retour ou un aller-simple ? (vooh-ley-vooh uhN nah-ley-ruh-toohr ooh uhN nah-ley-saN-pluh?) (*Do you want a round trip or one way?*)

Pour combien de personnes ? (poohr kohN-byaN duh pehr-suhhn?) (*For how many people?*)

Similarly, you may have some questions of your own:

À quelle heure y a-t-il un train pour . . . ? (ah kehl uhr yah-teel uhN traN poohr . . . ?) (*What time is there a train for . . . ?*)

Est-ce que le train est à l'heure ? (ehs kuh luh traN ey tah luhr?) (*Is the train on schedule/time?*)

To this last question, you may get any of the following answers: **Le train est à l'heure/en avance/en retard** (luh traN ey tah luhr/ahN nah-vahNs/ahN ruh-tahr) (*The train is on time/early/late*).

Talkin' the Talk

Julie, a young Canadian woman touring Paris, wants to visit Versailles, where Louis XIV's famous castle is located. She takes a day off from her group and heads to the train station, where she's about to try her luck on her own and buy a ticket for the ride to Versailles. (Track 30)

L'employé: **Bonjour, madame. Vous désirez ?**
bohN-zhoohr, mah-dahm. vooh dey-zee-rey?
Good morning, ma'am. Can I help you?

Julie: **Je voudrais un billet pour Versailles, s'il vous plaît.**
zhuh vooh-drey uhN bee-yey poohr vehr-sahy, seel vooh pley.
I'd like a ticket to Versailles, please.

L'employé:	**Aller-simple ou aller-retour ?** ah-ley-saN-pluh ooh ah-ley-ruh-toohr? *One way or round trip?*
Julie:	**Aller-retour, s'il vous plaît. Deuxième classe.** ah-ley-ruh-toohr, seel vooh pley. duh-zyehm klahs. *Round trip, please. Second class.*
L'employé:	**C'est pour combien de personnes ?** sey poohr kohN-byaN duh pehr-suhhn? *For how many people?*
Julie:	**Pour une personne, monsieur.** poohr ewn pehr-suhhn, muh-syuh. *For one person, sir.*
L'employé:	**Vous avez de la chance. J'ai encore une place. Ça fait douze euros.** vooh zah-vey duh lah shahNs. zhey ahN-kohr ewn plahs. sah fey doohz uh-roh. *You're lucky. I still have one seat. That'll be 12 euros.*
Julie:	**Est-ce que je dois changer de train ?** ehs kuh zhuh dwah shahN-zhey duh traN? *Do I have to change trains?*
L'employé:	**Oui, vous avez une correspondance à Issy.** wee, vooh zah-vey ewn koh-reh-spohN-dahNs ah ee-see. *Yes, you have a connecting train in Issy.*
Julie:	**Et de quel quai part le train ?** ey duh kehl key pahr luh traN? *And from which platform does the train leave?*
L'employé:	**Quai 12A [douze A].** key doohz ah. *Platform 12A.*
Julie:	**Merci. Au revoir.** mehr-see. ohr-vwahr. *Thank you. Good-bye.*

Book II

Exploring and Wandering About

Cruising Around by Car

If convenience and fast service are more important to you than economy, taking a taxi is a good way to get around. Or if you're more adventurous and like driving, you may want to rent a car. That way, you can stop wherever you want, visit local towns, meander through the **marchés** (mahr-shey) (*outdoor markets*), and change plans according to the weather or your mood. This section tells you what you need to know if a car is your vehicle of choice.

Hailing a taxi

Taxis are readily available at all airports and train stations as well as all over major cities. Although taxis come in all colors, depending on the country you're visiting, they're easily recognizable because of the international word on them: **Taxi.** Be prepared to pay in cash because some taxis don't take credit or debit cards. Here are some taxi-related terms:

- **le chauffeur de taxi** (luh shoh-fuhr duh tahk-see) (*cab driver*)
- **Je voudrais aller à . . .** (zhuh vooh-drey zah-ley ah . . .) (*I'd like to go to . . .*)
- **Où voulez-vous aller ?** (ooh vooh-ley-vooh zah-ley?) (*Where do you want to go?*)
- **le tarif** (luh tah-reef) (*fare*)
- **la station de taxi** (lah stah-syohN duh tahk-see) (*taxi stand*)

Although many taxi drivers in large international cities have a basic knowledge of English, have your destination address printed out to avoid any misunderstandings. Keep in mind that taxis have a passenger limit as well as a luggage limit.

In most European countries, expect to leave about a 10 percent tip on top of your taxi fare. Tipping is optional in Belgium, although rounding up to the nearest euro is customary.

Talkin' the Talk

Karen and Derek want to take a taxi from the airport to their hotel. They were lucky enough to get the attention of a taxi driver right away.

Le chauffeur de taxi: **Où voulez-vous aller ?**
ooh vooh-ley-vooh zah-ley?
Where do you want to go?

Karen: **Bruxelles, Hôtel Gillon, s'il vous plaît.**
brewk-sehl, oh-tehl zhee-lohN, seel vooh pley.
Brussels, Hotel Gillon, please.

Book II

Exploring and Wandering About

Le chauffeur de taxi: **Avec plaisir. C'est dans quelle rue ?**
ah-vehk pley-zeer. sey dahN kehl rew?
With pleasure. Which street is that on?

Derek: **Voyons . . . c'est 22 [vingt-deux] rue Albert. C'est combien ?**
vwah-yohN . . . sey vaNt-duh rew ahl-behr. sey kohN-byaN?
Let's see . . . it's 22 Albert Street. How much is it?

Le chauffeur de taxi: **Trente-cinq euros. C'est le tarif normal. Est-ce que je mets les valises dans le coffre ?**
trahNt-saNk uh-roh. sey luh tah-reef nohr-mahl. ehs kuh zhuh mey ley vah-leez dahN luh kuhh-fruh?
Thirty-five euros. That's the normal fare. Shall I put the suitcases in the trunk?

Karen: **Très bien, mais je garde mon sac à dos avec moi.**
trey byaN, mey zhuh gahrd mohN sahk ah doh ah-vehk mwah.
Very well, but I'm keeping my backpack with me.

Words to Know

la rue	lah rew	the street
C'est combien ?	sey kohN-byaN?	How much is it?
je mets	zhuh mey	I put
le coffre	luh kuhh-fruh	the trunk (of a vehicle)
garder	gahr-dey	to keep
le sac à dos	luh sahk ah doh	the backpack

Driving in a foreign land

Louer une voiture (looh-ey ewn vwah-tewr) (*renting a car*) in Europe may be a little more expensive than renting one in the United States. However, if you share the car with two or three others, this option may be less expensive than purchasing individual rail passes. If you decide to rent a car and drive yourself, do your research. Keep these points in mind:

✔ The minimum driving age for car rentals in Europe is between 21 and 25, and the maximum age is usually 70. If you're a younger or older driver, you may be asked to pay additional insurance against collision damage. Purchasing additional insurance anyway just for your peace of mind may be a good idea, but that's totally up to you. Check with your credit card company to see whether it covers the insurance on rental cars.

✔ When you're renting a car, make sure you tell the agency about your travel plans. Some agencies may have border restrictions or limits, so you may need to pay extra insurance fees for this travel. If you're renting a car in one country and want to drop it off in another, you may also be required to pay drop-off fees.

✔ In most countries, the only documentation you need to drive is your normal, valid driver's license. Some countries, though, may ask you for your *International Driving Permit,* or IDP, which is basically a translation of your license in many different languages. Getting an IDP is a good idea, especially if you aren't certain where your car travels may take you or if you find yourself stopped by the police. You can purchase an IDP for about $15 at any automobile association that's authorized by the Department of State to issue IDPs, such as AAA or CAA (Canadian Automobile Association). You need two passport-type photos as well as your valid driver's license to get an IDP.

✔ To avoid **une contravention** (ewn kohN-trah-vahN-syohN) (*a ticket*), keep in mind that **les limitations de vitesse** (ley lee-mee-tah-syohN duh vee-tehs) (*speed limits*) in France are approximately 130 kilometers per hour (80 miles per hour) on the highways, 90 kilometers per hour (55 miles per hour) on open roads, and 50 kilometers per hour (30 miles per hour) in the city. Speed limits — which are indicated by a round sign with a red border — are strictly enforced, and you pay a speeding fine on the spot. Also, the traffic arriving on the right always has **la priorité à droite** (lah pree-oh-ree-tey ah drwaht) (*the right of way* [Literally: *priority to the right*]).

✔ Many French **autoroutes** (oh-toh-rooht) (*highways*) require **des péages** (dey pey-ahzh) (*tolls*), and they aren't cheap. Always have coins handy, although most of the time you pick up a ticket at the point of entry and pay at the exit. In France, tollbooths usually accept credit cards: Just insert your ticket and then your credit card into a machine at the tollbooth, wait, get your receipt, and make sure you pull your card out again.

Here are some terms related to driving and **la circulation** (lah seer-kew-lah-syohN) (*traffic*):

✔ **le carrefour** (luh kahr-foohr) (*intersection*)

✔ **le demi-tour** (luh duh-mee-toohr) (*U-turn*)

✔ **l'embouteillage** (m) (lahN-booh-teh-yahzh) (*traffic jam*)

✔ **le piéton/la piétonne** (luh pyey-tohN/lah pyey-tuhhn) (*pedestrian*)

✔ **le pont** (luh pohN) (*bridge*)

✔ **ralentir** (rah-lahN-teer) (*to slow down*)

✔ **le rond-point** (luh rohN-pwaN) (*roundabout*)

✔ **rouler vite** (rooh-ley veet) (*to drive fast*)

✔ **le sens unique** (luh sahNs ew-neek) (*one way*)

✔ **la sortie** (lah sohr-tee) (*exit*)

✔ **le stationnement/le stationnement interdit** (luh stah-syuhhn-mahN/ luh stah-syuhhn-mahN aN-tehr-dee) (*parking/no parking*)

✔ **le trottoir** (luh troh-twahr) (*sidewalk*)

Filling up at the gas station

As you're probably aware, **faire le plein** (fehr luh plaN) (*to fill the gas tank*) in Europe — and specifically in France — costs more than it does in the United States. Don't get too excited when you see prices of 1.55 at the **station-service** (stah-syohN-sehr-vees) (*gas station*); that's in euros and per liter, not per gallon. A gallon is 3.78 liters. Although prices fluctuate, **l'essence** (ley-sahNs) (*gas*) is usually cheaper at supermarkets and hypermarkets than it is on major highways.

Just like in North America, in France you can decide which grade of **carburant** (kahr-bew-rahN) (*fuel*) you want: **sans-plomb** (sahN-plohN) (*unleaded*), **ordinaire** (ohr-dee-nehr) (*regular unleaded*), **super** (sew-pehr) (*super unleaded*), and **gazole/diesel** (gah-zuhhl/dyey-zehl) (*diesel*).

Gas stations on the major highways have **des pompistes** (dey pohN-peest) (*gas station attendants*), but others may not. Generally, you pump your gas first and then pay. Although you can pay a cashier with a credit card, a card may not work in the automated machines. Some European countries, including France, have adopted chip-and-pin cards, which are the only ones accepted at self-serve, pay-at-the-pump stations.

The following phrases can help you when you're looking to fill up the tank:

> **Où est-ce qu'il y a une station-service ?** (ooh ehs keel ee ah ewn stah-syohN-sehr-vees?) (*Where is there a gas station?*)
>
> **Est-ce qu'il y a une station-service près d'ici ?** (ehs keel ee ah ewn stah-syohN sehr-vees preh dee-see?) (*Is there a gas station near here?*)
>
> **Le plein, s'il vous plaît.** (luh plaN, seel vooh pley.) (*Fill it up, please.*)

When talking about unspecified quantities, French uses an article called the **partitif** (pahr-tee-teef) (*partitive*) because it describes a part of a quantity. You construct it by combining the preposition **de** (duh) (*of*) and the definite article **le**, **la**, or **le**, as follows:

- ✔ **de + le = du** (dew)
- ✔ **de + la = de la** (duh lah)
- ✔ **de + les = des** (dey)
- ✔ **de + l' = de l'** (duhl)

You can translate these constructions as *some,* as in **Je voudrais du carburant** (zhuh vooh-drey dew kahr-bew-rahN) (*I'd like some fuel*). Check out Chapter 2 of Book III for more info on partitive articles.

Here's a little advice: Fill up during the day at an attended station and keep some cash on hand in case the automated machines don't accept your credit card. Also, be aware that unlike gas stations on the highways, stations in town may be closed on Sundays.

Getting help when you have car trouble

Hopefully, your journey will be smooth, but if you have car trouble or see **un avertisseur lumineux** (uhN ah-vehr-tee-suhr lew-mee-nuh) (*a warning light*), you may need to talk to **un mécanicien** (uhN mey-kah-nee-syaN) (*a mechanic*). Here are some words and phrases that can help you identify what the trouble is:

- **la batterie** (lah bah-tree) (*battery*)
- **l'essuie-glace** (m) (ley-swee-glahs) (*windshield wiper*)
- **les freins** (m) (ley fraN) (*the brakes*)
- **le pare-brise** (luh pahr-breez) (*windshield*)
- **les phares** (m) (ley fahr) (*headlights*)
- **le pneu/le pneu crevé** (luh pnuh/luh pnuh kruh-vey) (*tire/flat tire*)
- **tomber (être) en panne** (tohN-bey [eh-truh] ahN pahn) (*to break down [car]*)
- **vérifier (les niveaux)** (vey-ree-fyey [ley nee-voh]) (*check [the levels]*)

Deciphering road signs

You can't drive safely without being able to understand **les panneaux routiers** (ley pah-noh rooh-tyey) (*road signs*). Although many signs are easily recognizable, others have less obvious meanings. Here are some important road signs:

- **arrêt** (m) (ah-rey) (*stop*)
- **cédez le passage** (sey-dey luh pah-sahzh) (*yield*)
- **chaussée glissante** (f) (shoh-sey glee-sahNt) (*slippery road*)
- **chaussée rétrécie** (f) (shoh-sey rey-trey-see) (*road narrows*)
- **interdiction** (f) **de faire demi-tour** (aN-tehr-deek-syohN duh fehr duh-mee-toohr) (*no U-turn*)
- **obligation** (f) **de tourner à gauche** (oh-blee-gah-syohN duh toohr-ney ah gohsh) (*left turn only*)

- ✔ **passage interdit** (m) (pah-sahzh aN-tehr-dee) (*no entry*)

- ✔ **passage piéton** (m) (pah-sahzh pyey-tohN) (*pedestrian crossing*)

- ✔ **risque** (m) **de chutes de pierre** (reesk duh shewt duh pyehr) (*falling rocks*)

- ✔ **sens unique** (m) (sahNs ew-neek) (*one way*)

- ✔ **travaux** (m) (trah-voh) (*road work*)

- ✔ **virage** (m) **à droite/gauche** (vee-rahzh ah drwaht/gohsh) (*bend to the right/left*)

Road signs are distinguishable by shape, by color, and by graphics. Here are a few visuals you should become familiar with:

- ✔ Triangles with a red border indicate a warning or a danger. Example: **Chaussée glissante**.

- ✔ Round signs with a thick red border indicate restrictions, including speed limits. Example: **Interdiction de faire demi-tour**.

- ✔ Round signs with blue background indicate what you're required to do. Example: **Obligation de tourner à gauche**.

- ✔ Square and rectangular signs guide you. Example: **Autoroute** (f) (oh-toh-rooht) (*highway*), which, in France, always begins with a capital **A** (for **Autoroute**) followed by the highway number.

Chapter 6

Dealing with Emergencies

In This Chapter

▶ Addressing health issues

▶ Handling police matters

*H*opefully, the only help you'll ever need to ask for when you're traveling is where the nearest bus terminal is or what local cuisine your hosts recommend. But if you do find yourself in an emergency situation, you can use the information in this chapter to get the help you need.

Getting Help Fast

If you're ever in an accident or have an emergency, use the following French phrases to call for help:

- ✔ **À l'aide ! Vite !** (ah lehd! veet!) (*Help! Fast!*)
- ✔ **Au secours !** (oh skoohr!) (*Help!*)
- ✔ **Au feu !** (oh fuh!) (*Fire!*)
- ✔ **Au voleur !** (oh voh-luhr!) (*Catch the thief!*)
- ✔ **Police !** (poh-lees!) (*Police!*)

The emergency phone number for the entire European Union is 112. It works from all phones in France, including cell phones, and it's free. When you call this number, it connects you to the local first responders, much like 911 does in the United States. Be sure you give the operator your location, the type of emergency, and your telephone number. (See more on placing calls in Chapter 5 of Book I)

You may find that knowing specific emergency numbers for the country you're visiting is helpful. In France, the numbers are as follows (in the provinces, all the emergency numbers are on one page of the phone book):

- **La police** (lah poh-lees) (*police*): 17
- **Le SAMU** (luh sah-mew) (*Urgent Medical Aid Service*): 15
- **les (sapeurs-)pompiers** (m) (ley [sah-puhr]-pohN-pyey) (*the firemen*): 18

French emergency medical care is provided by several organizations under public health control and under the leadership of **le SAMU (Service d'Aide Médicale Urgente)** (luh sah-mew [sehr-vees dehd mey-dee-kahl ewr-zhahNt]) (*Urgent Medical Aid Service*). **Le SAMU** has a mix of resources, such as first response vehicles, ambulances, and mobile intensive care units with physicians on board.

Chances are that one of the first responders called to the scene will speak enough English to communicate with you. Just in case, you can always ask for someone who speaks English by saying **Est-ce qu'il y a quelqu'un qui parle anglais ?** (ehs keel ee ah kehl-kuhN kee pahrl ahN-gley?) (*Is there someone who speaks English?*)

The French are required by law to provide assistance in an emergency. **La non-assistance à personne en danger** (lah nuhh-nah-sees-tahNs ah pehr-suhhn ahN dahN-zhey) (*failure to assist a person in danger*) is a punishable crime.

Fixing What Ails You: Receiving Medical Attention

France has one of the best healthcare systems in the world. Rest assured that you'll receive world-class care, whether you're simply not feeling well and want to discuss your symptoms with **un médecin/un docteur** (uhN meyd-saN/ uhN dohk-tuhr) (*a doctor*) or you've been hurt in an accident.

If you have a medical concern — you have **une maladie** (ewn mah-lah-dee) (*an illness*), for example — you may simply need to go **chez le médecin** (shey luh meyd-saN) (*to the doctor's office*) or **au cabinet médical** (oh kah-bee-ney mey-dee-kahl) (*to the medical office*). To do so, you need to **prendre rendez-vous** (prahN-druh rahN-dey-vooh) (*make an appointment*). Although doctors usually have consultation hours for patients who don't have appointments, you may have to wait a long time. (If you're too ill to go to the doctor, don't worry. Doctors can come to your hotel room or wherever you're staying.)

Your hotel can provide the addresses and phone numbers of local doctors or specialists. You can also get this information from a pharmacist. After hours or on Sundays or holidays, the local **gendarmerie** (zhahN-dahr-muh-ree) (*police station*) can provide the number of **le médecin de garde** (luh meyd-saN duh gahrd) (*the doctor on duty*) or **la pharmacie de garde** (lah fahr-mah-see duh gahrd) (*the 24-hour pharmacy*).

If you've been in an accident, you may need to go to **un hôpital** (uhN noh-pee-tahl) (*a hospital*) or **les urgences** (f) (ley zewr-zhahNs) (*the emergency room*). In such an emergency, you can use the following phrases:

Book II

Exploring and Wandering About

- ✔ **Il me faut un docteur.** (eel muh foh uhN dohk-tuhr.) (*I need a doctor.*)

- ✔ **Il lui faut une ambulance.** (eel lwee foh ewn ahN-bew-lahNs.) (*He/She needs an ambulance.*)

Before leaving home, check with your insurance provider to see whether your policy covers emergencies or doctor visits abroad. If emergencies or medical treatments abroad aren't covered, you may need to purchase coverage for the dates you're traveling. If you need any sort of medical services while abroad, simply show your U.S. provider's proof of your insurance. Also be sure to call your insurance company to explain what's happening. Usually, you have to pay your bill (with your credit card) when you receive medical care, but your insurance company will reimburse you when you present the detailed bill back home. Remember to keep all your receipts and any **feuilles de soins** (fuhy duh swaN) (*medical claim forms*) that you sign.

Getting the preliminaries out of the way

When you go to the doctor, he or she will undoubtedly ask you a few questions, such as **Où avez-vous mal ?** (ooh ah-vey-vooh mahl?) (*Where does it hurt?*) or **Quels sont vos symptômes ?** (kehl sohN voh saNp-tohm?) (*What are your symptoms?*).

To ask how you feel, a doctor may say **Comment vous sentez-vous ?** (koh-mahN vooh sahN-tey vooh?). You can answer **Je me sens (très) mal** (zhuh muh sahN [trey] mahl) (*I feel [very] bad*). The verb **se sentir** (suh sahN-teer) is an irregular verb that requires reflexive pronouns. Here's how to conjugate it in the present tense:

Conjugated Form	Pronunciation	Translation
je me sens	zhuh muh sahN	*I feel*
tu te sens	tew tuh sahN	*you feel*
il/elle/on se sent	eel/ehl/ohN suh sahN	*he/she/it/one feels*
nous nous sentons	nooh nooh sahN-tohN	*we feel*
vous vous sentez	vooh vooh sahN-tey	*you feel*
ils/elles se sentent	eel/ehl suh sahnt	*they feel*

If you've been involved in an accident and hurt yourself, a frequently used idiomatic expression is the question **Qu'est-ce qui s'est passé ?** (kehs kee sey pah-sey?) (*What happened?*). Another common expression is **Ça fait mal !** (sah fey mahl!) (*That hurts!*) You'll want to memorize both of these.

The doctor may ask you questions, such as the following, to determine whether you have other conditions he or she needs to know about:

- **Êtes-vous cardiaque ?** (eht-vooh kahr-dyahk?) (*Do you have a heart condition?*)

- **Êtes-vous diabétique ?** (eht-vooh dyah-bey-teek?) (*Are you a diabetic?*)

- **Avez-vous de l'hypertension ?** (ah-vey-vooh duh lee-pehr-tahN-syohN?) (*Do you have high blood pressure?*)

- **Avez-vous des allergies ?** (ah-vey-vooh dey zah-lehr-zhee?) (*Do you have any allergies ?*)

- **Prenez-vous des médicaments ?** (pruh-ney-vooh dey mey-dee-kah-mahN?) (*Are you taking any medications?*)

Of course, you can also offer this information before you're asked by using these phrases:

- **Je suis cardiaque.** (zhuh swee kahr-dyahk.) (*I have a heart condition.*)

- **J'ai de l'hypertension.** (zhey duh lee-pehr-tahN-syohN.) (*I have high blood pressure.*)

- **Je suis diabétique/allergique à . . .** (zhuh swee dyah-bey-teek/ah-lehr-zheek ah . . .) (*I'm diabetic/allergic to . . .*)

Talking about your specific complaint

With your basic information squared away, the doctor will want to hear about the particular issue that brings you to the office. This section helps you explain the problem.

Telling the doctor where it hurts

To describe what's bothering you, you need to be able to note which body part hurts or feels uncomfortable:

- **la bouche** (lah boohsh) (*mouth*)
- **le bras** (luh brah) (*arm*)
- **la cheville** (lah shuh-veey) (*ankle*)
- **les côtes** (f) (ley koht) (*ribs*)
- **le cou** (luh kooh) (*neck*)
- **le doigt** (luh dwah) (*finger*)
- **le dos** (luh doh) (*back*)
- **l'épaule** (f) (ley-pohl) (*shoulder*)
- **le ventre/l'estomac** (m) (luh vahN-truh/leh-stoh-mah) (*stomach*)
- **la figure** (lah fee-gewr) (*face*)
- **le genou** (luh zhuh-nooh) (*knee*)
- **la gorge** (lah guhhrzh) (*throat*)
- **la jambe** (lah zhahNb) (*leg*)
- **la main** (lah maN) (*hand*)
- **le nez** (luh ney) (*nose*)
- **le pied** (luh pyey) (*foot*)
- **la poitrine** (lah pwah-treen) (*chest*)
- **l'œil/les yeux** (m) (luhy/ley zyuh) (*eye/eyes*)
- **l'oreille** (f) (loh-rehy) (*ear*)
- **l'orteil** (m) (lohr-tehy) (*toe*)
- **la tête** (lah teht) (*head*)

To tell the doctor that something hurts, use the expression **J'ai mal à . . .** (zhey mahl ah . . .) (*My . . . hurts*) and insert the word for the body part. Note that **à** may contract to **au** (**à** + **le**) or **aux** (**à** + **les**): If the body part is masculine singular, use **au**; if it's masculine or feminine plural, use **aux**. (You can read about contractions in Chapter 2 of Book III.) Here are some examples:

J'ai mal au bras. (zhey mahl oh brah.) (*My arm hurts.*)

J'ai mal à la poitrine. (zhey mahl ah lah pwah-treen.) (*My chest hurts.*)

J'ai mal à l'oreille. (zhey mahl ah loh-rehy) (*My ear hurts.*)

J'ai mal aux pieds. (zhey mahl oh pyeh.) (*My feet hurt.*)

You can also indicate what hurts on someone else by changing the subject of the sentence and conjugating the verb **avoir** appropriately (check out Chapter 3 of Book III for info on subject pronouns and present tense verb conjugations):

Il a mal au dos. (eel ah mahl oh doh.) (*His back hurts.*)

Nous avons mal à la tête. (nooh zah-vohN mahl ah lah teht.) (*We have headaches.*)

Describing other symptoms

If you don't feel well — you have a fever or feel nauseous or faint, for example — you use the verb **avoir** (*to have*). You can say **j'ai . . .** (zhey . . .) (*I have . . .*) and follow it with the appropriate symptom, such as the following:

- ✔ **de l'asthme** (duh lahs-muh) (*asthma*)
- ✔ **de la fièvre** (duh lah fyeh-vruh) (*a fever*)
- ✔ **de la température** (duh lah tahN-pey-rah-tewr) (*a temperature*)
- ✔ **des problèmes à respirer** (dey proh-blehm ah reh-spee-rey) (*problems breathing*)
- ✔ **une coupure** (ewn kooh-pewr) (*a cut*)
- ✔ **la diarrhée** (lah dyah-rey) (*diarrhea*)
- ✔ **une éruption** (ewn ey-rewp-syohN) (*a rash*)
- ✔ **la grippe** (lah greep) (*the flu*)
- ✔ **des vomissements** (dey voh-mees-mahN) (*vomiting*)
- ✔ **une migraine** (ewn mee-grehn) (*a migraine*)
- ✔ **le nez bouché** (luh ney booh-shey) (*a stuffy nose*)
- ✔ **le nez qui coule** (luh ney kee koohl) (*a runny nose*)
- ✔ **un (gros) rhume** (uhN [groh] rewm) (*an [awful] cold*)
- ✔ **des taches rouges** (dey tahsh roohzh) (*red spots*)
- ✔ **la toux** (lah tooh) (*a cough*)

Keep in mind that the English translation may not actually include the verb *to have,* as these examples show:

J'ai de la nausée/J'ai mal au cœur. (zhey duh lah noh-zey/zhey mahl oh kuhr.) (*I'm nauseous.*)

J'ai des vertiges. (zhey dey vehr-teezh.) (*I'm dizzy.*)

Talkin' the Talk

Julia hasn't been feeling well, so she calls her doctor's office to make an appointment. She explains her symptoms to the receptionist. (Track 31)

Julia:	**Bonjour. C'est Julia Mills au téléphone. Est-ce que je pourrais prendre rendez-vous le plus tôt possible ?** bohN-zhoohr. sey zhew-lyah meels oh tey-ley-fuhhn. ehs kuh zhuh pooh-rey prahN-druh rahN-dey-vooh luh plew toh poh-see-bluh? *Hello. This is Julia Mills calling. Could I have an appointment as soon as possible?*
La réceptionniste:	**De quoi souffrez-vous ?** duh kwah sooh-frey-vooh? *What are you suffering from?*
Julia:	**Je suis tombée et maintenant j'ai très mal à la tête.** zhuh swee tohN-bey ey maN-tuh-nahN zhey trey mahl ah lah teht. *I fell and now I have a bad headache.*
La réceptionniste:	**Avez-vous mal au cœur ?** ah-vey-vooh mahl oh kuhr? *Do you feel nauseous?*
Julia:	**Oui. Je ne me sens pas très bien.** Wee. zhuh nuh muh sahN pah trey byaN. *Yes. I don't feel very well.*
La réceptionniste:	**Pouvez-vous venir tout de suite ?** pooh-vey-vooh vuh-neer toohd-sweet? *Can you come in right away?*
Julia:	**Oui, merci. À tout à l'heure.** wee, mehr-see. ah tooh tah luhr. *Yes, thank you. See you shortly.*

Saying that you broke, sprained, twisted, or cut something

In English, you use possessive adjectives before body parts: For example, *I broke my foot*. But French instead uses definite articles — **le/la/les** (*the*) — before body parts. To express that you've cut a part of your body, sprained or twisted your ankle, or broken your arm, you use a reflexive verb, such as

se casser (suh kah-sey) (*to break [oneself]*). In French, you can say **je me suis cassé le pied** (zhuh muh swee kah-sey luh pyey), which translates literally as *I broke the foot to me* or *I broke myself the foot*.

Je me suis cassé is conjugated in the **passé composé** (pah-sey kohN-poh-zey), a compound past tense used for actions that happened at a precise moment and were completed in the past. This tense requires an auxiliary verb and a past participle. To form the past tense of reflexive verbs, take the present tense conjugation of the auxiliary verb **être** (eh-truh) (*to be*) and follow it with a past participle. The past participle of **casser** is **cassé**.

Here's the conjugation of the verb **se casser** in the **passé composé** (see Chapter 1 of Book V for more on the **passé composé** of reflexive verbs):

Conjugation	Pronunciation	Translation
je me suis cassé	zhuh muh swee kah-sey	*I broke my*
tu t'es cassé	tew tey kah-sey	*you broke your*
il/elle/on s'est cassé	eel/ehl/ohN sey kah-sey	*he/she/one broke his/her/one's*
nous nous sommes cassé	nooh nooh suhhm kah-sey	*we broke our*
vous vous êtes cassé	vooh vooh zeht kah-sey	*you broke your*
ils/elles se sont cassé	eel/ehl suh sohN kah-sey	*they broke their*

Here are some example sentences:

> **Je me suis cassé la jambe.** (zhuh muh swee kah-sey lah zhahNb.) (*I broke my leg.*)

> **Tu t'es cassé la cheville.** (tew tey kah-sey lah shuh-veey.) (*You broke your ankle.*)

> **Il/Elle s'est cassé le bras.** (eel/ehl sey kah-sey luh brah.) (*He/She broke his/her arm.*)

> **Nous nous sommes cassé les orteils.** (nooh nooh sohm kah-sey ley zohr-tehy.) (*We broke our toes.*)

> **Vous vous êtes cassé les doigts.** (vooh vooh zeht kah-sey ley dwah.) (*You broke your fingers.*)

> **Ils/Elles se sont cassé les côtes.** (eel/ehl suh sohN kah-sey ley koht.) (*They broke their ribs.*)

Follow this pattern with other reflexive verbs and then add the affected part of the body. Here are some examples:

✔ **Je me suis foulé . . .** (zhuh muh swee fooh-ley . . .) (*I sprained . . .*)

✔ **Je me suis tordu . . .** (zhuh muh swee tohr-dew . . .) (*I twisted . . .*)

✔ **Je me suis coupé . . .** (zhuh muh swee kooh-pey . . .) (*I cut . . .*)

Undergoing a medical examination

The doctor or nurse will examine you and may want to **prendre votre pouls** (prahN-druh vuhh-truh poohl) (*take your pulse*) and **ausculter votre cœur** (oh-skewl-tey vuhh-truh kuhr) (*listen to your heart*) or even do the following, as warranted:

✔ **prendre votre tension artérielle** (prahN-druh vuhh-truh tahN-syohN ahr-tey-ryehl) (*to take your blood pressure*)

✔ **faire une prise de sang** (fehr ewn preez duh sahN) (*to take/draw blood*)

✔ **faire une radiographie** (fehr ewn rah-dyoh-grah-fee) (*to do an X-ray*)

After the exam, the doctor may **prescrire des médicaments** (preh-skreer dey mey-dee-kah-mahN) (*prescribe medication*), which you can get at a pharmacy (head to the following section for details).

Book II

Exploring and Wandering About

Talkin' the Talk

Julia arrives at the doctor's office and is given an examination. (Track 32)

Le médecin: **Depuis quand vous sentez-vous comme ça ?**
duh-pwee kahN vooh sahN-tey-vooh kuhhm sah?
How long have you been feeling like this?

Julia: **Depuis hier, quand je suis tombée.**
duh-pwee yehr, kahN zhuh swee tohN-bey.
Since yesterday, when I fell.

Le médecin: **Avez-vous perdu l'appétit ?**
ah-vey-vooh pehr-dew lah-pey-tee?
Have you lost your appetite?

Julia: **Oui, et j'ai mal au cœur.**
wee, ey zhey mahl oh kuhr.
Yes, and I feel nauseous.

Le médecin: **Vous avez une légère commotion cérébrale. Reposez-vous bien pendant quelques jours. Est-ce que vous prenez des médicaments ?**
vooh zah-vey ewn ley-zhehr koh-moh-syohN sey-rey-brahl. ruh-poh-zey-vooh byaN pahN-dahN kehl-kuh zhoohr. ehs kuh vooh pruh-ney dey mey-dee-kah-mahN?
You have a mild concussion. Take it very easy for a few days. Are you taking any medication?

Julia: **Non. Mais je suis allergique à l'aspirine.**
nohN. mey zhuh swee ah-lehr-zheek ah lah-spee-reen.
No. But I'm allergic to aspirin.

Le médecin: **Bon. Voici une ordonnance en cas de douleur. Prenez un comprimé toutes les quatre heures et revenez dans trois jours.**
bohN. vwah-see ewn ohr-doh-nahNs ahN kah duh dooh-luhr. pruh-ney uhN kohN-pree-mey tooht ley kahtr uhr ey ruh-vuh-ney dahN trwah zhoohr.
Good. Here's a prescription in case of pain. Take one pill every four hours and come back in three days.

Julia: **Merci, docteur. Au revoir.**
mehr-see, dohk-tuhr. ohr-vwahr.
Thank you, doctor. Good-bye.

Words to Know

depuis quand ?	duh-pwee kahN?	since when?
depuis hier	duh-pwee yehr	since yesterday
Je suis tombé(e).	zhuh swee tohN-bey.	I fell.
perdre l'appétit	pehr-druh lah-pey-tee	to lose one's appetite
une commotion cérébrale	ewn koh-moh-syohN sey-rey-brahl	a concussion
pendant quelques jours	pahN-dahN kehl-kuh zhoohr	for a few days

Going to a pharmacy

A French pharmacy is easily recognizable by the big green cross on it. Pharmacies are usually open Monday through Saturday from 9:00 a.m. to 7:00 p.m. and are closed on Sundays. For night and Sunday hours, you can always find **une pharmacie de garde** (ewn fahr-mah-see duh gahrd) (*a 24-hour pharmacy*. Literally: *a pharmacy on duty*) nearby.

Seeing the pharmacist for minor ailments

French pharmacists' duties far surpass those of the pharmacists in the United States, so the pharmacy is often the first place you go in France for minor medical concerns. In addition to filling **des ordonnances** (dey zohr-doh-nahNs) (*prescriptions*), the highly trained **pharmacien/pharmacienne** (fahr-mah-syaN/fahr-mah-syehn) (*pharmacist*) can dress wounds; give advice on how to remedy a bad cold, a migraine, a sunburn, and so on; and provide nutritional advice.

When you go to a pharmacist for medical care, you can ask **Pourriez-vous me donner un conseil ?** (pooh-ryey-vooh muh duhh-ney uhN kohN-sehy?) (*Could you give me some advice?*). If the problem is more serious and requires further medical attention, the pharmacist will refer you to the doctors in the area.

Book II

Exploring and Wandering About

Picking up medications and medical supplies

In France, all **médicaments** (mey-dee-kah-mahN) (*medications*), even things like aspirin, are sold only in pharmacies, not in supermarkets or anywhere else. Use a phrase like **je voudrais . . .** (zhuh vooh-drey . . .) (*I would like . . .*) or **J'ai besoin de . . .** (zhey buh-zwaN duh . . .) (*I need . . .*) to request any of the following items:

- ✔ **les antalgiques** (m) (ley zahN-tahl-zheek) (*analgesics, mild pain relievers*)
- ✔ **les antibiotiques** (m) (ley zahN-tee-byoh-teek) (*antibiotics*)
- ✔ **les antihistaminiques** (m) (ley zahN-tee-ees-tah-mee-neek) (*antihistamines*)
- ✔ **l'aspirine** (f) (lah-spee-reen) (*aspirin*)
- ✔ **le décongestionnant** (f) (luh dey-kohN-zhes-tyoh-nahN) (*decongestant*)
- ✔ **les gouttes** (f) **pour les yeux secs** (ley gooht poohr ley zyuh sehk) (*drops for dry eyes*)
- ✔ **les pastilles** (f) (ley pah-steey) (*lozenges*)
- ✔ **le sirop (pour la toux)** (luh see-roh [poohr lah tooh]) (*syrup [cough syrup]*)
- ✔ **les vitamines** (f) (ley vee-tah-meen) (*vitamins*)

If you need medication, provide the generic name of the medication to the pharmacist because the name brand may not exist in the country where you're traveling. For example, you can say **acétaminophène** (ah-sey-tah-mee-noh-fehn) (*acetaminophen*) rather than Tylenol or **ibuprofène** (ee-bew-proh-fehn) (*ibuprofen*) rather than Advil or Motrin.

Even though you probably won't need a fully stocked **trousse de secours** (troohs duh suh-koohr) (*first-aid kit*), you can also get some basic items like **de l'alcool** (duh lahl-kuhhl) (*[rubbing] alcohol*) and **des pensements** (dey pahN-smahN) (*bandages*) at pharmacies, too.

Braving the dentist

Anything can happen while traveling. You may get **une rage de dents** (ewn razh duh dahN) (*a violent toothache*) or lose a filling. In these situations, you can ask for the name of a local **dentiste** (f) (dahN-teest) (*dentist*) at your hotel or inquire at the nearest pharmacy. Here's some dental vocabulary:

- ✔ **un abcès** (uhN nahp-sey) (*an abscess*)
- ✔ **une couronne cassée** (ewn kooh-ruhhn kah-sey) (*a broken crown*)
- ✔ **la dent (sensible)** (lah dahN [sahN-see-bluh]) (*[sensitive] tooth*)
- ✔ **les gencives saignantes** (f) (ley zhahN-seev seh-nyahNt) (*bleeding gums*)
- ✔ **le plombage est tombé** (luh plohN-bahzh ey tohN-bey) (*the filling fell out*)

Handling Legal Matters

Most vacations and trips take place without any issues that would require you to talk to the police or need help from your consulate. But you may find yourself in a situation where such conversations are necessary. Perhaps your wallet or purse has been stolen, you've witnessed an accident, or you've lost your passport. This section provides the information you need to deal with such incidents.

Talking to the police

You should report any accident, emergency, theft, and so on to **le commissariat de police** (luh koh-mee-sah-ryah duh poh-lees) (*the police station*) in major cities or to **la gendarmerie** (lah zhahN-dahr-muh-ree) in smaller towns. (See the earlier section "Getting Help Fast" for emergency numbers.) To find the nearest police station, you can say **Où est le commissariat de police le plus proche ?** (ooh ey luh koh-mee-sah-ryah duh poh-lees luh plew prohsh?).

There, you can explain your purpose by saying **Je veux signaler . . .** (zhuh vuh see-nyah-ley . . .) (*I want to report . . .*) and filling in with the following phrases:

- **un accident** (uhN nahk-see-dahN) (*an accident*)
- **une agression** (ewn ah-greh-syohN) (*a mugging*)
- **un cambriolage** (uhN kahN-bree-oh-lahzh) (*a burglary*)
- **un vol** (uhN vuhhl) (*a theft*)

At this point, the conversation is likely to go beyond the French you know. In that case, you can say **Est-ce qu'il y a quelqu'un qui parle anglais ?** (ehs keel ee ah kehl-kuhN kee pahrl ahN-gley?) (*Is there anyone who speaks English?*)

Book II

Exploring and Wandering About

Reporting an accident

In the event of an accident in a town or city, report the accident to **un agent de police** (uhN nah-zhahN duh poh-lees) (*a police officer*). Report an accident on a country road to **un gendarme** (uhN zhahN-dahrm) (*a police officer*). You can say **Il y a eu un accident . . .** (eel ee ah ew uhN nahk-see-dahN . . .) (*There has been an accident . . .*) and then follow up with these phrases:

- **sur l'autoroute** (sewr loh-toh-rooht) (*on the highway*)
- **sur la route** (sewr lah rooht) (*on the road*)
- **près de . . .** (preh duh . . .) (*near . . .*)

When the police arrive, they usually ask a great many questions, such as the following:

Est-ce que je peux voir votre . . . (ehs kuh zhuh puh vwahr vuhh-truh . . .) (*Can I see your . . .*)

- **permis de conduire ?** (pehr-mee duh kohN-dweer?) (*driver's license?*)
- **carte d'assurance ?** (kahrt dah-sew-rahNs?) (*insurance card?*)
- **carte grise ?** (kahrt greez?) (*vehicle registration document?* Literally: *gray card*)

Quel est votre nom ? (kehl ey vuhh-truh nohN) (*What is your name?*)

Quelle est votre adresse ? (kehl ey vuhh-trah-drehs?) (*What is your address?*)

À quelle heure est-ce que ça s'est passé ? (ah kehl uhr ehs kuh sah sey pah-sey?) (*At what time did this happen?*)

Est-ce qu'il y a des témoins ? (ehs keel ee ah dey tey-mwaN?) (*Are there any witnesses?*)

The following phrases may help you explain what happened:

> **Il m'est rentré dedans.** (eel mey rahN-trey duh-dahN.) (*He ran into me.*)

> **Elle a conduit trop vite/près.** (ehl ah kohN-dwee troh veet/preh.) (*She drove too fast/close.*)

> **Je faisais . . . kilomètres à l'heure.** (zhuh fuh-zey . . . kee-loh-mehtr ah luhr) (*I was doing . . . kilometers per hour.*)

The police may also say **Vous devez venir au commissariat pour faire une déposition** (vooh duh-vey vuh-neer oh koh-mee-sah-ryah poohr fehr ewn dey-poh-zee-syohN) (*You have to come to the station to make a statement*) or **Vous devez payer une amende** (vooh duh-vey pey-yey ewn ah-mahNd) (*You have to pay a fine*).

At any time, feel free to say **Je voudrais un interprète/un avocat** (zhuh vooh-drey zuhN naN-tehr-preht/zuhN nah-voh-kah) (*I'd like an interpreter/a lawyer*).

Talkin' the Talk

André stops at an intersection, and the driver behind him fails to stop and hits him. A police officer is called to the scene. (Track 33)

Le gendarme:	**Qu'est-ce qui s'est passé ?** kehs kee sey pah-sey? *What happened?*
André:	**Je m'arrêtais au feu rouge quand cette voiture m'est rentrée dedans.** zhuh mah-reh-tey oh fuh roohzh kahN seht vwah-tewr mey rahN-trey duh-dahN. *I was stopping at the red light when this car ran into me.*
Le gendarme:	**Êtes-vous blessé ?** eht-vooh bley-sey? *Are you hurt?*
André:	**Non, monsieur, mais le pare-chocs est bosselé.** nohN, muh-syuh, mey luh pahr-shohk ey buhhs-ley. *No, sir, but the bumper is dented.*

Le gendarme:	**Est-ce que je peux voir votre permis de conduire et votre carte grise ?**
	ehs kuh zhuh puh vwahr vuhh-truh pehr-mee duh kohN-dweer ey vuhh-truh kahrt greez?
	Can I see your license and your vehicle registration?
André:	**Les voici.**
	ley vwah-see.
	Here they are.

Book II

Exploring and Wandering About

Words to Know

s'arrêter au feu rouge	sah-reh-tey oh fuh roozh	to stop at a red light
blessé	bley-sey	hurt, wounded
le pare-chocs	luh pahr-shohk	bumper
bosselé	buhhs-ley	dented

Describing what was stolen

If things have been stolen from you, a police officer will ask **Qu'est-ce qui vous manque ?** (kehs kee vooh mahNk?) (*What is missing?*). You can say **On m'a volé . . .** (ohN mah voh-ley . . .) (*They stole . . .*) and add the item stolen. Here are some items that are commonly stolen:

- **mes cartes** (f) **de crédit** (mey kahrt duh krey-dee) (*my credit cards*)
- **mon appareil-photo** (mohN nah-pah-rehy-foh-toh) (*my camera*)
- **mon argent** (mohN nahr-zhahN) (*my money*)
- **mon passeport** (mohN pahs-pohr) (*my passport*)
- **mon porte-monnaie** (mohN pohrt-moh-ney) (*my wallet*)
- **mon sac** (mohN sahk) (*my bag*)

The officer may also ask **Pouvez-vous décrire la personne ?** (pooh-vey-vooh dey-kreer lah pehr-suhhn?) (*Can you describe the person?*). If you happened to see the culprit, you can say **C'était quelqu'un . . .** (sey-tey kehl-kuhN . . .) (*It was someone . . .*) and then fill in the following descriptors:

- **aux cheveux blonds/bruns/roux/noirs/gris** (oh shuh-vuh blohN/bruhN/rooh/nwahr/gree) (*with blond/brown/red/black/gray hair*)

- **d'environ . . . ans** (dahN-vee-rohN . . . ahN) (*of about . . . years [of age]*)

- **grand(e)/petit(e)** (grahN[d]/puh-tee[t]) (*tall/short*)

- **mince/gros(se)** (maNs/groh[s]) (*skinny/fat*)

- **un peu chauve** (uhN puh shohv) (*balding*)

You may also be able to describe what that person was wearing. Go to Chapter 6 of Book I for clothing-related vocabulary.

Getting legal help

As a foreigner, you may feel overwhelmed and welcome some legal help. You can make one of the following requests:

J'ai besoin d'un avocat qui parle anglais. (zhey buh-zwaN duhN nah-voh-kah kee pahrl ahN-gley.) (*I need a lawyer who speaks English.*)

Je voudrais téléphoner à un(e) ami(e) en ville. (zhuh vooh-drey tey-ley-fuhh-ney ah uhN/ewn ah-mee ahN veel.) (*I'd like to call a friend in town.*)

Je dois contacter le consulat. (zhuh dwah kohN-tahk-tey luh kohN-sew-lah.) (*I have to contact the consulate.*)

While you're in a foreign country, the laws of that country override the laws of your own. In an emergency, your embassy is the most appropriate place to get help. Its staff is on your side, more so than any local lawyer or police.

Book III
Building the Grammatical Foundation for Communication

The 5th Wave   By Rich Tennant

"What do you say – formal or informal greeting?"

In this book . . .

In this book, we lead you gently through the building blocks of French — mainly becoming familiar with the parts of speech and conjugating verbs in the present tense. We introduce you to nouns, gender, and number, which provide the foundation for grammatical agreement. Being able to talk about *my book* versus *this book* with possessive and demonstrative adjectives makes a big difference in your French skills, so we cover them, too. You also become adept at understanding instructions and instructing others on what to do in some common situations. You also find out how to ask and answer questions.

Here are the contents of Book III at a glance:

Chapter 1

Building Strong Sentences with the Parts of Speech

*W*ords are classified based on their *parts of speech* — verbs, nouns, pronouns, articles, adjectives, adverbs, prepositions, conjunctions, and interjections. A word's part of speech depends on how the word is used. Knowing which roles each word can play allows you to put words in the right order and make sure all the pieces fit together in a sentence.

This chapter familiarizes you with key grammatical words and concepts so that when you dig deeper into grammatical units, you recognize them easily. We provide a quick course on identifying and using various parts of speech that make French sentences grammatically correct. We also give you some guidance on finding the correct word — with the right meaning and part of speech — in a bilingual dictionary.

Action! Getting the Lowdown on Verbs

A *verb* is a word that indicates an action (for example, **je parle** means *I speak*) or a state of being (for example, **je suis optimiste** means *I am* optimistic). Verbs change in several ways for the following reasons:

✔ **Time:** Verbs change to indicate that the action or state of mind is in the present, the future, or the past. These time concepts are called *tenses*.

✔ **Person:** Verbs change according to who or what is performing the action of the verb. These variable forms are called *conjugated* forms of the verb.

✔ **Mood:** Verbs change to convey commands (the imperative mood), to suggest consequences to hypothetical situations (the conditional mood), and to suggest certainty (the indicative mood) or uncertainty (the subjunctive mood).

We explain various conjugations, tenses, and moods throughout Books III, IV, and V (check the index for specific tenses and moods).

To figure out which form of a French verb to use, you have to know whether the verb is regular, regular with a spelling change, or irregular. In the present tense, there are three types of regular verbs, several types of spelling-change verbs, and an assortment of irregular verbs:

✔ **Regular verbs:** These verbs shouldn't cause any undue stress. They follow standard conjugation rules for verbs that end in **-er**, **-ir**, or **-re**. You remove the ending from the _infinitive_ (the unconjugated form of the verb that you find in the dictionary) and then add a new ending.

✔ **Spelling-change verbs:** When studying French verbs, you encounter some verbs that undergo spelling changes in the _stem,_ the part of the word you're left with after you take off the **-er**, **-ir**, or **-re** ending. These spelling changes typically involve the doubling of a letter or the addition or change of an accent — for example, **e** may become **è**, or **é** may become **è**.

✔ **Irregular verbs:** With these verbs, you need to keep on your toes. They have irregular conjugations and don't follow a specific pattern like regular verbs do.

See Chapter 3 of Book III for details on all three types of verbs.

Reflexive verbs can be classified as regular, spelling-change, or irregular verbs. The one thing that makes _reflexive verbs_ different from other verbs is that you use them with reflexive pronouns, which correspond to the subject of a sentence. You use reflexive verbs when you do something to yourself. The action reflects back to the subject. For example, **Je me brosse les dents** means _I brush my teeth._ Reflexive verbs are also used to express reciprocal actions, where two or more people do the action to each other. For example, **Ils s'écrivent** means _They write to each other._ Some idiomatic expressions also use reflexive verbs. For example, **Nous nous entendons bien** means _We get along well._ Check out Chapter 3 of Book IV for more on reflexive verbs.

Naming Things with Nouns

Nouns name things: people, objects, places, concepts, and so on. _House_ is a noun. So is _Mary_ or _truth_ or _Polynesia._ There are a few key differences between French and English nouns, however, as this section explains.

Looking at types of nouns

Both French and English have common nouns, proper nouns, and compound nouns:

- ✔ **Common nouns:** Common nouns name things and people, like **maison** (*house*) and **fille** (*daughter*). They aren't capitalized.

- ✔ **Proper nouns:** Proper nouns name specific people, geographical places, and sites, such as Nicolas Sarkozy, **les Alpes** (*the Alps*), and Paris. Proper nouns are capitalized in both French and English, but there are some differences. Days, months, religions, and languages are capitalized in English but not in French. Look at these examples: **samedi** (*Saturday*), **janvier** (*January*), **le bouddhisme** (*Buddhism*), **le français** (*French language*).

- ✔ **Compound nouns:** Compound nouns are two or more nouns combined to name one thing or person. In French, the main idea is always stated first, followed by its attribute or an enhancing detail. In English, the attribute or detail usually comes first. **La Tour Eiffel** (*the Eiffel Tower*) is a compound proper noun including the main idea — the tower — accompanied by the name of the person after whom it was named (engineer Gustave Eiffel). Both French and English have compound nouns composed of common nouns as well, such as **l'arrêt de bus** (*the bus stop*).

Look at Table 1-1 for examples of French nouns.

Book III

Building the Grammatical Foundation for Communication

Table 1-1	Common, Proper, and Compound Nouns	
Common Nouns	*Proper Nouns*	*Compound Nouns*
la ville (*the city*)	**Montréal** (*Montreal*)	**les chutes du Niagara** (*Niagara Falls*)
le chef (*the chef*)	**Bocuse** (*[French chef Paul] Bocuse*)	**l'auberge du Pont de Collonges** (*the Bridge of Collonges Inn*)
l'île (*the island*)	**la Martinique** (*Martinique*)	**la mer des Caraïbes** (*the Caribbean Sea*)
la pluie (*the rain*)	**la Bretagne** (*Brittany*)	**le manteau de pluie** (*the raincoat*)
la province (*the province*)	**Québec** (*Quebec*)	**la ville de Québec** (*Quebec City*)
le musée (*the museum*)	**le Louvre** (*the Louvre*)	**la pyramide du Louvre** (*the Louvre Pyramid*)

(continued)

Table 1-1 *(continued)*

Common Nouns	Proper Nouns	Compound Nouns
le palais (*the palace*)	**l'Elysée** (*the Elysée* [presidential palace])	**les Champs-Elysées** (*the Elysian Fields* [an avenue in Paris])
la liberté (*the liberty*)	**Bartholdi** (*Bartholdi* [sculptor of the Statue of Liberty])	**la statue de la Liberté** (*the Statue of Liberty*)

Understanding gender

Unlike English nouns, all French nouns have a gender: Grammatically, they're either masculine or feminine. Knowing whether a noun is masculine or feminine is important because it impacts the sentence construction. For example, if the noun is feminine, the articles and adjectives that go with that noun must also be feminine.

Of course, if you're talking about the sex of a person or a specific animal such as **la vache** (*the cow*) or **le taureau** (*the bull*), the gender is usually obvious. But if the noun is a thing or an idea, how do you determine its gender? For the most part, just look at the word's ending. With a few exceptions, the ending of a noun is a rather good indication of its gender. We cover masculine and feminine endings in Chapter 2 of Book III. If you're in doubt, you can consult a French dictionary, which we discuss later in "Making the Most of Bilingual Dictionaries," to find the gender.

Making singular nouns plural

In French, as in English, nouns are either singular or plural. In other words, nouns have a *number*. To make most nouns plural, you simply add an **-s** to the end, just like in English. For example, **maison** (*house*) is singular, whereas **maisons** (*houses)* is plural.

Put a plural article before a plural noun. Because the **-s** at the end of a noun usually isn't pronounced, the word **les** (*the*) or **des** (*some*) may be the only thing that tells listeners that the noun is plural. For example, **maison** (*house*) and **maisons** (*houses*) sound the same, but **la maison** (lah mey-zohN) (*the house*) is clearly singular and **les maisons** (ley mey-zohN) (*the houses*) is clearly plural. We cover articles in the next section.

If a noun ends in **-ou**, **-eu**, or **-eau**, you add an **-x** instead of an **-s** to make it plural. Here are some examples:

Singular	Plural
le genou (*the knee*)	**les genoux** (*the knees*)
le feu (*the fire*)	**les feux** (*the fires*)
le bureau (*the desk*)	**les bureaux** (*the desks*)

If a noun ends in **-al**, you change **-al** to **-aux** to make it plural:

Singular	Plural
le journal (*the newspaper*)	**les journaux** (*the newspapers*)
l'hôpital (*the hospital*)	**les hôpitaux** (*the hospitals*)
le cheval (*the horse*)	**les chevaux** (*the horses*)

If a noun already ends in an **-s**, **-z**, or **-x**, you don't add anything to it. In these instances, the article (and the context) clearly tells people that the noun is plural:

Singular	Plural
le fils (*the son*)	**les fils** (*sons*)
le nez (*the nose*)	**les nez** (*noses*)
l'époux (*the husband, spouse*)	**les époux** (the *spouses, married couple*)

Getting the Genuine Articles: Definite, Indefinite, and Partitive

Unlike English nouns, which don't necessarily need articles, French nouns are almost always preceded by definite articles (which translate as *the*), indefinite articles (*a/an, some*), or partitive articles (*some*). The *partitive article* expresses an unspecified quantity of something, such as **de la farine** (*some* flour). Table 1-2 lists the variations of definite, indefinite, and partitive articles in French.

Table 1-2	Definite, Indefinite, and Partitive French Articles			
Type of Article	Masculine Singular	Feminine Singular	Singular Before a Vowel or Mute h	Plural
Definite (*the*)	le	la	l'	les
Indefinite (*a/an, one, some*)	un	une	un, une	des
Partitive (*some, any*)	du (a contraction of **de** + **le**)	de la	de l'	des (a contraction of **de** + **les**)

Unlike English articles, French articles indicate the gender and the number of nouns. To help you remember the gender of a noun, memorize the article that goes with it. Instead of memorizing **table** (*table*), for example, memorize **la table** (*the table*) or **une table** (*a table*). Instead of **livre** (*book*), think **le livre** (*the book*) or **un livre** (*a book*).

For details on how to use these articles, keep reading.

Defining definite articles

The definite article refers to a specific noun and has only one form in English: *the*. In French, it's used with countries, religions, abstract concepts, and references to things and people in general:

- ✔ Countries: **le Canada** (*Canada*)

- ✔ Religions: **l'islam** (*Islam*)

- ✔ Abstract concept: **la beauté** (*beauty*)

- ✔ Generalities: **les fromages** (*cheeses*)

French also uses definite articles after verbs of preference, such as **aimer** (*to like, to love*), **détester** (*to hate*), and **préférer** (*to prefer*). For example, **j'aime le café** (*I like coffee.* Literally: *I like the coffee*).

Because French nouns have a gender, the article has to take the gender of the noun as well as its number (singular or plural). Here are the definite articles in French:

✔ **le** (*the*) — masculine singular

✔ **la** (*the*) — feminine singular

✔ **l'** (*the*) — singular, used in front of nouns that start with a vowel or mute **h**

✔ **les** (*the*) — plural

For example, the word **nuage** is masculine singular; therefore, you add a masculine, singular article in front of it: **le nuage** (*the cloud*). You follow the same pattern for a feminine singular noun: Simply add the feminine singular article **la** in front of **maison**, for example, and you have **la maison** (*the house*). If the noun is plural, regardless of whether it's masculine or feminine, the article is always **les**: **les nuages** (*the clouds*), **les maisons** (*the houses*).

If a singular noun begins with a vowel sound, then **le** or **la** usually changes to **l'**:

l'idée (f) (lee-dey) (*the idea*)

l'hôtel (m) (loh-tehl) (*the hotel*)

If a plural noun begins with a vowel sound, just use **les**. But remember to pronounce the **s** at the end of **les** — that is, make a **liaison** by voicing a *z* sound. (We explain pronunciation in Chapter 1 of Book I.) Here are some examples:

les idées (ley zee-dey) (*the ideas*)

les hôtels (ley zoh-tehl) (*the hotels*)

You occasionally come across nouns that start with what the French call *h* **aspiré**, an *aspirated* h, as opposed to a *mute* h. The **h** isn't pronounced in either case. The aspirated **h** supposedly requires a short breath before it, but for practical purposes, it means that **le/la** doesn't change to **l'** before those words and that you don't pronounce the **s** at the end of **les**. Examples of these nouns are **le hamster** (luh ahm-stehr) (*the hamster*), **la hauteur** (lah oh-tuhr) (*the height*), and **les haricot** (ley ah-ree-koh) (*the green beans*).

One of many: Generalizing with the indefinite article

When referring to an undetermined object, you use indefinite articles, equivalent to the English words *a/an, one,* and *some*. In French, the indefinite articles are

✔ **un** (*a/an, one*) — masculine singular

✔ **une** (*a/an, one*) — feminine singular

✔ **des** (*some, any*) — plural

The singular indefinite article is used as in English to say *a/an* or *one:*

> Paris est **une** grande ville. (*Paris is a big city.*)
>
> Je voudrais **un** café. (*I would like a coffee.*)
>
> Tu as **une** sœur ? (*Do you have a/one sister?*)

The plural indefinite article **des** (*some*) is used in French even when it's simply implied in English:

> Il y a **des** enfants dans le parc. (*There are [some] children in the park.*)
>
> Je voudrais prendre **des** photos. (*I would like to take [some] pictures.*)

Taking part: Choosing the partitive

The French language has a specific article that refers to a part of something as opposed to the whole. You can sometimes translate this *partitive* article as *some* or *any,* but it's frequently omitted in English.

The partitive article is the preposition **de** (*of*) followed by the definite article, **le/la/l'/les** (*the*). The article has a masculine form, **du** (the contraction of **de + le**); a feminine form, **de la**; and a plural form, **des** (the contraction of **de + les**). There's also a singular form for when the noun that follows starts with a vowel or a mute **h**: **de l'**. Here are a few examples:

> **Je voudrais du pain et du fromage.** (*I would like [some] bread and [some] cheese.*)
>
> **Si tu as soif, bois de l'eau !** (*If you're thirsty, drink [some] water!*)
>
> **Il mange souvent de la salade.** (*He often eats [some] salad.*)

Describing with Adjectives

Adjectives are a noun's best friend. They either accompany a noun, as in the noun phrase **un plat canadien** (*a Canadian dish*), or they describe the noun, as in the sentence **Ce monsieur est poli** (*This gentleman is polite*). Adjectives include words that indicate colors, sizes, nationalities, personality traits, and other attributes. In contrast to English, adjectives that refer to nationalities, languages, and religions aren't capitalized in French: **américain** (*American*), **français** (*French*), **chrétien** (*Christian*), and so on.

When the adjective is part of a noun phrase, as in **un livre intéressant** (*an interesting book*), the adjective usually comes after the noun. However, a few adjectives — namely the ones that deal with beauty, age, goodness or badness, and size — are placed before the noun in French. We discuss those adjectives in Chapter 2 of Book IV.

Adjectives have to match the nouns they modify in gender and number. You can change the ending of an adjective so that it agrees in gender and number with the noun. Table 1-3 shows some of the most frequent adjective endings as well as examples using these endings. Of course, there are irregular endings as well. Check out Chapter 2 of Book IV for details on changing adjective forms from masculine to feminine and singular to plural.

Regardless of the pattern of change, the feminine singular form of an adjective will end in **-e**, and a plural adjective will end in **-s** or **-x**.

Table 1-3	Endings of French Adjectives		
Masculine Singular	*Feminine Singular*	*Masculine Plural*	*Feminine Plural*
-e Example: **calme** (*calm*)	-e calme	-es calmes	-es calmes
-é Example: **fatigué** (*tired*)	-ée fatiguée	-és fatigués	-ées fatiguées
-[consonant] Example: **grand** (*big, tall*)	-[consonant] + e grande	-[consonant] + s grands	-[consonant] + es grandes
-eux Example: **heureux** (*happy*)	-euse heureuse	-eux heureux	-euses heureuses
-eur Example: **travailleur** (*hard working*)	-euse travailleuse	-eurs travailleurs	-euses travailleuses
-teur Example: **conservateur** (*conservative*)	-trice conservatrice	-teurs conservateurs	-trices conservatrices
-f Example: **sportif** (*athletic*)	-ve sportive	-fs sportifs	-ves sportives

(continued)

Table 1-3 (continued)

Masculine Singular	Feminine Singular	Masculine Plural	Feminine Plural
-ien Example: **canadien** (*Canadian*)	-ienne canadienne	-iens canadiens	-iennes canadiennes
-on Example: **bon** (*good*)	-onne bonne	-ons bons	-onnes bonnes
-er Example: **fier** (*proud*)	-ère fière	-ers fiers	-ères fières

For example, to describe your new car, you can say things like

> **Ma nouvelle voiture est belle, rouge et rapide, et c'est une voiture américaine.** (*My new car is beautiful, red, and fast, and it's an American car.*)

You just described your car with the following adjectives: **nouvelle**, **belle**, **rouge**, **rapide**, and **américaine**. The adjectives used to describe the feminine noun **la voiture** are a little different from the way they appear in a dictionary (except for **rouge** and **rapide**, which end in the silent letter **e** in their original masculine form).

Some adjectives have irregular feminine forms. For example, the masculine form of the adjective *beautiful* is **beau**, but it changes to **belle** to match the feminine gender of the noun **voiture**. Similarly, the masculine form of the adjective *new* is **nouveau**, but it changes to **nouvelle** to become feminine.

Minding Manners: Adding Meaning with Adverbs

An *adverb* is a word that modifies (describes) a verb, an adjective, or another adverb. In English, many adverbs end with *-ly: quickly, nervously, slowly,* and so on. In French, similar adverbs end in **-ment**, and they usually follow the verb. Here are some rules for forming adverbs from adjectives:

✔ If the masculine form of an adjective ends in a vowel, add **-ment**. For example, **vrai** (*true*) becomes **vraiment** (*truly, really*), and **absolu** (*absolute*) becomes **absolument** (*absolutely*).

✔ If the masculine form of an adjective ends in a consonant, take the adjective's feminine form and add **-ment**. **Sérieuse** (*serious*) becomes **sérieusement** (*seriously*), and **active** (*active*) becomes **activement** (*actively*).

✔ If the masculine form of an adjective ends in **-ent** or **-ant**, drop the **nt** and add **–mment**. **Constant** (*constant*) becomes **constamment** (*constantly*), and **évident** (*evident*) becomes **évidemment** (*evidently, obviously*). *Exception:* The adjective **lent** (*slow*) follows the usual rules for adverb formation and simply becomes **lentement**.

French and English also have many adverbs that aren't formed from adjectives. They can be classified as adverbs of time, such as **demain** (*tomorrow*); of frequency, such as **toujours** (*always*); of manner, such as **bien** (*well*) and **mal** (*badly*); of place, such as **ici** (*here*); of quantity, such as **trop** (*too much*); of negation, such as **jamais** (*never*); and of comparison, such as **moins** (*less*).

The position of an adverb in a French sentence depends on the type of adverb you're using, but most adverbs come right after the verb, as in the following examples:

Parlez **lentement**, s'il vous plaît. (*Speak <u>slowly</u>, please.*)

Les petits oiseaux chantent **joyeusement**. (*The little birds sing <u>happily</u>.*)

Elle parle **mal**. (*She speaks <u>badly</u>.*)

See Chapter 2 of Book IV for more info on the types and placement of adverbs.

Book III

Building the Grammatical Foundation for Communication

Solving the Pronoun Puzzle

A *pronoun* is first of all a word that replaces a noun or a noun phrase. There are many types of pronouns. Some pronouns are the *subject;* they're in charge of performing the action of the verb. Other pronouns are the *object* of the verb: They receive the action of the verb. On top of these, French has possessive pronouns, which indicate ownership; demonstrative pronouns, which help you compare and point at things and people; interrogative pronouns, which help you in questioning; and relative pronouns, which allow you to link two ideas within a sentence. Look at the following sections for an introduction to various pronouns, and check out Chapter 3 of Book IV for more information.

The actors: Subject pronouns

Subject pronouns act as the agents who perform an action. Here are the French subject pronouns:

Singular	*Plural*
je/j' (*I*)	**nous** (*we*)
tu (*you* — singular familiar)	**vous** (*you* — plural or singular formal)
il (*he/it*)	**ils** (*they* — masculine or mixed male and
elle (*she/it*)	female)
on (*one/we, they, people*)	**elles** (*they* — feminine)

Note that **tu** is a singular familiar form of *you* that you use with a friend, child, or person you know well. Although **vous** is the plural form of *you,* it's also a formal way to address a single person, such as a stranger or your boss.

You use subject pronouns before the appropriate conjugated form of a verb, as in <u>**Nous** aimons le français</u> (<u>*We* love French</u>).

The pronoun **je** changes to **j'** before a vowel or a mute **h**. Look at these examples:

> **Je** fais du ski. (*I ski.*)

> **J'**habite en Suisse. (*I live in Switzerland.*)

A French sentence doesn't contain pauses between words — the sounds flow together. This idea is especially important when the verb starts with a vowel or a mute **h**, because you link the sound of the subject pronoun to the first sound in the verb without any interruption. For example, say **Il arrive** (eel-ah-reev) (*He's arriving*) or **Elles arrivent** (ehl-zah-reev) (*They [females] are arriving*).

The emphasizers: Stress pronouns

Stress pronouns usually appear before a subject pronoun and, as their name indicates, serve to stress the importance of the subject. Instead of using your voice to say an emphatic *I* or *you* as you do in English, add one of the appropriate pronouns before **je** or **tu** or any other subject pronoun to get the same effect. Look at Table 1-4 to see the stress pronouns.

Table 1-4	**Stress Pronouns**
Singular	*Plural*
moi (*me*)	**nous** (*us*)
toi (*you* — singular familiar)	**vous** (*you* — plural or singular formal)
lui (*him*)	**eux** (*them* masculine)
elle (*her*)	**elles** (*them* feminine)

Here are some example sentences that emphasize the subject. Notice how most stress pronouns come right before the subject pronouns. This is the most common place for a stress pronoun in a sentence; however, you can also place the stress pronoun at the end of your sentence for additional emphasis:

Je reste, **moi.** (*I'm staying. [No ifs, ands, or buts.]*)

Toi, tu sors ? (*You're going out?*)

Lui, il travaille. (*He works.*)

Elle, elle mange. (*She's eating.*)

Nous, nous dansons. (*We are dancing.*)

Vous, vous lisez ? (*You're reading?*)

Eux, ils exagèrent ! (*They exaggerate!*)

Elles, elles sont gentilles. (*They are nice.*)

After prepositions such as **pour**, **avec**, **sans**, and so on, French uses stress pronouns to refer to people: **pour elles** (*for them*), **avec moi** (*with me*), **sans lui** (*without him*).

The recipients: Object pronouns

Pronouns that receive the action of the verb directly are called *direct-object pronouns.* The pronouns **me**, **te**, **nous**, and **vous** replace people, and the pronouns **le**, **la**, **l'**, and **les** can replace people or things. See Table 1-5.

Book III

Building the Grammatical Foundation for Communication

Table 1-5	Direct-Object Pronouns
Singular	*Plural*
me (*me*)	**nous** (*us*)
te (*you* — singular familiar)	**vous** (*you* — plural or singular formal)
le (*him/it*) **la** (*her/it*) **l'** (*him/her/it* before a vowel or a mute **h**)	**les** (*them*)

Les enfants ? Je **les** adore. (*Children? I love <u>them</u>.*)

Les romans canadiens ? Je **les** dévore. (*Canadian novels? I devour <u>them</u>.*)

Je **vous** comprends bien. (*I understand <u>you</u> well.*)

Pronouns that receive the action of the verb indirectly are called *indirect-object pronouns.* They can only replace people, and some of them are the same as the direct object pronouns. See Table 1-6.

Table 1-6	Indirect-Object Pronouns
Singular	*Plural*
me (*to/for me*)	**nous** (*to/for us*)
te (familiar *to/for you*)	**vous** (*to/for you* — plural or singular formal)
lui (*to/for him or her*)	**leur** (*to/for them*)

For example, you can say

Il **me** parle. (*He is talking to me.*)

Il **leur** parle. (*He is talking to them.*)

The owned: Possessive pronouns

Possessive pronouns help express *mine, yours, his, hers, ours, yours,* and *theirs.* For example, to say *Your car is here; mine is in the garage,* you'd use **la mienne** (*mine*) to stand in for **ma voiture** (*my car*): **Ta voiture est ici; la mienne est au garage.** Table 1-7 lists the various possessive pronouns, which, of course, must match the noun they replace in gender and number.

Table 1-7	Possessive Pronouns			
Meaning	*Masculine Singular*	*Feminine Singular*	*Masculine Plural*	*Feminine Plural*
mine	**le mien**	**la mienne**	**les miens**	**les miennes**
yours (singular familiar)	**le tien**	**la tienne**	**les tiens**	**les tiennes**
his/hers	**le sien**	**la sienne**	**les siens**	**les siennes**
ours	**le nôtre**	**la nôtre**	**les nôtres**	**les nôtres**
yours (plural or singular formal)	**le vôtre**	**la vôtre**	**les vôtres**	**les vôtres**
theirs	**le leur**	**la leur**	**les leurs**	**les leurs**

A little of this and that: Demonstrative pronouns

Demonstrative pronouns help express *this/that one* or *these/those (ones)*. For example, to say *This hat is too small; that one fits me,* you would replace **le chapeau** (*the hat*) with **celui-là** (*that one*): **Ce chapeau est trop petit; celui-là me va.** Table 1-8 lists the demonstrative pronouns, which match in gender and number the noun (and demonstrative adjective) they replace.

Table 1-8	French Demonstrative Pronouns	
Demonstrative Pronouns	**Gender and Number**	**Example**
celui-ci (*this one*) **celui-là** (*that one*)	Masculine singular	**ce chemisier-ci** (*this blouse*) becomes **celui-ci** (*this one*)
celle-ci (*this one*) **celle-là** (*that one*)	Feminine singular	**cette chemise-là** (*that shirt*) becomes **celle-là** (*that one*)
ceux-ci (*these ones*) **ceux-là** (*those ones*)	Masculine plural	**ces vêtements-ci** (*these clothes*) becomes **ceux-ci** (suh-see) (*these ones*)
celles-ci (*these ones*) **celles-là** (*those ones*)	Feminine plural	**ces bottes-là** (*those boots*) becomes **celles-là** (*those ones*)

Book III

Building the Grammatical Foundation for Communication

The questioners: Interrogative pronouns

Interrogative pronouns help express *who, whom, what,* and *which one:*

- ✔ **Qui** (*who*) can be the subject of the verb. It can be followed by **est-ce qui**.

    Qui est le monsieur ? (<u>*Who's*</u> *the gentleman?*)

    Qui est-ce qui veut ça ? (<u>*Who*</u> *wants this?*)

- ✔ **Qui** (*whom*) can be the object of the verb. It can be followed by **est-ce que**.

    Qui aimez-vous ? (<u>*Whom*</u> *do you like?*)

    Qui est-ce que tu invites ? (<u>*Whom*</u> *are you inviting?*)

- ✔ **Que** (*what*) can be subject or object of the verb and can be followed by **est-ce que**. You must then contract **que** and **est-ce que** into **Qu'est-ce que**.

    Que désirez-vous ? (<u>*What*</u> *would you like?*)

    Qu'est-ce que tu voudrais ? (<u>*What*</u> *would you like?*)

✔ **Lequel/laquelle** (*which one*) and **lesquels/lesquelles** (*which ones*) must match the noun they replace in gender and number. They can be subject or object of the verb.

> Les deux maisons sont jolies, alors **laquelle** est-ce que tu veux ? (*The two houses are nice, so <u>which one</u> do you want?*)

Check Chapter 5 of Book III for more on interrogative pronouns.

The connectors: Relative pronouns

French relative pronouns include **qui** (*who/which*), **que** (*whom/which*), **lequel** (*which*), **dont** (*of whom/whose/of which*), and **où** (*where*). Relative pronouns replace a word from the main clause and introduce a new clause. For example, in **La personne qui parle est mon père** (*The person who is talking is my father*), **qui** stands in for **la personne** in the second clause. And in **La bicyclette que je veux est fantastique** (*The bike [that] I want is fantastic*), **que** stands in for **le vélo**. Here are a few more examples that use relative pronouns:

> La voiture dans **laquelle** il est arrivé est neuve. (*The car in <u>which</u> he arrived is brand new.*)

> C'est le film **dont** je parlais. (*That's the movie [<u>that</u>] I was talking <u>about</u>. Literally: That's the movie <u>of which</u> I was talking.*)

> C'est la ville **où** il est né. (*That's the city <u>where</u> he was born.*)

Check Chapter 4 of Book IV for more on relative pronouns.

Joining Together with Prepositions

Prepositions are *joining* words — they connect nouns to other nouns or to verbs in order to show the relationship between those words, such as what something is *about*, whom someone is working *for*, or how your keys always manage to hide *from* you.

Sometimes French and English use corresponding prepositions, sometimes one language omits the preposition the other language uses, and other times, the two languages use totally different prepositions:

✔ **Same preposition in both French and English:** Here, you can simply translate a preposition from one language into another.

> Je parle **à** mes amis. (*I'm talking <u>to</u> my friends.*)

> La pyramide est **devant** le musée. (*The pyramid is <u>in front of</u> the museum.*)

✔ **Omitted preposition:** Here are a couple of examples. Note that the English preposition *to* is absent from the French sentence in the first example, and the French preposition **dans** (*in*) is absent from the English sentence in the next example.

> J'écoute la radio. (*I'm listening <u>to</u> the radio.*)

> J'entre **dans** la salle. (*I enter the room.*)

✔ **Different prepositions:** Prepositions don't always translate literally from one language to another. Consider the prepositions **sur** (*on*) and **dans** (*in*) in the following examples:

> Je suis **sur** le bus. (*I'm on [top of] the bus.*)

> Je suis **dans** le bus. (*I'm on the bus.* Literally: *I'm in the bus.*)

When you follow the prepositions **à** and **de** with the definite articles **le** and **les** (*the*), you have to form contractions (but you don't form contractions with **la** and **l'**):

✔ **à** + **le** becomes **au**

✔ **à** + **les** becomes **aux**

✔ **de** + **le** becomes **du**

✔ **de** + **les** becomes **des**

Here are a few examples that use contractions:

> Je vais **au** marché. (*I'm going to the store.*)

> Il se plaint **des** mouches. (*He's complaining about the flies.*)

Check out Chapter 1 of Book IV for more on prepositions.

Book III

Building the Grammatical Foundation for Communication

Adding and Explaining with Conjunctions

Conjunctions are words that link ideas or groups of words within the same sentence. The most important conjunctions you need to know are the following *coordinating conjunctions,* which you use to join words and phrases of equal value:

✔ **et** (*and*)

✔ **ou** (*or*)

✔ **mais** (*but*)

✔ **car** (*for/because*)

✔ **ni . . . ni** (*neither . . . nor*)

Throwing in some interjections? Eh oui !

Interjections don't play a grammatical role in sentences, but they're still super useful. These words and phrases help you express reactions and emotions as well as fill those pauses when you're thinking about to say next. Here are some French interjections:

- ✔ **Ah !** (*Ah!*)
- ✔ **Aïe !** (*Ouch!*)
- ✔ **Beurk !** (*Yuck!*)
- ✔ **Ça alors !** (*No kidding! Well, well!*)
- ✔ **C'est tannant !** (*That's a pain! — Québec*)
- ✔ **Chut !** (*Hush!*)
- ✔ **Eh ?** (*How about that? What's your opinion? — Québec*)
- ✔ **Eh oui !** (*You bet!*)

- ✔ **Eh non !** (*Not at all!*)
- ✔ **Envoie-donc !** (*Do it! — Québec*)
- ✔ **Euh . . .** (*Um . . .*)
- ✔ **Hein ! Hein ?** (*Huh! Huh?*)
- ✔ **Oh là là !** (*Wow!*)
- ✔ **Oups !** (*Oops!*)
- ✔ **Pouah !** (*Poo!*)
- ✔ **Tu crois ?** (*Really?*)
- ✔ **Tu dis pas ?** (*You don't say?*)
- ✔ **T'sais ?** (*You know? — Québec*)
- ✔ **Voyons !** (*Let's see!*)
- ✔ **Zut ! Zut alors ! Zut de zut !** (*Darn!*)

Look at the following examples:

> **J'aime faire du ski nautique et de la planche à voile.** (*I like to go waterskiing and windsurfing.*)

> **Est-ce que tu veux aller au restaurant ou manger à la maison ?** (*Do you want to go to the restaurant or eat at home?*)

> **Ils n'aiment ni l'automne ni l'hiver.** (*They like neither fall nor winter.*)

> **Il neige mais la neige fond tout de suite.** (*It snows, but the snow melts right away.*)

Other conjunctions that join ideas and groups of words in the same sentence are *subordinating conjunctions*. These conjunctions are words like **quand** (*when*) or **parce que** (*because*), which join dependent clauses (clauses that can't stand alone) to main clauses (clauses that make sense on their own). For example, in the following sentence, the conjunction **puisque** (*since, because*) joins the main clause **je voudrais aller en France** to the dependent clause **j'ai de la famille là-bas**:

> **Je voudrais aller en France puisque j'ai de la famille là-bas.** (*I would like to go to France since I have family there.*)

Find out a lot more about conjunctions in Chapters 4 and 5 of Book IV.

Making the Most of Bilingual Dictionaries

A bilingual dictionary can be a wonderful tool or a terrible crutch. When you don't know what a word means or how to say something in another language, a bilingual dictionary can give you the answer. But using the dictionary isn't as simple as just looking something up and taking the first thing you see. You have to know what to look up, how to interpret the information provided, and how much you can depend on the answer you get. This section can help you make a bilingual dictionary a helpful tool and not a hindrance.

Figuring out what to look up

Although dictionaries have thousands of entries, you can't find every word you want just by looking it up. Different versions of words, including plurals, feminines, and verb conjugations, for example, aren't listed separately, so you need to know where to find these words. You can find them only by looking for the main dictionary entry: a singular, masculine, infinitive (unconjugated), unmodified version of the word.

For example, suppose you see the word **mettez** for the first time and you want to know what it means. You grab your bilingual dictionary and discover there's no entry for **mettez**. Instead of giving up, do a little grammatical analysis. **Mettez** ends in **-ez**, which is a common French verb ending, so conjugate backwards — the infinitive is likely to be **metter**, **mettir**, or **mettre**. Look those up, and voilà! You discover that **mettre** means *to put*.

Likewise, if you can't find **traductrice**, replace the feminine ending **-trice** with the masculine **-teur**. The word in the dictionary is the default, masculine form **traducteur** (*translator*).

If you're trying to look up an expression, such as **Qui se ressemble s'assemble**, you can start by looking up the first word, **qui**, but you may not have any luck. The dictionary may include the expression under that entry, or it may list it under a different word that the dictionary editors thought was more of a key to the phrase, such as **ressembler**. Check the **ressembler** entry, and sure enough, you discover that the phrase means *Those who resemble each other assemble* — or rather, that it's the French equivalent of the proverb *Birds of a feather flock together*.

Note: Reflexive verbs, such as **se ressembler** and **se souvenir**, are listed in the dictionary under the verb, not the reflexive pronoun. So you'd look up **ressembler** and **souvenir**, not **se**.

Choosing the right word based on context and part of speech

Finding the dictionary entry for the word you want is only half the battle. You also need to think about what the word means, which is why you have to understand *context* — the situation in which you're using the word. Context can tell you which definition is correct.

For example, suppose someone tells you that he dislikes **les avocats**. When you look up **avocat**, you find two translations: *avocado* and *lawyer*. You need to figure out from his other words whether his **avocats** are food or people. The context obviously makes a big difference in which translation is correct. Look at Figure 1-1 to see a dictionary entry for **avocat**.

Figure 1-1:
A French-English dictionary entry for **avocat**.

AVOCAT
[a vɔ ka] m subst
(person) lawyer,
(fruit) avocado

*Illustration by Wiley,
Composition Services Graphics*

Context also helps you choose a word with the correct part of speech. If you want to know how to say *play* in French, you need to know whether you're looking for the noun, as in *I'm going to see a play,* or the verb, as in *I want to play tennis*. When you look up *play* in the dictionary, you see two translations: **une pièce** and **jouer**. The correct choice depends on context and on your knowing the difference between a noun and a verb.

Some people like to keep a list of words to look up later instead of putting the book down every two minutes to look up the words right away. If you're one of these people, be sure to jot down the phrase or sentence rather than just the word. Otherwise, when you get the dictionary out, you'll find that you can't figure out which translation is best because you have no context to fit it into.

Understanding symbols and terminology

Dictionaries save space by using symbols and abbreviations, and these short forms aren't necessarily standard from one dictionary to the next. Your best bet is to check the first few pages of the dictionary — you should see some kind of key that lists the abbreviations used throughout the book, the pronunciation notation, and symbols that indicate things such as formality or informality, archaic words, silent letters, and so on.

The *International Phonetic Alphabet,* or *IPA,* is a standard system for showing how to pronounce words in any language. However, many dictionaries either don't use it or adapt the alphabet with their own symbols, so you always need to check your dictionary to see which system they're using to explain pronunciation. The second line in Figure 1-1 shows the IPA spelling for the word **avocat** (*lawyer, avocado*).

The symbols and abbreviations aren't there just to look pretty! If a word is listed as archaic, you don't want to use it (unless you happen to be translating 14th-century poetry). If a term is starred three times, indicating that it's vulgar slang, you definitely don't want to say that to your boss. As we explain in the preceding section, you need to think about how you're using a particular word before you make your selection from the translations offered.

Interpreting figurative language and idioms

Book III

Building the Grammatical Foundation for Communication

When using a bilingual dictionary to determine a word's meaning, you also need to understand whether a term is being used literally or figuratively. French and English are both rich in figurative language, and translating can be tricky. Take the expression *Guy is hot.* Literally, this means that Guy is very warm — he's wearing too many clothes, say, or he has a fever. Figuratively (and informally), it means that Guy is extremely good looking. If you want to translate this sentence into French, you need to figure out which meaning you're after and then make sure you find the correct French translation for that meaning. When you look up the word, in this case, *hot,* literal meanings are normally listed first, followed by any figurative meanings. The latter has a notation such as *fig.* (short for *figurative*). For the record, the literal translation of *Guy is hot* is **Guy a chaud**, and the figurative is **Guy est sexy**.

You may run across figurative language when you translate into English, too. The French expression **connaître la musique** literally means to *know the music,* such as an actual song. Figuratively, it means *to know the routine.* You have to think about which of these English meanings is right for the context in which you saw or heard the French expression.

An *idiom* is an expression that can't be translated literally into another language because one or more words in it are used figuratively. *It's raining cats and dogs* doesn't really mean that animals are falling from the sky; it just means that it's raining really hard. You absolutely can't look up the individual words to come up with **Il pleut des chats et des chiens** — that makes no sense at all. The French equivalent of *It's raining cats and dogs* is also an idiom: **Il pleut des cordes** (*It's raining ropes*). The French-Canadian equivalent is even more difficult to translate: **Il mouille à boire debout** (*It's raining so much you can drink standing up*).

Automated translators, such as online translation websites, translate very literally, which is why you should never use them to translate something that you plan to say to someone or write in a letter. Be especially cautious when dealing with idioms. Imagine trying to translate the saying "Liar, liar, pants on fire" into French. You'd be better off expressing the main message by saying something like "You're such a liar."

Verifying your findings

After you've found your word or expression and have considered the context you'll be using it in, verifying what you've found is a good idea. We suggest you use the following ideas to double-check that you're using the right meaning:

- ✔ **Ask a native.** The best way to verify that you're using the right word is to ask a native speaker. Dictionaries are wonderful tools, but they're not infallible. Language changes — particularly informal language — and dictionaries change constantly. Even if they didn't, they still couldn't tell you that a certain expression or way of using a particular word "just doesn't sound right." Native speakers are the experts. To find a native speaker, ask your professor whether he or she knows anyone. If there's a local branch of the **Alliance française** near you, find out the time of the next meeting. Or you can try an online forum.

- ✔ **Do a reverse look-up.** One quick and easy way to check whether the word you found is the right one is to do reverse look-up, which is when you look up the translation that the dictionary just gave you. For example, if you've looked up *anger* in the English-French part of the dictionary and found that it means **colère** or **fureur**, you can then look up those two words in the French-English dictionary. You'll see that **colère** says *anger* and **fureur** says *fury,* which indicates that **colère** is probably the better translation for *anger*.

  Another way to confirm a translation is by looking up anger in an English dictionary and **colère** in a French dictionary and comparing the definitions.

Chapter 2

All Agreed? Matching Gender and Number of Nouns and Articles

. . . .

In This Chapter

▶ Naming things and people with nouns

▶ Identifying the gender and number of a noun

▶ Expressing gender and number with definite, indefinite, and partitive articles

▶ Getting particular with demonstrative, possessive, and interrogative adjectives

. . . .

*I*n this chapter, you discover how to demystify genders of nouns as masculine or feminine by looking at their endings. You also figure out how to use the appropriate singular and plural accompaniments in front of nouns — definite articles (*the*), indefinite articles (*a, an,* or *some*), partitive articles (*some*), possessive adjectives (*my, your, his, her,* and so on), demonstrative adjectives (*this, that, these,* or *those*), and interrogative adjectives (*which* or *what*).

That Whole Gender Thing

There are a few key differences between French and English nouns. In English, only nouns referring to people, certain animals, and some boats have gender. But in French, all nouns have a gender, which changes everything. A noun's gender determines which form of articles, adjectives, pronouns, and sometimes past participles you have to use, so knowing the gender is vital to speaking and writing French.

When you're working with compound and multiple nouns, figuring out which noun the other words have to agree with can be tricky:

✔ **Compound nouns:** The compound noun **la pyramide du Louvre** (*the pyramid of the Louvre*) is feminine because **la pyramide** is the main noun, even though **le Louvre** is masculine. Similarly, **l'omelette au fromage** (*the cheese omelet*) is feminine because **l'omelette** is the main noun, even though **fromage** is a masculine noun.

✔ **Multiple nouns:** In the sentence **Marc et Lucie sont gentils** (*Marc and Lucie are nice*), one subject (**Marc**) is masculine, and the other (**Lucie**) is feminine. If at least one of the subject nouns is masculine, consider the entire subject masculine. Here, the adjective **gentils**, which describes **Marc** and **Lucie**, must be in the masculine form so that it agrees with the gender of the subjects. Similarly, to say *They are nice,* you'd say **Ils sont gentils**, replacing **Marc et Lucie** with the masculine pronoun **ils**.

Determining a noun's gender

Luckily, most nouns that refer to people have a logical gender. **Homme** (*man*), **garçon** (*boy*), and **serveur** (*waiter*) are masculine, and **femme** (*woman*), **fille** (*girl*), and **serveuse** (*waitress*) are feminine. Animals and inanimate objects, however, are altogether another kettle (**poissonière** — feminine) of fish (**poisson** — masculine).

Memorizing gender

The gender of objects and many animals in French is arbitrary — or at least it seems that way to English speakers. In most cases, there's no way to just look at a word and know which gender it is — you just have to memorize the gender of each word as you learn it.

The best way to remember the gender of nouns is to make sure your vocabulary lists include an article for each noun (see "Expressing Gender and Number with Articles," later in this chapter). Then when you look at your list, the gender of the article tells you the gender of the noun. For example, you can see that **un ordinateur** (*a computer*) is masculine due to the masculine article **un** and that **une télévision** (*a television*) is feminine due to the feminine article **une**. If possible, use the indefinite articles **un/une** (*a*) rather than the definite articles **le/la** (*the*). **Le** and **la** contract to **l'** in front of a vowel or mute **h**, and **l'** doesn't give you gender information.

Finding hints at gender in word endings

A few word endings tend to indicate whether a noun is masculine or feminine. For example, words that end in **-age**, as in **message** and **mirage**, or **-eau**, like **manteau** (*coat*) and **chapeau** (*hat*), are usually masculine. On the other hand, most words that end in **-ion**, like **libération** and **possession**, and **-té**, such as **liberté** (*freedom*) and **égalité** (*equality*), are feminine.

Table 2-1 shows some common noun endings and likely genders. But remember that you can find exceptions to all these rules, and thousands of nouns don't end with these letters.

Table 2-1	Common Masculine and Feminine Noun Endings		
Masculine Endings	**Example**	**Feminine Endings**	**Example**
-eur	**l'auteur** (*author*) **le bonheur** (*happiness*)	-ade	**la promenade** (*walk*) **la limonade** (*lemon soda*)
-eau	**le chapeau** (*hat*) **le manteau** (*coat*)	-ance -ence	**la naissance** (*birth*) **la différence** (*difference*)
-isme	**le capitalisme** (*capitalism*) **le féminisme** (*feminism*)	-oire	**la mémoire** (*memory*) **la victoire** (*victory*)
-ment	**l'appartement** (*apartment*) **le logement** (*lodging, place of residence*)	-sion -tion	**l'impression** (*impression*) **la condition** (*condition*)
-ail	**le travail** (*work*) **le détail** (*detail*)	-son	**la saison** (*season*) **la maison** (*house*)
Final vowels other than -e	**le cinéma** (*movies*) **le piano** (*piano*) **le genou** (*knee*)	-té -ée	**la liberté** (*freedom*) **l'égalité** (*equality*) **l'idée** (*idea*) **la pensée** (*thought*)
-al	**le journal** (*newspaper*) **le festival** (*festival*)	-ie	**la boulangerie** (*bakery*) **l'épicerie** (*grocery store*)

Book III

Building the Grammatical Foundation for Communication

Throwing groups into the mix

French is a bit sexist when referring to groups of people. If you have a group of mixed masculine and feminine nouns, you always default to the masculine plural: **des amis** (*some friends*). The only time you can say **des amies** is when you're talking about a group of female friends, with not a single male in the bunch. However, if you have 65 girls and just 1 boy, you use **des amis**.

The same idea applies if you're talking about one person whose gender you don't know, such as *one tourist*. If you don't know whether it's a man or woman, you always default to the masculine: **un touriste**.

Noting nouns that are always masculine or feminine

A number of French nouns have only a masculine form or only a feminine form, regardless of the gender of the person they refer to. Many of the masculine nouns refer to professions that were once considered to be "for men."

In Canada and some other French-speaking countries, most nouns that refer to professions have both masculine and feminine forms. But in France, the dynamic nature of language is the object of much controversy. Changes to the French language are slow to occur because the **Académie française**, composed of 40 members elected to this body for life, regulates language usage.

The following nouns are always masculine:

- ✔ **un auteur** (*author*)
- ✔ **un charpentier** (*carpenter*)
- ✔ **un écrivain** (*writer*)
- ✔ **un ingénieur** (*engineer*)
- ✔ **un maire** (*mayor*)
- ✔ **un médecin** (*doctor*)
- ✔ **un ministre** (*minister*)
- ✔ **un policier** (*police officer*)
- ✔ **un pompier** (*firefighter*)
- ✔ **un président** (*president*)
- ✔ **un professeur** (*teacher*)

And these nouns are always feminine:

- ✔ **une brute** (*boor, lout*)
- ✔ **une connaissance** (*acquaintance*)
- ✔ **une idole** (*idol*)
- ✔ **une personne** (*person*)
- ✔ **une vedette** (*movie star*)
- ✔ **une victime** (*victim*)

People in mainstream society and in the media make some traditionally masculine nouns feminine. You'll hear students, even in France, refer to **la prof/la professeur** for the female teacher. In Québec, a male writer is **l'écrivain**, and a female writer is **l'écrivaine**.

Changing meaning

Some words have different meanings depending on their gender, like **un tour** (*a tour*) and **une tour** (*a tower*). Using the wrong gender for such a noun may lead to serious misunderstanding. For example, if you're talking to a police officer, be sure to use the masculine article when telling him that your **mari**

(*husband*) is at home. Otherwise, you may just find a search warrant waiting for you when you get there, because **la mari** is marijuana.

Table 2-2 gives you a list of nouns that can have either gender. Note how the gender determines the meaning of the noun.

Table 2-2	Nouns Whose Meaning Changes with Gender
Masculine Noun	*Feminine Noun*
le livre (*book*)	**la livre** (*pound*)
l'aide (*helper or assistant*)	**l'aide** (*help*)
le mémoire (*memoirs/written document*)	**la mémoire** (*memory*)
le/la critique (*author of a critique*)	**la critique** (*the actual critique, as in a movie critique or review*)
le mode (*manner/style*)	**la mode** (*fashion*)
le voile (*veil*)	**la voile** (*sail*)

Gender swap: Making masculine nouns feminine

Nouns that refer to people often have a masculine default form that you can make feminine. Table 2-3 shows how to make the gender switch:

Book III

Building the Grammatical Foundation for Communication

Table 2-3	Masculine and Feminine Nouns		
Rule	*Masculine Noun*	*Feminine Noun*	*Translation*
To make most nouns feminine, add **-e** to the end.	**un** étudi**ant** **un** avoc**at**	**une** étudi**ante** **une** avoc**ate**	*student* *lawyer*
If a masculine noun ends in **-en** or **-on**, add **-ne** for the feminine form.	**un** électrici**en** **un** patr**on**	**une** électrici**enne** **une** patr**onne**	*electrician* *boss*
Nouns that end in **-er** change the ending to **-ère** for the feminine.	**un** caissi**er** **un** boulang**er**	**une** caissi**ère** **une** boulang**ère**	*cashier* *baker*
Nouns that end in **-eur** may become feminine with **-euse** or **-rice**.	**un** vend**eur** **un** traduct**eur**	**une** vend**euse** **une** traduct**rice**	*vendor* *translator*

(continued)

Table 2-3 *(continued)*			
Rule	*Masculine Noun*	*Feminine Noun*	*Translation*
Nouns that end in **-e** in the masculine form have no change for the feminine (other than in the article, which changes to **une** or **la**).	**un** artiste **un** touriste	**une** artiste **une** touriste	*artist* *tourist*

That Whole Number Thing

In addition to masculine and feminine forms, most French nouns also have singular and plural forms. Making a noun plural in French is very similar to making a noun plural in English.

Looking at regular plurals

To make a noun plural, you usually just add an **-s**, as with changing **un homme** (*a man*) to **deux hommes** (*two men*) and **la femme** (*the woman*) to **les femmes** (*the women*). The final **s** is silent, which means that the singular and plural forms of these nouns are pronounced the same way. In speech, you can tell that the noun is plural because the article or other word before the noun changes. Look at the examples of plural nouns (and their accompanying articles/adjectives) in Table 2-4.

Table 2-4	Regular Plurals
Singular	*Plural*
le magasin (*the store*) **la robe** (*the dress*)	**les magasins** (*the stores*) **les robes** (*the dresses*)
un ami (*a friend*) **une copine** (*a female friend*)	**des amis** (*some friends*) **des copines** (*some female friends*)
ce quartier (*this neighborhood*) **cette ville** (*this town/city*)	**ces quartiers** (*these neighborhoods*) **ces villes** (*these/those towns/cities*)
mon sac (*my bag*) **ma valise** (*my suitcase*)	**mes sacs** (*my bags*) **mes valises** (*my suitcases*)

Forming irregular plurals

Here are some ways to form a plural in French when you can't simply add an **-s**:

- ✔ For nouns that end in **-s**, **-x**, or **-z**, don't make any changes to the noun. However, be sure to use a plural article before the noun to indicate the plural. For example **le mois** (*the month*) becomes **les mois** (*the months*) in the plural, **le choix** (*the choices*) becomes **les choix** (*the choices*), and **le gaz** (*the gas*) becomes **les gaz** (*the gases*).

- ✔ Singular nouns that end in **-ail** change the ending to **-aux** in the plural. For example, **vitrail** (*stained glass window*) becomes **vitraux** (*stained glass windows*).

  Notable exceptions: **détails** (*details*) and **chandails** (*sweaters*)

- ✔ Singular nouns that end in **-al** change their ending to **-aux** in the plural. For example, **hôpital** (*hospital*) becomes **hôpitaux** (*hospitals*).

  Notable exceptions: **bals** (*balls/dances*), **carnavals** (*carnivals*), **récitals** (*recitals*), **festivals** (*festivals*)

- ✔ Singular nouns that end in **-eau** add **-x** for the plural. For example, **château** (*castle*) becomes **châteaux** (*castles*).

- ✔ Singular nouns that end in **-eu** add **-x** for the plural. For example, **feu** (*fire*) becomes **feux** (*fires*).

  Notable exception: **pneus** (*tires*)

- ✔ Most of the time, a noun ending in **-ou**, like **le clou** (*the nail*), simply adds an **-s** in the plural (becoming **les clous**). However, a few rebels add an **-x**. For example, **bijou** (*jewel*) becomes **bijoux** (*jewels*).

See Table 2-5 for an overview of these patterns.

Book III

Building the Grammatical Foundation for Communication

Table 2-5	French Plural Patterns			
English	*French Singular*	*Singular Ending*	*French Plural*	*Plural Ending*
son	le fils	**-s**	les fils	**-s**
nose	le nez	**-z**	les nez	**-z**
voice	la voi**x**	**-x**	les voi**x**	**-x**
work	le trav**ail**	**-ail**	les trav**aux**	**-aux**
newspaper	le journ**al**	**-al**	les journ**aux**	**-aux**
coat	le mant**eau**	**-eau**	les mant**eaux**	**-eaux**
game	le j**eu**	**-eu**	les j**eux**	**-eux**
owl	le hib**ou**	**-ou**	les hib**oux**	**-oux**

A few French nouns have unpredictably irregular plurals — see Table 2-6 for some of the most common ones.

Table 2-6	Irregular French Plurals	
English	*French Singular*	*French Plural*
eye	un œil	des yeux
ma'am	madame	mesdames
miss	mademoiselle	mesdemoiselles
sir	monsieur	messieurs
sky	le ciel	les cieux

To make **madame**, **mademoiselle**, and **monsieur** plural, not only do you add an **-s** to the end, but you also change the beginnings of these words. Each of these forms of address is essentially made of two words: **ma dame** (*my lady*), **ma demoiselle** (*my young lady*), and **mon seigneur [mon sieur]** (*my lord*). When you form the plural, you have to change the built-in singular possessive adjective (**ma** or **mon**, which means *my*) to the plural possessive adjective **mes** (which also means *my*). See the section "Showing possession" later in this chapter for more info on possessives.

Expressing Gender and Number with Articles

Articles are small words that you can use only with nouns, and they have two purposes:

- ✔ Presenting a noun
- ✔ Indicating the gender and number of a noun

French articles may be definite, indefinite, or partitive. This section describes these three types of articles and identifies when and how to use them in your French writing and speech.

Identifying definite articles

Definite articles indicate that the noun they're presenting is specific. In English, the definite article is *the*. French has three different definite articles, which tell you that the noun is masculine, feminine, or plural. If the noun is singular, the article is **le**, which is masculine, or **la**, which is feminine. If the noun is plural, the article is **les**, no matter which gender the noun is.

If a singular noun begins with a vowel or silent **h**, the definite article **le** or **la** contracts to **l'**:

> **l'ami** (m) (*the friend*)
>
> **l'avocate** (f) (*the female lawyer*)
>
> **l'homme** (m) (*the man*)

Knowing when to use the definite articles

The French definite article is much more common than its English counterpart. In addition to referring to a specific noun, as in **le livre que j'ai acheté** (*the book I bought*), you use the French definite article to talk about the general sense of a noun, as in **J'aime le chocolat** (*I like chocolate*).

Look at Table 2-7, which shows you some examples of when French uses the definite article even though English does not.

Table 2-7   Circumstances That Call for French Definite Articles

Category	French	English
Abstracted ideas	**La** liberté est un droit essentiel.	*Freedom is an essential right.*
Generalization	**Les** êtres humains sont bizarres.	*Human beings are bizarre.*
Titles	**Le** professeur Curie est célèbre.	*Professor Curie is famous.*
Languages	**L'**anglais est la langue de l'Internet.	*English is the language of Internet.*
Continents	**L'**Europe est un grand continent.	*Europe is a big continent.*
Countries/states/regions	**La** Floride est une péninsule.	*Florida is a peninsula.*
Disciplines	**Les** arts martiaux sont populaires.	*Martial arts are popular.*
Parts of days	**Le** matin est beau ici.	*Morning is beautiful here.*
Days (on Sundays, on Mondays, and so on)	**Le** dimanche, je vais à la piscine.	*On Sundays, I go to the pool.*
Seasons	**Le** printemps est magnifique.	*Spring is magnificent.*

Book III

Building the Grammatical Foundation for Communication

On the other hand, you omit the definite article in French on the following occasions:

- When the day is a specific day:

    Je vais à un concert dimanche. (*I'm going to a concert on Sunday.*)

- Before titles, when you address the person:

    Bonjour, monsieur. (*Hello, sir.*)

- With seasons, after the preposition **en**:

    Je nage même en hiver. (*I swim even in winter.*)

Using contractions with definite articles

Whenever the definite article **le** or **les** follows the preposition **à** (*at, in, to*), or **de** (*of, from*), then the preposition and the article contract into a single word. See Table 2-8 for the contractions.

Table 2-8	Contractions of Prepositions and Definite Articles	
Preposition + Article	*Contraction*	*Example*
à + le	au	Je vais **au** stade. (*I'm going <u>to the</u> stadium.*)
à + les	aux	Je vais **aux** champs. (*I'm going <u>to the</u> fields.*)
de + le	du	Elle vient **du** magasin. (*She's coming <u>from the</u> store.*)
de + les	des	Elle vient **des** Antilles. (*She comes <u>from the</u> Antilles.*)

Although English often uses *'s* or just an apostrophe to express ownership — *the cat's paw, the emperor's boots, Jules' submarine* — you use the preposition **de** to express ownership in French. Make sure you use the contracted definite article when necessary, as in these examples:

C'est **le bureau du professeur.** (*This is <u>the teachers' office.</u> Literally: This is <u>the office of the teacher.</u>*)

Tu veux savoir **le prix de la maison.** (*You want to know <u>the price of the house.</u>*)

C'est **la femme du maire.** (*This is <u>the mayor's wife.</u> Literally: This is the wife of the mayor.*)

Identifying indefinite articles

An indefinite article refers to an unspecific noun. The singular English indefinite articles are *a* and *an*. French also has two singular indefinite articles, but the one you use depends on the gender of the noun: **un** is for masculine nouns, **une**, for feminine. The plural English indefinite article is *some,* which is often implied in English but must be expressed in French, as in **J'achète des cerises** (*I'm buying [some] cherries*).

Knowing when to use indefinite articles

You use the indefinite article basically the same way in French and English — to refer to an unspecific noun, as in **J'ai acheté une voiture** (*I bought a car*) or **Je veux voir un film** (*I want to see a movie*). Note that **un** and **une** can also mean *one*: **J'ai un frère** (*I have one brother*).

Des is the plural indefinite article, which you use for two or more masculine and/or feminine nouns: **J'ai des idées** (*I have some ideas*), **Nous avons vu des oiseaux** (*We saw some birds*). The indefinite article is necessary in French even when it's omitted but implied in English:

> J'ai acheté **des** chaussures chères. (*I bought [some] expensive shoes.*)

> Je cherche **des** baskets blancs. (*I'm looking for [some] white sneakers.*)

When you ask a question, the plural article **des** translates as *any:*

> **Tu as des questions ?** (*Do you have any questions?*)

The indefinite article **un**, **une**, or **des** changes to **de**, meaning *(not) any,* after a negated verb (with the exception of **être**). Note how **des** changes to **de** when you put **ne . . . pas** (*not*) in this sentence:

> J'ai **des** questions. (*I have [some] questions.*)

> Je **n'**ai **pas de** questions. (*I don't have any questions.*)

You omit the indefinite article at times, such as when you state someone's occupation or after the adjective **quel** used in exclamations. Look at the examples:

> **Il est serveur**. (*He is a server.*)

> **Elle est avocate.** (*She is a lawyer.*)

> **Quel animal !** (*What an animal!*)

> **Quelle histoire !** (*What a story!*)

Book III

Building the Grammatical Foundation for Communication

Approaching indefinite adjectives

Indefinite articles are kind of vague — you may be talking about *a book* or *some books* rather than a specific book — but French has indefinite adjectives that convey even more of an idea of vagueness. These adjectives can act like regular, descriptive adjectives, but some of them also function as articles, which accompany the noun. Some of them match the gender and number of the noun.

The adjective **certain** (*certain*), for example, has four forms: **certain** (masculine singular), **certaine** (feminine singular), **certains** (masculine plural), and **certaines** (feminine plural). Here are a couple of ways to use **certain**:

- **As a descriptive adjective:** J'ai un **certain** malaise. (*I'm feeling a certain discomfort/uneasiness.*)
- **As an indefinite article: Certains** jours, elle est vraiment triste. (*On certain days, she is really sad.*)

The adjective **quelques** (*a few, some*) exists only in the plural, with no differences in gender. It can act as a descriptive adjective or an indefinite article:

- **As a descriptive adjective:** Tu veux les **quelques** dollars que j'ai ? (*You want the few dollars I have?*)
- **As an indefinite article:** Ils ont **quelques** bons amis. (*They have a few good friends.*)

The adjective **aucun** (*no, not any*) has a feminine form, **aucune**, but no plural form because of its meaning. It functions as an article:

Nous n'avons **aucun** souci. (*We have no worry.*)

Vous n'avez **aucune** angoisse. (*You don't have any anguish.*)

Weighing in on some partitive articles

Partitive articles are used with things that you take only a part of. They don't exist in English, so the best translation is the word *some*. As with the definite articles, French has three partitive articles, depending on the gender and number of the noun:

- Masculine: **du** (a contraction of **de** + **le**)
- Feminine : **de la**
- Plural: **des** (a contraction of **de** + **les**)

When a singular noun begins with a vowel or mute **h**, the partitive article **du** or **de la** has to contract to **de l'**:

> **de l'oignon** (*some onion*)
>
> **de l'eau** (*some water*)
>
> **de l'hélium** (*some helium*)

You use the partitive article with food, drink, and other uncountable things that you take or use only a part of, such as air and money, as well as with abstract things, such as intelligence and patience. If you do eat or use all of something, and if it's countable, then you need the definite or indefinite article (see the preceding sections for details). Compare the following sentence pairs — the first sentence uses the partitive article, and the second uses the definite article:

> **J'ai acheté du chocolat.** (*I bought some chocolate* — 1 pound.)
>
> **J'ai acheté le chocolat.** (*I bought the chocolate* — that you like so much, or that Jacques told me about.)
>
> **Je veux de la tarte.** (*I want some pie* — such as one piece, or the part that's in the bakery display case.)
>
> **Je veux la tarte.** (*I want the pie* — the whole one at the bakery, or the one that Annette baked this morning.)

Getting Particular with Article-Like Adjectives

To say *my*, you use a possessive adjective. To say *this* thing, you use a demonstrative adjective. These words are like articles, but they're called adjectives because they give the noun they precede a particular attribute, specifying who owns the noun or which one it is. Like other adjectives and articles, possessive and demonstrative articles change to match the gender and the number of the noun they describe.

Showing possession

Possessive adjectives help assign ownership. In English, the possessive adjectives are *my, your, his, her, our,* and *their*.

In French, because every noun has a gender, the possessive adjectives must agree in gender and in number with the possessed object, not with the person possessing the object. For example, in French, there's no difference between *his* hat and *her* hat — both are **son chapeau**. Table 2-9 lists the owners of the objects followed by the possessive adjectives you use for masculine, feminine, and plural objects.

Here are a couple of examples:

> **Elle a un chien. C'est son chien.** (*She has a dog. It's her dog.*) Notice that the possessive adjective **son** agrees not with **elle**, the feminine subject, but with **chien**, a masculine, singular noun.
>
> **Il a une maison. C'est sa maison.** (*He has a house. It's his house.*) Here, the possessive adjective **sa** agrees with **maison**, which is feminine singular, not with the masculine subject **il**.

Table 2-9	French Possessive Adjectives		
Owner of the Objects	*Possessive Adjective for Masculine Singular Objects*	*Possessive Adjective for Feminine Singular Objects*	*Possessive Adjective for Plural Objects*
je (*I*)	**mon** (*my*)	**ma** (*my*)	**mes** (*my*)
tu (*you — singular familiar*)	**ton** (*your*)	**ta** (*your*)	**tes** (*your*)
il/elle/on (*he/she/one*)	**son** (*his/her*)	**sa** (*his/her*)	**ses** (*his/her*)
nous (*we*)	**notre** (*our*)	**notre** (*our*)	**nos** (*our*)
vous (*you — plural or singular formal*)	**votre** (*your*)	**votre** (*your*)	**vos** (*your*)
ils/elles (*they*)	**leur** (*their*)	**leur** (*their*)	**leurs** (*their*)

The possessive adjectives for *my*, *your* (singular informal), and *his/her* have three forms, depending on the gender, number, and first letter of the noun they're used with. Note that if a feminine singular noun begins with a vowel or mute **h**, you use the masculine singular possessive adjective. Here are a few examples:

> **J'ai un vélo, une moto et des chevaux. Ce sont mon vélo, ma moto et mes chevaux.** (*I have a bike, a motorcycle, and some horses. They are my bike, my motorcycle, and my horses.*)

> **Il a une idée. Son idée est très bonne.** (*He has an idea. His idea is very good.*) Even though **idée** is feminine, you use **son** because **idée** starts with a vowel.

The possessive adjectives for *our, your* (plural or singular formal), and *their* have only two forms, one for the singular (**notre, votre,** or **leur**) and one for the plural (**nos, vos,** or **leurs**), regardless of gender:

> **Où est notre voiture ?** (*Where is our car?*)

> **Où sont nos billets ?** (*Where are our tickets?*)

Being demonstrative: This one, that one

You use demonstrative adjectives before nouns to indicate specific nouns, such as *this book* or *these people*. Demonstrative adjectives agree in gender and number with the nouns they accompany. In French, the singular demonstrative adjectives are **ce, cet,** and **cette** (*this, that*), depending on whether the noun is masculine starting with a consonant, masculine starting with a vowel or mute **h**, or feminine. There's only one plural demonstrative adjective: **ces** (*these, those*). Table 2-10 summarizes the uses of these adjectives.

Table 2-10	Demonstrative Adjectives	
Masculine Singular	*Feminine Singular*	*Masculine/Feminine Plural*
ce (*this/that* — followed by a consonant) **cet** (*this/that* — followed by a vowel or mute **h**)	**cette** (*this/that*)	**ces** (*these/those*)

Look at these examples of demonstrative adjectives:

> **ce billet** (*this/that ticket*)

> **cet après-midi** (*this/that afternoon*)

> **cette promenade** (*this/that walk*)

> **ces tableaux** (*these/those paintings*)

To mark a sharp contrast between things or people you're comparing, you can add **-ci** or **-là** after a noun to express *here* or *there*:

> **Ce** tableau-**ci** est moderne mais **ce** tableau-**là** est du 17e siècle. (*This painting here is modern, but that painting there is from the 17th century.*)

> **Ces** manteaux-**ci** sont à la mode. **Ces** manteaux-**là** sont démodés. (*These coats are in style. Those coats are out of style.*)

Which one? Asking with interrogative adjectives

The interrogative adjective **quel** means *which* or *what* and acts a lot like an article. However, you use it to ask questions, as in **Quelle est la date?** (*What is the date?*). This adjective has four forms to match the gender and number of a noun it accompanies:

- Masculine singular: **quel** film (*which movie*)
- Feminine singular: **quelle** amie (*which friend*)
- Masculine plural: **quels** châteaux (*which castles*)
- Feminine plural: **quelles** images (*which images/pictures*)

Look at some example sentences that use **quel** as an interrogative adjective:

> **Quelles** réponses sont correctes ? (*Which answers are correct?*)

> J'ai rendez-vous chez le médecin. Mais **quel** jour est-ce ? (*I have an appointment at the doctor's. But which day is it?*)

You can also use **quel** to exclaim about something or someone, as in the following examples:

> **Quel** malheur ! (*What a misfortune/pity!*)

> J'ai tellement de choses à faire ! **Quelle** corvée ! (*I have so many things to do! What a chore!*)

Chapter 3

Dealing with the Here and Now: The Present Tense

In This Chapter

▶ Familiarizing yourself with subject pronouns and subject-verb agreement

▶ Looking at regular verb endings and conjugations

▶ Conjugating stem-changers and flat-out irregular verbs

*V*erbs express actions and states of being. They state, command, and question. They're the biggest key to revealing the meaning of a sentence. Here's your chance to get a handle on the present tense of verbs to describe what's happening, what people's routines are, or what a current situation is like. This most common French verb tense performs triple duty, because it can represent three different constructions in English: *I* [verb], *I do* [verb], and *I am* [*-ing* form of verb]. For example, **je mange** means *I eat, I do eat,* and *I am eating.*

In this chapter, we show you how to conjugate French verbs in the present tense. *Conjugating* a verb means changing the ending of the verb when the subject changes (for example, from *I* to *you*). Putting the correct subject with the correct verb ending is called *subject-verb agreement,* and we cover that topic here, too. Consider reading this chapter a huge investment in your French training, because you'll pick up skills that will help you far and wide and for a long time.

Understanding Subject Pronouns and Subject-Verb Agreement

The *subject* of a sentence is the person, place, or thing that's doing something. In the sentence *My dog has fleas,* for example, *my dog* is the subject. A *subject pronoun* can replace a subject so that if you've already mentioned your dog, you can just say *he* when you refer to your dog again.

Subject pronouns are important in French because each one requires a specific conjugated verb form. In a verb conjugation table, each subject pronoun represents any noun that plays the subject's role in the conversation. Subject pronouns may be singular or plural, and they may be *first person* (the speaker), *second person* (whoever's being addressed), or *third person* (everyone else). Table 3-1 breaks down the pronouns so you can better understand them.

Not every sentence or phrase uses a pronoun as the subject, but we use subject pronouns when showing verb conjugations because pronouns automatically give you information on number and person. Knowing the number and person of the subject is vital for knowing which conjugated form to use.

Table 3-1	French Subject Pronouns and Their English Cohorts	
Person	**Singular**	**Plural**
1st person	**je** (*I*)	**nous** (*we*)
2nd person	**tu** (*you*)	**vous** (*you*)
3rd person	**il** (*he, it*) **elle** (*she, it*) **on** (*one, people, they, we*)	**ils** (*they* — masculine) **elles** (*they* — feminine)

Note: In formal situations, **vous** can have a singular meaning — see "Tu or vous: The second person" for details.

Je or nous: The first person

Je is the first-person singular. Unlike its English equivalent, *I*, you don't capitalize **je** unless it begins a sentence:

> **Demain, je vais en France.** (*Tomorrow, I'm going to France.*)
>
> **Je suis américain.** (*I am American.*)

Note that when **je** is followed by word beginning with a vowel or mute **h**, the **je** contracts to **j'**: **Maintenant, j'habite en Californie** (*Now I live in California*).

Nous is the first-person plural, and it means *we*. You use it the same way in French and English:

> **Nous allons en France.** (*We're going to France.*)
>
> **Nous mangeons à midi.** (*We eat at noon.*)

Tu or vous: The second person

Tu and **vous** both mean *you,* but French distinguishes between different kinds of *you:*

- ✔ **Tu** is singular and informal (familiar), meaning that you use it only when you're talking to one person you know well — such as a family member, friend, classmate, or colleague — or to a child or animal.

- ✔ **Vous** is plural (regardless of formality) or formal singular. You use it

  - Whenever you're talking to more than one person, whether you know them or not. It then means *you both* or *you all.*

  - When you're talking to someone you don't know or you want to show respect to, such as your teacher, doctor, or boss. It still means *you,* of course, but it's a formal *you* addressed to one person.

Note that for the sake of keeping conjugation tables simple, we include the conjugated **vous** form of a verb on the plural side of the table only, even though it sometimes has a singular meaning.

If you're not sure whether to use **tu** or **vous**, be respectful and opt for **vous.** Except for when a close friend introduces you, you normally start out using **vous** with everyone you meet, except children. At some point, if you become friends, a new person may ask you to use **tu** by saying something like **On peut se tutoyer** (*We can use* tu *with one another*). English has no real equivalent to this invitation — "Call me John" comes close, but it doesn't indicate the same shift to intimacy as switching from **vous** to **tu** does. Using **tu** without this sort of invitation can be offensive, but the French usually make allowances for nonnative speakers.

Here are some examples that use **tu** and **vous**:

> **Tu peux commencer maintenant.** (*You can begin now.*)
>
> **Vous pouvez commencer.** (*You can start.*)

Il, elle, or on: The third-person singular

Il and **elle** mean *he* and *she*, respectively. When you want to say *it*, you have to figure out the gender of the subject because you use **il** to refer to a masculine subject and **elle** to refer to a feminine subject (see Chapter 2 of Book III for details on noun gender).

> **Il** a deux sœurs. (*He has two sisters.*)
>
> Où est mon livre ? **Il** est sur la table. (*Where is my book? It's on the table.*)
>
> **Elle** veut travailler ici. (*She wants to work here.*)
>
> Je vois la voiture. **Elle** est dans la rue. (*I see the car. It's in the street.*)

On is an indefinite pronoun that literally means *one:*

> **On ne doit pas dire cela.** (*One shouldn't say that.*)

But **on** can also mean *you, people* in general, or *we* informally. In any case, the word **on** is considered singular:

> **On ne sait jamais.** (*You never know.*)
>
> **On ne fait plus attention.** (*People don't pay attention anymore.*)
>
> **On va partir à midi.** (*We're going to leave at noon.*)

Ils or elles: The third-person plural

Ils and **elles** mean *they*. **Ils** is used for

- Groups of men or masculine nouns
- Mixed groups of men and women
- Masculine and feminine nouns together

Elles is used only for groups of women or feminine nouns. Even with only one man in a group of a thousand women, you have to use **ils**.

Here are some examples using **ils** and **elles**. The subject pronouns are in bold, and the words they stand in for are underlined:

> <u>Paul et David</u> **[ils]** habitent à Bruxelles. (*Paul and David [they] live in Brussels.*)

> Où sont <u>mes livres</u> ? **Ils** sont dans ta chambre. (*Where are my books? They're in your room.*)

> <u>Lise, Marie-Laure, Robert et Anne</u> **[ils]** partent ensemble. (*Lise, Marie-Laure, Robert, and Anne [they] are leaving together.*)

> <u>Ma mère et ma sœur</u> **[elles]** aiment danser. (*My mother and sister [they] like to dance.*)

> Je vois <u>tes clés</u>. **Elles** sont sur mon bureau. (*I see your keys. They're on my desk.*)

Conjugating Regular French Verbs

The French language classifies verbs to make them easier to conjugate. For example, if you know the conjugation of one verb in a given category, you can conjugate many verbs of the same type effortlessly because they follow the same pattern.

Verbs are classified according to the endings of their infinitives. All French verb infinitives end in **-er**, **-ir**, **-re**, or **-oir**. Within those four categories are regular and irregular verbs.

French has three groups of regular verbs:

- ✔ Verbs whose infinitive ends in **-er**, such as **parler** (*to speak*)
- ✔ Verbs whose infinitive ends in **-ir**, such as **finir** (*to finish*)
- ✔ Verbs whose infinitive ends in **-re**, such as **vendre** (*to sell*)

This section focuses on each group of regular verbs. We cover stem-change and irregular verbs (including verbs whose infinitives end in **-oir**) later in the chapter. If you can master the conjugation of regular verbs, you can express yourself in many everyday situations.

Book III

Building the Grammatical Foundation for Communication

Exploring -er verbs

The **-er** verbs are the most common group of French verbs, so knowing how to conjugate the present tense of one regular **-er** verb allows you to conjugate hundreds of **-er** verbs and express hundreds of ideas.

The verb **parler** (*to speak*) serves as an example in this group. Take **parler** and drop the **-er**, which leaves you with the stem, **parl-**. Then add the appropriate ending (**-e**, **-es**, **-e**, **-ons**, **-ez**, or **-ent**) depending on the subject pronoun. For example, if you start a sentence with **je** (*I*), you need the **-e** ending. Use the following endings to correctly conjugate a regular, present-tense **-er** verb.

Regular Present-Tense -er Verb Endings	
je **-e**	nous **-ons**
tu **-es**	vous **-ez**
il/elle/on **-e**	ils/elles **-ent**

The present-tense conjugations for a regular **-er** verb such as **parler** (*to speak*) are as follows:

parler (*to speak*)	
je parl**e**	nous parl**ons**
tu parl**es**	vous parl**ez**
il/elle/on parl**e**	ils/elles parl**ent**
Je **parle** français. (*I speak French.* OR *I am speaking French.* OR *I do speak French.*)	

This pattern applies to all regular **-er** verbs. Table 3-2 lists some common **-er** verbs that you may encounter in your everyday French-speaking life. You can also check out Appendix A for more regular **-er** verbs.

Table 3-2	Common Regular -er Verbs
-er Verb	*Translation*
adorer	*to adore*
aimer	*to like, to love*
arriver	*to arrive*

-er Verb	Translation
chanter	to sing
chercher	to look for
danser	to dance
demander	to ask
écouter	to listen to
enseigner	to teach
étudier	to study
habiter	to live (somewhere)
jouer jouer à jouer de	to play to play a sport or game to play an instrument
marcher	to walk
regarder	to watch/look at
rencontrer	to meet
téléphoner	to call
tomber	to fall
travailler	to work
trouver	to find
visiter	to visit (a place, not people)

If the verb begins with a vowel or a mute **h**, drop the **e** of **je** and add an apostrophe. For example, **j'aime** (*I like/love*) or **j'habite** (*I live*). However, the **u** in **tu** is never dropped, so you still have **tu aimes** or **tu habites**.

Introducing -ir verbs

After you understand how to conjugate regular **-er** verbs, you can easily use that skill to form the present tense for **-ir** verbs. Simply drop the final **-ir** of the infinitive and add the following endings to the stem:

Regular Present-Tense -ir Verb Endings	
je **-is**	nous **-issons**
tu **-is**	vous **-issez**
il/elle/on **-it**	ils/elles **-issent**

Book III

Building the Grammatical Foundation for Communication

Here are the present-tense conjugations for a regular **-ir** verb such as **finir** (*to finish*):

finir (*to finish*)	
je fin**is**	nous fin**issons**
tu fin**is**	vous fin**issez**
il/elle/on fin**it**	ils/elles fin**issent**
Je **finis** mes devoirs. (*I finish my homework*. OR *I am finishing my homework*. OR *I do finish my homework*.)	

Table 3-3 lists some common **-ir** verbs. Choose a verb from the list and try it out with the present-tense conjugation. You can also check out Appendix A for more regular **-ir** verbs.

Table 3-3	Common Regular -ir Verbs
-ir Verb	*Translation*
applaudir	*to applaud*
bâtir	*to build*
choisir	*to choose*
établir	*to establish*
finir	*to finish*
grandir	*to grow (up)*
grossir	*to gain weight*
maigrir	*to lose weight*
obéir à	*to obey*
pâlir	*to turn pale*
punir	*to punish*
réagir	*to react*
réfléchir à	*to reflect, to think (about)*
remplir	*to fill (out)*
réunir	*to unite, to gather, to assemble, to meet*
réussir (à)	*to succeed (in)/to pass a test*
vieillir	*to grow old*

Focusing on -re verbs

The third group of regular verbs is the **-re** group. This verb form is also easy to conjugate. Just drop the **-re** from the infinitive and add the appropriate endings to the stem. Use the following chart to conjugate these verbs.

Regular Present-Tense **-re** Verb Endings	
je **-s**	nous **-ons**
tu **-s**	vous **-ez**
il/elle/on -[nothing]	ils/elles **-ent**

You don't add any endings to the third-person singular **il**, **elle**, or **on** form. The stem is enough. For example, **il attend** means *he waits, he's waiting,* or *he does wait.*

Here's **vendre** (*to sell*), a regular **-re** verb, conjugated in the present tense:

vendre (*to sell*)	
je vend**s**	nous vend**ons**
tu vend**s**	vous vend**ez**
il/elle/on vend	ils/elles vend**ent**
Je **vends** la maison. (*I sell the house.* OR *I'm selling the house.* OR *I do sell the house.*)	

Table 3-4 provides some more examples of common **-re** verbs that you conjugate exactly like **vendre**.

Book III

Building the Grammatical Foundation for Communication

Table 3-4	Common Regular -re Verbs
-re Verbs	***Translation***
attendre	*to wait for*
descendre	*to go down (the stairs)*
entendre	*to hear*
fondre	*to melt*
perdre	*to lose, to waste time*
rendre rendre visite à quelqu'un	*to give back, to return* *to pay a visit to someone (to visit someone)*

Dealing with Present-Tense Irregularities

Two types of regular **-er** verbs require tiny adjustments in the **nous** form of the present tense. They're conjugated just like any other **-er** verb in all forms except for **nous** and **vous**. This section gives you the lowdown on these irregular changes, including alterations to the spellings and stems of some words.

Preserving pronunciation in -cer and -ger verbs

For pronunciation reasons, regular **-er** verbs ending in **-cer** and **-ger** have a slight spelling change in certain conjugations. In French (as in English), the letter *c* has two sounds: *hard,* like the *c* in *coal,* and *soft,* like the *c* in *celery.* The French **c** is

- ✔ Hard when it precedes the vowels **a**, **o**, or **u**
- ✔ Soft when it precedes **e**, **i**, or **y**

The last **c** in **-cer** verbs is soft because it precedes **e**, which means it needs to be soft in all conjugated forms. For example, take the verb **prononcer** (*to pronounce*), which is conjugated like a regular **-er** verb with one exception. In the **nous** form of the verb **prononcer**, the **c** would become hard before the vowel **o**: **nous prononcons**. To avoid that, the **c** changes to **ç**. (The little tail is called a *cedilla,* or *cédille* in French.) Now you have **nous prononçons**, and the **c** is soft, just like in the infinitive and all the other conjugated forms of the verb. Take a look at the conjugated forms of the verb **prononcer**:

prononcer (*to pronounce*)	
je prononc**e**	nous prononç**ons**
tu prononc**es**	vous prononc**ez**
il/elle/on prononc**e**	ils/elles prononc**ent**
Nous **prononçons** bien. (*We are pronouncing well.*)	

Table 3-5 shows you some common **-cer** verbs.

Table 3-5	Common -cer Verbs
-cer Verbs	**Translation**
annoncer	*to announce*
avancer	*to advance*
balancer	*to sway*
commencer	*to begin*
dénoncer	*to denounce*
divorcer	*to divorce*
effacer	*to erase*
influencer	*to influence*
lancer	*to throw*
remplacer	*to replace*

Like *c,* the letter *g* also has two sounds in French: hard, like the *g* in *glass,* and soft, like the *g* in *massage.* The French **g** is

- ✔ Hard when it precedes **a**, **o**, or **u**
- ✔ Soft when it precedes **e**, **i**, or **y**

The last **g** in **-ger** verbs is soft, so it has to be soft in all its conjugated forms. For example, you conjugate the verb **bouger** (*to move*) like a regular **-er** verb except for in the **nous** form. There, to avoid the hard **g**, you add an **e**: **bougeons**. This change makes the **g** soft, like in the infinitive and all the other conjugated forms. Take a look at the conjugated forms of the verb **bouger**.

bouger (*to move*)	
je boug**e**	nous boug**eons**
tu boug**es**	vous boug**ez**
il/elle/on boug**e**	ils/elles boug**ent**
Nous **bougeons** nos doigts. (*We're moving our fingers.*)	

You can see some common **-ger** verbs in Table 3-6.

Book III

Building the Grammatical Foundation for Communication

Table 3-6	Common -ger Verbs
-ger Verbs	*Translation*
arranger	to arrange
changer	to change
corriger	to correct
déménager	to move (residence)
déranger	to disturb
diriger	to direct
exiger	to demand, insist
loger	to lodge
manger	to eat
mélanger	to mix
partager	to share
plonger	to dive
voyager	to travel

Getting some stem-changing verbs to boot

For phonetic reasons, some verbs have a stem change in all forms except for **nous** and **vous**.

For example, the verb **acheter** (*to buy*) has a mute **e** in its infinitive stem and in its **nous** and **vous** stems. In forms other than **nous** and **vous**, the **e** of the stem is pronounced; therefore, you must add an **accent grave** to the **e**. The resulting letter **è** gives an open *eh* sound, as in the English words *set* and *met*. So you say, **J'achète un souvenir** (zhah-sheht uhN sooh-vuh-neer) for *I'm buying a souvenir.*

Similarly, the verb **espérer** (*to hope*) has an **accent aigu** in the infinitive stem and in the **nous** and **vous** stems. The letter **é** resembles the sound *ey* in the words *make* and *lake*. So you say **Nous espérons venir** (nooh zey-spey-rohN vuh-neer) for *We hope to come.* However, the pronunciation of forms other than **nous** and **vous** require that you change the **accent aigu** to **grave**. So you say **J'espère aussi** (zhey-spehr oh-see) for *I hope so, too.*

Verbs like **appeler** (*to call*) and **jeter** (*to throw*) have a silent **e** in the infinitive stem and in their **nous** and **vous** stems. However, in forms other than **nous** and **vous**, the **e** is pronounced, so you have to double the **l** of **appeler** and the **t** of **jeter** to render the appropriate sound.

Here's a summary of possible stem changes, which we discuss in the following subsections:

- e → è
- é → è
- eter → ett
- eler → ell
- y → i

Verbs that have a stem change in all conjugated forms except for the **nous** and **vous** forms are called *boot verbs* because if you take their verb conjugation tables and trace around everything except the **nous** and **vous** forms, you end up with the shape of a boot. (You can try this trick right now with the verbs **acheter**, **espérer**, **jeter**, and **essayer**, which appear in the following sections). The stems in this boot are all similar to each other, and the **nous** and **vous** forms resemble the infinitive.

The endings of stem-changing verbs are like all regular **-er** verbs. Head to the earlier section "Exploring -er verbs" to see these endings.

Tackling e → è stem-changing verbs

For verbs that have a mute **e** in the second-to-last syllable in their infinitive forms, you add the accent grave in all conjugated forms except the **nous** and **vous** forms. Look at the conjugation of the verb **acheter** (ahsh-tey) (*to buy*).

acheter (*to buy*)	
j'achè**te**	nous achet**ons**
tu achè**tes**	vous achet**ez**
il/elle/on achè**te**	ils/elles achè**tent**
J'**achète** des légumes. (*I'm buying vegetables.*)	

Check out Table 3-7 for other verbs like **acheter**.

Table 3-7	Adding an Accent Grave (è) to the Mute e
Verb	*Translation*
amener	*to bring*
geler	*to freeze*

(continued)

Book III

Building the Grammatical Foundation for Communication

Table 3-7 *(continued)*

Verb	Translation
lever	to raise
mener	to lead, to take along
peser	to weigh
promener	to take a person or a pet for a walk
se lever*	to get up, to stand
se promener*	to take a stroll, to take a walk

*Se lever and *se promener* are reflexive verbs; see Chapter 3 in Book IV for details on reflexive verbs and pronouns.

Taking a grave turn: é → è stem-changing verbs

Verbs that have an **é** (an **e** with an **accent aigu**) in the second-to-last syllable in their infinitive also undergo stem changes. The **accent aigu** (**é**) changes to an **accent grave** (**è**) in all the conjugated forms except for the **nous** and **vous** forms. Check out the conjugation of the verb **espérer**.

espérer (*to hope*)	
j'esp**è**re	nous esp**é**r**ons**
tu esp**è**res	vous esp**é**r**ez**
il/elle/on esp**è**re	ils/elles esp**è**r**ent**
J'**espè**re que tu vas bien. (*I hope you're doing well.*)	

Table 3-8 gives you a list of verbs that are similar to **espérer.**

Table 3-8	Changing the é to è
Verb	Translation
céder	to give up, to yield
exagérer	to exaggerate
préférer*	to prefer
protéger	to protect
répéter*	to repeat
suggérer	to suggest

*Note: The first *é* in the verbs *préférer* and *répéter* never changes; the last *é* changes to *è* in all forms except for *nous* and *vous*.

Examining -eler and -eter stem-changing verbs

Some verbs that end in **-eter** and **-eler** double the **t** or **l** after the mute **e** within the boot forms (excluding the **nous** and **vous** forms) to indicate that you pronounce the **e**. Consider the following example of **jeter**.

jeter (*to throw*)	
je je**tte**	nous jet**ons**
tu je**ttes**	vous jet**ez**
il/elle/on je**tte**	ils/elles je**ttent**
Je **jette** la balle. (*I'm throwing the ball.*)	

For a list of some common **-eter** and **-eler** verbs, check out Table 3-9.

Table 3-9	Common -eter and -eler Verbs
Verb	**Translation**
appeler	*to call*
épeler	*to spell*
rappeler	*to call back*
rejeter	*to reject*
***s'appeler**	*to be called (to be named)*
***se rappeler**	*to remember*

Refer to Chapter 3 of Book IV for details on reflexive verbs and pronouns.

Book III

Building the Grammatical Foundation for Communication

Mastering y → i stem-changing verbs

Another group of stem-changing verbs with regular endings involves infinitives that end in **-yer**. In this group, the **y** changes to an **i** in front of a mute **e** in all conjugated forms within the boot (that is, except for in the **nous** and **vous** forms). Here's the conjugation of the verb **envoyer** (*to send*).

envoyer (*to send*)	
j'envo**ie**	nous envoy**ons**
tu envo**ies**	vous envoy**ez**
il/elle/on envo**ie**	ils/elles envo**ient**
J'**envoie** une lettre. (*I'm sending a letter.*)	

Note that although this stem change is required for verbs that end in **-oyer** and **-uyer,** it's optional for verbs that end in **-ayer.** You can conjugate verbs such as **payer** (*to pay*) with or without the stem change: **Je paie** and **je paye** are both acceptable.

Examine Table 3-10 for other common verbs of this type.

Table 3-10	Common -yer Verbs
Verb	*Translation*
effrayer	*to scare, to frighten*
employer	*to use*
ennuyer	*to bother*
essayer	*to try*
essuyer	*to wipe*
nettoyer	*to clean*
payer	*to pay*
s'ennuyer*	*to be bored*
tutoyer	*to address someone informally by using the **tu** form*
vouvoyer	*to address someone formally by using the vous form*

For info on reflexive pronouns and reflexive verbs like **s'ennuyer, check out Chapter 3 of Book IV.*

Wrestling with Some Irregular Conjugations

French has numerous irregular verbs that have unique conjugation patterns limited to just a few verbs. In some cases, you just have to practice these conjugations until they feel natural, but in others, you can group verb families by their common irregular pattern. This section looks at several types of irregular French verbs and helps you keep track of them.

To get better at conjugating irregular verbs, try this quick exercise. Choose a verb and practice writing and reciting the forms of the verb for each subject pronoun. Take ten minutes to do this drill every day, and the conjugations should become second nature in no time.

Deceptive -ir verbs: Different stems, irregular endings

The conjugations for **venir** (*to come*), **tenir** (*to hold*), and all their derivatives have a stem change as well as irregular endings. In the singular conjugations and the third-person plural, the **e** in the stem changes to **ie**. However, the **nous** and **vous** forms keep their normal stems — the infinitive minus **-ir**. You can see the special endings for these verbs in the following table. The best way to understand these verbs is to look at the table, memorize the pattern, and apply it to related verbs.

venir (*to come*)	
je v**iens**	nous ven**ons**
tu v**iens**	vous ven**ez**
il/elle/on v**ient**	ils v**iennent**
Il **vient** dans deux heures. (*He's coming in two hours.*)	

Other verbs that follow this pattern include **revenir** (*to come back*), **devenir** (*to become*), **se souvenir** (*to remember*), **tenir** (*to hold*), **contenir** (*to contain*), and **maintenir** (*to maintain*).

Pseudo -ir verbs

Most verbs that end in **-tir**, like **sortir** (*to go out*), are conjugated with the endings of regular **-re** verbs, except for in the third-person singular. In the singular conjugations, you drop the **-ir** and the consonant just before it and add the endings **-s**, **-s**, and **-t**. In the plural forms, you just drop the **-ir** and use the endings **-ons**, **-ez**, and **-ent**. Commit the pattern in the following table to memory so that you can easily apply it to similar verbs.

sortir (*to go out*)	
je sor**s**	nous sort**ons**
tu sor**s**	vous sort**ez**
il/elle/on sor**t**	ils/elles sort**ent**
Nous **sortons** ce soir. (*We're going out tonight.*)	

Book III

Building the Grammatical Foundation for Communication

Other verbs that follow the same pattern as **sortir** include **mentir** (*to lie*), **sentir** (*to smell, to feel*), and **partir** (*to leave*).

Similarly, the verb **dormir** (*to sleep*) drops **-mir** from the infinitive for the singular forms and **-ir** for the plural forms. The verb **servir** (*to serve*) drops the **-vir** from the infinitive for the singular forms and **-ir** for the plural forms. Both verbs, like the **-tir** verbs, add the endings **-s**, **-s**, and **-t** in the singular conjugated forms and **-ons**, **-ez**, and **-ent** in the plural forms.

dormir (*to sleep*)	
je dor**s**	nous dorm**ons**
tu dor**s**	vous dorm**ez**
il/elle/on dor**t**	ils/elles dorm**ent**
Nous **dormons** comme des anges. (*We sleep like angels.*)	

servir (*to serve*)	
je ser**s**	nous serv**ons**
tu ser**s**	vous serv**ez**
il/elle/on ser**t**	ils/elles serv**ent**
Ils **servent** du Champagne pour fêter notre anniversaire de mariage. (*They're serving Champagne to celebrate our wedding anniversary.*)	

The -er-wannabe -ir verbs

Verbs that end in **-ffrir** and **-vrir**, like **offrir** (*to offer*) and **ouvrir** (*to open*), as well as the verb **accueillir** (*to welcome*), are conjugated with the same endings as regular **-er** verbs. To conjugate these verbs, just drop the **-ir** ending to find the stem and add then the following **-er** verb endings: **-e**, **-es**, **-e**, **-ons**, **-ez**, and **-ent**. Here's a look at **ouvrir** and **offrir**.

ouvrir (*to open*)	
j'ouvr**e**	nous ouvr**ons**
tu ouvr**es**	vous ouvr**ez**
il/elle/on ouvr**e**	ils/elles ouvr**ent**
Elles **ouvrent** la porte. (*They're opening the door.*)	

offrir (*to offer*)	
j'offre	nous offrons
tu offres	vous offrez
il/elle/on offre	ils/elles offrent
Elles **offrent** du parfum. (*They're offering perfume.*)	

Other verbs that follow this pattern include **découvrir** (*to discover*), **couvrir** (*to cover*), and **souffrir** (*to suffer*).

The take-charge prendre family

Prendre (*to take*) and all its derivatives are conjugated like regular **-re** verbs in the singular conjugated forms (with the endings **-s**, **-s**, and nothing). The plural forms, however, drop the **d** from the stem, and the third-person plural also takes on an extra **n**; these forms then take the regular **-re** verb endings: **-ons**, **-ez**, and **-ent**.

prendre (*to take*)	
je prends	nous prenons
tu prends	vous prenez
il/elle/on prend	ils/elles prennent
Ils **prennent** beaucoup de photos. (*They take a lot of pictures.*)	

Book III

Building the Grammatical Foundation for Communication

Similarly conjugated verbs include **apprendre** (*to learn*), **comprendre** (*to understand*), **entreprendre** (*to undertake*), **reprendre** (*to take back*), and **surprendre** (*to surprise*).

The mettre family

Like the verb **prendre** in the preceding section, the verb **mettre** (*to put/to put on*) and its derivatives have one stem in the singular and another stem in the plural. To form the singular conjugated forms, just drop the **-tre** from the infinitive and add **-s**, **-s**, and nothing. For the plural, bring back the **t** and add **-ons**, **-ez**, and **-ent**.

mettre (*to put, to put on*)	
je met**s**	nous mett**ons**
tu met**s**	vous mett**ez**
il/elle/on me**t**	ils/elles mett**ent**
Je **mets** mon manteau. (*I put my coat on.*)	

Similarly conjugated verbs include **admettre** (*to admit*), **permettre** (*to allow*), **promettre** (*to promise*), **soumettre** (*to submit/to subject*) and **transmettre** (*to transmit, to convey*).

The well-read family

The verbs **lire** (*to read*) and **dire** (*to tell, to say*) have similar patterns of conjugation, with one exception: The **vous** form of **dire** ends in **-tes**, just like the verbs **être** (*to be*), as in **vous êtes**, and **faire** (*to do, to make*), as in **vous faites**. (For details on **être** and **faire**, see the later section "Verbs of being and having.") The verb **lire**, on the other hand, has an **-s** in the stem in all its plural forms.

dire (*to say, to tell*)	
je di**s**	nous di**sons**
tu di**s**	vous di**tes**
il/elle/on di**t**	ils/elles di**sent**
Ils **disent** bonjour. (*They say hello.*)	

Other verbs conjugated like **dire** include **contredire** (*to contradict*), **interdire** (*to forbid*), **prédire** (*to predict*), and **redire** (*to repeat*). However, the **vous** forms of **contredire**, **interdire**, and **prédire** end in **-disez**.

lire (*to read*)	
je li**s**	nous li**sons**
tu li**s**	vous li**sez**
il/elle/on li**t**	ils/elles li**sent**
Ils **lisent** le journal. (*They read the newspaper.*)	

You conjugate **élire** (*to elect*), **relire** (*to reread*), **traduire** (*to translate*), and **conduire** (*to drive*) like you do **lire**.

The verb **écrire** (*to write*) has a conjugation similar to that of **lire**; drop the **-re** from the infinitive and add **-s**, **-s**, and **-t** for the singular. For the plural, add a **v** before the **-ons**, **-ez**, or **-ent**.

écrire (*to write*)	
j'écri**s**	nous écri**vons**
tu écri**s**	vous écri**vez**
il/elle/on écri**t**	ils/elles écri**vent**
Ils **écrivent** un courriel. (*They're writing an e-mail.*)	

Other verbs with conjugations like **écrire** include **décrire** (*to describe*), **inscrire** (*to inscribe*), **récrire** (*to rewrite*), and **transcrire** (*to transcribe*).

The recevoir family

Don't be fooled by the verb **recevoir** (*to receive*). It contains the verb **voir**, but it's conjugated very differently. (We show you the conjugated forms of **voir** in the later section "Seeing is believing: Voir and croire.") The endings of **recevoir** are regular, but look at the stem. You have to add a cedilla to the **c** in order to preserve the soft *s* sound of the **c** before **a**, **o**, or **u**. That way, the **c** is always pronounced *s* and not *k*. Look at the conjugation of **recevoir**.

Book III

Building the Grammatical Foundation for Communication

recevoir (*to receive*)	
je re**çois**	nous rece**vons**
tu re**çois**	vous rece**vez**
il/elle/on re**çoit**	ils/elles re**çoivent**
Elle **reçoit** un cadeau. (*She receives a present.*)	

Verbs conjugated like **recevoir** include **apercevoir** (*to notice, to perceive*), **concevoir** (*to conceive*), **décevoir** (*to disappoint, to deceive*), and **percevoir** (*to perceive*).

Remembering Notorious Irregular Pairs

Just like in life, where you may know a few eccentric people, French has some pairs of irregular verbs that are in worlds of their own; they're even more off-the-beaten-path than the irregular verbs we describe in the earlier section "Wrestling with Some Irregular Conjugations." However, they happen to be extremely useful. This section introduces them.

Wanting to do what you can: vouloir and pouvoir

The conjugated forms of **vouloir** (*to want*) and **pouvoir** (*to be able to*) are very similar. They have both stem changes and irregular endings. Check out the tables that follow.

vouloir (*to want to*)	
je v**eux**	nous v**oulons**
tu v**eux**	vous v**oulez**
il/elle/on v**eut**	ils/elles v**eulent**
Elles **veulent** danser. (*They want to dance.*)	

pouvoir (*to be able to, can, may*)	
je p**eux**	nous p**ouvons**
tu p**eux**	vous p**ouvez**
il/elle/on p**eut**	ils/elles p**euvent**
Tu **peux** partir. (*You may leave.*)	

Seeing is believing: Voir and croire

Voir (*to see*) and **croire** (*to believe*) are conjugated the same way. Take a look.

voir (*to see*)	
je v**ois**	nous v**oyons**
tu v**ois**	vous v**oyez**
il/elle/on v**oit**	ils/elles v**oient**
Nous **voyons** le volcan. (*We see the volcano.*)	

croire (*to believe*)	
je cr**ois**	nous cr**oyons**
tu cr**ois**	vous cr**oyez**
il/elle/on cr**oit**	ils/elles cr**oient**
Il **croit** au Père Noël. (*He believes in Santa Claus.*)	

Appreciating Uniquely Irregular Verbs

Some of the most important French verbs — those for being, doing, and other pivotal actions — have truly unique conjugations. Luckily, you'll encounter these verbs so often that you'll learn them quickly.

Putting in the time is the best way to master the everyday verbs in this section. Write out the conjugations and practice saying them. As you expand your vocabulary, use these verbs to discuss the cool things you have, talk about where your neighbor is going, or tell other people what they absolutely have to do.

Book III

Building the Grammatical Foundation for Communication

In the midst of these erratic conjugations, look for the following consistencies:

- ✔ The **nous** form almost always ends in **-ons**. (The exception is the verb **être**.)

- ✔ The **vous** form almost always ends in **-ez**. (Exceptions include **être**, **dire**, and **faire**, whose **vous** forms end in **-tes** instead.)

Verbs of being and having

In English, think of the countless times you use the verbs *to be* and *to have* in any kind of conversation. Obviously, you want to get up to speed on conjugating these verbs — **avoir** (*to have*) and **être** (*to be*) — stat! Because the forms of the verbs change almost completely every time you change the subject, you have to memorize each conjugated form of the verb. Look at the following tables.

avoir (*to have*)	
j'**ai**	nous **avons**
tu **as**	vous **avez**
il/elle/on **a**	ils/elles **ont**
J'**ai** une idée. (*I have an idea.*)	

être (*to be*)	
je **suis**	nous **sommes**
tu **es**	vous **êtes**
il/elle/on **est**	ils/elles **sont**
Tu **es** très intelligent. (*You're very smart.*)	

English language speakers use the progressive present tense much more frequently than the simple present: For example, "I'*m singing*" is more common than "I *sing*." Speakers of English have to resist the temptation to translate "I'm singing" as **je suis chanter**. Instead, just say **je chante**. These two words (subject and conjugated verb) translate as *I sing, I'm singing,* and *I do sing.* In some instances, though, when you really want to stress that something is happening *right now,* you can use the construction **être en train de**: **Je suis en train de chanter** (*I am [in the process of] singing [right now]*).

Verbs of going and doing

Going and doing may be regular topics of conversation, but conjugating the verbs **aller** (*to go*) and **faire** (*to do*) is anything but regular. Observe them closely in the following tables.

aller (*to go*)	
je **vais**	nous **allons**
tu **vas**	vous **allez**
il/elle/on **va**	ils/elles **vont**
Nous **allons** en France. (*We're going to France.*)	

faire (*to do, to make*)	
je **fais**	nous **faisons**
tu **fais**	vous **faites**
il/elle/on **fait**	ils/elles **font**
Il **fait** le lit. (*He's making the bed.*)	

Other verbs conjugated like **faire** are **refaire** (*to redo*), **défaire** (*to dismantle*), and **satisfaire** (*to satisfy*).

Verbs of knowledge

Do you know that I know Paris well? To say that sentence in French, you have to use two different verbs to account for the different meanings of *to know:* **savoir** (*to know [a fact], to know how*) and **connaître** (*to be familiar*). The sentence in French is **Savez-vous que je connais bien Paris ?** Here are the conjugations of the two verbs about knowing.

savoir (*to know, to know how*)	
je **sais**	nous **savons**
tu **sais**	vous **savez**
il/elle/on **sait**	ils/elles **savent**
Elles **savent** nager. (*They know how to swim.*)	

connaître (*to be familiar*)	
je **connais**	nous **connaissons**
tu **connais**	vous **connaissez**
il/elle/on **connaît**	ils/elles **connaissent**
Vous **connaissez** mon cousin ? (*Do you know my cousin?*)	

Verbs expressing necessity

The two verbs expressing necessity are indispensible, so you really need to know them. In fact, you can't express the "need to" concept without them. I'm referring to **devoir** (*should, to have to*) and **falloir** (*to be necessary*). Check out **devoir** in the following table:

devoir (*should, to have to*)	
je **dois**	nous **devons**
tu **dois**	vous **devez**
il/elle/on **doit**	ils/elles **doivent**
Vous **devez** essayer. (*You have to try.*)	

Falloir actually exists only in one conjugated form: **il faut** (*it's necessary/ one must*):

Il **faut** manger. (*It's necessary to eat.* OR *One must eat.*)

Chapter 4

Commanding and Instructing with the Imperative Mood

The *imperative* is the verb mood for giving orders, making suggestions, and offering advice. For example, when you say, "Close your eyes," "Stop that," or "Let's leave," you're using the imperative mood. The imperative is the only time that you don't name the subject along with the conjugated verb, but it's still *personal* because it has different forms for each of the three grammatical persons that you can order around: **tu**, **nous**, and **vous**.

The imperative is a mood, not a tense. Conjugating a verb in a certain *mood* allows the speaker to indicate how he or she feels about the action of the verb, whether it's real (the indicative mood), conditional (the conditional mood), subjective (the subjunctive mood), or a command (the imperative mood). The imperative mood indicates something that you're telling someone to do, but because that person may or may not actually do it, you don't use the indicative.

This chapter explains how to conjugate a verb in the imperative, covering the differences between affirmative commands ("Do it!") and negative commands ("Don't do it!"). We also show you how to add object pronouns to your commands, and we explore ways to give clear orders and instructions without using the imperative mood.

Made to Order: Conjugating in the Imperative

The imperative mood has only three conjugated forms because you can only command or instruct another person or other persons. You address **tu** (*you* singular familiar) or **vous** (*you* plural or singular formal), and occasionally you include yourself in the command and address **nous** (*us,* as in *Let's*).

Because there's no subject pronoun before the verb to guide you, getting the right form of the verb is extra important, because the verb is the only thing that tells you who's being ordered to do something. This section shows you how to go from a conjugated form of the present tense to the corresponding command form.

Making regular verbs imperative

The imperative forms of many French verbs are almost exactly the same as the present tense, except you don't use a subject pronoun with them. (Check out Chapter 3 of Book III for present-tense conjugations.) This section tells you how to conjugate regular verbs in the imperative. The patterns here also hold for stem-changing and spelling-change verbs.

Later, in "Personally Telling People What to Do," we present some examples that show how to use the familiar and formal commands as well as the inclusive *let's do it!* form of these verbs.

Imperative of -er verbs

When you want the imperative, you use the **nous** and **vous** forms of **-er** verbs exactly the way they are in the present indicative: Just drop the **-er** from the infinitive and then add **-ons** to the **nous** form or **-ez** to the **vous** form. For the **tu** form, however, **-er** verbs use the form they have in the present tense of the indicative minus the final **s**.

See Table 4-1 for the present tense indicative and imperative of **parler** (*to speak*). The subject pronouns are in parentheses in the right column to remind you that you don't use them with the imperative.

Table 4-1	Imperative of Parler (to talk, to speak), a Regular -er Verb
Present Tense Indicative	*Imperative*
tu parles (*you talk, you speak*)	(tu) **parle** (*talk, speak*)
nous parlons (*we talk, we speak*)	(nous) **parlons** (*let's talk, let's speak*)
vous parlez (*you talk, you speak*)	(vous) **parlez** (*talk, speak*)

Imperative of -ir and -re verbs

You use the **tu**, **nous**, and **vous** forms of **-ir** and **-re** verbs exactly the way they are in the present indicative when you want imperative forms. For **-ir** verbs, drop the **-ir** from the infinitive and then add **-is** to the **tu** form, **-issons** to the **nous** form, or **-issez** to the **vous** form. Table 4-2 shows the conjugation of a regular **-ir** verb.

Table 4-2	Imperative of Choisir (to choose), a Regular -ir Verb
Present Tense Indicative	*Imperative*
tu choisis (*you choose*)	(tu) **choisis** (*choose*)
nous choisissons (*we choose*)	(nous) **choisissons** (*let's choose*)
vous choisissez (*you choose*)	(vous) **choisissez** (*choose*)

For **-re** verbs, drop the **-re** from the infinitive and add **-s** to the **tu** form, **-ons** to the **nous** form, or **-ez** to the **vous** form. See Table 4-3 for the imperative form of a regular **-re** verb.

Table 4-3	Imperative of Vendre (to sell), a Regular -re Verb
Present Tense Indicative	*Imperative*
tu vends (*you sell*)	(tu) **vends** (*sell*)
nous vendons (*we sell*)	(nous) **vendons** (*let's sell*)
vous vendez (*you sell*)	(vous) **vendez** (*sell*)

The **tu** imperative of **-er** verbs doesn't end in **s**, but the **tu** imperative of **-ir** and **-re** verbs does.

Imperative of spelling-change verbs

Spelling-change verbs follow the same pattern in the imperative as regular verbs. For example, the **tu** form of **acheter** (*to buy*) in the imperative is **achète** (*buy*), the present tense **tu** form minus the **-s** ending. The other imperative forms match the present tense of the indicative: **achetez** (*buy* — singular formal or plural) and **achetons** (*let's buy*).

Making irregular commands

As long as you know how to conjugate irregular verbs in the present tense, you shouldn't have any trouble figuring out their imperative conjugations, because most irregular verbs use the same conjugations for the present tense and the imperative. (Check out Chapter 3 of Book III to see how to conjugate irregular verbs in the present tense.)

For example, the imperative forms of **partir** (*to leave*) match the present tense conjugations without the subject pronouns **tu**, **nous**, and **vous**. Take a look at Table 4-4.

Table 4-4   Imperative of Partir (to leave), an Irregular -ir Verb

Present Tense Indicative	Imperative
tu pars (*you leave*)	(tu) **pars** (*leave*)
nous partons (*we leave*)	(nous) **partons** (*let's leave*)
vous partez (*you leave*)	(vous) **partez** (*leave*)

The verb **aller** (*to go*), like regular **-er** verbs, loses its **-s** ending in the **tu** form of the imperative. Look at Table 4-5.

Table 4-5   Imperative of the Irregular Verb Aller (to go)

Present Tense Indicative	Imperative
tu vas (*you go*)	(tu) **va** (*go*)
nous allons (*we go*)	(nous) **allons** (*let's go*)
vous allez (*you go*)	(vous) **allez** (*go*)

The verb **ouvrir** (*to open*) — and related verbs conjugated like **-er** verbs in the present tense — likewise lose the **-s** ending in the **tu** form of the imperative.

Four French verbs — **avoir** (Table 4-6), **être** (Table 4-7), **savoir** (Table 4-8), and **vouloir** (Table 4-9) — have irregular imperative conjugations. (**Note:** The imperative forms for these four irregular verbs are similar to their subjunctive forms, which you can read about in Chapter 5 of Book IV.)

Table 4-6	Imperative of Avoir (to have)
Present Tense Indicative	*Imperative*
tu as (*you have*)	(tu) **aie** (*have*)
nous avons (*we have*)	(nous) **ayons** (*let's have*)
vous avez (*you have*)	(vous) **ayez** (*have*)

Table 4-7	Imperative of Être (to be)
Present Tense Indicative	*Imperative*
tu es (*you are*)	(tu) **sois** (*be*)
nous sommes (*we are*)	(nous) **soyons** (*let's be*)
vous êtes (*you are*)	(vous) **soyez** (*be*)

Table 4-8	Imperative of Savoir (to know)
Present Tense Indicative	*Imperative*
tu sais (*you know*)	(tu) **sache** (*know*)
nous savons (*we know*)	(nous) **sachons** (*let's know*)
vous savez (*you know*)	(vous) **sachez** (*know*)

Vouloir in the imperative isn't a command for someone to *want* something but rather a way of making a very polite request, as in **Veuillez m'excuser** (*Please excuse me*) or **Veuillez me répondre** (*Please answer me*). **Vouloir** is used only in the **vous** form because it's very formal. It also doesn't make much sense to say, "Let's want!" or "Let's excuse ourselves!" See Table 4-9.

Table 4-9	Imperative of Vouloir (to want)
Present Tense Indicative	*Imperative*
tu veux (*you want*)	not applicable
nous voulons (*we want*)	not applicable
vous voulez (*you want*)	(vous) **veuillez** (*please*)

Conjugating commands with reflexive verbs

To use reflexive verbs in the affirmative imperative — "Look at *yourself*," "Introduce *yourself*," "Sit *(yourself)* down" — you start by conjugating the verb according to whether it's a regular or irregular verb in the imperative (see the preceding sections). Then you attach the correct form of the reflexive pronoun — **toi**, **nous**, or **vous** — to the end of the verb with a hyphen, as in Tables 4-10 and 4-11. Note that the reflexive pronoun **tu** becomes **toi** when it follows the verb in this way. See Chapter 3 of Book III and Chapter 3 of Book IV for details on reflexive verbs.

Table 4-10	Imperative of Se Coucher (to go to bed), a Reflexive Verb
Present Tense Indicative	*Imperative*
tu te couches (*you go to bed*)	(tu) **couche-toi** (*go to bed*)
nous nous couchons (*we go to bed*)	(nous) **couchons-nous** (*let's go to bed*)
vous vous couchez (*you go to bed*)	(vous) **couchez-vous** (*go to bed*)

Table 4-11	Imperative of Se Taire (to be quiet), a Reflexive Verb
Present Tense Indicative	*Imperative*
tu te tais (*you are being quiet*)	(tu) **tais-toi** (*be quiet*)
nous nous taisons (*we are being quiet*)	(nous) **taisons-nous** (*let's be quiet*)
vous vous taisez (*you are being quiet*)	(vous) **taisez-vous** (*be quiet*)

Personally Telling People What to Do

With the imperative, you can give firm commands and lay down the law when talking to one of your children or another relative or a very good friend, especially when there's a sense of urgency. On the other hand, you may be talking to a new acquaintance and trying to inform and advise the person, in which case you need to be more formal. Or you may be advising several people. Finally, you can give advice or instructions that include you, as in *let's get something to eat* (see Chapter 7 of Book I for your snack options). This section explores all those scenarios — which call for the personal **tu**, **nous**, and **vous** forms of the imperative — in greater detail.

That sounds familiar: Bossing around someone you're close to

When you're in a hurry or want something done right away, use the familiar imperative with one of your loved ones or a good friend or a kid or pet. Here are some commands and instructions in the **tu** form:

Johnny, range tes vêtements ! (*Johnny, tidy up your clothes!*)

Commence ce devoir ! (*Start this assignment!*)

Obéis, Johnny ! (*Obey, Johnny!*)

Attends, Eric ! (*Wait, Eric!*)

Va à l'école, Eric ! (*Go to school, Eric!*)

Marie, fais ton travail tout de suite ! (*Marie, do your work right away!*)

Ecoute ta mère, Marie ! (*Listen to your mother, Marie!*)

Sors de la salle de bains ! (*Come out of the bathroom!*)

Oh là là, dépêche-toi, ma chérie ! (*Oh goodness, hurry up, my darling!*)

Rappelle-toi l'adresse ! (*Remember the address!*)

Book III

Building the Grammatical Foundation for Communication

Giving formal orders or instructing others

When you're in a hurry or need something done right away by a colleague or someone who isn't a close friend or relative, you use the formal imperative that comes from the **vous** form. You can include an additional **s'il vous plaît** (*please*) to show your good manners:

Venez tout de suite, s'il vous plaît ! (*Please come right away!*)

Regardez ce fax ! Je crois que c'est urgent. (*Look at this fax! I think it's urgent.*)

Prenez cette pile de factures ! (*Take this pile of bills!*)

Allez voir M. Dupont ! (*Go see Mr. Dupont!*)

Choisissez votre bureau ! (*Choose your desk!*)

Répondez à cette lettre, s'il vous plaît ! (*Please reply to this letter!*)

Veuillez prendre des notes ! (*Please take notes!*)

When you need something done by several people — regardless of whether they're family, friends, or colleagues and strangers — you use the same **vous** imperative form:

Mangez plus lentement, les enfants. (*Eat more slowly, children.*)

Tournez à gauche, puis allez tout droit ! (*Turn left, [and] then go straight!*)

Fermez la porte. (*Close the door.*)

Suivez bien mes instructions. (*Follow my instructions well.*)

The imperative makes a very polite request in the **vous** form when you make expressions like **avoir la bonté** or **être gentil** (*to be so kind*) imperative or when the imperative is followed by **je vous en prie** or **s'il vous plaît** (*please*):

Ayez la bonté de fermer la porte. (*Please be so kind as to close the door.*)

Asseyez-vous, s'il vous plaît. (*Sit down, please.*)

Reposez-vous, je vous en prie. (*Please rest.*)

Let's do it! Showing esprit de corps (team spirit or solidarity)

One way to offer suggestions or make requests is to include yourself. Then you use the **nous** form of the imperative, suggesting that you're willing to be a part of what needs to get done:

Levons-nous ! (*Let's get up!*)

Habillons-nous ! (*Let's get dressed!*)

Partons à midi. (*Let's leave at noon.*)

Sortons ce soir ! (*Let's go out tonight!*)

Allons au cinéma. (*Let's go to the movies.*)

Amusons-nous ! (*Let's have fun!*)

Tacking objects and other pronouns onto commands

In nearly all tenses and moods, any object pronoun, reflexive pronoun, or adverbial pronoun comes before the verb. However, in the affirmative imperative (that is, not in negative commands), these pronouns have to follow the verb, attached by hyphens. Here are a few examples that show the placement of pronouns in positive and negative commands:

Parle-**nous** ! (*Talk to us!*)

Ne **nous** parle pas ! (*Don't speak to us!*)

Achète-**moi** ce chien ! (*Buy me this dog!*)

Ne **m'**achète pas ce hamster ! (*Don't buy me this hamster!*)

Retourne-**toi** ! (*Turn [yourself] around!*)

Ne **te** retourne pas ! (*Don't turn [yourself] around!*)

The object pronoun **me** changes to **moi** and the reflexive pronoun **te** changes to **toi** after the hyphen when you use it in an affirmative imperative. For example, *Watch me* is **Regarde-moi**, and *Wash yourself* is **Lave-toi**.

A couple of pronouns — **y** and **en** — affect the conjugation of the imperative **tu** form of -**er** verbs. The object pronoun **y** replaces a phrase that begins with a preposition such as **à** (*at, in, to*) or with a prepositional phrase such as **en face de** (*across from*), and the object pronoun **en** replaces a phrase that begins with the preposition **de**. When the **tu** form of the imperative of an -**er** verb is followed by **y** or **en**, the verb ends in an -**s**, just like the present tense **tu** form of the verb. You pronounce this **s** because it's followed by a vowel, making the words more distinct and easier to hear.

Tes copains partent à la patinoire ? **Vas-y !** (*Your friends are leaving to the skating ring? Go ahead!*)

J'ai de la glace. **Manges-en !** (*I have [some] ice cream. Eat some!*)

See the next section for info on using pronouns with negative commands, and see Chapter 3 of Book IV for details on object and adverbial pronouns, including which order they go in when you have two in the same sentence.

Giving Negative Commands

You use affirmative commands to tell people to do something and negative commands to tell them not to do something. The difference between the affirmative and negative imperative is the word order you use when the command includes certain pronouns. This section helps you keep everything straight.

Just don't! Negative commands

When you tell someone not to do something, you use a negative command by putting **ne** in front of the verb and the second part of the negative structure — **pas** (*not*), **rien** (*nothing*), **plus** (*no more*), **jamais** (*never*), and so on — after the verb. See Chapter 5 of Book III for info about making French verbs negative.

> **Ne parle pas comme ça.** (*Don't talk like that.*)
>
> **Ne sois pas impoli, mon coco !** (*Don't be rude, my love!*)
>
> **Ne faites pas de bêtises, les enfants !** (*Don't get into any mischief, children!*)
>
> **N'allez pas là-bas !** (*Don't go there!*)
>
> **Ne désobéissons pas aux ordres !** (*Let's not disobey orders!*)
>
> **Ne revenons pas ici.** (*Let's not come back here.*)

If the verb requires a preposition after it, the word order depends on which kind of negation you're using. If you're using a negative adverb, such as **pas**, the preposition goes after the negative adverb, as in **Ne demandons pas à Pierre** (*Let's not ask Pierre*). But if you're using a negative pronoun, such as **rien**, the preposition goes before the negative pronoun, as in **N'aie peur de rien** (*Don't be afraid of anything*). See Chapter 5 of Book III to read about negation and Chapter 1 of Book IV for information about verbs that have to be followed by a preposition.

Don't do it! Negative commands with pronouns

Object and reflexive pronouns aren't in the same place in a negative command as they are in a command to do something. Although the pronouns follow the noun in affirmative commands, the pronouns go in front of the verb in negative commands. This section shows you where to place the pronouns in commands not to do something. Table 4-12 lists the various object and reflexive pronouns for reference. (See more on these pronouns in Chapter 3 of Book IV.)

Table 4-12	Direct- and Indirect-Object Pronouns	
Direct/Indirect Object (Replacing People)	*Indirect-Object Pronouns (Replacing People)*	*Direct-Object Pronouns (Replacing People or Objects)*
me (*me, to me*)	**lui** (*to him/to her*)	**le** (*him/it*)
te (*you, to you*)	**leur** (*to them*)	**la** (*her/it*)
nous (*us/ourselves, to us/to ourselves*)		**l'** (*him/her/it*)
vous (*you/yourselves, to you/to yourselves*)		**les** (*them*)

The object pronouns **me** and **te**, like **le** and **la**, lose their ending **-e/-a** before a vowel or mute **h**. **Me** becomes **m'**, **te** becomes **t'**, and **le** and **la** become **l'**.

Note the placement of the pronoun before the verb in the following sentences. We highlight the pronouns in bold.

> Ne **me** dérangez pas ! (*Don't disturb me!*)
>
> Ne **m'**attends pas, Marianne ! (*Don't wait for me, Marianne!*)
>
> Ne **vous** couchez pas si tôt ! (*Don't go to bed so early!*) ***Note:*** **Se coucher** is a reflexive verb; the literal meaning of this example is "Don't put yourself to bed so early!"
>
> Ne **lui** parlez pas ! Il travaille. (*Don't speak to him! He's working.*)
>
> Ne **leur** téléphonez pas ce soir ! (*Don't call them tonight!*)
>
> Ne **l'**écoutez pas ! Il est sot, votre petit frère. (*Don't listen to him! He's silly, your little brother.*)
>
> Ne **la** mangez pas. Elle est trop salée, cette soupe. (*Don't eat it. This soup is too salty.*)
>
> Ne **le leur** montrez pas encore ! Il n'est pas prêt, ce film ! (*Don't show it to them yet! This movie isn't ready!*) ***Note:*** This sentence contains both a direct object (**le**, *it*) and an indirect object (**leur**, *to them*).

Book III

Building the Grammatical Foundation for Communication

Finding Other Ways to Give Commands

The imperative is the most common way to give orders and make suggestions in French, but you have a few other options as well. This section gives you a quick overview.

Instructing with the infinitive

You can use the infinitive for impersonal orders when you're giving instructions to an unknown audience, such as on signs, in use-and-care instructions for appliances or clothes, in recipes, and in guide books. The infinitive is the unconjugated form of the verb that ends in **-er**, **-ir**, or **-re**, the form you find in a dictionary.

Object, reflexive, and adverbial pronouns precede the infinitive verb, as in **nous contacter** (*contact us*), **s'abonner** (*subscribe*), and **en ajouter** (*add some*).

Signs

In tourist sites and in hotels, you see instructions such as these:

> **Fermer la porte et les fenêtres la nuit.** (*Close the door and windows at night.*)
>
> **Quitter la chambre avant midi.** (*Leave the room before noon.*)
>
> **Éteindre la lumière en partant.** (*Turn off the light when leaving.*)
>
> **Composter le billet.** (*Validate the ticket.*)
>
> **Ne pas utiliser de flash.** (*Do not use a flash*).
>
> **Laisser les sacs au vestiaire.** (*Leave bags at the coat check.*)
>
> **Ne pas toucher.** (*Do not touch.*)

Appliance manuals

You may find these instructions to clean a coffee maker:

> **mettre de l'eau tiède** (*put in some warm water*)
>
> **ajouter du vinaigre** (*add some vinegar*)
>
> **allumer la cafetière** (*turn on the coffee maker*)
>
> **jeter le liquide** (*throw away the liquid*)
>
> **rincer à fond** (*rinse thoroughly*)

Care instructions

You can find these instructions to wash and care for clothes:

> **laver à la machine** (*machine wash*)
>
> **laver à l'eau froide** (*wash in cold water*)
>
> **laver à la main** (*wash by hand*)
>
> **ne pas repasser à chaud** (*do not press/iron with heat*)
>
> **ne pas utiliser de chlore** (*do not use chlorine*)

> **éviter le séchoir** (*avoid dryer*)
>
> **ne pas suspendre** (*do not hang*)
>
> **nettoyer à sec** (*dry clean*)

Recipes

You sometimes find recipes with instructions like these:

> **casser les œufs** (*break the eggs*)
>
> **battre les œufs** (*beat the eggs*)
>
> **ajouter le lait** (*add milk*)
>
> **graisser la poêle** (*grease the pan*)
>
> **faire cuire** (*cook*)
>
> **retourner** (*turn over*)
>
> **servir chaud** (*serve hot*)

Guides

If you were to look up how to fill out a résumé, you'd find some instructions like the following examples:

> **présenter ses qualifications** (*present qualifications*)
>
> **se concentrer sur ses qualifications essentielles** (*focus on essential qualifications*)
>
> **justifier les interruptions dans ses études** (*justify/explain interruptions in studies*)
>
> **mettre en valeur ses expériences professionnelles** (*highlight professional experiences*)
>
> **conserver la police de caractères dans tout le document** (*keep the same font throughout the document*)
>
> **faire l'inventaire de ses aptitudes et de ses compétences** (*give inventory of aptitudes and abilities*)

Textbooks

If you use a French textbook or workbook, you find instructions like these:

> **lire le passage** (*read the passage*)
>
> **répondre aux questions** (*answer the questions*)
>
> **remplir les trous** (*fill in the blanks*)
>
> **trouver le mot qui convient** (*find the word that fits*)
>
> **choisir la bonne reponse** (*choose the right answer*)

Book III

Building the Grammatical Foundation for Communication

analyser la phrase (*analyze the sentence*)

justifier la réponse (*justify/explain the answer*)

Online

In surfing the **francophone** web, you find instructions like the following:

rechercher (*search*)

continuer (*continue*)

accepter (*accept*)

annuler (*cancel*)

modifier (*modify*)

voir (*see*)

commander (*order*)

imprimer votre facture (*print your bill*)

valider (*validate*)

consulter le suivi des commandes (*follow up on orders*)

changer le mot de passe (*change the password*)

sélectionner (*select*)

renvoyer (*send back*)

Ordering or forbidding with "il faut"

The impersonal phrase **Il faut** (*It's necessary*) followed by an infinitive verb tells you what's expected of you:

Il faut arriver à l'heure. (*You must arrive on time.*)

Il faut se doucher avant d'aller à la piscine. (*You must take a shower before going to the pool.*) ***Note:*** **Se doucher** is a reflexive verb. Notice the position of the reflexive pronoun **se** before the infinitive.

Il ne faut pas followed by an infinitive verb tells you what's forbidden:

Il ne faut pas tourner à droite au feu rouge. (*Do not turn right at the red light.*)

Il ne faut pas stationner ici le dimanche. (*Do not park here on Sundays.*)

Urging, encouraging, or asking with "prière de"

The phrase **prière de** followed by an infinitive verb tells you that you're politely asked to do or not to do something. Look at the examples:

> **Prière de frapper avant d'entrer.** (*Please knock before entering.*)
>
> **Prière de garder le silence.** (*Please remain silent.*)
>
> **Prière de faire un don.** (*Please make a donation.*)
>
> **Prière de ne pas s'asseoir sur l'herbe.** (*Please do not sit on the lawn.*)

Forbidding with "défense de"

The expression **défense de** (*prohibited from*), gives short, impersonal *do not do this* orders on signs. You probably won't use it yourself, unless you're in charge of making signs to post on doors and windows.

If you see a sign that's round and red, pay close attention to it because it's a warning sign. Warning signs may say things like the following:

> **Défense d'entrer. Propriété privée.** (*Do not enter. Private property.*)
>
> **Défense de passer. Passage fermé.** (*Do not go through. Closed passage.*)
>
> **Défense de stationner.** (*Do not park.*)
>
> **Défense de faire demi-tour.** (*Do not make a U-turn.*)
>
> **Défense de pêcher.** (*Do not fish.*)
>
> **Défense d'entrer sur le chantier.** (*Do not enter the construction site.*)
>
> **Défense de se baigner.** (*Do not swim.*)
>
> **Défense de jeter des ordures.** (*No littering.*)
>
> **Defense de nourrir les animaux.** (*Do not feed the animals.*)
>
> **Défense de fumer.** (*No smoking.*)

Requesting with the future

To make polite requests, you can use the future tense instead of using the **vous** imperative. For example, you may use the future when giving instructions to people you don't know, as in a meeting or interview:

Vous travaillerez ensemble, s'il vous plaît. (*[You will] Work together, please.*)

Vous ferez la pause à 10h00. (*[You will please] Take a break at 10:00 a.m.*)

Vous le compléterez avant vendredi, s'il vous plaît. (*[You will] Finish it by Friday, please.*)

Chapter 6 of Book IV explains how to conjugate and use the French future tense.

Politely demanding with the subjunctive

Using certain verbs and expressions that require the subjunctive mood is equivalent to giving commands or making requests. You can use these expressions to soften the command while being clear that it's very much an order. The verb that follows **que** (*that*) in each phrase needs to be in the subjunctive mood, which we cover in Chapter 5 of Book IV.

Here are some impersonal expressions that you can use to give commands or make requests.

- **il faut que** (*it's necessary that*)
- **il est essentiel que** (*it's essential that*)
- **il est nécessaire que** (*it's necessary that*)
- **il est urgent que** (*it's urgent that*)

Here are some verbs that you can use to give commands or make requests:

- **demander que** (*to ask that*)
- **souhaiter que** (*to wish that*)
- **conseiller que** (*to advise that*)
- **exiger que** (*to demand that*)
- **ordonner que** (*to order that*)
- **vouloir que** (*to want that*)
- **préférer que** (*to prefer that*)

Here's a list of instructions you may hear in the classroom, using the subjunctive mood:

Il faut que nous discutions de ce sujet. (*It's necessary that we discuss this topic.*)

Il est indispensable que vous compreniez cette analyse. (*It is essential that you understand this analysis.*)

Il est essentiel que tout le monde fasse attention. (*It's essential that everyone pay attention.*)

J'exige que vous vous taisiez ! (*I demand that you be quiet!*)

Je demande que vous écoutiez attentivement. (*I ask that you listen attentively.*)

Je préfère que nous commencions tout de suite. (*I prefer that we start right away.*)

Chapter 5

Asking and Answering Questions

*Q*uestions are one of the foundations of a good conversation or letter, and knowing how to ask and answer questions greatly improves both your spoken and written French. When you exchange letters with your friend in Brussels and your colleague in Montréal, you can show interest in their activities and get information by asking lots of questions.

This chapter explains how to ask and answer different types of questions, and it provides all the interrogative vocabulary that goes along with them.

Oui ou Non: Asking Yes-or-No Questions

A sentence consists of at least a subject and a verb. The sentence **Elle porte une jolie robe** (*She is wearing a pretty dress*) has the subject **elle** (*she*) and the verb **porte** (*is wearing*). The rest of the sentence is the *complement* of the sentence: It completes it. This section focuses on the subject-verb unit because that's where the changes may occur when you go from a statement to a question.

You can ask yes-or-no questions in various ways, and which one you use depends on what kind of a conversation you're having or the type of letter you're writing. In most cases, you choose between the less-formal intonation or **est-ce que** method and the more-formal inversion method. This section helps you make the right decision and shows you how to use each form.

Posing informal questions

In French, you can easily transform a simple statement into a question in a few ways. We cover these informal question methods next.

Intoning

One way to ask questions is just to tack a question mark at the end of a statement, as in **Tu veux venir avec nous ?** (*You want to come with us?*). **Tu pars** means *you're leaving,* but **Tu pars ?** means *Are you leaving?* Here are a couple of other examples:

> **Vous avez froid.** (*You're cold.*)
>
> **Vous avez froid ?** (*Are you cold?*)

> **Jonas est absent.** (*Jonas is absent.*)
>
> **Jonas est absent ?** (*Jonas is absent?*)

When speaking, you raise the pitch of your voice at the end of the sentence — it automatically sounds like a question. To hear how these informal questions sound, play some of the audio tracks for the Talkin' the Talk dialogues, such as the train station scene in Chapter 5 of Book II (Track 30).

Raising the pitch is the most informal way of asking a question. Never use this method to ask a question in anything official or business-related. Inversion (see the section "Asking formal questions with inversion") is the best way to ask questions in any kind of formal situation.

Making use of est-ce que

Tacking the phrase **est-ce que** (ehs kuh) (Literally: *is it that . . . ?*) to the beginning of a statement is another informal way of asking a question in French. It's as easy as placing a *do* or a *does* before a statement in English, as in *Do you see?* For example, start with a statement like **Tu vas** (*You go*) and place **est-ce que** before it to get the question **Est-ce que tu vas ?** (*Do you go?* OR *Are you going?*). This method is rarely written — it's used mainly when speaking.

Typing the French question mark

In French texts, the question mark and all other two-part punctuation marks — exclamation points, **guillemets** (French quotation marks), colons, and semicolons — must be preceded by a space. When typing, use a nonbreaking space in front of the punctuation mark to keep it from wrapping to the next line. Or if you set the language of your word-processing program to French, it should add the spaces for you.

In English, a question doesn't always start with *do* or *does* because sometimes the verb *is* or *are* is part of the verb form, as in *Are you going somewhere?* It's impossible to translate this question literally from English to French, because French doesn't have a special tense for actions in progress: *you go, you're going,* and *you do go* are all the present tense in French. Remember to think of the statement first: **tu vas** (*you go, you're going, you do go*) and then add **est-ce que** before that statement (or use intonation) to make an informal question:

> **Vous restez à la maison.** (*You stay home.* OR *You're staying home.*)

> **Est-ce que vous restez à la maison ?** (*Do you stay home?* OR *Are you staying home?*)

> **Il va se marier en janvier.** (*He's getting married in January.*)

> **Est-ce qu'il va se marier en janvier ?** (*Is he going to get married in January ?*)

The phrase **est-ce que** changes to **est-ce qu'** before a vowel or a mute **h**, as in **Est-ce qu'elle est grande ?** (*Is she tall?*).

You can tack on n'est-ce pas, right?

If all you want to do is make a point and you're expecting the other person to agree with you, then you make your statement and tack on the phrase **n'est-ce pas** (nehs pah) (Literally: *isn't it so?*):

> **Il fait beau, n'est-ce pas ?** (*The weather is nice, isn't it ?*)

> **Vous allez rentrer tard, n'est-ce pas ?** (*You're going to come home late, aren't you?*)

> **Ils choisissent toujours ce restaurant, n'est-ce pas ?** (*They always choose this restaurant, don't they?*)

Asking formal questions with inversion

Inversion is a little bit more complicated than the informal methods. Whereas you can ask any question using intonation or **est-ce que**, inversion works only with a subject pronoun (**je**, **tu**, **il/elle/on**, **nous**, **vous**, or **ils/elles**), not a noun or a name. Inversion is also more formal, so in a business setting, such as a job interview or conversation with your boss, it's the best option.

To ask a question with inversion, you switch the order of the subject pronoun and verb and join them with a hyphen:

> **Tu es prêt.** (*You are ready.*)

> **Es-tu prêt ?** (*Are you ready?*)

Book III

Building the Grammatical Foundation for Communication

Il sait nager. (*He knows how to swim.*)

Sait-il nager ? (*Does he know how to swim?*)

You can invert only subject pronouns, not actual nouns. So when you ask a question with a subject such as **Pierre** or **l'enfant** (*the child*), you have to either replace the subject with a pronoun or start the question with the subject, followed by the inverted verb and subject pronoun:

Tes amis sont français. (*Your friends are French.*)

Tes amis sont-ils français ? (*Are your friends French?* Literally: *Your friends, are they French?*)

Pierre est prêt. (*Pierre is ready*)

Pierre est-il prêt ? (*Is Pierre ready?*)

Les professeurs vont faire grève. (*The teachers are going to strike.*)

Les professeurs vont-ils faire grève ? (*Are the teachers going to strike?*)

L'enfant sait nager. (*The child knows how to swim.*)

L'enfant sait-il nager ? (*Does the child know how to swim?*)

When the verb ends in a vowel and is followed by a third-person singular pronoun (**il/elle/on**), add **-t-** between the verb and pronoun. The **t** prevents back-to-back vowel sounds, making pronunciation easier. You have to do this for all regular **-er** verbs and some irregular verbs. Look at these examples:

Parle-t-elle français ? (*Does she speak French?*)

Cherche-t-il son hôtel ? (*Is he looking for his hotel?*)

Va-t-on au cirque ? (*Are we going to the circus ?*)

A-t-on de l'argent ? (*Do we have any money?*)

You never have to worry about inserting **-t-** when the verb is an **-ir** or **-re** verb because the **il/elle/on** form of such a verb ends in **-t** or **-d**. Both consonants are pronounced as a *t* sound in the liaison (linking a consonant to a vowel sound). For example:

Rose perd-elle souvent ses affaires ? (rohz pehr-tehl sooh-vahN seyz ah-fehr?) (*Does Rose often lose her things?*)

Charles grossit-il ? (shahrl groh-see-teel ?) (*Is Charles gaining weight?*)

Question Words: Probing for More Information

Questions that ask for information, such as *who, when, why,* and *how,* are sometimes called *wh* questions in English because all these question words begin with *w* or *h.* French has three types of question words, and you need to understand how they differ in order to ask *wh* questions.

Which one? Interrogative adjectives

In English, when you ask a question about two or more similar objects, you can just use *what* plus the noun, even though *which* may be the grammatically correct option, as in *What (Which) shirt do you like better?* But in French, you have to use **quel** (*which*) whenever you're asking someone to make a distinction between two or more nouns, as in **Quelle chemise préfères-tu ?** (*What/which shirt do you prefer?*) Interrogative adjectives offer a little challenge because they must reflect the gender (masculine or feminine) and number (singular or plural) of the noun they accompany:

- ✔ Masculine singular: **quel homme** (*what/which man*)
- ✔ Feminine singular: **quelle femme** (*what/which woman*)
- ✔ Masculine plural: **quels hommes** (*what/which men*)
- ✔ Feminine plural: **quelles femmes** (*what/which women*)

When, where, why, and how? Interrogative adverbs

Interrogative adverbs ask for more information about something that happens. French has five important interrogative adverbs:

- ✔ **comment** (*how*)
- ✔ **combien (de)** (*how much/many*)
- ✔ **quand** (*when*)
- ✔ **où** (*where*)
- ✔ **pourquoi** (*why*)

Comment means *how,* as in **Comment as-tu fait ça ?** (*How did you do that?*). However, used alone, **Comment ?** means *What?* — for example, ask **Comment ?** when you need someone to repeat what he or she just said.

Quand means *when,* and the answer can be a time or date: **Quand vas-tu en France ? —Dans deux semaines.** (*When are you going to France? —In two weeks.*) If you want to know at what time something happens, use **à quelle heure** (*at what time*).

Who or what? Interrogative pronouns qui and que

Interrogative pronouns ask *who, whom,* or *what,* and because they're pronouns, you can't use them in front of a noun. *Who* or *whom* in French is pretty easy — it's usually translated as **qui:**

> **Qui fait ce travail ?** (*Who does this work?*)
>
> **Qui invitez-vous ?** (*Whom are you inviting?*)

The word *what* is more complicated. If it's at the beginning of a question, the French translation is **que** (or **qu'** before a vowel or a mute **h**):

> **Que désirez-vous ?** (*What would you like?*)
>
> **Qu'avez-vous fait ?** (*What have you done?*)

But if *what* is after a preposition, the word is **quoi** (see Chapter 1 of Book IV for details on prepositions):

> **Avec quoi est-ce que tu écris ?** (*With what do you write?*)
>
> **Sur quoi est-ce que tu écris ?** (*About what [On what topic] are you writing?*)

If you're asking a *what* question in which *what* is followed by and describes a noun, you want an interrogative adjective, **quel,** as in **Quelle heure est-il ?** (*What time is it?*). We cover interrogative adjectives in the preceding section.

Don't get too attached to the idea that **que** means *what* and **qui** means *who.* They usually do but not always. When asking questions, **qui** and **que** also indicate whether you're using *who* or *what* as the subject or object of the question — see the next section for details.

Constructing Wh Questions

You need to know where to place all the words you need in a *wh* question. Using intonation poses no problem, but it's very informal. When you have to be less informal, use **est-ce que**, and when you have to be very formal, use inversion. This section helps get it all straight.

Asking wh questions using intonation

Qui, **où**, **quand**, **comment**, **combien**, **pourquoi**, and **quel** phrases often appear at the beginning or at the end of a question in which intonation indicates that it's a question rather than a statement. Placing the question word at the beginning is really quite informal:

Qui tu cherches ? OR **Tu cherches qui ?** (*Whom are you looking for?*)

Où tu vas ? OR **Tu vas où ?** (*Where are you going?*)

Pourquoi elle répond comme ça ? OR **Elle répond comme ça pourquoi ?** (*Why does she answer like that?*)

Quand vous allez revenir ? OR **Vous allez revenir quand ?** (*When are you going to come back?*)

Combien je te dois ? OR **Je te dois combien ?** (*How much do I owe you?*)

Quel bus tu prends ? OR **Tu prends quel bus ?** (*Which bus do you take?*)

Book III

Building the Grammatical Foundation for Communication

Asking wh questions with est-ce que

You can ask *wh* questions with **est-ce que** by putting the question word at the beginning of the question, followed by **est-ce que**, the subject, and the verb:

Où est-ce que tu vas ? (*Where are you going?*)

Pourquoi est-ce qu'il aime le jazz ? (*Why does he like jazz?*)

Quand est-ce que Laure va arriver ? (*When is Laure going to arrive?*)

Here's how these example questions break down:

Question Word	Est-ce que	Subject	Verb
Où (*Where*)	**est-ce que** (*is it that*)	**tu** (*you*)	**vas ?** (*are going?*)
Pourquoi (*Why*)	**est-ce qu'** (*is it that*)	**il** (*he*)	**aime . . . ?** (*likes . . . ?*)
Quand (*When*)	**est-ce que** (*is it that*)	**Laure**	**va arriver ?** (*is going to arrive?*)

Sometimes a question starts with a question phrase, such as **quel livre** (*which book*) or **combien d'argent** (*how much money*) rather than a question word. Don't forget that **quel** has to be followed by a noun and that it has to agree with that noun in gender and number:

> **Quel livre est-ce que** tu veux ? (*Which book do you want?*)

> **Combien d'argent est-ce que** vous avez ? (*How much money do you have?*)

Using the interrogative pronouns **que** (*what*) and **qui** (*who/whom*) with **est-ce que** can be tricky because **est-ce que** sometimes changes to **est-ce qui**. The choice depends on whether the pronoun is the subject or the direct object of the question. Here are some guidelines:

- ✔ When *what* is the subject of the question, use **que** + **est-ce qui** + the verb. **Que** contracts to **qu'** before a vowel, giving you **qu'est-ce qui**:

  > **Qu'est-ce qui** se passe ? (*What is happening?*)

- ✔ When *what* is the direct object of the question, use **que** + **est-ce que** + the subject + the verb:

  > **Qu'est-ce que** tu veux ? (*What do you want?*)

- ✔ When *who* is the subject of a question, use **qui** + **est-ce qui** + the verb. Note that **qui** never contracts:

  > **Qui est-ce qui** fait ce bruit ? (*Who is making this noise?*)

- ✔ When *whom* is the direct object of a question, use **qui** + **est-ce que** + the subject + the verb:

  > **Qui est-ce que** tu préfères ? (*Whom do you prefer?*)

Here's how the preceding example questions break down:

Question Word	Est-ce que/qui	Subject	Verb
Qu' (*What*)	**est-ce qui** (*is it that*)		**se passe ?** (*is happening?*)
Qu' (*What*)	**est-ce que** (*is it that*)	**tu** (*you*)	**veux ?** (*want?*)
Qui (*Who*)	**est-ce qui** (*is it that*)		**fait . . . ?** (*makes . . . ?*)
Qui (*Whom*)	**est-ce que** (*is it that*)	**tu** (*you*)	**préfères ?** (*prefer?*)

Table 5-1 summarizes where to use **que** and **qui** in your questions. Note that the first word — **que** or **qui** — tells you whether the question word is *what* or *who/whom*. The word after **est-ce** indicates whether you're asking about a subject or direct object. (*Note:* The **que** or **qui** after the **est-ce** is actually a relative pronoun meaning *that* or *who.* We cover relative pronouns in Chapter 4 of Book IV.)

If you're not sure how to tell whether something is a subject or object, try reordering the words. When you rearrange *What do you want to do?* you get *You want to do what?* which makes it easier to see that *you* is the subject and *what* is the object. On the other hand, you find out that *What is happening?* can't be rearranged because *what* is the subject.

Table 5-1	Asking Who/Whom or What with Est-ce Que/Qui	
Pronoun	*Subject of the Question*	*Object of the Question*
What	Qu'est-ce qui	Qu'est-ce que
Who/whom	Qui est-ce qui	Qui est-ce que

Asking wh questions with inversion

To ask a *wh* question using inversion, just put the interrogative word at the beginning and follow it with the inverted verb and subject:

Que veux-tu ? (*What do you want?*)

Qui préfèrent-ils ? (*Whom do they prefer?*)

Although most yes-or-no and *wh* questions can be asked with either **est-ce que** or inversion, certain common questions are virtually always asked with inversion. Table 5-2 lists these fixed questions. Use the **tu** forms with a person you know well, and use **vous** in more formal settings or when addressing a group.

Table 5-2	Common Questions with Inversion
English	*French*
Do you speak French/English?	**Parles-tu français/anglais ?** **Parlez-vous français/anglais ?**
How are you?	**Comment vas-tu ?** **Comment allez-vous ?**
How old are you?	**Quel âge as-tu ?** **Quel âge avez-vous ?**
How's the weather?	**Quel temps fait-il ?**
What day is it?	**Quel jour sommes-nous ?**

(continued)

Table 5-2 *(continued)*	
English	*French*
What is your name?	**Comment t'appelles-tu ?**
	Comment vous appelez-vous ?
What time is it?	**Quelle heure est-il ?**
Where are you going?	**Où vas-tu ?**
	Où allez-vous ?
Who is it?	**Qui est-ce ?**

Answering Questions Affirmatively

Knowing how to ask questions is only half the battle. What kind of world would it be if questions were never answered? Would that make them rhetorical? What good would that do? Are we annoying you yet? So you see, you also have to know how to answer questions — and understand other people's answers, too. This section gives you an overview of responding to different types of questions.

Answering yes-or-no questions

Yes-or-no questions aren't just easy to ask — they're also easy to answer. You can take the easy road and just answer **oui** (*yes*):

> **Est-ce que tu es prêt ? —Oui.** (*Are you ready? —Yes.*)

> **Elle joue bien ? —Ah oui !** (*Does she play well? —Oh yes!*)

You can also repeat the question as a statement after you say *yes:*

> **Oui, je suis prêt.** (*Yes, I'm ready.*)

> **Oui, elle joue bien.** (*Yes, she plays well.*)

 French has two words for *yes,* **oui** and **si**. Use **oui** when someone asks you an affirmative question, but use **si** when a person asks a question in the negative and you want to respond in the affirmative. For example, if someone says, "Don't you like to swim?" and you do like to swim, in English, you have to say, "Yes, I like to swim." But in French, someone can ask **N'aimes-tu pas nager ?** and you can just answer **Si**.

We cover negative answers later in "Just Say No: Answering Negatively." Of course, not all questions merit a simple *yes* or *no*. The following are some useful ways to answer questions:

- **oui** (*yes*)
- **si** (*yes* — in response to a negative)
- **bien sûr** (*of course*)
- **peut-être** (*maybe*)
- **ça m'est égal** (*I don't care*)

Answering wh questions

The answers to *wh* questions are quite a bit different from responses to yes-or-no questions. Because they're asking for information, you have to respond with that information in place of the question words. You can use the following words to help you answer *wh* questions (see Chapter 2 of Book I for details on numbers, dates, and times):

- **à** (*at, in, to*)
- **c'est**, **on est** (*it is* — with dates)
- **il est** (*it is* — with time)
- **parce que** (*because*)
- **pendant** (*for* — with time)

Book III

Building the Grammatical Foundation for Communication

Here are some examples of answers to *wh* questions:

Comment t'appelles-tu ? —Je m'appelle Jean. (*What's your name? —My name is Jean.*)

Combien de frères est-ce que tu as ? —J'ai deux frères. (*How many brothers do you have? —I have two brothers.*)

C'est quand, ton anniversaire ? —C'est le 30 janvier. (*When is your birthday? —It's on January 30.*)

Quelle heure est-il ? —Il est midi. (*What time is it? —It's noon.*)

Pourquoi es-tu en retard ? —Parce qu'il y a de la circulation. (*Why are you late? —Because there's traffic.*)

Quand va-t-elle faire son travail ? —Pendant la classe. (*When is she going to do her work? —During class.*)

Just Say No: Answering Negatively

Even if you'd rather be a yes-man or yes-woman, sometimes you've just got to say no. Otherwise, you may discover that you've accepted a weekend work assignment with no extra pay. In French, being negative is twice as hard as it is in English because French requires at least two words, whereas English needs only one. This section explains various ways to be negative in French, as well as how to respond — whether you agree or disagree — when someone says something negative to you.

Never say never: Negative adverbs

When someone asks you if you smoke and you answer *never* or *not anymore*, you're using the negative adverb *never* or the adverbial phrase *not anymore*. Similarly, if someone asks you how often you go to the movies and you say you don't go at all, you're using the negative adverbial phrase *not at all*. This section introduces French negative adverbs and tells you where they fit in a sentence.

Knowing common negative adverbs

The French equivalent of *not*, as in *I do not sing*, is **ne . . . pas**. These two words have to surround the verb — you put **ne** in front of it and **pas** after. When you have **ne** + a vowel or mute **h**, it contracts to **n'**.

Even when **ne** doesn't contract, it's often pronounced as just an **n** sound:

> **Je ne suis pas prêt.** (zhuhn swee pah preh.) (*I'm not ready.*)
>
> **Nous ne voulons pas partir.** (noohn vooh-lohN pah pahr-teer.) (*We don't want to leave.*)
>
> **Elle n'est pas là.** (ehl neh pah lah.) (*She's not there.*)

In informal spoken French, **ne** is often only partially pronounced or even dropped entirely, so **pas** negates the verb all on its own:

> **Je ne sais pas.** → **Je sais pas.** (*I don't know.*)
>
> **Il ne veut pas étudier.** → **Il veut pas étudier.** (*He doesn't want to study.*)

Remember that partitive articles (**du**, **de la**, **des**) and indefinite articles (**un**, **une**, **des**) change to **de** after a negation. (See Chapter 2 of Book III for info on articles.)

> **J'ai un frère.** → **Je n'ai pas de frère.** (*I have a brother.* → *I don't have any brothers.*)

Although **ne . . . pas** is the most common negative adverb, several others are also very useful:

- ✔ **ne . . . jamais** (*never*)
- ✔ **ne . . . nulle part** (*nowhere*)
- ✔ **ne . . . pas du tout** (*not at all*)
- ✔ **ne . . . pas encore** (*not yet*)
- ✔ **ne . . . pas que** (*not only*)
- ✔ **ne . . . pas toujours** (*not always*)
- ✔ **ne . . . plus** (*not anymore, no more, no longer*)
- ✔ **ne . . . que** (*only*)

As with **ne . . . pas**, you can often drop the **ne** in informal spoken French:

> **Je ne fume plus.** → **Je fume plus.** (*I don't smoke any more.*)

> **Je n'y suis jamais allé.** → **J'y suis jamais allé.** (*I've never gone there.*)

Be careful when dropping **ne**, because the second part of the adverb can have a different meaning when used affirmatively. **Plus**, for example, can mean *more* when it's not used with **ne**, so make sure that you add any other info necessary to get your point across. Similarly, **jamais** used in questions without **ne** means *ever*, such as with **As-tu jamais vu ce film ?** (*Have you ever seen this movie?*).

Book III

Building the Grammatical Foundation for Communication

Putting negative adverbs in their place

Negative adverbs usually surround a conjugated verb, though sometimes a few other words get in the way.

When you have two verbs in a sentence — one conjugated and one in infinitive form — **ne** and **pas** surround just the conjugated verb:

> Il **ne** va **pas** travailler. (*He isn't going to work.*)

> Ils **ne** savent **pas** jouer à ça. (*They don't know how to play that.*)

> Tu **ne** dois **pas** venir. (*You don't have to come.*)

Similarly, in compound tenses like the **passé composé** (a tense that requires an auxiliary verb — **avoir** or **être** — and a past participle; see Chapter 1 of Book V), the negative adverb surrounds the conjugated auxiliary verb, and the past participle comes after **pas**:

> Elles **ne** sont **pas** arrivées. (*They didn't arrive.*)

> Je **n'**ai **pas** mangé. (*I didn't eat.*)

When your negative statement or question has reflexive, object, or adverbial pronouns (see Chapter 3 of Book IV), they have to stay directly in front of the verb. So **ne** precedes the whole group of them, and **pas** follows the conjugated verb as usual:

> Je **ne** te crois **pas.** (*I don't believe you.*)
>
> Tu **ne** me l'as **pas** donné. (*You didn't give it to me.*)
>
> Vous **ne** vous êtes **pas** trompé. (*You didn't make a mistake.*)

For questions with inversion, the **ne . . . pas** surrounds the inverted verb-subject unit:

> **Ne** viennent-ils **pas ?** (*Aren't they coming?*)
>
> **N'**as-tu **pas** faim **?** (*Aren't you hungry?*)

All negative adverbs follow the same placement rules as **ne . . . pas**, with **ne** preceding the conjugated verb and with **plus, jamais**, or whatever else following it:

> Elle **ne** ment **jamais.** (*She never lies.*)
>
> Je **ne** suis **pas encore** prêt. (*I'm not ready yet.*)
>
> Nous **n'**avons **que** 5 euros. (*We have only 5 euros.*)

Getting really negative with adjectives

Like negative adverbs, French negative adjectives also have two parts. But instead of negating verbs — the actions — negative adjectives negate nouns in a very emphatic way that leaves no room for uncertainty.

The placement of negative adjectives is pretty much the same as for negative adverbs: **ne** goes in front of the conjugated verb, and the second part of the negative construction goes after the verb. Here's a list of negative adjectives:

- ✔ **ne . . . aucun(e)** (*no, not any, not one*)
- ✔ **ne . . . nul(le)** (*no, not any*)
- ✔ **ne . . . pas un(e)** (*no, not one*)
- ✔ **ne . . . pas un seul(e)** (*not a single*)

Like other kinds of French adjectives, negative adjectives have to agree in gender with the nouns they're negating (feminine endings are in parentheses in the preceding list). However, negative adjectives are never plural, because you're saying there's not even one of the noun.

Even though there are four different negative adjectives, they all mean pretty much the same thing — *no* or *not any,* with the exception of **ne . . . pas un seul**, which is a bit stronger than the others — *not a single one.* But there is a difference in how you use them.

You can use **ne . . . pas un** and **ne . . . pas un seul** only for *countable* nouns (such as books, employees, and houses), and you can use **ne . . . nul** only for *uncountable* nouns (such as intelligence, money, and furniture).

> Je **n'**ai **pas une seule** idée. (*I don't have a single idea.*)
>
> Il **ne** connaît **pas un seul** bon resto. (*He doesn't know one single good restaurant.*)
>
> Ils **n'**ont **nulle** foi. (*They have no faith.*)

The last negative adjective, **ne . . . aucun**, is less picky — you can use it with countable and uncountable nouns:

> Je **n'**ai **aucune** solution. (*I have no solution, I have not one solution.*)
>
> Il **ne** connaît **aucun** bon café. (*He doesn't know any good cafés.*)
>
> Ils **n'**ont **aucune** intégrité. (*They have no integrity.*)

You can start a sentence with a negative adjective by putting the second part of the adjective at the beginning, followed by the noun, **ne**, and the verb:

> **Nul** argent **ne** sera remboursé. (*No money will be reimbursed.*)
>
> **Aucun** bruit **ne** parvenait à mes oreilles. (*Not a sound reached my ears.*)
>
> **Pas un seul** client **n'**est resté. (*Not a single client stayed.*)

We got nothing: Using negative pronouns

Negative adjectives (see the preceding section) and negative pronouns are a lot alike. In fact, you can use all the adjectives as pronouns. The difference between these two negative structures is that negative adjectives are used *with* the nouns they negate, and negative pronouns *replace* the nouns.

Identifying negative pronouns

Here are the French negative pronouns:

- ✔ **ne . . . aucun(e) (de)** (*none [of], not any [of]*)
- ✔ **ne . . . nul(le)** (*no one*)
- ✔ **ne . . . pas un(e) (de)** (*not one [of]*)
- ✔ **ne . . . pas un seul(e) (de)** (*not a single one [of]*)

Book III

Building the Grammatical Foundation for Communication

> ✔ **ne . . . personne** (*no one*)
>
> ✔ **ne . . . rien** (*nothing, not anything*)

The opposite of negative pronouns are indefinite pronouns, as Table 5-3 shows.

Table 5-3	Negative and Indefinite Pronouns
Negative Pronouns	*Indefinite Pronouns*
ne . . . aucun(e) (*none, not any*) ne . . . pas un(e) (*not one*)	quelques (*some, any*)
ne . . . personne (*no one*)	quelqu'un (*someone*)
ne . . . rien (*nothing*)	quelque chose (*something*)

Like other pronouns, negative pronouns have to agree in gender with the nouns they replace:

> **Tu as quelques euros ? —Non, je n'en ai aucun.** (*Do you have any euros ? —No, I don't have any [of them].*)

Because **euros** is masculine, you use the masculine form of **aucun**. (The pronoun **en** here replaces "some quantity" here. To read more about it, see Chapter 3 of Book IV.)

Working with negative pronouns

You can use **ne . . . pas un** and **ne . . . pas un seul** only for countable nouns, and you can use **ne . . . aucun** for countable or uncountable nouns. These three negative pronouns work in one of two ways. In the first way, the pronoun is followed by **de** + some additional information about what you're negating:

> **Je n'aime aucune de ces idées.** (*I don't like any of these ideas.*)

> **Pas un des employés n'est arrivé.** (*Not one of the employees has arrived.*)

In the second way, the pronoun has an *antecedent* (a noun that you're referring back to) and the pronoun **en** (we explain **en**, which replaces **de** + noun, further in Chapter 3 of Book IV):

> **Il a trois voitures et moi, je n'en ai pas une seule.** (*He has three cars, and I don't have a single one.*)

> **Ils ont apporté trois CD et je n'en trouve pas un seul.** (*They brought three CDs, and I'm not finding a single one of them.*)

Ne . . . nul means *no, not one* as a negative adjective and *no one* as a negative pronoun:

✔ Adjective: **Je n'ai nulle idée.** (*I don't have any ideas.*)

✔ Pronoun: **J'ai deux options mais nulle ne m'inspire.** (*I have two options but neither one inspires me.*)

The negative pronouns **personne** (*no one*) and **rien** (*nothing*) can be a subject, a direct object, or the object of a preposition:

✔ Subject:

> **Personne n'**est venu à la fête. (*No one came to the party.*)

> **Rien ne** m'intéresse. (*Nothing interests me.*)

✔ Direct object:

> Je **ne** connais **personne.** (*I don't know anyone.*)

> Je **ne** vois **rien** sans mes lunettes. (*I don't see anything without my glasses.*)

✔ Object of a preposition:

> Je **ne** parle **à personne.** (*I'm not talking to anyone.*)

> Je **ne** pense **à rien** quand je fais de l'exercice. (*I think about nothing when I exercise.*)

The pronoun **personne** (*no one*) is always masculine, unlike the noun **une personne** (*person*), which is always feminine.

You can modify negative pronouns with **d'entre** + **nous/vous/eux/elles** to mean *of us/you/them:*

> **Aucun d'entre nous ne** peut y aller. (*None of us can go.*)

> **Nul d'entre eux n'**est innocent. (*None of them is innocent.*)

You can answer questions with just the negative pronoun:

> **Combien d'enfants avez-vous ? —Aucun.** (*How many kids do you have? —None.*)

> **Qui as-tu vu à la fête ? —Personne.** (*Whom did you see at the party? —No one.*)

Book III

Building the Grammatical Foundation for Communication

Getting down to the essentials with negative phrases

Just like in English, speakers of French don't always answer questions in complete sentences. Sometimes a shorter message goes right to the point. Try the following negative phrases, which include **pas** (*not*) and another adverb. (Check out Chapter 2 of Book IV for more on adverbs.)

- **Pas tout de suite** (*Not right away*)
- **Pas ici** (*Not here*)
- **Pas si vite** (*Not so fast*)
- **Pas comme ça** (*Not like that*)
- **Pas tout à fait** (*Not quite*)
- **Pas vraiment** (*Not really*)
- **Pas encore** (*Not yet*)
- **Pas tous les jours** (*Not every day*)
- **Pas assez** (*Not enough*)
- **Pas tellement** (*Not so many*)
- **Pas trop** (*Not too much*)

Here's a list of examples in which you answer negatively with a short phrase:

Tu veux un peu de vin ? —Non merci, pas tout de suite. (*Do you want a little wine?— No thank you, not right away.*)

Ils ont fini leur projet ? —Pas tout à fait. (*Did they finish their project? — Not quite.*)

Elle sait bien parler français ? —Pas vraiment. (*Does she speak French well? —Not really.*)

Tu aimes le sel ? —Pas trop ! (*Do you like salt? —Not too much!*)

Absolutely not: Inflating with double negatives

You often encounter double negatives in French, either with or without a verb. You can use them to have a strong effect or dramatize a situation or simply state a fact. Here are some examples:

Il te reste quelques dollars ? —Non, plus rien. (*Do you have a few dollars left? —No, nothing at all.*)

Tu vas retourner dans cette boutique ? —Plus jamais ! (*Are you going to return to this boutique? —No, never again!*)

Il y a encore des clients au bar ? —Non, plus personne. (*Are there any clients left at the bar? —No, no one anymore. [Not a soul]*)

Tu veux parler de l'accident ? —Non, je ne veux plus jamais en entendre parler. (*Do you want to talk about the accident? —No, I never want to hear anything about it again.*)

Tu as du travail à finir ? Oui, mais je ne veux plus rien faire ce soir. (*Do you have work to finish? —Yes, but I don't want to do anything more tonight.*)

Book III

Building the Grammatical Foundation for Communication

Chapter 6

Communicating Clearly with Infinitives and Present Participles

••

••

*I*nfinitives and present participles are *impersonal* verb forms, but that doesn't mean they don't have any friends. It just means that they each have only one form — you don't conjugate them for the different grammatical persons like you do with other verb tenses and moods. In English, the infinitive is the word *to* + a verb, as in *to go* or *to sing,* and the present participle ends in *-ing,* as in *going* or *singing.* In French, the infinitive is a single word ending in **-er**, **-ir**, or **-re**, like the verbs **aller** (*to go*) and **chanter** (*to sing*), and the present participle ends in **-ant**, as in **allant** (*going*).

Although infinitives and present participles exist in both French and English, you use them differently in the two languages. The French present participle is much less common than its English counterpart; in French, the infinitive often takes the place of the present participle in English. However, both verb forms can act as other parts of speech, such as nouns.

This chapter explains how to recognize infinitives and present participles, how to form present participles, and how to use both forms.

Infinitive Possibilities: Putting Infinitives to Work

The *infinitive* is the default form of a verb, its basic, unconjugated state. When you don't know what a verb means, you look up the infinitive in the dictionary, and when you need to conjugate a verb, you usually start with the infinitive.

In English, the infinitive has two parts — *to* + a verb — as in *to go, to choose,* and *to hear.* In French, the infinitive is a single word that ends in **-er, -ir,** or **-re,** such as **aller, choisir,** and **entendre.**

You can often translate the French infinitive as either the English present participle (an *-ing* verb) or the English infinitive (*to* + a verb):

> **J'aime chanter.** (*I like singing.* OR *I like to sing.*)

> **Il préfère marcher.** (*He prefers walking.* OR *He prefers to walk.*)

In addition to using the infinitive as a base to conjugate many verb tenses, you can use the infinitive as a verb or noun. This section shows you how.

Expressing more action

You use the French infinitive most often as a verb. To do this, you conjugate a verb according to the subject (as in **je veux** or **il faut**) and follow that with an infinitive (such as **aller, commander, choisir,** or **vendre**):

> Je **veux aller** en France. (*I want to go to France.*)

> Nous **voudrions commander**. (*We would like to order.*)

> **Peux**-tu **nager** ? (*Can you swim?*)

> Il **faut voyager** ? (*Is it necessary to travel ?*)

You can use the infinitive after the conjugated form of the verb **aller** (*to go*) to express that you're going to do something. This tense is called the near future tense. (See Chapter 6 of Book IV for more on this tense.)

> Nous **allons vendre** notre maison. (*We're going to sell our house.*)

> Tu **vas répondre** tout de suite ? (*Are you going to answer right away?*)

Even though the French infinitive already includes the idea of *to,* many French verbs require a preposition (usually **à** or **de**) between the conjugated verb and the infinitive. When you translate this into English, the extra preposition has no English equivalent:

> **J'hésite à parler.** (*I hesitate to speak.*)

> **J'ai décidé de partir.** (*I decided to leave.*)

The preposition you have to use in French — if any — depends on the conjugated verb, not on the infinitive that follows. In other words, you don't have to precede **partir** with **de**; rather, you have to follow **décider** with **de**.

Likewise, **hésiter** has to be followed by **à**. On the other hand, some verbs such as **vouloir** (*to want*) don't need a preposition. You say **Elle veut boire de l'eau** (*She wants to drink some water*). See Chapter 1 of Book IV for an explanation of prepositions and verbs that require them.

Look at the following sentences, noting that the verbs **aimer** and **défendre** are not followed by a preposition, whereas the verb **hésiter** is followed by **à**, and the verb **essayer** is followed by **de**:

> Nous **aimons regarder** des films d'amour. (*We like to watch romantic movies.*)

> Nous **hésitons à regarder** des films de guerre. (*We hesitate to watch war movies.*)

> Les chiens **défendent** leurs maîtres. (*Dogs defend their masters.*)

> Les chiens **essaient de défendre** leurs maîtres. (*Dogs try to defend their masters.*)

When the infinitive is a reflexive verb (that is, a verb that needs a reflexive pronoun — see Chapter 3 of Book IV), the reflexive pronoun has to agree with the subject. Look at the following examples. We put the subject of the sentence and the reflexive pronoun (before each infinitive verb) in bold.

> **Je** dois **me** coucher. (*I must go to bed.* Literally: *I must put myself to bed.*)

> **Nous** devons **nous** coucher. (*We must go to bed.*)

> **Ils/elles** doivent **se** coucher. (*They must go to bed.*)

TIP

In French, people also use the infinitive to give *impersonal* commands, such as on signs and in instructions (Chapter 4 of Book III explains more about the ways to give orders and instructions in French):

> **Marcher lentement.** (*Walk slowly.*)

> **Agiter bien avant l'emploi.** (*Shake well before use.*)

Standing as subjects and objects

The infinitive is the only French verb form that can act as the subject of a sentence. When you use the infinitive as a subject, the conjugated verb always takes on the third-person singular form, as if you were using **il/elle/on** as the subject. Just put the infinitive in your sentence where you'd put any other noun and follow it with a verb conjugated in the third-person singular. The French infinitive in this construction is equivalent to the *-ing* verb form in English:

Book III

Building the Grammatical Foundation for Communication

Avoir des amis **est** important. (*Having friends is important.*)

Pleurer ne **sert** à rien. (*Crying doesn't do any good.*)

Voir, c'**est croire.** (*Seeing is believing.*)

Even though you're using these French infinitives as nouns in these sentences, they still have to act like verbs: You can't use them with articles or adjectives or make them plural. However, some French infinitives are also legitimate nouns with non-verb-like meanings. These nouns act just like regular nouns, meaning you can modify them with articles and adjectives and use them as plurals. See Table 6-1 for some common examples.

Table 6-1	French Infinitive Nouns
French Verb	*French Noun*
déjeuner (*to have lunch*)	**le déjeuner** (*lunch*)
devoir (*to have to*)	**le devoir** (*duty*)
dîner (*to have dinner*)	**le dîner** (*dinner*)
être (*to be*)	**l'être** *(the [human] being)*
goûter (*to taste*)	**le goûter** (*the snack*)
pouvoir (*to be able to*)	**le pouvoir** (*power*)
rire *(to laugh)*	**le rire** (*the laugh, laughter*)
savoir (*to know*)	**le savoir** (*knowledge*)
sourire (*to smile*)	**le sourire** (*the smile*)

You also use the French infinitive after prepositions, where you'd use the *-ing* form in English, as in **sans attendre** (*without waiting*) and **avant de manger** (*before eating*). The French preposition **à** + an infinitive often means *for,* as in **à vendre** (*for sale*) and **à louer** (*for rent*).

Understanding word order with infinitives

When your sentence has a conjugated verb followed by an infinitive, you have to pay attention to where you put some of the smaller sentence elements. For example, object and adverbial pronouns such as **le** (*it*) and **y** (*there*) always come right before the infinitive, not the conjugated verb (see Chapter 3 of Book IV for info on pronouns):

Je peux **le** faire. (*I can do <u>it</u>.*)

Il va **nous** téléphoner. (*He's going to call <u>us</u>.*)

In a negative sentence (see Chapter 5 of Book III) with an infinitive, you have to consider the meaning of your sentence: Are you negating the conjugated verb or the infinitive verb? If it's the conjugated verb, the negative structure (such as **ne . . . pas**) surrounds that. Think about where you'd put the negative word in English:

✔ If *not* or another negative word goes with the conjugated verb, including a form of *be* or *do,* you're negating the conjugated verb in French:

> **Il n'aime pas lire.** (*He doesn't like to read.*)
>
> **Je ne peux pas trouver mon portefeuille.** (*I can't find my wallet.*)

✔ If you're using a verb followed by *not to* in English, you're negating the French infinitive. In that case, both parts of the negative structure (**ne pas, ne rien, ne jamais**) stay together in front of the infinitive:

> **Je t'ai dit de ne pas commencer sans moi.** (*I told you not to start without me.*)
>
> **Il préfère ne pas parler.** (*He prefers not to talk.*)
>
> **Nous décidons de ne rien faire aujourd'hui.** (*We decide not to do anything today.*)
>
> **J'ai décidé de ne jamais voyager sans mon chien.** (*I decided never to travel without my dog.*)
>
> **Être ou ne pas être . . .** (*To be or not to be . . .*)

When you make an infinitive negative and use it as the subject of a sentence, both negative adverbs also stay together in front of the infinitive:

> **Ne plus inviter Marie serait cruel.** (*Not inviting Marie anymore would be cruel.*)
>
> **Ne rien faire est quelquefois le meilleur passe-temps.** (*Doing nothing is sometimes the best pastime.*)

Book III

Building the Grammatical Foundation for Communication

Presenting Present Participles

In English, the present participle ends in *-ing,* and in French, it ends in **-ant.** It's less common in French than in English, because French often uses infinitives where English uses present participles.

The present participle form can act as a verb, adjective, or noun. It's also something of a misnomer because the *present* participle doesn't actually have a tense; you can use it along with another main verb that's in the present, past, or future.

In French, the present participle is *variable* (it has different forms for masculine, feminine, singular, and plural) when it's an adjective or noun and is *invariable* when it's a verb. In this section, we discuss how to create the present participle and how to use it.

Forming present participles

For nearly all verbs — regular, stem-changing, spelling-change, and irregular — you form the French present participle by taking the present-tense **nous** form of the verb, dropping **-ons**, and adding **-ant**. See Table 6-2.

Table 6-2	Creating Present Participles	
Infinitive	*Nous Form*	*Present Participle*
parler (*to talk, speak*)	parl**ons**	parl**ant** (talking, speaking)
choisir (*to choose*)	choisiss**ons**	choisiss**ant** (choosing)
entendre (*to hear*)	entend**ons**	entend**ant** (hearing)
aller (*to go*)	all**ons**	all**ant** (going)
commencer (*to begin*)	commenç**ons**	commenç**ant** (beginning)
voir (*to see*)	voy**ons**	voy**ant** (*seeing*)

This rule has only three exceptions. These three present participles still end in **-ant**, but they're not obtained from the **nous** form of the verb:

- **avoir** (*to have*): **ayant**
- **être** (*to be*): **étant**
- **savoir** (*to know*): **sachant**

The present participle of reflexive verbs (see Chapter 3 of Book IV) is preceded by the reflexive pronoun:

- **se lever** (*to get up*): **se levant**
- **se coucher** (*to go to bed*): **se couchant**
- **s'habiller** (*to get dressed*): **s'habillant**

Note that the reflexive pronoun always changes to agree with the subject:

> **En me levant, j'ai vu les fleurs.** (*Upon getting [myself] up, I saw the flowers.*)

> **Nous parlions en nous habillant.** (*We talked while getting [ourselves] dressed.*)

Using French present participles

In both French and English, you can use the present participle as an adjective, noun, or verb. But the use of the present participle in the two languages is very different. This section shows how to use present participles in various situations.

Present participles as adjectives

When you use the French present participle as an adjective, it acts just like any other adjective, meaning that it usually follows the noun it modifies and that it has to agree in gender and number. Remember that you add **-e** to make an adjective feminine and **-s** to make an adjective plural. (See Chapter 2 of Book IV for details on adjectives.) Here are some present participles acting as adjectives:

> un livre **intéressant** (*an interesting book*)

> une soucoupe **volante** (*a flying saucer*)

> des appartements **charmants** (*some charming apartments*)

> des tables **pliantes** (*some folding tables*)

You can't turn just any French verb into a present-participle adjective. This form is far less common in French than in English — if you want to use a present participle as an adjective, always check your adjectives in a French dictionary.

Nouns that are present participles

Some French nouns that refer to people happen to be present participles. You can think of these words as "nouns that end in **-ant**," or simply "nouns." You probably won't start with a French infinitive and form the present participle to use it as a noun — you'll just recognize the word as a noun.

Naturally, the present participle as a noun has different forms for masculine, feminine, singular, and plural. You follow the same rules for making these words feminine and plural as for other nouns: For example, **assistant** is masculine, **assistante** is feminine, **assistants** is masculine plural, and **assistantes** is feminine plural. (See Chapter 1 of Book III for more info on nouns.)

> **un assistant, une assistante** (*an assistant*)
>
> **un dirigeant, une dirigeante** (*a leader*)
>
> **un étudiant, une étudiante** (*a student*)
>
> **un participant, une participante** (*a participant*)
>
> **un survivant, une survivante** (*a survivor*)

The French present participle is much rarer than the English one, and its use as a noun is extremely limited. If you have any doubts at all about whether to use the French present participle as a noun in a particular sentence, don't — it would likely be wrong. For information on the English present participle used as a noun, see the later section "Translating -ing words into French."

Verbs: Describing action with present participles

French uses present participles to indicate an action that's happening at the same time as another action. To do this, use the present participle followed by an adjective or other descriptive information:

> **Étant** fatigué, il voulait rentrer. (*Being tired, he wanted to go home.*)
>
> J'ai vu un homme **marchant** très vite. (*I saw a man walking very quickly.*)

When you have two nouns in a sentence, as in the second example, the meaning of the present participle can be ambiguous. Was I walking very quickly, or was the man? To avoid confusion, think about whether you're modifying the subject of the sentence or the object. If it's the subject, use the **gérondif** (explained in the next section), as in **En marchant très vite, j'ai vu un homme** (*While [I was] walking very quickly, I saw a man*). If it's the object, use **qui** (*who*) + verb, as in **J'ai vu un homme qui marchait très vite** (*I saw a man who was walking very quickly*). Note that the verb **marchait** (*was walking*) is in the **imparfait** tense because it explains what was happening when something else happened. You can read about the **imparfait** in Chapter 2 of Book V.

While, as, and by: Expressing simultaneous action with the gérondif

A **gérondif** in French is the present participle preceded by **en**, which means *while, as,* or *by* in English. Because the **gérondif** modifies another verb, it's essentially acting as an adverb. To use the present participle as a **gérondif**, just put **en** in front of it and put any descriptive information after:

> **En quittant** le bâtiment, j'ai vu mon frère. (*While leaving [As I left] the building, I saw my brother.*)
>
> Je l'ai fait **en rêvant** de mes vacances. (*I did it while dreaming of my vacation.*)

En me brossant les dents, j'ai avalé du dentifrice. (*While brushing my teeth, I swallowed some toothpaste.*)

The English *gerund* is simply the *-ing* form of a verb that you use as a noun. The French **gérondif** is the **en** + verb + **-ant** construction that you use to express something that was happening at the same time as something else.

You can add **tout** (*all*) in front of the **gérondif** to obtain one of two effects:

✔ To emphasize the simultaneity of the **gérondif** and main verb:

Je me suis habillé(e) **tout en mangeant**. (I got dressed while eating [at the same time].)

✔ To contrast the meanings of the **gérondif** and main verb:

Tout en acceptant ton invitation, je ne te pardonne pas. (*While I accept your invitation, I don't forgive you.*)

French present participles as verbs and as **gérondifs** are both *invariable* — they never change in gender or number to agree with anything else. The **gérondif** includes **en** and can modify only a verb, whereas the participle can modify a noun:

J'ai rencontré un voisin allant au marché. (*I met a neighbor [who was] going to the market.*) The participle, **allant**, modifies the noun **voisin**.

J'ai rencontré un voisin en allant au marché. (*I met a neighbor while [I was] going to the market.*) The gérondif, **en allant**, modifies the verb **ai rencontré**.

Translating -ing words into French

In English, you can use an *-ing* verb as a noun that refers to the action of a verb, as in *Running is good exercise* or *Smoking is bad for you.* An *-ing* verb used as a noun is called a *gerund* in English, and it's identical to the present participle. However, you can't use the French present participle this way. You can translate this use of the English gerund only with the French infinitive or an equivalent French noun:

J'aime la pêche. OR **J'aime pêcher.** (*I like fishing.* OR *I like to fish.*)

L'écriture est difficile. OR **Écrire est difficile.** (*Writing is difficult.*)

See Table 6-3 for some examples of words you'd use to replace an English gerund.

Table 6-3	English -ing Nouns and Their French Counterparts	
English Noun	*French Noun*	*Infinitive*
dancing	**la danse**	**danser**
fishing	**la pêche**	**pêcher**
hunting	**la chasse**	**chasser**
reading	**la lecture**	**lire**
running	**la course**	**courir**
smoking	**le tabagisme**	**fumer**
swimming	**la natation**	**nager**
writing	**l'écriture**	**écrire**

In English, you often use a conjugated verb followed by the present participle, as in *I am thinking.* You can't do this in French — that grammatical structure simply doesn't exist, so something like **je suis pensant** (*I* + *am* + the present participle of **penser**) doesn't make sense. You'd use the present tense instead, saying **je pense** (*I'm thinking, I think, I do think*).

Here are some considerations to remember when translating the English present participle into French:

✔ If the verb is *is/am/are + -ing,* the French equivalent is the simple present tense verb (see Chapter 3 of Book III).

> **J'écris** une lettre. (*I'm writing a letter.*)
>
> Ils **vont** en vacances. (*They're going on vacation.*)
>
> Tu **lis** encore ? (*You're still reading?*)

✔ If the verb is *was/were + -ing,* the French equivalent is the **imparfait** (*imperfect tense*). Check out Chapter 2 of Book V for info on this tense.

> Nous **faisions** tout le travail. (*We were doing all the work.*)
>
> Les gens **attendaient**. (*People were waiting.*)
>
> **Dormais**-tu ? (*Were you sleeping?*)

✔ If the conjugated verb is something other than *to be* and is introducing the verb in the present participle, the French equivalent is the infinitive.

> J'aime **voyager.** (*I like traveling.*)
>
> Nous détestons **faire la cuisine.** (*We hate cooking.*)

Book IV

Getting Down to Detail and Precision in Your Communication

The 5th Wave — By Rich Tennant

©RICHTENNANT

"I'm not sure whether I'm stressing the right syllable in the wrong word, or stressing the wrong syllable in the right word, but it's starting to stress me out."

In this book . . .

Communicating well in French requires not only good grammar but also a certain flair for description. This book gives you insight into how adjectives and adverbs dress up sentences and paint a detailed picture of things, people, and events. This book also tells you how to avoid repeating things by using object pronouns and how to reflect back on the subject with reflexive pronouns and pronominal verbs. In addition, you discover how to link ideas with prepositions, conjunctions, and relative pronouns. Finally, you explore the use of the present subjunctive to express feelings, wishes, and possibilities and the use of the future indicative and present conditional to speculate on what lies ahead or what could still happen.

Here are the contents of Book IV at a glance:

Chapter 1

Specifying Relationships with Prepositions

In This Chapter

▶ Understanding common prepositions

▶ Making contractions

▶ Using prepositions with cities, states, and countries

▶ Recognizing verbs that need prepositions

*P*repositions are joining words — they connect nouns to other nouns or to verbs in order to show the relationship between those words, such as what something is *about*, whom someone is working *for*, or how your keys always manage to hide *from* you. Look at the difference the preposition makes in these examples: *I'm talking to my friend* and *I'm talking about my friend*.

Prepositions can be tricky in foreign languages because you can't memorize them like you do vocabulary lists. Many French prepositions have more than one English translation and vice versa. Simply knowing what they mean isn't enough; you have to know how you use them in each language. This chapter explains the most common French prepositions and how to use them to indicate possession, place, time, frequency, sequence, manner, and more.

Using the Most Common Prepositions

The most-used French prepositions are **à** and **de**. The word **à** often means *to, at,* or *in,* and **de** usually means *of, from,* or *about.* But you also use these prepositions to indicate other concepts, such as ownership or purpose. This section identifies the most common prepositions — **à, de,** and others — and explains their usage.

The preposition à

À is the French equivalent of *to, at,* or *in* — at least most of the time. It often indicates current location or future destination:

> **Je vais à la banque.** (*I'm going to the bank.*)
>
> **Je suis à l'hôpital.** (*I'm at/in the hospital.*)

English makes a distinction between whether you're going *to* a place or are currently *at* or *in* it, but French doesn't. À covers both of those concepts.

You can also use **à** to mean at a point in time (see Chapter 2 of Book I for more on time):

> **Notre vol est à 14h00.** (*Our flight is at 2:00 p.m.*)
>
> **Je suis parti à 5h30.** (*I left at 5:30 a.m.*)

The preposition **à** + the article **le** (*the*) contracts into **au**, as in **Je suis au concert** (*I'm at the concert*). Similarly, **à** + **les** contracts into **aux**, as in **aux États-Unis** (*in the United States*).

The preposition **à** has other uses as well — you can read about them in the sections "When to use **à** versus **de**" and "Looking at Verbs That Need Prepositions" later in this chapter.

The preposition de

De is the French equivalent of *from, of,* and *about* — usually. You use **de** for all these meanings:

- Cause: **Je meurs de soif !** (*I'm dying of thirst!*)
- Description: **un guide de voyage** (*a travel guide*)
- Origin: **Il est de Dakar.** (*He is from Dakar.*)
- Possession/ownership: **le voyage de Simone** (*Simone's trip*)
- Way of doing something: **un choc de front** (*head-on crash*)

Here's a quick note on using **de** to signal possession: In English, you use *'s* or just an apostrophe: *Jean's book, the students' books.* To translate this concept into French, you have to reverse the words and say *the book of Jean* and *the books of the students.* Look at these examples:

> **le livre de Jean** (*Jean's book*)
>
> **le pull d'Anne** (*Anne's sweater*)

la femme de l'acteur (*the actor's wife*)

le chien de la dame (*the lady's dog*)

les horaires du pharmacien (*the pharmacist's work hours*)

la chambre des enfants (*the children's room*)

You may notice a slightly different form of **de** in the second example, **le pull d'Anne.** That's a contraction of **de,** which we cover in the next section.

You need the preposition **de** in other constructions as well. See the later sections "Distinguishing between Prepositions" and "Looking at Verbs That Need Prepositions."

Forming contractions with prepositions

When you follow the prepositions **à** and **de** with the definite articles **le** and **les** (*the*), you have to form contractions. But you don't form contractions with the definite articles **la** and **l'** — see Table 1-1.

Table 1-1		Preposition Contractions	
à + Article	*Does It Contract?*	*de + Article*	*Does It Contract?*
à + le	Yes: **au**	de + le	Yes: **du**
à + la	No: **à la**	de + la	No: **de la**
à + l'	No: **à l'**	de + l'	No: **de l'**
à + les	Yes: **aux**	de + les	Yes: **des**

Here are some examples:

Je vais au marché. (*I'm going to the market.*)

Il se plaint des mouches. (*He's complaining about the flies.*)

À and **de** contract only with the definite articles **le** and **les.** They don't contract with the direct objects **le** and **les** (see Chapter 2 of Book III for information about definite articles and Chapter 3 of Book IV for information on direct objects). Here are some examples:

Je parle du problème. (*I'm talking about the problem.*) Here, **du** [de + le] means *about the.*

Il m'a dit de le faire. (*He told me to do it.*) *It* is what's being done, so **le** is the direct object of **faire** and doesn't contract.

Book IV

Getting Down to Detail and Precision in Your Communication

Identifying other useful prepositions

Though **à** and **de** are the most common French prepositions, you may hear, read, and use many others on a daily basis. Here are a couple of other useful prepositions:

- **Chez** is one of the most interesting French prepositions. It has several meanings and no simple English equivalent — in different contexts, you can translate it as *at/to the home of, at/to the office of, in the mind of,* or *among:*

  Je suis rentré chez moi. (*I went back [to my] home.*)

  Elle va chez le dentiste. (*She's going to the dentist's office.*)

  Chez Sartre, l'enfer, c'est les autres. (*In Sartre's mind/According to Sartre, hell is other people.*)

  Manger en famille est très important chez les Français. (*Eating as a family is very important to/among the French.*)

- **En** is another preposition with multiple meanings — you may translate it as *in* or *to* (for more-detailed information about **en**, check out "When to use dans versus en" later in this chapter):

  Je l'ai fait en 5 minutes. (*I did it in 5 minutes.*)

  Je suis en France. (*I'm in France.*)

  Nous allons en Algérie. (*We're going to Algeria.*)

Other important French prepositions tend to be used much like their English equivalents as Table 1-2 shows.

Table 1-2	French Prepositions		
French Preposition	*English Preposition*	*Example*	*Translation*
après	*after*	Je suis parti **après** minuit.	I left *after* midnight.
avant	*before*	J'ai mangé **avant** la fête.	I ate *before* the party.
avec	*with*	Il voyage **avec** sa copine.	He's traveling *with* his girlfriend.
contre	*against*	J'ai voté **contre** lui.	I voted *against* him.
dans	*in*	Mets-le **dans** le tiroir.	Put it *in* the drawer.

French Preposition	English Preposition	Example	Translation
pour	for	Je l'ai acheté **pour** vous.	I bought it *for* you.
sans	without	Elle mange **sans** parler.	She eats *without* speaking.
sous	under	Cet animal habite **sous** terre.	This animal lives *under* the ground.
sur	on	Il y a un carton **sur** mon lit.	There's a box *on* my bed.
vers	toward	Conduisons **vers** la plage.	Let's drive *toward* the beach.

Distinguishing between Prepositions

Part of the difficulty with French prepositions is that some of them have more than one meaning, and some of them share a meaning with other prepositions — at least when you translate them into English. In fact, French prepositions are very precise. The ones that seem to share a meaning have specific rules governing their uses. This section helps you determine how to use the right preposition.

When to use à versus de

The French prepositions **à** and **de** have overlapping or complementary meanings, which can be confusing. The key is to understand what they mean in French before you try to translate them into English. The following list spells out when to use each one:

- **Location:** **À** tells you where something is or will be, and **de** tells you where it was.

    Je suis à Paris. (*I'm in Paris.*)

    Je vais à Marseille. (*I'm going to Marseilles.*)

    Il est de Québec. (*He is from Quebec City.*)

    Il arrive de Montréal. (*He is arriving from Montreal.*)

Book IV

Getting Down to Detail and Precision in Your Communication

✔ **Description:** When you use **à** between two nouns, the second noun explains what the first noun is *for*. In comparison, when **de** goes between two nouns, the second noun tells you what is *in* the first noun.

> **une cuiller à thé** (*a teaspoon, a spoon for tea*)
>
> **un verre à eau** (*a water glass, a glass for water*)
>
> **une cuiller de thé** (*a spoonful of tea*)
>
> **un verre d'eau** (*a glass of water*)

In addition, many French verbs require either **à** or **de** — go to "Looking at Verbs That Need Prepositions," later in this chapter.

When to use dans versus en

Dans and **en** both mean *in,* but they're not interchangeable. **Dans** means *in* in both location and time, but **en** has some restrictions in these categories. The following guide spells out when to use **dans** and when to use **en**:

✔ **Location: Dans** means inside of something, such as a box, bag, or house.

> **Il y a une souris dans ma chambre !** (*There's a mouse in my bedroom!*)
>
> **As-tu un stylo dans ton sac ?** (*Do you have a pen in your bag?*)

En can't mean *in* something concrete, like a box or a bag. It can only mean in a country, which you can read about in the later section "Prepositions with countries."

✔ **Time:** When you use **dans** followed by a period of time, you're saying that you'll do something that far in the future.

> **Je le ferai dans dix minutes.** (*I'll do it in ten minutes [ten minutes from now].*)
>
> **Nous partons dans un mois.** (*We're leaving in a month.*)

In reference to time, **en** explains duration, or how long something takes.

> **Je l'ai fait en dix minutes.** (*I did it in ten minutes.* OR *It took me ten minutes to do it.*)
>
> **Je peux écrire cet article en un mois.** (*I can write this article in a month.* OR *It will take me a month to write this article.*)

En can also tell you when something happens or happened — in which month, season, or year.

> **Nous ne travaillons pas en été.** (*We don't work in the summer.*)
>
> **Il a écrit cet article en 2007.** (*He wrote this article in 2007.*)

Using Prepositions with Places

In French, you use all kinds of prepositions with places depending on whether you're talking about a city or a country — and in the case of a country, depending on the gender, number, and first letter of that country. This section clarifies the rules so you know which preposition to use the next time you're traveling or talking about a specific place.

Prepositions with countries

When choosing prepositions to use with countries, you can't just put your hand in the preposition grab bag and pull one out. You have to look at the gender (masculine or feminine) and the number of the country (singular or plural) to determine which preposition to use.

Countries that end in **e** are usually feminine: **la France**, **l'Italie**, and so on. The following four countries are exceptions; they end in **e** but are masculine:

- **le Cambodge** (*Cambodia*)
- **le Mexique** (*Mexico*)
- **le Mozambique** (*Mozambique*)
- **le Zimbabwe** (*Zimbabwe*)

Masculine countries are the four countries listed plus all countries that don't end in **e**: **le Canada**, **l'Iran**, and so on.

Plural countries in French are the same as in English: **les États-Unis** (*the United States*), **les Pays-bas** (*the Netherlands*), **les Philippines** (*the Philippines*), **les Seychelles** (*the Seychelles islands*), **les Emirats Arabes Unis** (*the United Arab Emirates*), and so on.

Going to or being in a country

Use the following info to decide which preposition to use when talking about going to or being in a country:

- Masculine singular country: **au**
- Feminine singular country: **en**
- Plural country: **aux**

Check out these prepositions in action:

Nous voyageons au Maroc. (*We're traveling to Morocco.*)

Il veut rester au Sénégal. (*He wants to stay in Senegal.*)

Je vais en France. (*I'm going to France.*)

Il habite en Côte d'Ivoire. (*He lives in Côte d'Ivoire.*)

Nous habitons aux États-Unis. (*We live in the United States.*)

Il va aux Seychelles. (*He's going to the Seychelles.*)

English has different prepositions depending on whether you're on your way somewhere (*to*) or you're already there (*in*), but French doesn't. The same preposition expresses both of these ideas.

If the masculine country begins with a vowel or mute **h**, you have to use either **à l'** (rather than **au**) or use **en** to say to the country:

Quand vas-tu à l'Angola/en Angola ? (*When are you going to Angola?*)

Je veux bien voyager à l'Ouganda/en Ouganda. (*I'd really like to travel to Uganda.*)

Coming from or being from a country

To say that you're arriving from, or are originally from, a country, you need the preposition **de.** You have to look at the gender and the number of the country to determine the correct form of **de**:

- ✔ Masculine singular country: **du**
- ✔ Feminine singular country: **de**
- ✔ Plural country: **des**

Here are some examples:

Elle est du Canada. (*She's from Canada.*)

Nous revenons de Suisse. (*We're coming back from Switzerland.*)

Nous sommes des États-Unis. (*We're from the United States.*)

If the feminine country begins with a vowel or mute **h**, **de** contracts to **d'**:

Êtes-vous d'Égypte ? (*Are you from Egypt?*)

Il vient d'Hongrie. (*He's coming from Hungary.*)

When you're arriving or are originally from a masculine country that begins with a vowel or mute **h**, use **de l'** or **d'**:

J'arrive de l'/d'Oman. (*I'm arriving from Oman.*)

Je reviens de l'/d'Oregon. (*I'm back from Oregon.*)

Prepositions with cities

The prepositions you use with cities are much more straightforward than the country-related ones in the preceding sections. You use **à** to mean *in* or *to* a city and **de** to mean *from:*

> **Nous allons à Genève.** (*We're going to Geneva.*)
>
> **Ils sont à Casablanca.** (*They're in Casablanca.*)
>
> **Elle est de Bruxelles.** (*She's from Brussels.*)
>
> **Il est arrivé d'Alger.** (*He arrived from Algiers.*)

Prepositions with states, regions, continents, and islands

The prepositions used with regions such **la Bretagne** (*Brittany*), with continents such as **l'Europe** (*Europe*), and states such as **le Kansas** (*Kansas*) follow the same rules as the ones for countries. Use **au** or **du** for masculine places, **en** or **de** for feminine places, **en** or **d'** for places that start with a vowel or mute **h**, and **aux** or **des** for plural places.

Here's how you say *in, to,* or *from* a state when referring to some of the states that make up the United States.

Name of the State	*In/To the State*	*From the State*
l'Alaska (m)	en Alaska	d'Alaska
l'Arizona (m)	en Arizona	d'Arizona
la Californie	en Californie	de Californie
le Colorado	au Colorado	du Colorado
la Floride	en Floride	de Floride
la Louisiane	en Louisiane	de Lousiane
le Missouri	au Missouri	du Missouri
l'Illinois (m)	en Illinois	d'Illinois
le Texas	au Texas	du Texas

Book IV

Getting Down to Detail and Precision in Your Communication

The prepositions used with islands are sometimes unpredictable. For example, *in Cuba* is **à Cuba**, but *in Corsica* is **en Corse**. Islands are best considered on a one-by-one basis. Here's a list of French islands or groups of islands. Note that **Haïti** (in the Caribbean Sea), **Tahiti** (in the South Pacific Ocean), **Mayotte** (in the Indian Ocean), and **Saint Pierre et Miquelon** (in the Atlantic Ocean) don't include an article in their names. Therefore, use the preposition **à** or **de/d'** with these islands, as if they were cities (see preceding section).

The following table shows you how to express *in, to,* and *from* with some French or French-speaking islands.

Name	In/To the Island	From the Island
le Mont Saint-Michel	au Mont Saint-Michel	du Mont Saint-Michel
la Corse	en Corse	de Corse
les Antilles	aux Antilles	des Antilles
Haïti	à/en Haïti	d'Haïti
Saint Martin	à Saint Martin	de Saint Martin
la Guadeloupe	en/ à la Guadeloupe	de la/de Guadeloupe
la Martinique	en/ à la Martinique	de la/de Martinique
Tahiti	à Tahiti	de Tahiti
la Nouvelle Calédonie	en/ à la Nouvelle Calédonie	de la/de Nouvelle Calédonie
Madagascar	à Madagascar	de Madagascar
Mayotte	à Mayotte	de Mayotte
les Seychelles	aux Seychelles	des Seychelles
la Réunion	en/à la Réunion	de la/de Réunion
Saint Pierre et Miquelon	à Saint Pierre et Miquelon	de Saint Pierre et Miquelon

Looking at Verbs That Need Prepositions

Many French verbs need a preposition when they're followed by an object or an infinitive. English has some verbs that need prepositions, called *phrasal verbs,* but they're not the same thing. Phrasal verbs in English require different prepositions depending on meaning, as in *to move on* and *to move in.*

French has a few verbs that have different meanings depending on which preposition follows, but most verbs just require a certain preposition that, confusingly, often has no English translation or has a meaning that doesn't correspond to the "normal" meaning of the preposition. This section points out some of the more common verbs and the prepositions that go with them.

Verbs with à

Hundreds of French verbs require the preposition à. The preposition doesn't make any difference in the verb conjugation, so just conjugate the verb and then follow with the preposition.

Some French verbs have to be followed by a preposition even though their English equivalents are not:

- **apprendre à** + infinitive (*to learn [to do something]*)

- **commencer à** + infinitive (*to begin [to do something]*)

- **continuer à** + infinitive (*to continue [doing something]*)

- **tenir à** + infinitive (*to insist on [doing something]*)

- **jouer à** + noun (*to play [a game or sport]*)

- **désobéir à** + noun (*to disobey [someone]*)

- **obéir à** + person (*to obey [someone]*)

- **ressembler à** + person (*to resemble/to look like [someone]*)

- **plaire à** + person (*to please [someone]*)

- **téléphoner à** + person (*to call [someone]*)

Look at some example sentences:

Ils **apprennent à** parler francais. (*They learn to speak French.*)

Tu **commences à** m'amuser. (*You're beginning to amuse me.*)

Tu **joues aux** cartes ? (*Do you play cards?*)

Il ne **désobéit** jamais **à** ses professeurs. (*He never disobeys his teachers.*)

Je **téléphone à** une amie. (*I'm calling a friend.*)

Table 1-3 gives you a variety of verbs followed by the preposition **à** in French. Some of the verbs can be used with or without the preposition **à**. For example, the verb **chercher** can be used without a preposition to mean *to look for* or *to pick up,* as in **Nous cherchons une pharmacie** (*We're looking for a pharmacy*). With the preposition **à**, its meaning changes to *attempting to do something,* as in **Je cherche à plaire** (*I'm attempting to please*).

Book IV

Getting Down to Detail and Precision in Your Communication

Table 1-3		Verbs Followed by à	
Verb + à	*Translation*	*Verb + à*	*Translation*
aider à + infinitive	to help [to do something]	**s'intéresser à** + noun	to be interested in [something]
s'amuser à + infinitive	to enjoy [doing something]	**inviter** + person + **à** + noun	to invite [someone] to [something]
arriver à + infinitive	to manage/ succeed in [doing something]	**se mettre à** + infinitive	to start/to set about [doing something]
assister à + noun	to attend [something]	**persister à** + infinitive	to persist in [doing something]
s'attendre à + infinitive	to expect [to do something]	**plaire à** + person	to please [someone]
chercher à + infinitive	to attempt [to do something]	**se préparer à** + infinitive	to prepare oneself [to do something]
conseiller à + person	to advise [someone]	**réfléchir à** + noun	to think about [something]
consentir à + infinitive	to consent [to doing something]	**renoncer à** + infinitive	to give up [doing something]
se décider à + infinitive	to decide/to make up one's mind [to do something]	**répondre à** + person/noun	to answer [someone/ something]
demander à + person	to ask [someone]	**résister à** + infinitive	to resist [doing something]
dire à + person	to tell [someone]	**réussir à** + infinitive	to succeed in [doing something]
emprunter à + person	to borrow from [someone]	**serrer la main à** + person	to shake the hand of [someone]
encourager à + infinitive	to encourage [to do something]	**servir à** + infinitive	to be used [to do something] to be used as [something]
faire attention à + noun	to pay attention to [something]	**tarder à** + infinitive	to delay/to be late [in doing something]
s'habituer à + noun/infinitive	to get used to [something/doing something]	**téléphoner à** + person	to call [someone]
hésiter à + infinitive	to hesitate [to do something]	**voler à** + person	to steal from [someone]

These examples show some of these verbs at work:

> **Fais attention aux** instructions. (*Pay attention to the instructions.*)
>
> Vas-tu m'**inviter à** la fête ? (*Are you going to invite me to the party?*)
>
> Il a **volé** cette idée **à** son collègue. (*He stole this idea from his colleague.*)

Note that the French infinitive after **à** often translates more naturally as the present participle, an *-ing* word, in English: **Je m'amuse à regarder les touristes.** (*I enjoy watching the tourists.*) You can read about the difference between French and English infinitives and present participles in Chapter 6 of Book III.

Verbs with de

Hundreds of French verbs require the preposition **de**. To use these verbs, just conjugate them and follow them with the preposition **de**.

Here's a list of verbs that are followed by **de** even though their English equivalents aren't followed by *of* or *from:*

- ✔ **jouer de** + noun (*to play [an instrument]*)
- ✔ **manquer de** + noun (*to lack [something]*)
- ✔ **parler de** + noun (*to talk about [something or someone]*)
- ✔ **penser de** + noun (*to have an opinion of [something or someone]*)
- ✔ **servir de** + noun (*to function as [something]*)
- ✔ **se souvenir de** + noun (*to remember [something or someone]*)

Look at these examples of how these verbs and prepositions are used:

> Elle **joue du** violon. (*She plays the violin.*)
>
> Je ne **me souviens** pas **de** votre nom. (*I don't remember your name.*)
>
> Cette soupe **manque de** sel. (*This soup lacks salt.*)

Table 1-4 gives you a variety of verbs that are followed by the preposition **de** in French. Some of the verbs can be used with or without the preposition **de**. Without the preposition, the verb **accepter** means *to accept something,* as in **Nous acceptons ce cadeau** (*We're accepting this gift*). With the preposition **de**, it means *accepting to do something,* as in **J'accepte de faire ce travail** (*I accept doing this work*).

Book IV

Getting Down to Detail and Precision in Your Communication

Table 1-4		Verbs Followed by de	
Verb + de	*Translation*	*Verb + de*	*Translation*
accepter de + infinitive	*to accept/to agree [to do something]*	**finir de** + infinitive	*to finish [doing something]*
s'agir de + noun/ infinitive*	*to be a question of [something/doing something]*	**se méfier de** + infinitive	*to beware of [doing something]*
avoir besoin de + noun	*to need*	**mériter de** + infinitive	*to deserve [to do something]*
avoir envie de + noun	*to want*	**se moquer de** + noun	*to make fun of [something]*
avoir peur de + noun/infinitive	*to be afraid of [something/doing something]*	**offrir de** + infinitive	*to offer [to do something]*
cesser de + infinitive	*to stop/cease [doing something]*	**oublier de** + infinitive	*to forget [to do something]*
choisir de + infinitive	*to choose [to do something]*	**persuader de** + infinitive	*to persuade [to do something]*
conseiller de + infinitive	*to advise [to do something]*	**se plaindre de** + noun	*to complain about [something]*
craindre de + infinitive	*to fear [doing something]*	**prier de** + infinitive	*to beg [to do something]*
décider de + infinitive	*to decide [to do something]*	**promettre de** + infinitive	*to promise [to do something]*
défendre à + person + **de** + infinitive	*to forbid [someone] [to do something]*	**proposer de** + infinitive	*to suggest [doing something]*
demander à + person + **de** + infinitive	*to ask [someone] [to do something]*	**refuser de** + infinitive	*to refuse [to do something]*
se dépêcher de + infinitive	*to hurry [to do something]*	**regretter de** + infinitive	*to regret [doing something]*
dire à + person + **de** + infinitive	*to tell [someone] [to do something]*	**remercier de** + infinitive	*to thank for [doing something]*
empêcher de + infinitive	*to prevent keep from [doing something]*	**risquer de** + infinitive	*to risk [doing something]*
essayer de + infinitive	*to try [to do something]*	**se souvenir de** + noun/infinitive	*to remember [something/doing something]*

S'agir de is an impersonal verb, so use it only in the third-person singular. For example, **Dans cet article, il s'agit de la liberté d'expression (This article is about freedom of expression. Literally: In this article, it's about freedom of expression).*

Verb + de	Translation	Verb + de	Translation
s'excuser de + infinitive	to apologize for [doing something]	**venir de** + infinitive	to have just [done something]
féliciter de + infinitive	to congratulate for [doing something]		

Look at these examples of verbs followed by **de**:

> **Nous refusons de partir.** (*We're refusing to leave.*)

> **Il a oublié de se raser.** (*He forgot to shave.*)

> **Je viens de manger.** (*I just ate.*)

When you use the verb **venir** (*to come*) followed by **de** and an infinitive verb, you're forming the near past tense (**passé proche**), which helps you say that something just happened. The preposition **de** makes a big difference here, because **je viens manger** means *I'm coming to eat,* whereas **Je viens de manger** means *I just ate.* (See Chapter 1 of Book V for more on this past tense.)

Verbs with other prepositions

Though **à** and **de** are the most common prepositions after verbs, certain verbs require other French prepositions. Just conjugate these verbs, add the preposition, and go!

Verbs with **contre**:

- ✔ **s'asseoir contre** + person (*to sit next to [someone]*)
- ✔ **se battre contre** + noun/person (*to fight against [something/someone]*)
- ✔ **échanger** (noun) **contre** (noun) (*to exchange [something] for [something else]*)
- ✔ **se fâcher contre** + person (*to get mad at [someone]*)

Verbs with **dans**:

- ✔ **boire quelque chose dans** + noun (*to drink something out of [something]*)
- ✔ **courir dans** + noun (*to run through [something]*)
- ✔ **coûter dans** + amount (*to cost [about]*)
- ✔ **entrer dans** + noun (*to enter [something]*)
- ✔ **fouiller dans** + noun (*to look through [something]*)

Book IV

Getting Down to Detail and Precision in Your Communication

✔ **lire dans** + noun (*to read in [a publication]*)

✔ **manger dans** + noun (*to eat out/off of [something]*)

✔ **prendre quelque chose dans** + noun (*to take something from [something]*)

✔ **regarder dans** + noun (*to look in [something]*)

✔ **vivre dans** + noun (*to live in [something]*)

Verbs with **en**:

✔ **agir en** + noun (*to act like [something]*)

✔ **casser en** + noun/number (*to break in/into [something/a certain number of pieces]*)

✔ **se changer en** + noun (*to change/to turn into [something]*)

✔ **couper en** + number (*to cut in [some number of pieces]*)

✔ **croire en** + noun (*to believe in [something]*)

✔ **écrire en** + language (*to write in a language*)

✔ **transformer** + noun + **en** + noun (*to change [something] into [something else]*)

✔ **se vendre en** + noun (*to be sold in/by [bottle, kilo]*)

✔ **voyager en** + noun (*to travel by [train, car]*)

Verbs with **par**:

✔ **commencer par** + infinitive (*to begin by [doing something]*)

✔ **finir par** + infinitive (*to end up [doing something], to finally [do something]*)

✔ **sortir par** + noun (*to leave by way of [something]*)

✔ **jurer par** + noun (*to swear by [something]*)

✔ **obtenir quelque chose par** + infinitive (*to obtain something [by doing something]*)

Verbs with **pour**:

✔ **creuser pour** + noun (*to dig for [something]*)

✔ **être pour** + noun (*to be in favor of [something]*)

✔ **parler pour** + person (*to speak on behalf of [someone]*)

✔ **payer pour** + person (*to pay for [someone]*)

✔ **signer pour** + person (*to sign on behalf of [someone]*)

Verbs with **sur**:

- ✔ **acheter** (noun) **sur le marché** (*to buy [something] at the market*)
- ✔ **appuyer sur** + noun (*to press [something]*)
- ✔ **arriver sur** + time (*to arrive around [sometime]*)
- ✔ **compter sur** + noun/person (*to count on [something/someone]*)
- ✔ **concentrer sur** + noun (*to concentrate on [something]*)
- ✔ **copier sur** + person (*to copy from [someone]*)
- ✔ **s'endormir sur** + noun (*to fall asleep over [something]*)
- ✔ **s'étendre sur** + noun (*to spread out over [something]*)
- ✔ **interroger** (someone) **sur** + noun (*to question someone about [something]*)
- ✔ **se jeter sur** + person (*to throw oneself upon [someone]*)
- ✔ **prendre modèle sur** + person (*to model oneself on [someone]*)
- ✔ **réfléchir sur** + noun (*to study/to examine [something]*)
- ✔ **revenir sur** + noun (*to go back over [something]*)

Verbs with **vers**:

- ✔ **se diriger vers** + noun (*to move toward/make/head for [something]*)
- ✔ **regarder vers** + noun (*to face/look toward [something]*)
- ✔ **tourner vers** + noun (*to turn toward [something]*)

Verbs whose meanings change with different prepositions

Although most verbs always require one specific preposition, a few have different meanings according to which preposition you use. See Table 1-5 for some examples. Just conjugate these verbs and follow with the appropriate preposition. No simple shortcut exists to know which verb uses which preposition, but you'll have an easier time remembering them if you make your vocabulary lists with the prepositions each verb needs and the different translations.

Table 1-5	Verb Meanings with Different Prepositions		
Verb + à	*Translation*	*Verb + Another Preposition*	*Translation*
aller à	*to go to*	**aller vers**	*to go toward/in the direction of*
donner à	*to give to*	**donner contre**	*to trade for/to exchange*
être à	*to be at/to belong to*	**être vers**	*to be near/ around*
jouer à	*to play [a game/ sport]*	**jouer de**	*to play [an instrument]*
manquer à	*to miss someone*	**manquer de**	*to fail to do something/to lack*
parler à	*to talk to*	**parler de**	*to talk about*
penser à	*to think about/to reflect on*	**penser de**	*to have an opinion on*
profiter à	*to benefit/to be profitable to*	**profiter de**	*to make the most of*
téléphoner à	*to call someone*	**téléphoner pour**	*to phone about/ regarding [something]*
tenir à	*to insist on*	**tenir de**	*to resemble*

Look at these examples:

> Je **parle à** mon frère. (*I'm talking to my brother.*)
>
> Nous **parlons de** la France. (*We're talking about France.*)
>
> Il **va à** Paris. (*He's going to Paris.*)
>
> Elle **va vers** le musée. (*She's going toward the museum.*)

You can translate both **penser à** and **penser de** as *to think about,* but their precise meanings differ. **Penser à** means *to have in mind* or *to consider,* and **penser de** means *to have an opinion on:*

Je **pense à** mes vacances. (*I'm thinking about my vacation.*)

Que **penses**-tu de cette idée ? (*What do you think about this idea?*)

A few French verbs can be used with two different prepositions with no difference in meaning:

✔ **commencer à/de** + infinitive (*to begin [doing something]*)

✔ **continuer à/de** + infinitive (*to continue [doing something]*)

✔ **rêver à/de** + noun/infinitive (*to dream of/about [something/doing something]*)

✔ **traduire en/vers le** + language (*to translate into [a language]*)

Verbs with no French preposition

Some French verbs are followed directly by the infinitive or direct object, even though their English equivalents need a preposition. For example, **attendre** means *to wait for* + noun, not *to wait*. To remember these verbs, include the English preposition and whether it's followed by a noun or verb in your vocabulary list.

Here's a list of such French verbs and examples of how they're used:

✔ **attendre** + noun (*to wait for [something or someone]*)

✔ **chercher** + noun (*to look for [something or someone]*)

✔ **demander** + noun (*to ask for [something]*)

✔ **écouter** + noun (*to listen to [something or someone]*)

✔ **payer** + noun (*to pay for [something]*)

✔ **regarder** + noun (*to look at [something or someone]*)

Here are a few examples:

Vous attendez le bus ? (*Are you waiting for the bus?*)

Vous payez tout ça ? (*Are you paying for all this?*)

Elles écoutent une chanson. (*They're listening to a song.*)

Table 1-6 lists verbs that require prepositions in English but not in French.

Table 1-6	Verbs with Prepositions in English but Not in French		
Verb	*Translation*	*Verb*	*Translation*
aller + infinitive	*to be going to [do something]*	**habiter** + noun	*to live in [some place]*
approuver + noun	*to approve of [something]*	**ignorer** + noun	*to be unaware of [something]*
attendre + noun	*to wait for [something]*	**mettre** + noun	*to put [something] on*
chercher + noun	*to look for [something]*	**payer** + noun	*to pay for [something]*
demander + noun	*to ask for [something]*	**penser** + infinitive	*to think about [doing something]*
devoir + infinitive	*to have to/be obliged to [do something]*	**pouvoir** + infinitive	*to be able to [do something]*
écouter + noun	*to listen to [something]*	**regarder** + noun	*to look at [something]*
envoyer chercher + noun	*to send for [something]*	**sentir** + noun	*to smell of [something]*
essayer + noun	*to try [something] on*	**soigner** + person	*to take care of [someone]*

Here are a few examples of verbs that are followed by prepositions in English but not in French:

Je **cherche** mon sac à dos. (*I'm looking for my backpack.*)

Il **ignore** mon dilemme. (*He's unaware of my dilemma.*)

Je **pense** passer chez toi. (*I'm thinking about stopping by at your place.*)

Chapter 2

Describing with Flair: Adjectives and Adverbs

Adjectives are descriptive words, and adverbs sometimes help them out. Whereas nouns and verbs are the building blocks and actions of language, adjectives and adverbs are the colors, shapes, sizes, speeds, frequencies, and styles that bring those blocks and actions to life. For example, in the first sentence in this chapter, *descriptive* is an adjective and *sometimes* is an adverb. Without them, the sentence would've been missing some important information: "Adjectives are words, and adverbs help them out." So adjectives and adverbs provide detail and clarification to the nouns, verbs, and other words they modify.

This chapter explains all about adjectives and adverbs, including how to use them, where to put them in a French sentence, the different types, and how to make comparisons.

Coloring Your Language with Adjectives

Adjectives describe nouns and pronouns. They can tell you what something looks, tastes, feels, sounds, and smells like as well as how smart it is, where it's from, what it's for, and sometimes even why you should or shouldn't care about it. This section focuses on what you need to know about adjectives to use them correctly in your French writing and speaking.

Making your adjectives agree

In French, most adjectives come after the noun they modify rather than before, and they have to agree with the noun in gender and number. To make adjectives *agree,* you need to add and/or change certain letters. Most of the rules for making adjectives feminine and plural are the same as the rules for making nouns feminine and plural. (Chapter 2 of Book III explains noun gender and number in detail.)

Most French adjectives have four forms: masculine singular, feminine singular, masculine plural, and feminine plural. The masculine singular is the default form of the adjective — that's what you'd look up in the dictionary. For example, **vert** (*green*) and **beau** (*beautiful*) are masculine; your dictionary likely doesn't have entries for the feminine equivalents, **verte** and **belle**; the masculine plural, **verts** and **beaux**; or the feminine plural, **vertes** and **belles**.

Making adjectives feminine

To make a masculine adjective feminine, all you have to do for many adjectives is add an **-e** to the end:

> **petit** (*small*) becomes **petite**
>
> **joli** (*pretty*) becomes **jolie**
>
> **préféré** (*favorite*) becomes **préférée**
>
> **bleu** (*blue*) becomes **bleue**

If the masculine adjective already ends in a silent **-e** (one without any accent), you don't make any changes at all to get the feminine form:

> **grave** (*serious*) remains **grave**
>
> **rouge** (*red*) remains **rouge**

Like nouns, certain adjective endings have irregular feminine forms. For many of these words, you double the final consonant before adding the **-e**:

- ✔ For masculine adjectives that end in **-el**, **-il**, or **-ul**, add **-le** for the feminine:

  > **formel** (*formal*) becomes **formelle**
  >
  > **pareil** (*similar*) becomes **pareille**
  >
  > **nul** (*none*) becomes **nulle**

- ✔ For adjectives that end in **-en** or **-on**, add **-ne** for the feminine form:

  > **tunisien** (*Tunisian*) becomes **tunisienne**
  >
  > **bon** (*good*) becomes **bonne**

✔ For most adjectives that end in **-s**, add **-se** for the feminine:

    bas (*low*) becomes **basse**

However, for adjectives that refer to nationalities, just add **-e** without doubling the **s**:

    chinois (*Chinese*) becomes **chinoise**

French also has several other irregular feminine forms, which follow these patterns:

✔ **-c** to **-che**: **blanc** (*white*) becomes **blanche**

✔ **-eau** to **-elle**: **nouveau** (*new*) becomes **nouvelle**

✔ **-er** to **-ère**: **cher** (*expensive*) becomes **chère**

✔ **-et** to **-ète**: **secret** (*secret*) becomes **secrète**

✔ **-eux** to **-euse**: **heureux** (*happy*) becomes **heureuse**

✔ **-f** to **-ve**: **vif** (*lively*) becomes **vive**

✔ **-is** to **-îche**: **frais** (*fresh*) becomes **fraîche**

✔ **-x** to **-ce**: **doux** (*sweet*) becomes **douce**

Making adjectives plural

To make most French adjectives plural, all you do is add an **-s**. For instance, **joli** (*pretty*) becomes **jolis**, **blanc** (*white*) changes to **blancs**, and **triste** (*sad*) becomes **tristes**. If you need a feminine plural form, add an **-s** to the feminine form: **jolie** becomes **jolies**, **blanche** becomes **blanches**, and **triste** becomes **tristes**.

If the masculine adjective ends in **-s** or **-x**, the plural form is the same as the singular. For example, **français** (*French*) and **vieux** (*old*) can modify both singular and plural nouns. Here are a couple of other situations to remember:

✔ Masculine adjectives that end in **-al** become plural with **-aux**: **social** (*social*) becomes **sociaux**, and **idéal** (*ideal*) changes to **idéaux**.

✔ Masculine adjectives that end in **-eau** add an **-x** for the plural: **nouveau** (*new*) becomes **nouveaux**, and **beau** (*beautiful*) switches to **beaux**.

Feminine adjectives always end in **-e**, so all you have to do to make them plural is add an **-s**. Table 2-1 shows some French adjectives in all four forms.

Book IV

Getting Down to Detail and Precision in Your Communication

Table 2-1	French Adjectives, Ready to Agree			
English	*Masculine Singular*	*Feminine Singular*	*Masculine Plural*	*Feminine Plural*
green	vert	verte	verts	vertes
gray	gris	grise	gris	grises
red	rouge	rouge	rouges	rouges
white	blanc	blanche	blancs	blanches

Adjectives that end in **-s**, like **gris**, have only three forms because the masculine singular and plural are the same. Adjectives that end in **-e**, like **rouge**, have only two forms because the masculine and feminine forms are the same.

Color adjectives that come from the names of fruit or nuts, such as the color orange, which comes from **l'orange** (*the orange*), and the color brown, which comes from **le marron** (*the chestnut*), have only one form. They're invariable, never changing to agree with the noun.

Aiding pronunciation with special masculine singular forms

Most French adjectives have four forms: masculine singular, feminine singular, masculine plural, and feminine plural. But six French adjectives that go in front of nouns have an extra form: a masculine singular form that you use in front of a vowel or mute **h**. The goal of this form is to make pronunciation easier so you don't have to say back-to-back vowel sounds.

See Table 2-2 for these adjectives. (***Note:*** Unlike most French adjectives, these adjectives go in front of the noun. See the next section for details on word order.)

Table 2-2	Adjectives with Special Masculine Singular Forms				
English	*Masculine Singular*	*Masculine Singular before a Vowel or Mute h*	*Feminine Singular*	*Masculine Plural*	*Feminine Plural*
beautiful	beau	bel	belle	beaux	belles
this	ce	cet	cette	ces	ces
new	nouveau	nouvel	nouvelle	nouveaux	nouvelles
crazy	fou	fol	folle	fous	folles
soft	mou	mol	molle	mous	molles
old	vieux	vieil	vieille	vieux	vieilles

You use this special form only with masculine nouns and only when the adjective directly precedes a vowel or mute **h**:

> **mon nouvel avocat** (*my new lawyer*)
>
> **un bel homme** (*a handsome man*)

The letter the noun actually starts with doesn't necessarily tell you whether you have to use the special form. If the adjective directly precedes **ingénieur** (*engineer*) or **architecte** (*architect*), for example, you use the special form. And if the adjective precedes another adjective that starts with a vowel or mute **h**, such as **ancien** (*former*), you use the special form as long as the noun is masculine (even if the noun itself begins with a consonant). But if another adjective like **grand** (*great*) comes before the noun, you don't use the special form — even if the noun begins with a vowel or mute **h**:

> **cet ingénieur** (*this engineer*)
>
> **cet ancien maire** (*this former mayor*)
>
> **ce grand architecte** (*this great engineer*)

You use the special adjective form only if all three of these conditions are met:

- ✔ The noun is masculine.
- ✔ The noun is singular.
- ✔ The word that actually follows the adjective — whether it's the noun itself or another adjective — begins with a vowel or mute **h**.

Correctly positioning adjectives with nouns

Using adjectives with nouns is a great way to add description to a sentence. But to put adjectives in their correct places, you need to think about the type of adjective and what it means. Most *descriptive* French adjectives — that is, adjectives that describe the nature or appearance of a noun, such as color, shape, or origin — follow the nouns they modify:

> **une voiture verte** (*a green car*)
>
> **un garçon mince** (*a slender boy*)
>
> **des vêtements européens** (*European clothing*)
>
> **une fille heureuse** (*a happy girl*)

Book IV

Getting Down to Detail and Precision in Your Communication

In addition, present and past participles (verb forms) used as adjectives always follow nouns (see Chapter 6 of Book III for info on present participles and Chapter 1 of Book V for details on past participles):

des yeux étincelants (*sparkling eyes*)

une histoire compliquée (*a complicated story*)

Common descriptive adjectives that refer to the following qualities have to come in front of the nouns they modify (you can remember these qualities with the acronym *BAGS*):

- ✔ Beauty: **une jolie femme** (*a pretty woman*), **un beau pays** (*a beautiful country*)

- ✔ Age: **un jeune homme** (*a young man*, **une nouvelle voiture** (*a new car*), **une vieille maison** (*an old house*)

- ✔ Goodness and badness: **une bonne idée** (*a good idea*), **un mauvais rhume** (*a bad cold*)

- ✔ Size: **un petit appartement** (*a small apartment*), **une grande montagne** (*a big mountain*)

The meaning of **grand** depends on where you put it. When it precedes the noun, it means *big* (for an object) or *great* (for a person): **une grande maison** (*a big house*), **un grand homme** (*a great man*). But to say that a person is *tall*, **grand** has to follow the noun it modifies: **un homme grand** (*a tall man*). See the next section for details.

All nondescriptive adjectives — possessive, demonstrative, interrogative, indefinite, negative, and numerical adjectives — come before the noun. (You can read about possessives, demonstratives, and interrogatives in Chapter 2 of Book III; negatives in Chapter 5 of Book III; and numbers in Chapter 2 of Book I.)

ma fille (*my daughter*)

cette voiture (*this car*)

Quelle maison ? (*Which house?*)

certains livres (*certain books*)

aucune idée (*no idea*)

quatre-vingts jours (*eighty days*)

Identifying adjectives with meaning changes

Some French adjectives, like **grand** or **ancien**, have different meanings depending on whether they precede or follow the noun. When these adjectives have a figurative meaning, you place them before the noun. When they have a literal meaning, you place them after the noun.

Figurative Meaning	Literal Meaning
l'ancien monument (*the former monument*)	**le monument ancien** (*the ancient monument*)
la pauvre femme (*the poor, wretched woman*)	**la femme pauvre** (*the poor, penniless woman*)
un grand ami (*a great friend*)	**un ami grand** (*a tall friend*)

See Table 2-3 for some common French adjectives with meaning changes.

Table 2-3	Adjectives with Meaning Changes	
Adjective	**Meaning before Noun (Figurative)**	**Meaning after Noun (Literal)**
brave	*good, decent*	*brave*
cher	*dear*	*expensive*
curieux	*odd, strange*	*inquisitive*
dernier	*final*	*previous*
franc	*real, genuine*	*frank*
grand	*great*	*tall*
premier	*first*	*basic, primary*
prochain	*following*	*next*
propre	*(my, his, our) own*	*clean*
triste	*sorry, pathetic*	*sad*

Book IV

Getting Down to Detail and Precision in Your Communication

Using Adverbs Correctly

Like adjectives, adverbs are descriptive words. But instead of modifying nouns, *adverbs* modify verbs, adjectives, or other adverbs. Adverbs tell you when, where, why, how, how often, and how much.

Adverbs are invariable: They have only one form, and they don't have to agree with anything. This section covers what you need to know, including how to recognize types of adverbs, form adverbs, and position them, so you can correctly use adverbs in your writing and speech.

Identifying types of adverbs

Different types of adverbs have different purposes, and the type you want to use depends on what you want to say. Are you talking about how often something happens, where it happens, when? Adverb position, which we cover later in the chapter, depends in part on the type of adverb you're using.

Adverbs of frequency

Adverbs of frequency express how often or how consistently something happens:

- **encore** (*again*)
- **jamais** (*ever*)
- **parfois** (*sometimes*)
- **quelquefois** (*sometimes*)
- **rarement** (*rarely*)
- **souvent** (*often*)
- **toujours** (*always, still*)

Je vais souvent aux musées. (*I often go to museums.*)

Habites-tu toujours au Québec ? (*Do you still live in Quebec?*)

Adverbs of place

Adverbs of place tell you where something happens:

- **dedans** (*inside*)
- **dehors** (*outside*)
- **derrière** (*behind, in back*)
- **dessous** (*below*)
- **dessus** (*above*)
- **devant** (*in front*)
- **en bas** (*below, down[stairs]*)
- **en haut** (*up[stairs]*)
- **ici** (*here*)
- **là** (*there*)
- **loin** (*far away*)
- **partout** (*everywhere*)
- **près** (*near*)
- **quelque part** (*somewhere*)

Take a look at some example sentences:

> **Je préfère m'asseoir derrière.** (*I prefer sitting in back.*)
>
> **Qui habite en haut ?** (*Who lives upstairs?*)

Many adverbs of place are also prepositions. The difference is that an adverb acts by itself to modify a verb — **J'habite en bas** (*I live below*) — and a preposition joins its object (the noun that follows it) with another word — **J'habite en bas de Michel** (*I live below Michel*). See Chapter 1 of Book IV for more information on French prepositions.

Adverbs of time

Adverbs of time explain when something happens:

- **actuellement** (*currently*)
- **après** (*after*)
- **aujourd'hui** (*today*)
- **aussitôt** (*immediately*)
- **autrefois** (*formerly, in the past*)
- **avant** (*before*)
- **bientôt** (*soon*)
- **d'abord** (*first, at first*)
- **déjà** (*already*)
- **demain** (*tomorrow*)
- **depuis** (*since*)
- **enfin** (*at last, finally*)
- **ensuite** (*next*)
- **hier** (*yesterday*)
- **immédiatement** (*immediately*)
- **longtemps** (*for a long time*)
- **maintenant** (*now*)
- **récemment** (*recently*)
- **tard** (*late*)
- **tôt** (*early*)

Actuellement is a false friend; it means *currently,* not *actually.* **En fait** and **en réalité** mean *actually.* (See Chapter 1 of Book I for more on words that look similar but have different meanings in French and English.)

Here are some sentences that use adverbs of time:

> **Nous allons partir demain.** (*We're going to leave tomorrow.*)
>
> **J'ai enfin visité Paris.** (*I finally visited Paris.*)

Adverbs of quantity

Adverbs of quantity tell you how many or how much of something:

Book IV

Getting
Down to
Detail and
Precision
in Your
Communication

- ✓ **assez (de)** (*quite, fairly, enough*)
- ✓ **autant (de)** (*as much, as many*)
- ✓ **beaucoup (de)** (*a lot, many*)
- ✓ **bien de** (*quite a few*)
- ✓ **combien (de)** (*how many, how much*)
- ✓ **encore de** (*more*)

- ✓ **moins (de)** (*less, fewer*)
- ✓ **pas mal de** (*quite a few*)
- ✓ **(un) peu (de)** (*few, little, not very*)
- ✓ **la plupart de** (*most*)
- ✓ **plus (de)** (*more*)
- ✓ **tant (de)** (*so much, so many*)
- ✓ **très** (*very*)
- ✓ **trop (de)** (*too much, too many*)

The parentheses around **de** in many of these phrases indicate that the **de** is required only if a noun follows the adverb. For example, **J'ai assez mangé** (*I ate enough*) doesn't need **de** because **assez** is followed by a verb, but **j'ai mangé assez de riz** (*I ate enough rice*) does because *rice* is a noun. Look at some more examples:

> **C'est combien ?** (*How much is it?*)

> **Combien d'argent est-ce qu'il gagne ?** (*How much money does he earn?*)

> **C'est trop.** (*It's too much.*)

> **Il y a trop de circulation.** (*There's too much traffic.*)

When a noun follows an adverb of quantity, you need to include the preposition **de** between the two words, and you don't use an article (**le**, **la**, or **les**) in front of the noun. However, there are exceptions: **bien de**, **encore de**, and **la plupart de** always need to be followed by an article, as in **La plupart de la plage est rocheuse** (*Most of the beach is rocky*). That means you may have to use the contractions of **de** + **le** (**du**) and **de** + **les** (**des**) after the adverb, as in **J'ai dit ça bien des fois** (*I said that many times*). See Chapter 2 of Book III for more on contractions.

You can use these adverbs of quantity to modify adjectives, as in the following examples:

> **Je suis encore fatigué.** (*I'm still tired.*) Here, **encore** (*still*) modifies **fatigué**.

> **Elle est très aimable.** (*She is very nice.*) **Très** (*very*) modifies **aimable**.

> **Ils sont trop impatients.** (*They are too impatient.*) **Trop** (*too*) modifies **impatients**.

You can use also these adverbs of quantity to modify other adverbs:

> **Je parle très vite.** (*I speak very quickly.*) Here, **très** (*very*) modifies **vite**.

> **Elle vient moins fréquemment.** (*She comes less frequently.*) **Moins** (*less*) modifies **fréquemment**.

> **Ils font beaucoup trop de fautes.** (*They make far too many mistakes.*) **Beaucoup** (*many*) modifies **trop**.

French has three other types of adverbs that you need to know about. They include interrogative adverbs (Chapter 5 of Book III), negative adverbs (Chapter 5 of Book III), and adverbs of manner (see the next section).

Forming adverbs of manner

Many adverbs are formed from adjectives. These *adverbs of manner* express how something happens, and they usually end in *-ly* in English (*clearly, quickly, frankly*), whereas their French equivalents end in **-ment** (**clairement, rapidement, franchement**).

The rules for turning adjectives into adverbs are fairly straightforward. For masculine adjectives that end in a single vowel, just add **-ment**:

> **poli** (*polite*) becomes **poliment** (*politely*)

> **carré** (*square*) becomes **carrément** (*squarely*)

> **triste** (*sad*) becomes **tristement** (*sadly*)

Other words need a little more tweaking:

- ✔ When the masculine adjective ends in a consonant (other than **-ant** or **-ent**) or multiple vowels, take the feminine form of the adjective and add **-ment**. Most French adjectives of manner are formed like this:

  > **certain** (m) (*certain*)/**certaine** (f) becomes **certainement** (*certainly*)

  > **heureux** (m) (*happy*)/**heureuse** (f) becomes **heureusement** (*happily, fortunately*)

  > **dernier** (m) (*last*)/**dernière** (f) becomes **dernièrement** (*lastly*)

  > **nouveau** (m) (*new*)/**nouvelle** (f) becomes **nouvellement** (*newly*)

- ✔ For adjectives that end in **-ant** or **-ent**, replace that ending with **-amment** or **-emment**:

  > **constant** (*constant*) becomes **constamment** (*constantly*)

  > **intelligent** (*intelligent*) becomes **intelligemment** (*intelligently*)

However, remember a few specific exceptions to the preceding rules:

- **continu** (*continuous*) becomes **continûment** (*continuously*)
- **énorme** (*enormous*) becomes **énormément** (*enormously*)
- **gentil** (*nice, kind*) becomes **gentiment** (*nicely, kindly*)
- **lent** (*slow*) becomes **lentement** (*slowly*)
- **vrai** (*true*) becomes **vraiment** (*truly*)

Some French adverbs of manner aren't formed from adjectives and therefore don't end in -**ment**:

- **bien** (*well*)
- **debout** (*standing up*)
- **exprès** (*on purpose*)
- **mal** (*poorly, badly*)
- **mieux** (*better*)
- **vite** (*quickly*)
- **volontiers** (*gladly*)

Here are some sentences that use adverbs of manner:

> **Elle parle très poliment.** (*She speaks very politely.*)
>
> **Tu l'as fait exprès !** (*You did it on purpose!*)

Positioning adverbs

The position of French adverbs depends on what they're modifying and on the type of adverb. Read on.

After the verb

When French adverbs modify a verb, they usually follow it:

> Je le ferai **volontiers !** (*I'll gladly do it/I'll be glad to do it!*)
>
> Nous voyageons **souvent** en été. (*We often travel in the summer.*)

For sentences with a conjugated verb followed by an infinitive, the adverb goes after the conjugated verb. In the following example, the adverb **beau-coup** (*a lot*) goes after **aime** (*like*), not after the infinitive **nager** (*to swim*).

> J'aime **beaucoup** nager. (*I love swimming.*)

For sentences with a verb conjugated in a *compound tense,* which includes a conjugated auxiliary (helping) verb and a past participle, the adverb goes after the conjugated auxiliary verb. In the following example, the adverb **déjà** (*already*) goes after **ai** (*has*), not after the past participle **mangé** (*eaten*). (See Chapter 1 of Book V for details on the **passé composé**, the compound tense used here):

> Il a **déjà** mangé. (*He already ate.* Literally: *He has already eaten.*)
>
> Je ne me sens **pas** bien. (*I don't feel well.*) Here, **pas** (*not*) comes before **bien** (*well*).
>
> Il ne travaille **jamais** vite. (*He never works quickly.*) Here, **jamais** (*never*) comes before **vite** (*quickly*).

Other places for adverbs

You can usually put adverbs that refer to a point in time like **aujourd'hui** (*today*) and **hier** (*yesterday*) at the beginning or end of the sentence, as in **Je dois travailler aujourd'hui** (*I have to work today*).

The same placement at the beginning or end of a sentence works for long adverbs, as in **Normalement, je me lève à 7h00** (*Usually, I get up at 7 a.m.*). However, when you want to stress the meaning of the adverb, you put it after the conjugated verb, as in **Il a violemment critiqué la nouvelle loi** (*He strongly criticized the new law*).

The best place for adverbs of place is, just like in English, after the direct object or, if there isn't one, after the verb:

> Tu trouveras tes valises **en haut.** (*You'll find your suitcases upstairs.*)
>
> J'aimerais vivre **ici.** (*I'd like to live here.*)

Adverbs that modify adjectives or other adverbs go in front of those words. In the following example, the adverb **très** (*very*) modifies the adjective **belle** (*beautiful*), and in the next one, the adverb **vraiment** (*really*) modifies the adverb **bien** (*well*):

> **Elle est très belle.** (*She is very beautiful.*)
>
> **Elle parle vraiment bien.** (*She speaks really well.*)

Book IV

Getting Down to Detail and Precision in Your Communication

Comparing with Comparatives and Superlatives

The two kinds of comparisons you can make in French are comparative and superlative. *Comparatives* say that something is *more ____ than, less ____ than,* or *as ____ as* something else; *superlatives* proclaim that something is the *most ____* or *least ____* of all.

More or less, equal: Relating two things with comparatives

Comparatives can indicate one of three things: superiority, inferiority, or equality. You use the comparative **plus ____ que** in French to indicate superiority — that something is *more ____ than* or *____-er than* something else. The construction works for both adjectives, such as **beau/belle** (*beautiful*), and adverbs, such as **rapidement** (*quickly*):

> Elle est **plus** belle **que** moi. (*She is more beautiful than I am.*)

> Jacques parle **plus** rapidement **que** toi. (*Jacques speaks more quickly than you.*)

In French comparatives and superlatives, you use stress pronouns after **que** (*than, as*), as in the preceding examples. *Stress pronouns* are special forms that you use after prepositions and in comparatives or superlatives. See Table 2-4.

Table 2-4	Stress Pronouns that Follow Que in Comparatives and Superlatives
Singular	*Plural*
moi (*I, me*)	**nous** (*we, us*)
toi (*you*)	**vous** (*you*)
lui/elle (*he/she, him/her*)	**eux/elles** (*they, them*)

Here are some examples:

> Jean est **aussi** attentif **que moi.** (*Jean is as attentive as I.*)

> Tu es **plus** bavarde **qu'elle.** (*You're more talkative than she.*)

> Vous êtes **moins** raisonnable **qu'eux.** (*You are less reasonable than they.*)

Although the English translations here are grammatically correct, saying "more talkative than *me*" or "less reasonable than *them*" may sound more natural. Don't worry too much about which type of pronoun you'd use in English — French just sticks with the stress pronouns.

When using an adjective in a comparative structure, make it agree with the noun it follows. To do so, follow the agreement rules in "Making your adjectives agree" (as always, adverbs don't agree):

> **Paul** est **plus grand que** Camille. (*Paul is taller than Camille.*)
>
> **Camille** est **plus grande que** Paul. (*Camille is taller than Paul.*)

To say that something is inferior (*less _____ than*), use the comparative **moins _____ que**:

> Yvette est **moins** aventureuse **que** son frère. (*Yvette is less adventurous than her brother.*)
>
> Ce livre est **moins** intéressant **que** l'autre. (*This book is less interesting than the other one.*)
>
> Il chante **moins** distinctement **que** son frère. (*He sings less distinctly than his brother.*)

You express equality with **aussi _____ que** in French, which is equivalent to *as _____ as* in English:

> L'exercice est **aussi** important **que** la nutrition. (*Exercise is as important as nutrition.*)
>
> Ma mère est **aussi** grande **que** mon père. (*My mother is as tall as my father.*)
>
> Vous vivez **aussi** bien **qu'**un roi. (*You live as well as a king.*)

All these comparatives are between two people or things, but you can also make comparisons with two adjectives:

> Je suis **plus agacé que fâché.** (*I'm more annoyed than angry.*)
>
> Il est **aussi audacieux que courageux.** (*He's as audacious as [he is] courageous.*)

You can also make comparisons with **plus de** (*more of something*), **moins de** (*less of something*), and **autant de** (*as much of something*) followed by a stress pronoun or a noun; note that the preposition **de** that follows each adverb **plus/moins/autant** is invariable, regardless of whether the noun is masculine or feminine, singular or plural:

> Il a **plus de poils** aux jambes **que moi.** (*He has more hair on his legs than I.*)

Cette mère fait **autant de sports que sa fille.** (*This mother does as many sports as her daughter.*)

Elle boit **moins de café que son copain.** (*She drinks less coffee than her boyfriend.*)

Supersizing with superlatives

Superlatives talk about the two extremes: *the most (the _____-est)* and *the least.* To form the superlative in French, you need to know the three parts involved:

- ✔ The definite article **le/la/les** (*the*)
- ✔ **Plus** (*most*) or **moins** (*least*)
- ✔ The adjective or adverb

Adjectives

To form the superlative, use the definite article + **plus** or **moins** + the adjective. The definite article (**le**, **la**, or **les**) and the adjective both have to agree with the noun they're modifying (that is, be masculine or feminine and singular or plural).

Before you can use superlatives, you have to know whether the adjective you're using goes before or after the verb (see the section "Correctly positioning adjectives with nouns," earlier in this chapter):

- ✔ When the superlative adjective follows the noun, you have to use the definite article twice — it precedes both the noun and the superlative **plus/moins**:

    C'est **la solution la plus équitable.** (*That's the fairest solution.*)

    Mon frère est **l'homme le moins sportif** du monde. (*My brother is the least athletic man in the world.*)

- ✔ Adjectives that precede the noun can either precede or follow the noun in superlatives. When they precede the noun, you use only one definite article, and when they follow it, you use two:

    C'est **le plus bel homme** du monde. OR C'est **l'homme le plus beau** du monde. (*He is the handsomest [most handsome] man in the world.*)

    Voilà une liste **des moins mauvais films.** OR Voilà une liste **des films les moins mauvais.** (*There's a list of the least bad movies.*)

Note that when you single one thing out of many or one person out of many, as in *the handsomest man in the world,* the French translation of *in* is **de**, which may contract with **le** to form **du** or with **les** to form **des**. (See more on contractions in Chapter 2 of Book III.)

Adverbs

Superlatives with adverbs are a little different from superlatives with adjectives. Because adverbs don't agree with the words they modify, the definite article in superlatives doesn't, either — it's always **le**. Superlatives with adverbs simply take the form **le** + **plus** or **moins** + the adverb:

Elle danse **le plus parfaitement.** (*She dances the most perfectly.*)

Ils agissent **le moins passionnément.** (*They act the least passionately.*)

For better or worse: Special comparative and superlative forms

Two French adjectives have special forms in the comparative and superlative: **bon** (*good*) and **mauvais** (*bad*).

Just as in English, where one thing is *good,* another is *better* (not *more good*), and another yet is the *best* (not the *most good*), the comparative of **bon** is **meilleur** (*better*), and the superlative is **le meilleur** (*the best*). Like all adjectives, **bon** and **meilleur** have to agree with the nouns they modify:

Ton nouveau vélo est **meilleur que** l'ancien. (*Your new bike is better than the old one.*)

Ma question est **la meilleure**. (*My question is the best.*)

In English, you say that one thing is *bad,* another is *worse* (not *more bad*), and another one yet is *the worst* (not the *most bad*). But in French, the adjective **mauvais** has two comparative and superlative forms. You can say **plus mauvais** (*more bad*) or **pire** (*worse*), and you can say **le plus mauvais** or **le pire** (*the worst*).

Cette décision est **plus mauvaise que** l'autre. OR Cette décision est **pire que** l'autre. (*This decision is worse than the other one.*)

C'est **la pire** de toutes les idées présentées jusqu'à présent. OR C'est **la plus mauvaise** idée de toutes les idées présentées jusqu'à présent. (*This is the worst of all ideas presented so far.*)

French also has special forms for the comparative and superlative of the adverb **bien** (*well*). The comparative is **mieux** (*better*), and the superlative is **le mieux** (*the best*):

Philippe comprend **mieux que** moi. (*Philippe understands better than I do.*)

C'est en France que je me sens **le mieux.** (*It's in France that I feel best.*)

Chapter 3

Taking Shortcuts with Object Pronouns

*O*bject and adverbial pronouns are little words that provide a lot of information. Direct and indirect objects tell you *who* or *what* is being looked at, spoken to, or otherwise acted upon, as in *I gave Tim the book —* *book* is the direct object and *Tim* is the indirect object. *Object pronouns* replace the direct and indirect objects to keep you from repeating the same words over and over (and over and over), as in *I gave it to him — it* and *him* are object pronouns. Similarly, adverbial pronouns replace certain phrases to give you the same amount of information in less space. For instance, in *We went to France and lived there for two months,* the word *there* would be translated as the adverbial pronoun **y** in French. With **y**, you don't have to repeat *in France*.

To use object and adverbial pronouns effectively, you have to understand what they mean and where they go in the sentence as well as which order they go in when you use two at once. This chapter explains direct object, indirect object, adverbial, and reflexive pronouns as well as the correct order for two pronouns working together.

Using Object Pronouns

Just as pronouns replace nouns, *object pronouns* replace objects. In a convenient case of linguistic logic, direct-object pronouns replace direct objects, and indirect-object pronouns replace indirect objects. Despite the name *object,* objects aren't always things like books and trees — they can, and often do, refer to people and animals.

If you don't know your French object pronouns, you may end up saying something like "I ate you" instead of "I ate it"! This section spells out how to use direct-object and indirect-object pronouns so everyone knows what you're talking about.

Direct-object pronouns

A *direct object* is a person or thing that a verb is acting on. When it isn't in the form of a pronoun, the direct object usually follows the verb in both French and English. You can tell it's a direct object because it comes right after the verb, with no preposition in front of it.

Transitive verbs, such as *to like* and *to watch,* are verbs that need direct objects. You can't say *I like* without a direct object — the sentence isn't complete. You have to say *I like you, I like chocolate, I like polka-dot slippers.* Verbs that don't need direct objects, such as *to walk* and *to travel,* are *intransitive* verbs. Of course, some verbs, like *to read,* can be both transitive and intransitive: *I read the newspaper* (transitive) versus *I read daily* (intransitive). Knowing the difference between transitive and intransitive helps you choose the right translation when you look up verbs in a dictionary (see Chapter 1 of Book III).

Replacing direct objects with pronouns

To use a direct-object pronoun, you first need to identify the object. To figure out the direct object, ask yourself who or what is receiving the effect of the action expressed in the verb. For example, in the sentence **Lise connaît les athlètes** (*Lise knows the athletes*), you can tell that **Lise** is the subject of the sentence because she's the person who knows. To find the direct object, you'd then ask, "Whom does she know?" **Athlètes** is the object — the people she knows. Or in the sentence **Mon frère déteste la glace** (*My brother hates ice cream*), *you can tell that* **mon frère** is the subject because he's the person who hates. Then ask, "What does he hate?" **La glace** is the object — the thing that he hates.

Just as you can replace the subjects **Lise** and **mon frère** with the subject pronouns **elle** (*she*) and **il** (*he*), you can replace the direct objects **les athlètes** and **la glace** with direct-object pronouns. When you choose a direct-object pronoun, you have to consider the gender and number of the object you're replacing as well as the grammatical person, because there are different pronoun forms for each of these. See Table 3-1 for the French direct-object pronouns.

Table 3-1	Direct-Object Pronouns	
Subject Pronoun	*Direct-Object Pronoun*	*Translation*
je	me (m', moi)	me
tu	te (t', toi)	you
il	le (l')	him/it
elle	la (l')	her/it
nous	nous	us
vous	vous	you
ils, elles	les	them

The following examples use direct-object pronouns to replace the direct objects:

> Lise connaît **les athlètes**. → Lise **les** connaît. (*Lise knows <u>the athletes</u>.* → *Lise knows <u>them</u>.*)

> Mon frère déteste **la glace**. → Mon frère **la** déteste. (*My brother hates <u>ice cream</u>.* → *My brother hates <u>it</u>.*)

Me, **te**, **le**, and **la** contract to **m'**, **t'**, and **l'** whenever they precede a vowel, a mute **h**, or the adverbial pronoun **y**:

> Tu **m'aimes** ? (*Do you like/love me?*)

> Viens à ma soirée. Je **t'y** invite. (*Come to my party. I'm inviting you to it.*)

Understanding word order with direct-object pronouns

The word order differs in French and English. Although English direct-object pronouns follow the verb — *knows them, hates it* — French direct-object pronouns go before the verb:

> On lave **le chien**. → On **le** lave. (*We wash <u>the dog</u>.* → *We wash <u>him</u>.*)

"Before the verb" isn't as clear-cut when you have multiple verbs or compound tenses. Here's where to put the direct-object pronoun in these cases:

✔ Conjugated verb + infinitive: When two verbs that have the same subject follow each other in French — as in **On va laver le chien** (*We're going to wash the dog*) — the first verb (**va**) is conjugated and the second one (**laver**) remains in its infinitive form. In such a sentence, the direct-object pronoun goes right before the infinitive verb:

> **On va le laver.** (*We're going to wash him.*)

✔ Conjugated verb + past participle: In the **passé composé** (Chapter 1 of Book V) and other compound tenses (see Chapter 3 of Book V), the direct-object pronoun precedes the conjugated auxiliary (helping) verb:

>   **Je l'ai lavé.** (*I washed him.*)

When you're telling someone to do something (with the affirmative imperative — see Chapter 4 of Book III), the word order is different: the direct-object pronoun follows the verb and attaches to it with a hyphen; in addition, **me** changes to **moi** and **te** changes to **toi**. Look at these examples:

>   **Trouvez-le.** (*Find it.*)
>
>   **Écoute-moi !** (*Listen to me!*)
>
>   **Lave-toi !** (*Wash yourself!*)

Indirect-object pronouns

Indirect objects are the people that a verb is happening to or for. Indirect objects usually follow a preposition, such as **à** (*to*) or **pour** (*for*). (See Chapter 1 of Book IV to read more about prepositions.)

To figure out the French indirect object, you can ask, "To whom?" or "For whom?" In the example **Elle parle à ses amis** (*She's talking to her friends*), **elle** is the subject of the sentence — she's the person who's talking. **Ses amis** is the indirect object — the people she's talking to. In **J'achète des livres pour ma nièce** (*I'm buying some books for my niece* OR *I'm buying my niece some books*), **je** is the subject — the person who's buying. **Ma nièce** is the indirect object — the person I'm buying books for. Ask your questions to find the indirect object: To whom is she talking? Her friends. For whom am I buying books? My niece.

Note that indirect-object pronouns apply to people, not things. If you want to say that your dad is talking to your mom, you can refer to your mom with an indirect-object pronoun. But if you want to say that he's talking to the television, "to the television" requires a different pronoun. See the later section "Getting there with the adverbial pronoun y" for details.

Distinguishing between direct and indirect objects

Before you can correctly use an indirect-object pronoun, you need to make sure that what you're replacing is really an indirect object. Here are some tips for distinguishing a direct object from an indirect object in French:

✔ When a noun such as **le cadeau** (*the gift*) receives the action of a verb and it's not preceded by a preposition of any kind, then it's a direct object:

> J'ai trouvé **le meilleur cadeau**. (*I found the best gift.*)

✔ When a noun such as **mon professeur** (*my teacher*) represents a person and is preceded by the preposition **à**, then it's an indirect object:

> J'ai parlé **à mon ancien professeur** hier soir. (*I spoke to my former teacher last night.*)

Consider the following sentence, noting that **son papa** (*her dad*) is preceded by the preposition **à** (*to*). This indicates that **son papa** is an indirect object in the French sentence.

> Elle montre ses boucles d'oreille **à son papa**. (*She shows her earrings to her dad.* OR *She shows her dad her earrings.*)

Don't rely on seeing *to + somebody* in the English translation when deciding whether you have an indirect object. Instead, look for **à/pour** + [a person] in the French, and make sure it answers the question "To whom?" or "For whom?" Here's why the English translation isn't always reliable:

✔ In English, you can say *I gave John the money* to mean *I gave the money to John.* So you can use *John* as an indirect object without using the preposition *to*. However, in French, the indirect object John must appear after the direct object with **à** or **pour**:

> J'ai donné l'argent à John. (*I gave John the money.* OR *I gave the money to John.*)

✔ Some verbs followed by *to + somebody* in English take direct objects, not indirect objects, in French. For example, you don't use a preposition after the French verb **écouter** (*to listen to*), even though *listen* is followed by the preposition *to* in English. So if you're listening *to your teacher,* your teacher is actually a direct object in French. Note the absence of the preposition **à** here:

> J'écoute le prof. (*I listen to the teacher.*)

✔ Some French verbs have to be followed by the preposition **à**, even though you wouldn't use a preposition there in the English. In those cases, French may use an indirect object where English uses a direct object. For example, the verb **conseiller** (*to advise*) has to be followed by **à**, even though you wouldn't say *advise to* someone in English; you'd simply say *advise* someone. In this next example, **aux jeunes gens** (*to the young people*) is an indirect object in the French sentence (note that **aux** is a contraction of **à + les**):

Book IV

Getting Down to Detail and Precision in Your Communication

> **On conseille aux jeunes gens de ne pas boire trop d'alcool.** (*We advise young people not to drink too much alcohol.*)

See Chapter 1 of Book IV for details on verbs that require **à**.

Replacing indirect objects with pronouns

Most of the French indirect-object pronouns are the same as the direct ones: **me** can mean *me* (direct object) or *to/for me* (indirect object), **te** can mean *you* or *to/for you* (singular familiar), **nous** can mean *us* or *to/for us*, and **vous** can mean *you* or *to/for you* (plural or singular formal). Only the third-person pronouns used to say *to/for him/her* (**lui**) and *to/for them* (**leur**) are different. Look at Table 3-2.

The word order for indirect-object pronouns is exactly the same as for direct-object pronouns:

- ✔ An object pronoun goes in front of the verb.

- ✔ When a subject is followed by two verbs, the object pronoun goes in front of the second verb which is in the infinitive form.

- ✔ In the **passé composé**, the pronoun goes in front of the auxiliary verb.

- ✔ In a command to do something (the affirmative imperative), the pronoun goes after the verb, joined by a hyphen.

Table 3-2	Indirect-Object Pronouns	
Subject Pronoun	*Direct-Object Pronoun*	*Indirect-Object Pronoun*
je	**me (m', moi)** (*me*)	**me (m', moi)** (*to/for me*)
tu	**te (t', toi)** (*you*)	**te (t', toi)** (*to/for you*)
il, elle	**le, la (l')** (*it/him/her*)	**lui** (*to him, her*)
nous	**nous** (*us*)	**nous** (*to us*)
vous	**vous** (*you*)	**vous** (*to you*)
ils, elles	**les** (*them*)	**leur** (*to them*)

Lui is the indirect-object pronoun that replaces the preposition **à** + a person, male or female:

> Il téléphone **à David**. → Il **lui** téléphone. (*He's calling David.* → *He's calling him.*)

> Je parle **à ma mère**. → Je **lui** parle. (*I'm talking to my mother.* → *I'm talking to her.*)

Leur is the indirect-object pronoun that replaces the preposition **à** and two or more people:

> Nous **leur** écrivons tous les jours. (*We write to them every day.*)
>
> Tu vas **leur** poser une question ? (*Are you going to ask them a question?*)

Note that the pronoun **leur** (*to them*) is invariable. It should not to be confused with the possessive adjective **leur** (*their*), which has a singular and a plural form (see Chapter 2 of Book III). The first example here shows **leur** as a pronoun, and the next two show it as a possessive adjective.

> Elle **leur** parle. (*She's talking to them.*)
>
> Elles adorent **leur université**. (*They adore their university.*)
>
> Elles adorent **leurs profs**. (*They adore their professors.*)

Understanding Adverbial Pronouns

Adverbial pronouns are similar to indirect-object pronouns in that they replace a preposition + noun. However, the nouns that adverbial pronouns replace aren't indirect objects — they're *prepositional phrases*. Prepositional phrases provide additional information about the verb — for example, *to the movies* is a prepositional phrase. But the verb doesn't act on prepositional phrases like verbs act on indirect objects. This section gives you the lowdown on the different adverbial pronouns and how to use them.

Getting there with the adverbial pronoun y

You can use the adverbial pronoun **y** to replace any prepositional phrase that indicates in, at, or to a location — such as **à la plage** (*at/to the beach*), **chez le docteur** (*at/to the doctor's*), **dans la salle d'attente** (*in the waiting room*), or **en France** (*in/to France*) — to mean *there*.

The adverbial pronoun **y** goes in exactly the same place as direct- and indirect-object pronouns — usually before the verb:

> Je vais **à la plage**. → J'**y** vais. (*I'm going to the beach. → I'm going there.*)
>
> Elle a passé deux jours **en France**. → Elle **y** a passé deux jours. (*She spent two days in France. → She spent two days there.*)

Book IV

Getting Down to Detail and Precision in Your Communication

You can also use **y** to replace **à** + [a thing] with verbs that require the preposition **à**. Earlier in this chapter, we note that you can replace **à** + [a noun] with an indirect-object pronoun, so what's the difference? The indirect object tells you *whom* something is being done to or for, but **y** tells you *what* something is being done to. In French, indirect-object pronouns can replace only people; you have to replace places and things with the adverbial pronoun **y**. (See Chapter 1 of Book IV to read about verbs that need a preposition.) The first example here uses **y**, and the next uses the indirect object **leur**:

> Nous obéissons **aux lois**. → Nous **y** obéissons. (*We obey the laws.* → *We obey them.*)

> Nous obéissons **à nos parents**. → Nous **leur** obéissons. (*We obey our parents.* → *We obey them.*)

Just as transitive verbs need a direct object to be complete, French verbs that need the preposition **à**, such as **aller** (*to go*), need either **à** + [a noun] or the adverbial pronoun **y** to be complete. In English, you can simply say, "I'm going," but in French, you can't — either you have to say where you're going, as in **Je vais chez moi** (*I'm going to my place*), or you have to use **y**: **J'y vais** (*I'm going there*).

Replacing some of it with the pronoun en

The adverbial pronoun **en** usually translates to *some* or *of it/them*. To use the adverbial pronoun **en**, you replace one or more words with **en**. The word order for **en** is the same as for object pronouns and the adverbial pronoun **y** (see "Direct-object pronouns" for details).

You can use **en** to replace

- **De** + noun
- Partitive article **du**, **de la**, or **des** + noun
- A noun after a number
- A noun after an adverb of quantity
- A noun after an indefinite or negative adjective

Remember that **en** isn't always a pronoun. It can also be a preposition, as in **en France** (*in/to France*) — see Chapter 1 of Book IV for details. **En** can also mean *from a location*. For example, in **Mes amis sont allés en Corse. Ils y sont restés deux semaines et ils en reviennent aujourd'hui**, the pronoun **y** replaces *in Corsica*, whereas the pronoun **en** replaces *from Corsica*.

En replaces de + noun

With the preposition **de** (*of, from*) or with the partitive article **du/de la/de l'/des** (*some*), **en** replaces **de** as well as the noun following it:

>Nous parlons **d'amour**. → Nous **en** parlons. (*We're talking about love. → We're talking about it.*)

>Je veux **des fraises**. → J'**en** veux. (*I want [some] strawberries. → I want some [of them].*)

In English, *of them* or *of it* is usually optional — as long as everyone knows you're talking about strawberries, you can just say, "I want some." In French, however, **Je veux des** is incomplete — if you don't include the noun **fraises**, then you have to replace **des fraises** with **en**.

En with numbers

When you use **en** with a number, it replaces only the noun — you still need to put the number after the verb:

>Il a **trois voitures**. → Il **en** a **trois**. (*He has three cars. → He has three [of them].*)

>J'ai acheté **une dizaine de livres**. → J'**en** ai acheté **une dizaine**. (*I bought about ten books. → I bought about ten [of them].*)

En with adverbs of quantity

With adverbs of quantity such as **beaucoup** (*a lot*), **trop** (*too much/too many*), **assez** (*enough*), and **peu** (*little/few*), **en** replaces **de** and the noun, but you still need the adverb of quantity, so you tack it on the end (see Chapter 2 of Book IV for info on adverbs):

>Avez-vous **beaucoup de temps** ? → **En** avez-vous **beaucoup** ? (*Do you have a lot of time? → Do you have a lot [of it]?*)

>Je mange **très peu d'avocats**. → J'**en** mange **très peu**. (*I eat very few avocados. → I eat very few [of them].*)

En with indefinite and negative adjectives

You can use **en** with indefinite and negative adjectives. Indefinite adjectives express an unspecific quantity, such as **quelques** (*some*) and **plusieurs** (*several*). Negative adjectives negate a noun — they're terms like **ne . . . aucun** (*not any*) and **ne . . . nul** (*none*).

As with adverbs of quantity, you replace the noun with **en** and tack the indefinite adjective or the second part of the negative adjective on the end of the sentence. When you do this, the adjective technically becomes a pronoun, but you don't need to remember that; because indefinite and negative adjectives and pronouns are identical, you don't need to change anything.

> J'ai **d'autres idées**. → J'**en** ai **d'autres**. (*I have other ideas.* → *I have others.*)

> Il cherche **plusieurs amis**, mais il **n'en** a trouvé **aucun**. → Il **en** cherche **plusieurs**, mais il **n'en** a trouvé **aucun**. (*He's looking for several friends, but he hasn't found any [of them]. → He's looking for several [of them], but he hasn't found any [of them].*)

Positioning Double Pronouns

In English, you can't say, "I bought for him it" — you have to say, "I bought it for him." This word order is nonnegotiable. The same is true in French: Pronouns have to go in a certain order.

Object pronouns and adverbial pronouns as well as reflexive pronouns (see the later section "When Object Pronouns Double Up as Reflexive Pronouns") all go in the same place: in front of the verb — except in the affirmative imperative. But something happens when you have two of these pronouns in the same sentence: They both go in front of the verb, but in which order? This section clarifies the order.

Lining up: Standard pronoun order

Using any two object, adverbial, or reflexive pronouns together requires a very specific word order. But before we tell you the order, check out Table 3-3 for a review of the reflexive and object pronouns.

Table 3-3	Object and Reflexive Pronouns		
Subject Pronoun	*Reflexive Pronoun*	*Direct-Object Pronoun*	*Indirect-Object Pronoun*
je	me	me	me
tu	te	te	te
il/elle/on	se	le/la	lui
nous	nous	nous	nous
vous	vous	vous	vous
ils/elles	se	les	leur

Here's the pronoun order for all verb tenses, moods, and constructions except the affirmative imperative (see the next section for info on commands):

1. **Me**, **te**, **se**, **nous**, or **vous** always comes first.

2. **Le**, **la**, or **les** comes second.

3. **Lui** or **leur** is next.

4. **Y** comes later.

5. **En** is last.

Of course, you can't have five pronouns in the same sentence — two is the maximum. Check out the following examples of pronouns correctly placed in front of the verbs:

> Elle **nous en** parle. (*She's talking to us about it.*)
>
> Il **me l'**a donné. (*He gave it to me.*)
>
> Je vais **le lui** montrer. (*I'm going to show it to him.*)

Note that in the last example, the pronouns go before the infinitive rather than before the conjugated verb **vais**. We discuss object-pronoun placement with multiple verbs and compound tenses earlier in "Understanding word order with direct-object pronouns."

Me, **te**, **nous**, and **vous** are identical as direct, indirect, and reflexive pronouns, and they all come first when you have double pronouns. If you do have a sentence with more than two things that could be replaced with object or adverbial pronouns, just pick two to replace and leave the other as is. Here are two ways to rewrite **J'ai acheté des vêtements pour moi-même en France** (*I bought some clothes for myself in France*) with pronouns:

> Je **m'y** suis acheté des vêtements. (*I bought myself some clothes there.*) Here, **me** replaces **pour moi-même**, and **y** replaces **en France**.
>
> Je **m'en** suis acheté en France. (*I bought myself some in France.*) **Me** replaces **pour moi-même**, and **en** replaces **des vêtements**.

Using pronouns in commands

In the affirmative imperative — commands to do something — the pronouns follow the verb and are joined to it with hyphens. Here's the slightly different double-pronoun order that applies:

1. **Le**, **la**, or **les** comes first.

2. **Moi**, **toi**, **lui**, **nous**, **vous**, or **leur** is next.

Book IV

Getting Down to Detail and Precision in Your Communication

3. Y comes later.

4. En is last.

Here are some examples:

> **Montre-le-moi !** (*Show it to me!*)
>
> **Présente-la-leur !** (*Present her to them!*)
>
> **Laisse-les-y !** (*Leave them there!*)
>
> **Donne-m'en un peu !** (*Give me some [of it]!*)

The pronouns **me** and **te** change to **moi** and **toi** in affirmative commands (see Chapter 4 of Book III) unless they're followed by the pronoun **y** or **en**, in which case they're **m'** and **t'**.

When Object Pronouns Double Up as Reflexive Pronouns

The pronouns **me**, **te**, **nous**, and **vous**, which can act as direct- and indirect-object pronouns, also serve as reflexive pronouns for pronominal verbs. *Pronominal verbs* are verbs that have a reflexive pronoun as part of their structure. The pronoun tells you that the verb you're using has a special meaning. You can use most pronominal verbs without the reflexive pronoun, but then the meaning changes — sometimes slightly, sometimes significantly.

Pronominal verbs need a reflexive pronoun to tell you one of three things:

✔ The subject is performing the action of the verb on himself or herself, as in as in **Je me lave** (*I wash myself*).

✔ Two or more subjects are performing the action on each other, as in **Ils se regardent** (*They're looking at each other*).

✔ The verb has a special meaning, unrelated to the one it has without the pronoun, as in **Je me rends compte . . .** (*I realize . . .*). Without the reflexive pronoun, the verb **rendre** means *to give back, to return.*

Reflexive pronouns can shorten the way you say something in French. For example, in French, **je me peigne** is sufficient to say *I comb my hair,* and **il se baigne** is sufficient to say *He's taking a bath.*

This section explains the types of pronominal verbs, how to correctly use reflexive pronouns with pronominal verbs, and how to use pronominal verbs effectively.

Understanding the types of pronominal verbs

You can recognize a pronominal verb by the reflexive pronoun **se** that precedes the infinitive in the dictionary or your vocab lists: **se coucher** (*to go to bed*), **se laver** (*to wash oneself*), and so on. Within sentences, you can tell a verb is pronominal when you see **se** or one of the other reflexive pronouns, which we list later in Table 3-5.

Although you can use most pronominal verbs without the reflexive pronoun, the meaning changes: Alone, **coucher** means *to put (someone else) to bed*, and **laver** means *to wash (someone/something else)*. So knowing when to use the reflexive pronoun and when not to is very important. This section covers the three types of pronominal verbs.

Reflexive verbs: Acting on oneself

Reflexive verbs tell you that someone is doing something to himself or herself. The following list shows some common reflexive verbs. Note that many of them have something to do with parts of the body or clothing, and the others have to do with personal circumstance or position:

- **s'approcher de** (*to approach*)
- **s'asseoir** (*to sit down*)
- **se baigner** (*to bathe, swim*)
- **se brosser (les dents, les cheveux)** (*to brush [one's teeth, hair]*)
- **se casser (le bras, le doigt)** (*to break [one's arm, finger]*)
- **se coiffer** (*to fix one's hair*)
- **se coucher** (*to go to bed*)
- **se couper** (*to cut oneself*)
- **se déshabiller** (*to get undressed*)
- **se doucher** (*to take a shower*)
- **se fâcher** (*to get angry*)
- **s'habiller** (*to get dressed*)
- **s'inquiéter** (*to worry*)
- **se laver (les mains, les cheveux)** (*to wash [one's hands, hair]*)
- **se lever** (*to get up*)
- **se maquiller** (*to put on makeup*)
- **se marier (avec)** (*to get married [to]*)
- **se moucher** (*to blow one's nose*)
- **se peigner** (*to comb one's hair*)
- **se promener** (*to go for a walk*)
- **se raser** (*to shave*)
- **se regarder** (*to look at oneself*)
- **se reposer** (*to rest*)
- **se réveiller** (*to wake up*)
- **se souvenir de** (*to remember*)

Book IV

Getting Down to Detail and Precision in Your Communication

Here are a couple of example sentences:

> Je **me marie** avec Thérèse demain. (*I'm marrying Thérèse tomorrow.*)
>
> Il **se rase** une fois par semaine. (*He shaves once a week.*)

Reflexive verbs don't really exist in English — you just use regular verbs, and if you want to stress that you're doing something to yourself, you can tack on *myself,* as in *I got dressed by myself* or *I dressed myself.* In French, though, the idea of *by myself,* represented by the reflexive pronoun **me**, is not optional — you have to use it to distinguish from the nonreflexive meaning. See "Deciding whether to make a verb pronominal," later in this chapter, for more information.

Reciprocal verbs: What you do to each other

Reciprocal verbs are any verbs that you use reflexively to mean that two or more subjects are doing something to, at, or with each other. Here are some common reciprocal verbs.

- **s'aimer** (*to love [each other]*)
- **se comprendre** (*to understand [each other]*)
- **se connaître** (*to know [each other]*)
- **se détester** (*to hate [each other]*)
- **se dire** (*to tell [each other]*)
- **se disputer** (*to argue [with each other]*)
- **s'écrire** (*to write [to each other]*)
- **s'embrasser** (*to kiss [each other]*)
- **se parler** (*to talk [to each other]*)
- **se promettre** (*to promise [each other]*)
- **se quitter** (*to leave [each other]*)
- **se regarder** (*to look [at each other]*)
- **se rencontrer** (*to meet [each other]*)
- **se sourire** (*to smile [at each other]*)
- **se téléphoner** (*to call [each other]*)
- **se voir** (*to see [each other]*)

The following sentence indicates reciprocal action:

> Nous **nous connaissons** bien. (*We know each other well.*)

Many reciprocal verbs can also be used reflexively: **Je me parle** (*I'm talking to myself*), **Elle se regarde** (*She's looking at herself*), and so on.

Figuratively speaking: Idiomatic pronominal verbs

Idiomatic pronominal verbs sound exciting, but *idiomatic* just means that the verbs' meanings with the reflexive pronouns are distinct from their meanings without reflexive pronouns. An *idiom* is an expression whose meaning you can't determine just by literally translating the individual words. Table 3-4 shows some common idiomatic pronominal verbs and their nonpronominal equivalents.

Table 3-4	Idiomatic Pronominal Verbs
Nonpronominal Verb	*Pronominal Verb*
amuser (*to amuse*)	**s'amuser** (*to have a good time*)
appeler (*to call*)	**s'appeler** (*to be named*)
débrouiller (*to untangle*)	**se débrouiller** (*to manage, get by*)
décider (*to decide*)	**se décider** (*to make up one's mind*)
demander (*to ask*)	**se demander** (*to wonder*)
dépêcher (*to send, to dispatch*)	**se dépêcher** (*to hurry*)
endormir (*to put to sleep*)	**s'endormir** (*to fall asleep*)
ennuyer (*to bother, to annoy*)	**s'ennuyer** (*to be bored*)
entendre (*to hear*)	**s'entendre** (*to get along*)
installer (*to install*)	**s'installer** (*to settle in [a home]*)
mettre (*to place, put*)	**se mettre à** (*to begin to*)
rappeler (*to call back*)	**se rappeler** (*to recall, remember*)
rendre compte de (*to account for*)	**se rendre compte de** (*to realize, take into account*)
réunir (*to gather, collect*)	**se réunir** (*to meet, get together*)
tromper (*to deceive*)	**se tromper** (*to be mistaken*)
trouver (*to find*)	**se trouver** (*to be located*)

Here's what these verbs look like pronominally:

Je **m'appelle** Laura. (*My name is Laura. Literally: I call myself Laura.*)

Il **s'est** bien **amusé.** (*He had a really good time. Literally: He amused himself well.*)

Using reflexive pronouns

Reflexive pronouns are *personal*, meaning that you use a different one for each grammatical person, such as *I, you, he, she,* and so on. For all practical purposes, the reflexive pronouns **me, te, nous,** and **vous** are the same pronouns you know as direct- or indirect-object pronouns. But you now need to also know the pronoun **se,** which accompanies the third-person singular **il/elle/on** as well as the third person plural **ils/elles.** See Table 3-5 for the French reflexive pronouns in all their forms.

Table 3-5	Reflexive Pronouns		
Subject Pronoun	*Reflexive Pronoun*	*Before a Vowel or Mute h*	*Affirmative Imperative*
je	me	m'	
tu	te	t'	toi
il, elle, on	se	s'	
nous	nous	nous	nous
vous	vous	vous	vous
ils, elles	se	s'	

The reflexive pronoun usually goes in front of the verb. (For info on different word-order situations, check out the next section.) For example, the pronominal verb **se doucher** means *to take a shower*. **Doucher** is a regular **-er** verb, so you'd conjugate the pronominal form in the present tense like this.

se doucher (*to take a shower*)	
je **me douche**	nous **nous douchons**
tu **te douches**	vous **vous douchez**
il/elle/on **se douche**	ils/elles **se douchent**
Je **me douche** le soir. (*I shower at night.*)	

Don't let the **nous** and **vous** forms of pronominal verbs weird you out. Yes, the subject and object pronoun are identical, but they're both required.

When **me**, **te**, or **se** is followed by a word that begins with a vowel or mute **h**, you have to drop the **-e** and make a contraction. For example, the pronominal verb **s'habiller** (*to get dressed*) is also a regular **-er** verb, so your present tense conjugated forms look like this.

s'habiller (*to get dressed*)	
je **m'habille**	nous **nous habillons**
tu **t'habilles**	vous **vous habillez**
il/elle/on **s'habille**	ils/elles **s'habillent**
Elle **s'habille** dans ta chambre. (*She's getting dressed in your room.*)	

The reflexive pronoun always has to agree with the subject in all tenses and moods, including the present participle and the infinitive (see Chapter 6 of Book III). In compound tenses such as the **passé composé**, reflexive verbs are conjugated with the helping verb **être** (See Chapter 1 of Book V). Table 3-6 gives some example sentences in which **je** is the subject.

Table 3-6	Reflexive Pronouns with Different Verb Forms	
Verb Form	*French*	*Translation*
Present tense	Je **me couche**.	*I'm going to bed.*
Passé composé	Je **me suis douché(e)**.	*I took a shower.*
Present participle	En **m'habillant**, je suis tombé(e).	*While getting dressed, I fell.*
Infinitive	Je n'ai pas besoin de **me dépêcher**.	*I don't need to hurry.*

When using pronominal verbs, you need to make sure you use the correct word order with the reflexive pronoun. If you don't, the person you're talking to may not understand who's doing what to whom. Word order with the reflexive pronoun is very simple: You put the pronoun directly in front of the pronominal verb in nearly all tenses, moods, and constructions. For example, **Je me lève à 9h00** (*I get up at 9:00 a.m.*).

When you have a conjugated verb followed by an infinitive, the reflexive pronoun goes in front of the infinitive because the infinitive is the pronominal verb. For example, **Nous allons nous acheter de la glace** (*We're going to buy ourselves some ice cream*).

Even if you're using inversion to ask a question, the reflexive pronoun still goes in front of the verb. The reflexive pronoun precedes the inverted verb-subject, which means it usually goes at the beginning of the sentence. (See Chapter 5 of Book III for information about asking questions.)

> **Te douches**-tu le matin ou le soir ? (*Do you shower in the morning or at night?*)
>
> **Vous êtes**-vous levés avant 7h00 ? (*Did you get up before 7:00 a.m.?*)

The only times you don't put the reflexive pronoun right in front of the pronominal verb are in the following situations:

✔ Commands (the a**ffirmative imperative):** In the affirmative imperative, you place the reflexive pronoun *after* the verb and connect the two words with hyphens. Note that **te** changes to **toi**. (See Chapter 4 of Book III for more information about the imperative.)

> **Lève-toi.** (*Get up.*)

> **Dépêchez-vous.** (*Hurry up.*)

✔ **Compound tenses:** In the **passé composé** and other compound tenses (tenses that use an auxiliary verb plus the past participle), the reflexive pronoun precedes the helping verb **être**. (Go to Chapter 1 of Book V to read up on the **passé composé**.)

> Je **me suis levé(e)** très tôt. (*I got up really early.*)

> Vous **vous êtes trompés,** mes amis. (*You made a mistake, my friends.*)

> Elle ne **s'est** pas **fâchée.** (*She did not get angry.*)

Deciding whether to make a verb pronominal

Pronominal verbs tell you that the action is being done to the subject, two or more subjects are doing something to each other, or the verb has an idiomatic meaning. You can use the great majority of pronominal verbs without the reflexive pronoun, but they'll have a different meaning. The extent of the difference in meaning depends on the type of pronominal verb. This section discusses the correct ways to use pronominal verbs.

Reflexive verbs: Oneself or something else?

Reflexive verbs indicate that the subject is doing something to itself — usually something to do with parts of the body (washing, brushing), clothing (dressing, undressing), personal circumstance (marriage, divorce), or position (sitting, waking up). Using those verbs without the reflexive pronoun means that the subject is doing something to someone or something else. Compare the following sentences:

> Yvette **se marie** avec François demain. (*Yvette is marrying François tomorrow.*)

> Le prêtre **marie** trois couples par semaine. (*The priest marries three couples a week.*)

In the first sentence, Yvette herself is getting married, but in the second, the priest is performing the ceremony that joins two people — not including himself — to one another. Here are a couple more examples:

Je **me lave** les mains. (*I'm washing my hands.*)

Je **lave** la voiture. (*I'm washing the car.*)

In the first sentence, the subject is washing a part of himself or herself; in the second sentence, the subject is washing something else. So the difference in meaning has nothing to do with the verb, which describes the same action in both sentences; the difference is just in who or what is affected by the verb.

When you use reflexive verbs like **se laver** (*to wash*), **se brosser** (*to brush*), and **se casser** (*to break*) with body parts, you use the definite article (*the*) — not the possessive adjective (*my, your, his, her, our, their*) — in front of the body part, because the reflexive pronoun tells you whom it belongs to:

> **Je me suis cassé la jambe**. (*I broke my leg.*)

> **Il se brosse les dents.** (*He's brushing his teeth.*)

If you've broken someone else's leg or broken something nonhuman, you don't use the verb reflexively:

> **J'ai cassé la jambe de mon frère.** (*I broke my brother's leg.*)

> **J'ai cassé une assiette.** (*I broke a plate.*)

You can't use all pronominal verbs without the reflexive pronoun. **Se souvenir** (*to remember*), for example, is always reflexive. There's no nonreflexive equivalent.

Reciprocal verbs: Returning the favor?

Reciprocal verbs tell you that two or more people are doing something to each other, sort of a grammatical mutual admiration society. Reciprocal verbs usually have to do with communication (reading or writing to each other), feeling (loving or hating each other), and being together or apart.

You use reciprocal verbs when you want to be clear that the subjects are both doing the same thing to each other. All reciprocal verbs can be used without the reflexive pronoun. Compare these sentences:

> **Nous nous promettons.** (*We promise each other.*)

> **Je te promets.** (*I promise you.*)

> **Ils se sourient.** (*They're smiling at each other.*)

> **Il a souri en voyant le chiot.** (*He smiled upon seeing the puppy.*)

The difference in meaning here isn't huge. The reciprocal verb indicates that multiple subjects are all treating each other the same way: They're making promises to each other, smiling at each other, and so on. The nonreciprocal verb indicates the same activity, but it's not returned.

Book IV

Getting Down to Detail and Precision in Your Communication

Idiomatic verbs: What's the meaning of all this?

Idiomatic pronominal verbs have the biggest difference in meaning between the pronominal and nonpronominal forms. Although reflexive and reciprocal verbs used without the reflexive pronoun just change who receives the action of the verb and whether the action is reciprocated, idiomatic pronominal verbs have a meaning that's completely different from that of their nonpronominal counterparts. Check Table 3-4, earlier in this chapter, to be sure you're saying the right thing. Compare these sentence pairs:

> Je **m'entends** bien avec mes parents. (*I get along well with my parents.*)
>
> J'**entends** bien mes parents. (*I hear my parents well.*)
>
> **Te rappelles**-tu de son prénom ? (*Do you remember his name?*)
>
> Tu peux me **rappeler** demain. (*You can call me back tomorrow.*)

Even though the verb itself is the same, the meanings of these sentence pairs have nothing in common because the reflexive pronoun changes the literal meaning of the verb into an idiomatic meaning.

Chapter 4

Tying Ideas Together with Conjunctions and Relative Pronouns

Conjunctions and relative pronouns help you join words and sentences. They can make your speech and writing much more elegant, so instead of saying, "I like coffee. I like tea. I drink coffee in the morning. I drink tea at night," you can say, "I like coffee, which I drink in the morning, and tea, which I drink at night."

Conjunctions make some kind of a connection between two words (as in *this and that*), between phrases (as in *not right now but perhaps tomorrow*), or between clauses (as in *I'll do it, but it has to be reasonable*). *Phrases* are groups of words that together make up an idea, as in **le marché de fruits** (*the fruit market*) or **pas maintenant** (*not now*). Clauses are groupings of words that include at least a subject and a verb. For example, **Nous allons au marché parce que je veux acheter des fruits frais** (*We're going to the market because I want to buy fresh fruit*) has one main clause, which makes sense all by itself (**Nous allons au marché**), and one subordinate clause, which makes sense only when attached to the main clause (**parce que je veux acheter des fruits frais**).

When the words, phrases, or clauses have a parallel function, you join them with coordinating conjunctions, as in "coffee *or* tea" or "funny stories *and* good food." When you have two clauses that aren't equal, you use subordinating conjunctions, as in "I think *that* you're right." *Relative pronouns* are like subordinating conjunctions in that they join two unequal clauses, but relative pronouns, like all pronouns, replace nouns, which means they can be subjects or objects in the joined clause. This chapter discusses the most common conjunctions and relative pronouns and how to use them effectively.

Joining with Conjunctions

Conjunctions are joining words, and the type of conjunction you use depends on equality. We're not talking about equal rights for parts of speech but rather an equality of purpose for the words you're joining. If you have a verb that has two direct objects, a noun with two adjectives, or even an adjective describing two nouns, those two things are equal because they're modifying or being modified by the same word, so you connect them with a coordinating conjunction. If, on the other hand, you have one phrase that depends on another, those phrases aren't equal, so you need a subordinating conjunction. This section spells out the different ways to use coordinating and subordinating conjunctions in French.

Staying on equal footing with coordinating conjunctions

Coordinating conjunctions join two words, phrases, or clauses that are equal. That is, the words are the same part of speech and are modifying the same thing, or they're two similarly constructed and equally important words, phrases, or clauses.

To correctly use a coordinating conjunction, just place it between the words you want to join. The items linked by coordinating conjunctions can usually be reversed with little or no difference in meaning. Here are some examples:

✔ **Joining two nouns:**

> **Nous aimons bien la plage et les montagnes.** (*We love the beach and the mountains.*)

In this example, the coordinating conjunction **et** (*and*) joins two nouns, **la plage** and **les montagnes**. The nouns are equal because they serve the same purpose in the sentence: They're both direct objects of the verb **aimer** (*to love*). We love the beach, and we love the mountains. And two objects can be reversed: There's no difference between *We love the beach and the mountains* and *We love the mountains and the beach*.

✔ **Joining two adjectives:**

> **Je veux une robe bleue ou verte.** (*I want a blue or green dress.*)

Here, the coordinating conjunction **ou** (*or*) joins two adjectives, **bleue** and **verte**, which are both modifying **robe**. Both colors are equally important — I want a blue dress, or I want a green dress; it doesn't matter which.

✔ **Joining two clauses:**

> **Le chat a miaulé, et puis le chien a aboyé.** (*The cat meowed, and then the dog barked.*)

In this case, the coordinating conjunction **et puis** (*and then*) is joining two clauses. The cat meowed, the dog barked — both of these can stand alone as complete sentences, and neither one is modifying the other, so they, too, are equal.

See Table 4-1 for a list of the most common French coordinating conjunctions.

Table 4-1	Coordinating Conjunctions
French Conjunction	*Translation*
donc	*so*
et	*and*
et . . . et	*both . . . and*
et/ou	*and/or*
et puis	*and then*
mais	*but*
ne . . . ni . . . ni	*neither . . . nor*
ou	*or*
ou bien	*or else*
ou . . . ou	*either . . . or*
soit . . . soit	*either . . . or*

You use the conjunctions **et . . . et, ou . . . ou, ne . . . ni . . . ni,** and **soit . . . soit** when you want to emphasize the relationship between the joined items, as in the following examples:

> **Il veut et un vélo et une mobylette.** (*He wants both a bike and a moped.*) This structure stresses the fact that he wants not just one or the other but both.

> **Je peux voyager ou en France ou en Suisse.** OR **Je peux voyager soit en France soit en Suisse.** (*I can travel either to France or to Switzerland.*) With **ou . . . ou** or **soit . . . soit** rather than just **ou,** you emphasize that you can't go to both places, only to one or the other.

> **Elle ne peut ni lire ni écrire.** (*She can neither read nor write.*) The negative conjunction **ne . . . ni . . . ni** stresses the negative aspect of both verbs — she can't read, nor can she write.

Depending on subordinating conjunctions

You use subordinating conjunctions to combine two clauses. A *clause* is a part of a sentence that has both a subject and a verb. The conjunction tells you that the clause after it is *subordinate*, meaning that it's dependent on the *main clause;* the subordinate clause can't stand alone.

To correctly use a subordinating conjunction, you have to determine which clause is the main clause and which is the subordinate clause. Then put the subordinating conjunction at the beginning of the subordinate clause and join the two clauses:

> **Je pense que tu peux le faire.** (*I think that you can do it.*)

> **Il veut que je travaille.** (*He wants me to work.*)

In the first example, **tu peux le faire** is the subordinate clause — the idea that you can do it is not a fact, the way it would be if the clause were a complete sentence. The subordinating conjunction **que** tells you that these words are dependent on the main clause **je pense**. Though I think you can do it, in reality, you may or may not be able to. In the second example, **je travaille** is the subordinate clause — I may or may not work, because the subordinating conjunction **que** is explaining that he wants me to work, but that doesn't necessarily mean I am working or will work.

Que is the most common subordinating conjunction, and it's required in French. In English, you can often drop its equivalent *that:* **Je pense que tu as raison** (*I think [that] you're right*). In many constructions, it's more natural to reword the English with a direct object + infinitive: **Il veut que je travaille** becomes *He wants me to work* rather than the literal translation *He wants that I work.*

See Table 4-2 for some other common subordinating conjunctions. *Note:* The starred conjunctions require the subjunctive mood (see Chapter 5 of Book IV) in the subordinate clause.

Table 4-2	Subordinating Conjunctions
Conjunction	*Translation*
afin que*	so that
ainsi que	just as, so as
alors que	while, whereas
à moins que*	unless

Conjunction	Translation
après que	after, when
avant que*	before
bien que*	although
de crainte/peur que*	for fear that
en attendant que*	while, until
jusqu'à ce que*	until
lorsque	when
parce que	because
pendant que	while
pour que*	so that
pourvu que*	provided that
puisque	since, as
quand	when
quoique*	even though
quoi que*	whatever, no matter what
sans que*	without
tandis que	while, whereas

Here's a sentence that uses a subordinating conjunction:

Il est parti parce qu'il doit travailler. (*He left because he has to work.*)

The important information in this sentence is in the main clause **il est parti**. Why did he leave? The subordinating conjunction **parce que** (*because*) introduces the subordinate clause to tell you that **il doit travailler** — he has to work.

If you get confused between the conjunction **parce que** (*because*) and the expression **à cause de** (*because of, due to*), remember that **parce que** has to go in front of a clause with a subject and a verb: **J'ai froid parce qu'il neige** (*I'm cold because it's snowing*). **À cause de** goes in front of a noun: **J'ai froid à cause de la neige** (*I'm cold due to the snow*).

Here's another example:

Je ne lis pas quand j'ai sommeil. (*I don't read when I'm sleepy.*)

The main clause is **je ne lis pas**, but the idea isn't complete because I do read sometimes. I just don't read *when,* as the subordinating conjunction **quand** tells you, **j'ai sommeil**.

You can't reverse the clauses joined by subordinating conjunctions, because they either make no sense or the meaning changes. **Tu peux le faire que je pense** (*You can do it that I think*) is nonsense, and **J'ai sommeil quand je ne lis pas** (*I'm sleepy when I don't read*) changes the meaning entirely.

Grasping Relative Pronouns

Relative pronouns and subordinating conjunctions are somewhat similar because they both link subordinate clauses to main clauses. An example of a relative pronoun in English is *who*, as in *I'm not who you think I am*.

Relative pronouns let you introduce additional information about something you just mentioned. For example, you may show a friend a beautiful vase but explain that you just broke it: **Regarde le joli vase que je viens de casser !** (*Look at the pretty vase [that] I just broke!*). **Regarde le joli vase** is the main clause, and the relative clause **que je viens de casser** gives additional information: which vase I want you to look at.

This section squares away relative pronouns and explains how to use them correctly in your writing and speech.

To remember the French word order for relative pronouns, follow the English rule about not ending a sentence with a preposition, as in *Here is the engineer with whom I work* and *Do you know the girl to whom I talked yesterday?* The English sounds a bit stilted, but following this rule is a good reminder that French word order is stricter; you literally can't end a sentence with a preposition. Using the formal English order also helps you choose the right relative pronoun.

Pronouns that join: Sizing up relative pronouns

Relative pronouns join two clauses and become the subject or object of the clause they begin. When you join *I know someone* and *He lives in Tunisia,* you use the relative pronoun *who* to replace the subject of the second sentence: *I know someone who lives in Tunisia*. French is very similar: **Je connais quelqu'un. Il habite en Tunisie** becomes **Je connais quelqu'un qui habite en Tunisie.** Because the relative pronoun **qui** (*who*) replaces the subject of the second sentence, it's the subject of the second clause.

French has five relative pronouns:

- **qui**
- **que**

    ✔ **lequel**

    ✔ **dont**

    ✔ **où**

You don't see translations for them here because the definitions depend on how you use them in your sentences. (Note that **qui** and **que** are also interrogative pronouns, which you can read about in Chapter 5 of Book III.) This section gives you some more direction and helps you figure out when you need to use these pronouns.

Using qui

Qui is the relative pronoun that you use to replace the *subject* of a subordinate clause when you join two sentences. **Qui** can replace any subject: masculine or feminine, singular or plural, human or inanimate. **Qui** loosely translates as *who* or *that:*

> **Nous connaissons un boulanger. Il fait du très bon pain.** → **Nous connaissons un boulanger qui fait du très bon pain.** (*We know a baker. He makes very good bread.* → *We know a baker who makes very good bread.*) Here, **qui** replaces **il**, the subject of **fait** (*makes*).

> **J'ai trouvé des livres. Ils ne sont pas très chers.** → **J'ai trouvé des livres qui ne sont pas très chers.** (*I found some books. They're not very expensive.* → *I found some books that are not very expensive.*) In this example, **qui** replaces **ils**, the subject of **ne sont pas** (*are not*).

You know that **qui** is the subject of the subordinate clause because it replaces the subject of the verb in the second clause. Notice that **qui** is followed by a verb (which can be in a negative form, as in the second example). If **qui** were not the subject, you'd see another subject — a noun or pronoun — there.

You also use **qui** to replace the indirect object or the *object of a preposition* (the noun or pronoun after a preposition):

> **Je voudrais te présenter le nouvel élève. Je viens de lui parler.** → **Je voudrais te présenter le nouvel élève à qui je viens de parler.** (*I would like to introduce you to the new student. I just spoke to him.* → *I would like to introduce to you the new student to whom I just spoke. OR I would like to introduce to you the new student I just spoke to.*) In this example, you replace the indirect object **lui** (*to him*) with **à qui** (*to whom*).

> **Voici Madame Rousseau. Je vais travailler avec elle.** → **Voici Madame Rousseau avec qui je vais travailler.** (*Here is Mrs. Rousseau. I'm going to work with her.* → *Here is Mrs. Rousseau, with whom I'm going to work. OR Here is Mrs. Rousseau, [whom] I'm going to work with.*) Here, you replace **avec elle** with **avec qui**.

Book IV

Getting Down to Detail and Precision in Your Communication

You can use **qui** as an indirect object (*to/for* + [someone]) or object of a preposition only when it refers to a person. If it's a thing, use **lequel**. In addition, you can't use **qui** after the preposition **de** — you have to use **dont**. You can read more about direct and indirect objects in Chapter 3 of Book IV.

Using que

Que replaces the direct object of the subordinate clause. **Que** loosely translates as *whom, that,* or *which,* and it can replace any direct object: a person or thing of any gender or number. **Que** contracts to **qu'** in front of a vowel or mute **h**. Check out the following examples:

> **Je mange au restaurant. Mon frère l'a acheté. → Je mange au restaurant que mon frère a acheté.** (*I'm eating at the restaurant. My brother bought it. → I'm eating at the restaurant that my brother bought.*)

> **Nous cherchons la ville. Étienne la visite chaque été. → Nous cherchons la ville qu'Étienne visite chaque été.** (*We're looking for the town. Étienne visits it every summer. → We're looking for the town [that] Étienne visits every summer.*)

> **Je ne connais pas l'homme. Je l'ai vu hier. → Je ne connais pas l'homme que j'ai vu hier.** (*I don't know the man. I saw him yesterday. → I don't know the man [whom] I saw yesterday.*)

Que replaces the direct object in these sentences. You know it's the direct object because it answers the question "Who or what is the verb acting on?" What did my brother buy? The restaurant. What are we looking for? The town. Whom did I see? The man.

In the example **Je ne connais pas l'homme que j'ai vu hier**, the relative pronoun that replaces **l'homme** cannot be **qui**. Although the pronoun does replace a person just like **qui** does, it's not the subject of the verb **ai vu**, because **j'** (*I*) is the subject. The correct relative pronoun to use in this example is **que**, which receives the action of the verb **ai vu** (*saw*) and is therefore its object. (See Chapter 3 of Book IV for details on direct and indirect objects.)

A quick rule of thumb to distinguish **qui** from **que** is that **qui** is followed by the conjugated form of a verb (sometimes a negative verb), but **que** is followed by a subject noun or pronoun (**je, tu, il, elle, on, nous, vous, ils,** or **elles**). This rule can help you after you've eliminated the possibility that you need a preposition before the relative pronoun (in which case you may need **lequel, dont,** or **où** instead — see the next sections).

In French, relative pronouns are required, but in English, they're sometimes optional, as in *the book you wrote* or *the book that you wrote;* both constructions are acceptable in English. But in French, you can't say **le livre tu as écrit** — you have to say **le livre que tu as écrit**.

Using lequel

Lequel is the pronoun you use when the indirect object or object of the preposition of the subordinate clause isn't a person. (When the indirect object or object of the preposition is a person, you use **qui**.) **Lequel** loosely translates as *which:*

> **J'ai acheté un livre. Il y a un billet de loterie dans le livre. → J'ai acheté un livre dans lequel il y a un billet de loterie.** (*I bought a book. There's a lottery ticket in the book. → I bought a book in which there's a lottery ticket.*) In this example, you replace **dans le livre** (*in the book*) with **dans lequel** (*in which*) and place this phrase at the beginning of the second clause.

> **Gérard travaille pour cette entreprise. Cette entreprise vend des appareils électroménagers. → L'entreprise pour laquelle Gérard travaille vend des appareils électroménagers.** (*Gérard works for this company. This company sells appliances. → The company for which Gérard works sells appliances. OR The company [that] Gérard works for sells appliances.*) Here, you replace **pour cette entreprise** (*for this company*) with **pour laquelle** (*for which*).

Unlike the other relative pronouns, **lequel** has different forms for masculine, feminine, singular, and plural. In addition, the masculine singular and both plural forms contract with the prepositions **à** and **de**, just like the definite articles **le** and **les** do (you can read about that in Chapter 1 of Book IV). Take a look at Table 4-3 for the different forms of **lequel**.

Table 4-3	Forms of Lequel		
Form	*No Preposition*	*à + a form of lequel*	*de + a form of lequel*
Masculine singular	**lequel**	**auquel**	**duquel**
Feminine singular	**laquelle**	**à laquelle**	**de laquelle**
Masculine plural	**lesquels**	**auxquels**	**desquels**
Feminine plural	**lesquelles**	**auxquelles**	**desquelles**

For example, when you say *to think about* in the sense of *to have on one's mind,* you need the French verb **penser** followed by the preposition **à**. In the following example, **à** contracts with **lesquelles**, which replaces the feminine plural noun **les villes**:

> **Les villes auxquelles je pense sont en Europe.** (*The towns about which I'm thinking are in Europe. OR The towns I'm thinking about are in Europe.*)

Many French prepositional phrases, such as **à cause de** (*because of*), **loin de** (*far from*), and **avant de** (*before*), include **de**. (See Chapter 1 of Book IV for info on prepositions.) In the next example, **à côté de** (*next to*) contracts with **lequel**, which replaces the masculine singular noun **le musée**:

> **Le musée à côté duquel il travaille est fermé.** (*The museum next to which he works is closed.* OR *The museum he works next to is closed.*)

Using dont

Dont is the relative pronoun that replaces **de** + [an object (person or thing)] (unless **de** is part of a prepositional phrase such as **à côté de**, as in the preceding section). **Dont** loosely translates as *about, of whom,* or *what:*

> **Je parle d'un ami. Il habite en Tunisie. → L'ami dont je parle habite en Tunisie.** (*I'm talking about a friend. He lives in Tunisia. → The friend about whom I'm talking lives in Tunisia.* OR *The friend [whom] I'm talking about lives in Tunisia.*)

> **Nous rêvons d'une plage. Le sable de cette plage est noir. → Nous rêvons d'une plage dont le sable est noir.** (*We're dreaming about a beach. The sand of this beach is black. → We're dreaming about a beach whose sand is black.*)

If the preposition is just **de**, use **dont**. If it's one or more words plus **de** — **loin de** (*far from*), **près de** (*near*), and so on — use **duquel, de laquelle, desquels,** or **desquelles,** depending on the gender and number of the noun you're replacing. See Table 4-3 in the preceding section.

Using où

You use the relative pronoun **où** to refer to a place or time. It loosely translates as *where* or *when:*

> **J'habite dans un village. Il est très touristique. → Le village où j'habite est très touristique.** (*I live in a village. It's very touristy. → The village where I live is very touristy.*)

> **C'était le moment où elle est tombée amoureuse de la France.** (*That was the moment [when] she fell in love with France.*)

Quand is the normal translation of *when* in questions, as in **Quand vas-tu arriver ?** (*When are you going to arrive?*), and after a main clause, as in **Je ne sais pas quand il va arriver** (*I don't know when he's going to arrive*). But after a noun that indicates time such as **le jour** (*the day*), **l'année** (*the year*), **le mois** (*the month*), **le moment** (*the moment*), or **la minute** (*the minute*), you have to use **où**, as in **le jour où il est né** (*the day when he was born*), **l'année où elle s'est mariée** (*the year when she got married*), or **le moment où il l'a remarquée** (*the moment when he noticed her*).

What you need to know: Identifying indefinite relative pronouns

Unlike standard relative pronouns, indefinite relative pronouns don't have a specific antecedent (something they replace) — they refer back to something unknown. When you say, "What I like" or "That's what we think," *what* is an indefinite relative pronoun. It's a sort of dummy subject of the clause.

- **ce qui** (*what*)
- **ce que** (*what*)
- **ce dont** (*about what*)
- **quoi** (*what*)

You see that the English translations for three of the French indefinite relative pronouns are identical. That's because in French, you need different pronouns depending on how you're using those words (as a subject, direct object, or object of a preposition), whereas in English, you just need *what*.

Using ce qui

You use **ce qui** as the subject of a relative clause:

> **Ce qui me dérange le plus, c'est la malhonnêteté.** (*What bothers me the most is dishonesty.*)

> **Vois-tu ce qui fait ce bruit ?** (*Do you see what's making that noise?*)

In these examples, you know **ce qui** is the subject because it tells you what's performing the action of the verb (*what bothers me, worries me, is making that noise*). The verb used with **ce qui** takes the third-person singular (**il/elle/on**) ending.

Note that **ce qui** is the subject of a relative clause, not the subject of the entire sentence. You can rearrange the last example to say **Tu vois ce qui fait ce bruit** (*You see what is making that noise*). *You* is the subject of the sentence, *see* is the verb, and *what is making that noise* is the thing that's seen. Altogether, the entire clause *what is making that noise* acts like a direct object, but that doesn't matter. Instead, pay attention to the role **ce qui** plays within its own clause. **Ce qui** is followed by a verb rather than a subject noun or pronoun, so **ce qui** is likely acting as a subject.

Using ce que

The relative pronoun **ce que** serves as the indefinite direct object of a relative clause:

Book IV

Getting Down to Detail and Precision in Your Communication

Ce que nous avons, c'est impossible à expliquer. (*What we have is impossible to explain.*)

C'est ce que j'aimerais savoir. (*That's what I'd like to know.*)

Savez-vous ce que Philippe a acheté ? (*Do you know what Philippe bought?*)

In contrast to the *subject,* which performs the action of the verb, the *direct object* receives the action of the verb and is impacted by it. Here are some guidelines for choosing between **ce qui** and **ce que**:

- Use **ce qui**, the subject form, before a verb or verb phrase:

    Ce qui ne va pas, c'est cette couleur. (*What does not work is this color.*)

    C'est **ce qui m'inquiète**. (*That's what worries me.*)

    The verb after **ce qui** may be negative or come with a reflexive pronoun or object pronoun, but you don't see a noun/subject pronoun between **ce qui** and the verb.

- Use **ce que**, the direct-object form, before a noun/subject pronoun + verb:

    Ce que maman veut, elle le reçoit. (*What Mom wants, she gets [it].*)

    Ce que tu racontes est vrai. (*What you're telling is true.*)

Before using this rule of thumb, check that the verb in the relative clause doesn't require the preposition **à** or **de** — you may need one of the indefinite relative pronouns from the next two sections.

Using ce dont

You use the indefinite relative pronoun **ce dont** to replace the preposition **de** + [its object]:

Ce dont j'ai envie, c'est une nouvelle voiture. (*What I want is a new car.*) **Avoir envie de** means *to want.*

C'est ce dont il parlait. (*That's what he was talking about.*) **Parler de** means *to talk about.*

Sais-tu ce dont elles rêvent ? (*Do you know what they dream about?*) **Rêver de** means *to dream about.*

Whenever you use a verb that requires **de** (see Chapter 1 of Book IV), the indefinite relative pronoun is **ce dont**. **Avoir envie de** (*to want*), **parler de** (*to talk about*), and **rêver de** (*to dream about*) all require **de**, so when you use an indefinite relative pronoun with them, it has to be **ce dont**.

Using quoi

After any preposition except **de**, you use the indefinite relative pronoun **quoi** in relative clauses:

> **Sur quoi pouvons-nous écrire ?** (*On what can we write?* OR *What can we write on?*)

> **Je ne sais pas à quoi ils s'intéressent.** (*I don't know what they're interested in.*)

When you use **à quoi** at the beginning of the clause or after the expression **c'est**, you need to add **ce** in front of the preposition:

> **Ce à quoi nous nous attendons, c'est une lettre d'excuses.** (*What we're expecting is a letter of apology.*)

> **C'est ce à quoi je m'intéresse.** (*That's what I'm interested in.*)

In order to pick the correct indefinite relative pronoun, determine first whether the verb or expression in the relative clause requires the pronoun **à** or **de**. For example, if the relative clause has the verb **penser à** (*to think about*), then you say **Ce à quoi je pense constamment, c'est mes vacances** (*What I constantly think about is my vacation*). If the relative clause has the phrase **avoir besoin de** (*to need*), you say **Ce dont j'ai besoin, c'est un bon verre de vin** (*What I need is a good glass of wine*). If the verb or expression in the relative clause does not require **à** or **de**, then apply the rule of thumb: **ce qui** + [verb] or **ce que** + [subject pronoun/noun].

Book IV

Getting Down to Detail and Precision in Your Communication

Chapter 5

Getting That Subjunctive Feeling

The **subjonctif** (*subjunctive*) may make you tense, but it's not a verb tense — it's a mood, with an attitude. The difference between a tense and a mood is that a *tense* tells you when something is happening, and a *mood* tells you the speaker's attitude toward the action of the verb. The subjunctive mood indicates subjectivity — the speaker may want something to happen or think it's important for something to happen, but the subjunctive tells you that this something may or may not actually happen. In contrast, the *indicative* is the "normal" verb mood that indicates the way something actually is.

The subjunctive exists in English, but it's so rare and so easily avoided that many native speakers aren't even aware of it. For example, in the sentence *It's important that you be good,* the verb *be* is in the subjunctive. But English speakers are far more likely to say *It's important for you to be good.* The only real holdouts are a few verbs like *suggest, recommend,* and *demand* as well as the expressions *If I were you* and *I wish I were. I were* is the subjunctive; the indicative is *I was.*

In fact, the subjunctive is so rarely used in English that referring to it in translations is pretty useless. Instead, focus on when and how the French use it. This chapter tells you all about the French subjunctive: how to conjugate verbs in it, when to use it, and how and when to avoid it.

Conjugating in the Present Subjunctive

The subjunctive mood includes only two time frames or tenses: the present, which takes care of anything present and future, and the past. The present subjunctive is one of the easier verb conjugations. All regular verbs, no matter which endings they have, are conjugated the same way. Stem-changing verbs and all but seven irregular verbs are conjugated in a second way. That leaves just a handful of verbs that are irregular in the subjunctive, making the subjunctive conjugations (if not the uses) relatively easy to master. This section covers conjugations in the present subjunctive.

Regular verbs

All regular **-er**, **-ir**, and **-re** verbs use the third-person plural (**ils**) present indicative as the root for present subjunctive conjugations. To conjugate any regular verb, just take the **ils/elles** form of the present tense, drop **-ent**, and add the subjunctive ending **-e**, **-es**, **-e**, **-ions**, **-iez**, or **-ent**. (See Chapter 3 of Book III for info on present-tense conjugations.) These subjunctive endings are the same for all regular verbs, all stem-changing verbs, all spelling-change verbs, and nearly all irregular verbs.

The present subjunctive endings of verbs are the present indicative endings of **-er** verbs in all forms, except in the **nous** and **vous** forms, for which the endings are **-ions** and **-iez**. Look at Table 5-1.

Table 5-1	Comparing Present Indicative and Present Subjunctive Endings	
Person	*Present Indicative Ending*	*Present Subjunctive Ending*
je	-e	-e
tu	-es	-es
il/elle/on	-e	-e
nous	-ons	-ions
vous	-ez	-iez
ils/elles	-ent	-ent

The present indicative **ils/elles** form of the regular **-er** verb **parler** (*to speak*), for instance, is **[ils/elles] parlent**, so the subjunctive stem is **parl-**. The following table shows what **parler** looks like in the subjunctive.

parler (to speak)	
je parl**e**	nous parl**ions**
tu parl**es**	vous parl**iez**
il/elle/on parl**e**	ils/elles parl**ent**
Il veut que nous **parlions** en français. (*He wants us to speak in French.*)	

Spelling-change verbs have no spelling change in the subjunctive because all the subjunctive endings begin with soft vowels (**e** or **i**). The present-tense **ils** form of **manger** (*to eat*) is **mangent**, so the stem is **mang-**.

manger (to eat)	
je mang**e**	nous mang**ions**
tu mang**es**	vous mang**iez**
il/elle/on mang**e**	ils/elles mang**ent**
Il faut que tu **manges** immédiatement. (*You have to eat immediately.*)	

You'd say **ils/elles finissent** in the present indicative, so the subjunctive stem of **finir** (*to finish*) is **finiss-**.

finir (to finish)	
je finiss**e**	nous finiss**ions**
tu finiss**es**	vous finiss**iez**
il/elle/on finiss**e**	ils/elles finiss**ent**
Il faut que tu **finisses** avant midi. (*You have to finish before noon.*)	

The subjunctive stem of **vendre** (*to sell*) is **vend-**.

vendre (to sell)	
je vend**e**	nous vend**ions**
tu vend**es**	vous vend**iez**
il/elle/on vend**e**	ils/elles vend**ent**
Penses-tu qu'il **vende** des fraises ? (*Do you think he sells strawberries?*)	

Stem-changing and most irregular verbs

Stem-changing verbs and all but seven irregular verbs enjoy a little variety — they have two subjunctive stems. Like regular verbs, stem-changing and irregular verbs use the **ils/elles** conjugation minus **-ent** as the stem — but only for the **je**, **tu**, **il/elle/on**, and **ils/elles** subjunctive forms (the "boot" forms). For **nous** and **vous**, the verbs use the present-tense **nous** form minus **-ons**. Regardless of the stem, these verbs all take the same subjunctive endings as regular verbs: **-e**, **-es**, **-e**, **-ions**, **-iez**, and **-ent**.

With **envoyer** (*to send*), for example, you write **ils/elles envoient** or **nous envoyons** in the normal present tense. So in the subjunctive, the two stems are **envoi-** and **envoy-**.

envoyer (*to send*)	
j'envoi**e**	nous envoy**ions**
tu envoi**es**	vous envoy**iez**
il/elle/on envoi**e**	ils/elles envoi**ent**
Il est bon que vous **envoyiez** le chèque. (*It's good that you're sending the check.*)	

For the subjunctive stems of **lever** (*to lift*), write **ils/elles lèvent** minus **-ent** to get **lèv-** and **nous levons** minus **-ons** to get **lev-**.

lever (*to lift*)	
je lèv**e**	nous lev**ions**
tu lèv**es**	vous lev**iez**
il/elle/on lèv**e**	ils/elles lèv**ent**
Il ne faut pas que vous **leviez** la main. (*You must not raise your hand.*)	

For the irregular verb **devoir** (*to have to*), **ils/elles doivent** minus **-ent** is **doiv-**, and **nous devons** minus **-ons** is **dev-**.

devoir (*to have to*)	
je doiv**e**	nous dev**ions**
tu doiv**es**	vous dev**iez**
il/elle/on doiv**e**	ils/elles doiv**ent**
Penses-tu que je **doive** partir ? (*Do you think I have to leave?*)	

Really irregular verbs

The conjugation rules in the preceding sections apply to all but seven irregular verbs. The seven irregular verbs that are also irregular in the subjunctive are **aller**, **avoir**, **être**, **faire**, **pouvoir**, **savoir**, and **vouloir**.

Faire (*to do, to make*), **pouvoir** (*to be able*), and **savoir** (*to know*) have a single irregular stem for all conjugated forms: **fass-**, **puiss-**, and **sach-**, respectively. **Vouloir** (*to want*) and **aller** (*to have*) have two irregular stems each: **veuill-** and **aill-** for the boot forms (the third-person plural and all the singular conjugations) and **voul-** and **all-** for the **nous** and **vous** forms. These five verbs take the same subjunctive endings as the rest: **-e**, **-es**, **-e**, **-ions**, **-iez**, and **-ent**.

faire (to do, make)	
je fass**e**	nous fass**ions**
tu fass**es**	vous fass**iez**
il/elle/on fass**e**	ils/elles fass**ent**
Il est bon que tu le **fasses**. (*It's good [that] you're doing it.*)	

pouvoir (to be able)	
je puiss**e**	nous puiss**ions**
tu puiss**es**	vous puiss**iez**
il/elle/on puiss**e**	ils/elles puiss**ent**
Elle ne croit pas que je **puisse** nager. (*She doesn't believe that I can swim.*)	

savoir (to know)	
je sach**e**	nous sach**ions**
tu sach**es**	vous sach**iez**
il/elle/on sach**e**	ils/elles sach**ent**
Il est important que vous **sachiez** lire. (*It's important that you know how to read.*)	

vouloir (*to want*)	
je veuill**e**	nous voul**ions**
tu veuill**es**	vous voul**iez**
il/elle/on veuill**e**	ils/elles veuill**ent**
Il est possible qu'elles **veuillent** partir tôt. (*It's possible that they want to leave early.*)	

aller (*to go*)	
j'aill**e**	nous all**ions**
tu aill**es**	vous all**iez**
il/elle/on aill**e**	ils/elles aill**ent**
Veux-tu que j'**aille** avec toi ? (*Do you want me to go with you?*)	

Finally, **être** (*to be*) and **avoir** (*to have*) have completely irregular subjunctive conjugations. See the following tables.

être (*to be*)	
je **sois**	nous **soyons**
tu **sois**	vous **soyez**
il/elle/on **soit**	ils/elles **soient**
Nous avons peur qu'elle **soit** malade. (*We're afraid she's sick.*)	

avoir (*to have*)	
j'**aie**	nous **ayons**
tu **aies**	vous **ayez**
il/elle/on **ait**	ils/elles **aient**
Je suis heureux que tu **aies** une nouvelle voiture. (*I'm happy [that] you have a new car.*)	

In your pronunciation, make sure you distinguish between the subjunctive forms of **aller** (*to go*) and **avoir** (*to have*). Mispronouncing them could lead you to utter sentences that make no sense. For example, if you mean to say that *they must go to the bank,* say **Il faut qu'ils aillent à la banque** (eel foh keel zahy ah lah bahNk). Don't say **Il faut qu'ils aient à la banque** (eel foh keel zey ah lah bahNk), which would mean that *they must have at the bank.* Here's some pronunciation info:

✔ **Aller:** The singular subjunctive forms of the verb **aller** (**aille**, **ailles**, and **aille**) are pronounced *ahy*. For the **nous** and **vous** forms, remember to include the **liaison** and say **nous allions** (nooh zah-lyohN) and **vous alliez** (vooh zah-lyey) — that is, pronounce the **s** at the end of **nous** or **vous** because the next word starts with a vowel. The third-person plural is pronounced like the singular forms (ahy), but you must make the liaison and say **ils/elles aillent** (eel/ehl zahy).

✔ **Avoir:** The singular subjunctive forms of the verb **avoir** (**aie**, **aies**, and **ait**) are pronounced *ey*. For the **nous** and **vous** forms, include the liaison and say **nous ayons** (nooh zey-yohN) and **vous ayez** (vooh zey-yey). The third-person plural is pronounced like the singular forms (ey), but you must make the liaison, so you say **ils/elles aient** (eel/ehl zey).

Getting Unreal: Using the Subjunctive

The most important thing to understand about the subjunctive mood is that, as its name suggests, it expresses subjectivity. When any desire, doubt, emotion, judgment, or necessity is expressed in a sentence, you have to use the subjunctive to show that the action of the verb isn't a fact but rather is based on the subjective notion in the phrase that precedes it. The verb in the subjunctive tells you about what someone wants, needs, or feels but not whether that's actually going to happen. It may be good, bad, important, necessary, or doubtful, but is it real? Will it actually happen? The subjunctive indicates the unreality or uncertainty of the situation.

The subjunctive is nearly always found in a dependent clause preceded by **que**. This **que** is required, unlike its English equivalent *that*, which is often optional:

> **Il est bon que tu partes.** (*It's good [that] you're leaving.*)

> **Je suggère que nous mangions à midi.** (*I suggest [that] we eat at noon.*)

The French subjunctive is required after many expressions, verbs, and conjunctions, and it's optional after others. This section explains when you need to use the subjunctive and how to use it correctly.

There's a present subjunctive and a past subjunctive but no future subjunctive. If the action is supposed to happen in the future, you use the present subjunctive: **Je te téléphonerai bien que tu sois en France la semaine prochaine** (*I'll call you even though you'll be in France next week*).

Book IV

Getting
Down to
Detail and
Precision
in Your
Communication

With impersonal expressions

Impersonal expressions require the subjunctive when they indicate some kind of subjectivity, will, possibility, or judgment, whether on the part of the speaker or of society as a whole. Impersonal expressions include the following:

- ✓ **il est bon que** (*it's good that*)
- ✓ **il est dommage que** (*it's too bad that*)
- ✓ **il est douteux que** (*it's doubtful that*)
- ✓ **il est étonnant que** (*it's amazing that*)
- ✓ **il est important que** (*it's important that*)
- ✓ **il est impossible que** (*it's impossible that*)
- ✓ **il est improbable que** (*it's improbable that*)
- ✓ **il est naturel que** (*it's natural that*)
- ✓ **il est nécessaire que** (*it's necessary that*)
- ✓ **il est normal que** (*it's normal that*)
- ✓ **il est possible que** (*it's possible that*)
- ✓ **il est rare que** (*it's rare that*)
- ✓ **il est regrettable que** (*it's regrettable that*)
- ✓ **il est surprenant que** (*it's surprising that*)
- ✓ **il est urgent que** (*it's urgent that*)

Check out some examples, noting the subjunctive verb in the clause after the **que** (*that*):

Il est bon que tu travailles pour ton père. (*It's good that you work for your father.*)

Il est important que tout le monde fasse de l'exercice. (*It's important that everyone exercise.*)

Il est impossible qu'il ait autant de temps libre que moi. (*It's impossible that he has as much free time as me.*)

In English, you can often more naturally translate a French impersonal expression + subjunctive as *for* + a subject and infinitive:

Il est normal que tu aies peur. (*It's normal for you to be afraid.*)

Il est rare qu'il mente. (*It's rare for him to lie.*)

You can also begin impersonal expressions with **c'est**: **c'est dommage** (*it's too bad*), **c'est bon** (*it's good*), and so on. The meaning is the same, but **c'est** is slightly informal.

Once more, with feelings (and orders and opinions)

Because feelings — such as fear, doubt, regret, surprise, and happiness — are subjective, they require the subjunctive. Here are some common phrases that express feelings and opinions:

- **avoir peur que** (*to be afraid that*)

- **craindre que** (*to fear that*)

- **détester que** (*to hate that*)

- **douter que** (*to doubt that*)

- **être content que** (*to be happy that*)

- **être désolé que** (*to be sorry that*)

- **être étonné que** (*to be amazed that*)

- **être heureux que** (*to be happy that*)

- **être surpris que** (*to be surprised that*)

- **être triste que** (*to be sad that*)

- **regretter que** (*to regret that*)

Consider these examples:

J'ai peur qu'il soit blessé. (*I'm afraid that he's wounded.*)

Nous sommes contents que tu veuilles voyager. (*We're happy you want to travel.*)

In the examples, the words following **être** (**contents**, **désolé**, and so on), are adjectives. Like all adjectives, they have to agree with the nouns or pronouns they modify, which in this case is the subject of the verb **être**. See Chapter 2 of Book IV for info on adjectives.

When you use **douter** (*to doubt*) in the negative, it doesn't take the subjunctive because saying that you don't doubt something means that you believe it to be true; when you believe something, you can't use the subjunctive. Compare the following sentences — only the first requires the subjunctive:

Je doute qu'il ait raison. (*I doubt that he's right.*)

Je ne doute pas qu'il a raison. (*I don't doubt that he's right.*)

Verbs that indicate the speaker's will, wants, or opinions express something that may or may not happen and therefore require the subjunctive. Some common phrases include

- **demander que** (*to ask that [someone do something]*)
- **désirer que** (*to desire that*)
- **exiger que** (*to demand that*)
- **ordonner que** (*to order that*)
- **préférer que** (*to prefer that*)
- **proposer que** (*to propose that*)
- **souhaiter que** (*to wish that*)
- **suggérer que** (*to suggest that*)
- **vouloir que** (*to want that*)

Here are some examples:

J'exige que vous partiez. (*I demand that you leave.*)

Il veut que je fasse moins. (*He wants me to do less.*)

Why not? With certain verbs in the negative or interrogative

Verbs and expressions that indicate what a person believes, a general statement of fact, or something that's probable don't take the subjunctive when you use them in a statement, because they indicate something that's reality, at least in the mind of the speaker. However, these same terms do require the subjunctive when you use them in a question or negation because that question or negation indicates doubt, which requires the subjunctive. Some examples include the following:

- **croire que** (*to believe that*)
- **dire que** (*to say that*)
- **espérer que** (*to hope that*)
- **être certain que** (*to be certain that*)
- **être clair que** (*to be clear/obvious that*)
- **être sûr que** (*to be sure that*)
- **être évident que** (*to be obvious that*)
- **être probable que** (*to be probable that*)
- **être vrai que** (*to be true that*)
- **paraître que** (*to appear that*)
- **penser que** (*to think that*)
- **savoir que** (*to know that*)
- **trouver que** (*to find/think that*)

Check out the following sentences. Notice that the last two use the subjunctive:

> **Je pense que tu as raison.** (*I think you're right.*)
>
> **Je ne pense pas que tu aies raison.** (*I don't think you're right.*)
>
> **Penses-tu que j'aie raison ?** (*Do you think I'm right?*)

And with conjunctions

Conjunctions that express some sort of condition, concession, or feeling require the subjunctive. Some common conjunctions include

- **à moins que** (*unless*)
- **afin que** (*so that*)
- **avant que** (*before*)
- **bien que** (*although*)
- **de crainte/peur que** (*for fear that*)
- **en attendant que** (*while, until*)

- **jusqu'à ce que** (*until*)
- **pour que** (*so that*)
- **pourvu que** (*provided that*)
- **quoi que** (*whatever, no matter what*)
- **quoique** (*even though*)
- **sans que** (*without*)

Here are some examples:

> **Je suis parti(e) pour qu'il puisse se concentrer.** (*I left so that he could concentrate.*)
>
> **Il travaille bien que sa famille soit riche.** (*He works even though his family is rich.*)

Conjunctions such as the following that express anything considered real aren't followed by the subjunctive:

- **ainsi que** (*just as, so as*)
- **alors que** (*while, whereas*)
- **après que** (*after, when*)
- **aussitôt que** (*as soon as*)
- **depuis que** (*since*)
- **dès que** (*as soon as, immediately*)
- **en même temps que** (*at the same time that*)

- **parce que** (*because*)
- **pendant que** (*while*)
- **plutôt que** (*instead of, rather than*)
- **puisque** (*since, as*)
- **quand** (*when*)
- **tandis que** (*while, whereas*)

When you use **après que**, **aussitôt que**, **depuis que**, or **dès que** after a verb in the **futur** (*future tense*), the verb in the clause following the conjunction must also be in the **futur**. (For more on the **futur**, see Chapter 6 of Book IV.)

The following sentences use the normal, indicative mood after the conjunctions. The first example has the **passé composé** (*past tense;* see Chapter 1 of Book V) in the first clause and the **imparfait** (*imperfect*) in the second (see Chapter 2 of Book V); and the second sentence has the **futur** in both clauses:

> **Il est tombé parce que le trottoir était glissant.** (*He fell because the sidewalk was slippery.*)

> **Nous en parlerons dès que tu seras prêt.** (*We'll talk about it as soon as you're ready.*)

With superlatives: Simply the best

When you use superlatives, such as *best, worst, nicest,* and so on, you need to use the subjunctive. Superlatives (see Chapter 2 of Book IV) are subjective notions and therefore require the subjunctive:

> **C'est le meilleur médecin que je connaisse.** (*He's the best doctor I know.*)

> **Voici le plus bel appartement que je puisse trouver.** (*Here's the prettiest apartment I can find.*)

Words referring to something unique, such as only, first, and last, are optional subjunctives. You use the subjunctive when you're talking about something that you're claiming is unique: the first ever, the only one in the world. However, you use the subjunctive only when you're expressing a subjective opinion. You don't use it when talking about something factual. Consider these pairs of sentences:

> **C'est le premier livre que je comprenne.** (*That's the first book I understand.*) This book is unique in that it's the first — and so far only — one that I'm able to understand. But I may be able to understand other books out there, too, and I express this possibility with the subjunctive.

> **C'est le premier livre que j'ai lu.** (*That's the first book I read.*) This is a fact — I know it's the first book that I read, and no other book can possibly show up claiming that I read it first. Because the statement is factual, I use the indicative.

> **Ma voiture est la seule qui soit verte à pois jaunes.** (*My car is the only one that's green with yellow polka dots.*) It's the only car like this in the world — at least I think so. I can't know for sure because I haven't seen every car in the world, so I use the subjunctive.

> **C'est la seule voiture que j'ai.** (*That's the only car I have.*) I have just one car — this one. It's a fact, so I use the indicative.

Something else: Words with indefinite and negative pronouns

The indefinite pronouns **quelqu'un** (*someone*) and **quelque chose** (*something*) and the negative pronouns **ne . . . personne** (*no one*) and **ne . . . rien** (*nothing*) plus **qui** are optional subjunctives. You use the subjunctive when you're not sure whether something exists or when you're sure that it doesn't, but you don't use the subjunctive when you're sure that it does exist. Here's how that distinction breaks down:

✔ **Positive it doesn't exist:** Subjunctive

✔ **Not sure it exists:** Subjunctive

✔ **Sure it exists:** Indicative

Look at two pairs of example sentences:

Je ne connais personne qui sache pourquoi. (*I don't know anyone who knows why.*) I don't believe that anyone in the world knows why, so I use the subjunctive.

Je ne connais personne qui sait conduire. (*I don't know anyone who knows how to drive.*) Many people know how to drive. I know they exist; I just don't happen to know any of them. Therefore, I don't use the subjunctive.

Je cherche un traducteur qui sache toutes les langues africaines. (*I'm looking for a translator who knows all African languages.*) I'm not sure such a person exists, so I use the subjunctive.

Je cherche un traducteur qui sait l'Alsacien. (*I'm looking for a translator who knows Alsatian.*) Some translators know Alsatian, a dialect spoken in the Alsace region, but I don't happen to know any of them. Therefore, I don't use the subjunctive.

All by itself

The subjunctive usually goes in a subordinate clause after a verb, expression, or conjunction, but it also has a few solo tricks up its sleeve. On its own, the subjunctive can express certain kinds of commands. When you take **que** and add the subjunctive, you get a third-person command:

Qu'il se taise ! (*Make him shut up!* OR *If only he'd shut up!*)

Que tout le monde me laisse en paix ! (*I wish everyone would leave me alone!*)

Qu'ils mangent de la brioche ! (*Let them eat brioche!* — Marie Antoinette's legendary exclamation, which is commonly translated as *Let them eat cake!*)

A few verbs in the subjunctive can make third-person commands without **que** (Chapter 4 of Book III explains more about giving orders):

- ✔ **Être** (*to be*): **Soit !** (*So be it!*)
- ✔ **Pouvoir** (*to be able to*): **Puisse Dieu vous aider !** (*May God help you!*)
- ✔ **Vivre** (*to live*): **Vive la France !** (*Long live France!*)

Savoir (*to know*) has a special formal meaning as a main-clause subjunctive:

Pas que je sache. (*Not as far as I know.* OR *Not to my knowledge.*)

Expressing Opinions, Doubts, or Regrets about the Past

You use the past subjunctive for the same reasons you use the present subjunctive: The main clause of your sentence has a verb, an adjective, or a structure that triggers doubt or uncertainty in the dependent clause. However, when the action of the dependent clause precedes the action or state of mind expressed in the main clause, you must use the past tense of the subjunctive mood. For example, if you're sorry that your friend missed a train, you're sorry about something that's already happened; therefore, you say **Je suis désolé(e) que tu aies raté ton train.** (*I'm sorry that you missed your train.*)

In structure, the past subjunctive is a compound tense that resembles the **passé composé**, the past tense you use for completed actions in the past (see Chapter 1 of Book V). The sentence **Tu as raté ton train** (*You missed your train*) is in the **passé composé**.

Both past tenses use a conjugated auxiliary (helping) verb — either **avoir** or **être** — as well as a past participle. For the past subjunctive, you just put the auxiliary verb in the present subjunctive instead of the present indicative (the regular present tense). Tables 5-2 and 5-3 compare the **passé composé** and past subjunctive tenses. Head to Chapter 3 of Book V for more info on how and when to conjugate a verb in the past subjunctive.

Table 5-2	Passé Composé and Past Subjunctive of Chanter (To Sing)
Passé Composé	*Past Subjunctive*
j'ai chanté	j'aie chanté
tu as chanté	tu aies chanté
il/elle/on a chanté	il/elle/on ait chanté
nous avons chanté	nous ayons chanté
vous avez chanté	vous ayez chanté
ils/elles ont chanté	ils/elles aient chanté

Table 5-3	Passé Composé and Past Subjunctive of Aller (To Go)
Passé Composé	*Past Subjunctive*
je suis allé(e)	je sois allé(e)
tu es allé(e)	tu sois allé(e)
il, elle, on est allé(e)	il, elle, on soit allé(e)
nous sommes allé(s/es)	nous soyons allé(s/es)
vous êtes allé(e/s/es)	vous soyez allé(e/s/es)
ils, elles sont allé(s/es)	ils, elles soient allé(s/es)

Look at a few examples of the past subjunctive in sentences:

> **Maman est surprise que tu sois arrivé à l'heure, Jean.** (*Mom is surprised that you arrived on time, Jean.*)
>
> **Je regrette que tu n'aies pas téléphoné.** (*I'm sorry [that] you did not call.*)
>
> **Tu as peur que Josée se soit perdue ?** (*Are you afraid [that] Josée got lost?*)

Avoiding the Subjunctive

The subjunctive is an essential verb mood that expresses subjectivity, but you can avoid it in some instances, with the potential for some variation in meaning. Of course, this sidestep doesn't mean that you can ignore the subjunctive entirely, but knowing how to express something in different ways is always good. Plus, you can express different nuances by using different constructions. In this section, we help you run some of these bypasses.

Book IV

Getting Down to Detail and Precision in Your Communication

Shared and implied subjects: Using de + infinitive

When you use the subjunctive verbs and expressions in this chapter in English, you may use them with the same subject in both clauses. For example, *I* is the subject of both clauses in *I'm sad that I don't have time to meet you.* In French, however, when the main clause and the subordinate clause have the same subject, you don't use the subjunctive. Instead, you use **de** in place of **que** and follow it with the infinitive (the dictionary form of the verb):

> **Je suis content que j'habite à la plage.** → **Je suis content d'habiter à la plage.** (*I'm happy that I live at the beach.* → *I'm happy to live at the beach.*)
>
> **Es-tu surpris que tu aies raison ?** → **Es-tu surpris d'avoir raison ?** (*Are you surprised that you're right?* → *Are you surprised to be right?*)
>
> **Tu dois manger avant que tu partes.** → **Tu dois manger avant de partir.** (*You have to eat before you leave.* → *You have to eat before leaving.*)

When you have an impersonal expression with an implied subject, you can again replace **que** with **de** and follow it with the infinitive. Note that doing so in the second example turns something specific (it's good for *you* to be happy) into a general statement of fact (it's good to be happy):

> **Il est important que tout le monde travaille.** → **Il est important de travailler.** (*It's important for everyone to work.* → *It's important to work.*)
>
> **Il est bon que vous soyez content.** → **Il est bon d'être content.** (*It's good that you're happy.* → *It's good to be happy.*)

Slipping in some indirect objects

You can avoid the subjunctive with orders and requests by changing the subject of the subjunctive clause to an indirect object, replacing **que** with **de**, and turning the subjunctive into an infinitive.

In the following example, **que tu fasses** turns into **de faire**; the indirect-object pronoun **te** becomes necessary after the subject **tu** is gone:

> **J'ordonne que tu le fasses.** → **Je t'ordonne de le faire.** (*I order that you do it.* → *I order you to do it.*)

In the next example, **que je voyage** turns into **de voyager**; the indirect-object pronoun **me** becomes necessary after the subject (**je** is gone:

> **Il propose que je voyage avec lui.** → **Il me propose de voyager avec lui.**
> (*He proposes that I travel with him.* → *He asks me to travel with him.*)

You can rewrite subjunctive sentences that have impersonal verbs, such as **falloir** (*to be necessary*), with no change in meaning. Just replace the subject after **que** with an indirect object and replace the subjunctive with an infinitive:

> **Il faut que tu le fasses.** → **Il te faut le faire.** (*You have to do it.*)

> **Il arrive que j'aie tort.** → **Il m'arrive d'avoir tort.** (*It sometimes happens that I am wrong.*)

You can read more about indirect objects in Chapter 3 of Book IV.

Swapping the subjunctive for a noun

With time-related conjunctions like **avant que** (*before*), you can sometimes replace the subjunctive clause with a noun with little or no change in meaning. Note that you have to drop **que**:

> **Nous allons manger avant que tu arrives.** → **Nous allons manger avant ton arrivée.** (*We're going to eat before you arrive* → *We're going to eat before your arrival.*)

> **Je travaille en attendant que le film commence.** → **Je travaille en attendant le début du film.** (*I'm working until the film starts* → *I'm working until the start of the film.*)

Casting a doubt with "if"

With verbs like **douter** (*to doubt*), you can replace **que** with **si** (*if*), which can't be followed by the subjunctive. This change makes the meaning a bit more doubtful:

> **Je doute qu'il soit là.** → **Je doute s'il est là.** (*I doubt that he's there.* → *I doubt if he's there.*)

Chapter 6

What Lies Ahead and What Could Happen: Simple Future and Present Conditional

▶ Conjugating and using the **futur simple** (*simple future*) tense

▶ Considering other ways to talk about the future

▶ Using the **conditionnel** (*conditional*) with *if* clauses

*W*hen planning for or dreaming about the future, you use the French **futur** (*future*) tense. Whether you're organizing a trip, figuring out a five-year plan, or deciding what to do next Friday night, you'll use the future to explain what will happen.

The **conditionnel** (*conditional*) is a verb mood that expresses something that could or would happen, usually depending on whether something else does or doesn't happen, as in *I could travel around the world if I were rich* or *He would go swimming if he didn't have to work*. The **conditionnel** lets you ask people whether they'd be happier living somewhere else, and it helps you tell people whether you'd date someone if he or she were the last person on Earth.

The French future tense and present conditional are easy to conjugate. You use the same stem for both of them, usually the infinitive form of the verb. Only the endings are slightly different as you compare the simple future with the present conditional. This chapter explains how to conjugate and use these verb forms and offers some other ways to talk about the future in French.

The Infinitive and Beyond: Conjugating the Futur

Telling the future in French can be a snap, even without a crystal ball. The basic future tense — the **futur simple** — is one of the easiest French verb conjugations because all verbs take the same endings, no matter what the future stem is, and only a few verbs are irregular in the future. For most verbs, you just do the following:

1. **Take the infinitive, dropping the final -e if it's an -re verb.**

   The future stem for all verbs — regular, stem-changing, spelling-change, and irregular — always ends in **r**.

2. **Add -ai, -as, -a, -ons, -ez, or -ont.**

   The future endings for the singular conjugations and the third-person plural (the boot forms in a verb conjugation chart) are the same as the present-tense conjugations of **avoir** (*to have*): **j'ai**, **tu as**, **il/elle/on a**, and **ils/elles ont**. The **nous** and **vous** future endings are the **avoir** conjugations (**nous avons**, **vous avez**) minus **av-**.

This section covers what you need to know when conjugating verbs in the future tense so you can correctly say and write what you mean.

Regular and spelling-change verbs

Regular and spelling-change verbs stick with simplicity. Regular **-er** verbs use their infinitive as the future stem, so just add the appropriate ending right on the end of the infinitive: **-ai**, **-as**, **-a**, **-ons**, **-ez**, or **-ont**.

parler (*to talk*)	
je parler**ai**	nous parler**ons**
tu parler**as**	vous parler**ez**
il/elle/on parler**a**	ils/elles parler**ont**
Je te **parlerai** demain. (*I'll talk to you tomorrow.*)	

Spelling-change verbs like **commencer** (*to begin*) and **manger** (*to eat*) have no spelling change in the future tense. Just take the infinitive and add the appropriate future ending.

commencer (*to begin*)	
je commenc**erai**	nous commenc**erons**
tu commenc**eras**	vous commenc**erez**
il/elle/on commenc**era**	ils/elles commenc**eront**
Nous **commencerons** dans cinq minutes. (*We'll begin in five minutes.*)	

Regular **-ir** verbs also use their infinitives as the future stem. Just add the appropriate ending: **-ai**, **-as**, **-a**, **-ons**, **-ez**, or **-ont**.

finir (*to finish*)	
je finir**ai**	nous finir**ons**
tu finir**as**	vous finir**ez**
il/elle/on finir**a**	ils/elles finir**ont**
Ils **finiront** bientôt. (*They'll finish soon.*)	

For regular **-re** verbs, drop the final **-e** from the infinitive before adding the future ending: **-ai**, **-as**, **-a**, **-ons**, **-ez**, or **-ont**.

vendre (*to sell*)	
je vendr**ai**	nous vendr**ons**
tu vendr**as**	vous vendr**ez**
il/elle/on vendr**a**	ils/elles vendr**ont**
Vendras-tu ta voiture ? (*Will you sell your car?*)	

Stem-changing verbs

Most stem-changing verbs need the same stem change in the future as they do in the present tense. (See Chapter 3 of Book III for conjugations of stem-changing verbs as well as lists of verbs in each category.) This section shows you how to create the future with different types of stem-changing verbs.

Verbs with -yer

Verbs that end in **-oyer** and **-uyer** have a required **y**-to-**i** stem change in all the future conjugations. So you take the infinitive, change the **y** to an **i**, and add the future ending: **-ai**, **-as**, **-a**, **-ons**, **-ez**, or **-ont**.

employer (*to use*)	
j'emploier**ai**	nous emploier**ons**
tu emploier**as**	vous emploier**ez**
il/elle/on emploier**a**	ils/elles emploier**ont**
Nous **emploierons** notre argent. (*We'll use our money.*)	

However, there are exceptions to this rule. The stem-changing verbs **envoyer** (*to send*) and **renvoyer** (*to fire, to send back*) have irregular future stems: **enverr-** and **renverr-**. Just take these irregular stems and add the appropriate ending.

envoyer (*to send*)	
j'enverr**ai**	nous enverr**ons**
tu enverr**as**	vous enverr**ez**
il/elle/on enverr**a**	ils/elles enverr**ont**
Elle **enverra** la lettre. (*She'll send the letter.*)	

Verbs that end in **-ayer** have an optional **y**-to-**i** stem change in the future. There's absolutely no difference between these two conjugations — they're equally acceptable, though you should be consistent. So for example, you may use the infinitive **payer** or the stem-changed infinitive **paier** and add the ending **-ai**, **-as**, **-a**, **-ons**, **-ez**, or **-ont**.

payer (*to pay*)	
je payer**ai**/paier**ai**	nous payer**ons**/paier**ons**
tu payer**as**/paier**as**	vous payer**ez**/paier**ez**
il/elle/on payer**a**/paier**a**	ils/elles payer**ont**/paier**ont**
Je **payerai/paierai** demain. (*I'll pay tomorrow.*)	

Verbs with double consonants

Verbs that end in **-eler** need a double **l** in the future, so the future stem for **appeler** is **appeller-**. Just add the ending **-ai**, **-as**, **-a**, **-ons**, **-ez**, or **-ont**.

appeler (*to call*)	
j'appeller**ai**	nous appeller**ons**
tu appeller**as**	vous appeller**ez**
il/elle/on appeller**a**	ils/elles appeller**ont**
Il **appellera** Marc. (*He'll call Marc.*)	

Verbs that end in **-eter** double the **t** for the future stem, making the future stem for **jeter** (*to throw*) **jetter-**, to which you add the ending **-ai**, **-as**, **-a**, **-ons**, **-ez**, or **-ont**.

jeter (*to throw*)	
je jetter**ai**	nous jetter**ons**
tu jetter**as**	vous jetter**ez**
il/elle/on jetter**a**	ils/elles jetter**ont**
Ils **jetteront** la balle de tennis. (*They'll throw the tennis ball.*)	

Verbs with accent changes

Verbs that end in **-e*er** (see Chapter 3 of Book III) need an **accent grave** on the first **e** for the future stem, so **mener** becomes **mèner-**, and then you add the future ending **-ai**, **-as**, **-a**, **-ons**, **-ez**, or **-ont**.

mener (*to lead*)	
je mèner**ai**	nous mèner**ons**
tu mèner**as**	vous mèner**ez**
il/elle/on mèner**a**	ils/elles mèner**ont**
Je **mènerai** l'enquête. (*I'll lead the investigation.*)	

The only stem-changing verbs that don't have a stem-change in the future are **-é*er** verbs, such as **gérer** (*to manage*). You keep the **accent aigu** on the first **e** and just add the future ending to the infinitive to get the future tense.

gérer (*to manage*)	
je gérer**ai**	nous gérer**ons**
tu géreras	vous gérer**ez**
il/elle/on gérera	ils/elles gérer**ont**
Vous **gérerez** la crise. (*You'll handle the crisis.*)	

Irregular verbs

Irregular verbs can make the future a bit interesting, but everything works out in the end. Many irregular verbs follow the same future conjugation rules as regular verbs, but other irregular verbs have irregular stems. Either way, all these verbs take the same future endings. This section points out how to conjugate irregular verbs in the future tense.

Aller

The only irregular **-er** verb, **aller** (*to go*), has an irregular future stem: **ir-**. Start with that stem and add the appropriate ending: **-ai**, **-as**, **-a**, **-ons**, **-ez**, or **-ont**.

aller (*to go*)	
j'ir**ai**	nous ir**ons**
tu ir**as**	vous ir**ez**
il/elle/on ir**a**	ils/elles ir**ont**
J'**irai** à la banque demain. (*I'll go to the bank tomorrow.*)	

Irregular -ir verbs

Like the regular **-ir** verbs, most irregular **-ir** verbs, including **sortir** (*to go out*), **ouvrir** (*to open*), and all verbs conjugated like them (see Chapter 3 of Book III), use their infinitives as the future stem. No need to change anything — just add the appropriate future ending.

sortir (*to go out*)	
je sortir**ai**	nous sortir**ons**
tu sortir**as**	vous sortir**ez**
il/elle/on sortir**a**	ils/elles sortir**ont**
Nous **sortirons** ce soir. (*We'll go out tonight.*)	

A few irregular **-ir** verbs have irregular future stems. To form the future tense, take the stems in Table 6-1 and add the ending: **-ai**, **-as**, **-a**, **-ons**, **-ez**, or **-ont**.

Table 6-1	Irregular Future Stems on -ir Verbs
Infinitive	*Future Stem*
avoir (*to have*)	**aur-**
devoir (*to have to*)	**devr-**
mourir (*to die*)	**mourr-**
pleuvoir (*to rain*)	**pleuvr-**
pouvoir (*to be able to*)	**pourr-**
recevoir (*to receive*)	**recevr-**
savoir (*to know*)	**saur-**
tenir (*to hold*)	**tiendr-**
valoir (*to be worth*)	**vaudr-**
venir (*to come*)	**viendr-**
voir (*to see*)	**verr-**
vouloir (*to want*)	**voudr-**

For example, here's what **avoir** (*to have*) looks like in the future tense.

avoir (*to have*)	
j'aur**ai**	nous aur**ons**
tu aur**as**	vous aur**ez**
il/elle/on aur**a**	ils/elles aur**ont**
Elle **aura** beaucoup d'argent. (*She'll have a lot of money.*)	

Irregular -re verbs

Most irregular **-re** verbs, like the regular **-re** verbs, use the infinitive forms minus **-e** as the future stems. This set of verbs includes **prendre** (*to take*), **mettre** (*to put*), **craindre** (*to fear*), and all verbs conjugated like them.

Book IV

Getting
Down to
Detail and
Precision
in Your
Communication

prendre (*to take*)	
je prendr**ai**	nous prendr**ons**
tu prendr**as**	vous prendr**ez**
il/elle/on prendr**a**	ils/elles prendr**ont**
Vous **prendrez** des photos. (*You'll take some pictures.*)	

Two irregular **-re** verbs have irregular future stems. The future stem for **être** is **ser-**, and the future stem for **faire** is **fer-**. To form the future, just take the stem and add the appropriate ending: **-ai**, **-as**, **-a**, **-ons**, **-ez**, or **-ont**.

être (*to be*)	
je ser**ai**	nous ser**ons**
tu ser**as**	vous ser**ez**
il/elle/on ser**a**	ils/elles ser**ont**
Tu **seras** en retard. (*You'll be late.*)	

faire (*to do, make*)	
je fer**ai**	nous fer**ons**
tu fer**as**	vous fer**ez**
il/elle/on fer**a**	ils/elles fer**ont**
Nous **ferons** le lit. (*We'll make the bed.*)	

Looking Ahead with the Future Tense

Say you're writing an e-mail to your best friend in Nice and you want to talk about what's going to happen next Sunday, such as the launch of your 80-day trip around the globe. In that case, you use the future tense to let her know whether you'll cross the Atlantic Ocean by boat or hot-air balloon. After you master how to conjugate the future tense (see the previous sections), you can use this tense to talk about when you'll be doing something in the future:

Je ferai la lessive plus tard. (*I'll do the laundry later.*)

Nous voyagerons en France dans deux semaines. (*We'll travel to France in two weeks.*)

In French, you also use the future tense after certain conjunctions when they indicate something that's going to happen in the future, even though you use the present tense for the corresponding expressions in English. Those conjunctions include the following:

- **après que** (*after*)
- **aussitôt que** (*as soon as*)
- **dès que** (*as soon as*)
- **lorsque** (*when*)
- **quand** (*when*)

For example, you may say the following:

> **Je te téléphonerai quand j'arriverai à l'hôtel.** (*I'll call you when I arrive at the hotel.*)

> **Il le fera dès qu'il finira son travail.** (*He'll do it as soon as he finishes his work.*)

You use the present tense after these expressions in English, but in French, the future is required because the action after the expression hasn't yet occurred.

You can also use the future tense to talk about something that will happen in the future if a certain condition is met. ***Remember:*** The condition after **si** (*if*) has to be in the present tense; you use the future tense only in the main clause:

> **J'irai en France si tu viens avec moi.** (*I'll go to France if you come with me.*)

> **Si tu viens chez moi, nous regarderons le film ensemble.** (*If you come to my house, we'll watch the movie together.*)

You can also give polite requests using the future tense. Using the future tense is more polite than using the imperative, making the statement more of a request than a demand. (See Chapter 4 of Book III for information on giving orders in French.)

> **Vous me suivrez, s'il vous plaît.** (*Follow me, please.*)

Book IV

Getting Down to Detail and Precision in Your Communication

Talking about the Near Future in Other Ways

The future tense can have a slightly formal feel to it. If you want to lighten your conversation and make it a bit less formal, you can talk about the future in a couple of other ways, especially if you're discussing something that will happen soon (like what you'll do to your little brother if he changes the channel *one more time*). This section helps you add a little casualness to your words when referring to the future.

Making the future into a present

In both French and English, you can use the present tense to talk about something that's in the future. When you're going to do something in just a few minutes or in the next few days, the present tense helps bring that event just a little closer. It's slightly less formal than the future:

Je vais à la plage demain. (*I'm going to the beach tomorrow.*)

Nous partons dans dix minutes. (*We're leaving in ten minutes.*)

Where there's a will, there's a vais: Using the futur proche

You can talk about the near future with the present tense of **aller** + the infinitive. This **futur proche** (*near future*) construction is equivalent to *to be going to do something* in English. Like the present tense, the **futur proche** is just slightly informal. It's become the tense of choice in conversation to refer to what's going to happen soon and even what will happen in the distant future.

Here's the verb **travailler** (*to work*) in the **futur proche**.

travailler (*to work*)	
je **vais travailler**	nous **allons travailler**
tu **vas travailler**	vous **allez travailler**
il/elle/on **va travailler**	ils/elles **vont travailler**
Il **va travailler** pendant toute la journée. (*He's going to work all day.*)	

Here's another example of the **futur proche**:

> **Alexandre et Laurent vont être déçus.** (*Alexandre and Laurent are going to be disappointed.*)

With reflexive verbs (see Chapter 3 of Book IV), the reflexive pronoun goes in front of the infinitive:

> **Nous allons nous promener sur la plage.** (*We're going to walk on the beach.*)

> **Vas-tu t'habiller ?** (*Are you going to get dressed?*)

Object and adverbial pronouns, such as **le** (*it/him*), **la** (*it/her*), **lui** (*to him/her*), **leur** (*to them*), **y** (*there*), and **en** (*some of it/them*), also precede the infinitive:

> **Je vais le faire demain.** (*I'm going to do it tomorrow.*)

> **Ils vont en avoir envie.** (*They're going to want some.*)

You can read more about word order with pronouns in Chapter 3 of Book IV.

Setting the Mood with Conditional Conjugations

The present conditional helps you hypothesize about events that aren't guaranteed to take place. You use it to express a sense of possibility or to say that you'd do something if something else were to occur. The "something else" is either stated with an *if* clause or just implied.

Conjugating verbs in the present conditional

The present tense of the conditional mood uses the exact same stem as the simple future. When you compare the simple future and present conditional, only the endings are different.

To conjugate a verb in the present conditional, you usually just take the infinitive of an **-er** or **-ir** verb, or the infinitive minus **-e** of an **-re** verb, and add the appropriate ending: **-ais**, **-ais**, **-ait**, **-ions**, **-iez**, or **-aient**. Check out the earlier section "The Infinitive and Beyond: Conjugating the Futur" for info on the stems of stem-changing and irregular verbs.

The conditional stem for all verbs — regular, stem-changing, spelling-change, and irregular — always ends in **r**.

Regular **-er** verbs use their infinitive as the conditional stem, so the regular **-er** verb **parler** looks like the following in the conditional. The stem is **parler-**, and the endings are **-ais**, **-ais**, **-ait**, **-ions**, **-iez**, and **-aient**.

parler (*to talk*)	
je parler**ais**	nous parler**ions**
tu parler**ais**	vous parler**iez**
il/elle/on parler**ait**	ils/elles parler**aient**
Je **parlerais** plus lentement. (*I would speak more slowly.*)	

Here are some example sentences with verbs in the present conditional:

Cette robe t'irait bien. (*This dress would suit you well.*)

Laquelle choisirais-tu à ma place ? (*Which one would you choose in my place?*)

Ils voudraient vendre leur maison. (*They would like to sell their house.*)

Tu aurais encore de l'énergie après une si longue promenade ? (*Would you have any energy left after such a long walk?*)

The verbs **pouvoir** (*to be able to/can*), **vouloir** (*to want*), and **devoir** (*to have to/must*) have special meanings in the present conditional. You can't just translate their conjugated forms as *would* + infinitive. Conjugated in the conditional, **pouvoir** translates as *could* (*would be able to*), **vouloir** translates as *would like,* and **devoir** translates as *should:*

Elle pourrait t'accompagner. (*She could [would be able to] accompany you.*)

Voudriez-vous venir dîner ? (*Would you like to come for dinner?*)

Les enfants devraient se coucher. (*The children should go to bed.*)

Je voudrais (*I would like*) is a handy phrase for making reservations, ordering tickets, or telling the server at the restaurant that you'd like a ham and cheese sandwich. Check out Chapter 2 of Book II for details on dining out and making reservations.

Getting the hang of si clauses: If only

As the name indicates, the *conditional mood* usually involves a condition — it tells you that something would or could happen only if something else does or does not happen. The "if something happens" part is an *if* clause.

Hand in hand: Using the conditional and the imparfait

You use the conditional most commonly with **si** (*if*) clauses or in *if-then* statements. The conditional goes in the *then* clause. Here are the tenses and moods you use in each part of the sentence:

✔ The **si** clause, which is the *if* clause describing the condition, uses the **imparfait** tense. This tense is a past tense used for description and for regular occurrences. (See Chapter 2 of Book V.)

✔ The main clause — the *then* part — uses the present tense of the conditional mood.

For example, if a friend asks you to go France with him but you can go only if you find a babysitter, you use the conditional to respond to the invitation:

J'irais en France si je trouvais un babysitter. (*I would go to France if I found a babysitter.*) Here, **irais** is in the conditional and **trouvais** is in the **imparfait**.

Or say you want to buy a car, but whether you can buy a new or used one depends on how much money you earn. Although you're hoping for a raise, you're not sure you'll get it. Here's what you may say:

J'achèterais une nouvelle voiture si j'obtenais une augmentation de salaire. (*I would buy a new car if I got a raise.*) The verb **achèterais** is in the conditional and **obtenais** is in the **imparfait**.

Note that the present conditional endings and the **imparfait** endings are the same: **-ais, -ais, -ait, -ions, -iez,** or **-aient.** Only the stems differ. The conditional stem is usually the infinitive, and the **imparfait** stem is usually the present-tense **nous** form minus **-ons.**

Book IV

Getting Down to Detail and Precision in Your Communication

Putting if clauses in the present tense

An *if-then* statement with the conditional and **imparfait** indicates an unlikely situation. When you talk about something that is more likely to occur, you don't use the conditional. Instead, you use the present tense in the **si**/*if* clause and the present or future in the *then* clause. So if you think there's a pretty good chance that you'll get that raise, you can say this:

> **J'achèterai une nouvelle voiture si j'obtiens une augmentation de salaire.** (*I'll buy a new car if I get a raise.*) Here, **achèterai** is in the future and **obtiens** is in the present.

In English, you can sometimes use the conditional after *if,* as in *If you would like to go* or *I don't know if I should go.* You can't do this in French — the French conditional can't follow the word **si** (*if*) — you have to use the present tense instead:

> **Si vous voulez manger avec nous, vous devez vous laver les mains.** (*If you would like to eat with us, you have to wash your hands.*)

> **Je ne sais pas si je dois y aller.** (*I don't know if I should go.*)

Interpreting "would": Distinguishing between the conditional and the habitual

In English, you can use *would* in the sense of *used to* in talking about something habitual in the past, as in *When I lived in Paris, I would go to the bakery every day.* You can't use the French conditional here — this English construction is equivalent to the French **imparfait**: **Quand j'habitais à Paris, j'allais à la boulangerie tous les jours**. You can read about the **imparfait** in Chapter 2 of Book V.

Book V
Going Back in Time

"Here's an idea, let's practice conjugating verbs
in French. Last night, you 'as bu beaucoup
de vin.' But this morning, you 'bois beaucoup
de Pepto Bismol.'"

In this book . . .

Although staying current with the present and preparing for the future are important, questioning and explaining the past is equally worthwhile. What you did a short while ago or last week impacts now and tomorrow. This book tells you how to narrate, explain, and question past occurrences. In addition, we show you how to navigate various conversational past tenses: the **passé proche** (*near past*) for things that just happened, the **passé composé** (*compound past*) for things that took place and were completed at specific moments, and the **imparfait** (*imperfect*) for things that were happening for an indefinite period of time or on a regular basis. You also look over tenses that preceded other actions that are either past or future (**plus-que-parfait**, or *pluperfect,* and **futur antérieur**, or *future perfect*) and go over the **passé du conditionnel** (*past conditional*), which helps you talk about what could have happened but didn't.

Here are the contents of Book V at a glance:

Chapter 1

Been There, Done That: Passé Proche and Passé Composé

*W*hen you want to say that something just happened, you need the **passé proche** (*near past*). This tense uses the verb **venir** (*to come*) followed by the preposition **de** and an infinitive verb. However, when you want to tell someone what you've accomplished, where you've been, and whom you met yesterday, last week, last month, or even years ago, then you need the **passé composé**. This tense recounts events that were completed at a specific time in the past. The **passé composé** is conjugated with an auxiliary verb — either **avoir** or **être** — plus the past participle. This chapter explains all about auxiliary verbs and how to say you just did something or that you did something at a precise point of time.

We cover other ways to talk about the past in the next two chapters. Chapter 2 of Book V covers what used to happen, and Chapter 3 of Book V covers what had happened, would have happened, or will have happened.

Just Finished: Creating the Near Past Tense

When you want to emphasize that something just occurred, form the near past tense with the following:

✔ The verb **venir** conjugated in the present tense

✔ The preposition **de**

✔ An infinitive verb

Venir by itself means *to come,* but when it's followed by **de** + infinitive, it means *to have just done something.* The following table shows the verb **acheter** (*to buy*) in the near past tense.

acheter (*to buy*)	
je **viens d'acheter**	nous **venons d'acheter**
tu **viens d'acheter**	vous **venez d'acheter**
il/elle/on **vient d'acheter**	ils/elles **viennent d'acheter**
Nous **venons d'acheter** les billets. (*We just bought the tickets.*)	

To construct the immediate past with reflexive verbs, just place the reflexive pronoun before the infinitive, like so (check out Chapter 3 of Book IV for details on reflexive verbs):

Je viens de me réveiller. (*I just woke up.*)

Elle vient de se coucher. (*She has just gone to bed.*)

To make the immediate past negative, simply place **ne** before the conjugated verb (**venir**) and put **pas** (or any other negative word you want to use) after the conjugated verb:

Ils ne viennent pas de manger ? (*Didn't they just eat?*)

Explaining What Happened: Forming the Passé Composé

The **passé composé** is a compound tense that has three meanings in English. **J'ai parlé**, for example, means *I spoke, I have spoken,* and *I did speak.* Here's how to form the **passé composé**:

- ✔ Conjugate the auxiliary verb in the present tense
- ✔ Add the past participle

The French language has only two auxiliary verbs for the **passé composé**: **avoir** (*to have*) and **être** (*to be*). Most verbs take the auxiliary **avoir**; however, certain verbs take **être**, especially those that express motion, such as **aller** (*to go*), **partir** (*to leave*), and **venir** (*to come*).

Sounds simple enough, right? In this section, we start with verbs that take **avoir** as their auxiliary (we cover the other verbs later in "Creating the Passé Composé with Être"). See the following table for a review of **avoir** in the present tense, and read on for info on forming past participles and sorting out agreement.

avoir (to have)	
j'**ai**	nous **avons**
tu **as**	vous **avez**
il/elle/on **a**	ils/elles **ont**

Creating past participles

To form the **passé composé**, you take the present tense of the auxiliary verb and add the appropriate past participle. This section explains how to form the past participles of regular and irregular verbs.

Past participles of regular verbs

Here's how to form the past participles of regular verbs:

- ✔ **Regular -er verbs:** To form the past participle of a regular **-er** verb, such as **parler** (*to speak*), simply drop the **-er** and add an **-é**, like so: **parlé**.

  Even verbs with spelling changes in the present tense, such as **jeter** (*to throw*), **acheter** (*to buy*), **essayer** (*to try*), and **espérer** (*to hope*), have regular past participles: **jeté**, **acheté**, **essayé**, and **espéré**. (See Chapter 3 of Book III for info on spelling-change verbs.)

- ✔ **Regular -ir verbs:** For the regular **-ir** verbs, such as **finir** (*to finish*), simply drop the **-r**, and voilà: **fini**.

- ✔ **Regular -re verbs:** Regular **-re** verbs, like **vendre** (*to sell*), drop the **-re** and add a **-u**: **vendu**.

The following tables show three regular verbs conjugated in the **passé composé** (a present-tense auxiliary verb + the past participle). Note that each verb has **avoir** as its auxiliary.

parler (*to speak*)	
j'**ai parlé**	nous **avons parlé**
tu **as parlé**	vous **avez parlé**
il/elle/on **a parlé**	ils/elles **ont parlé**
Nous **avons parlé** aux enfants. (*We spoke/have spoken/did speak to the children.*)	

finir (*to finish*)	
j'**ai fini**	nous **avons fini**
tu **as fini**	vous **avez fini**
il/elle/on **a fini**	ils/elles **ont fini**
Elle **a fini** ses devoirs. (*She finished/has finished/did finish her homework.*)	

vendre (*to sell*)	
j'**ai vendu**	nous **avons vendu**
tu **as vendu**	vous **avez vendu**
il/elle/on **a vendu**	ils/elles **ont vendu**
Les étudiants **ont vendu** leurs livres. (*The students sold/have sold/did sell their books.*)	

Past participles of irregular verbs

Many French verbs have an irregular past participle. Usually, if a verb is irregular in the present tense (see Chapter 3 of Book III), then it also has an irregular past participle.

However, irregular verbs that follow the same conjugation pattern as **partir** (*to leave*) have regular past participles. These verbs include **sortir** (*to go out*), **dormir** (*to sleep*), **mentir** (*to lie*), and **servir** (*to serve*). For the **-ir** verbs like **partir**, just drop the **-r**. Similarly, **aller** (*to go*) has a regular past participle: Just drop the **-er** and add **-é**.

In the following tables, we've grouped the verbs with irregular past participles according to their endings. Many irregular verbs (those ending in **-oir**, **-re**, or **-ir**) have a past participle that ends in **u** — see Table 1-1.

Table 1-1	Irregular Verbs and Their Past Participles Ending in u
Infinitive	*Past Participle*
apercevoir (*to see, to perceive*)	**aperçu**
appartenir (*to belong to*)	**appartenu**
avoir (*to have*)	**eu**
battre (*to beat*)	**battu**
boire (*to drink*)	**bu**
connaître (*to know*)	**connu**
convaincre (*to convince*)	**convaincu**
courir (*to run*)	**couru**
croire (*to believe*)	**cru**
décevoir (to disappoint)	**déçu**
devenir (*to become*)	**devenu**
devoir (*to owe, to have to*)	**dû**
falloir (*to be necessary, to have to*)	**fallu**
lire (*to read*)	**lu**
paraître (*to appear*)	**paru**
plaire (*to please*)	**plu**
pleuvoir (*to rain*)	**plu**
pouvoir (*to be able to*)	**pu**
recevoir (*to receive*)	**reçu**
revenir (*to come back*)	**revenu**
savoir (*to know*)	**su**
tenir (*to hold*)	**tenu**
venir (*to come*)	**venu**
vivre (*to live*)	**vécu**
voir (*to see*)	**vu**
vouloir (*to want*)	**voulu**

Some past participles end in **t**. Table 1-2 shows some of those verbs along with their past participles.

Table 1-2   Irregular Verbs and Their Past Participles Ending in t

Infinitive	Past Participle
conduire (*to drive*)	**conduit**
construire (*to construct, to build*)	**construit**
couvrir (*to cover*)	**couvert**
dire (*to say*)	**dit**
écrire (*to write*)	**écrit**
faire (*to do, to make*)	**fait**
inscrire (*to note, to write down*)	**inscrit**
offrir (*to offer*)	**offert**
ouvrir (*to open*)	**ouvert**
souffrir (*to suffer*)	**souffert**

Table 1-3 lists some irregular verbs whose past participles end in **s**. Note the pattern for verbs that end in **-mettre** or **-prendre**.

Table 1-3   Irregular Verbs and Their Past Participles Ending in s

Infinitive	Past Participle
mettre (*to put, to place*)	**mis**
admettre (*to admit*)	**admis**
prendre (*to take*)	**pris**
apprendre (*to learn*)	**appris**

Some past participles of irregular verbs end in **i**. See Table 1-4.

Table 1-4   Irregular Verbs and Their Past Participles Ending in i

Infinitive	Past Participle
rire (*to laugh*)	**ri**
sourire (*to smile*)	**souri**
suivre (*to follow, to take a course*)	**suivi**

Table 1-5 shows four other irregular verbs whose past participles you're likely to encounter.

Table 1-5	Other Irregular Verbs and Their Past Participles
Infinitive	*Past Participle*
avoir (*to have*)	**eu**
être (*to be*)	**été**
mourir (*to die*)	**mort**
naître (*to be born*)	**né**

Making past participles agree with direct objects

If a verb is conjugated in the **passé composé** with the auxiliary **avoir** and there happens to be a direct object before that verb, then the past participle needs to agree with the direct object. Make the following changes to the past participle, depending on the direct object's gender and number:

- If the preceding direct object is masculine singular, then leave the past participle alone.
- If it's feminine singular, add an **-e** to the past participle.
- If it's masculine plural, add an **-s** to the past participle.
- If it's feminine plural, add an **-es** to the past participle.

Check out the following example to see how the past participle can change:

> **J'ai mis les fleurs dans le vase.** (*I put the flowers in the vase.*) In this example, the past participle doesn't need to agree because the direct object, **les fleurs**, comes after the verb.

> **Je les ai mises dans le vase.** (*I put them in the vase.*) Here you replace the direct object **les fleurs**, which is feminine plural, with the direct-object pronoun **les**. Because the direct object now comes before the verb, you have to make the past participle **mis** agree with **les** (feminine plural) by adding **-e** for feminine and **-s** for plural; therefore, the past participle is spelled **mises**.

Here's another example:

> **Il a vu Nicole.** (*He saw Nicole.*) The direct object **Nicole** comes after the verb, so the past participle **vu** doesn't need to agree with it.

Il l'a vue. (*He saw her.*) To replace the direct object **Nicole**, which is feminine singular, with the direct object pronoun **la**, which means *her*, place the direct-object pronoun **la** before the verb (**la** contracts to **l'** because it's before a vowel). Then make the past participle **vu** agree with **l'** (feminine singular) by adding **e** to it; therefore, it's spelled **vue.**

Table 1-6 lists direct-object pronouns always placed before the verb, except in the affirmative imperative (commands to do something).

Drop the vowel of **me**, **te**, **le**, and **la** and add an apostrophe when the verb begins with a vowel or a mute **h**. In the **passé composé** when the auxiliary is **avoir**, this is always the case.

Table 1-6	Direct-Object Pronouns
French Pronoun	*English Equivalent*
me (m')	*me*
te (t')	*you*
le (l')	*him/it*
la (l')	*her/it*
nous	*us*
vous	*you*
les	*them*

The pronouns **me**, **te**, **nous**, and **vous** sometimes act as indirect objects instead of direct objects, so be careful — the past participle that follows the auxiliary **avoir** must agree with these pronouns only if they're direct objects. Look at the following sentences in the **passé composé** and notice where the past participle agrees:

Le travail, nous l'avons fini. (*The work, we finished it.*) — agrees with **le** (which refers to **le travail**)

La robe, nous l'avons finie. (*The dress, we finished it.*) — agrees with **la** (which refers to **la robe**)

Ils m'ont prévenu(e). (*They warned me.*) — agrees with **me**

Il nous a téléphoné. (*He called us.*) — does not agree

Remember that indirect objects mean *to/for someone*. To figure out whether the pronouns are direct or indirect objects of the verb, reason it out as follows: In the sentence **Ils m'ont prévenue** (*They warned me*), the verb **prévenir** is in the **passé composé** and follows the auxiliary verb **avoir**. Try rewriting the sentence to include a name instead of the pronoun **me**. For example, ask yourself whether the verb **prévenir** introduces a person like Jean directly or with the preposition **à**. In other words, is the sentence saying **Ils ont prévenu à Jean** or **Ils ont prévenu Jean**? The fact that the correct sentence is **Ils ont prévenu Jean** — without **à** — indicates that the verb **prévenir** introduces a direct object; therefore **me (m')** is a direct object. The past participle **prévenu** must agree with **me (m')** in this sentence. If you're male, the past participle remains the same, but if you're female, it takes an **e**.

In the sentence **Il nous a téléphoné** (*He called us*), the verb **téléphoner** is in the **passé composé** and follows the auxiliary verb **avoir**. Ask yourself whether the verb **téléphoner** introduces a person like Jean directly or with the preposition **à**. In other words, is the sentence **Il téléphone à Jean** or **Il téléphone Jean**? The fact that the correct sentence is **Il téléphone à Jean** indicates that the verb **téléphoner** introduces an indirect object; therefore, **nous** is an indirect object. The past participle **téléphoné** doesn't agree with **nous** (plural) in this sentence.

To check whether a verb is followed by **à**, look at a dictionary or see Chapter 1 of Book IV.

Creating the Passé Composé with Être

Some specific verbs, such as verbs of motion, are intransitive and take the auxiliary verb **être** (*to be*). An *intransitive verb* is one that isn't followed by a direct object. To form the **passé composé** with these verbs, conjugate the verb **être** in the present tense and add the past participle of the verb you want:

> **Il est arrivé à 9 heures.** (*He arrived at 9 o'clock.*)

> **Elle est montée dans sa chambre.** (*She went up to her room.*)

Note that with **être** verbs, the past participle agrees in gender and number with the subject.

See the following table for a review of **être** in the present tense. Then read on for info on which verbs take **être** in the **passé composé** and how to make past participles agree.

être (*to be*)	
je **suis**	nous **sommes**
tu **es**	vous **êtes**
il/elle/on **est**	ils/elles **sont**

Knowing which verbs take être

TIP

To remember which verbs take the auxiliary verb **être** in the **passé composé** (and other compound tenses), visualize the **Maison d'être,** or *House of Être* (see Figure 5-1). Picture a huge door and an elegant staircase. Many of the verbs that take **être** are what we call "door" verbs. You can *go, come, return, enter, arrive,* and *pass* through the door in the House of **Être**. What about the staircase? You can *go up* or *go down,* and if you aren't careful, you can *fall.* Now think of the house as your world and of **naître** and **mourir** as coming into and leaving that world, and you will have a visual image of all **être** verbs. The French equivalents of all these verbs take **être**.

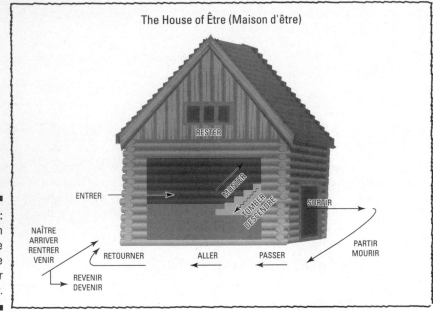

The House of Être (Maison d'être)

RESTER

MONTER

ENTRER

TOMBER
DESCENDRE

SORTIR

NAÎTRE
ARRIVER
RENTRER
VENIR

RETOURNER   ALLER   PASSER

PARTIR
MOURIR

REVENIR
DEVENIR

Figure 1-1: Verbs in the House of **Être** use **être** as their auxiliary.

Illustration by Wiley, Composition Services Graphics

Table 1-7 shows the verbs that use **être** when forming the **passé composé** along with the past participles of these verbs. The verbs marked with an asterisk can take either **avoir** or **être**. They take the auxiliary **avoir** when they're followed by a direct object and **être** when they aren't. We further explain the difference in the later section "Flexible Verbs: Using Either Avoir or Être"

Besides the verbs in the House of Être, all reflexive verbs use **être** as their auxiliary. See the later section "Understanding agreement with pronominal verbs" for details.

Table 1-7	Past Participles of the Verbs in the House of Être
Infinitive	*Past Participle*
aller (*to go*)	**allé**
arriver (*to arrive*)	**arrivé**
descendre* (*to go down stairs, to descend*)	**descendu**
devenir (*to become*)	**devenu**
entrer (*to enter*)	**entré**
monter* (*to go up stairs, to climb*)	**monté**
mourir (*to die*)	**mort**
naître (*to be born*)	**né**
partir (*to leave*)	**parti**
passer* (*to pass, to spend*)	**passé**
rentrer* (*to come back home*)	**rentré**
rester (*to stay*)	**resté**
retourner* (*to return*)	**retourné**
revenir (*to come back*)	**revenu**
sortir* (*to go out*)	**sorti**
tomber (*to fall*)	**tombé**
venir (*to come*)	**venu**

Making the subject and past participle agree

The past participles of **être** verbs usually agree with the subject. If the subject is masculine singular, leave the past participle alone. Otherwise, add **-e** to make the participle feminine, **-s** to make it masculine plural, or **-es** to make it feminine plural.

Look at the verb **partir** (*to leave*) conjugated in the **passé composé**. You conjugate **être** in the present tense, add the past partciple **parti** (the infinitive **partir** minus **-r**), and make the participle agree with the subject.

partir (*to leave*)	
je **suis parti(e)**	nous **sommes parti(s/es)**
tu **es parti(e)**	vous êtes **parti(e/s/es)**
il/elle/on **est parti(e)**	ils/elles **sont parti(s/es)**
Phillipe et moi, nous **sommes partis** à midi. (*We left at noon.*)	

Understanding agreement with pronominal verbs

All pronominal verbs — verbs that take reflexive pronouns — take **être** as their auxiliary in the **passé composé**. However, the past participle follows that same rule of agreement as the verbs taking **avoir**: The past participle agrees with the preceding direct object if the sentence has one. Read on for details on agreement. (For more info on reflexive pronouns and pronominal verbs, flip to Chapter 3 of Book IV.)

Agreeing with the reflexive pronoun

In most sentences with pronominal verbs, the reflexive pronoun (which corresponds to the subject) acts as the direct object. If this is the case, add **-e** to the past participle if the pronoun is feminine, **-s** if it's plural, or **-es** if it's feminine plural.

The following example conjugates **se coucher** (*to go to bed*) in the **passé composé**.

se coucher (*to go to bed*)	
je **me suis couché(e)**	nous **nous sommes couché(s/es)**
tu **t'es couché(e)**	vous **vous êtes couché(e/s/es)**
il/elle/on **s'est couché(e)**	ils/elles **se sont couché(s/es)**
Les filles **se sont couchées** à dix heures. (*The girls went to bed at 10 o'clock.*)	

Avoiding agreement with other direct objects

If the sentence has a direct object other than the reflexive pronoun, then the reflexive pronoun is an indirect object and the past participle doesn't have to agree with it. Take the verb **se laver** (*to wash oneself*). When the verb isn't followed by a direct object, the past participle agrees with the reflexive pronoun. However, when the same verb is followed by a direct object, the reflexive pronoun is acting as the indirect object and you don't have agreement. Check out the following examples:

Je **me suis lavé(e).** (*I washed myself.*)

Je **me suis lavé** les cheveux. (*I washed my hair.*)

Elle **s'est lavée.** (*She washed herself.*)

Elle **s'est lavé** les cheveux. (*She washed her hair.*)

Past participles don't agree with indirect objects. This rule applies to verbs taking the auxiliary **avoir** as well as to pronominal verbs. Table 1-8 shows the indirect-object pronouns.

Table 1-8	Indirect-Object Pronouns
French Pronoun	*English Equivalent*
me	*to me*
te	*to you*
se	*to himself/herself/themselves* (for pronominal verbs only)
lui	*to him/her*
nous	*to us*
vous	*to you*
leur	*to them*

Lui and **leur** are always indirect objects, but the reflexive pronouns **me, te, se, nous,** and **vous** can be direct- or indirect-object pronouns.

To figure out whether these pronouns are direct or indirect objects of the verb, reason it out as follows: In the sentence **Marie et Jean se sont parlé** (*Marie and Jean spoke to each other*), the verb **parler** is in the **passé composé** and in the reflexive form. It's conjugated with the auxiliary verb **être**. Ask yourself whether the verb **parler** introduces a person like Jean directly or with the preposition **à**. In other words, is the sentence saying **Marie parle à Jean** or **Marie parle Jean**? The fact that the correct sentence includes **à Jean** indicates that the verb **parler** introduces an indirect object; therefore, **se** is an indirect object, so the past participle **parlé** doesn't agree with **se** in this sentence.

In the sentence **Marie et Jean se sont regardés** (*Marie and Jean looked at each other*), the verb **regarder** is in the **passé composé** and in the reflexive form. It's conjugated with the auxiliary verb **être**. Ask yourself whether the verb **regarder** introduces a person like Jean directly or with the preposition **à**. In other words, would you say **Marie regarde à Jean** or **Marie regarde Jean**? The fact that the correct sentence is **Marie regarde Jean** indicates that the verb **regarder** introduces a direct object; therefore, **se** is the direct object, and the past participle **regardés** must agree with **se** (plural) in this sentence.

The following examples in the **passé composé** all have indirect objects rather than direct objects before the verbs, so the past participles don't agree:

> **Vous vous êtes dit au revoir.** (*You said goodbye to each other.*) **Dire à** is to say something to someone, so **vous** is an indirect object.

> **Ils se sont juré de toujours dire la vérité.** (*They swore each other to always tell the truth.*) **Jurer à** is to swear something to someone, so **se** is an indirect object.

> **Elle s'est rendu compte que la nuit tombait.** (*She realized that night was falling.*) Within the expression **se rendre compte** (*to account for something*), the word **compte** (the something to account for) is the direct object of **rendre**, so **s'** is an indirect object.

To check whether a French verb has to be followed by an indirect object (**à** + a person), see Chapter 1 of Book IV or use a dictionary.

Some pronominal verbs have reflexive pronouns that are always indirect-object pronouns. In this case, the past participle doesn't ever agree with the pronouns. Table 1-9 shows these verbs.

Table 1-9	Pronominal Verbs with Indirect-Object Pronouns
Verb	*Translation*
s'acheter	to buy for oneself or for each other
s'écrire	to write for oneself or to each other
se demander	to wonder
se dire	to say to oneself or to each other
se donner	to give to oneself or to each other
se parler	to speak to oneself or to each other
se promettre	to promise oneself or each other
se rendre compte de + [noun] se rendre compte que + [subject + verb]	to realize [something] to realize that [subject + verb]
se rendre visite	to visit each other
se ressembler	to look alike, to resemble each other
se sourire	to smile to oneself or at each other
se téléphoner	to call each other

Flexible Verbs: Using Either Avoir or Être

The verbs **descendre**, **monter**, **passer**, **rentrer**, **retourner**, and **sortir** can take either auxiliary — avoir or être in the **passé composé**. The choice depends on how you're using the verb. If the verb is followed by a direct object, then it's transitive and it takes **avoir** as its auxiliary. If it isn't followed by a direct object, then it's intransitive and takes **être** as its auxiliary. The verbs translate differently into English depending on your choice of auxiliary. See the examples in Table 1-10.

Table 1-10	Verbs That Take Either Auxiliary	
Verb	*Transitive (Avoir)*	*Intransitive (Être)*
passer	Elle **a passé** un examen. (*She took an exam.*)	Elle **est passée** par la bibliothèque. (*She passed by the library.*)
descendre	Elle **a descendu** les livres. (*She brought down the books.*)	Elle **est descendue** au sous-sol. (*She went down to the basement.*)
monter	Elle **a monté** la valise. (*She brought up the suitcase.*)	Elle **est montée** dans un taxi. (*She got in a taxi.*)
sortir	Elle **a sorti** le chien. (*She took out the dog.*)	Elle **est sortie** avec ses amis. (*She went out with her friends.*)
rentrer	Elle **a rentré** la voiture. (*She put the car in.*)	Elle **est rentrée** à minuit. (*She came home at midnight.*)
retourner	Elle **a retourné** les crêpes. (*She turned over the crepes.*)	Elle **est retournée** à son livre. (*She returned to her book/ reading.*)

Didn't Happen: Making the Passé Composé Negative

If you want to say that you didn't do something or you didn't go anywhere, you make the **passé composé** negative. Just place **ne** before the auxiliary, which is the conjugated verb, and **pas** after the auxiliary:

Je n'ai pas voyagé. (*I didn't travel.*)

Nous n'avons pas lu le journal. (*We didn't read the newspaper.*)

For pronominal verbs, the **ne** precedes not only the auxiliary verb but also the reflexive pronoun, and the **pas** follows the auxiliary:

Tu ne t'es pas couché(e). (*You didn't go to bed.*)

Nous ne nous sommes pas amusés. (*We didn't have fun.*)

Check Chapter 5 of Book III for more on negatives.

Chapter 2

How Was It? What Was Going On? The Imparfait

Do you ever get nostalgic about the past? Do you want to be able to say what you used to do when you were a child, to describe a wonderful family tradition, or to recall how blue the sky was on your favorite vacation and what feelings you experienced? Well, you can with the **imparfait** — the imperfect tense. You use the imperfect tense to describe a continuous or habitual action in the past, an action that you did a nonspecific number of times, or what things used to be like and how you felt.

Grammatically speaking, *perfect* means complete, and the **imparfait** tells you that an action wasn't completed — it was an ongoing state of being (*it was hot, I was hungry*) — or that something happened repeatedly (*I used to go to the beach every weekend*). You often use the **imparfait** in conjunction with the **passé composé** to describe some action (in the **imparfait**) that got interrupted by some other action (in the **passé composé**), as in *I was eating when you called.* (Check out Chapter 1 of Book V for details on the **passé composé**.)

This chapter explains how to conjugate regular and irregular verbs in the **imparfait** and how and when to use the **imparfait**. It also covers the difference between the **imparfait** and **passé composé** and how to use them together.

Conjugating the Imparfait

You conjugate virtually all verbs exactly the same way in the **imparfait**: You take the present-tense **nous** form of the verb, drop **-ons**, and add the **imparfait** endings: **-ais**, **-ais**, **-ait**, **-ions**, **-iez**, and **-aient**. These endings are the same for all verbs in the **imparfait**. This section shows how to conjugate all the different verb types — regular, stem-changing, spelling-change, and irregular — to illustrate how easy forming this tense is.

Regular verbs

To conjugate regular verbs in the **imparfait**, just find the present-tense **nous** form of the verb, drop **-ons**, and add the **imparfait** endings. The **nous** form of the regular **-er** verb **parler** (*to speak*) is **parlons**, so the stem is **parl-**. Then add **-ais**, **-ais**, **-ait**, **-ions**, **-iez**, or **-aient**. The conjugations for all regular **-er** verbs follow this pattern:

parler (*to speak*)	
je parl**ais**	nous parl**ions**
tu parl**ais**	vous parl**iez**
il/elle/on parl**ait**	ils/elles parl**aient**
Il **parlait** trop vite. (*He was speaking too quickly.*)	

The singular and third-person plural conjugated forms — which together make a boot shape in the chart — all sound identical. The subject pronoun lets you know who the subject is.

Verbs that end in **-ier**, like **étudier** (*to study*), can look a little strange in the **imparfait**. When you drop **-ons** from the **nous** form **étudions**, you find a stem than ends in **i**: **étudi-**. Because the **nous** and **vous imparfait** endings begin with **i**, you end up with a double **i** in those conjugations.

étudier (*to study*)	
j'étudi**ais**	nous étudi**ions**
tu étudi**ais**	vous étudi**iez**
il/elle/on étudi**ait**	ils/elles étudi**aient**
Nous **étudiions** hier soir. (*We were studying yesterday evening.*)	

The **nous** and **vous** forms of the **imparfait** end in **-ions** and **-iez** for all verbs: **nous parlions** (*we were talking*), **vous fermiez** (*you were closing*). But verbs that end in **-ier** also end in **-ions** and **-iez** in the present tense: **nous étudions** (*we study*), **vous skiez** (*you ski*). Therefore, the double **i** tells you that **-ier** verbs are in the **imparfait**: **nous étudiions** (*we were studying*), **vous skiiez** (*you were skiing*). You don't really hear this difference in speech, though.

The **nous** form of the regular **-ir** verb **finir** (*to finish*) is **finissons**, so the stem for all the **imparfait** conjugations is **finiss-**. Add the **imparfait** endings to the stem: **-ais**, **-ais**, **-ait**, **-ions**, **-iez**, and **-aient**.

finir (*to finish*)	
je finiss**ais**	nous finiss**ions**
tu finiss**ais**	vous finiss**iez**
il/elle/on finiss**ait**	ils/elles finiss**aient**
Elles **finissaient** leurs études au Canada. (*They were finishing their studies in Canada.*)	

Vendons is the **nous** form of the regular **-re** verb **vendre** (*to sell*), so the root is **vend-**. Here's **vendre** in the **imparfait**.

vendre (*to sell*)	
je vend**ais**	nous vend**ions**
tu vend**ais**	vous vend**iez**
il/elle/on vend**ait**	ils/elles vend**aient**
Je **vendais** ma voiture. (*I was selling my car.*)	

Stem-changing verbs

A stem-changing verb doesn't have a stem change in the **nous** form of the present tense, so the **imparfait** doesn't, either. The **nous** form of **payer** (*to pay*) is **payons**, so the stem is **pay-**. The **nous** form of **acheter** (*to buy*) is **achetons**, so the stem is **achet-**. To conjugate these verbs, add the **imparfait** endings to the stems: **-ais**, **-ais**, **-ait**, **-ions**, **-iez**, and **-aient**.

payer (*to pay*)	
je pay**ais**	nous pay**ions**
tu pay**ais**	vous pay**iez**
il/elle/on pay**ait**	ils/elles pay**aient**
Vous **payiez** trop. (*You were paying too much.*)	

acheter (*to buy*)	
j'achet**ais**	nous achet**ions**
tu achet**ais**	vous achet**iez**
il/elle/on achet**ait**	ils/elles achet**aient**
Tu **achetais** beaucoup de pain. (*You were buying a lot of bread.*)	

Spelling-change verbs

The present-tense **nous** form of spelling-change verbs has a spelling change for pronunciation reasons, and you keep that change for most of the **imparfait** conjugations. The **nous** form of **commencer** (*to begin*) is **commençons**, giving you the stem **commenç-**, and the **nous** form of **manger** (*to eat*) is **mangeons**, so the stem is **mange-**. You use these stems for the singular and the third-person plural conjugations (the boot forms in the conjugation table).

The spelling changes in these verbs occur to maintain the pronunciation of **c** and **g**. The **imparfait** endings for the **nous** and **vous** forms begin with the soft vowel **i**, so you don't need the spelling change in those conjugations. The stems for the **nous** and **vous** forms are therefore **commenc-** and **mang-**, simply the infinitives minus **-er**. To the stems, add the **imparfait** endings: **-ais**, **-ais**, **-ait**, **-ions**, **-iez**, and **-aient**.

See Chapter 3 of Book III for more information about spelling-change verbs.

commencer (*to begin*)	
je commen**çais**	nous commen**cions**
tu commen**çais**	vous commen**ciez**
il/elle/on commen**çait**	ils/elles commen**çaient**
Il **commençait** à lire. (*He was beginning to read.*)	

manger (*to eat*)	
je mang**eais**	nous mang**ions**
tu mang**eais**	vous mang**iez**
il/elle/on mang**eait**	ils/elles mang**eaient**
Nous **mangions** ensemble. (*We were eating together.*)	

Irregular verbs

With one exception, you conjugate irregular verbs just like regular verbs in the **imparfait**: with the present-tense **nous** form minus **-ons**. Then you add the imperfect endings. **-ais**, **-ais**, **-ait**, **-ions**, **-iez**, and **-aient**. Here are **aller** (*to go*), **venir** (*to come*), and **écrire** (*to write*) in the **imparfait**.

aller (*to go*)	
j'all**ais**	nous all**ions**
tu all**ais**	vous all**iez**
il/elle/on all**ait**	ils/elles all**aient**
Ils **allaient** au parc. (*They were going to the park.*)	

venir (*to come*)	
je ven**ais**	nous ven**ions**
tu ven**ais**	vous ven**iez**
il/elle/on ven**ait**	ils/elles ven**aient**
Tu **venais** seul. (*You were coming alone.*)	

écrire (*to write*)	
j'écriv**ais**	nous écriv**ions**
tu écriv**ais**	vous écriv**iez**
il/elle/on écriv**ait**	ils/elles écriv**aient**
Elle **écrivait** une longue lettre. (*She was writing a long letter.*)	

French does have one irregular present-tense verb — **être** (*to be*) — that's also irregular in the **imparfait**. The present-tense **nous** form of **être** is **sommes**, so it has no **-ons** to drop. Instead, you use the stem **ét-** and add the **imparfait** endings to that.

être (*to be*)	
j'ét**ais**	nous ét**ions**
tu ét**ais**	vous ét**iez**
il/elle/on ét**ait**	ils/elles ét**aient**
Vous **étiez** en retard. (*You were late.*)	

Using the Imparfait

The **imparfait** explains that something happened or was happening in the past with no precise beginning or ending. You often translate it as *was/were doing* or *used to do* in English. Another translation of the imperfect tense in English is *would,* as in **Quand j'habitais à Paris, je prenais souvent le métro** (*When I lived in Paris, I would often take the metro*).

Don't confuse the *would* translation of the **imparfait**, which expresses a recurring action in the past, with the *would* of the conditional tense, which is used in a hypothetical sense. Here's an example of the conditional: **Si j'habitais à Paris, je prendrais le metro** (*If I lived in Paris, I would take the metro*). See Chapter 6 of Book IV for details on the conditional tense.

You can use the **imparfait** to express a number of things that happened or existed in the past:

- ✔ Something that happened an unknown number of times, especially habitual actions:

    Je visitais le Louvre tous les jours. (*I visited/used to visit the Louvre every day.*)

    L'année dernière, il lisait régulièrement. (*Last year, he read regularly.*)

- ✔ States of being and descriptions:

    Quand j'étais petit, j'aimais danser. (*When I was little, I liked to dance.*)

    La voiture faisait du bruit. (*The car was making noise.*)

✔ Actions or states of being with no specific beginning or end:

> **Je regardais la télé pendant le petit déjeuner.** (*I watched/was watching TV during breakfast.*)

> **Nous avions besoin de tomates.** (*We needed tomatoes.*)

✔ Two things that were happening at the same time:

> **Il travaillait et j'étudiais.** (*He was working, and I was studying.*)

> **Je lisais pendant que mon frère jouait au tennis.** (*I read while my brother played tennis.*)

✔ Background information and actions or states of being that got interrupted:

> **Travaillais-tu quand je t'ai téléphoné ?** (*Were you working when I called you?*)

> **J'avais faim, donc j'ai acheté un sandwich.** (*I was hungry, so I bought a sandwich.*)

Note that the interruption is expressed with the **passé composé**. See the following section for more information on figuring out which tense to use.

✔ Time, date, and age:

> **Il était lundi quand . . .** (*It was Monday when . . .*)

> **Tu étais trop jeune.** (*You were too young.*)

> **Il y avait/était une fois . . .** (*Once upon a time . . .*)

✔ Wishes, suggestions, and conditions after **si** (*if*):

> **Si seulement elle venait avec nous.** (*If only she were coming with us.*)

> **Si on allait au ciné ce soir ?** (*How about going to the movies tonight?*)

When the **imparfait** is used to express wishes and make suggestions, it doesn't refer to a past action or circumstance. The **imparfait** and present conditional are used together in conditional sentences such as **Si on allait au cinéma ce soir, ce serait sympa** (*If we went to the movies tonight, it would be nice*). Here, the **imparfait** appears in **si on allait** (*if we went*), which expresses a wish, a desire that may or may not be realized. The present conditional is in **ce serait sympa** (*it would be nice*), which is the anticipated result of the wish if it's realized. (See Chapter 6 of Book IV to read about the conditional.)

Similarly, when you ask a question using **si** and the **imparfait**, as in **Si on allait au cinéma ce soir ?** you're making a wish or a suggestion. You just don't bother to state the anticipated result.

Choosing Past Times: The Imparfait versus the Passé Composé

The **imparfait** and the **passé composé** express the past differently, and only by working together can they can fully express what happened in the past. To use the right one at the right time, you need to know what each tense describes. Table 2-1 spells out their differences. (You can read more about the **passé composé** in Chapter 1 of Book V.)

Table 2-1	Functions of the Imparfait and Passé Composé
Uses of the Imparfait	*Uses of the Passé Composé*
Actions that *were happening* (no definite beginning or end is indicated)	Actions that *happened* (a definite beginning and/or end or state of completion is indicated)
Habitual or repeated actions	Single events
Simultaneous ongoing or habitual actions	Sequential actions
Actions that got interrupted	Actions that interrupted other actions
Background information	Changes in physical or mental states
General descriptions	

In a nutshell, the **imparfait** usually describes the background state of being, and the **passé composé** explains the actions and events. This section breaks down the situations in which you have to choose between the **imparfait** and the **passé composé**. We also give you hints to help you make that decision.

Getting help from key words

Certain words or phrases in a sentence can help you decide whether to use the **imparfait** or **passé composé** because they tell you whether the past action was habitual or took place only once, for example. The following terms are usually used with the **imparfait** because they point to regularly performed acts:

- **chaque fois que** (*each time that*)
- **chaque semaine/mois/année** (*each week/month/year*)
- **d'habitude, normalement** (*usually*)
- **de temps en temps** (*from time to time*)
- **en général** (*in general*)

- ✔ **généralement** (*generally*)
- ✔ **le lundi, le mardi** (*on Mondays, on Tuesdays*)
- ✔ **le matin, le soir** (*in the mornings, in the evenings*)
- ✔ **parfois, quelquefois** (*sometimes*)
- ✔ **pendant que** (*while*)
- ✔ **régulièrement** (*regularly*)
- ✔ **souvent** (*often*)
- ✔ **tous les jours, toutes les semaines** (*every day, every week*)
- ✔ **toujours** (*always*)
- ✔ **le week-end** (*on the weekends*)

The terms in the following list tell you that you probably need the **passé composé** because they point to a completed action that happened at a precise moment and/or suddenly:

- ✔ **une fois, deux fois, trois fois** (*once, twice, three times*)
- ✔ **un jour** (*one day*)
- ✔ **lundi, mardi** (*on Monday, on Tuesday*)
- ✔ **plusieurs fois** (*several times*)
- ✔ **quand** (*when*)
- ✔ **soudainement** (*suddenly*)
- ✔ **tout d'un coup** (*all of a sudden*)
- ✔ **un week-end** (*one weekend*)

Considering the context

In the absence of key words like the ones in the preceding section, follow other clues. For example, ask yourself whether the past action was incomplete or habitual. Also keep an eye open for verbs that indicate state of being, such as **être** (*to be*), and state of mind, such as **penser** (*to think*), which tend to be used in the **imparfait**. This section looks at these and other helpful context clues.

Actions with no end in sight

When you use the **imparfait** to describe an action, you're saying that it had no precise beginning or end:

> **J'écrivais une lettre.** (*I was writing a letter.*)

This action is incomplete, so you use the **imparfait**. You know that at some point I was in the process of writing a letter, but you don't know whether I ever finished it or when I started or stopped. On the other hand, the **passé composé** says that an action did have a specific end. Compare the preceding example to this sentence:

J'ai écrit une lettre. (*I wrote a letter.*)

This act has a definite ending; the letter is written. The action is complete, so you use the **passé composé**.

Making a habit of something

When an act happened a specific number of times, use the **passé composé**. If the act was habitual or repeated, use the **imparfait**:

Elle écrivait des lettres le samedi. (*She used to write letters on Saturdays.*)

Here, you don't know how many times she wrote letters or how many letters she wrote. Writing letters is something she habitually did on Saturdays, so use the **imparfait**. Compare this usage to

Elle a écrit trois lettres samedi. (*She wrote three letters on Saturday.*)

This action is complete, so you use the **passé composé**. On Saturday, she sat down and wrote three letters. It's done.

The way we were

When in doubt, use verbs like **être** (*to be*), **avoir** (*to have*), **pouvoir** (*to be able to*), **vouloir** (*to want to*), **penser** (*to think*), **croire** (*to believe*), and **espérer** (*to hope*) in the **imparfait** because they tend to indicate a state of being or a state of mind.

However, when you want to emphasize a change in someone's state of being, you can use them in the **passé composé**. Take a look at these examples:

Étienne avait faim. (*Étienne was hungry.*)

Quand il a vu les frites, Étienne a eu faim. (*When he saw the french fries, Étienne was/got/became hungry.*)

The first sentence just describes the way Étienne felt — he was hungry, for no particular reason. In this instance, you use the **imparfait**. In the second sentence, Étienne hadn't been hungry, but then he saw those delicious-looking fries and suddenly was hungry. In this case, you use the **passé composé**.

Here are some more examples. The following sentences, using the **imparfait**, describe a state of being:

> **J'espérais passer une nuit mémorable.** (*I was hoping to spend a memorable night.*)
>
> **J'étais trop loin de la scène et je ne pouvais pas voir l'acteur principal.** (*I was too far from the stage and couldn't see the main actor.*)
>
> **J'avais pourtant très envie de le voir.** (*Yet I really wanted to see him.*)

This next sentence, using the **passé composé**, illustrates a change in state of being:

> **Quand l'homme devant moi a enlevé son chapeau, j'ai pu voir tous les acteurs.** (*When the man in front of me took off his hat, I could see all the actors.*)

French has many **avoir** idioms that indicate a state of being and therefore are usually used in the **imparfait**. Here's the short list:

- ✔ **avoir besoin de** (*to need*)
- ✔ **avoir chaud/froid** (*to be hot/cold*)
- ✔ **avoir envie de** (*to feel like/want*)
- ✔ **avoir faim/soif** (*to be hungry/thirsty*)
- ✔ **avoir hâte de** (*to be in a hurry*)
- ✔ **avoir l'intention de** (*to intend*)
- ✔ **avoir peur** (*to be afraid*)
- ✔ **avoir raison/tort** (*to be right/wrong*)
- ✔ **avoir sommeil** (*to be sleepy*)

Check out a couple of examples using the **imparfait**:

> **Elle avait besoin d'un verre d'eau.** (*She needed a glass of water.*)
>
> **Nous avions hâte d'arriver.** (*We were in a hurry to arrive.*)

Describing weather conditions

When you tell your friends about a vacation you went on, the weather almost always comes up. Was it just as expected (warm, sunny days), or did it unexpectedly change (tropical storm) and put a dent in your plans?

You use the **imparfait** to talk casually about how the weather was:

> **Il faisait chaud et il y avait une douce brise.** (*It was hot, and there was a gentle breeze.*)

Use the **passé composé** to indicate a change in the weather:

> **L'hiver a été très doux contrairement à ce qu'on attendait. Il a neigé une seule fois en décembre.** (*Winter was very mild, contrary to what we expected. It snowed only once.*)

Two (or more) acts at a time

When you have two or more actions, the tense you use depends on whether the actions are simultaneous or sequential. You use the **imparfait** to express two or more things that were happening at the same time and the **passé composé** to indicate things that happened one after the other without a clear sense of when they ended:

> **Henriette conduisait pendant que Thierry chantait.** (*Henriette drove while Thierry sang.*)

> **Ils sont partis, et puis Viviane a commencé à pleurer.** (*They left, and then Viviane started to cry.*)

In the first example, the two actions were occurring at the same time, so you use the **imparfait**. In the second, they left first, and Viviane started to cry afterward. Because these actions are sequential, you use the **passé composé**.

Getting interrupted

The **imparfait** and **passé composé** work together to express something that interrupted something else. The **imparfait** gives you the background info — what was happening when something else (expressed with the **passé composé**) occurred. In the following examples, the verbs in the **imparfait** tell you what was happening, and the verbs in the **passé composé** tell you what interrupted:

> **Je lisais quand quelqu'un a frappé à la porte.** (*I was reading when someone knocked on the door.*)

> **Quand nous sommes arrivés, tout le monde mangeait.** (*When we arrived, everyone was eating.*)

> **Il marchait quand il a trouvé le chien.** (*He was walking when he found the dog.*)

Chapter 3

To the Past and Beyond: Other Past Tenses

French has several compound tenses for talking about the past. All these tenses use a conjugated auxiliary verb — **avoir** or **être** — and the past participle. Simply by changing the tense of the auxiliary, you can talk about what *had* happened, *would have* happened, *will have* happened, and more.

All the tenses we introduce in this chapter are closely related to the **passé composé**, which we cover in Chapter 1 of Book V. There, we explain which auxiliary to use, tell you how to form past participles, and give you rules of agreement. This chapter shows you how to form four new compound past tenses and when to use them.

Remembering Common Rules for Compound Tenses

You form a compound past tense by conjugating an auxiliary (helping) verb and adding a past participle. All the compound tenses look similar — the only difference is in the auxiliary verb. You just need to know how to conjugate **avoir** (*to have*) and **être** (*to be*), particularly in the simple tenses and moods from the past few chapters. The choice between **avoir** and **être** depends on the main verb.

Table 3-1 shows how the compound past tenses compare. Don't worry if you don't understand it all yet — we cover the **passé composé** in detail in Chapter 1 of Book V and the rest of the compound tenses in this chapter.

Table 3-1	Auxiliary Verb Differences in Compound Past Tenses		
Compound Tense	*Tense and Mood of the Auxiliary Verb*	*Sample Conjugated Auxiliary + Past Participle*	*Meaning*
passé composé	present indicative (regular present tense)	**a** + past participle **est** + past participle	*has [happened]*
pluperfect	**imparfait** indicative	**avait** + past participle **était** + past participle	*had [happened]*
past conditional	present conditional	**aurait** + past participle **serait** + past participle	*would have [happened]*
future perfect	**futur simple** indicative	**aura** + past participle **sera** + past participle	*will have [happened]*
past subjunctive	present subjunctive	**ait** + past participle **soit** + past participle	*[that something happened]*

You get the past participles of regular **-er** verbs by dropping **-er** from the infinitive and adding an **-é**: **chanter** → **chanté** (*sung*). You get the past participles of regular **-ir** verbs by dropping **-r** from the infinitive: **finir** → **fini** (*finished*). And you get the past participles of regular **-re** verbs by dropping **-re** from the infinitive and adding **-u**: **vendre** → **vendu** (*sold*). Just memorize the past participles of irregular verbs, which we note in Chapter 1 of Book V.

You may need to make the past participle agree with a noun or pronoun. The rules of agreement for past participles are the same for all compound tenses:

- ✔ The past participle agrees with the preceding direct object — if there is one — when a verb is conjugated with the auxiliary **avoir**.

- ✔ The past participle agrees with the subject when a verb is conjugated with the auxiliary **être**.

- ✔ The past participle of a pronominal verb agrees with the preceding direct object of the verb, which is often the reflexive pronoun, even though the verb is conjugated with the auxiliary **être**.

You add **-e** to make the participle feminine, **-s** to make it plural, or **-es** to make it feminine plural. Check out Chapter 1 of Book V for details.

What Had Happened: Stepping Further Back with the Pluperfect

You use the pluperfect (the **plus-que-parfait**) to recount an action that happened before something else. Not only was the action completed in the past, but it took place even before the **passé composé**.

The meaning of the pluperfect in English is *had done, had been,* and so on. For example, **Les enfants avaient déjà fini leurs devoirs quand ils ont commencé à regarder la télé** means *The children had already finished their homework when they started watching TV.* **Avaient fini** (*had finished*) is in the pluperfect and **ont commencé** (*started*) is in the **passé composé** because one action happened before the other.

In this section, we show you how to form the pluperfect and how to use it.

Forming the pluperfect perfectly

You form the pluperfect just like the **passé composé**, except you conjugate the auxiliaries **avoir** and **être** in the **imparfait** rather than the present tense before adding the past participle of the verb. Chapter 1 of Book V tells you which auxiliary verb to use, how to form past participles, and how to make past participle agreements. The following tables show the auxiliaries **avoir** and **être** in the **imparfait**. (See Chapter 2 of Book V for details on the **imparfait**.)

avoir (*to have*)	
j'**avais**	nous **avions**
tu **avais**	vous **aviez**
il/elle/on **avait**	ils/elles **avaient**

être (*to be*)	
j'**étais**	nous **étions**
tu **étais**	vous **étiez**
il/elle/on **était**	ils/elles **étaient**

The next two tables show an **avoir** verb and an **être** verb conjugated in the pluperfect. The past participle agrees with the subject when the auxiliary is **être**.

manger (*to eat*)	
j'**avais mangé**	nous **avions mangé**
tu **avais mangé**	vous **aviez mangé**
il/elle/on **avait mangé**	ils/elles **avaient mangé**
Nous **avions** déjà **mangé** quand tu es arrivé. (*We had already eaten when you arrived.*)	

partir (*to leave*)	
j'**étais parti(e)**	nous **étions parti(s/es)**
tu **étais parti(e)**	vous **étiez parti(e/s/es)**
il/elle/on **était parti(e)**	ils/elles **étaient parti(s/es)**
Ils **étaient partis** quand nous avons téléphoné. (*They had left when we called.*)	

Saving the pluperfect for just the right time

Use the pluperfect to say that something had already happened by a certain point of time or by the time something else happened. The *something else* is in the **passé composé**, but what had happened is in the pluperfect. Look at these examples:

Je suis allé(e) au théâtre hier, mais j'**avais acheté** mon billet le mois dernier. (*I went to the theater yesterday, but I had bought my ticket last month.*)

À neuf heures du matin, ils **étaient** déjà **allés** faire les courses. (*At nine in the morning, they had already gone shopping.*)

Il **avait préparé** le dîner quand sa femme est rentrée. (*He had prepared dinner when his wife came home.*)

Il **avait atteint** le sommet de la montagne quand il a commencé à neiger. (*He had reached the top of the mountain when it started snowing.*)

Il **était** heureusement **retourné** au refuge avant l'avalanche. (*He had luckily gone back to the refuge before the avalanche.*)

You also use the pluperfect to express regret with the condition **si** (*if only*); you then express the result of the condition set with a verb in the past conditional (see the next section). For example, **Nous aurions attendu si nous avions pu** means *We would've waited if we had been able to*. The condition in the *if* clause is in the pluperfect (**avions pu**), and the result is in the past conditional (**aurions attendu**). This type of sentence always contains unrealized conditions and unmet expectations. The following examples use the pluperfect in a **si** clause:

> Si j'**étais arrivé(e)** plus tôt, je n'aurais pas raté l'avion. (*If I had arrived earlier, I wouldn't have missed the plane.*)

> Si nous **avions su,** nous serions resté(s/es) à la maison. (*If we had known, we would've stayed home.*)

Woulda, Coulda, Shoulda: Adding the Past Conditional

You use the past conditional tense in all those situations when you could just kick yourself because you should've said this or should've done that. For example, you may say *I should have locked the door* when a thief takes your car stereo or *I shouldn't have locked the door* when you lock your keys inside your car. You may tell your friend *you should've gone out with him,* or you may say *you wouldn't have said that* in her place. This section shows you how to form and when to use the past conditional tense.

Forming the past conditional

You form the past conditional (the **conditionnel passé**) by putting the auxiliary **avoir** (*to have*) or **être** (*to be*) in the present conditional tense and adding the past participle of the main verb. The following tables conjugate just the auxiliaries in the conditional. (See Chapter 6 of Book IV for details on the present conditional.)

avoir (*to have*)	
j'**aurais**	nous **aurions**
tu **aurais**	vous **auriez**
il/elle/on **aurait**	ils/elles **auraient**

être (to be)	
je **serais**	nous **serions**
tu **serais**	vous **seriez**
il/elle/on **serait**	ils/elles **seraient**

The following tables show a couple of verbs in the past conditional. **Étudier** (*to study*) takes the auxiliary **avoir**, and **partir** (*to leave*) takes **être**. The past participle of verbs taking **être** as their auxiliary agrees with the subject (unless the verb is pronominal). If you aren't sure about the past participle of verbs, look at Chapter 1 of Book V.

étudier (to study)	
j'**aurais étudié**	nous **aurions étudié**
tu **aurais étudié**	vous **auriez étudié**
il/elle/on **aurait étudié**	ils/elles **auraient étudié**
Elle **aurait étudié**. (*She would have studied.*)	

partir (to leave)	
je **serais parti(e)**	nous **serions parti(s/es)**
tu **serais parti(e)**	vous **seriez parti(e/s/es)**
il/elle/on **serait parti(e)**	ils/elles **seraient parti(s/es)**
Nous **serions partis**. (*We would have left.*)	

For pronominal verbs, place the reflexive pronoun in front of the auxiliary **être**, which is followed by the past participle of the verb. Remember that all pronominal verbs are conjugated with the auxiliary **être**. The past participle of pronominal verbs agrees not with the subject but with the direct object, which is usually the reflexive pronoun (see Chapter 1 of Book V for details). Here's **se lever** (*to get up*) in the past conditional.

se lever (to get up)	
je **me serais levé(e)**	nous **nous serions levé(s/es)**
tu **te serais levé(e)**	vous **vous seriez levé(e/s/es)**
il/elle/on **se serait levé(e)**	ils/elles **se seraient levé(s/es)**
Vous **vous seriez levés**. (*You would have gotten up.*)	

To make any compound tense negative, place **ne** in front of the auxiliary and **pas** after the auxiliary. For pronominal verbs, place **ne** in front of the reflexive pronoun and **pas** after the auxiliary:

> **Je n'aurais pas fini.** (*I would not have finished.*)
>
> **Benjamin ne se serait pas réveillé.** (*Benjamin would not have woken up.*)

Hypothesizing with the past conditional

In English, the past conditional is usually translated as *would have done something*. The past conditional often expresses a missed opportunity in the past, a wish that could've been realized but wasn't, or a regret. Look at these examples:

> **Nous aurions voulu vous aider.** (*We would have liked to help you.*)
>
> **Elle aurait voulu voyager mais elle n'avait pas assez d'argent.** (*She would have liked to travel, but she didn't have enough money.*)
>
> **Avec un peu de chance, ils seraient arrivés.** (*With a little luck, they would have arrived.*)
>
> **Ils auraient dû s'arrêter avant midi.** (*They should have stopped before noon.*)

In English, you use the past conditional to express what *would have* or *would not have* occurred if something had happened or had not happened. In French, the *if* condition is in the pluperfect, and the result is the in the past conditional (we cover the pluperfect earlier in "What Had Happened: Stepping Further Back with the Pluperfect"). Look at these examples:

> **On aurait écrit plus tôt si on avait trouvé votre adresse.** (*We would have written earlier if we had found your address.*) Here, **aurait écrit** is in the past conditional, and **avait trouvé** is in the pluperfect.
>
> **S'il avait réussi à ses examens, il serait allé en Europe.** (*If he had passed his exams, he would have gone to Europe.*) **Avait réussi** is in the pluperfect, and **serait allé** is in the past conditional.
>
> **S'ils avaient voulu, ils auraient pu venir.** (*If they had wanted to, they could have come.*) **Avaient voulu** is in the pluperfect, and **auraient pu** is in the past conditional.

What Will Have Happened: Completing the Future Perfect

Do you ever say to yourself, "I'll have this or that done by a certain time," such as before you leave the office or by Friday? If so, you use the *future perfect tense,* or **futur antérieur**. The meaning of this tense in English is *will have done something.* You use the future perfect tense for something that will happen in the future before something else. For example, **À la fin de ce chapitre, vous aurez appris quatre nouvelles conjugaisons** means *By the end of this chapter, you will have learned four more conjugations.* **Aurez appris** (*will have learned*) is in the future perfect. This section shows you how to form the future perfect and when to use it.

Managing the future perfect

Like any compound tense, you form the future perfect by using an auxiliary verb and a past participle. You put the auxiliaries in the future tense before adding the past participle of the verb of your choice.

First, you need to conjugate **avoir** and **être** in the future tense, as the following tables show. (We introduce the future tense in Chapter 6 of Book IV.) After you conjugate the auxiliary in the future tense, you add the past participle. (See Chapter 1 of Book V for details on **avoir** and **être** verbs, formation of the past participles, and agreement of past participles.)

avoir (*to have*)	
j'**aurai**	nous **aurons**
tu **auras**	vous **aurez**
il/elle/on **aura**	ils/elles **auront**

être (*to be*)	
je **serai**	nous **serons**
tu **seras**	vous **serez**
il/elle/on **sera**	ils/elles **seront**

The following tables show three examples of verbs in the future perfect: **finir** (*to finish*), **arriver** (*to arrive*), and **se réveiller** (*to wake up*). **Finir** takes the auxiliary **avoir**, **arriver** takes **être**, and **se réveiller**, like all pronominal verbs, also takes **être**.

For pronominal verbs, place the reflexive pronoun in front of the auxiliary **être**, which is followed by the past participle of the verb.

finir (*to finish*)	
j'**aurai fini**	nous **aurons fini**
tu **auras fini**	vous **aurez fini**
il/elle/on **aura fini**	ils/elles **auront fini**
Ils **auront fini** avant le weekend. (*They will have finished before the weekend.*)	

arriver (*to arrive*)	
je **serai arrivé(e)**	nous **serons arrivé(s/es)**
tu **seras arrivé(e)**	vous **serez arrivé(s/e/es)**
il/elle/on **sera arrivé(e)**	ils/elles **seront arrivé(s/es)**
Nous **serons arrivés** avant le 5 août. (*We will have arrived before the 5th of August.*)	

se réveiller (*to wake up*)	
je **me serai réveillé(e)**	nous **nous serons réveillé(s/es)**
tu **te seras réveillé(e)**	vous **vous serez réveillé(s/e/es)**
il/elle/on **se sera réveillé(e)**	ils/elles **se seront réveillé(s/es)**
Ils ne **se seront** sûrement pas encore **réveillés** à six heures du matin. (*They will surely not have awakened yet at 6 a.m.*)	

Meeting the deadline with future perfect

You use the future perfect to describe events that will have taken place before another future action. You can also use the future perfect alone to express that a future action will have been completed by a certain time in the future:

Nous **aurons économisé** une bonne somme d'argent avant la fin de l'année. (*We'll have saved a good amount of money before the end of the year.*)

Tu **auras obtenu** ton diplôme quand tu commenceras à travailler. (*You'll have obtained your diploma when you start to work.*)

You can also use the future perfect to express a probability or a supposition that you're pretty certain about, as in the following example: **Il y a un embouteillage. Il y aura eu un accident.** (*There's a traffic jam. There must have been an accident.*) **Aura eu** (*must have been*) is in the future perfect.

Like the simple future tense (see Chapter 6 of Book IV), you use the future perfect with expressions that imply a future action, such as *when* and *as soon as*. You can also use the future or future perfect after the expressions **après que** (*after*), **tant que** (*as long as*), or **une fois que** (*once*) if future action is implied. Compare the following examples:

Je réchaufferai la soupe une fois que tu seras là. (*I will heat up the soup once you're here.*) The expression **une fois que** is followed by the simple future because *being here* will take place in the future, at the same time as something else worth mentioning (heating the soup).

Une fois que j'aurai réchauffé la soupe, nous nous mettrons à table. (*Once I have heated the soup, we'll sit down to eat.*) Here, **une fois que** is followed by the future perfect because heating up the soup will take place in the future but before something else worth mentioning — the act of sitting down to eat.

Table 3-2 lists some common French expressions of the future. If you see one of these expressions, you may need either the future or the future perfect.

Table 3-2	Common Future Perfect Expressions
French Expression	*English Translation*
après que	*after*
aussitôt que	*as soon as*
dès que	*as soon as*
lorsque	*when*
quand	*when*
tant que	*as long as*
une fois que	*once*

Here are some examples that use future perfect expressions. The English translations are in the present tense, but the French uses the future perfect here:

> **Quand tu auras atterri à Paris,** appelle-moi ! (*When you land in Paris, call me.*)

> **Dès que tu seras rentré(e) à la maison,** change-toi et viens ! (*As soon as you get home, change and come!*)

> **Après que mes invités seront arrivés,** je servirai l'apéritif. (*After my guests arrive, I'll serve the aperitif.*)

Looking Back: Getting Emotional with the Past Subjunctive

You use the past tense of the subjunctive mood when you're happy or sad about something that happened. The *past subjunctive* (**subjonctif passé**), also known as the *perfect subjunctive,* is a compound tense that expresses a completed action in the past. You use the past subjunctive in French much more often than in English. It's common in both speaking and writing.

The choice between the present and past subjunctive depends on the time relationship between the main clause and the subordinate clause. Use the past subjunctive when the action of the verb in the subordinate clause takes place before the action of the main verb. For example, **Je suis triste que mon ami ne soit pas venu à ma boom hier** means *I'm sad that my friend didn't come to my party yesterday.* **Ne soit pas venu** (*didn't come*) is in the past subjunctive.

The past subjunctive follows the same rules as the present subjunctive, which we talk about in Chapter 5 of Book IV. In this section, we show you how to form the past subjunctive and how to make the right choice about using past rather than present subjunctive.

Forming the past subjunctive

Like all compound tenses in French, the past subjunctive needs an auxiliary verb and the past participle of a verb of your choice. To form the past subjunctive, put **avoir** or **être** in the present subjunctive and add the past participle. The following tables show the auxiliaries in the present subjunctive. For details on verbs taking **avoir** and **être** as auxiliaries as well as how to form past participles of various verbs, see Chapter 1 of Book V.

avoir (*to have*)	
que j'**aie**	que nous **ayons**
que tu **aies**	que vous **ayez**
qu'il/elle/on **ait**	qu'ils/elles **aient**

être (*to be*)	
que je **sois**	que nous **soyons**
que tu **sois**	que vous **soyez**
qu'il/elle/on **soit**	qu'ils/elles **soient**

The past participle in the past subjunctive follows the standard rules of agreement for compound tenses: If the auxiliary is **être** and the verb is not reflexive, then the past participle agrees with the subject. If the auxiliary is **avoir**, then the past participle agrees with the preceding direct object if the sentence has one. If the sentence doesn't have a preceding direct object, then the past participle doesn't change. The past participle of pronominal verbs agrees with the preceding direct object — usually the reflexive pronoun — if the sentence has one.

In the following examples, we conjugate an **avoir** verb (**voir**), an **être** verb (**partir**), and a pronominal verb (**se lever**) in the past subjunctive tense.

voir (*to see*)	
que j'**aie vu**	que nous **ayons vu**
que tu **aies vu**	que vous **ayez vu**
qu'il/elle/on **ait vu**	qu'ils/elles **aient vu**
C'est le meilleur film que j'**aie vu**. (*It's the best film that I've seen.*)	

partir (*to leave*)	
que je **sois parti(e)**	que nous **soyons parti(s/es)**
que tu **sois parti(e)**	que vous **soyez parti(s/e/es)**
qu'il/elle/on **soit parti(e)**	qu'ils/elles **soient parti(s/es)**
Il est triste que tu **sois parti**. (*He's sad that you left.*)	

se lever (*to get up*)	
que je **me sois levé(e)**	que nous **nous soyons levé(s/es)**
que tu **te sois levé(e)**	que vous **vous soyez levé(s/e/es)**
qu'il/elle/on **se sois levé(e)**	qu'ils/elles **se soient levé(s/es)**
Il est surprenant que vous **vous soyez levés** si tôt, mes enfants. (*It's surprising that you got up so early, my children.*)	

Reflecting on what happened with the past subjunctive

In order for the verb in the subordinate clause to be in the subjunctive, the verb (or verbal expression) in the main clause must express a wish, will, command, emotion, doubt, or subjective point of view (see Chapter 5 of Book IV for details on the subjunctive mood). You use the past subjunctive when the action of the verb in the subordinate clause comes *before* the action of the verb in the main clause, which expresses a wish, will, command, emotion, and so on. In the following examples, the clause after **que** (*that*) is in the past subjunctive:

> Je suis triste **que tu sois parti(e).** (*I am sad that you left.*)
>
> J'étais triste **que tu sois parti(e).** (*I was sad that you left.*)
>
> Je serai triste **que tu sois parti(e).** (*I will be sad that you left.*)

The choice between the present and past subjunctive doesn't depend on the tense of the verb in the main clause. The verb in the main clause can be in the present, the past, the future, or even the conditional.

In the following sentence, the verb in the dependent clause is in the past subjunctive only because the action of not going preceded the state of surprise that Granddad experienced:

> **Mon grand-père était surpris que je ne sois pas allé le voir.** (*My grandfather was surprised that I did not go to see him.*) Here, **était** is in the **imparfait**, and **ne sois pas allée** is in the past subjunctive.

In this next example, the verb in the dependent clause is in the past subjunctive because the action of helping preceded the state she should be in right now: happy. Note that the past participle **aidée** agrees with the feminine preceding direct object **l'** (*her*), which is necessary for verbs conjugated with **avoir** (see Chapter 1 of Book V for agreements of past participles):

> **Elle devrait être contente que nous l'ayons aidée à finir ce gros travail.**
> (*She should be happy that we helped her finish this big job.*) Here, **devrait** is in the present conditional, and **ayons aidée** is in the past subjunctive.

In the following sentence, the verb in the dependent clause is in the past subjunctive because the action of quarreling precedes the regrets he'll have tomorrow. Note that the past participle **disputés** agrees with the preceding direct object — the reflexive pronoun **se**, which represents the masculine plural noun **amis** — as is necessary for pronominal or reflexive verbs (see Chapter 1 of Book V for more on agreement of past participles):

> **Demain il regrettera que ses amis se soient disputés chez lui.**
> (*Tomorrow he'll regret that his friends quarreled at his house.*) Here, **regrettera** is in the simple future and **se soient disputés** is in the past subjunctive.

Book VI
Appendixes

"Honey, please! Be patient! How's anyone going to know what's wrong unless I find the French word for 'alligator?'"

In this book . . .

These last pages give you the opportunity to skip over explanations and find the facts you want at a glance; just flip open the book, find what you need, and go on your merry way. Use these appendixes to conjugate French verbs (Appendix A), discover what French words mean in English (Appendix B), and find French translations of English words (Appendix C). Head to Appendix D to take a break from reading and engage in fun, game-like activities, and check out Appendix E for details on making the most of the accompanying CD, as well as a complete track listing of the CD contents.

Here are the contents of Book VI at a glance:

Appendix A

Verb Tables

In this appendix, we provide the conjugations of commonly used verbs in various tenses of the indicative, conditional, and subjunctive moods so that you can quickly find the verb form you're looking for to produce a sentence. This appendix first shows you the past and present participle forms of a verb, followed by the conjugation of the verb in various tenses and moods, including the present indicative (something happens, is happening, or does happen); **imparfait**, or imperfect (something happened, was happening, or used to happen); simple future (something will happen); and present conditional (something would happen). Then we show you compound tenses, including the **passé composé** (something happened or has happened); pluperfect (something had happened); future perfect (something will have happened); and past conditional (something would have happened). Finally, we present the subjunctive ([that] something happens) and past subjunctive ([that] something happened) tenses of the same verb.

The following table shows how we've arranged the verb tenses and moods within the verb tables. The simple tenses come first, followed by the compound past tenses that build off them; we've included some construction notes for the compound tenses in parentheses. The subjunctive mood is in the last row only because we didn't want to overcrowd the tables with another column. For more on these verb forms and tenses, refer to Books III, IV, and V.

Simple Tenses	Present Indicative	**Imparfait**	Future	Present Conditional
Compound Tenses (Conjugated Auxiliary Verb + Past Participle of the Main Verb)	**Passé Composé** (Present Auxiliary + Past Participle)	Pluperfect (**Imparfait** Auxiliary + Past Participle)	Future Perfect (Future Auxiliary + Past Participle)	Past Conditional (Present Conditional Auxiliary + Past Participle)
Subjunctive Tenses (Simple and Compound)	Present Subjunctive	Past Subjunctive (Present Subjunctive Auxiliary + Past Participle)		

Regular French Verbs

In this section, the tables first show you the conjugations of some regular verbs in simple tenses, which require the stem of the verb and a specific ending. The tables then give you conjugations in compound tenses, which require an auxiliary verb (**avoir** or **être**) and a past participle. Chapter 1 of Book V tells you how to figure out which auxiliary is necessary.

You can follow the patterns you see here to conjugate all regular **-er**, **-ir**, and **-re** verbs. This section also includes an example of a regular *pronominal verb,* a verb that has to be conjugated with a reflexive pronoun. Pronominal verbs use **être** as their auxiliary in compound tenses, and the past participle may have to agree in number and gender with the subject or direct object. See Chapter 1 of Book V for details.

As you read through this appendix, look for patterns. For example, notice how the **imparfait** and present conditional use the same endings, and note how the future and present conditional have the same stems.

Regular Verbs Ending with -er
For example: parler (to speak)

Past Participle: parlé (spoken); Present Participle: parlant (speaking)

	Present Indicative	Imparfait	Future	Present Conditional
je/j' (I)	parle	parlais	parlerai	parlerais
tu (you, fam.)	parles	parlais	parleras	parlerais
il/elle/on (he/she/it/one)	parle	parlait	parlera	parlerait
nous (we)	parlons	parlions	parlerons	parlerions
vous (you, form./pl.)	parlez	parliez	parlerez	parleriez
ils/elles (they)	parlent	parlaient	parleront	parleraient

	Passé Composé	Pluperfect	Future Perfect	Past Conditional
je/j' (I)	ai parlé	avais parlé	aurai parlé	aurais parlé
tu (you, fam.)	as parlé	avais parlé	auras parlé	aurais parlć
il/elle/on (he/she/it/one)	a parlé	avait parlé	aura parlé	aurait parlé
nous (we)	avons parlé	avions parlé	aurons parlé	aurions parlé
vous (you, form./pl.)	avez parlé	aviez parlé	aurez parlé	auriez parlé
ils/elles (they)	ont parlé	avaient parlé	auront parlé	auraient parlé

	Present Subjunctive	Past Subjunctive
je/j' (I)	parle	aie parlé
tu (you, fam.)	parles	aies parlé
il/elle/on (he/she/it/one)	parle	ait parlé
nous (we)	parlions	ayons parlé
vous (you, form./pl.)	parliez	ayez parlé
ils/elles (they)	parlent	aient parlé

Regular Verbs Ending with -ir
For example: finir (to finish)

Past Participle: fini (finished); Present Participle: finissant (finishing)

	Present Indicative	Imparfait	Future	Present Conditional
je/j' (I)	finis	finissais	finirai	finirais
tu (you, fam.)	finis	finissais	finiras	finirais
il/elle/on (he/she/it/one)	finit	finissait	finira	finirait
nous (we)	finissons	finissions	finirons	finirions
vous (you, form./pl.)	finissez	finissiez	finirez	finiriez
ils/elles (they)	finissent	finissaient	finiront	finiraient

	Passé Composé	Pluperfect	Future Perfect	Past Conditional
je/j' (I)	ai fini	avais fini	aurai fini	aurais fini
tu (you, fam.)	as fini	avais fini	auras fini	aurais fini
il/elle/on (he/she/it/one)	a fini	avait fini	aura fini	aurait fini
nous (we)	avons fini	avions fini	aurons fini	aurions fini
vous (you, form./pl.)	avez fini	aviez fini	aurez fini	auriez fini
ils/elles (they)	ont fini	avaient fini	auront fini	auraient fini

	Present Subjunctive	Past Subjunctive
je/j' (I)	finisse	aie fini
tu (you, fam.)	finisses	aies fini
il/elle/on (he/she/it/one)	finisse	ait fini
nous (we)	finissions	ayons fini
vous (you, form./pl.)	finissiez	ayez fini
ils/elles (they)	finissent	aient fini

Regular Verbs Ending with -re
For example: vendre (to sell)

Past Participle: vendu (sold); Present Participle: vendant (selling)

	Present Indicative	Imparfait	Future	Present Conditional
je/j' (I)	vends	vendais	vendrai	vendrais
tu (you, fam.)	vends	vendais	vendras	vendrais
il/elle/on (he/she/it/one)	vend	vendait	vendra	vendrait
nous (we)	vendons	vendions	vendrons	vendrions
vous (you, form./pl.)	vendez	vendiez	vendrez	vendriez
ils/elles (they)	vendent	vendaient	vendront	vendraient

	Passé Composé	Pluperfect	Future Perfect	Past Conditional
je/j' (I)	ai vendu	avais vendu	aurai vendu	aurais vendu
tu (you, fam.)	as vendu	avais vendu	auras vendu	aurais vendu
il/elle/on (he/she/it/one)	a vendu	avait vendu	aura vendu	aurait vendu
nous (we)	avons vendu	avions vendu	aurons vendu	aurions vendu
vous (you, form./pl.)	avez vendu	aviez vendu	aurez vendu	auriez vendu
ils/elles (they)	ont vendu	avaient vendu	auront vendu	auraient vendu

	Present Subjunctive	Past Subjunctive
je/j' (I)	vende	aie vendu
tu (you, fam.)	vendes	aies vendu
il/elle/on (he/she/it/one)	vende	ait vendu
nous (we)	vendions	ayons vendu
vous (you, form./pl.)	vendiez	ayez vendu
ils/elles (they)	vendent	aient vendu

Book VI

Appendixes

Reflexive/Pronominal Verbs
For example: se laver (to wash oneself)

Past Participle: lavé (washed); Present participle: lavant (washing)

	Present Indicative	Imparfait	Future	Present Conditional
je/j' (I)	me lave	me lavais	me laverai	me laverais
tu (you, fam.)	te laves	te lavais	te laveras	te laverais
il/elle/on (he/she/it/one)	se lave	se lavait	se lavera	se laverait
nous (we)	nous lavons	nous lavions	nous laverons	nous laverions
vous (you, form./pl.)	vous lavez	vous laviez	vous laverez	vous laveriez
ils/elles (they)	se lavent	se lavaient	se laveront	se laveraient

	Passé Composé	Pluperfect	Future Perfect	Past Conditional
je/j' (I)	me suis lavé(e)	m'étais lavé(e)	me serai lavé(e)	me serais lavé(e)
tu (you, fam.)	t'es lavé(e)	t'étais lavé(e)	te seras lavé(e)	te serais lavé(e)
il/elle/on (he/she/it/one)	s'est lavé(e)	s'était lavé(e)	se sera lavé(e)	se serait lavé(e)
nous (we)	nous sommes lavé(s/es)	nous étions lavé(s/es)	nous serons lavé(s/es)	nous serions lavé(s/es)
vous (you, form./pl.)	vous êtes lavé(e/s/es)	vous étiez lavé(e/s/es)	vous serez lavé(e/s/es)	vous seriez lavé(e/s/es)
ils/elles (they)	se sont lavé(s/es)	s'étaient lavé(s/es)	se seront lavé(s/es)	se seraient lavé(s/es)

	Present Subjunctive	Past Subjunctive
je/j' (I)	me laves	me sois lavé(e)
tu (you, fam.)	te laves	te sois lavé(e)
il/elle/on (he/she/it/one)	se lave	se soit lavé(e)
nous (we)	nous lavions	nous soyons lavé(s/es)
vous (you, form./pl.)	vous laviez	vous soyez lavé(e/s/es)
ils/elles (they)	se lavent	se soient lavé(s/es)

Stem-Changing French Verbs

Some regular **-er** verbs are called *stem-changing* verbs because in the present indicative, their stem is the usual infinitive form minus the **-er** ending only in the **nous** and **vous** forms. For the **je**, **tu**, **il/elle/on**, and **ils/elles** forms, the stem is slightly different. For example, the verb **acheter** has its regular stem (**achet-**) in the **nous** and **vous** forms, but it adds an **accent grave** over the **e** (**achèt-**) in all other forms. The verbs in this section show five types of stem changes. See Chapter 3 of Book III for more details.

e → è Stem-Changing Verbs
For example: acheter (to buy)

Past Participle: acheté (bought); Present Participle: achetant (buying)

	Present Indicative	Imparfait	Future	Present Conditional
je/j' (I)	achète	achetais	achèterai	achèterais
tu (you, fam.)	achètes	achetais	achèteras	achèterais
il/elle/on (he/she/it/one)	achète	achetait	achètera	achèterait
nous (we)	achetons	achetions	achèterons	achèterions
vous (you, form./pl.)	achetez	achetiez	achèterez	achèteriez
ils/elles (they)	achètent	achetaient	achèteront	achèteraient

	Passé Composé	Pluperfect	Future Perfect	Past Conditional
je/j' (I)	ai acheté	avais acheté	aurai acheté	aurais acheté
tu (you, fam.)	as acheté	avais acheté	auras acheté	aurais acheté
il/elle/on (he/she/it/one)	a acheté	avait acheté	aura acheté	aurait acheté
nous (we)	avons acheté	avions acheté	aurons acheté	aurions acheté
vous (you, form./pl.)	avez acheté	aviez acheté	aurez acheté	auriez acheté
ils/elles (they)	ont acheté	avaient acheté	auront acheté	auraient acheté

	Present Subjunctive	Past Subjunctive
je/j' (I)	achète	aie acheté
tu (you, fam.)	achètes	aies acheté
il/elle/on (he/she/it/one)	achète	ait acheté
nous (we)	achetions	ayons acheté
vous (you, form./pl.)	achetiez	ayez acheté
ils/elles (they)	achètent	aient acheté

é → è Stem-Changing Verbs
For example: **répéter** (to repeat)

Past Participle: **répété** (repeated);
Present Participle: **répétant** (repeating)

	Present Indicative	Imparfait	Future	Present Conditional
je/j' (I)	répète	répétais	répéterai	répéterais
tu (you, fam.)	répètes	répétais	répéteras	répéterais
il/elle/on (he/she/it/one)	répète	répétait	répétera	répéterait
nous (we)	répétons	répétions	répéterons	répéterions
vous (you, form./pl.)	répétez	répétiez	répéterez	répéteriez
ils/elles (they)	répètent	répétaient	répéteront	répéteraient

	Passé Composé	Pluperfect	Future Perfect	Past Conditional
je/j' (I)	ai répété	avais répété	aurai répété	aurais répété
tu (you, fam.)	as répété	avais répété	auras répété	aurais répété
il/elle/on (he/she/it/one)	a répété	avait répété	aura répété	aurait répété
nous (we)	avons répété	avions répété	aurons répété	aurions répété
vous (you, form./pl.)	avez répété	aviez répété	aurez répété	auriez répété
ils/elles (they)	ont répété	avaient répété	auront répété	auraient répété

	Present Subjunctive	Past Subjunctive
je/j' (I)	répète	aie répété
tu (you, fam.)	répètes	aies répété
il/elle/on (he/she/it/one)	répète	ait répété
nous (we)	répétions	ayons répété
vous (you, form./pl.)	répétiez	ayez répété
ils/elles (they)	répètent	aient répété

y → i Stem-Changing Verbs
For example: essuyer (to wipe)

Past Participle: essuyé (wiped); Present Participle: essuyant (wiping)

	Present Indicative	Imparfait	Future	Present Conditional
je/j' (I)	essuie	essuyais	essuierai	essuierais
tu (you, fam.)	essuies	essuyais	essuieras	essuierais
il/elle/on (he/she/it/one)	essuie	essuyait	essuiera	essuierait
nous (we)	essuyons	essuyions	essuierons	essuierions
vous (you, form./pl.)	essuyez	essuyiez	essuierez	essuieriez
ils/elles (they)	essuient	essuyaient	essuieront	essuieraient

	Passé Composé	Pluperfect	Future Perfect	Past Conditional
je/j' (I)	ai essuyé	avais essuyé	aurai essuyé	aurais essuyé
tu (you, fam.)	as essuyé	avais essuyé	auras essuyé	aurais essuyé
il/elle/on (he/she/it/one)	a essuyé	avait essuyé	aura essuyé	aurait essuyé
nous (we)	avons essuyé	avions essuyé	aurons essuyé	aurions essuyé
vous (you, form./pl.)	avez essuyé	aviez essuyé	aurez essuyé	auriez essuyé
ils/elles (they)	ont essuyé	avaient essuyé	auront essuyé	auraient essuyé

	Present Subjunctive	Past Subjunctive
je/j' (I)	essuie	aie essuyé
tu (you, fam.)	essuies	aies essuyé
il/elle/on (he/she/it/one)	essuie	ait essuyé
nous (we)	essuyions	ayons essuyé
vous (you, form./pl.)	essuyiez	ayez essuyé
ils/elles (they)	essuient	aient essuyé

l → ll Stem-Changing Verbs
For example: appeler (to call)

Past Participle: appelé (called); Present Participle: appelant (calling)

	Present Indicative	Imparfait	Future	Present Conditional
je/j' (I)	appelle	appelais	appellerai	appellerais
tu (you, fam.)	appelles	appelais	appelleras	appellerais
il/elle/on (he/she/it/one)	appelle	appelait	appellera	appellerait
nous (we)	appelons	appelions	appellerons	appellerions
vous (you, form./pl.)	appelez	appeliez	appellerez	appelleriez
ils/elles (they)	appellent	appelaient	appelleront	appelleraient

	Passé Composé	Pluperfect	Future Perfect	Past Conditional
je/j' (I)	ai appelé	avais appelé	aurai appelé	aurais appelé
tu (you, fam.)	as appelé	avais appelé	auras appelé	aurais appelé
il/elle/on (he/she/it/one)	a appelé	avait appelé	aura appelé	aurait appelé
nous (we)	avons appelé	avions appelé	aurons appelé	aurions appelé
vous (you, form./pl.)	avez appelé	aviez appelé	aurez appelé	auriez appelé
ils/elles (they)	ont appelé	avaient appelé	auront appelé	auraient appelé

	Present Subjunctive	Past Subjunctive
je/j' (I)	appelle	aie appelé
tu (you, fam.)	appelles	aies appelé
il/elle/on (he/she/it/one)	appelle	ait appelé
nous (we)	appelions	ayons appelé
vous (you, form./pl.)	appeliez	ayez appelé
ils/elles (they)	appellent	aient appelé

Book VI

Appendixes

t → tt Stem-Changing Verbs
For example: jeter (to throw, to throw away)

Past Participle: jeté (thrown); Present Participle: jetant (throwing)

	Present Indicative	Imparfait	Future	Present Conditional
je/j' (I)	jette	jetais	jetterai	jetterais
tu (you, fam.)	jettes	jetais	jetteras	jetterais
il/elle/on (he/she/it/one)	jette	jetait	jettera	jetterait
nous (we)	jetons	jetions	jetterons	jetterions
vous (you, form./pl.)	jetez	jetiez	jetterez	jetteriez
ils/elles (they)	jettent	jetaient	jetteront	jetteraient

	Passé Composé	Pluperfect	Future Perfect	Past Conditional
je/j' (I)	ai jeté	avais jeté	aurai jeté	aurais jeté
tu (you, fam.)	as jeté	avais jeté	auras jeté	aurais jeté
il/elle/on (he/she/it/one)	a jeté	avait jeté	aura jeté	aurait jeté
nous (we)	avons jeté	avions jeté	aurons jeté	aurions jeté
vous (you, form./pl.)	avez jeté	aviez jeté	aurez jeté	auriez jeté
ils/elles (they)	ont jeté	avaient jeté	auront jeté	auraient jeté

	Present Subjunctive	Past Subjunctive
je/j' (I)	jette	aie jeté
tu (you, fam.)	jettes	aies jeté
il/elle/on (he/she/it/one)	jette	ait jeté
nous (we)	jetions	ayons jeté
vous (you, form./pl.)	jetiez	ayez jeté
ils/elles (they)	jettent	aient jeté

Irregular French Verbs

This portion of the appendix contains the conjugations of common irregular verbs in alphabetical order. A few of these verbs are also reflexive.

accueillir (to welcome)
Past Participle: accueilli (welcomed);
Present Participle: accueillant (welcoming)

	Present Indicative	Imparfait	Future	Present Conditional
je/j' (I)	accueille	accueillais	accueillerai	accueillerais
tu (you, fam.)	accueilles	accueillais	accueilleras	accueillerais
il/elle/on (he/she/it/one)	accueille	accueillait	accueillera	accueillerait
nous (we)	accueillons	accueillions	accueillerons	accueillerions
vous (you, form./pl.)	accueillez	accueilliez	accueillerez	accueilleriez
ils/elles (they)	accueillent	accueillaient	accueilleront	accueilleraient

	Passé Composé	Pluperfect	Future Perfect	Past Conditional
je/j' (I)	ai accueilli	avais accueilli	aurai accueilli	aurais accueilli
tu (you, fam.)	as accueilli	avais accueilli	auras accueilli	aurais accueilli
il/elle/on (he/she/it/one)	a accueilli	avait accueilli	aura accueilli	aurait accueilli
nous (we)	avons accueilli	avions accueilli	aurons accueilli	aurions accueilli
vous (you, form./pl.)	avez accueilli	aviez accueilli	aurez accueilli	auriez accueilli
ils/elles (they)	ont accueilli	avaient accueilli	auront accueilli	auraient accueilli

	Present Subjunctive	Past Subjunctive
je/j' (I)	accueille	aie accueilli
tu (you, fam.)	accueilles	aies accueilli
il/elle/on (he/she/it/one)	accueille	ait accueilli
nous (we)	accueillions	ayons accueilli
vous (you, form./pl.)	accueilliez	ayez accueilli
ils/elles (they)	accueillent	aient accueilli

aller (to go)
Past Participle: allé (gone); Present Participle: allant (going)

	Present Indicative	Imparfait	Future	Present Conditional
je/j' (I)	vais	allais	irai	irais
tu (you, fam.)	vas	allais	iras	irais
il/elle/on (he/she/it/one)	va	allait	ira	irait
nous (we)	allons	allions	irons	irions
vous (you, form./pl.)	allez	alliez	irez	iriez
ils/elles (they)	vont	allaient	iront	iraient

	Passé Composé	Pluperfect	Future Perfect	Past Conditional
je/j' (I)	suis allé(e)	étais allé(e)	serai allé(e)	serais allé(e)
tu (you, fam.)	es allé(e)	étais allé(e)	seras allé(e)	serais allé(e)
il/elle/on (he/she/it/one)	est allé(e)	était allé(e)	sera allé(e)	serait allé(e)
nous (we)	sommes allé(s/es)	étions allé(s/es)	serons allé(s/es)	serions allé(s/es)
vous (you, form./pl.)	êtes allé(e/s/es)	étiez allé(e/s/es)	serez allé(e/s/es)	seriez allé(e/s/es)
ils/elles (they)	sont allé(s/es)	étaient allé(s/es)	seront allé(s/es)	seraient allé(s/es)

	Present Subjunctive	Past Subjunctive
je/j' (I)	aille	sois allé(e)
tu (you, fam.)	ailles	sois allé(e)
il/elle/on (he/she/it/one)	aille	soit allé(e)
nous (we)	allions	soyons allé(s/es)
vous (you, form./pl.)	alliez	soyez allé(e/s/es)
ils/elles (they)	aillent	soient allé(s/es)

s'asseoir (to sit)
Past Participle: assis (sat); Present Participle: asseyant (sitting)

	Present Indicative	**Imparfait**	**Future**	**Present Conditional**
je/j' (I)	m'assieds	m'asseyais	m'assiérai	m'assiérais
tu (you, fam.)	t'assieds	t'asseyais	t'assiéras	t'assiérais
il/elle/on (he/she/it/one)	s'assied	s'asseyait	s'assiéra	s'assiérait
nous (we)	nous asseyons	nous asseyions	nous assiérons	nous assiérions
vous (you, form./pl.)	vous asseyez	vous asseyiez	vous assiérez	vous assiériez
ils/elles (they)	s'asseyent	s'asseyaient	s'assiéront	s'assiéraient

	Passé Composé	**Pluperfect**	**Future Perfect**	**Past Conditional**
je/j' (I)	me suis assis(e)	m'étais assis(e)	me serai assis(e)	me serais assis(e)
tu (you, fam.)	t'es assis(e)	t'étais assis(e)	te seras assis(e)	te serais assis(e)
il/elle/on (he/she/it/one)	s'est assis(e)	s'était assis(e)	se sera assis(e)	se serait assis(e)
nous (we)	nous sommes assis(es)	nous étions assis(es)	nous serons assis(es)	nous serions assis(es)
vous (you, form./pl.)	vous êtes assis(e/es)	vous étiez assis(e/es)	vous serez assis(e/es)	vous seriez assis(e/es)
ils/elles (they)	se sont assis(es)	s'étaient assis(es)	se seront assis(es)	se seraient assis(es)

	Present Subjunctive	**Past Subjunctive**
je/j' (I)	m'asseye	me sois assis(e)
tu (you, fam.)	t'asseyes	te sois assis(e)
il/elle/on (he/she/it/one)	s'asseye	se soit assis(e)
nous (we)	nous asseyions	nous soyons assis(es)
vous (you, form./pl.)	vous asseyiez	vous soyez assis(e/es)
ils/elles (they)	s'asseyent	se soient assis(es)

avoir (to have)
Past Participle: eu (had); Present Participle: ayant (having)

	Present Indicative	Imparfait	Future	Present Conditional
je/j' (I)	ai	avais	aurai	aurais
tu (you, fam.)	as	avais	auras	aurais
il/elle/on (he/she/it/one)	a	avait	aura	aurait
nous (we)	avons	avions	aurons	aurions
vous (you, form./pl.)	avez	aviez	aurez	auriez
ils/elles (they)	ont	avaient	auront	auraient

	Passé Composé	Pluperfect	Future Perfect	Past Conditional
je/j' (I)	ai eu	avais eu	aurai eu	aurais eu
tu (you, fam.)	as eu	avais eu	auras eu	aurais eu
il/elle/on (he/she/it/one)	a eu	avait eu	aura eu	aurait eu
nous (we)	avons eu	avions eu	aurons eu	aurions eu
vous (you, form./pl.)	avez eu	aviez eu	aurez eu	auriez eu
ils/elles (they)	ont eu	avaient eu	auront eu	auraient eu

	Present Subjunctive	Past Subjunctive
je/j' (I)	aie	aie eu
tu (you, fam.)	aies	aies eu
il/elle/on (he/she/it/one)	ait	ait eu
nous (we)	ayons	ayons eu
vous (you, form./pl.)	ayez	ayez eu
ils/elles (they)	aient	aient eu

boire (to drink)
Past Participle: bu (drunk); Present Participle: buvant (drinking)

	Present Indicative	Imparfait	Future	Present Conditional
je/j' (I)	bois	buvais	boirai	boirais
tu (you, fam.)	bois	buvais	boiras	boirais
il/elle/on (he/she/it/one)	boit	buvait	boira	boirait
nous (we)	buvons	buvions	boirons	boirions
vous (you, form./pl.)	buvez	buviez	boirez	boiriez
ils/elles (they)	boivent	buvaient	boiront	boiraient

	Passé Composé	Pluperfect	Future Perfect	Past Conditional
je/j' (I)	ai bu	avais bu	aurai bu	aurais bu
tu (you, fam.)	as bu	avais bu	auras bu	aurais bu
il/elle/on (he/she/it/one)	a bu	avait bu	aura bu	aurait bu
nous (we)	avons bu	avions bu	aurons bu	aurions bu
vous (you, form./pl.)	avez bu	aviez bu	aurez bu	auriez bu
ils/elles (they)	ont bu	avaient bu	auront bu	auraient bu

	Present Subjunctive	Past Subjunctive
je/j' (I)	boive	aie bu
tu (you, fam.)	boives	aies bu
il/elle/on (he/she/it/one)	boive	ait bu
nous (we)	buvions	ayons bu
vous (you, form./pl.)	buviez	ayez bu
ils/elles (they)	boivent	aient bu

conduire (to drive)
Past Participle: conduit (driven);
Present Participle: conduisant (driving)

	Present Indicative	Imparfait	Future	Present Conditional
je/j' (I)	conduis	conduisais	conduirai	conduirais
tu (you, fam.)	conduis	conduisais	conduiras	conduirais
il/elle/on (he/she/it/one)	conduit	conduisait	conduira	conduirait
nous (we)	conduisons	conduisions	conduirons	conduirions
vous (you, form./pl.)	conduisez	conduisiez	conduirez	conduiriez
ils/elles (they)	conduisent	conduisaient	conduiront	conduiraient

	Passé Composé	Pluperfect	Future Perfect	Past Conditional
je/j' (I)	ai conduit	avais conduit	aurai conduit	aurais conduit
tu (you, fam.)	as conduit	avais conduit	auras conduit	aurais conduit
il/elle/on (he/she/it/one)	a conduit	avait conduit	aura conduit	aurait conduit
nous (we)	avons conduit	avions conduit	aurons conduit	aurions conduit
vous (you, form./pl.)	avez conduit	aviez conduit	aurez conduit	auriez conduit
ils/elles (they)	ont conduit	avaient conduit	auront conduit	auraient conduit

	Present Subjunctive	Past Subjunctive
je/j' (I)	conduise	aie conduit
tu (you, fam.)	conduises	aies conduit
il/elle/on (he/she/it/one)	conduise	ait conduit
nous (we)	conduisions	ayons conduit
vous (you, form./pl.)	conduisiez	ayez conduit
ils/elles (they)	conduisent	aient conduit

connaître (to know)
Past Participle: connu (known);
Present Participle: connaissant (knowing)

	Present Indicative	Imparfait	Future	Present Conditional
je/j' (I)	connais	connaissais	connaîtrai	connaîtrais
tu (you, fam.)	connais	connaissais	connaîtras	connaîtrais
il/elle/on (he/she/it/one)	connaît	connaissait	connaîtra	connaîtrait
nous (we)	connaissons	connaissions	connaîtrons	connaîtrions
vous (you, form./pl.)	connaissez	connaissiez	connaîtrez	connaîtriez
ils/elles (they)	connaissent	connaissaient	connaîtront	connaîtraient

	Passé Composé	Pluperfect	Future Perfect	Past Conditional
je/j' (I)	ai connu	avais connu	aurai connu	aurais connu
tu (you, fam.)	as connu	avais connu	auras connu	aurais connu
il/elle/on (he/she/it/one)	a connu	avait connu	aura connu	aurait connu
nous (we)	avons connu	avions connu	aurons connu	aurions connu
vous (you, form./pl.)	avez connu	aviez connu	aurez connu	auriez connu
ils/elles (they)	ont connu	avaient connu	auront connu	auraient connu

	Present Subjunctive	Past Subjunctive
je/j' (I)	connaisse	aie connu
tu (you, fam.)	connaisses	aies connu
il/elle/on (he/she/it/one)	connaisse	ait connu
nous (we)	connaissions	ayons connu
vous (you, form./pl.)	connaissiez	ayez connu
ils/elles (they)	connaissent	aient connu

construire (to build)
Past Participle: construit (built);
Present Participle: construisant (building)

	Present Indicative	Imparfait	Future	Present Conditional
je/j' (I)	construis	construisais	construirai	construirais
tu (you, fam.)	construis	construisais	construiras	construirais
il/elle/on (he/she/it/one)	construit	construisait	construira	construirait
nous (we)	construisons	construisions	construirons	construirions
vous (you, form./pl.)	construisez	construisiez	construirez	construiriez
ils/elles (they)	construisent	construisaient	construiront	construiraient

	Passé Composé	Pluperfect	Future Perfect	Past Conditional
je/j' (I)	ai construit	avais construit	aurai construit	aurais construit
tu (you, fam.)	as construit	avais construit	auras construit	aurais construit
il/elle/on (he/she/it/one)	a construit	avait construit	aura construit	aurait construit
nous (we)	avons construit	avions construit	aurons construit	aurions construit
vous (you, form./pl.)	avez construit	aviez construit	aurez construit	auriez construit
ils/elles (they)	ont construit	avaient construit	auront construit	auraient construit

	Present Subjunctive	Past Subjunctive
je/j' (I)	construise	aie construit
tu (you, fam.)	construises	aies construit
il/elle/on (he/she/it/one)	construise	ait construit
nous (we)	construisions	ayons construit
vous (you, form./pl.)	construisiez	ayez construit
ils/elles (they)	construisent	aient construit

courir (to run)
Past Participle: couru (run); Present Participle: courant (running)

	Present Indicative	Imparfait	Future	Present Conditional
je/j' (I)	cours	courais	courrai	courrais
tu (you, fam.)	cours	courais	courras	courrais
il/elle/on (he/she/it/one)	court	courait	courra	courrait
nous (we)	courons	courions	courrons	courrions
vous (you, form./pl.)	courez	couriez	courrez	courriez
ils/elles (they)	courent	couraient	courront	courraient

	Passé Composé	Pluperfect	Future Perfect	Past Conditional
je/j' (I)	ai couru	avais couru	aurai couru	aurais couru
tu (you, fam.)	as couru	avais couru	auras couru	aurais couru
il/elle/on (he/she/it/one)	a couru	avait couru	aura couru	aurait couru
nous (we)	avons couru	avions couru	aurons couru	aurions couru
vous (you, form./pl.)	avez couru	aviez couru	aurez couru	auriez couru
ils/elles (they)	ont couru	avaient couru	auront couru	auraient couru

	Present Subjunctive	Past Subjunctive
je/j' (I)	coure	aie couru
tu (you, fam.)	coures	aies couru
il/elle/on (he/she/it/one)	coure	ait couru
nous (we)	courions	ayons couru
vous (you, form./pl.)	couriez	ayez couru
ils/elles (they)	courent	aient couru

Book VI

Appendixes

craindre (to fear)
Past Participle: craint (feared); Present Participle: craignant (fearing)

	Present Indicative	Imparfait	Future	Present Conditional
je/j' (I)	crains	craignais	craindrai	craindrais
tu (you, fam.)	crains	craignais	craindras	craindrais
il/elle/on (he/she/it/one)	craint	craignait	craindra	craindrait
nous (we)	craignons	craignions	craindrons	craindrions
vous (you, form./pl.)	craignez	craigniez	craindrez	craindriez
ils/elles (they)	craignent	craignaient	craindront	craindraient

	Passé Composé	Pluperfect	Future Perfect	Past Conditional
je/j' (I)	ai craint	avais craint	aurai craint	aurais craint
tu (you, fam.)	as craint	avais craint	auras craint	aurais craint
il/elle/on (he/she/it/one)	a craint	avait craint	aura craint	aurait craint
nous (we)	avons craint	avions craint	aurons craint	aurions craint
vous (you, form./pl.)	avez craint	aviez craint	aurez craint	auriez craint
ils/elles (they)	ont craint	avaient craint	auront craint	auraient craint

	Present Subjunctive	Past Subjunctive
je/j' (I)	craigne	aie craint
tu (you, fam.)	craignes	aies craint
il/elle/on (he/she/it/one)	craigne	ait craint
nous (we)	craignions	ayons craint
vous (you, form./pl.)	craigniez	ayez craint
ils/elles (they)	craignent	aient craint

croire (to believe)
Past Participle: cru (believed); Present Participle: croyant (believing)

	Present Indicative	Imparfait	Future	Present Conditional
je/j' (I)	crois	croyais	croirai	croirais
tu (you, fam.)	crois	croyais	croiras	croirais
il/elle/on (he/she/it/one)	croit	croyait	croira	croirait
nous (we)	croyons	croyions	croirons	croirions
vous (you, form./pl.)	croyez	croyiez	croirez	croiriez
ils/elles (they)	croient	croyaient	croiront	croiraient

	Passé Composé	Pluperfect	Future Perfect	Past Conditional
je/j' (I)	ai cru	avais cru	aurai cru	aurais cru
tu (you, fam.)	as cru	avais cru	auras cru	aurais cru
il/elle/on (he/she/it/one)	a cru	avait cru	aura cru	aurait cru
nous (we)	avons cru	avions cru	aurons cru	aurions cru
vous (you, form./pl.)	avez cru	aviez cru	aurez cru	auriez cru
ils/elles (they)	ont cru	avaient cru	auront cru	auraient cru

	Present Subjunctive	Past Subjunctive
je/j' (I)	croie	aie cru
tu (you, fam.)	croies	aies cru
il/elle/on (he/she/it/one)	croie	ait cru
nous (we)	croyions	ayons cru
vous (you, form./pl.)	croyiez	ayez cru
ils/elles (they)	croient	aient cru

devoir (to have to)

Past Participle: dû (had to); Present Participle: devant (having to)

	Present Indicative	Imparfait	Future	Present Conditional
je/j' (I)	dois	devais	devrai	devrais
tu (you, fam.)	dois	devais	devras	devrais
il/elle/on (he/she/it/one)	doit	devait	devra	devrait
nous (we)	devons	devions	devrons	devrions
vous (you, form./pl.)	devez	deviez	devrez	devriez
ils/elles (they)	doivent	devaient	devront	devraient

	Passé Composé	Pluperfect	Future Perfect	Past Conditional
je/j' (I)	ai dû	avais dû	aurai dû	aurais dû
tu (you, fam.)	as dû	avais dû	auras dû	aurais dû
il/elle/on (he/she/it/one)	a dû	avait dû	aura dû	aurait dû
nous (we)	avons dû	avions dû	aurons dû	aurions dû
vous (you, form./pl.)	avez dû	aviez dû	aurez dû	auriez dû
ils/elles (they)	ont dû	avaient dû	auront dû	auraient dû

	Present Subjunctive	Past Subjunctive
je/j' (I)	doive	aie dû
tu (you, fam.)	doives	aies dû
il/elle/on (he/she/it/one)	doive	ait dû
nous (we)	devions	ayons dû
vous (you, form./pl.)	deviez	ayez dû
ils/elles (they)	doivent	aient dû

dire (to say)
Past Participle: dit (said); Present Participle: disant (saying)

	Present Indicative	Imparfait	Future	Present Conditional
je/j' (I)	dis	disais	dirai	dirais
tu (you, fam.)	dis	disais	diras	dirais
il/elle/on (he/she/it/one)	dit	disait	dira	dirait
nous (we)	disons	disions	dirons	dirions
vous (you, form./pl.)	dites	disiez	direz	diriez
ils/elles (they)	disent	disaient	diront	diraient

	Passé Composé	Pluperfect	Future Perfect	Past Conditional
je/j' (I)	ai dit	avais dit	aurai dit	aurais dit
tu (you, fam)	as dit	avais dit	auras dit	aurais dit
il/elle/on (he/she/it/one)	a dit	avait dit	aura dit	aurait dit
nous (we)	avons dit	avions dit	aurons dit	aurions dit
vous (you, form./pl.)	avez dit	aviez dit	aurez dit	auriez dit
ils/elles (they)	ont dit	avaient dit	auront dit	auraient dit

	Present Subjunctive	Past Subjunctive
je/j' (I)	dise	aie dit
tu (you, fam.)	dises	aies dit
il/elle/on (he/she/it/one)	dise	ait dit
nous (we)	disions	ayons dit
vous (you, form./pl.)	disiez	ayez dit
ils/elles (they)	disent	aient dit

Book VI

Appendixes

dormir (to sleep)
Past Participle: dormi (slept); Present Participle: dormant (sleeping)

	Present Indicative	Imparfait	Future	Present Conditional
je/j' (I)	dors	dormais	dormirai	dormirais
tu (you, fam.)	dors	dormais	dormiras	dormirais
il/elle/on (he/she/it/one)	dort	dormait	dormira	dormirait
nous (we)	dormons	dormions	dormirons	dormirions
vous (you, form./pl.)	dormez	dormiez	dormirez	dormiriez
ils/elles (they)	dorment	dorment	dormiront	dormiraient

	Passé Composé	Pluperfect	Future Perfect	Past Conditional
je/j' (I)	ai dormi	avais dormi	aurai dormi	aurais dormi
tu (you, fam.)	as dormi	avais dormi	auras dormi	aurais dormi
il/elle/on (he/she/it/one)	a dormi	avait dormi	aura dormi	aurait dormi
nous (we)	avons dormi	avions dormi	aurons dormi	aurions dormi
vous (you, form./pl.)	avez dormi	aviez dormi	aurez dormi	auriez dormi
ils/elles (they)	ont dormi	avaient dormi	auront dormi	auraient dormi

	Present Subjunctive	Past Subjunctive
je/j' (I)	dorme	aie dormi
tu (you, fam.)	dormes	aies dormi
il/elle/on (he/she/it/one)	dorme	ait dormi
nous (we)	dormions	ayons dormi
vous (you, form./pl.)	dormiez	ayez dormi
ils/elles (they)	dorment	aient dormi

écrire (to write)
Past Participle: écrit (written); Present Participle: écrivant (writing)

	Present Indicative	Imparfait	Future	Present Conditional
je/j' (I)	écris	écrivais	écrirai	écrirais
tu (you, fam.)	écris	écrivais	écriras	écrirais
il/elle/on (he/she/it/one)	écrit	écrivait	écrira	écrirait
nous (we)	écrivons	écrivions	écrirons	écririons
vous (you, form./pl.)	écrivez	écriviez	écrirez	écririez
ils/elles (they)	écrivent	écrivaient	écriront	écriraient

	Passé Composé	Pluperfect	Future Perfect	Past Conditional
je/j' (I)	ai écrit	avais écrit	aurai écrit	aurais écrit
tu (you, fam.)	as écrit	avais écrit	auras écrit	aurais écrit
il/elle/on (he/she/it/one)	a écrit	avait écrit	aura écrit	aurait écrit
nous (we)	avons écrit	avions écrit	aurons écrit	aurions écrit
vous (you, form./pl.)	avez écrit	aviez écrit	aurez écrit	auriez écrit
ils/elles (they)	ont écrit	avaient écrit	auront écrit	auraient écrit

	Present Subjunctive	Past Subjunctive
je/j' (I)	écrive	aie écrit
tu (you, fam.)	écrives	aies écrit
il/elle/on (he/she/it/one)	écrive	ait écrit
nous (we)	écrivions	ayons écrit
vous (you, form./pl.)	écriviez	ayez écrit
ils/elles (they)	écrivent	aient écrit

Book VI

Appendixes

éteindre (to turn off)
Past Participle: éteint (turned off);
Present Participle: éteignant (turning off)

	Present Indicative	Imparfait	Future	Present Conditional
je/j' (I)	éteins	éteignais	éteindrai	éteindrais
tu (you, fam.)	éteins	éteignais	éteindras	éteindrais
il/elle/on (he/she/it/one)	éteint	éteignait	éteindra	éteindrait
nous (we)	éteignons	éteignions	éteindrons	éteindrions
vous (you, form./pl.)	éteignez	éteigniez	éteindrez	éteindriez
ils/elles (they)	éteignent	éteignaient	éteindront	éteindraient

	Passé Composé	Pluperfect	Future Perfect	Past Conditional
je/j' (I)	ai éteint	avais éteint	aurai éteint	aurais éteint
tu (you, fam.)	as éteint	avais éteint	auras éteint	aurais éteint
il/elle/on (he/she/it/one)	a éteint	avait éteint	aura éteint	aurait éteint
nous (we)	avons éteint	avions éteint	aurons éteint	aurions éteint
vous (you, form./pl.)	avez éteint	aviez éteint	aurez éteint	auriez éteint
ils/elles (they)	ont éteint	avaient éteint	auront éteint	auraient éteint

	Present Subjunctive	Past Subjunctive
je/j' (I)	éteigne	aie éteint
tu (you, fam.)	éteignes	aies éteint
il/elle/on (he/she/it/one)	éteigne	ait éteint
nous (we)	éteignions	ayons éteint
vous (you, form./pl.)	éteigniez	ayez éteint
ils/elles (they)	éteignent	aient éteint

être (to be)
Past Participle: été (been); Present Participle: étant (being)

	Present Indicative	Imparfait	Future	Present Conditional
je/j' (I)	suis	étais	serai	serais
tu (you, fam.)	es	étais	seras	serais
il/elle/on (he/she/it/one)	est	était	sera	serait
nous (we)	sommes	étions	serons	serions
vous (you, form./pl.)	êtes	étiez	serez	seriez
ils/elles (they)	sont	étaient	seront	seraient

	Passé Composé	Pluperfect	Future Perfect	Past Conditional
je/j' (I)	ai été	avais été	aurai été	aurais été
tu (you, fam.)	as été	avais été	auras été	aurais été
il/elle/on (he/she/it/one)	a été	avait été	aura été	aurait été
nous (we)	avons été	avions été	aurons été	aurions été
nous (you, form./pl.)	avez été	aviez ete	aurez été	auriez été
ils/elles (they)	ont été	avaient été	auront été	auraient été

	Present Subjunctive	Past Subjunctive
je/j' (I)	sois	aie été
tu (you, fam.)	sois	aies été
il/elle/on (he/she/it/one)	soit	ait été
nous (we)	soyons	ayons été
vous (you, form./pl.)	soyez	ayez été
ils/elles (they)	soient	aient été

faire (to make, to do)
Past Participle: fait (made, done);
Present Participle: faisant (making, doing)

	Present Indicative	Imparfait	Future	Present Conditional
je/j' (I)	fais	faisais	ferai	ferais
tu (you, fam.)	fais	faisais	feras	ferais
il/elle/on (he/she/it/one)	fait	faisait	fera	ferait
nous (we)	faisons	faisions	ferons	ferions
vous (you, form./pl.)	faites	faisiez	ferez	feriez
ils/elles (they)	font	faisaient	feront	feraient

	Passé Composé	Pluperfect	Future Perfect	Past Conditional
je/j' (I)	ai fait	avais fait	aurai fait	aurais fait
tu (you, fam.)	as fait	avais fait	auras fait	aurais fait
il/elle/on (he/she/it/one)	a fait	avait fait	aura fait	aurait fait
nous (we)	avons fait	avions fait	aurons fait	aurions fait
vous (you, form./pl.)	avez fait	aviez fait	aurez fait	auriez fait
ils/elles (they)	ont fait	avaient fait	auront fait	auraient fait

	Present Subjunctive	Past Subjunctive
je/j' (I)	fasse	aie fait
tu (you, fam.)	fasses	aies fait
il/elle/on (he/she/it/one)	fasse	ait fait
nous (we)	fassions	ayons fait
vous (you, form./pl.)	fassiez	ayez fait
ils/elles (they)	fassent	aient fait

interdire (to forbid)
Past Participle: interdit (forbidden);
Present Participle: interdisant (forbidding)

	Present Indicative	Imparfait	Future	Present Conditional
je/j' (I)	interdis	interdisais	interdirai	interdirais
tu (you, fam.)	interdis	interdisais	interdiras	interdirais
il/elle/on (he/she/it/one)	interdit	interdisait	interdira	interdirait
nous (we)	interdisons	interdisions	interdirons	interdirions
vous (you, form./pl.)	interdisez	interdisiez	interdirez	interdiriez
ils/elles (they)	interdisent	interdisaient	interdiront	interdiraient

	Passé Composé	Pluperfect	Future Perfect	Past Conditional
je/j' (I)	ai interdit	avais interdit	aurai interdit	aurais interdit
tu (you, fam.)	as interdit	avais interdit	auras interdit	aurais interdit
il/elle/on (he/she/it/one)	a interdit	avait interdit	aura interdit	aurait interdit
nous (we)	avons interdit	avions interdit	aurons interdit	aurions interdit
vous (you, form./pl.)	avez interdit	aviez interdit	aurez interdit	auriez interdit
ils/elles (they)	ont interdit	avaient interdit	auront interdit	auraient interdit

	Present Subjunctive	Past Subjunctive
je/j' (I)	interdise	aie interdit
tu (you, fam.)	interdises	aies interdit
il/elle/on (he/she/it/one)	interdise	ait interdit
nous (we)	interdisions	ayons interdit
vous (you, form./pl.)	interdisiez	ayez interdit
ils/elles (they)	interdisent	aient interdit

Book VI

Appendixes

lire (to read)
Past Participle: lu (read); Present Participle: lisant (reading)

	Present Indicative	Imparfait	Future	Present Conditional
je/j' (I)	lis	lisais	lirai	lirais
tu (you, fam.)	lis	lisais	liras	lirais
il/elle/on (he/she/it/one)	lit	lisait	lira	lirait
nous (we)	lisons	lisions	lirons	lirions
vous (you, form./pl.)	lisez	lisiez	lirez	liriez
ils/elles (they)	lisent	lisaient	liront	liraient

	Passé Composé	Pluperfect	Future Perfect	Past Conditional
je/j' (I)	ai lu	avais lu	aurai lu	aurais lu
tu (you, fam.)	as lu	avais lu	auras lu	aurais lu
il/elle/on (he/she/it/one)	a lu	avait lu	aura lu	aurait lu
nous (we)	avons lu	avions lu	aurons lu	aurions lu
vous (you, form./pl.)	avez lu	aviez lu	aurez lu	auriez lu
ils/elles (they)	ont lu	avaient lu	auront lu	auraient lu

	Present Subjunctive	Past Subjunctive
je/j' (I)	lise	aie lu
tu (you, fam.)	lises	aies lu
il/elle/on (he/she/it/one)	lise	ait lu
nous (we)	lisions	ayons lu
vous (you, form./pl.)	lisiez	ayez lu
ils/elles (they)	lisent	aient lu

mentir (to lie, tell untruths)
Past Participle: menti (lied); Present Participle: mentant (lying)

	Present Indicative	Imparfait	Future	Present Conditional
je/j' (I)	mens	mentais	mentirai	mentirais
tu (you, fam.)	mens	mentais	mentiras	mentirais
il/elle/on (he/she/it/one)	ment	mentait	mentira	mentirait
nous (we)	mentons	mentions	mentirons	mentirions
vous (you, form./pl.)	mentez	mentiez	mentirez	mentiriez
ils/elles (they)	mentent	mentaient	mentiront	mentiraient

	Passé Composé	Pluperfect	Future Perfect	Past Conditional
je/j' (I)	ai menti	avais menti	aurai menti	aurais menti
tu (you, fam.)	as menti	avais menti	auras menti	aurais menti
il/elle/on (he/she/it/one)	a menti	avait menti	aura menti	aurait menti
nous (we)	avons menti	avions menti	aurons menti	aurions menti
vous (you, form./pl.)	avez menti	aviez menti	aurez menti	auriez menti
ils/elles (they)	ont menti	avaient menti	auront menti	auraient menti

	Present Subjunctive	Past Subjunctive
je/j' (I)	mente	aie menti
tu (you, fam.)	mentes	aies menti
il/elle/on (he/she/it/one)	mente	ait menti
nous (we)	mentions	ayons menti
vous (you, form./pl.)	mentiez	ayez menti
ils/elles (they)	mentent	aient menti

Book VI

Appendixes

mettre (to put, to put on, to place)
Past Participle: mis (put, put on, placed);
Present Participle: mettant (putting, putting on, placing)

	Present Indicative	Imparfait	Future	Present Conditional
je/j' (I)	mets	mettais	mettrai	mettrais
tu (you, fam.)	mets	mettais	mettras	mettrais
il/elle/on (he/she/it/one)	met	mettait	mettra	mettrait
nous (we)	mettons	mettions	mettrons	mettrions
vous (you, form./pl.)	mettez	mettiez	mettrez	mettriez
ils/elles (they)	mettent	mettaient	mettront	mettraient

	Passé Composé	Pluperfect	Future Perfect	Past Conditional
je/j' (I)	ai mis	avais mis	aurai mis	aurais mis
tu (you, fam.)	as mis	avais mis	auras mis	aurais mis
il/elle/on (he/she/it/one)	a mis	avait mis	aura mis	aurait mis
nous (we)	avons mis	avions mis	aurons mis	aurions mis
vous (you, form./pl.)	avez mis	aviez mis	aurez mis	auriez mis
ils/elles (they)	ont mis	avaient mis	auront mis	auraient mis

	Present Subjunctive	Past Subjunctive
je/j' (I)	mette	aie mis
tu (you, fam.)	mettes	aies mis
il/elle/on (he/she/it/one)	mette	ait mis
nous (we)	mettions	ayons mis
vous (you, form./pl.)	mettiez	ayez mis
ils/elles (they)	mettent	aient mis

mourir (to die)
Past Participle: mort (died); Present Participle: mourant (dying)

	Present Indicative	Imparfait	Future	Present Conditional
je/j' (I)	meurs	mourais	mourrai	mourrais
tu (you, fam.)	meurs	mourais	mourras	mourrais
il/elle/on (he/she/it/one)	meurt	mourait	mourra	mourrait
nous (we)	mourons	mourions	mourrons	mourrions
vous (you, form./pl.)	mourez	mouriez	mourrez	mourriez
ils/elles (they)	meurent	mouraient	mourront	mourraient

	Passé Composé	Pluperfect	Future Perfect	Past Conditional
je/j' (I)	suis mort(e)	étais mort(e)	serai mort(e)	serais mort(e)
tu (you, fam.)	es mort(e)	étais mort(e)	seras mort(e)	serais mort(e)
il/elle/on (he/she/it/one)	est mort(e)	était mort(e)	sera mort(e)	serait mort(e)
nous (we)	sommes mort(s/es)	étions mort(s/es)	serons mort(s/es)	serions mort(s/es)
vous (you, form./pl.)	êtes mort(e/s/es)	étiez mort(e/s/es)	serez mort(e/s/es)	seriez mort(e/s/es)
ils/elles (they)	sont mort(s/es)	étaient mort(s/es)	seront mort(s/es)	seraient mort(s/es)

	Present Subjunctive	Past Subjunctive
je/j' (I)	meure	sois mort(e)
tu (you, fam.)	meures	sois mort(e)
il/elle/on (he/she/it/one)	meure	soit mort(e)
nous (we)	mourions	soyons mort(s/es)
vous (you, form./pl.)	mouriez	soyez mort(e/s/es)
ils/elles (they)	meurent	soient mort(s/es)

Book VI

Appendixes

naître (to be born)
Past Participle: né ([been] born);
Present Participle: naissant (being born)

	Present Indicative	Imparfait	Future	Present Conditional
je/j' (I)	nais	naissais	naîtrai	naîtrais
tu (you, fam.)	nais	naissais	naîtras	naîtrais
il/elle/on (he/she/it/one)	naît	naissait	naîtra	naîtrait
nous (we)	naissons	naissions	naîtrons	naîtrions
vous (you, form./pl.)	naissez	naissiez	naîtrez	naîtriez
ils/elles (they)	naissent	naissaient	naîtront	naîtraient

	Passé Composé	Pluperfect	Future Perfect	Past Conditional
je/j' (I)	suis né(e)	étais né(e)	serai né(e)	serais né(e)
tu (you, fam.)	es né(e)	étais né(e)	seras né(e)	serais né(e)
il/elle/on (he/she/it/one)	est né(e)	était né(e)	sera né(e)	serait né(e)
nous (we)	sommes né(s/es)	étions né(s/es)	serons né(s/es)	serions né(s/es)
vous (you, form./pl.)	êtes né(e/s/es)	étiez né(e/s/es)	serez né(e/s/es)	seriez né(e/s/es)
ils/elles (they)	sont né(s/es)	étaient né(s/es)	seront né(s/es)	seraient né(s/es)

	Present Subjunctive	Past Subjunctive
je/j' (I)	naisse	sois né(e)
tu (you, fam.)	naisses	sois né(e)
il/elle/on (he/she/it/one)	naisse	soit né(e)
nous (we)	naissions	soyons né(s/es)
vous (you, form./pl.)	naissiez	soyez né(e/s/es)
ils/elles (they)	naissent	soient né(s/es)

obtenir (to obtain)
Past Participle: obtenu (obtained);
Present Participle: obtenant (obtaining)

	Present Indicative	Imparfait	Future	Present Conditional
je/j' (I)	obtiens	obtenais	obtiendrai	obtiendrais
tu (you, fam.)	obtiens	obtenais	obtiendras	obtiendrais
il/elle/on (he/she/it/one)	obtient	obtenait	obtiendra	obtiendrait
nous (we)	obtenons	obtenions	obtiendrons	obtiendrions
vous (you, form./pl.)	obtenez	obteniez	obtiendrez	obtiendriez
ils/elles (they)	obtiennent	obtenaient	obtiendront	obtiendraient

	Passé Composé	Pluperfect	Future Perfect	Past Conditional
je/j' (I)	ai obtenu	avais obtenu	aurai obtenu	aurais obtenu
tu (you, fam.)	as obtenu	avais obtenu	auras obtenu	aurais obtenu
il/elle/on (he/she/it/one)	a obtenu	avait obtenu	aura obtenu	aurait obtenu
nous (we)	avons obtenu	avions obtenu	aurons obtenu	aurions obtenu
vous (you, form./pl.)	avez obtenu	aviez obtenu	aurez obtenu	auriez obtenu
ils/elles (they)	ont obtenu	avaient obtenu	auront obtenu	auraient obtenu

	Present Subjunctive	Past Subjunctive
je/j' (I)	obtienne	aie obtenu
tu (you, fam.)	obtiennes	aies obtenu
il/elle/on (he/she/it/one)	obtienne	ait obtenu
nous (we)	obtenions	ayons obtenu
vous (you, form./pl.)	obteniez	ayez obtenu
ils/elles (they)	obtiennent	aient obtenu

Book VI

Appendixes

offrir (to offer)
Past Participle: offert (offered); Present Participle: offrant (offering)

	Present Indicative	Imparfait	Future	Present Conditional
je/j' (I)	offre	offrais	offrirai	offrirais
tu (you, fam.)	offres	offrais	offriras	offrirais
il/elle/on (he/she/it/one)	offre	offrait	offrira	offrirait
nous (we)	offrons	offrions	offrirons	offririons
vous (you, form./pl.)	offrez	offriez	offrirez	offririez
ils/elles (they)	offrent	offraient	offriront	offriraient

	Passé Composé	Pluperfect	Future Perfect	Past Conditional
je/j' (I)	ai offert	avais offert	aurai offert	aurais offert
tu (you, fam.)	as offert	avais offert	auras offert	aurais offert
il/elle/on (he/she/it/one)	a offert	avait offert	aura offert	aurait offert
nous (we)	avons offert	avions offert	aurons offert	aurions offert
vous (you, form./pl.)	avez offert	aviez offert	aurez offert	auriez offert
ils/elles (they)	ont offert	avaient offert	auront offert	auraient offert

	Present Subjunctive	Past Subjunctive
je/j' (I)	offre	aie offert
tu (you, fam.)	offres	aies offert
il/elle/on (he/she/it/one)	offre	ait offert
nous (we)	offrions	ayons offert
vous (you, form./pl.)	offriez	ayez offert
ils/elles (they)	offrent	aient offert

ouvrir (to open)
Past Participle: ouvert (opened);
Present Participle: ouvrant (opening)

	Present Indicative	Imparfait	Future	Present Conditional
je/j' (I)	ouvre	ouvrais	ouvrirai	ouvrirais
tu (you, fam.)	ouvres	ouvrais	ouvriras	ouvrirais
il/elle/on (he/she/it/one)	ouvre	ouvrait	ouvrira	ouvrirait
nous (we)	ouvrons	ouvrions	ouvrirons	ouvririons
vous (you, form./pl.)	ouvrez	ouvriez	ouvrirez	ouvririez
ils/elles (they)	ouvrent	ouvraient	ouvriront	ouvriraient

	Passé Composé	Pluperfect	Future Perfect	Past Conditional
je/j' (I)	ai ouvert	avais ouvert	aurai ouvert	aurais ouvert
tu (you, fam.)	as ouvert	avais ouvert	auras ouvert	aurais ouvert
il/elle/on (he/she/it/one)	a ouvert	avait ouvert	aura ouvert	aurait ouvert
nous (we)	avons ouvert	avions ouvert	aurons ouvert	aurions ouvert
vous (you, form./pl.)	avez ouvert	aviez ouvert	aurez ouvert	auriez ouvert
ils/elles (they)	ont ouvert	avaient ouvert	auront ouvert	auraient ouvert

	Present Subjunctive	Past Subjunctive
je/j' (I)	ouvre	aie ouvert
tu (you, fam.)	ouvres	aies ouvert
il/elle/on (he/she/it/one)	ouvre	ait ouvert
nous (we)	ouvrions	ayons ouvert
vous (you, form./pl.)	ouvriez	ayez ouvert
ils/elles (they)	ouvrent	aient ouvert

paraître (to appear, to seem)
Past Participle: paru (appeared, seemed);
Present Participle: paraissant (appearing, seeming)

	Present Indicative	Imparfait	Future	Present Conditional
je/j' (I)	parais	paraissais	paraîtrai	paraîtrais
tu (you, fam.)	parais	paraissais	paraîtras	paraîtrais
il/elle/on (he/she/it/one)	paraît	paraissait	paraîtra	paraîtrait
nous (we)	paraissons	paraissions	paraîtrons	paraîtrions
vous (you, form./pl.)	paraissez	paraissiez	paraîtrez	paraîtriez
ils/elles (they)	paraissent	paraissaient	paraîtront	paraîtraient

	Passé Composé	Pluperfect	Future Perfect	Past Conditional
je/j' (I)	ai paru	avais paru	aurai paru	aurais paru
tu (you, fam.)	as paru	avais paru	auras paru	aurais paru
il/elle/on (he/she/it/one)	a paru	avait paru	aura paru	aurait paru
nous (we)	avons paru	avions paru	aurons paru	aurions paru
vous (you, form./pl.)	avez paru	aviez paru	aurez paru	auriez paru
ils/elles (they)	ont paru	avaient paru	auront paru	auraient paru

	Present Subjunctive	Past Subjunctive
je/j' (I)	paraisse	aie paru
tu (you, fam.)	paraisses	aies paru
il/elle/on (he/she/it/one)	paraisse	ait paru
nous (we)	paraissions	ayons paru
vous (you, form./pl.)	paraissiez	ayez paru
ils/elles (they)	paraissent	aient paru

partir (to leave)
Past Participle: parti (left); Present Participle: partant (leaving)

	Present Indicative	Imparfait	Future	Present Conditional
je/j' (I)	pars	partais	partirai	partirais
tu (you, fam.)	pars	partais	partiras	partirais
il/elle/on (he/she/it/one)	part	partait	partira	partirait
nous (we)	partons	partions	partirons	partirions
vous (you, form./pl.)	partez	partiez	partirez	partiriez
ils/elles (they)	partent	partaient	partiront	partiraient

	Passé Composé	Pluperfect	Future Perfect	Past Conditional
je/j' (I)	suis parti(e)	étais parti(e)	serai parti(e)	serais parti(e)
tu (you, fam.)	es parti(e)	étais parti(e)	seras parti(e)	serais parti(e)
il/elle/on (he/she/it/one)	est parti(e)	était parti(e)	sera parti(e)	serait parti(e)
nous (we)	sommes parti(s/es)	étions parti(s/es)	serons parti(s/es)	serions parti(s/es)
vous (you, form./pl.)	êtes parti(e/s/es)	étiez parti(e/s/es)	serez parti(e/s/es)	seriez parti(e/s/es)
ils/elles (they)	sont parti(s/es)	étaient parti(s/es)	seront parti(s/es)	seraient parti(s/es)

	Present Subjunctive	Past Subjunctive
je/j' (I)	parte	sois parti(e)
tu (you, fam.)	partes	sois parti(e)
il/elle/on (he/she/it/one)	parte	soit parti(e)
nous (we)	partions	soyons parti(s/es)
vous (you, form./pl.)	partiez	soyez parti(e/s/es)
ils/elles (they)	partent	soient parti(s/es)

Book VI

Appendixes

plaire (to please)
Past Participle: plu (pleased); Present Participle: plaisant (pleasing)

	Present Indicative	Imparfait	Future	Present Conditional
je/j' (I)	plais	plaisais	plairai	plairais
tu (you, fam.)	plais	plaisais	plairas	plairais
il/elle/on (he/she/it/one)	plaît	plaisait	plaira	plairait
nous (we)	plaisons	plaisions	plairons	plairions
vous (you, form./pl.)	plaisez	plaisiez	plairez	plairiez
ils/elles (they)	plaisent	plaisaient	plairont	plairaient

	Passé Composé	Pluperfect	Future Perfect	Past Conditional
je/j' (I)	ai plu	avais plu	aurai plu	aurais plu
tu (you, fam.)	as plu	avais plu	auras plu	aurais plu
il/elle/on (he/she/it/one)	a plu	avait plu	aura plu	aurait plu
nous (we)	avons plu	avions plu	aurons plu	aurions plu
vous (you, form./pl.)	avez plu	aviez plu	aurez plu	auriez plu
ils/elles (they)	ont plu	avaient plu	auront plu	auraient plu

	Present Subjunctive	Past Subjunctive
je/j' (I)	plaise	aie plu
tu (you, fam.)	plaises	aies plu
il/elle/on (he/she/it/one)	plaise	ait plu
nous (we)	plaisions	ayons plu
vous (you, form./pl.)	plaisiez	ayez plu
ils/elles (they)	plaisent	aient plu

pouvoir (to be able to)
Past Participle: pu (been able to);
Present Participle: pouvant (being able to)

	Present Indicative	Imparfait	Future	Present Conditional
je/j' (I)	peux	pouvais	pourrai	pourrais
tu (you, fam.)	peux	pouvais	pourras	pourrais
il/elle/on (he/she/it/one)	peut	pouvait	pourra	pourrait
nous (we)	pouvons	pouvions	pourrons	pourrions
vous (you, form./pl.)	pouvez	pouviez	pourrez	pourriez
ils/elles (they)	peuvent	pouvaient	pourront	pourraient

	Passé Composé	Pluperfect	Future Perfect	Past Conditional
je/j' (I)	ai pu	avais pu	aurai pu	aurais pu
tu (you, fam.)	as pu	avais pu	auras pu	aurais pu
il/elle/on (he/she/it/one)	a pu	avait pu	aura pu	aurait pu
nous (we)	avons pu	avions pu	aurons pu	aurions pu
vous (you, form./pl.)	avez pu	aviez pu	aurez pu	auriez pu
ils/elles (they)	ont pu	avaient pu	auront pu	auraient pu

	Present Subjunctive	Past Subjunctive
je/j' (I)	puisse	aie pu
tu (you, fam.)	puisses	aies pu
il/elle/on (he/she/it/one)	puisse	ait pu
nous (we)	puissions	ayons pu
vous (you, form./pl.)	puissiez	ayez pu
ils/elles (they)	puissent	aient pu

Book VI

Appendixes

prendre (to take)
Past Participle: pris (taken); Present Participle: prenant (taking)

	Present Indicative	Imparfait	Future	Present Conditional
je/j' (I)	prends	prenais	prendrai	prendrais
tu (you, fam.)	prends	prenais	prendras	prendrais
il/elle/on (he/she/it/one)	prend	prenait	prendra	prendrait
nous (we)	prenons	prenions	prendrons	prendrions
vous (you, form./pl.)	prenez	preniez	prendrez	prendriez
ils/elles (they)	prennent	prenaient	prendront	prendraient

	Passé Composé	Pluperfect	Future Perfect	Past Conditional
je/j' (I)	ai pris	avais pris	aurai pris	aurais pris
tu (you, fam.)	as pris	avais pris	auras pris	aurais pris
il/elle/on (he/she/it/one)	a pris	avait pris	aura pris	aurait pris
nous (we)	avons pris	avions pris	aurons pris	aurions pris
vous (you, form./pl.)	avez pris	aviez pris	aurez pris	auriez pris
ils/elles (they)	ont pris	avaient pris	auront pris	auraient pris

	Present Subjunctive	Past Subjunctive
je/j' (I)	prenne	aie pris
tu (you, fam.)	prennes	aies pris
il/elle/on (he/she/it/one)	prenne	ait pris
nous (we)	prenions	ayons pris
vous (you, form./pl.)	preniez	ayez pris
ils/elles (they)	prennent	aient pris

recevoir (to receive)
Past Participle: reçu (received);
Present Participle: recevant (receiving)

	Present Indicative	Imparfait	Future	Present Conditional
je/j' (I)	reçois	recevais	recevrai	recevrais
tu (you, fam.)	reçois	recevais	recevras	recevrais
il/elle/on (he/she/it/one)	reçoit	recevait	recevra	recevrait
nous (we)	recevons	recevions	recevrons	recevrions
vous (you, form./pl.)	recevez	receviez	recevrez	recevriez
ils/elles (they)	reçoivent	recevaient	recevront	recevraient

	Passé Composé	Pluperfect	Future Perfect	Past Conditional
je/j' (I)	ai reçu	avais reçu	aurai reçu	aurais reçu
tu (you, fam.)	as reçu	avais reçu	auras reçu	aurais reçu
il/elle/on (he/she/it/one)	a reçu	avait reçu	aura reçu	aurait reçu
nous (we)	avons reçu	avions reçu	aurons reçu	aurions reçu
vous (you, form./pl.)	avez reçu	aviez reçu	aurez reçu	auriez reçu
ils/elles (they)	ont reçu	avaient reçu	auront reçu	auraient reçu

	Present Subjunctive	Past Subjunctive
je/j' (I)	reçoive	aie reçu
tu (you, fam.)	reçoives	aies reçu
il/elle/on (he/she/it/one)	reçoive	ait reçu
nous (we)	recevions	ayons reçu
vous (you, form./pl.)	receviez	ayez reçu
ils/elles (they)	reçoivent	aient reçu

rire (to laugh)
Past Participle: ri (laughed); Present Participle: riant (laughing)

	Present Indicative	Imparfait	Future	Present Conditional
je/j' (I)	ris	riais	rirai	rirais
tu (you, fam.)	ris	riais	riras	rirais
il/elle/on (he/she/it/one)	rit	riait	rira	rirait
nous (we)	rions	riions	rirons	ririons
vous (you, form./pl.)	riez	riiez	rirez	ririez
ils/elles (they)	rient	riaient	riront	riraient

	Passé Composé	Pluperfect	Future Perfect	Past Conditional
je/j' (I)	ai ri	avais ri	aurai ri	aurais ri
tu (you, fam.)	as ri	avais ri	auras ri	aurais ri
il/elle/on (he/she/it/one)	a ri	avait ri	aura ri	aurait ri
nous (we)	avons ri	avions ri	aurons ri	aurions ri
vous (you, form./pl.)	avez ri	aviez ri	aurez ri	auriez ri
ils/elles (they)	ont ri	avaient ri	auront ri	auraient ri

	Present Subjunctive	Past Subjunctive
je/j' (I)	rie	aie ri
tu (you, fam.)	ries	aies ri
il/elle/on (he/she/it/one)	rie	ait ri
nous (we)	riions	ayons ri
vous (you, form./pl.)	riiez	ayez ri
ils/elles (they)	rient	aient ri

savoir (to know)
Past Participle: su (known); Present Participle: sachant (knowing)

	Present Indicative	Imparfait	Future	Present Conditional
je/j' (I)	sais	savais	saurai	saurais
tu (you, fam.)	sais	savais	sauras	saurais
il/elle/on (he/she/it/one)	sait	savait	saura	saurait
nous (we)	savons	savions	saurons	saurions
vous (you, form./pl.)	savez	saviez	saurez	sauriez
ils/elles (they)	savent	savaient	sauront	sauraient

	Passé Composé	Pluperfect	Future Perfect	Past Conditional
je/j' (I)	ai su	avais su	aurai su	aurais su
tu (you, fam.)	as su	avais su	auras su	aurais su
il/elle/on (he/she/it/one)	a su	avait su	aura su	aurait su
nous (we)	avons su	avions su	aurons su	aurions su
vous (you, form./pl.)	avez su	avions su	aurez su	auriez su
ils/elles (they)	ont su	avaient su	auront su	auraient su

	Present Subjunctive	Past Subjunctive
je/j' (I)	sache	aie su
tu (you, fam.)	saches	aies su
il/elle/on (he/she/it/one)	sache	ait su
nous (we)	sachions	ayons su
vous (you, form./pl.)	sachiez	ayez su
ils/elles (they)	sachent	aient su

servir (to serve)
Past Participle: servi (served); Present Participle: servant (serving)

	Present Indicative	Imparfait	Future	Present Conditional
je/j' (I)	sers	servais	servirai	servirais
tu (you, fam.)	sers	servais	serviras	servirais
il/elle/on (he/she/it/one)	sert	servait	servira	servirait
nous (we)	servons	servions	servirons	servirions
vous (you, form./pl.)	servez	serviez	servirez	serviriez
ils/elles (they)	servent	servaient	serviront	serviraient

	Passé Composé	Pluperfect	Future Perfect	Past Conditional
je/j' (I)	ai servi	avais servi	aurai servi	aurais servi
tu (you, fam.)	as servi	avais servi	auras servi	aurais servi
il/elle/on (he/she/it/one)	a servi	avait servi	aura servi	aurait servi
nous (we)	avons servi	avions servi	aurons servi	aurions servi
vous (you, form./pl.)	avez servi	aviez servi	aurez servi	auriez servi
ils/elles (they)	ont servi	avaient servi	auront servi	auraient servi

	Present Subjunctive	Past Subjunctive
je/j' (I)	serve	aie servi
tu (you, fam.)	serves	aies servi
il/elle/on (he/she/it/one)	serve	ait servi
nous (we)	servions	ayons servi
vous (you, form./pl.)	serviez	ayez servi
ils/elles (they)	servent	aient servi

suivre (to follow)
Past Participle: suivi (followed);
Present Participle: suivant (following)

	Present Indicative	Imparfait	Future	Present Conditional
je/j' (I)	suis	suivais	suivrai	suivrais
tu (you, fam.)	suis	suivais	suivras	suivrais
il/elle/on (he/she/it/one)	suit	suivait	suivra	suivrait
nous (we)	suivons	suivions	suivrons	suivrions
vous (you, form./pl.)	suivez	suiviez	suivrez	suivriez
ils/elles (they)	suivent	suivaient	suivront	suivraient
	Passé Composé	**Pluperfect**	**Future Perfect**	**Past Conditional**
je/j' (I)	ai suivi	avais suivi	aurai suivi	aurais suivi
tu (you, fam.)	as suivi	avais suivi	auras suivi	aurais suivi
il/elle/on (he/she/it/one)	a suivi	avait suivi	aura suivi	aurait suivi
nous (we)	avons suivi	avions suivi	aurons suivi	aurions suivi
vous (you, form./pl.)	avez suivi	aviez suivi	aurez suivi	auriez suivi
ils/elles (they)	ont suivi	avaient suivi	auront suivi	auraient suivi
	Present Subjunctive	**Past Subjunctive**		
je/j' (I)	suive	aie suivi		
tu (you, fam.)	suives	aies suivi		
il/elle/on (he/she/it/one)	suive	ait suivi		
nous (we)	suivions	ayons suivi		
vous (you, form./pl.)	suiviez	ayez suivi		
ils/elles (they)	suivent	aient suivi		

Book VI

Appendixes

se taire (to be quiet)
Past Participle: tu (been quiet); Present Participle: taisant (being quiet)

	Present Indicative	Imparfait	Future	Present Conditional
je/j' (I)	me tais	me taisais	me tairai	me tairais
tu (you, fam.)	te tais	te taisais	te tairas	te tairais
il/elle/on (he/she/it/one)	se tait	se taisait	se taira	se tairait
nous (we)	nous taisons	nous taisions	nous tairons	nous tairions
vous (you, form./pl.)	vous taisez	vous taisiez	vous tairez	vous tairiez
ils/elles (they)	se taisent	se taisaient	se tairont	se tairaient

	Passé Composé	Pluperfect	Future Perfect	Past Conditional
je/j' (I)	me suis tu(e)	m'étais tu(e)	me serai tu(e)	me serais tu(e)
tu (you, fam.)	t'es tu(e)	t'étais tu(e)	te seras tu(e)	te serais tu(e)
il/elle/on (he/she/it/one)	s'est tu(e)	s'était tu(e)	se sera tu(e)	se serait tu(e)
nous (we)	nous sommes tu(s/es)	nous étions tu(s/es)	nous serons tu(s/es)	nous serions tu(s/es)
vous (you, form./pl.)	vous êtes tu(e/s/es)	vous étiez tu(e/s/es)	vous serez tu(e/s/es)	vous seriez tu(e/s/es)
ils/elles (they)	se sont tu(s/es)	s'étaient tu(s/es)	se seront tu(s/es)	se seraient tu(s/es)

	Present Subjunctive	Past Subjunctive
je/j' (I)	me taise	me sois tu(e)
tu (you, fam.)	te taises	te sois tu(e)
il/elle/on (he/she/it/one)	se taise	se soit tu(e)
nous (we)	nous taisions	nous soyons tu(s/es)
vous (you, form./pl.)	vous taisiez	vous soyez tu(e/s/es)
ils/elles (they)	se taisent	se soient tu(s/es)

tenir (to hold)
Past Participle: tenu (held); Present Participle: tenant (holding)

	Present Indicative	Imparfait	Future	Present Conditional
je/j' (I)	tiens	tenais	tiendrai	tiendrais
tu (you, fam.)	tiens	tenais	tiendras	tiendrais
il/elle/on (he/she/it/one)	tient	tenait	tiendra	tiendrait
nous (we)	tenons	tenions	tiendrons	tiendrions
vous (you, form./pl.)	tenez	teniez	tiendrez	tiendriez
ils/elles (they)	tiennent	tenaient	tiendront	tiendraient

	Passé Composé	Pluperfect	Future Perfect	Past Conditional
je/j' (I)	ai tenu	avais tenu	aurai tenu	aurais tenu
tu (you, fam.)	as tenu	avais tenu	auras tenu	aurais tenu
il/elle/on (he/she/it/one)	a tenu	avait tenu	aura tenu	aurait tenu
nous (we)	avons tenu	avions tenu	aurons tenu	aurions tenu
vous (you, form./pl.)	avez tenu	aviez tenu	aurez tenu	auriez tenu
ils/elles (they)	ont tenu	avaient tenu	auront tenu	auraient tenu

	Present Subjunctive	Past Subjunctive
je/j' (I)	tienne	aie tenu
tu (you, fam.)	tiennes	aies tenu
il/elle/on (he/she/it/one)	tienne	ait tenu
nous (we)	tenions	ayons tenu
vous (you, form./pl.)	teniez	ayez tenu
ils/elles (they)	tiennent	aient tenu

Book VI

Appendixes

venir (to come)
Past Participle: venu (come); Present Participle: venant (coming)

	Present Indicative	Imparfait	Future	Present Conditional
je/j' (I)	viens	venais	viendrai	viendrais
tu (you, fam.)	viens	venais	viendras	viendrais
il/elle/on (he/she/it/one)	vient	venait	viendra	viendrait
nous (we)	venons	venions	viendrons	viendrions
vous (you, form./pl.)	venez	veniez	viendrez	viendriez
ils/elles (they)	viennent	venaient	viendront	viendraient

	Passé Composé	Pluperfect	Future Perfect	Past Conditional
je/j' (I)	suis venu(e)	étais venu(e)	serai venu(e)	serais venu(e)
tu (you, fam.)	es venu(e)	étais venu(e)	seras venu(e)	serais venu(e)
il/elle/on (he/she/it/one)	est venu(e)	était venu(e)	sera venu(e)	serait venu(e)
nous (we)	sommes venu(s/es)	étions venu(s/es)	serons venu(s/es)	serions venu(s/es)
vous (you, form./pl.)	êtes venu(e/s/es)	étiez venu(e/s/es)	serez venu(e/s/es)	seriez venu(e/s/es)
ils/elles (they)	sont venu(s/es)	étaient venu(s/es)	seront venu(s/es)	seraient venu(s/es)

	Present Subjunctive	Past Subjunctive
je/j' (I)	vienne	sois venu(e)
tu (you, fam.)	viennes	sois venu(e)
il/elle/on (he/she/it/one)	vienne	soit venu(e)
nous (we)	venions	soyons venu(s/es)
vous (you, form./pl.)	veniez	soyez venu(e/s/es)
ils/elles (they)	viennent	soient venu(s/es)

vivre (to live, to exist)
Past Participle: vécu (lived, existed);
Present Participle: vivant (living, existing)

	Present Indicative	Imparfait	Future	Present Conditional
je/j' (I)	vis	vivais	vivrai	vivrais
tu (you, fam.)	vis	vivais	vivras	vivrais
il/elle/on (he/she/it/one)	vit	vivait	vivra	vivrait
nous (we)	vivons	vivions	vivrons	vivrions
vous (you, form./pl.)	vivez	viviez	vivrez	vivriez
ils/elles (they)	vivent	vivaient	vivront	vivraient

	Passé Composé	Pluperfect	Future Perfect	Past Conditional
je/j' (I)	ai vécu	avais vécu	aurai vécu	aurais vécu
tu (you, fam.)	as vécu	avais vécu	auras vécu	aurais vécu
il/elle/on (he/she/it/one)	a vécu	avait vécu	aura vécu	aurait vécu
nous (we)	avons vécu	avions vécu	aurons vécu	aurions vécu
vous (you, form./pl.)	avez vécu	aviez vécu	aurez vécu	auriez vécu
ils/elles (they)	ont vécu	avaient vécu	auront vécu	auraient vécu

	Present Subjunctive	Past Subjunctive
je/j' (I)	vive	aie vécu
tu (you, fam.)	vives	aies vécu
il/elle/on (he/she/it/one)	vive	ait vécu
nous (we)	vivions	ayons vécu
vous (you, form./pl.)	viviez	ayez vécu
ils/elles (they)	vivent	aient vécu

voir (to see)
Past Participle: vu (seen); Present Participle: voyant (seeing)

	Present Indicative	Imparfait	Future	Present Conditional
je/j' (I)	vois	voyais	verrai	verrais
tu (you, fam.)	vois	voyais	verras	verrais
il/elle/on (he/she/it/one)	voit	voyait	verra	verrait
nous (we)	voyons	voyions	verrons	verrions
vous (you, form./pl.)	voyez	voyiez	verrez	verriez
ils/elles (they)	voient	voyaient	verront	verraient

	Passé Composé	Pluperfect	Future Perfect	Past Conditional
je/j' (I)	ai vu	avais vu	aurai vu	aurais vu
tu (you, fam.)	as vu	avais vu	auras vu	aurais vu
il/elle/on (he/she/it/one)	a vu	avait vu	aura vu	aurait vu
nous (we)	avons vu	avions vu	aurons vu	aurions vu
vous (you, form./pl.)	avez vu	aviez vu	aurez vu	auriez vu
ils/elles (they)	ont vu	avaient vu	auront vu	auraient vu

	Present Subjunctive	Past Subjunctive
je/j' (I)	voie	aie vu
tu (you, fam.)	voies	aies vu
il/elle/on (he/she/it/one)	voie	ait vu
nous (we)	voyions	ayons vu
vous (you, form./pl.)	voyiez	ayez vu
ils/elles (they)	voient	aient vu

vouloir (to want)
Past Participle: voulu (wanted); Present Participle: voulant (wanting)

	Present Indicative	Imparfait	Future	Present Conditional
je/j' (I)	veux	voulais	voudrai	voudrais
tu (you, fam.)	veux	voulais	voudras	voudrais
il/elle/on (he/she/it/one)	veut	voulait	voudra	voudrait
nous (we)	voulons	voulions	voudrons	voudrions
vous (you, form./pl.)	voulez	vouliez	voudrez	voudriez
ils/elles (they)	veulent	voulaient	voudront	voudraient

	Passé Composé	Pluperfect	Future Perfect	Past Conditional
je/j' (I)	ai voulu	avais voulu	aurai voulu	aurais voulu
tu (you, fam.)	as voulu	avais voulu	auras voulu	aurais voulu
il/elle/on (he/she/it/one)	a voulu	avait voulu	aura voulu	aurait voulu
nous (we)	avons voulu	avions voulu	aurons voulu	aurions voulu
vous (you, form./pl.)	avez voulu	aviez voulu	aurez voulu	auriez voulu
ils/elles (they)	ont voulu	avaient voulu	auront voulu	auraient voulu

	Present Subjunctive	Past Subjunctive
je/j' (I)	veuille	aie voulu
tu (you, fam.)	veuilles	aies voulu
il/elle/on (he/she/it/one)	veuille	ait voulu
nous (we)	voulions	ayons voulu
vous (you, form./pl.)	vouliez	ayez voulu
ils/elles (they)	veuillent	aient voulu

Book VI

Appendixes

Appendix B

French-English Mini-Dictionary

*K*ey: m = masculine, f = feminine, s = singular, pl = plural

A

à (ah): to, at, in

à bientôt (ah byaN-toh): see you soon

à côté de (ah koh-tey duh): next to

à demain (ah duh-maN): see you tomorrow

à droite (ah drwaht): on the right

à gauche (ah gohsh): on the left

à l'heure (ah luhr): on time

à moins que (ah mwaN kuh): unless

s'abonner (sah-boh-ney): to subscribe

abricot (ah-bree-koh) m: apricot

absolument (ahp-soh-lew-mahN): absolutely

accepter (ahk-sehp-tey): to accept

accuser (ah-kew-zey): to accuse

acheter (ahsh-tey): to buy

actuellement (ahk-tew-ehl-mahN): currently

addition (ah-dee-syohN) f: check

admettre (ahd-meh-truh): to admit

admirer (ahd-mee-rey): to admire

adorer (ah-doh-rey): to love, to adore

adresse (ah-drehs) f: address

adresse électronique (ah-drehs ey-lehk-troh-neek) f: e-mail address

aérogare (ah-ey-roh-gahr) f: airport terminal

affaires (ah-fehr) fpl: business

affranchissement (ah-frahN-shee-smahN) m: postage

afin que (ah-faN kuh): so that

agacer (ah-gah-sey): to annoy, irritate

agneau (ah-nyoh) m: lamb

agrafe (ah-grahf) f: staple

agrafeuse (ah-grah-fuhz) f: stapler

agréable (ah-grey-ah-bluh): pleasant

aider (ey-dey): to help

aimer (ey-mey): to like, to love

ainsi que (aN-see kuh): just as, so as, as well as

aller (ah-ley): to go

aller-retour (ah-ley-ruh-toohr) m: round trip

aller-simple (ah-ley-saN-pluh) m: one-way (ticket)

allumette (ah-lew-meht) f: match

alors que (ah-lohr kuh): while, whereas

amener (ah-muh-ney): to bring (people)

ami/amie (ah-mee) m/f: friend

amuser/s'amuser (ah-mew-zey/sah-mew-zey): to amuse/to have fun

ananas (ah-nah-nah) m: pineapple

aneth (ah-neht) m: dill

annoncer (ah-nohN-sey): to announce

antibiotique (ahN-tee-bee-oh-teek) m: antibiotic

août (ooht) m: August

appareil-photo (ah-pah-rehy-foh-toh) m: camera

appartenir (ah-pahr-tuh-neer): to belong

appeler/s'appeler (ah-pley/sah-pley): to call/to call oneself, to be named

apporter (ah-pohr-tey): to bring (things)

apprendre (ah-prahN-druh): to learn

après (ah-prey): after

architecte (ahr-shee-tehkt) m/f: architect

argent (ahr-zhahN) m: money

armoire (ahr-mwahr) f: armoire

arranger (ah-rahN-zhey): to arrange

arrêt (ah-rey) m: stop

arrêter/s'arrêter (ah-rey-tey/sah-rey-tey): to stop/to stop oneself

arrivée (ah-ree-vey) f: arrival

arriver (ah-ree-vey): to arrive

arroser (ah-roh-zey): to water

ascenseur (ah-sahN-suhr) m: elevator

asperge (ah-spehrzh) f: asparagus

assez (ah-sey): enough

assiette (ah-syeht) f: plate

assister (ah-sees-tey): to attend

attacher (ah-tah-shey): to attach

attendre (ah-tahN-druh): to wait for

attrapper (ah-trah-pey): to catch

au (oh) ms: to the, at the, in the

au fond (oh fohN): in the back

au revoir (ohr-vwahr): goodbye

aubaine (oh-behn) f: sales [Québec]

aujourd'hui (oh-zhoohr-dwee): today

aussi (oh-see): also

aussitôt (oh-see-toh): as soon as

autant (oh-tahN): as much

auteur (oh-tuhr) m: author

automne (oh-tuhhn) m: fall

autour (oh-toohr): around

autrefois (oh-truh-fwah): formerly

aux (oh) pl: to the, at the, in the

avancer/s'avancer (ah-vahN-sey/sah-vahN-sey): to advance, to move forward

avant (ah-vahN): before

avec (ah-vehk): with

avertir (ah-vehr-teer): to warn

avion (ah-vyohN) m: plane

avocat/avocate (ah-voh-kah/ah-voh-kaht) m/f: lawyer; m: avocado

avoir (ah-vwahr): to have

avoir faim (ah-vwahr faN): to be hungry

avoir soif (ah-vwahr swahf): to be thirsty

avril (ah-vreel) m: April

B

baigner/se baigner (beh-nyey/suh beh-nyey): to bathe

baignoire (beh-nywahr) f: bathtub

balance (bah-lahNs) f: scale

balancer/se balancer (bah-lahN-sey/suh bah-lahN-sey): to swing

balayer (bah-leh-yey): to sweep

banane (bah-nahn) f: banana

bande dessinée (bahNd deh-see-ney) f: comic strip

banque (bahNk) f: bank

basilic (bah-zee-leek) m: basil

basket (bah-skeht) m: basketball

baskets (bah-skeht) fpl: sneakers

bâtir (bah-teer): to build

bavarder (bah-vahr-dey): to chat, talk

beau/belle (boh/behl) m/f: nice, beautiful, handsome

beaucoup (boh-kooh): a lot

bercer (behr-sey): to rock, to cradle

beurre (buhr) m: butter

bicyclette (bee-see-kleht) f: bicycle

bien (byaN): well

bien des (byaN dey): quite a few

bien que (byaN kuh): although

bien sûr (byaN sewr): of course

bientôt (byaN-toh): soon

bière (byehr) f: beer

bifteck (beef-tehk) m: steak

bijouterie (bee-zhooh-tree) f: jewelry store

billet (bee-yey) m: ticket

bizarre (bee-zahr): weird, bizarre

blanc/blanche (blahN/blahNsh) m/f: white

blazer (blah-zehr) m: blazer

blesser/se blesser (bleh-sey/suh bleh-sey): to hurt, to wound

bleu/blcue (bluh) m/f: blue

bœuf (buhf) m: beef

boire (bwahr): to drink

boîte aux lettres (bwaht oh leh-truh) f: mailbox

bon/bonne (bohN/buhhn) m/f: good

bonheur (buhh-nuhr) m: happiness

bonjour (bohN-zhoohr): hello, good day

bonne nuit (buhhn nwee) f: good night (when going to bed)

bonsoir (bohN-swahr) m: good evening, good night

bottes (buhht) fpl: boots

bouche (boohsh) f: mouth

boucherie (booh-shree) f: butcher shop

bouger (booh-zhey): to move

boulangerie (booh-lahN-zhree) f: bakery

bras (brah) m: arm

bronzer/se bronzer (brohN-zey/suh brohN-zey): to tan

brosse (bruhhs) f: brush

brosser/se brosser (bruhh-sey/suh bruhh-sey): to brush

bruyant/bruyante (brwee-ahN/brwee-ahNt) m/f: noisy

bureau (bew-roh) m: office, desk

bureau de change (bew-roh duh shahNzh) m: currency exchange office

C

ça va (sah vah): okay

cabine d'essayage (kah-been dey-sey-ahzh) f: fitting room

cacher/se cacher (kah-shey/suh kah-shey): to hide

café (kah-fey) m: coffee, café

caisse (kehs) f: cash register

caissier/caissière (key-syey/key-syehr) m/f: cashier

calendrier (kah-lahN-dree-yey) m: calendar

cambriolage (kahN-bree-oh-lahzh) m: burglary

campagne (kahN-pah-nyuh) f: countryside

canapé (kah-nah-pey) m: sofa

canard (kah-nahr) m: duck

canne à pêche (kahn ah pehsh) f: fishing pole

capot (kah-poh) m: hood (of a car)

carotte (kah-ruhht) f: carrot

carrefour (kahr-foohr) m: intersection

carrément (kah-rey-mahN): squarely

carte d'embarquement (kahrt dahN-bahr-kuh-mahN) f: boarding pass

carte de crédit (kahrt duh krey-dee) f: credit card

carte postale (kahrt poh-stahl) f: postcard

casse-croûte (kahs-krooht) m: snack

ce (suh) m: this

ceinture (saN-tewr) f: belt

célébrer (sey-ley-brey): to celebrate

celui-ci/celle-ci (suh-lwee-see/sehl-see) m/f: this one

celui-là/celle-là (suh-lwee-lah/sehl-lah) m/f: that one

centre commercial (sahN-truh koh-mehr-syahl) m: mall, shopping center

cerfeuil (sehr-fuhy) m: chervil

cerise (suh-reez) f: cherry

certainement (sehr-tehn-mahN): certainly

ces (sey): these

cette (seht) f: this

champignon (shahN-pee-nyohN) m: mushroom

changer (shahN-zhey): to change

chanter (shahN-tey): to sing

chapeau (shah-poh) m: hat

charmant/charmante (shahr-mahN/shahr-mahNt) m/f: charming

château (shah-toh) m: castle

chaud/chaude (shoh/shohd) m/f: warm, hot

chaussettes (shoh-seht) fpl: socks

chaussons (shoh-sohN) mpl: slippers

chaussures (shoh-sewr) fpl: shoes

chemise (shuh-meez) f: button-down shirt

chemisier (shuh-mee-zyey) m: blouse

cher/chère (shehr) m/f: expensive, dear

chercher (sher-shey): to look for

cheville (shuh-veey) f: ankle

choisir (shwah-zeer): to choose

chou (shooh) m: cabbage

chou-fleur (shooh-fluhr) m: cauliflower

choux de Bruxelles (shooh duh brewk-sehl) mpl: Brussels sprouts

cinéaste (see-ney-ahst) m/f: filmmaker

cinéma (see-ney-mah) m: movies, movie theater

cinq (saNk): five

ciseaux (see-zoh) mpl: scissors

citron pressé (see-trohN prey-sey) m: lemonade

clair/claire (klehr) m/f: light-colored, clear

classeur à tiroirs (klah-suhr ah tee-rwahr) m: file cabinet

clavier (klah-vyey) m: keyboard

climatisation (klee-mah-tee-zah-syohN) f: air conditioning

code postal (kohd puh-stahl) m: zip code, postal code

coffre (kuh-fruh) m: trunk

coiffer/se coiffer (kwah-fey/suh kwah-fey): to style hair

colis (koh-lee) m: package

collègue (koh-lehg) m/f: colleague, coworker

combien (kohN-byaN): how much

commencer (koh-mahN-sey): to begin

comment (koh-mahN): how

commettre (koh-meh-truh): to commit

commode (koh-muhd) f: dresser

compagnie (kohN-pah-nyee) f: company

comparer (kohN-pah-rey): to compare

complet (kohN-pleh) m: suit [France]

compléter (kohN-pley-tey): to complete

composter (kohN-poh-stey): to validate a ticket

comprendre (kohN-prahN-druh): to understand

comptoir (kohN-twahr) m: counter

conduire (kohN-dweer): to drive

confiture (kohN-fee-tewr) f: jam

connaître (koh-neh-truh): to know, to be familiar with

conseiller (kohN-sey-yey): to advise

consentir (kohN-sahN-teer): to consent

considérer (kohN-see-dey-rey): to consider

consigne (kohN-see-nyuh) f: baggage room

construire (kohN-strweer): to construct, build

conte de fée (kohNt duh fey) m: fairy tale

contenir (kohN-tuh-neer): to contain

continuellement (kohN-tee-new-ehl-mahN): continually

continuer (kohN-tee-new-ey): to continue

contravention (kohN-trah-vahN-syohN) f: traffic ticket

contre (kohN-truh): against

contredire (kohN-truh-deer): to contradict

coquilles Saint-Jacques (koh-keey saN zhahk) fpl: scallops

corbeille à papiers (kohr-behy ah pah-pyey) m: wastepaper basket

coriandre (koh-ree-ahN-druh) m: coriander

corriger/se corriger (koh-ree-zhey/suh koh-ree-zhey): to correct/to correct oneself

costume de bains (koh-stewm duh baN) m: bathing suit [Québec]

côte (koht) f: coast

côtes (koht) fpl: ribs

cou (kooh) m: neck

coucher/se coucher (kooh-shey/suh kooh-shey): to put to bed/to go to bed

couleur (kooh-luhr) f: color

couper/se couper (kooh-pey/suh kooh-pey): to cut/to cut oneself

cour (koohr) f: courtyard

couramment (kooh-rah-mahN): fluently

courir (kooh-reer): to run

couteau (kooh-toh) m: knife

couverts (kooh-vehr) mpl: silverware

couverture (kooh-vehr-tewr) f: blanket

couvrir (kooh-vrecr): to cover

craindre (kraN-druh): to fear

cravate (krah-vaht) f: tie

crayon (krey-ohN) m: pencil

crème (krehm) f: cream

crémerie (kreym-ree) f: dairy product and cheese store

crevettes (kruh-veht) fpl: shrimp

croire (krwahr): to believe

crudités (krew-dee-tey) fpl: raw vegetables, mixed greens

cuillère (kwee-yehr) f: spoon, teaspoon

cuir (kweer) m: leather

cuire (kweer): to cook

cuisinière (kwee-zee-nyehr) f: stove

Book VI

Appendixes

D

d'accord (dah-kohr): all right, okay

dans (dahN): in, inside

danser (dahN-sey): to dance

de (duh): of, from

de crainte que (duh kraNt kuh): for fear that

de la (duh lah) fs: some

de peur que (duh puhr kuh): for fear that

se débrouiller (suh dey-brooh-yey): to manage

décembre (dey-sahN-bruh) m: December

décevoir (dey-suh-vwahr): to disappoint

décider (dey-see-dey): to decide

décourager (dey-kooh-rah-zhey): to discourage

découvrir (dey-kooh-vreer): to discover

décrire (dey-kreer): to describe

dedans (duh-dahN): inside

défendre/se défendre (dey-fahN-druh/ suh dey-fahN-druh): to defend or forbid/to defend oneself

dehors (duh-ohr): outside

déjà (dey-zhah): already

déjeuner (dey-zhuh-ney) m: lunch; verb: to have lunch

demain (duh-maN): tomorrow

demander/se demander (duh-mahN-dey/ suh duh-mahN-dey): to ask/to wonder

déménager (dey-mey-nah-zhey): to move (to a different house/apartment/etc.)

demi-tour (duh-mee-toohr) m: U-turn

dénoncer (dey-nohN-sey): to denounce

dent (dahN) f: tooth

dentifrice (dahN-tee-frees) m: toothpaste

dentiste (dahN-teest) m/f: dentist

départ (dey-pahr) m: departure

se dépêcher (suh dey-pey-shey): to hurry

depuis (duh-pwee): since

déranger (dey-rahN-zhey): to disturb

dernièrement (dehr-nyehr-mahN) : lately, lastly

derrière (deh-ryehr): behind

des (dey) pl: some

descendre (dey-sahN-druh): to go down, to get off

désirer (dey-zee-rey): to desire, to wish

désolé/désolée (dey-zoh-ley) m/f: sorry

dessert (deh-sehr) m: dessert

dessin animé (deh-saN ah-nee-mey) m: cartoon

dessous (duh-sooh): underneath, below

dessus (duh-sew): above

détester (dey-teh-stey): to hate

deux (duh): two

devant (duh-vahN): in front of

devenir (duh-vuh-neer): to become

devoir (duh-vwahr): to have to

difficile (dee-fee-seel): difficult

dinde (daNd) f: turkey

dire (deer): to say

directeur/directrice (dee-rehk-tuhr/ dee-rehk-trees) m/f: manager (of a company, business)

diriger (dee-ree-zhey): to direct

disparaître (dee-spah-reh-truh): to disappear

disputer/se disputer (dee-spew-tey/suh dee-spew-tey): to argue

distributeur (de billets) (dee-stree-bew-tuhr [duh bee-yey]) m: ATM

divorcer/se divorcer (dee-vohr-sey/suh dee-vohr-sey): to divorce

dix (dees): ten

dix-huit (dee-zweet): eighteen

dix-neuf (dee-znuhf): nineteen

dix-sept (dee-seht): seventeen

docteur (dohk-tuhr) m: doctor

documentaire (doh-kew-mahN-tehr) m: documentary

doigt (dwah) m: finger

donc (dohNk): so, therefore

donner (duhh-ney): to give

dormir (dohr-meer): to sleep

dos (doh) m: back

se doucher (suh dooh-shey): to shower

doux/douce (dooh/doohs) m/f: mild, sweet

douze (doohz): twelve

draps (drah) mpl: sheets

du (dew) ms: some; from, about

E

eau (oh) f: water

échecs (ey-shehk) mpl: chess

éclairage (ey-kleh-rahzh) m: lighting

écouter (ey-kooh-tey): to listen (to)

écrire (ey-kreer): to write

effacer (ey-fah-sey): to erase

effets spéciaux (ey-feh spey-syoh) mpl: special effects

effrayer (ey-freh-yey): to scare, to frighten

égalité (ey-gah-lee-tey) f: equality

élastique (cy-lah-steek) m: rubber band

élever (ey-luh-vey): to raise (children, animals)

elle/elles (ehl) f: she/they

embouteillage (ahN-booh-teh-yahz) m: traffic jam

embrasser (ahN-brah-sey): to kiss

employé/employée (ahN-plwah-yey) m/f: employee

employer (ahN-plwah-yey): to employ

en (ahN): in, to, by, upon

s'en aller (sahN-nah-ley): to go away

en attendant que (ahN-nah-tahN-dahN kuh): while, until

en bas (ahN-bah): down

en face de (ahN fahs duh): across from, in front of

en haut (ahN oh): up, upstairs

en retard (ahN ruh-tahr): late

enchanté/enchantée (ahN-shahN-tey) m/f: delighted

encore (ahN-kohr): again, still

encourager (ahN-kooh-rah-zhey): to encourage

s'endormir (sahN-dohr-meer): to fall asleep

s'énerver (sey-nehr-vey): to become irritated

enfant (ahN-fahN) m/f: child

enfin (ahN-faN): finally

enlever (ahN-luh-vey): to remove

ennuyer/s'ennuyer (ahN-nwee-yey/ sahN-nwee-yey): to bore, annoy/to be bored, be annoyed

ennuyeux/ennuyeuse (ahN-nwee-yuh/ ahN-nwee-yuhz): m/f: boring

énormément (ey-nohr-mey-mahN): enormously

enseigner (ahN-sey-nyey): to teach

ensuite (ahN-sweet): then, next

entendre/s'entendre (ahN-tahN-druh/ sahN-tahN-druh): to hear/to get along

entre (ahN-truh): between

entrée (ahN-trey) f: appetizer, entrance

entrer (ahN-trey): to enter

enveloppe (ahN-vluhhp) f: envelope

envoyer (ahN-vwah-yey): to send

épaule (ey-pohl) f: shoulder

épeler (eyp-ley): to spell

épicerie (ey-pee-sree) f: grocery store, general store

épinards (ey-pee-nahr) mpl: spinach

époux/épouse (ey-pooh/ey-poohz) m/f: spouse

Book VI

Appendixes

escalier roulant (eh-skah-lyey rooh-lahN) m: escalator

espérer (eh-spey-rey): to hope

essayer (ey-sey-yey): to try, to try on

essence (ey-sahNs) f: gas

essuie-glace (ey-swee-glahs) m: windshield wiper

essuyer (ey-swee-yey): to wipe

est (ehst) m: east

estragon (eh-strah-gohN) m: tarragon

et (ey): and

établir (ey-tah-bleer): to establish

été (ey-tey) m: summer

être (eh-truh): to be

étroit/étroite (ey-trwah/ey-trwaht) m/f: narrow

étudier (ey-tew-dyey): to study

évier (ey-vyey) m: kitchen sink

s'excuser (seyk-skew-zey): to apologize, to excuse oneself

exiger (ehg-zee-zhey): to demand

exprès (eyk-sprey): on purpose

F

facile (fah-seel): easy

faire (fehr): to do, to make

faire du jardinage (fehr dew zhahr-dee-nahzh): to garden

faire le plein (fehr luh plaN): to fill the gas tank

fatigué/fatiguée (fah-tee-gey) m/f: tired

femme (fahm) f: woman, wife

fenêtre (fuh-neh-truh) f: window

fêtes (feht) fpl: holidays

feuilleter (fuhy-tey): to leaf through

février (fey-vryey) m: February

se fiancer (suh fee-ahN-sey): to get engaged

fichier (fee-shyey) m: file

fier/fière (fyehr) m/f: proud

figue (feeg) f: fig

figure (fee-gewr) f: face

fille (feey) f: daughter, girl

film d'amour (feelm dah-moohr) m: romance film

film d'aventures (feelm dah-vahN-tewr) m: adventure film

film d'épouvante/d'horreur (feelm dey-pooh-vahNt/doh-ruhr) m: horror film

film d'espionnage (feelm deh-spee-oh-nahzh) m: spy film

film de science-fiction (feelm duh syahNs feek-syohN) m: science-fiction film

film policier (feelm poh-lee-syey) m: detective film

fils (fees) m: son

fin (faN) f: end

finir (fee-neer): to finish

flanelle (flah-nehl) f: flannel

fleur (fluhr) f: flower

foncé/foncée (fohN-sey) m/f: dark

fondre (fohN-druh): to melt

football (fooht-buhhl) m: soccer

football américain (fooht-buhhl ah-mey-ree-kaN) m: (American) football

formel/formelle (fohr-mehl) m/f: formal

foulard (fooh-lahr) m: scarf

four à micro-ondes (foohr ah mee-kroh-ohNd) m: microwave

fourchette (foohr-sheht) f: fork

frais/fraîche (frey/frehsh): fresh, cool

fraise (frehz) f: strawberry

framboise (frahN-bwahz) f: raspberry

freins (fraN) mpl: brakes (of a car)

frère (frehr) m: brother

froid/froide (frwah/frwahd) m/f: cold

fromage (froh-mahzh) m: cheese

fruits (frwee) mpl: fruit

G

gagner (gah-nyey): to win

garçon (gahr-sohN) m: boy

gare (gahr) f: train station

gâteau (gah-toh) m: cake

geler (zhuh-ley): to freeze

générique (zhey-ney-reek) m: credits

genou (zhuh-nooh) m: knee

gentil/gentille (zhahN-teey) m/f: kind, nice

gentiment (zhaN-tee-mahN): kindly, nicely

gérant/gérante (zhey-rahN/zhey-rahNt) m/f: manager (of a restaurant, hotel, shop)

gérer (zhcy-rey): to manage

gigot d'agneau (zhee-goh dah-nyoh) m: leg of lamb

glace (glahs) f: ice cream

gomme (guhhm) f: eraser

goûter (gooh-tey) m: snack; verb: to taste

graine (grehn) f: seed

grand/grande (grahN/grahNd) m/f: big, tall, large

grand magasin (grahN mah-gah-zaN) m: department store

grandir (grahN-deer): to grow

gras/grasse (grah/grahs) m/f: fat

grave (grahv): serious

grippe (greep) f: flu

gros/grosse (groh/gruhhs) m/f: large, fat, thick

grossir (groh-seer): to gain weight

guérir (gey-reer): to cure, heal

guichet (gee-shey) m: ticket window

guitare (gee-tahr) f: guitar

H

s'habiller (sah-bee-yey): to get dressed

habit (ah-bee) m: suit [Québec]

habiter (ah-bee-tey): to live

haricots verts (ah-ree-koh vehr) mpl: green beans

hésiter (ey-zee-tey): to hesitate

heure de pointe (uhr duh pwaNt) f: rush hour, peak

heureusement (uh-ruhz-mahN): fortunately

heureux/heureuse (uh-ruh/uh-ruhz) m/f: happy

hiver (ee-vehr) m: winter

homard (oh-mahr) m: lobster

hoqueter (oh-kuh-tey): to hiccup

horaire (oh-rehr) m: schedule

horloge (ohr-luhhzh) f: clock

hortensia (ohr-tahN-syah) m: hydrangea

hôtel (oh-tehl) m: hotel

hôtesse de l'air (oh-tehs duh lehr) f: female flight attendant

huit (weet): eight

huitres (wee-truh) fpl: oysters

Book VI

Appendixes

I

ici (ee-see): here

icône (ee-kohn) f: icon

idée (ee-dey) f: idea

il (eel) m: he

il y a (eel ee ah): there is, there are

ils (eel) mpl: they

immédiatement (ee-mey-dyaht-mahN): immediately

imperméable (aN-pehr-mey-ah-bluh) m: raincoat, rainproof

imprimante (aN-pree-mahNt) f: printer

infirmier/infirmière (aN-feer-myey/aN-feer-myehr) m/f: nurse

influencer (aN-flew-ahN-sey): to influence

informaticien/informaticienne (aN-fohr-mah-tee-syaN/aN-fohr-mah-tee-syehn) m/f: computer scientist

ingénieur (aN-zhey-nyuhr) m: engineer

s'inquiéter (saN-kyey -tey): to worry

intelligemment (aN-tey-lee-zhah-mahN): intelligently

interdire (aN-tehr-deer): to forbid

intéressant/intéressante (aN-tey-rey-sahN/aN-tey-rey-sahNt): interesting

inviter (aN-vee-tey): to invite

J

jamais (zhah-mey): never

jambe (zhahNb) f: leg

jambon (zhahN-bohN) m: ham

janvier (zhahN-vyey) m: January

jardin (zhahr-daN) m: yard, garden

jardin d'agrément (zhahr-daN dah-grey-mahN) m: flower garden

jardin potager (zhahr-daN poh-tah-zhey) m: vegetable garden

jaune (zhohn): yellow

je (zhuh): I

jean (jeen) m: jeans

jeter (zhuh-tey): to throw, throw away

joindre (zhwaN-druh): to attach

joli/jolie (zhoh-lee) m/f: pretty

jonquille (zhohN-keey) f: daffodil

jouer (zhooh-ey): to play

jour (zhoohr) m: day

journal (zhoohr-nahl) m: newspaper, journal

juillet (zhwee-yeh) m: July

juin (zhwaN) m: June

jupe (zhewp) f: skirt

jusqu'à (ce que) (zhews-kah [suh kuh]): until

L

la (lah) f: the

là (lah): there

là-bas (lah-bah): over there

lac (lahk) m: lake

laine (lehn) f: wool

laisser (leh-sey): to leave behind, to let, to allow

lait (leh) m: milk

laitue (ley-tew) f: lettuce

lancer (lahN-sey): to launch, to throw

large (lahrzh): large, wide

lavabo (lah-vah-boh) m: bathroom sink

lave-vaisselle (lahv veh-sehl) m: dishwasher

laver/se laver (lah-vey/suh lah-vey): to wash/to wash oneself

le (luh) m: the

lecteur de CD/de DVD (lehk-tuhr duh sey dey/duh dey vey dey) m: CD/DVD player

légumes (ley-gewm) mpl: vegetables

lendemain (lahN-duh-mahN) m: next day

lentement (lahN-tuh-mahN): slowly

lequel (luh-kehl): which one

les (ley) pl: the

leur (luhr): to them

leur/leurs (luhr) s/pl: their

lever/se lever (luh-vey/suh luh-vey): to lift, to raise/to get up

liberté (lee-behr-tey) f: freedom

librairie (lee-brey-ree) f: bookstore

limonade (lee-moh-nahd) f: lemonade [Québec], lemon-flavored drink [France]

lin (laN) m: linen

lire (leer): to read

lit (lee) m: bed

livre (lee-vruh) m: book; f: pound

loger/se loger (loh-zhey/suh loh-zhey): to lodge

logiciel (loh-zhee-syehl) m: software

loin (lwaN): far

long-métrage (lohN mey-trahzh) m: feature film

longtemps (lohN-tahN): for a long time

lorsque (lohr-skuh): when

lui (lwee) m: him

lunettes de soleil (lew-neht duh soh-lehy) fpl: sunglasses

M

ma (mah) f: my

madame (mah-dahm) f: ma'am, missus

mademoiselle (mahd-mwah-zehl) f: miss

magasin (mah-gah-zaN) m: store

mai (mey) m: May

maigrir (mey-greer): to lose weight

maillot de bains (mah-yoh duh baN) m: bathing suit

main (maN) f: hand

maintenant (maN-tuh-nahN): now

mais (mey): but

maison (meh-zohN) f: house

mal (mahl): badly

maladie (mah-lah-dee) f: illness

manger (mahN-zhey): to eat

manquer (mahN-key): to miss

manteau (mahN-toh) m: coat

maquiller/se maquiller (mah-kee-yey/ suh mah-kee-yey): to put on make-up

marchand/marchande (mahr-shahN/ mahr-shahNd) m/f: vendor

marcher (mahr-shey): to walk; to work

margarine (mahr-gah-reen) f: margarine

marguerite (mahr-guh-reet) f: daisy

mari (mah-ree) m: husband

se marier (suh mah-ree-yey): to get married

marron (mah-rohN): brown

mars (mahrs) m: March

matériel (mah-tey-ryehl) m: equipment, material

mauvais/mauvaise (moh-veh/moh-vehz) m/f: bad

médecin (meyd-saN) m: physician

mél (mehl) m: e-mail

mélanger (mey-lahN-zhey): to mix

même (mehm): even, same

mémoire (mey-mwahr) f: memory

mener (muh-ney): to lead

menthe (mahNt) f: mint

mentir (mahN-teer): to lie

mer (mehr) f: ocean

merci (mehr-see): thank you

mère (mehr) f: mother

mes (mey) pl: my

messagerie (mey-sah-zhree) f: voice mail

metteur-en-scène (meh-tuhr-ahN-sehn) m: theater or film director

mettre/se mettre à (meh-truh/suh meh-truh): to put, to place/to start to

mien/mienne/miens/miennes (myaN/ myehn) ms/fs/mpl/fpl: mine

mieux (myuh): better

mille (meel) m: thousand

mince (maNs): thin

miroir (mee-rwahr) m: mirror

mobile (moh-beel) m: cell phone

modérer (moh-dey-rey): to moderate

moderne (moh-dehrn) m/f: modern

moi (mwah): me

moins (mwaN): less

mois (mwah) m: month

mon (mohN): my

moniteur (moh-nee-tuhr) m: monitor

monsieur (muh-syuh) m: sir, mister

montagne (mohN-tah-nyuh) f: mountain

monter (mohN-tey): to go up, to climb, to get on

montre (mohN-truh) f: watch

montrer (mohN-trey): to show

moquette (moh-keht) f: carpet

mot de passe (moh duh pahs) m: password

mourir (mooh-reer): to die

moyen/moyenne (mwah-yaN/mwah-yehn) m/f: average

N

nager (nah-zhey): to swim

naissance (neh-sahNs) f: birth

naître (neh-truh): to be born

natation (nah-tah-syohN) f: swimming

navigateur (nah-vee-gah-tuhr) m: web browser

ne . . . aucun (nuh . . . oh-kuhN): none

ne . . . jamais (nuh . . . zhah-mey): never

ne . . . ni . . . ni (nuh . . . nee . . . nee): neither . . . nor

ne . . . nul (nuh . . . newl): none

ne . . . nulle part (nuh . . . newl pahr): nowhere

ne . . . pas (nuh pah): not

ne . . . pas du tout (nuh . . . pah dew tew): not at all

ne . . . pas encore (nuh . . . pah zahN-kuhhr): not yet

ne . . . pas toujours (nuh . . . pah tooh-zhoohr): not always

ne . . . personne (nuh . . . pehr-suhhn): no one

ne . . . plus (nuh . . . plew): not any-more, no more

ne . . . que (nuh . . . kuh): only

neige (nehzh) f: snow

nettoyer (neh-twah-yey): to clean

neuf (nuhf): nine

neuf/neuve (nuhf/nuhv) m/f: brand new

nez (ney) m: nose

noir/noire (nwahr) m/f: black

nom (nohN) m: last name

non (nohN): no

nord (nohr) m: north

notre/nos (nuhh-truh/noh) s/pl: our

nôtre/nôtres (noh-truh) s/pl: ours

nous (nooh): we

nouveau/nouvelle (nooh-voh/nooh-vehl) m/f: new

nouvellement (nooh-vehl-mahN): newly

novembre (noh-vahN-bruh) m: November

nuage (new-ahzh) m: cloud

numéro de téléphone (new-mey-roh duh tey-ley-fuhhn) m: phone number

O

obéir (oh-bey-eer): to obey

obliger (oh-blee-zhey): to force

obtenir (uhhp-tuh-neer): to obtain

octobre (uhhk-toh-bruh) m: October

œil/yeux (uhy/yuh) m: eye/eyes

œillet (uh-yeh) m: carnation

offrir (oh-freer): to offer

oignon (uhh-nyohN) m: onion

oiseau (wah-zoh) m: bird

on (ohN): one, we, they

oncle (ohN-kluh) m: uncle

onze (ohNz): eleven

orange (oh-rahNzh) f: orange

ordinateur (ohr-dee-nah-tuhr) m: computer

oreille (oh-rehy) f: ear

oreiller (oh-reh-yey) m: pillow

orteil (ohr-tehy) m: toe

oseille (oh-zehy) f: sorrel

où (ooh): where

ou (ooh): or

ou bien (ooh byaN): or else

ou . . . ou (ooh . . . ooh): either . . .or

oublier (ooh-blee-yey): to forget

ouest (ooh-wehst) m: west

oui (wee): yes

ouvrir (ooh-vreer): to open

P

page d'accueil (pahzh dah-kuhy) f: home page

pain (paN) m: bread

pâlir (pah-leer): to turn pale

pansement (pahNs-mahN) m: bandage

pantalon (pahN-tah-lohN) m: pants, slacks

pantoufles (pahN-tooh-fluh) fpl: slippers

par (pahr): by

paraître (pah-reh-truh): to appear

parce que (pahr-suh kuh): because

pardessus (pahr-duh-sew) m: overcoat

pare-brise (pahr-breez) m: windshield

pareil (pah-rehy): similar

parfait/parfaite (pahr-feh/pahr-feht) m/f: perfect

parfois (pahr-fwah): sometimes

parler (pahr-ley): to speak, to talk

partager (pahr-tah-zhey): to share

partir (pahr-teer): to leave

partout (pahr-tooh): everywhere

pas du tout (pah dew tooh): not at all

pas mal de (pah mahl duh): quite a bit of, quite a few

passeport (pahs-pohr) m: passport

passer (pah-sey): to pass (by), (to) spend [time]

pastèque (pah-stehk) f: watermelon

pastille (pah-steey) f: lozenge

pâte (paht) f: dough

pâtes (paht) fpl: pasta

pâtisserie (pah-tee-sree) f: pastry shop

payer (pey-yey): to pay

pays (pey-ee) m: country

PDG (pey dey zhey): CEO

pêche (pehsh) f: peach

pêcher (peh-shey): to go fishing

peigne (peh-nyuh) m: comb

peigner/se peigner (peh-nyey/suh peh-nyey): to comb someone's hair/to comb one's hair

pendant que (pahN-dahN kuh): while

pensée (pahN-sey) f: thought

penser (pahN-sey): to think

perdre (pehr-druh): to lose

père (pehr) m: father

période creuse (pey-ree-uhhd kruhz) f: off peak

permis de conduire (pehr-mee duh kohN-dweer) m: driver's license

persil (pehr-see) m: parsley

personne (pehr-suhhn) f: person

peser (puh-zey): to weigh

petit/petite (puh-tee/puh-teet) m/f: small, short

petit déjeuner (puh-tee dey-zhuh-ney) m: breakfast

petit-fils (puh-tee fees) m: grandson

petite-fille (puh-teet feey) f: granddaughter

petits-enfants (puh-tee-zahN-fahN) mpl: grandchildren

petits pois (puh-tee pwah) mpl: peas

peu de (puh duh): little of

photo (foh-toh) f: picture, photo

photocopieuse (foh-toh-koh-pyuhz) f: copy machine

piano (pyah-noh) m: piano

pièce (pyehs) f: room, theatrical play

pièce jointe (pyehs zhwaNt) f: attachment

pied (pyey) m: foot

piéton/piétonne (pyey-tohN/pyey-tuhhn) m/f: pedestrian

pire (peer): worse

piscine (pee-seen) f: swimming pool

place (plahs) f: seat, city or town square

placer (plah-sey): to place

plage (plahzh) f: beach

plan (plahN) m: map

planche à voile (plahNsh ah vwahl) f: windsurfing

plate-bande (plaht-bahNd) f: flowerbed

pleuvoir (pluh-vwar): to rain

plonger (plohN-zhey): to dive

plupart (plew-pahr): most

plus (de) (plew/plews [duh]): more (than)

pneu (pnuh) m: tire

pointure (pwaN-tewr) f: shoe size

poire (pwahr) f: pear

poireau (pwah-roh) m: leek

poisson (pwah-sohN) m: fish

poissonnerie (pwah-sohn-ree) f: fish store

poitrine (pwah-treen) f: chest

poivre (pwah-vruh) m: pepper

police (poh-lees) f: police

poliment (poh-lee-mahN): politely

pomme (puhhm) f: apple

pomme de terre (puhhm duh tehr) f: potato

pont (pohN) m: bridge

porc (pohr) m: pork

portable (pohr-tah-bluh) m: laptop

porte (pohrt) f: door

portefeuille (pohrt-fuhy) m: wallet

porter (pohr-tey): to wear, to carry

posséder (poh-sey-dey): to possess

poste (puhhst) f: post office

poulet (pooh-leh) m: chicken

pour (poohr): for, in order to

pour que (poohr kuh): so that

pourboire (poohr-bwahr) m: tip

pourquoi (poohr-kwah): why

pourvu que (poohr-vew kuh): provided that

pouvoir (pooh-vwahr): to be able to

préféré/préférée (prey-fey-rey): favorite

préférer (prey-fey-rey): to prefer

premier/première (pruh-myey/pruh-myehr): first

prendre (prahN-druh): to take

prénom (prey-nohN) m: first name

préparer (prey-pah-rey): to prepare

près (prey): near

présenter (prey-zahN-tey): to present, to introduce

prétendre (prey-tahN-druh): to pretend, to claim

printemps (praN-tahN) m: spring

professeur (proh-feh-suhr) m: high-school teacher, college professor

projeter (proh-zhuh-tey): to project, to plan

promenade (proh-muh-nahd) f: walk

promener/se promener (proh-muh-ney/suh proh-muh-ney): to walk (a dog)/to take a walk

promettre (proh-meh-truh): to promise

prononcer (proh-nohN-sey): to pronounce

proposer (proh-poh-zey): to propose

propriétaire (proh-pree-ey-tehr) m/f: owner

protéger (proh-tey-zhey): to protect

prune (prewn) f: plum

pseudo (psuh-doh) m: username

publicité (pew-blee-see-tey) f: advertisement

puis (pwee): then

puisque (pwee-skuh): since, as

pull (pewl) m: sweater

punir (pew-neer): to punish

Q

quai (key) m: platform

quand (kahN): when

quatorze (kah-tohrz): fourteen

quatre (kah-truh): four

quel/quelle (kehl) m/f: which

quelque chose (kehl-kuh shohz): something

quelque part (kehl-kuh pahr): somewhere

quelquefois (kehl-kuh-fwah): sometimes

qu'est-ce que (kehs-kuh): what

qui (kee): who

quinze (kaNz): fifteen

quitter (kee-tey): to leave

quoi (kwah): what

quoi que (kwah kuh): whatever, no matter what

quoique (kwah-kuh): even though

R

raisin (reh-zaN) m: grape

raisin sec (reh-zaN sehk) m: raisin

ralentir (rah-lahN-teer): to slow down

randonnée (rahN-doh-ney) f: hike

ranger (rahN-zhey): to tidy up

rappeler/se rappeler (rah-pley/suh rah-pley): to call back/to recall

rarement (rahr-mahN): rarely

raser/se raser (rah-zey/suh rah-zey): to shave/to shave oneself

rasoir (rah-zwahr) m: razor

réagir (rey-ah-zheer): to react

réalisateur/réalisatrice (rey-ah-lee-zah-tuhr/rey-ah-lee-zah-trees) m/f: director (of a film or play)

récemment (rey-sah-mahN): recently

recevoir (ruh-suh-vwahr): to receive

reconnaître (ruh-koh-neh-truh): to recognize

reçu (ruh-sew) m: receipt

réfléchir (rey-fley-sheer): to reflect, think

réfrigérateur (rey-free-zhey-rah-tuhr) m: refrigerator

refuser (ruh-few-zey): to refuse

regarder (ruh-gahr-dey): to watch

rejeter (ruh-zhuh-tey): to reject

se réjouir (suh rey-zhweer): to rejoice, delight

remplacer (rahN-plah-sey): to replace

remplir (rahN-pleer): to fill out/to fill in

rencontrer (rahN-kohN-trey): to meet

rendez-vous (rahN-dey-vooh) m: appointment

rendre (rahN-druh): to return (something)

rendre visite à (rahN-druh vee-zeet ah): to visit a person

renouveler (ruh-nooh-vley): to renew

renseignement (rahN-seh-nyuh-mahN) m: piece of information

rentrer (rahN-trey): to return, to go home

repas (ruh-pah) m: meal

répéter (rey-pey-tey): to repeat

répondre (rey-pohN-druh): to answer

se reposer (suh ruh-poh-zey): to rest

représentation (ruh-prey-zahN-tah-syohN) f: performance

réseau (rey-zoh) m: network

rester (reh-stey): to stay

retourner (ruh-toohr-ney): to return

retraité/retraitée (ruh-treh-tey) m/f: retiree

réunion (rey-ew-nyohN) f: reunion

réunir/se réunir (rey-ew-neer/suh rey-ew-neer): to meet together, to unite

réussir (rey-ew-seer): to succeed

réveil (rey-vehy) m: alarm clock

réveiller/se réveiller (rey-vey-yey/suh rey-vey-yey): to wake up

revenir (ruh-vuh-neer): to come back

rêver (rey-vey): to dream

revoir (ruh-vwahr): to see again

rez-de-chaussée (reyd-shoh-sey) m: ground (first) floor

rhume (rewm) m: a cold

rideau (ree-doh) m: curtain

rire (reer): to laugh

riz (ree) m: rice

robe (ruhhb) f: dress

roman (roh-mahN) m: novel

romarin (roh-mah-raN) m: rosemary

rouge (roohzh): red

rougir (rooh-zheer): to blush

ruban adhésif (rew-bahN ah-dey-zeef) m: tape

rue (rew) f: street

S

sa (sah) f: his, her, its

sable (sah-bluh) m: sand

sac (sahk) m: bag

sac de couchage (sahk duh kooh-shahzh) m: sleeping bag

saison (seh-zohN) f: season

salade verte (sah-lahd vehrt) f: green salad, salad with lettuce only

salle d'attente (sahl dah-tahNt) f: waiting room

salon de chat (sah-lohN duh chaht) m: chat room

salut (sah-lew): hi

sandales (sahN-dahl) fpl: sandals

sans (sahN): without

sauge (sohzh) f: sage

saumon (soh-mohN) m: salmon

savoir (sah-vwahr): to know a fact or how to do something

savon (sah-vohN) m: soap

séance (sey-ahNs) f: (a movie) showing

secret (suh-kreh) m: secret

secrétaire (suh-krey-tehr) m/f: secretary

seize (sehz): sixteen

séjour (sey-zhoohr) m: stay, living room

sel (sehl) m: salt

semaine (suh-mehn) f: week

sens unique (sahNs ew-neek) m: one way

sentir/se sentir (suh sahN-teer/suh sahN-teer): to feel

sept (seht): seven

septembre (sehp-tahN-bruh) m: September

serveur/serveuse (sehr-vuhr/sehr-vuhz) m/f: waiter/waitress

serviette (sehr-vyeht) f: napkin, towel

servir/se servir de (sehr-veer/suh sehr-veer duh): to serve/to use

ses (sey) pl: his, her, its

seulement (suhl-mahN): only

si (see): if, yes (in response to a negative statement or question)

siège (syehzh) m: seat

sien/siens/sienne/siennes (syaN/syaN/syehn/syehn) ms/mpl/fs/fpl: his, hers, its

siffler (see-fley): to whistle

six (sees): six

slip (sleep) m: underpants, briefs

soccer (soh-kehr) m: soccer

sœur (suhr) f: sister

soie (swah) f: silk

soirée (swah-rey) f: evening, party

soit . . . soit (swaht . . . swaht OR swah . . . swah): either . . . or

sol (suhhl) m: soil

soldes (suhhld) mpl: sales [France]

soleil (soh-lehy) m: sun

son (sohN) m: his, her, its

sortie (sohr-tee) f: exit

sortir (sohr-teer): to exit, to go out, to take out

soucoupe (sooh-koohp) f: saucer

souffrir (sooh-freer): to suffer

sourire (sooh-reer): to smile

souris (sooh-ree) f: mouse

sous (sooh): under, underneath

sous-vêtements (sooh-veht-mahN) m: underwear

se souvenir (suh sooh-vuh-neer): to remember

souvent (sooh-vahN): often

sportif/sportive (spohr-teef/spohr-teev) m/f: athletic

stationnement (stah-syuhhn-mahN) m: parking

station-service (stah-syohN-sehr-vees) f: gas station

steward (stee-wahr) m: flight attendant

stylo (stee-loh) m: pen

sucre (sew-kruh) m: sugar

sud (sewd) m: south

suffisamment (sew-fee-zah-mahN): sufficiently

suggérer (sewg-zhey-rey): to suggest

supermarché (sew-pehr-mahr-shey) m: supermarket

sur (sewr): on, on top of

surveillant/surveillante de plage, de baignade (sewr-vehy-ahN/sewr-vehy-ahNt duh plahzh, duh beh-nyahd) m/f: lifeguard

sweat (sweht) m: sweatshirt

T

ta (tah) f: your

tableau d'affichage (tah-bloh dah-fee-shahzh) m: bulletin board

tailleur (tahy-uhr) m: women's suit

tandis que (tahN-dee kuh): while, whereas

tant pis (tahN pee): too bad

tante (tahNt) f: aunt

tapis (tah-pee) m: rug

tard (tahr): late

tarif réduit (tah-reef rey-dwee) m: reduced fare

tarte aux pommes (tahr toh puhhm) f: apple tart

tasse (tahs) f: cup

taux de change (toh duh shahNzh) m: exchange rate

télécharger (tey-ley-shahr-zhey): to download

télécopie (tey-ley-koh-pee) f: fax

télécopieur (tey-ley-koh-pyuhr) m: fax machine

téléphoner (tey-ley-fuhh-ney): to telephone, to call

tenir (tuh-neer): to hold

tennis (tey-nees) m: tennis

tes (tey) pl: your

tête (teht) f: head

thé (tey) m: tea

thon (tohN) m: tuna

thym (taN) m: thyme

tien/tiens/tienne/tiennes (tyaN/tyaN/tyehn/tyehn) ms/mpl/fs/fpl: yours (familiar singular)

timbre (taN-bruh) m: stamp

toi (twah): you (familar singular)

tomate (toh-maht) f: tomato

tomber (tohN-bey): to fall

ton (tohN) m: your

tondeuse à gazon (tohN-duhz ah gah-zohN) f: lawn mower

tondre la pelouse/le gazon (tohN-druh lah puh-loohz/luh gah-zohN): to mow the lawn

tôt (toh): early

toujours (tooh-zhoohr): always, still

tous/toutes (tooh/tooht) mpl/fpl: all

tout/toute (tooh/tooht) ms/fs: all, whole

tout le monde (tooh luh mohNd): everyone, everybody

toux (tooh) f: a cough

train (traN) m: train

travailler (trah-vah-yey): to work

travailleur/travailleuse (trah-vah-yuhr/trah-vah-yuhz) m/f: hardworking

treize (trehz): thirteen

trois (trwah): three

trop (troh): too much

trottoir (troh-twahr) m: sidewalk

trouver (trooh-vey): to find

trucages (trew-kahzh) mpl: special effects

truite (trweet) f: trout

tu (tew): you (familiar singular)

tutoyer (tew-twah-yey): to use *tu*

tuyau d'arrosage (twee-yoh dah-roh-zahzh) m: garden hose

U

un/une (uhN/ewn) m/f: one

V

vague (vahg) f: wave

valoir (vah-lwar): to be worth

valise (vah-leez) f: suitcase

veau (voh) m: veal, calf

vedette (vuh-deht) f: movie star

vendre (vahN-druh): to sell

venir (vuh-neer): to come

verre (vehr) m: glass

vers (vehr): toward

vert/verte (vehr/vehrt) m/f: green

veste (vehst) f: jacket (for men and women)

veston (veh-stohN) m: man's suit jacket

viande (vyahNd) f: meat

victoire (veek-twahr) f: victory

vidange (vee-dahNzh) f: oil change

vieillir (vyey-eer): to grow old

vieux/vieille (vyuh/vyehy) m/f: old

vif/vive (veef/veev): lively

ville (veel) f: city/town

vin (vaN) m: wine

vingt (vaN): twenty

violon (vyoh-lohN) m: violin

visiter (vee-zee-tey): to visit (a place)

vite (veet): quickly

vitrine (vee-treen) f: store window

vivre (vee-vruh): to live

voie (vwah) f: track

voile (vwahl) m: veil, headscarf; f: sail (of a boat)

voir (vwahr): to see

voiture (vwah-tewr) f: car

vol (vuhhl) m: flight, theft

volontiers (voh-lohN-tyey): gladly

vos (voh) pl: your (formal or plural)

votre (vuhh-truh) s: your (formal or plural)

vôtre/vôtres (voh-truh) s/pl: yours (formal or plural)

vouloir (vooh-lwahr): to want

vous (vooh): you (formal or plural)

vouvoyer (vooh-vwah-yey): to use *vous*

voyage d'affaires (vwah-yahzh dah-fehr) m: business trip

voyager (vwah-yah-zhey): to travel

vrai/vraie (vrey): true

vraiment (vrey-mahN): really

W

week-end (wee-kehnd) m: weekend

Y

yaourt (yah-oohrt) m: yogurt

yeux (yuh) mpl: eyes

Z

zéro (zey-roh): zero

Appendix C

English-French Mini Dictionary

Key: m = masculine, f = feminine, s = singular, pl = plural, n = noun, adj = adjective

A

a, an, one: **un/une** (uhN/ewn) m/f

(to) be able to: **pouvoir** (pooh-vwahr)

about, of, from: **de** (duh)

above: **dessus** (duh-sew)

absolutely: **absolument** (ahp-soh-lew-mahN)

(to) accept: **accepter** (ahk-sehp-tey)

(to) accommodate/(to) lodge: **loger** (loh-zhey)

(to) accuse: **accuser** (ah-kew-zey)

across from, in front of: **en face de** (ahN fahs duh)

address: **adresse** (ah-drehs) f

(to) address someone as *tu*: **tutoyer** (tew-twah-yey)

(to) address someone as *vous*: **vouvoyer** (vooh-vwah-yey)

(to) admire: **admirer** (ahd-mee-rey)

(to) admit: **admettre** (ahd-meh-truh)

(to) adore: **adorer** (ah-doh-rey)

(to) advance: **avancer/s'avancer** (ah-vahN-sey/sah-vahN-sey)

(to) advise: **conseiller** (kohN-sey-yey)

adventure film: **film d'aventures** (feelm dah-vahN-tewr) m

advertisement: **publicité** (pew-blee-see-tey) f

after: **après** (ah-prey)

again: **encore** (ahN-kohr)

against: **contre** (kohN-truh)

air conditioning: **climatisation** (klee-mah-tee-zah-syohN) f

airport terminal: **aérogare** (ah-ey-roh-gahr) f

alarm clock: **réveil** (rey-vehy) m

all right, okay: **d'accord** (dah-kohr)

all: **tout/toute/tous/toutes** (tooh/tooht/tooh/tooht) ms/fs/mpl/fpl

(to) allow, let, permit, leave behind: **laisser** (leh-sey)

already: **déjà** (dey-zhah)

also: **aussi** (oh-see)

although: **bien que** (byaN kuh), **quoique** (kwah-kuh)

always: **toujours** (tooh-zhoohr)

American football: **foot(ball) américain** (fooht[-buhhl] ah-mey-ree-kaN) m

and: **et** (ey)

ankle: **cheville** (shuh-veey) f

(to) announce: **annoncer** (ah-nohN-sey)

(to) annoy, (to) bore: **ennuyer** (ahN-nwee-yey)

(to) answer: **répondre** (rey-pohN-druh)

antibiotic: **antibiotique** (ahN-tee-bee-oh-teek) m

(to) appear: **paraître** (pah-reh-truh)

(to) apologize: **s'excuser** (seyk-skew-zey)

appetizer, entrance: **entrée** (ahN-trey) f

apple: **pomme** (puhhm) f

apple tart: **tarte aux pommes** (tahrt oh puhhm) fpl

appointment: **rendez-vous** (rahN-dey-vooh) m

apricot: **abricot** (ah-bree-koh) m

April: **avril** (ah-vreel) m

architect: **architecte** (ahr-shee-tehkt) m/f

(to) argue: **se disputer** (suh dee-spew-tey)

arm: **bras** (brah) m

armoire: **armoire** (ahr-mwahr) f

around: **autour** (oh-toohr)

(to) arrange: **arranger** (ah-rahN-zhey)

arrival: **arrivée** (ah-ree-vey) f

(to) arrive: **arriver** (ah-ree-vey)

(to) ask: **demander** (duh-mahN-dey)

as much/many: **autant** (oh-tahN)

as soon as: **aussitôt que** (oh-see-toh kuh)

asparagus: **asperge** (ah-spehrzh) f

at, to, in: **à** (ah)

athletic: **sportif/sportive** (spohr-teef/spohr-teev) m/f

ATM: **distributeur (de billets)** (dee-stree-bew-tuhr [duh bee-yey]) m

(to) attach: **joindre** (zhwaN-druh)

attachment: **pièce jointe** (pyehs zhwaNt) f

(to) attend: **assister** (ah-sees-tey)

August: **août** (ooht) m

aunt: **tante** (tahNt) f

author: **auteur** (oh-tuhr) m

average: **moyen/moyenne** (mwah-yaN/mwah-yehn) m/f

B

back: **dos** (doh) m

bad: **mauvais/mauvaise** (moh-veh/moh-vehz) m/f

badly: **mal** (mahl)

bag: **sac** (sahk) m

baggage room: **consigne** (kohN-see-nyuh) f

bakery: **boulangerie** (booh-lahN-zhree) f

banana: **banane** (bah-nahn) f

bandage: **pansement** (pahNs-mahN) m

bank: **banque** (bahNk) f

basketball: **basket** (bah-skeht) m

(to) bathe: **baigner/se baigner** (beh-nyey/suh beh-nyey)

bathing suit, swimsuit: **maillot de bain** [France] (mah-yoh duh baN) m, **costume de bains** [Québec] (koh-stewm duh baN) m

bathroom sink: **lavabo** (lah-vah-boh) m

bathtub: **baignoire** (beh-nywahr) f

(to) be: **être** (eh-truh)

beach: **plage** (plahzh) f

because: **parce que** (pahr-suh kuh)

(to) become: **devenir** (duh-vuh-neer)

(to) become irritated: **s'énerver** (sey-nehr-vey)

bed: **lit** (lee) m

beef: **bœuf** (buhhf) m

beer: **bière** (byehr) f

before: **avant** (ah-vahN)

(to) begin (to): **commencer** (koh-mahN-sey)/**se mettre à** (suh meh-trah)

behind: **derrière** (deh-ryehr)

(to) believe: **croire** (krwahr)

(to) belong: **appartenir** (ah-pahr-tuh-neer)

below, underneath: **dessous** (duh-sooh)

belt: **ceinture** (saN-tewr) f

better: **mieux** (myuh), **meilleur** (mey-yuhr)

between: **entre** (ahN-truh)

bicycle: **vélo** (vey-loh) m, **bicyclette** (bee-see-kleht) f big, tall, large: **grand/grande** (grahN/grahNd) m/f

bird: **oiseau** (wah-zoh) m

birth: **naissance** (neh-sahNs) f

black: **noir/noire** (nwahr) m/f

blanket: **couverture** (kooh-vehr-tewr) f

blazer: **blazer** (blah-zehr) m

blouse: **chemisier** (shuh-mee-zyey) m

blue: **bleu/bleue** (bluh) m/f

boarding pass: **carte d'embarquement** (kahrt dahN-bahr-kuh-mahN) f

book: **livre** (lee-vruh) m

bookstore: **librairie** (lee-brey-ree) f

boot: **botte** (buhht) fpl

(to) bore, annoy: **ennuyer** (ahN-nwee-yey)

(to) be/get bored: **s'ennuyer** (sahN-nwee-yey)

boring: **ennuyeux/ennuyeuse** (ahN-nwee-yuh/ahN-nwee-yuhz) m/f

(to) be born: **naître** (neh-truh)

boy: **garçon** (gahr-sohN) m

brakes: **freins** (fraN) mpl

bread: **pain** (paN) m

breakfast: **petit déjeuner** (puh-tee dey-zhuh-ney) m

bridge: **pont** (pohN) m

(to) bring something: **apporter** (ah-pohr-tey)

(to) bring someone: **amener** (ah-muh-ney)

(to) bring up, (to) raise: **élever** (eyl-vey)

brother: **frère** (frehr) m

brown: **marron** (mah-rohN)

brush: **brosse** (bruhhs) f

(to) brush: **brosser/se brosser** (bruhh-sey/suh bruhh-sey)

Brussels sprouts: **choux de Bruxelles** (shooh duh brewk-sehl) mpl

(to) build: **bâtir** (bah-teer)

bulletin board: **tableau d'affichage** (tah-bloh dah-fee-shahzh) m

burglary: **cambriolage** (kahN-bree-oh-lahzh) m

business trip: **voyage d'affaires** (vwah-yahzh dah-fehr) m

business: **affaires** (ah-fehr) fpl

but: **mais** (mey)

butcher shop: **boucherie** (booh-shree) f

butter: **beurre** (buhr) m

(to) buy: **acheter** (ahsh-tey)

by: **par** (pahr), **en** (ahN)

C

cabbage: **chou** (shooh) m

café: **café** (kah-fey) m

cake: **gâteau** (gah-toh) m

calendar: **calendrier** (kah-lahN-dree-yey) m

(to) call/(to) call oneself, (to) be named: **appeler/s'appeler** (ah-pley/sah-pley)

(to) call back: **rappeler** (rah-pley)

camera: **appareil-photo** (ah-pah-rchy-foh-toh) m

can (to be able): **pouvoir** (pooh-vwahr)

car: **voiture** (vwah-tewr) f

carnation: **œillet** (uh-yeh) m

carpet: **moquette** (moh-keht) f

carrot: **carotte** (kah-ruhht) f

(to) carry: **porter** (pohr-tey)

cartoon: **dessin animé** (deh-saN ah-nee-mey) m

cashier: **caissier/caissière** (key-syeh/key-syehr) m/f

cash register: **caisse** (kehs) f

castle: **château** (shah-toh) m

(to) catch: **attraper** (ah-trah-pey)

cauliflower: **chou-fleur** (shooh-fluhr) m

Book VI

Appendixes

CD, DVD player: **lecteur de CD/de DVD** (lehk-tuhr duh sey dey/duh dey vey dey) m

(to) celebrate: **célébrer** (sey-ley-brey), **fêter** (feh-tey)

cell phone: **mobile** (moh-beel) m

certainly: **certainement** (sehr-tehn-mahN)

CEO: **PDG** (pey dey zhey)

(to) change: **changer** (shaN-zhey)

charming: **charmant/charmante** (shahr-mahN/shahr-mahNt) m/f

chat room: **salon de chat** (sah-lohN duh chaht) m

(to) chat: **bavarder** (bah-vahr-dey)

check: **addition** (ah-dee-syohN) f

cheese: **fromage** (froh-mahzh) m

cherry: **cerise** (suh-reez) f

chervil: **cerfeuil** (sehr-fuhy) m

chess: **échecs** (ey-shehk) mpl

chest: **poitrine** (pwah-treen) f

chicken: **poulet** (pooh-leh) m

child: **enfant** (ahN-fahN) m/f

(to) choose: **choisir** (shwah-zeer)

city/town: **ville** (veel) f

(to) claim: **prétendre** (prey-tahN-druh)

(to) clean: **nettoyer** (neh-twah-yey)

(to) climb: **monter** (mohN-tey)

clock: **horloge** (ohr-luhhzh) f

cloud: **nuage** (new-ahzh) m

coast: **côte** (koht) f

coat: **manteau** (mahN-toh) m

coffee: **café** (kah-fey) m

cold (n): **rhume** (rewm) m

cold (adj): **froid/froide** (frwah/frwahd) m/f

colleague, coworker: **collègue** (koh-lehg) m/f

color: **couleur** (kooh-luhr) f

comb: **peigne** (peh-nyuh) m

(to) comb: **peigner/se peigner** (peh-nyey/suh peh-nyey)

(to) come: **venir** (vuh-neer)

(to) come back: **revenir** (ruh-vuh-neer)

(to) come back home: **rentrer** (rahN-trey)

comic strip: **bande dessinée** (bahNd deh-see-ney) f

company: **compagnie** (kohN-pah-nyee) f

(to) compare: **comparer** (kohN-pah-rey)

(to) complete: **compléter** (kohN-pley-tey)

computer: **ordinateur** (ohr-dee-nah-tuhr) m

computer scientist: **informaticien/informaticienne** (aN-fohr-mah-tee-syaN/aN-fohr-mah-tee-syehn) m/f

(to) consent: **consentir** (kohN-sahN-teer)

(to) consider: **considérer** (kohN-see-dey-rey)

(to) construct, (to) build: **construire** (kohN-strweer)

continually: **continuellement** (kohN-tee-new-ehl-mahN)

(to) contain: **contenir** (kohN-tuh-neer)

(to) continue: **continuer** (kohN-tee-new-ey)

(to) contradict: **contredire** (kohN-truh-deer)

(to) cook: **faire la cuisine** (fehr lah kwee-zeen), **cuire** (kweer)

copy machine: **photocopieuse** (foh-toh-koh-pyuhz) f

coriander: **coriandre** (koh-ree-ahN-druh) m

(to) correct: **corriger** (koh-ree-zhey)

cough (n): **toux** (tooh) f

counter: **comptoir** (kohN-twahr) m

country: **pays** (pey-ee) m

countryside: **campagne** (kahN-pah-nyuh) f

courtyard: **cour** (koohr) f

(to) cover: **couvrir** (kooh-vreer)

cream: **crème** (krehm) f

credit card: **carte de crédit** (kahrt duh krey-dee) f

credits: **générique** (zhey-ney-reek) m

cup: **tasse** (tahs) f

(to) cure, (to) heal: **guérir** (gey-reer)

currency exchange office: **bureau de change** (bew-roh duh shahNzh) m

currently: **actuellement** (ahk-tew-ehl-mahN)

curtain: **rideau** (ree-doh) m

(to) cut: **couper/se couper** (kooh-pey/ suh kooh-pey)

D

daffodil: **jonquille** (zhohN-keey) f

dairy product and cheese store: **crémerie** (kreym-ree) f

daisy: **marguerite** (mahr-guh-reet) f

(to) dance: **danser** (dahN-sey)

dark: **foncé/foncée** (fohN-sey) m/f

daughter, girl: **fille** (feey) f

day: **jour** (zhoohr) m

dear, expensive: **cher/chère** (shehr) m/f

December: **décembre** (dey-sahN-bruh) m

(to) decide: **décider** (dey-see-dey)

(to) defend: **défendre** (dey-fahN-druh)

delighted: **enchanté/enchantée** (ahN-shahN-tey) m/f

(to) demand: **exiger** (eyg-zee-zhey)

(to) denounce: **dénoncer** (dey-nohN-sey)

dentist: **dentiste** (dahN-teest) m/f

department store: **grand magasin** (grahN mah-gah-zaN) m

departure: **départ** (dey-pahr) m

(to) descend: **descendre** (dey-sahN-druh)

(to) describe: **décrire** (dey-kreer)

(to) desire: **désirer** (dey-zee-rey)

desk: **bureau** (bew-roh) m

dessert: **dessert** (deh-sehr) m

detective film: **film policier** (feelm poh-lee-syey) m

(to) die: **mourir** (mooh-reer)

difficult: **difficile** (dee-fee-seel)

dill: **aneth** (ah-neht) m

(to) direct: **diriger** (dee-ree-zhey)

director (film): **metteur-en-scène/ réalisateur/réalisatrice** (meh-tuhr-ahN-sehn/rey-ah-lee-zah-tuhr/rey-ah-lee-zah-trees) m/m/f

director/manager (of a company or business): **directeur/directrice** (dee-rehk-tuhr/dee-rehk-trees) m/f

(to) disappear: **disparaître** (dee-spah-reh-truh)

(to) disappoint: **décevoir** (dey-suh-vwahr)

(to) discourage: **décourager** (dey-kooh-rah-zhey)

(to) discover: **découvrir** (dey-kooh-vreer)

(to) displace: **déplacer** (dey-plah-sey)

(to) dive: **plonger** (plohN-zhey)

(to) divorce: **(se) divorcer** ([suh] dee-vohr-sey)

dishwasher: **lave-vaisselle** (lahv veh-sehl) m

(to) do, (to) make: **faire** (fehr)

(to) do one's hair: **se coiffer** (suh kwah-fey)

doctor: **médecin** (meyd-saN), **docteur** (dohk-tuhr) m

Book VI

Appendixes

documentary: **documentaire** (doh-kew-mahN-tehr) m

door: **porte** (puhhrt) f

down: **en bas** (ahN bah)

(to) download: **télécharger** (tey-ley-shahr-zhey)

(to) dream: **rêver** (reh-vey)

dress: **robe** (ruhhb) f

(to get) dressed: **s'habiller** (sah-bee-yey)

dresser: **commode** (koh-muhhd) f

(to) drink: **boire** (bwahr)

(to) drive: **conduire** (kohN-dweer)

driver's license: **permis de conduire** (pehr-mee duh kohN-dweer) m

duck: **canard** (kah-nahr) m

E

ear: **oreille** (oh-rehy) f

early: **tôt** (toh)

easy: **facile** (fah-seel)

(to) eat: **manger** (mahN-zhey)

eight: **huit** (weet)

eighteen: **dix-huit** (dee-zweet)

either . . . or: **ou** (ooh) . . . **ou** (ooh)/**soit** (swaht) . . . **soit** (swaht)

elevator: **ascenseur** (ah-sahN-suhr) m

eleven: **onze** (ohNz)

e-mail: **e-mail** (ee-meyl) m, **courrier électronique** (kooh-ree-ey ey-lehk-troh-neek) m, **mél** (mehl) m

e-mail account: **messagerie** (mey-sah-zhree) f

e-mail address: **adresse électronique** (ah-drehs ey-lehk-troh-neek) f

(to) employ, use: **employer** (ahN-plwah-yey)

employee: **employé/employée** (ahN-plwah-yey) m/f

(to) encourage: **encourager** (ahN-kooh-rah-zhey)

end: **fin** (faN) f

(to get) engaged: **se fiancer** (suh fee-ahN-sey)

engineer: **ingénieur** (aN-zhey-nyuhr) m

enormously: **énormément** (ey-nohr-mey-mahN)

enough: **assez** (ah-sey)

(to) enter: **entrer** (ahN-trey)

envelope: **enveloppe** (ahN-vluhhp) f

equality: **égalité** (ey-gah-lee-tey) f

equipment, material: **matériel** (mah-tey-ryehl) m

(to) erase: **effacer** (ey-fah-sey)

eraser: **gomme** (guhhm) f

escalator: **escalier roulant** (eh-skah-lyey rooh-lahN) m

establish: **établir** (ey-tah-bleer)

even, same: **même** (mehm)

even though: **bien que** (byaN kuh)

evening, evening party: **soirée** (swah-rey) f

ever/never: **jamais** (zhah-mey)

everyone, everybody: **tout le monde** (tooh luh mohNd)

everywhere: **partout** (pahr-tooh)

exchange rate: **taux de change** (toh duh shahNzh) m

(to) excuse/(to) excuse oneself: **excuser/s'excuser** (eyk-skew-zey/seyk-skew-zey)

exit: **sortie** (sohr-tee) f

(to) exit, (to) go out: **sortir** (sohr-teer)

expensive, dear: **cher/chère** (shehr) m/f

eye/eyes: **œil /yeux** (uhy/yuh) m

F

face: **figure** (fee-gewr) f

to face, overlook: **donner sur** (duhh-ney sewr)

fairy tale: **conte de fée** (kohNt duh fey) m

fall: **automne** (oh-tuhhn) m

(to) fall: **tomber** (tohN-bey)

(to) fall asleep: **s'endormir** (sahN-dohr-meer)

(to) be familiar with: **connaître** (koh-neh-truh)

far: **loin** (lwaN)

fat, large: **gros/grosse** (groh/gruhhs) m/f

father: **père** (pehr) m

favorite: **préféré/préférée** (prey-fey-rey) m/f

fax: **télécopie** (tey-ley-koh-pee) f

fax machine: **télécopieur** (tey-ley-koh-pyuhr) m

(to) fear: **craindre** (kraN-druh)

feature film: **long-métrage** (lohN mey-trahzh) m

February: **février** (fey-vryey) m

(to) feel [an emotion or mood]: **sentir/se sentir** (sahN-teer/suh sahN-teer)

fifteen: **quinze** (kaNz)

fig: **figue** (feeg) f

file cabinet: **classeur à tiroirs** (klah-suhr ah tee-rwahr) m

file: **fichier** (fee-shyey) m

(to) fill: **remplir** (rahN-pleer)

(to) fill the gas tank: **faire le plein** (fehr luh plaN)

filmmaker: **cinéaste** (see-ney-ahst) m/f

finally: **finalement** (fee-nahl-mahN), **enfin** (ahN-faN)

(to) find: **trouver** (trooh-vey)

finger: **doigt** (dwah) m

(to) finish: **finir** (fee-neer)

first name: **prénom** (prey-nohN) m

fish: **poisson** (pwah-sohN) m

(to) fish, go fishing: **pêcher** (peh-shey)

fishing pole: **canne à pêche** (kahn ah pehsh) f

fish store: **poissonnerie** (pwah-suhhn-ree) f

fitting room: **cabine d'essayage** (kah-been dey-sey-ahzh) f

five: **cinq** (saNk)

flannel: **flanelle** (flah-nehl) f

flight: **vol** (vuhhl) m

flight attendant: **steward/hôtesse de l'air** (stee-wahr/oh-tehs duh lehr) m/f

flower: **fleur** (fluhr) f

flowerbed: **plate-bande** (plaht-bahNd) f

flower garden: **jardin d'agrément** (zhahr-daN dah-grey-mahN) m

flu: **grippe** (greep) f

fluently: **couramment** (kooh-rah-mahN)

foot: **pied** (pyey) m

for: **pour** (poohr)

for a long time: **longtemps** (lohN-tahN)

(to) forbid: **défendre** (dey-fahN-druh), **interdire** (aN-tehr-deer)

(to) force: **forcer** (fohr-sey)

(to) forget: **oublier** (ooh-blee-yey)

fork: **fourchette** (foohr-sheht) f

formal: **formel/formelle** (fohr-mehl) m/f

formerly: **autrefois** (oh-truh-fwah)

fortunately: **heureusement** (uh-ruhz-mahN)

four: **quatre** (kah-truh)

fourteen: **quatorze** (kah-tohrz)

freedom: **liberté** (lee-behr-tey) f

(to) freeze: **geler** (zhuh-ley)

fresh: **frais/fraîche** (frey/frehsh)

friend: **ami/amie** (ah-mee) m/f

(to) frighten, scare: **effrayer** (ey-frey-yey)

from, about, of: **de** (duh)

fruit: **fruits** (frwee) mpl

fun, funny: **amusant/amusante** (ah-mew-zahN/ah-mew-zahNt) m/f

(to have) fun: **s'amuser** (sah-mew-zey)

G

(to) gain weight: **grossir** (groh-seer)

(to) garden: **faire du jardinage** (fehr dew zhahr-dee-nahzh)

garden hose: **tuyau d'arrosage** (tew-yoh dah-roh-zahzh) m

gas station: **station-service** (stah-syohN-sehr-vees) f

gas: **essence** (ey-sahNs) f

glass: **verre** (vehr) m

(to) get along: **s'entendre** (sahN-tahN-druh)

(to) get dressed: **s'habiller** (sah-bee-yey)

(to) get engaged: **se fiancer** (suh fee-ahN-sey)

(to) get up: **se lever** (suh-luh-vey)

(to) give: **donner** (duhh-ney)

(to) give back: **rendre** (rahN-druh)

gladly: **volontiers** (voh-lohN-tyey)

(to) go: **aller** (ah-ley)

(to) go down, (to) get off: **descendre** (dey-sahN-druh)

(to) go out: **sortir** (sohr-teer)

(to) go up, (to) climb, (to) get on: **monter** (mohN-tey)

(to) grow: **grandir** (grahN-deer)

(to) grow old: **vieillir** (vyey-yeer)

good: **bon/bonne** (bohN/buhhn) m/f

goodbye: **au revoir** (ohr-vwahr)

good day, hello: **bonjour** (bohN-zhoohr)

good evening, good night: **bonsoir** (bohN-swahr) m

good night (when going to bed): **bonne nuit** (buhhn nwee) f

grandchildren: **petits-enfants** (puh-tee-zahN-fahN) mpl

granddaughter: **petite-fille** (puh-teet-feey)

grandson: **petit-fils** (puh-tee-fees) m

grape: **raisin** (reh-zaN) m

green: **vert/verte** (vehr/vehrt) m/f

green beans: **haricots verts** (ah-ree-koh vehr) mpl

green salad, salad with lettuce only: **salade verte** (sah-lahd vehrt) f

grocery store, general store: **épicerie** (ey-pees-ree) f

ground (first) floor: **rez-de-chaussée** (reyd shoh-sey) m

guitar: **guitare** (gee-tahr) f

H

ham: **jambon** (zhahN-bohN) m

hand: **main** (maN) f

happiness: **bonheur** (boh-nuhr) m

happy: **heureux/heureuse** (uh-ruh/uh-ruhz) m/f

hardworking: **travailleur/travailleuse** (trah-vah-yuhr/trah-vah-yuhz) m/f

hardware: **matériel** (mah-tey-ree-ehl) m

hat: **chapeau** (shah-poh) m

(to) hate: **détester** (dey-teh-stey)

(to) have: **avoir** (ah-vwahr)

(to) have fun: **s'amuser** (sah-mew-zey)

(to) have to: **devoir** (duh-vwahr)

he, it: **il** (eel) m

head: **tête** (teht) f

(to) hear: **entendre** (ahN-tahN-druh)

(to) help: **aider** (ey-dey)

here: **ici** (ee-see)

(to) hesitate: **hésiter** (ey-zee-tey)

hi: **salut** (sah-lew)

(to) hiccup: **hoqueter** (oh-kuh-tey)

(to) hide: **cacher/se cacher** (kah-shey/ suh kah-shey)

high-school teacher, college professor: **professeur** (proh-feh-suhr) m

hike: **randonnée** (rahN-doh-ney) f

his, her, its: **son** (sohN) ms/**sa** (sah) fs/ **ses** (sey) pl

his, hers, its: **sien/siens** (syaN) ms/mpl, **sienne/siennes** (syehn) fs/fpl

holidays: **fêtes** (feht) fpl

(to) hold: **tenir** (tuh-neer)

home page: **page d'accueil** (pahzh dah-kuhy) f

hood (of a car): **capot** (kah-poh) m

(to) hope: **espérer** (ey-spey-rey)

horror film: **film d'épouvante/ d'horreur** (feelm dey-pooh-vahnt/ doh-ruhr) m

hotel: **hôtel** (oh-tehl) m

house: **maison** (meh-zohN) f

how: **comment** (koh-mahN)

how much, how many: **combien** (kohN-byaN)

(to be) hungry: **avoir faim** (ah-vwahr faN)

(to) hurry: **se dépêcher** (suh dey-pey-shey)

(to) hurt/(to) hurt oneself: **blesser/se blesser** (bleh-sey/suh bleh-sey)

husband: **mari** (mah-ree) m

hydrangea: **hortensia** (ohr-tahN-syah) m

I

I: **je** (zhuh)

ice cream: **glace** (glahs) f

icon: **icône** (ee-kohn) f

idea: **idée** (ee-dey) f

illness: **maladie** (mah-lah-dee) f

immediately: **immédiatement** (ee-mey-dyaht-mahN)

in, inside: **dans** (dahN)

in the back: **au fond** (oh fohN)

in front of: **devant** (duh-vahN)

(to) influence: **influencer** (aN-flew-ahN-sey)

information: **renseignement** (rahN-sehn-yuh-mahN) m

inside (it): **dedans** (duh-daN)

intelligently: **intelligemment** (aN-tey-lee-zhah-mahN)

interesting: **intéressant** (aN-tey-rey-sahN)

intersection: **carrefour** (kahr-foohr) m

(to) introduce: **présenter** (prey-zahN-tey)

(to) invite: **inviter** (aN-vee-tey)

J

jacket (for men and women): **veste** (vehst) f

jam: **confiture** (kohN-fee-tewr) f

January: **janvier** (zhahN-vyey) m

jeans: **jean** (djeen) m

jewelry store: **bijouterie** (bee-zhooh-tree) f

(to) judge: **juger** (zhew-zhey)

July: **juillet** (zhwee-yeh) m

June: **juin** (zhwaN) m

just as, so as, as well as: **ainsi que** (aN-see kuh)

K

keyboard: **clavier** (klah-vyey) m

kind: **gentil/gentille** (zhahN-teey) m/f

kindly: **gentiment** (zhahN-tee-mahN)

kitchen sink: **évier** (ey-vyey) m

knee: **genou** (zhuh-nooh) m

knife: **couteau** (kooh-toh) m

(to) know, (to) be familiar with: **connaître** (koh-neh-truh)

(to) know (a fact/how to do something): **savoir** (sah-vwahr)

L

lake: **lac** (lahk) m

lamb: **agneau** (ah-nyoh) m

laptop: **portable** (pohr-tah-bluh) m

large, wide: **large** (lahrzh) m/f

last name: **nom** (nohN) m

lastly: **dernièrement** (dehr-nyehr-mahN)

late: **en retard** (ahN ruh-tahr)

(to) laugh: **rire** (reer)

(to) launch, (to) throw: **lancer** (lahN-sey)

lawn mower: **tondeuse à gazon** (tohN-duhz ah gah-zohN) f

lawyer: **avocat/avocate** (ah-voh-kah/ah-voh-kaht) m/f

(to) lead: **mener** (muh-ney)

(to) leaf through: **feuilleter** (fuhy-tey)

leak: **poireau** (pwah-roh) m

(to) learn: **apprendre** (ah-prahN-druh)

leather: **cuir** (kweer) m

(to) leave: **partir/s'en aller** (pahr-teer/sahN-nah-ley)

(to) leave, (to) abandon: **quitter** (kee-tey)

leg: **jambe** (zhahNb) f

leg of lamb: **gigot d'agneau** (zhee-goh dah-nyoh) m

lemonade: **citron pressé** (see-trohN preh-sey) m, **limonade** (lee-moh-nahd) f

less: **moins** (mwaN)

lettuce: **laitue** (ley-tew) f

(to) lie: **mentir** (mahN-teer)

(to) lift, (to) raise: **lever** (luh-vey)

lifeguard: **surveillant/surveillante de plage, de baignade** (sewr-vehy-ahN/sewr-vehy-ahNt duh plahzh, duh beh-nyahd) m/f

light-colored, clear: **clair/claire** (klehr) m/f

lighting: **éclairage** (ey-kleh-rahzh) m

(to) like, (to) love: **aimer** (eh-mey)

linen: **lin** (laN) m

(to) listen: **écouter** (ey-kooh-tey)

little of: **peu de** (puh duh)

(to) live, (to) exist: **vivre** (vee-vruh)

(to) live, (to) reside: **habiter** (ah-bee-tey)

lively: **vif/vive** (veef/veev)

lobster: **homard** (oh-mahr) m

(to) lodge: **loger** (loh-zhey)

(to) look for: **chercher** (shehr-shey)

(to) lose, (to) waste: **perdre** (pehr-druh)

(to) lose weight: **maigrir** (mey-greer)

a lot: **beaucoup** (boh-kooh)

(to) love, (to) adore: **adorer** (ah-doh-rey)

lozenge: **pastille** (pah-steey) f

lunch (noun), to have lunch (verb): **déjeuner** (dey-zhuh-ney) m

M

ma'am, missus: **madame** (mah-dahm) f

mailbox: **boîte aux lettres** (bwaht oh leh-truh) f

majority: **la plupart de** (lah plew-pahr duh)

(to) make, (to) do: **faire** (fehr)

mall, shopping center: **centre commercial** (sahN-truh koh-mehr-syahl) m

(to) manage, get by: **se débrouiller** (suh dey-brooh-yey)

(to) manage (things/business): **gérer** (zhey-rey)

man's suit jacket: **veston** (veh-stohN) m

manager (of a company, business): **directeur/directrice** (dee-rehk-tuhr/ dee-rehk-trees) m/f

manager (of a restaurant, hotel, shop): **gérant/gérante** (zhey-rahN/zhey-rahNt) m/f

map: **plan** (plahN) m

March: **mars** (mahrs) m

margarine: **margarine** (mahr-gah-reen) f

match: **allumette** (ah-lew-meht) f

May: **mai** (mey) m

me: **moi** (mwah)

meal: **repas** (ruh-pah) m

meat: **viande** (vyahNd) f

(to) meet: **rencontrer** (rahN-kohN-trey)/ **se réunir** (suh rey-ew-neer)

meeting: **réunion** (rey-ew-nyohN)

(to) melt: **fondre** (fohN-druh)

memory: **mémoire** (mey-mwahr) f, **souvenir** (sooh-vuh-neer) m

microwave: **four à micro-ondes** (foohr ah mee-kroh-ohNd) m

midnight: **minuit** (mee-nwee)

mild, sweet: **doux/douce** (dooh/doohs) m/f

milk: **lait** (leh) m

mine: **mien/miens** (myaN) ms/mpl, **mienne/ miennes** (myehn) fs/fpl

mint: **menthe** (mahNt) f

mirror: **miroir** (mee-rwahr) m

miss (title): **mademoiselle** (mahd-mwah-zehl) f

(to) miss: **manquer** (mahN-key)

mister, sir: **monsieur** (muh-syuh) m

(to) mix: **mélanger** (mey-lahN-zhey)

mixed greens, raw vegetables: **crudités** (krew-dee-tey) fpl

(to) moderate: **modérer** (moh-dey-rey)

modern: **moderne** (moh-dehrn) m/f

money: **argent** (ahr-zhahN) m

monitor: **moniteur** (moh-nee-tuhr) m

more than: **plus de/que** (plews duh/kuh)

mother: **mère** (mehr) f

mountain: **montagne** (mohN-tah-nyuh) f

mouse: **souris** (sooh-ree) f

mouth: **bouche** (boohsh) f

(to) move: **bouger** (booh-zhey)

(to) move, (to) change residence: **déménager** (dey-mey-nah-zhey)

movie star: **vedette** (vuh-deht) f

movies: **cinéma** (see-ney-mah) m

(to) mow the lawn: **tondre la pelouse/le gazon** (tohN-druh lah puh-loohz/luh gah-zohN)

mushroom: **champignon** (shahN-pee-nyohN) m

my: **mon** (mohN) ms/**ma** (mah) fs/**mes** (mey) pl

N

(to) be named: **s'appeler** (sah-pley)

napkin, towel: **serviette** (sehr-vyeht) f

narrow: **étroit/étroite** (ey-trwah/ey-trwaht) m/f

near: **près** (prey)

neck: **cou** (kooh) m

neither . . . nor: **ne . . . ni . . . ni** (nuh . . . nee . . . nee)

network: **réseau** (rey-zoh) m

never/ever: **jamais** (zhah-mey)

new: **nouveau/nouvelle** (nooh-voh/nooh-vehl) m/f

new, brand new: **neuf/neuve** (nuhf/nuhv) m/f

newly: **nouvellement** (nooh-vehl-mahN)

newspaper: **journal** (zhoohr-nahl) m

next: **ensuite** (ahN-sweet)

next day: **lendemain** (lahN-duh-maN) m

next to: **à côté de** (ah koh-tey duh)

nice, beautiful, handsome: **beau/belle** (boh/behl) m/f

nine: **neuf** (nuhf)

nineteen: **dix-neuf** (deez-nuhf)

no: **non** (nohN)

no one: **ne . . . personne** (nuh . . . pehr-suhhn)

noisy: **bruyant/bruyante** (brwee-yahN/brwee-yahNt) m/f

none: **ne . . . aucun/aucune** (nuh . . . oh-kuhN/oh-kewn) m/f, **ne . . . nul/nulle** (nuh . . . newl) m/f

noon: **midi** (mee-dee)

north: **nord** (nohr) m

nose: **nez** (ney) m

not: **ne . . . pas** (nuh . . . pah)

not always: **(ne . . .) pas toujours** ([nuh] pah tooh-zhoor)

not any more: **ne . . . plus** (nuh . . . plew)

not at all: **(ne . . .) pas du tout** ([nuh] pah dew tooh)

not yet: **(ne . . .) pas encore** ([nuh] pah zahN-kohr)

novel: **roman** (roh-mahN) m

November: **novembre** (noh-vahN-bruh) m

now: **maintenant** (maN-tuh-nahN)

nowhere: **(ne . . .) nulle part** ([nuh] newl pahr)

nurse: **infirmier/infirmière** (aN-feer-myey/aN-feer-myehr) m/f

O

(to) obey: **obéir** (oh-bey-eer)

(to) obtain: **obtenir** (uhhp-tuh-neer)

ocean: **mer** (mehr) f

October: **octobre** (uhhk-toh-bruh) m

of, from, about: **de** (duh)

of course: **bien sûr** (byaN sewr)

off peak: **période creuse** (pey-ree-uhhd kruhz) f

(to) offer: **offrir** (oh-freer)

office: **bureau** (bew-roh) m

often: **souvent** (sooh-vahN)

oil change: **vidange** (vee-dahNzh) f

okay: **ça va** (sah vah)

old: **vieux/vieille** (vyuh/vyehy) m/f

on, on top of: **sur** (sewr)

on the left: **à gauche** (ah gohsh)

on purpose: **exprès** (eyk-sprey)

on the right: **à droite** (ah drwaht)

on time: **à l'heure** (ah luhr)

one: **un/une** (uhN/ewn) m/f

one (impersonal subject), we, they: **on** (ohN)

one way: **sens unique** (sahNs ew-neek) m

one-way ticket: **aller-simple** (ah-ley saN-pluh) m

onion: **oignon** (uhh-nyohN) m

only: **seulement** (suhl-mahN)/**ne . . . que** (nuh . . . kuh)

(to) open: **ouvrir** (ooh-vreer)

or: **ou** (ooh)

or else: **ou bien** (ooh byaN)

orange: **orange** (oh-rahNzh) f

our: **notre** (nuhh-truh) s/**nos** (noh) pl

ours: **nôtre** (noh-truh) s/**nôtres** (noh-truh) pl

outside: **dehors** (duh-ohr)

over there: **là-bas** (lah-bah)

overcoat: **pardessus** (pahr-duh-sew) m

owner: **propriétaire** (proh-pree-ey-tehr) m/f

oysters: **huitres** (wee-truh) fpl

P

package: **colis** (koh-lee) m

pants, slacks: **pantalon** (pahN-tah-lohN) m

parking: **stationnement** (stah-syuhhn-mahN) m

parsley: **persil** (pehr-see) m

(to) pass (by): **passer** (pah-sey)

passport: **passeport** (pahs-pohr) m

password: **mot de passe** (moh duh pahs) m

pasta: **pâtes** (paht) fpl

pastry shop: **pâtisserie** (pah-tee-sree) f

(to) pay: **payer** (pey-yey)

peach: **pêche** (pehsh) f

pear: **poire** (pwahr) f

peas: **petits pois** (puh-tee pwah) mpl

pedestrian: **piéton/piétonne** (pyey-tohN/pyey-tuhhn) m/f

pen: **stylo** (stee-loh) m

pencil: **crayon** (krey-ohN) m

pepper: **poivre** (pwah-vruh) m

perfect: **parfait/parfaite** (pahr-feh/pahr-feht) m/f

performance: **représentation** (ruh-prey-zahN-tah-syohN) f

person: **personne** (pehr-suhhn) f

phone number: **numéro de téléphone** (new-mey-roh duh tey-ley-fuhhn) m

photograph: **photo** (foh-toh) f

physician: **médecin** (meyd-saN) m

piano: **piano** (pyah-noh) m

picture: **photo** (foh-toh) f

pillow: **oreiller** (oh-rehy-ey) m

pineapple: **ananas** (ah-nah-nah) m

(to) place: **placer** (plah-sey)

plane: **avion** (ah-vyohN) m

plate: **assiette** (ah-syeht) f

platform: **quai** (key) m

(to) play: **jouer** (zhooh-ey)

(theatrical) play, room: **pièce** (pyehs) f

pleasant: **agréable** (ah-grey-ah-bluh)

plum: **prune** (prewn) f

police: **police** (poh-lees) f

politely: **poliment** (poh-lee-mahN)

pork: **porc** (pohr) m

(to) possess: **posséder** (poh-sey-dey)

post office: **poste** (puhhst) f

postage: **affranchissement** (ah-frahN-shee-smahN) m

postcard: **carte postale** (kahrt puhh-stahl) f

potato: **pomme de terre** (puhhm duh tehr) fpl

pound: **livre** (lee-vruh) f

(to) prefer: **préférer** (prey-fey-rey)

(to) prepare: **préparer** (prey-pah-rey)

(to) present: **présenter** (prey- zahN-tey)

pretty: **joli/jolie** (zhoh-lee) m/f

printer: **imprimante** (aN-pree-mahnt) f

(to) project, plant: **projeter** (proh-zhuh-tey)

(to) promise: **promettre** (proh-meh-truh)

(to) pronounce: **prononcer** (proh-nohN-sey)

(to) propose: **proposer** (proh-poh-zey)

(to) protect: **protéger** (proh-tey-zhey)

proud: **fier/fière** (fyehr) m/f

provided that: **pourvu que** (poohr-vew kuh)

prune: **pruneau** (prew-noh) m

(to) punish: **punir** (pew-neer)

(to) put, (to) place: **mettre** (meh-truh)

(to) put on make-up: **se maquiller** (suh mah-kee-yey)

Q

quickly: **vite** (veet)

quite a bit of: **pas mal de** (pah mahl duh)

quite a few: **bien des** (byaN dey)

R

(to) rain: **pleuvoir** (pluh-vwahr)

raincoat (n), rainproof (adj): **imperméable** (aN-pehr-mey-ah-bluh) m

(to) raise, (to) lift: **lever** (luh-vey)

raisin: **raisin sec** (reh-zaN sehk) m

rarely: **rarement** (rahr-mahN)

raspberry: **framboise** (frahN-bwahz) f

razor: **rasoir** (rah-zwahr) m

(to) react: **réagir** (rey-ah-zheer)

(to) read: **lire** (leer)

receipt: **reçu** (ruh-sew) m

(to) receive: **recevoir** (ruh-suh-vwahr)

recently: **récemment** (rey-sah-mahN)

red: **rouge** (roohzh)

reduced fare: **tarif réduit** (tah-reef rey-dwee) m

(to) reflect, (to) think: **réfléchir** (rey-fley-sheer)

refrigerator: **réfrigérateur** (rey-free-zhey-rah-tuhr) m, **frigo** (free-goh) m

(to) refuse: **refuser** (ruh-few-zey)

(to) reject: **rejeter** (ruh-zhuh-tey)

(to) rejoice, (to) delight: **se réjouir** (suh rey-zhweer)

(to) remember: **se rappeler** (suh rah-pley), **se souvenir** (suh sooh-vuh-neer)

(to) remove: **enlever** (ahN-luh-vey)

(to) renew: **renouveler** (ruh-new-vuh-ley)

(to) repeat: **répéter** (rey-pey-tey)

(to) replace: **remplacer** (rahN-plah-sey)

(to) require, (to) demand: **exiger** (eyg-zee-zhey)

(to) rest: **se reposer** (suh ruh-poh-zey)

retiree: **retraité/retraitée** (ruh-treh-tey) m/f

(to) return, (to) go home: **rentrer** (rahN-trey)

(to) return (something): **rendre** (rahN-druh)

ribs: **côtes** (koht) fpl

rice: **riz** (ree) m

(to) rock, (to) cradle: **bercer** (behr-sey)

romance film: **film d'amour** (feelm dah-moohr) m

room: **pièce** (pyehs) f

rosemary: **romarin** (roh-mah-raN) m

round trip: **aller-retour** (ah-ley ruh-toohr) m

rubber band: **élastique** (ey-lah-steek) m

rug: **tapis** (tah-pee) m

(to) run: **courir** (kooh-reer)

rush hour: **heure de pointe** (uhr duh pwaNt) f

S

sad: **triste** (treest)

sadly: **tristement** (trees-tuh-mahN)

sage (n): **sauge** (sohzh) f

sailing: **voile** (vwahl) f

sales: **soldes** [France] (suhhld) mpl, **aubaine** [Québec] (oh-behn) fs

salmon: **saumon** (soh-mohN) m

salt: **sel** (sehl) m

sand: **sable** (sah-bluh) m

sandals: **sandales** (sahN-dahl) fpl

saucer: **soucoupe** (sooh-koohp) f

(to) say: **dire** (deer)

scale: **balance** (bah-lahNs) f

scallops: **coquilles Saint-Jacques** (koh-keey saN-zhahk) fpl

scarf: **foulard** (fooh-lahr) m

schedule: **horaire** (oh-rehr) m

science-fiction film: **film de science-fiction** (feelm duh syahNs feek-syohN) m

scissors: **ciseaux** (see-zoh) mpl

season: **saison** (seh-zohN) f

seat: **siège** (syehzh) m

secretary: **secrétaire** (suh-krey-tehr) m/f

(to) see: **voir** (vwahr)

(to) see again: **revoir** (ruh-vwahr)

see you soon: **à bientôt** (ah byaN-toh)

see you tomorrow: **à demain** (ah duh-maN)

seed: **graine** (grehn) f

(to) sell: **vendre** (vahN-druh)

September: **septembre** (sehp-tahN-bruh) m

(to) send: **envoyer** (ahN-vwah-yey)

serious: **sérieux** (seh-ryuh)

(to) serve: **servir** (sehr-veer)

seven: **sept** (seht)

seventeen: **dix-sept** (dee-seht)

(to) share: **partager** (pahr-tah-zhey)

(to) shave: **raser/se raser** (rah-zey/suh rah-zey)

she, it: **elle** (ehl) f

sheets: **draps** (drah) mpl

shirt: **chemise** (shuh-meez) f

shoe: **chaussure** (shoh-sewr) f

shoe size: **pointure** (pwaN-tewr) f

shoulder: **épaule** (ey-pohl) f

(to) show: **montrer** (mohN-trey)

(to) shower: **se doucher** (suh dooh-shey)

showing (of a movie): **séance** (sey-ahNs) f

shrimp: **crevettes** (kruh-veht) fpl

sidewalk: **trottoir** (troh-twahr) m

silk: **soie** (swah) f

silverware: **couverts** (kooh-vehr) mpl:

similar: **pareil/pareille** (pah-rehy) m/f

since: **depuis** (duh-pwee)

since, as: **puisque** (pwee-skuh)

(to) sing: **chanter** (shaN-tey)

sister: **sœur** (suhr) f

six: **six** (sees)

sixteen: **seize** (sehz)

skirt: **jupe** (zhewp) f

slacks, pants: **pantalon** (pahN-tah-lohN) m

(to) sleep: **dormir** (dohr-meer)

sleeping bag: **sac de couchage** (sahk duh kooh-shahzh) m

(to) sing: **chanter** (shahN-tey)

slippers: **chaussons/pantoufles** (shoh-sohN/pahN-tooh-fluh) mpl/fpl

(to) slow down: **ralentir** (rah-lahN-teer)

slowly: **lentement** (lahNt-mahN)

small, short: **petit/petite** (puh-tee/puh-teet) m/f

(to) smile: **sourire** (sooh-reer)

snack (noun), (to) taste (verb): **goûter** (gooh-tey) m

snack: **casse-croûte** (kahs-krooht) m

sneakers: **baskets** (bah-skeht) fpl

snow: **neige** (nehzh) f

so: **donc** (dohNk)

so that: **afin que/pour que** (ah-faN kuh/poohr kuh)

soap: **savon** (sah-vohN) m

soccer: **football** [France] (fooht-buhhl) m/**soccer** [Québec] (soh-kehr) m

sock: **chaussette** (shoh-seht) f

sofa: **canapé** (kah-nah-pey) m

software: **logiciel** (loh-zhee-syehl) m

soil: **sol** (suhhl) m

some: **du** (dew) m/**de la** (duh lah) f/**des** (dey) pl

something: **quelque chose** (kehl-kuh shohz)

sometimes: **parfois** (pahr-fwah)/**quelquefois** (kehl-kuh-fwah)

somewhere: **quelque part** (kehl-kuh pahr)

son: **fils** (fees) m

soon: **bientôt** (byaN-toh)

sorrel: **oseille** (oh-zehy) f

sorry: **désolé/désolée** (dey-zoh-ley) m/f

south: **sud** (sewd) m

(to) speak/(to) talk: **parler** (pahr-ley)

special effects: **effets spéciaux** (ey-feh spey-syoh) mpl, **trucages** (trew-kahzh) mpl

(to) spell: **épeler** (ey-puh-ley)

(to) spend (money): **dépenser** (dey-pahN-sey)

(to) spend (time): **passer** (pah-sey)

spinach: **épinards** (ey-pee-nahr) mpl

spoon, teaspoon: **cuillère** (kwee-yehr) f

spouse: **époux/épouse** (ey-pooh/ey-poohz) m/f

spring: **printemps** (praN-tahN) m

spy film: **film d'espionnage** (feelm deh-spyoh-nahzh) m

squarely: **carrément** (kah-rey-mahN)

stamp: **timbre** (taN-bruh) m

staple: **agrafe** (ah-grahf) f

stapler: **agrafeuse** (ah-grah-fuhz) f

stay: **séjour** (sey-zhoohr) m

(to) stay: **rester** (reh-stey)

steak: **bifteck** (beef-tehk) m

stop: **arrêt** (ah-rey) m

(to) stop: **arrêter/s'arrêter** (ah-reh-tey/sah-reh-tey)

store: **magasin** (mah-gah-zaN) m

store window: **vitrine** (vee-treen) f

stove: **cuisinière** (kwee-zee-nyehr) f

strawberry: **fraise** (frehz) f

street: **rue** (rew) f

(to) study: **étudier** (ey-tew-dyey)

(to) subscribe: **s'abonner** (sah-boh-ney)

(to) succeed **réussir** (rey-ew-seer)

(to) suffer: **souffrir** (sooh-freer)

sufficiently: **suffisamment** (sew-fee-zah-mahN)

sugar: **sucre** (sew-kruh) m

(to) suggest: **suggérer** (sewg-zhey-rey)

suit: **complet** [France] (kohN-pleh) m/**habit** [Québec] (ah-bee) m suitcase: **valise** (vah-leez) f

summer: **été** (ey-tey) m

sun: **soleil** (soh-lehy) m

sunglasses: **lunettes de soleil** (lew-neht duh soh-lehy) fpl

supermarket: **supermarché** (sew-pehr-mahr-shey) m

(to) surprise: **surprendre** (sewr-prahN-druh)

sweatshirt: **sweat** (sweht) m

sweater: **pull** (pewl) m

(to) sweep: **balayer** (bah-ley-yey)

(to) swim: **nager** (nah-zhey)

swimming: **natation** (nah-tah-syohN) f

swimming pool: **piscine** (pee-seen) f

swimsuit, bathing suit: **maillot de bain** [France] (mah-yoh duh baN) m, **costume de bains** [Québec] (koh-stewm duh baN) m

(to) swing: **balancer/se balancer** (bah-lahN-sey/suh bah-lahN-sey)

T

(to) take: **prendre** (prahN-druh)

(to) take, (to) bring someone along: **emmener** (ahN-muh-ney)

(to) take a walk, stroll: **se promener** (suh proh-muh-ney)

(to) talk, (to) speak: **parler** (pahr-ley)

(to) tan: **bronzer** (brohN-zey)

tape: **ruban adhésif** (rew-bahN ah-dey-zeef) m

tarragon: **estragon** (eh-strah-gohN) m

tea: **thé** (tey) m

(to) teach: **enseigner** (ahN-seh-nyey)

(to) telephone, (to) call: **téléphoner** (tey-ley-fuhh-ney)

telephone number: **numéro de téléphone** (new-mey-roh duh tey-ley-fuhhn) m

ten: **dix** (dees)

tennis: **tennis** (tey-nees) m

thank you: **merci** (mehr-see)

that one: **celui-là/celle-là** (suh-lwee-lah/sehl-lah) m/f

the: **le/la/les** (luh/lah/ley) ms/fs/pl

theatrical play: **pièce** (pyehs) f

theft: **vol** (vuhhl) m

their, theirs: **leur/leurs** (luhr)

then: **puis** (pwee)

there: **là** (lah)

there is, there are: **il y a** (eel ee ah)

these, those: **ces** (sey)

these ones: **ceux-ci/celles-ci** (suh-see/sehl-see) m/f

they: **elles** (ehl) fpl/**ils** (eel) mpl

thin: **mince** (maNs)

(to) think: **penser** (pahN-sey)

(to be) thirsty: **avoir soif** (ah-vwahr swahf)

thirteen: **treize** (trehz)

this, that: **ce/cette/cet** (suh/seht/seht) ms/fs/m before vowel or mute **h**

this one: **celui-ci/celle-ci** (suh-lwee-see/sehl-see) m/f

those ones: **ceux-là/celles-là** (suh-lah/sehl-lah) m/f

thought: **pensée** (pahN-sey) f

thousand: **mille** (meel) m

(to) threaten: **menacer** (muh-nah-sey)

three: **trois** (trwah)

(to) throw: **jeter** (zhuh-tey)/**lancer** (lahN-sey)

thyme: **thym** (taN) m

ticket: **billet** (bee-yey) m

ticket (traffic): **contravention** (kohN-trah-vahN-syohN) f

ticket window: **guichet** (gee-shey) m

tie: **cravate** (krah-vaht) f

tip: **pourboire** (poohr-bwahr) m

tire: **pneu** (pnuh) m

tired: **fatigué/fatiguée** (fah-tee-gey) m/f

to, at, in: **à** (ah)

to/at/in the: **au/à la/aux** (oh) ms/fs/pl

today: **aujourd'hui** (oh-zhoohr-dwee)

toe: **orteil** (ohr-tehy) m

tomato: **tomate** (toh-maht) f

too bad: **tant pis** (tahN pee)

too much: **trop** (troh)

tooth: **dent** (dahN) f

toothpaste: **dentifrice** (dahN-tee-frees) m

toward: **vers** (vehr)

track: **voie** (vwah) f

traffic jam: **embouteillage** (ahN-booh-teh-yahzh) m

train: **train** (traN) m

train station: **gare** (gahr) f

(to) travel: **voyager** (vwah-yah-zhey)

trout: **truite** (trweet) f

truly: **vraiment** (vrey-mahN)

trunk: **coffre** (koh-fruh) m

(to) try: **essayer** (ey-sey-yey)

tuna: **thon** (tohN) m

turkey: **dinde** (daNd) f

(to) turn pale: **pâlir** (pah-leer)

twelve: **douze** (doohz)

twenty: **vingt** (vaN)

two: **deux** (duh)

U

U-turn: **demi-tour** (duh-mee-toohr) m

uncle: **oncle** (ohN-kluh) m

under, underneath: **sous** (sooh)

underpants, briefs: **slip** (sleep) m

(to) understand: **comprendre** (kohN-prahN-druh)

underwear: **sous-vêtements** (sooh-veht-mahN) m

unless: **à moins que** (ah mwaN kuh)

(to) unite, (to) gather, (to) assemble: **réunir/se réunir** (rey-ew-neer/suh rey-ew-neer)

until: **jusqu'à** (zhew-skah), **jusqu'à ce que** (zhew-skah skuh), **en attendant que** (ahN nah-tahN-dahN kuh)

up: **en haut** (ahN oh)

(to) use: **employer** (ahN-plwah-yey)/**se servir de** (suh sehr-veer duh)

(to) use *tu*: **tutoyer** (tew-twah-yey)

(to) use *vous*: **vouvoyer** (vooh-vwah-yey)

username: **pseudo** (psuh-doh) m

V

(to) validate a ticket: **composter** (kohN-poh-stey)

veal, calf: **veau** (voh) m

vegetable garden: **jardin potager** (zhahr-daN poh-tah-zhey) m

vegetables: **légumes** (ley-gewm) mpl

vendor: **marchand/marchande** (mahr-shahN/mahr-shahNd) m/f

very: **très** (trey)

victory: **victoire** (veek-twahr) f

violin: **violon** (vyoh-lohN) m

(to) visit (a person): **rendre visite à** (rahN-druh vee-zeet ah)

(to) visit (a place): **visiter** (vee-zee-tey)

W

(to) wait (for): **attendre** (ah-tahN-druh)

waiter, waitress: **serveur/serveuse** (sehr-vuhr/sehr-vuhz) m/f

waiting room: **salle d'attente** (sahl dah-tahNt) f

(to) wake up: **se réveiller** (suh rey-vey-yey)

(to) walk: **marcher** (mahr-shey)

walk: **promenade** (pruhhm-nahd) f

wallet: **portefeuille** (pohrt-fuhy) m

(to) want: **vouloir** (vooh-lwahr)

warm/hot: **chaud/chaude** (shoh/shohd) m/f

(to) warn: **avertir** (ah-vehr-teer)

(to) wash: **laver/se laver** (lah-vey/suh lah-vey)

wastepaper basket: **corbeille à papiers** (kohr-behy ah pah-pyey) m

watch: **montre** (mohN-truh) f

(to) watch, (to) look at: **regarder** (ruh-gahr-dey)

water: **eau** (oh) f

(to) water: **arroser** (ah-roh-zey)

watermelon: **pastèque** (pah-stehk) f

wave: **vague** (vahg) f

we: **nous** (nooh)

(to) wear: **porter** (pohr-tey)

web browser: **navigateur** (nah-vee-gah-tuhr) m

week: **semaine** (suh-mehn) f

(to) weigh: **peser** (puh-zey)

weird, bizarre: **bizarre** (bee-zahr)

well: **bien** (byaN)

west: **ouest** (ooh-wehst) m

what: **qu'est-ce que/qui** (kehs kuh/kee), **quoi** (kwah)

whatever, no matter what: **quoi que** (kwah kuh)

what time: **quelle heure** (kehl uhr)

what weather: **quel temps** (kehl tahN)

when: **quand** (kahN)

where: **où** (ooh)

which: **quel/quelle/quels/quelles** (kehl)

which one: **lequel** (luh-kehl) ms/ **laquelle** (lah-kehl) fs

which ones: **lesquels/lesquelles** (ley-kehl) mpl/fpl

while, during the time that: **pendant que** (pahN-dahN kuh)

while, until: **en attendant que** (ahN nah-tahN-dahN kuh)

while, whereas: **alors que** (ah-lohr kuh), **tandis que** (tahN-dee kuh)

(to) whistle: **siffler** (see-fley)

white: **blanc/blanche** (blahN/blahNsh) m/f

who, whom: **qui** (kee)

why: **pourquoi** (poohr-kwah)

(to) win: **gagner** (gah-nyey)

window: **fenêtre** (fuh-neh-truh) f

windshield: **pare-brise** (pahr-breez) m

windshield wiper: **essuie-glace** (ey-swee-glahs) m

windsurfing: **planche à voile** (plahNsh ah vwahl) f

wine: **vin** (vaN) m

winter: **hiver** (ee-vehr) m

(to) wipe: **essuyer** (ey-swee-yey)

with: **avec** (ah-vehk)

without: **sans** (sahN)

woman, wife: **femme** (fahm) f

woman's suit: **tailleur** (tahy-uhr) m

(to) wonder: **se demander** (suh duh-mahN-dey)

wool: **laine** (lehn) f

(to) work: **travailler** (trah-vah-yey)

(to get) worried: **s'inquiéter** (saN-kyey-tey)

worse: **pire** (peer)

(to) be worth: **valoir** (vah-lwahr)

(to) write: **écrire** (ey-kreer)

Y

yard, garden: **jardin** (zhahr-daN) m

yellow: **jaune** (zhohn)

yes: **oui** (wee)

yes (in response to a negative comment or question): **si** (see)

you (plural or singular formal): **vous** (vooh)

you (singular familar): **tu** (tew)

your (plural or singular formal): **votre/vos** (vuhh-truh/voh) s/pl

your (singular familair): **ton/ta/tes** (tohN/tah/tey) ms/fs/pl

yours (plural or singular formal): **vôtre/vôtres** (voh-truh)

yours (singular familiar): **tien/tiens** (tyaN) ms/mpl, **tienne/tiennes** (tyehn) fs/fpl

Z

zip code, postal code: **code postal** (kohd puhh-stahl) m

Appendix D

Fun & Games

· ·

This appendix gives you the opportunity to challenge yourself and check how much info you took in from a given chapter. We hope the activities entertain you as you assess your skill. We provide you with translations and correct answers at the end of the chapter.

Book 1, Chapter 1: Warming Up with Some French Fundamentals

Read the following passage, saying the words aloud. Play with the possible meanings of words and see what you can understand of the passage. You can then check the translation in the answer key.

> Nick est américain. Sa famille habite en Louisiane, à Bâton-Rouge. Il a de la famille au Canada et en France. Il reste en contact avec ses cousins français et canadiens grâce à Facebook et il envoie souvent des e-mails à ses oncles qui ne sont pas sur Facebook. De cette manière, il partage des photos, des annonces et sa musique favorite sur Internet.
>
> Les membres les plus âgés de sa grande famille ne sont pas capables d'envoyer de courriels. Alors Nick assiste aux réunions de famille. Ces réunions lui permettent de rencontrer ces membres qui figurent sur les photos de famille mais n'utilisent pas les technologies actuelles.

Book 1, Chapter 2: Un, Deux, Trois: Numbers, Dates, and Times

You're placing bids for a collector's item at an auction. The bidding started at 200 euros. You place your bid, but someone else keeps outbidding you. Say the numbers aloud to play the game. See the key at the end of the appendix to check how your numbers should sound.

> **You #1:** 250 euros.
>> **Other:** 275 euros.
>
> **You #2:** 300 euros.
>> **Other:** 325 euros.
>
> **You #3:** 370 euros.
>> **Other:** 380 euros.
>
> **You #4:** 400 euros.
>> **Other:** 500 euros.
>
> **You #5:** 600 euros.
>> **Other:** 750 euros.
>
> **You #6:** 1,000 euros.

Book 1, Chapter 3: Greetings, Goodbyes, and Small Talk

For A–D, match each picture with one season and one activity from the following word bank:

- **Season:** C'est le printemps./C'est l'été./C'est l'automne./C'est l'hiver.
- **Activity:** On voit les premières fleurs./Les feuilles tombent des arbres./ On a soif./On fait des bonhommes de neige.

A. _____

_____

_____

B. _____

_____

_____

C. _____

_____

_____

D. _____

_____

_____

Illustration by Elizabeth Kurtzman

For E–H, match each picture with one type of weather and one activity from the following word bank:

✔ **Weather:** Il pleut./Il fait chaud./Il neige./Il fait du vent.

✔ **Activity:** On sort la luge./C'est le temps idéal pour la piscine et les baignades./C'est le temps idéal pour les cerfs-volants./On promène les chiens sous la pluie.

E. _____

_____

_____

F. _____

_____

_____

G. _____

_____

_____

H. _____

_____

_____

Illustration by Elizabeth Kurtzman

Book 1, Chapter 4: Getting Personal: Discussing Your Home, Family, and Daily Routine

Eloïse and Gustave have two grown children, Eric and Isabelle. They, in turn, are married and have two children each. In each box, write that person's role in the family, as indicated in English.

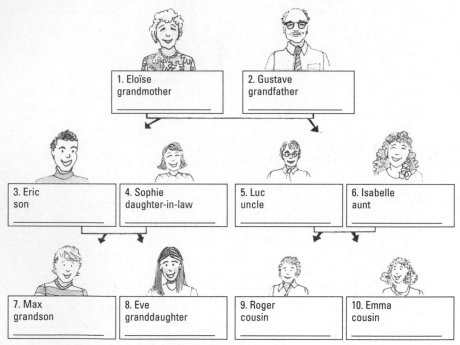

1. Eloïse grandmother
2. Gustave grandfather
3. Eric son
4. Sophie daughter-in-law
5. Luc uncle
6. Isabelle aunt
7. Max grandson
8. Eve granddaughter
9. Roger cousin
10. Emma cousin

Illustration by Elizabeth Kurtzman

Book 1, Chapter 5: Talking Business and Politics

You're reading the paper. In which sections would you find articles on the topics labeled A through E?

Article Topics:

    A. un nouveau président

    B. une avalanche dans les Alpes

    C. débats en Grande-Bretagne et en Irlande

    D. le nombre d'emplois

    E. le tournoi de rugby

Newspaper Sections:

    1. ____ L'actualité

    2. ____ Le sport en images

    3. ____ Les résultats des élections

    4. ____ Les nouvelles internationales

    5. ____ L'économie

Book VI

Appendixes

Book 1, Chapter 6: Shopping at a Store and Online

Pretend you're on a French-Canadian website and you see the following statements. Do you understand them? Take a guess. Then check your answers with the key at the end of the appendix.

1. Magasinez tôt pour assurer la livraison avant Noël.

2. Vous pouvez joindre le service à la clientèle du lundi au vendredi de 09h00 à 21h00 et les samedi-dimanche de 09h00 à 18h00.

3. Achetez vos cadeaux en ligne.

4. La valeur minimale des cartes-cadeaux est de 10,00 $, et la valeur maximale est de 500,00 $.

5. Recevez nos offres spéciales par courriel.

6. Economisez avec nos services en ligne.

7. Veuillez remplir votre adresse courriel et votre mot de passe.

8. C'est votre première visite ?

Book 1, Chapter 7: Buying, Preparing, and Tasting Foods

Categorize foods and drinks into breakfast foods (A), lunch foods (B), and desserts (C).

A. le petit déjeuner

B. le déjeuner

C. le dessert

1. ____ le croissant

2. ____ la crêpe à la confiture

3. ____ la salade

4. ____ la tartine au beurre

5. ____ la tarte à la pomme

6. ____ le sandwich au fromage

7. ____ les escargots

8. ____ les céréales aux fruits

9. ____ le vin

10. ____ la mousse au chocolat

Book 11, Chapter 1: Making Plans and Discovering New Places

Read the sentences and use the numbers in the pictures to locate various things relative to the **Arc de Triomphe** (*Arch of Triumph*). Then fill in the blank with one of the prepositions:

dans	devant	derrière	à droite de
à gauche de	près de	sur	sous

1. Il y a une voiture _____ l'Arc de Triomphe.

2. Il y a une grande avenue _____ l'Arc de Triomphe.

3. Il y a un réverbère (*street light*) _____ l'Arc de Triomphe.

4./5. Il y a des personnes _____ et _____ l'Arc de Triomphe.

6. Il y a des maisons _____ l'Arc de Triomphe.

7. Il y a une station de métro _____ l'Arc de Triomphe.

8. Il y a un escalier _____ l'Arc de Triomphe.

Illustration by Elizabeth Kurtzman

Book II, Chapter 2: Enjoying a Night on the Town

Jean-Marc and Lisette are dining out. Complete the conversation between the two of them by using the appropriate word or phrase from the bank for each blank.

bœuf   desserts   crudités   comme

commande   salade   compris

1. Jean-Marc : Je voudrais une assiette de _____ pour commencer. Et toi ?

2. Lisette : Moi aussi. Et _____ plat principal, le poulet provençal.

3. Jean-Marc : Bonne idée ! Pour moi, le _____ bourguignon.

4. Lisette : On _____ des légumes ?

5. Jean-Marc : Non, les légumes sont _____ .

6. Lisette : Ah oui, je vois. Et la _____ aussi.

7. Jean-Marc : Après le repas, on regardera la carte des _____ !

Book II, Chapter 3: Money Matters

Fill in the boxes with the correct French words.

Illustration by Wiley, Composition Services Graphics

Across

2. spare change

4. credit

5. cash

6. signature

8. receipt

9. bill, paper currency

10. money

Down

1. ATM

3. to insert

7. fees

Book 11, Chapter 4: Home Is Where Your Suitcase Is: Looking for Accommodations

In the following phone conversation, Ariane wants to verify that the hotel she has in mind for her upcoming stay in Quebec City is suitable. Can you reconstruct her discussion with the hotel receptionist by matching his lines, which follow, with hers?

A. Je suis sûr de pouvoir vous en trouver une, madame. Pour quelles dates est-ce que vous désirez une chambre ?

B. Le prix est trois cents dollars par jour avec le petit déjeuner inclus.

C. Oui, madame. Je me ferai un plaisir de vous donner les renseignements que vous demandez.

D. La suite réservée aux jeunes mariés est justement disponible pour ces dates. Voulez-vous faire votre réservation ?

E. Oui, madame. Je suis prêt à noter le numéro.

F. Certainement, madame. Nous sommes un hôtel de luxe.

Le réceptionniste : Allô. Ici l'hôtel Ma Blonde. George Lévêque à votre service.

1. Ariane : Bonjour, Monsieur. J'ai quelques questions à vous poser.

   Le réceptionniste : _____

2. Ariane : Votre hôtel est bien un hôtel à trois étoiles ?

   Le réceptionniste : _____

3. Ariane : Mon mari et moi voudrions fêter notre cinquième anniversaire de mariage à Québec. Avez-vous une belle chambre avec jacuzzi et avec vue sur la rivière ?

   Le réceptionniste : _____

4. Ariane : Nous voulons prendre la chambre le 3 mai et repartir le 6 mai.

   Le réceptionniste : _____

5. Ariane : D'abord, quel est le prix de la chambre et que comprend-il ?

   Le réceptionniste : _____

6. Ariane : Je voudrais effectivement réserver la chambre. Je vous donne le numéro de ma carte de crédit ?

   Le réceptionniste : _____

Book 11, Chapter 5: Getting Around

Louise is returning from a trip to Paris. Match her replies to the questions of a Canadian customs agent.

A. Ce foulard est un cadeau et le manteau vient des États-Unis. J'ai acheté les chaussures à très bon prix à Paris.

B. Au revoir, monsieur.

C. J'ai du parfum que j'ai acheté hors taxe en France, monsieur.

D. Oui, monsieur. Voilà.

1. L'agent de douane : Bonjour, madame. Vous avez quelque chose à déclarer ?

   Louise : _____

2. L'agent de douane : Pouvez-vous ouvrir votre sac, madame ?

   Louise : _____

3. L'agent de douane : Vous avez acheté ce foulard, ces chaussures et ce manteau en cuir en France ?

   Louise : _____

4. L'agent de douane : Merci, madame. Veuillez passer.

   Louise : _____

Book II, Chapter 6: Dealing with Emergencies

Your friend François, a daredevil snowboarder, crashed during one of his jumps. He seems okay, but just to make sure, you ask him about each one of his body parts. Start each question with **Tu as mal . . . ?** See the example for Number 1.

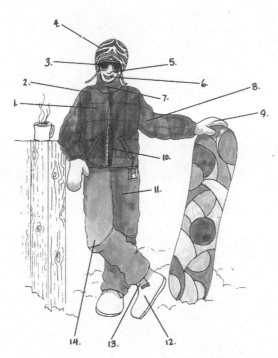

Illustration by Elizabeth Kurtzman

1. Tu as mal à la poitrine? (*Does your chest hurt?*)

2. _____

3. _____

4. _____

5. _____

6. _____

7. _____

8. _____

9. _____

10. _____

11. _____

12. _____

13. _____

14. _____

Book III, Chapter 1: Building Strong Sentences with the Parts of Speech

What follows is a short news article about the royal family of Monaco, but the words of the sentences got all scrambled. Restore each sentence by putting its various parts in the correct order.

1. est/le fils de Grace Kelly/le Prince Albert/une actrice américaine/de Monaco

_____

_____

2. s'appelle/la femme du/Charlène/Prince Albert

_____

_____

3. elle est/en Afrique/très belle/elle est née/et

_____

_____

4. sont/heureux/Albert et Charlène/et/les adore/la presse

_____

_____

5. et/à des fonctions officielles/à des charités/le couple/on voit

_____

_____

Book III, Chapter 2: All Agreed? Matching Gender and Number of Nouns and Articles

The police are making an inventory of stolen goods they have found in a burglar's studio. Provide the appropriate indefinite article (**un**, **une**) or the appropriate number (spelled out) for each item or set of items.

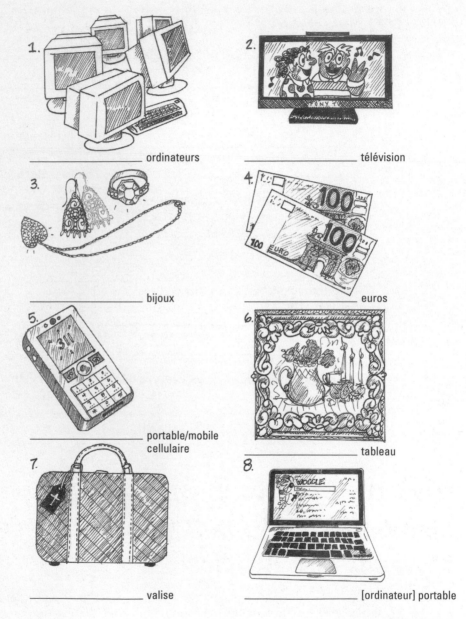

1. _____ ordinateurs

2. _____ télévision

3. _____ bijoux

4. _____ euros

5. _____ portable/mobile cellulaire

6. _____ tableau

7. _____ valise

8. _____ [ordinateur] portable

Illustration by Elizabeth Kurtzman

Book III, Chapter 3: Dealing with the Here and Now: The Present Tense

Write either the conjugated present tense form or the infinitive form of each verb in parentheses in the blank spaces.

Si on 1. _____ (faire) un sondage sur les activités de loisir des jeunes gens, on 2. _____ (remarquer) qu'il y 3. _____ (avoir) certaines tendances. Par exemple, beaucoup de jeunes 4. _____ (faire) des sports au lycée. Ils 5. _____ (jouer) au football américain, au football, au softball, etc. Ils 6. _____ (choisir) plus souvent des sports d'équipe que des sports individuels. En équipe, vous 7. _____ (pouvoir) gagner ou perdre — c' 8. _____ (être) l'esprit de corps qui 9. _____ (dominer) et qui 10. _____ (compter).

Les jeunes 11. _____ (passer) aussi beaucoup de temps à 12. _____ (écouter) de la musique, à 13. _____ (envoyer) des textos à leurs amis et à 14. _____ (partager) des photos sur les sites sociaux. Est-ce qu'ils 15. _____ (lire) ? Oui, surtout sur leurs lecteurs de livres numériques. Est-ce qu'ils ne 16. _____ (devoir) pas faire de devoirs ? Est-ce qu'ils ne 17. _____ (prendre) pas leurs repas en famille ? Si, bien sûr ! Mais tout 18. _____ (dépendre) de la famille !

Book III, Chapter 4: Commanding and Instructing with the Imperative Mood

Categorize the commands and instructions into the following four categories:

A. Boss to employee

B. Signs at a tourist site

C. A mother or father to a child

D. Instructions in a recipe

1. _____ Remplissez ce formulaire.

2. _____ Battre les œufs en neige.

3. _____ Verser dans un bol.

4. _____ Arrête de regarder la télévision.

5. _____ Prière de respecter les règles.

6. _____ Écrivez ce contrat, s'il vous plaît.

7. _____ Défense de passer dans ce corridor.

8. _____ Viens manger.

Book III, Chapter 5: Asking and Answering Questions

Virginie is going out, and Théo has a lot of questions for her. Match Virginie's replies to Théo's questions.

A. Je vais au grand marché au centre-ville.

B. Oui, je sais que tu les adores.

C. Je vais essayer d'être de retour vers 15 heures.

D. Je vais au marché acheter des fruits.

E. Non, je préfère aller toute seule et prendre mon temps.

1. Théo : Où est-ce que tu vas, Virginie ?

   Virginie : _____

2. Théo : À quel marché tu vas ? Le grand ou le petit ?

   Virginie : _____

3. Théo : Je viens avec toi ?

   Virginie : _____

4. Théo : Tu peux acheter des olives vertes et des olives noires ?

   Virginie : _____

5. Théo : Merci. Tu ne vas pas rester trop longtemps ?

   Virginie : _____

Book III, Chapter 6: Communicating Clearly with Infinitives and Present Participles

Complete each sentence with the present participle of the infinitive verb that best describes what is in the picture.

se bronzer   dormir   courir   faire

1.

2.

3.

4.

Illustration by Elizabeth Kurtzman

1. Luc réfléchit en _____ ses devoirs.

2. Maria se repose en _____.

3. Chloé sort en _____.

4. Papa ronfle (rrrrrr . . .) en _____.

Book IV, Chapter 1: Specifying Relationships with Prepositions

Jeannot est un petit garçon qui joue des mauvais tours (*Jeannot is a little boy who plays bad tricks*). Read about the jokes that Jeannot plays on his friends while inserting the appropriate preposition from the word bank.

    à   dans   de   derrière   en

1. Un jour, Jeannot apporte un cadeau _____ son copain Dodo. Mais quand son copain regarde _____ la boîte, il n'y a rien dedans !

2. Un autre jour, Jeannot donne une flûte _____ son copain Didi. Mais quand son copain essaie de jouer _____ la flûte, des abeilles en sortent !

3. Un autre jour, Jeannot donne un chocolat _____ son voisin. Mais quand le voisin met le chocolat _____ sa bouche, il éternue parce que le chocolat est plein _____ poivre !

4. Un autre jour, Jeannot est _____ classe _____ Riri et chaque fois que Riri parle, il souffle très fort _____ ses cheveux.

Book IV, Chapter 2: Describing with Flair: Adjectives and Adverbs

Translate the following segments of a weather report into French, being careful to make the adjectives and nouns agree and also placing the adjective appropriately before or after the noun. Write your answer under the matching picture.

1. (strong winds) vent/fort (100 km/h)

2. (torrential rains) pluie/torrentiel

3. (low temperatures) température/bas (5°C)

4. (beautiful moon) lune/beau

5. (torrid heat) chaleur/torride (30°C)

6. (high tide) marée/haut

_____
_____

_____
_____

Illustration by Elizabeth Kurtzman

Book IV, Chapter 3: Taking Shortcuts with Object Pronouns

Louis is flirting with Sylvie and asking her lots of questions. Complete her replies with an object pronoun from the list:

en   moi   y   t'   leur   la

1. Louis : Quand est-ce que tu portes cette jolie casquette ?

   Sylvie : Je _____ porte quand je vais à la plage.

2. Louis : Tu vas souvent à la plage ?

   Sylvie : J'_____ vais le samedi.

3. Louis : Tu emportes des sandwichs quand tu vas à la plage ?

   Sylvie : Non, j'_____ achète à la plage.

4. Louis : Tu vas m'inviter à venir avec toi ?

   Sylvie : Oui, bien sûr, je _____ invite cette semaine.

5. Louis : Je peux te chercher ?

   Sylvie : Certainement ! Cherche-_____ à la maison vers 11 heures.

6. Louis : Et tes parents ?

   Sylvie : Je vais _____ dire que je sors avec toi.

Book IV, Chapter 4: Tying Ideas Together with Conjunctions and Relative Pronouns

A very annoyed dad asks his wife questions about their daughter, Claudine. Find Mom's answers.

A. Après qu'elle aura fini ses études.

B. Lorsqu'elle va avoir un vrai travail.

C. Parce qu'elle se lève tard le matin.

D. Je la défends en attendant que tu te calmes, Henri.

E. Jusqu'à ce qu'elle trouve un bon emploi.

1. Papa : Pourquoi est-ce que Claudine est toujours en retard ?

   Maman : _____

2. Papa : Quand est-ce qu'elle va commencer à utiliser un réveil le matin ?

   Maman : _____

3. Papa : Et pendant combien de temps est-ce qu'elle va encore nous demander de l'argent ?

   Maman : _____

4. Papa : Mais quand est-ce qu'elle va trouver un emploi ?

   Maman : _____

5. Papa : Pourquoi est-ce que tu la défends toujours ?

   Maman : _____

Book IV, Chapter 5: Getting That Subjunctive Feeling

The mechanics say they have to change the oil, check the brakes, and repair the mirror on the car. Choose the right verb from the list and put it into the correct present subjunctive form:

   réparer   changer   vérifier

A. Il faut que nous 1. _____ l'huile, que nous 2. _____ les freins et que nous 3. _____ le miroir.

Then they say that they may have to put on new tires and order a new radio and that they need to keep the car till tomorrow. Choose the right verb from the list:

   garder   mettre   commander

B. Il est possible que nous 1. _____ de nouveaux pneus et que nous 2. _____ une nouvelle radio. Il faut que nous 3. _____ la voiture jusqu'à demain pour finir tout ça.

Book IV, Chapter 6: What Lies Ahead and What Could Happen: Simple Future and Present Conditional

The following ad promises many good things, but you have to buy this special shampoo and use it every day! Choose the appropriate verb from the list and conjugate it in the future tense to fill in each blank.

être   utiliser   avoir   acheter   tomber

Vous 1. _____ ce shampooing, vous l'2. _____ chaque jour ! Alors vos cheveux 3. _____ si brillants et si beaux que tout le monde 4. _____ amoureux de vous. Vous 5. _____ une belle vie !

Book V, Chapter 1: Been There, Done That: Passé Proche and Passé Composé

In which order did Marius do the following things yesterday? Restore the order by putting numbers 2 through 8 before the sentences (Number 1 is done).

_____ Ensuite il a téléphoné à des clients.

_____ Il a fait du café pour lui et ses collègues.

__1__ Il est allé au bureau.

_____ Il a passé l'après-midi à l'ordinateur.

_____ Après une douche, il a mis son sweat pour aller faire un jogging.

_____ À dix-sept heures, il a quitté le bureau.

_____ À dix-huit heures, il est rentré chez lui.

_____ À midi il est allé déjeuner dans un petit café.

Book V, Chapter 2: How Was It? What Was Going on? The Imparfait

Fill the boxes with the correct French verbs in the **imparfait.**

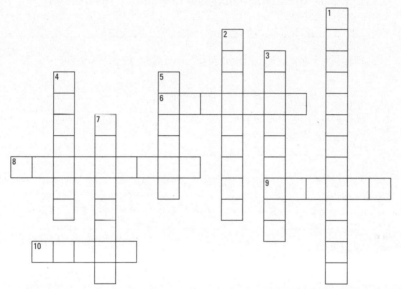

Illustration by Wiley, Composition Services Graphics

Across

6. (We) were coming

8. (They) used to do

9. (I) used to go

10. (I) was

Down

1. (They) were choosing

2. (He) was resisting

3. (You [singular familiar]) were finishing

4. (You [singular formal]) were taking

5. (We) had

7. (She) was singing

Book V, Chapter 3: To the Past and Beyond: Other Past Tenses

Express Sam's many regrets using the pluperfect tense.

1. If he had waited to get married (attendre de se marier)

   _____

2. If he had worked a little less (travailler un peu moins)

   _____

3. If he had come home more often (rentrer plus souvent)

   _____

4. If he done some cooking from time to time (faire la cuisine de temps en temps)

   _____

5. If he had brought some flowers to his wife (apporter des fleurs à sa femme)

   _____

6. If he had taken care of himself (se soigner)

   _____

7. If she had not been so understanding (être si indulgente)

   _____

8. If she had told him to be more romantic (lui dire d'être plus romantique)

   _____

9. If they had loved each other more (s'aimer davantage)

   _____

10. If she had not left (ne pas partir)

Answer Key

The following sections provide answers and translations for the games in this appendix. The answers appear in boldface.

Book 1, Chapter 1: Warming Up with Some French Fundamentals

Read the passage aloud. Here's the translation of the French:

Nick is American. His family lives in Louisiana, in Baton-Rouge (Literally: red stick). He has family in Canada and in France. He stays in contact with his French and Canadian cousins thanks to Facebook, and he often sends e-mails to his uncles who are not on Facebook. This way, he shares photos, announcements, and his favorite music on the Internet.

The older members of his family are not able to send e-mails. So Nick attends family reunions. These reunions allow him to meet those members who are in the family pictures but don't use current technology.

Book 1, Chapter 2: Un, Deux, Trois: Numbers, Dates, and Times

Say the auction bids aloud.

1. **duh sahN saN-kahNt uh-roh** (deux cent cinquante euros)
2. **trwah sahN zuh-roh** (trois cents euros)
3. **trwah sahN swah-sahNt-dees uh-roh** (trois cent soixante-dix euros)
4. **kah-truh sahN zuh-roh** (quatre cents euros)
5. **see sahN zuh-roh** (six cents euros)
6. **meel uh-roh** (mille euros)

Book 1, Chapter 3: Greetings, Goodbyes, and Small Talk

Match the pictures to the seasons, weather, and activities.

    A. **C'est l'hiver.** (*It's winter.*) **On fait des bonhommes de neige.** (*We make snowmen.*)

    B. **C'est l'été.** (*It's summer.*) **On a soif.** (*We're thirsty.*)

    C. **C'est le printemps.** (*It's spring.*) **On voit les premières fleurs.** (*We see the first flowers.*)

    D. **C'est l'automne.** (*It's fall.*) **Les feuilles tombent des arbres.** (*Leaves are falling from trees.*)

    E. **Il fait du vent.** (*It's windy.*) **C'est le temps idéal pour les cerfs-volants.** (*It's ideal weather for kites.*)

    F. **Il fait chaud.** (*It's hot.*) **C'est le temps idéal pour la piscine et les baignades.** (*It's the ideal weather for the pool and swimming.*)

    G. **Il pleut.** (*It's raining.*) **On promène les chiens sous la pluie.** (*We walk dogs in the rain.*)

    H. **Il neige.** (*It's snowing.*) **On sort la luge.** (*We get out the sled.*)

Book 1, Chapter 4: Getting Personal: Discussing Your Home, Family, and Daily Routine

Fill in the roles of the family members:

    1. Eloïse: **la grand-mère**

    2. Gustave: **le grand-père**

    3. Eric: **le fils**

    4. Sophie: **la belle-fille**

    5. Isabelle: **la tante**

    6. Luc: **l'oncle**

7. Max: **le petit-fils**

8. Eve: **la petite-fille**

9. Roger: **le cousin**

10. Emma: **la cousine**

Book 1, Chapter 5: Talking Business and Politics

Match the newspaper sections to the article topics.

1. **B.** Current events: an avalanche in the Alps

2. **E.** Sports in pictures: Rugby tournament

3. **A.** Election results: a new president

4. **C.** International news: Debates in Great Britain and Ireland

5. **D.** Economy: number of jobs

Book 1, Chapter 6: Shopping at a Store and Online

Translate the French statements from the French-Canadian website.

1. **Shop early to ensure delivery before Christmas.**

2. **You can reach customer service from Monday to Friday from 9:00 a.m. to 9:00 p.m. and on Saturday and Sunday from 9:00 am to 6:00 p.m.**

3. **Buy your gifts online.**

4. **The minimum value of gift cards is $10.00, and the maximum value is $500.00.**

5. **Receive our special offers by e-mail.**

6. **Save with our online services.**

7. **Please fill in your e-mail address and your password.**

8. **Is this your first visit?**

Book I, Chapter 7: Buying, Preparing, and Tasting Foods

Categorize foods and drinks into breakfast foods (A), lunch foods (B), and desserts (C).

1. **A** (croissant)

2. **A/C** (crêpe with jam or jelly)

3. **B** (salad)

4. **A** (slice of bread with butter)

5. **C** (apple tart)

6. **B** (cheese sandwich)

7. **B** (snails)

8. **A** (cereal with fruit)

9. **B** (wine)

10. **C** (chocolate mousse)

Book II, Chapter 1: Making Plans and Discovering New Places

Fill in the blanks to state the locations of various things relative to the Arc de Triomphe:

1. **devant** (*in front*). Sentence translation: *There's a car in front of the Arc de Triomphe.*

2. **derrière** (*behind*). Sentence translation: *There's a big avenue behind the Arc de Triomphe.*

3. **à droite de** (*to the right*). Sentence translation: *There's a street light to the right of the Arc de Triomphe.*

4./5. **sur** (*on*), **sous** (*under*). Sentence translation: *There are people on and under the Arc de Triomphe.*

6. **à gauche de** (*to the left of*). Sentence translation: *There are houses to the left of the Arc de Triomphe.*

7. **près de** (*near*). Sentence translation: *There's a subway station near the Arc de Triomphe.*

8. **dans** (*in/inside*). Sentence translation: *There's a staircase inside the Arc de Triomphe.*

Book 11, Chapter 2: Enjoying a Night on the Town

Complete the conversation between Jean-Marc and Lisette by filling in the blanks.

1. **crudités** (*raw vegetables*)
2. **comme** (*for*)
3. **boeuf** (*beef*)
4. **commande** (*order*)
5. **compris** (*included*)
6. **salade** (*salad*)
7. **desserts** (*desserts*)

Translation:

Jean-Marc: I would like a plate of crudités (raw vegetables) to start. And you?

Lisette: Me, too. And for the main course, chicken provençal.

Jean-Marc: Good idea! For me, beef bourguignon (Burgundy).

Lisette: Do we order vegetables?

Jean-Marc: No, the vegetables are included.

Lisette: Oh yes, I see. And the salad, too.

Jean-Marc: After the meal, we'll look at the dessert menu!

Book 11, Chapter 3: Money Matters

Fill in the crossword puzzle with the correct French words.

Across: **2. monnaie 4. crédit 5. espèces 6. signature 8. reçu 9. billet 10. argent**

Down: **1. distributeur 3. insérer 7. frais**

Book 11, Chapter 4: Home 1s Where Your Suitcase 1s: Looking for Accommodations

Reconstruct the conversation by matching the receptionist's lines with Ariane's.

> Receptionist: Hello. This is the Hôtel Ma Blonde. George Lévêque at your service.

1. **C.** Ariane: Hello, sir. I have a few questions to ask you.

   > Receptionist: Yes, ma'am. I will be happy to give you the information you are asking for.

2. **F.** Ariane: Your hotel is a three-star hotel, right?

   > Receptionist: Certainly, ma'am. We are a luxury hotel.

3. **A.** Ariane: My husband and I would like to celebrate our fifth anniversary in Québec. Do you have a beautiful room with a Jacuzzi and with a view of the river?

   > Receptionist: I'm sure I can find you one, ma'am. For which dates do you want a room?

4. **D.** Ariane: We want to check in on May 3 and leave on May 6.

   > Receptionist: The bridal suite happens to be available for those dates. Do you want to make your reservation?

5. **B.** Ariane: First, what is the price of the room and what is included?

   > Receptionist: The price is 300 dollars a day, and breakfast is included.

6. **E.** Ariane: I would indeed like to reserve the room. Shall I give you my credit card number?

   > Receptionist: Yes, ma'am. I'm ready to record the number.

Book 11, Chapter 5: Getting Around

Match Louise's replies to the questions of a Canadian customs agent.

1. **C.** Customs agent: Hello, ma'am. Do you have anything to declare?

   Louise: I have perfume I bought duty-free in France, sir.

2. **D.** Customs agent: Can you open your bag, ma'am?

   Louise: Yes, sir. There!

3. **A.** Customs agent: You bought this scarf, these shoes, and this leather coat in France?

   Louise: This scarf is a gift, and the coat comes from the United States. I bought the shoes at a very good price in Paris.

4. **B.** Customs agent: Thanks, ma'am. Please go through.

   Louise: Goodbye, sir.

Book II, Chapter 6: Dealing with Emergencies

Ask your friend François whether he's hurt anything after his snowboarding crash.

1. **Tu as mal à la poitrine ?** (*Does your chest hurt?*)
2. **Tu as mal à l'épaule ?** (*Does your shoulder hurt?*)
3. **Tu as mal à l'œil ?** (*Does your eye hurt?*)
4. **Tu as mal à la tête ?** (*Does your head hurt?*)
5. **Tu as mal au nez ?** (*Does your nose hurt?*)
6. **Tu as mal à la bouche ?** (*Does your mouth hurt?*)
7. **Tu as mal au cou ?** (*Does your neck hurt?*)
8. **Tu as mal au bras ?** (*Does your arm hurt?*)
9. **Tu as mal à la main ?** (*Does your hand hurt?*)
10. **Tu as mal à l'estomac/au ventre ?** (*Does your stomach hurt?*)
11. **Tu as mal à la jambe ?** (*Does your leg hurt?*)
12. **Tu as mal au pied ?** (*Does your foot hurt?*)
13. **Tu as mal à la cheville ?** (*Does your ankle hurt?*)
14. **Tu as mal au genou ?** (*Does your knee hurt?*)

Book III, Chapter 1: Building Strong Sentences with the Parts of Speech

Restore the sentences by putting the parts back in order.

1. **Le Prince Albert de Monaco est le fils de Grace Kelly, une actrice américaine.** (*Prince Albert of Monaco is the son of Grace Kelly, an American actress.*)

2. **La femme du Prince Albert s'appelle Charlène.** (*Prince Albert's wife is named Charlène.*)

3. **Elle est née en Afrique et elle est très belle.** (*She was born in Africa, and she is very beautiful.*)

4. **Albert et Charlène sont heureux et la presse les adore.** (*Albert and Charlène are happy, and the press adores them.*)

5. **On voit le couple à des fonctions officielles et à des charités** OR **On voit le couple à des charités et à des fonctions officielles.** (*One sees them at official functions and at charity events* OR *One sees them at charity events and official functions.*)

Book III, Chapter 2: All Agreed? Matching Gender and Number of Nouns and Articles

Fill in the articles and numbers for the inventory of stolen goods:

1. **cinq** ordinateurs (*five computers*)

2. **une** télévision (*one/a television*)

3. **trois** bijoux (*three pieces of jewelry*)

4. **deux cents** euros (*two hundred euros*)

5. **un** portable/mobile/cellulaire (*one/a cellphone*)

6. **un** tableau (*one/a painting*)

7. **une** valise (*one/a suitcase*)

8. **un** [ordinateur] portable (*one/a laptop*)

Book III, Chapter 3: Dealing with the Here and Now: The Present Tense

Fill in the blanks by writing the conjugated present tense or infinitive form of each verb.

1. **fait**

2. **remarque**

3. a

4. font

5. jouent

6. choisissent

7. pouvez

8. est

9. domine

10. compte

11. passent

12. écouter

13. envoyer

14. partager

15. lisent

16. doivent

17. prennent

18. dépend

Translation:

> If you do a poll on leisure activities of young people, you notice (that) there are certain tendencies. For example, a lot of young people do sports in high school. They play American football, soccer, softball, etc. They choose team sports more often than individual sports. On a team, you can win or lose — it's team spirit that dominates and counts.
>
> Young people also spend a lot of time listening to music, sending text messages to their friends, and sharing pictures on social networks. Do they read? Yes, especially on their e-book readers. Don't they have to do homework? Don't they eat meals with their families? Yes, of course! But it all depends on the family!

Book III, Chapter 4: Commanding and Instructing with the Imperative Mood

Categorize the commands, noting whether they're from a boss to an employee, from a sign at a tourist site, from a parent to a child, or from a recipe.

1. **A, boss to employee.** (Translation: *Fill out this form.*)

2. **D, instructions in a recipe.** (Translation: *Beat the egg whites until stiff.* Literally: *Beat the eggs into snow.*)

3. **D, instructions in a recipe.** (Translation: *Pour into a bowl.*)

4. **C, a mother or father to a child.** (Translation: *Stop watching TV.*)

5. **B, signs at a tourist site.** (Translation: *Please respect the rules.*)

6. **A, boss to employee.** (Translation: *Write this contract, please.*)

7. **B, signs at a tourist site.** (Translation: *Do not go through this corridor.*)

8. **C, a mother or father to a child.** (Translation: *Come eat.*)

Book III, Chapter 5: Asking and Answering Questions

Match Virginie's reply to each one of Théo's questions.

1. **D.** Théo: Where are you going, Virginie?

   Virginie: I'm going to the market to buy some fruit.

2. **A.** Théo: To which market are you going? The big one or the little one?

   Virginie: I'm going to the big market downtown.

3. **E.** Théo: Shall I come with you?

   Virginie: No, I prefer to go alone and take my time.

4. **B.** Théo: Can you buy some green and black olives?

   Virginie: Yes, I know you love them.

5. **C.** Théo: Thanks. You're not going to stay too long, are you?

   Virginie: I'm going to try to be back around 3 p.m.

Book III, Chapter 6: Communicating Clearly with Infinitives and Present Participles

Complete each sentence with the present participle of the infinitive verb that best describes what is in the picture.

1. **faisant** (Sentence translation: *Luc thinks while doing his homework.*)

2. **se bronzant** (Sentence translation: *Maria rests while getting a tan.*)

3. **courant** (Sentence translation: *Chloé goes out running.*)

4. **dormant** (Sentence translation: *Dad snores while sleeping.*)

Book IV, Chapter 1: Specifying Relationships with Prepositions

Fill in the appropriate preposition from the word bank.

1. **à, dans** (Sentence translation: *One day, Jeannot brings a gift to his friend Dodo. But when his friend looks inside the box, there's nothing inside.*)

2. **à, de** (Sentence translation: *Another day, Jeannot gives a flute to his friend Didi. But when his friend tries to play the flute, bees come out of it.*)

3. **à, dans, de** (Sentence translation: *Another day, Jeannot gives chocolate to his neighbor. But when the neighbor puts the chocolate into his mouth, he sneezes because the chocolate is full of pepper.*)

4. **en, derrière, dans** (Sentence translation: *Another day, Jeannot is in class behind Riri, and each time Riri speaks, he blows very hard into his hair.*)

Book IV, Chapter 2: Describing with Flair: Adjectives and Adverbs

Translate the segments of a weather report into French. Write your answer under the matching picture.

A. **6: marée haute** (*high tide*)

B. **5: chaleur torride** (*torrid heat*)

C. **3: températures basses** (*low temperatures*)

D. **4: belle lune** (*beautiful moon*)

E. **1: vents forts** (*strong winds*)

F. **2: pluies torrentielles** (*torrential rains*)

Book IV, Chapter 3: Taking Shortcuts with Object Pronouns

Complete Sylvie's replies to Louis with an object pronoun from the list.

1. **la.** Louis: When do you wear this pretty cap?

   Sylvie: I wear it when I go to the beach.

2. **y.** Louis: Do you often go to the beach?

   Sylvie: I go (there) on Saturdays.

3. **en.** Louis: Do you take sandwiches with you when you go to the beach?

   Sylvie: No, I buy some at the beach.

4. **t'.** Louis: Are you going to invite me to come with you?

   Sylvie: Yes, of course, I'll invite you this week.

5. **moi.** Louis: May I pick you up?

   Sylvie: Certainly! Come and get me at home around 11 a.m.

6. **leur.** Louis: How about your parents?

   Sylvie: I'll tell them I'm going out with you.

Book IV, Chapter 4: Tying Ideas Together with Conjunctions and Relative Pronouns

Match Mom's answers to Dad's questions.

1. **C.** Dad: Why is Claudine always late?

   Mom: Because she gets up late in the morning.

2. **B.** Dad: When is she going to start using an alarm clock in the morning?

   Mom: When she has real work.

3. **E.** Dad: And for how long is she still going to ask us for money?

   Mom: Until she finds a good job.

4. **A.** Dad: But when is she going to find a job?

   Mom: After she finishes her studies.

5. **D.** Dad: Why do you always defend her?

   Mom: I'll defend her until you calm down, Henri.

Book IV, Chapter 5: Getting That Subjunctive Feeling

Choose the right verb from the list and put it into the correct present subjunctive form.

> A. **1. changions, 2. vérifiions, 3. réparions** (Sentence translation: *We have to change the oil, check the brakes, and repair the mirror.*)
>
> B. **1. mettions, 2. commandions, 3. gardions** (Sentence translation: *We may put on new tires and order a new radio. We need to keep the car until tomorrow to finish all that.*)

Book IV, Chapter 6: What Lies Ahead and What Could Happen: Simple Future and Present Conditional

Choose the appropriate verb from the list to complete the shampoo ad.

1. **achèterez**
2. **utiliserez**
3. **seront**
4. **tombera**
5. **aurez**

Translation :

> You will buy this shampoo, you'll use it every day! Then your hair will be so shiny and so attractive that everybody will fall in love with you. You'll have a beautiful life!

Book V, Chapter 1: Been There, Done That: Passé Proche and Passé Composé

Put the sentences in the correct order.

1. **Il est allé au bureau.** (*He went to the office.*)
2. **Il a fait du café pour lui et ses collègues.** (*He made coffee for himself and his colleagues.*)

3. **Ensuite il a téléphoné à des clients.** (*Then he called some clients.*)

4. **A midi il est allé déjeuner dans un petit café.** (*At noon he went to have lunch in a little café.*)

5. **Il a passé l'après-midi à l'ordinateur.** (*He spent the afternoon at the computer.*)

6. **A dix-sept heures, il a quitté le bureau.** (*At 5 p.m., he left the office.*)

7. **A dix-huit heures, il est rentré chez lui.** (*At 6 p.m., he got home.*)

8. **Après une douche, il a mis son sweat pour aller faire un jogging.** (*After a shower, he put on his sweat suit to go jogging.*)

Book V, Chapter 2: How Was It? What Was Going on? The Imparfait

Fill in the crossword puzzle with verbs conjugated in the **imparfait**.

Across: **6. venions 8. faisaient 9. allais 10. étais**

Down: **1. choisissaient 2. résistait 3. finissais 4. preniez 5. avions 7. chantait**

Book V, Chapter 3: To the Past and Beyond: Other Past Tenses

Express Sam's many regrets using the pluperfect tense.

1. **s'il avait attendu pour se marier**

2. **s'il avait travaillé un peu moins**

3. **s'il était rentré plus souvent**

4. **s'il avait fait la cuisine de temps en temps**

5. **s'il avait apporté des fleurs à sa femme**

6. **s'il s'était soigné**

7. **si elle n'avait pas été si indulgente**

8. **si elle lui avait dit d'être plus romantique**

9. **s'ils s'étaient aimés davantage**

10. **si elle n'était pas partie**

Appendix E

About the CD

. . . .

*T*his appendix walks you through the CD that accompanies this book. The CD is audio-only, so it'll play in any standard CD player or in your computer's CD-ROM drive. ***Note:*** If you're using a digital version of this book, please go to http://booksupport.wiley.com for access to the additional content.

How to Use the CD

We recorded many of the Talkin' the Talk dialogues in this book to help you sharpen your listening skills. The written dialogues you encounter through-out the chapters will come to life when you listen to the CD. You're sure to discover more about pronunciation and oral communication by listening to these native speakers of French.

You can use the CD to practice both your listening comprehension and your speech. If your goal is to work on pronunciation, start by listening to the tracks that accompany the first chapter of Book I and learn all those funny new sounds. Imitate the speakers on the CD and start to sound French.

Here are a couple of ways you can practice your listening comprehension:

✔ First read a dialogue for comprehension. Then listen to the CD track without following the written script to see how much you understand without visual support. Repeat this exercise as many times as you like.

✔ Before you even read the dialogue, listen to it a couple of times and extract as many ideas as possible from it. Then check the written dia-logue in your book to confirm how much you understood.

And here are some ways to practice your speaking ability:

✔ Read the dialogue in the book. Say one sentence at a time aloud before listening to that sentence to check whether it sounds the way you thought it would.

✔ Pick one of the speakers and pretend to be that person, allowing you to interact with the other person(s) in the conversation. Say your lines aloud as you play the audio track. You can even take turns being different characters.

Track Listing

The following is a list of the tracks that appear on this book's audio CD.

Track 1: Introduction and the French alphabet

Track 2: Alphabet with Canadian pronunciation

Track 3: Making weekend plans (Chapter 1 of Book I)

Track 4: Talking about next weekend in Canada (Chapter 1 of Book I)

Track 5: Finding out when the wedding is (Chapter 2 of Book I)

Track 6: Running late (Chapter 2 of Book I)

Track 7: Greeting business associates (Chapter 3 of Book I)

Track 8: Meeting someone on a plane (Chapter 3 of Book I)

Track 9: Discussing work with someone new (Chapter 3 of Book I)

Track 10: Asking for a number and a dinner date (Chapter 3 of Book I)

Track 11: Looking for a roommate (Chapter 4 of Book I)

Track 12: Claiming possessions (Chapter 4 of Book I)

Track 13: Showing off a pet (Chapter 4 of Book I)

Track 14: Sending a contract to a prospective client (Chapter 5 of Book I)

Track 15: Discussing politics (Chapter 5 of Book I)

Track 16: Dress shopping (Chapter 6 of Book I)

Track 17: Buying a sports jacket (Chapter 6 of Book I)

Track 18: Visiting the fresh food market (Chapter 7 of Book I)

Track 19: Sharing a home-cooked meal with friends (Chapter 7 of Book I)

Track 20: Booking a flight (Chapter 1 of Book II)

Track 21: Packing for a trip (Chapter 1 of Book II)

Track 22: Visiting the Winter Festival in Quebec City (Chapter 1 of Book II)

Track 23: Going camping (Chapter 1 of Book II)

Track 24: Asking for directions (Chapter 1 of Book II)

Track 25: Deciding what to do for fun (Chapter 2 of Book II)

Track 26: Deciding what type of nightlife to pursue (Chapter 2 of Book II)

Track 27: Accessing an ATM (Chapter 3 of Book II)

Track 28: Checking in at the front desk (Chapter 4 Book II)

Track 29: Sorting out the bus schedule (Chapter 5 of Book II)

Track 30: Buying a train ticket (Chapter 5 of Book II)

Track 31: Making a doctor's appointment (Chapter 6 of Book II)

Track 32: Visiting the doctor (Chapter 6 of Book II)

Track 33: Reporting an accident (Chapter 6 of Book II)

Customer Care

If you have trouble with the CD, please call Wiley Product Technical Support at 877-762-2974. Outside the United States, call 317-572-3993. You can also contact Wiley Product Technical Support at http://support.wiley.com.

Wiley will provide technical support only for installation and other general quality control items.

To place additional orders or to request information about other Wiley products, please call 877-762-2974.

Index

• U •

• V •

Notes

John Wiley & Sons, Inc.
End-User License Agreement

READ THIS. You should carefully read these terms and conditions before opening the software packet(s) included with this book "Book". This is a license agreement "Agreement" between you and John Wiley & Sons, Inc. "WILEY". By opening the accompanying software packet(s), you acknowledge that you have read and accept the following terms and conditions. If you do not agree and do not want to be bound by such terms and conditions, promptly return the Book and the unopened software packet(s) to the place you obtained them for a full refund.

1. **License Grant.** WILEY grants to you (either an individual or entity) a nonexclusive license to use one copy of the enclosed software program(s) (collectively, the "Software") solely for your own personal or business purposes on a single computer (whether a standard computer or a workstation component of a multi-user network). The Software is in use on a computer when it is loaded into temporary memory (RAM) or installed into permanent memory (hard disk, CD-ROM, or other storage device). WILEY reserves all rights not expressly granted herein.

2. **Ownership.** WILEY is the owner of all right, title, and interest, including copyright, in and to the compilation of the Software recorded on the physical packet included with this Book "Software Media". Copyright to the individual programs recorded on the Software Media is owned by the author or other authorized copyright owner of each program. Ownership of the Software and all proprietary rights relating thereto remain with WILEY and its licensers.

3. **Restrictions on Use and Transfer.**

   (a) You may only (i) make one copy of the Software for backup or archival purposes, or (ii) transfer the Software to a single hard disk, provided that you keep the original for backup or archival purposes. You may not (i) rent or lease the Software, (ii) copy or reproduce the Software through a LAN or other network system or through any computer subscriber system or bulletin-board system, or (iii) modify, adapt, or create derivative works based on the Software.

   (b) You may not reverse engineer, decompile, or disassemble the Software. You may transfer the Software and user documentation on a permanent basis, provided that the transferee agrees to accept the terms and conditions of this Agreement and you retain no copies. If the Software is an update or has been updated, any transfer must include the most recent update and all prior versions.

4. **Restrictions on Use of Individual Programs.** You must follow the individual requirements and restrictions detailed for each individual program in the "About the CD" appendix of this Book or on the Software Media. These limitations are also contained in the individual license agreements recorded on the Software Media. These limitations may include a requirement that after using the program for a specified period of time, the user must pay a registration fee or discontinue use. By opening the Software packet(s), you agree to abide by the licenses and restrictions for these individual programs that are detailed in the "About the CD" appendix and/or on the Software Media. None of the material on this Software Media or listed in this Book may ever be redistributed, in original or modified form, for commercial purposes.

ple & Mac

d 2 For Dummies,
d Edition
3-1-118-17679-5

one 4S For Dummies,
d Edition
3-1-118-03671-6

d touch For Dummies,
d Edition
3-1-118-12960-9

c OS X Lion
Dummies
3-1-118-02205-4

ogging & Social Media

yVille For Dummies
3-1-118-08337-6

cebook For Dummies,
Edition
3-1-118-09562-1

m Blogging
Dummies
3-1-118-03843-7

itter For Dummies,
d Edition
3-0-470-76879-2

rdPress For Dummies,
Edition
3-1-118 07342-1

siness

sh Flow For Dummies
3-1-118-01850-7

esting For Dummies,
Edition
3-0-470-90545-6

Job Searching with Social Media For Dummies
978-0-470-93072-4

QuickBooks 2012
For Dummies
978-1-118-09120-3

Resumes For Dummies,
6th Edition
978-0-470-87361-8

Starting an Etsy Business
For Dummies
978-0-470-93067-0

Cooking & Entertaining

Cooking Basics
For Dummies, 4th Edition
978-0-470-91388-8

Wine For Dummies,
4th Edition
978-0-470-04579-4

Diet & Nutrition

Kettlebells For Dummies
978-0-470-59929-7

Nutrition For Dummies,
5th Edition
978-0-470-93231-5

Restaurant Calorie Counter
For Dummies,
2nd Edition
978-0-470-64405-8

Digital Photography

Digital SLR Cameras &
Photography For Dummies,
4th Edition
978-1-118-14489-3

Digital SLR Settings & Shortcuts
For Dummies
978-0-470-91763-3

Photoshop Elements 10
For Dummies
978-1-118-10742-3

Gardening

Gardening Basics
For Dummies
978-0-470-03749-2

Vegetable Gardening
For Dummies,
2nd Edition
978-0-470-49870-5

Green/Sustainable

Raising Chickens
For Dummies
978-0-470-46544-8

Green Cleaning
For Dummies
978-0-470-39106-8

Health

Diabetes For Dummies,
3rd Edition
978-0-470-27086-8

Food Allergies
For Dummies
978-0-470-09584-3

Living Gluten-Free
For Dummies,
2nd Edition
978-0-470-58589-4

Hobbies

Beekeeping
For Dummies,
2nd Edition
978-0-470-43065-1

Chess For Dummies,
3rd Edition
978-1-118-01695-4

Drawing For Dummies,
2nd Edition
978-0-470-61842-4

eBay For Dummies,
7th Edition
978-1-118-09806-6

Knitting For Dummies,
2nd Edition
978-0-470-28747-7

Language & Foreign Language

English Grammar
For Dummies,
2nd Edition
978-0-470-54664-2

French For Dummies,
2nd Edition
978-1-118-00464-7

German For Dummies,
2nd Edition
978-0-470-90101-4

Spanish Essentials
For Dummies
978-0-470-63751-7

Spanish For Dummies,
2nd Edition
978-0-470-87855-2

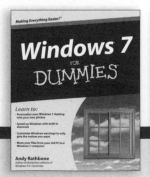

Math & Science

Algebra I For Dummies,
2nd Edition
978-0-470-55964-2

Biology For Dummies,
2nd Edition
978-0-470-59875-7

Chemistry For Dummies,
2nd Edition
978-1-1180-0730-3

Geometry For Dummies,
2nd Edition
978-0-470-08946-0

Pre-Algebra Essentials
For Dummies
978-0-470-61838-7

Microsoft Office

Excel 2010 For Dummies
978-0-470-48953-6

Office 2010 All-in-One
For Dummies
978-0-470-49748-7

Office 2011 for Mac
For Dummies
978-0-470-87869-9

Word 2010
For Dummies
978-0-470-48772-3

Music

Guitar For Dummies,
2nd Edition
978-0-7645-9904-0

Clarinet For Dummies
978-0-470-58477-4

iPod & iTunes
For Dummies,
9th Edition
978-1-118-13060-5

Pets

Cats For Dummies,
2nd Edition
978-0-7645-5275-5

Dogs All-in One
For Dummies
978-0470-52978-2

Saltwater Aquariums
For Dummies
978-0-470-06805-2

Religion & Inspiration

The Bible For Dummies
978-0-7645-5296-0

Catholicism For Dummies,
2nd Edition
978-1-118-07778-8

Spirituality For Dummies,
2nd Edition
978-0-470-19142-2

Self-Help & Relationships

Happiness For Dummies
978-0-470-28171-0

Overcoming Anxiety
For Dummies,
2nd Edition
978-0-470-57441-6

Seniors

Crosswords For Seniors
For Dummies
978-0-470-49157-7

iPad 2 For Seniors
For Dummies, 3rd Edition
978-1-118-17678-8

Laptops & Tablets
For Seniors For Dummies,
2nd Edition
978-1-118-09596-6

Smartphones & Tablets

BlackBerry For Dummies,
5th Edition
978-1-118-10035-6

Droid X2 For Dummies
978-1-118-14864-8

HTC ThunderBolt
For Dummies
978-1-118-07601-9

MOTOROLA XOOM
For Dummies
978-1-118-08835-7

Sports

Basketball For Dummies,
3rd Edition
978-1-118-07374-2

Football For Dummies,
2nd Edition
978-1-118-01261-1

Golf For Dummies,
4th Edition
978-0-470-88279-5

Test Prep

ACT For Dummies,
5th Edition
978-1-118-01259-8

ASVAB For Dummies,
3rd Edition
978-0-470-63760-9

The GRE Test For
Dummies, 7th Edition
978-0-470-00919-2

Police Officer Exam
For Dummies
978-0-470-88724-0

Series 7 Exam
For Dummies
978-0-470-09932-2

Web Development

HTML, CSS, & XHTML
For Dummies, 7th Edition
978-0-470-91659-9

Drupal For Dummies,
2nd Edition
978-1-118-08348-2

Windows 7

Windows 7
For Dummies
978-0-470-49743-2

Windows 7
For Dummies,
Book + DVD Bundle
978-0-470-52398-8

Windows 7 All-in-One
For Dummies
978-0-470-48763-1

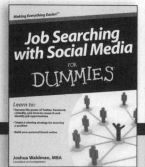

Available wherever books are sold. For mo ⬚ ⬚ ⬚ ⬚ ⬚ ⬚ customers visit www.dummies.com or call 1-877-762-29 ⬚
U.K. customers visit www.wileyeurop ⬚ ⬚ 3 1901 05366 4787 ⬚ customers visit www.wiley.ca or call 1-800-567-4797.

Connect with us online at www.facebook.com/fordummies or @fordummies